Jeep Patriot & Compass

Automotive Repair Manual

by Jeff Killingsworth and John H Haynes

Member of the Guild of Motoring Writers

Models covered:

Jeep Patriot and Compass
2007 through 2017

Does not include information specific to diesel models

Haynes Group Limited   *(50050-6X1)*
Sparkford Nr Yeovil
Somerset BA22 7JJ England

ABCDE
FGHIJ
KLMN

Haynes North America, Inc.
2801 Townsgate Road, Suite 340
Thousand Oaks, CA 91361 USA

www.haynes.com

Acknowledgements

Technical writer who contributed to this project is Demian Hurst and Scott "Gonzo" Weaver. Mechanical work and photography was provided by Mark Henderson.

A book in the Haynes Automotive Repair Manual Series

Printed in India

ISBN-13: 978-1-62092-286-6
ISBN-10: 1-62092-286-X

Library of Congress Control Number: 2017962269

While every attempt is made to ensure that the information in this manual is correct, no liability can be accepted by the authors or publishers for loss, damage or injury caused by any errors in, or omissions from, the information given.

17-288

Contents

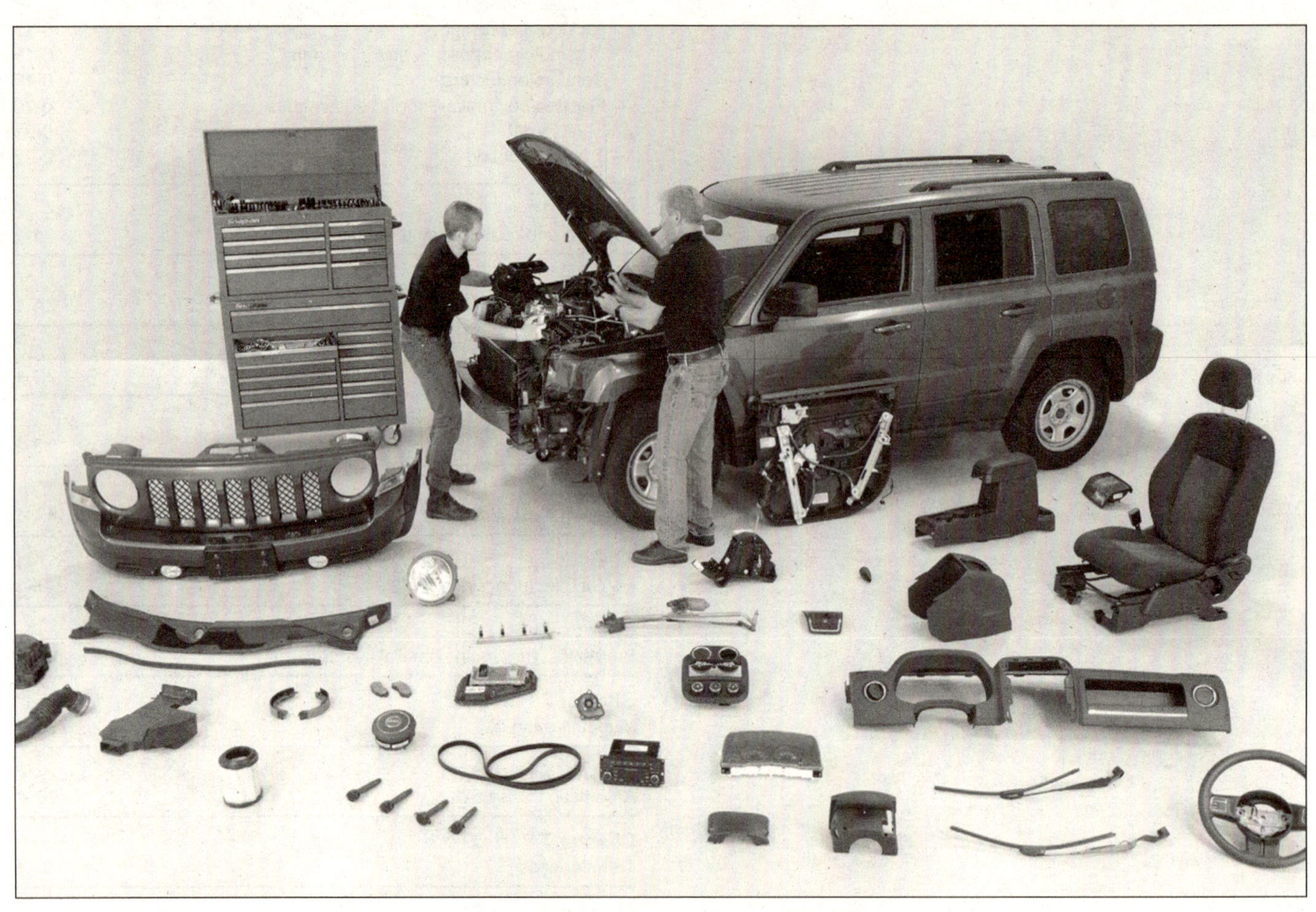

Haynes mechanic and photographer with a 2014 Jeep Patriot

About this manual

Its purpose

The purpose of this manual is to help you get the best value from your vehicle. It can do so in several ways. It can help you decide what work must be done, even if you choose to have it done by a dealer service department or a repair shop; it provides information and procedures for routine maintenance and servicing; and it offers diagnostic and repair procedures to follow when trouble occurs.

We hope you use the manual to tackle the work yourself. For many simpler jobs, doing it yourself may be quicker than arranging an appointment to get the vehicle into a shop and making the trips to leave it and pick it up. More importantly, a lot of money can be saved by avoiding the expense the shop must pass on to you to cover its labor and overhead costs. An added benefit is the sense of satisfaction and accomplishment that you feel after doing the job yourself.

Using the manual

The manual is divided into Chapters. Each Chapter is divided into numbered Sections, which are headed in bold type between horizontal lines. Each Section consists of consecutively numbered paragraphs.

The reference numbers used in illustration captions pinpoint the pertinent Section and the Step within that Section. That is, illustration 3.2 means the illustration refers to Section 3 and Step (or paragraph) 2 within that Section.

Procedures, once described in the text, are not normally repeated. When it's necessary to refer to another Chapter, the reference will be given as Chapter and Section number. Cross references given without use of the word "Chapter" apply to Sections and/or paragraphs in the same Chapter. For example, "see Section 8" means in the same Chapter.

References to the left or right side of the vehicle assume you are sitting in the driver's seat, facing forward.

Even though we have prepared this manual with extreme care, neither the publisher nor the author can accept responsibility for any errors in, or omissions from, the information given.

NOTE

A **Note** provides information necessary to properly complete a procedure or information which will make the procedure easier to understand.

CAUTION

A **Caution** provides a special procedure or special steps which must be taken while completing the procedure where the Caution is found. Not heeding a Caution can result in damage to the assembly being worked on.

WARNING

A **Warning** provides a special procedure or special steps which must be taken while completing the procedure where the Warning is found. Not heeding a Warning can result in personal injury.

Introduction

These models feature transversely mounted 2.0L or 2.4L in-line four cylinder engines, with double overhead camshafts and mechanical lash buckets. These engines have four valves per cylinder, Variable Valve Timing (VVT) and electronic multi-port fuel injection. The engine drives the front wheels through a five-speed manual, six-speed automatic transaxle or a CVT (continuously variable automatic transaxle) via independent driveaxles. 2.4L models are available with all-wheel drive, in which a transfer case, driveshaft, rear differential and rear driveaxles deliver power to the rear wheels.

The fully independent front suspension consists of coil spring/strut units, control arms and a stabilizer bar. The rear suspension uses a multi-link design that consists of a knuckle, stabilizer bar, upper control arms, trailing arms, toe links, lower control arms and coil-over shock absorber assemblies.

The power-assisted rack-and-pinion steering unit is mounted on the front suspension crossmember.

Front brakes are disc-type. Rear brakes are either disc- or drum-type. Power brake assist is standard, as is an Anti-lock Brake System (ABS).

Vehicle identification numbers

Modifications are a continuing and unpublicized process in vehicle manufacturing. Since spare parts manuals and lists are compiled on a numerical basis, the individual vehicle numbers are essential to correctly identify the component required.

Vehicle Identification Number (VIN)

This very important identification number is stamped on a plate attached to the left side of the dashboard just inside the windshield

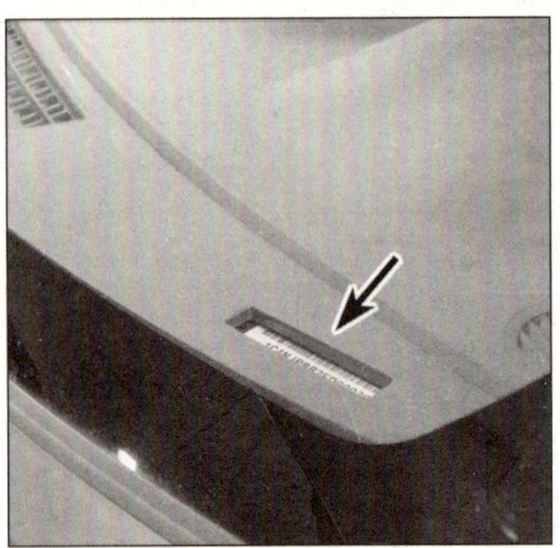

3.2 The VIN plate is visible from outside of the vehicle, through the driver's side of the windshield

(see illustration) . The VIN also appears on the Vehicle Certificate of Title and Registration. It contains information such as where and when the vehicle was manufactured, the model year and the body style.

VIN year and engine codes

Two particularly important pieces of information located in the VIN are the model year and engine codes. Counting from the left, the engine code is the eighth digit and the model year code is the 10th digit.

On the models covered by this manual the engine codes are:

0	2.0L (2008 and earlier)
W	2.4L (2008 and earlier)
A	2.0L (2009 and later)
B	2.4L (2009 and later)

On the models covered by this manual the model year codes are:

7	2007
8	2008
9	2009
A	2010
B	2011
C	2012
D	2013
E	2014
F	2015
G	2016
H	2017

Safety Certification label

The Safety Certification label is affixed to the end of the left front door (see illustration). The label contains the name of the manufacturer, the month and year of production, the Gross Vehicle Weight Rating (GVWR) and the safety certification statement. This label also contains the paint code. It is especially useful for matching the color and type of paint during repair work.

Engine identification number

The engine identification number is stamped into a machined pad on the bottom of the engine block, between the oil pan and the transaxle (see illustration).

Transaxle identification number

The ID number on the automatic transaxle is stamped into a pad on the top of the transaxle housing (see illustration).

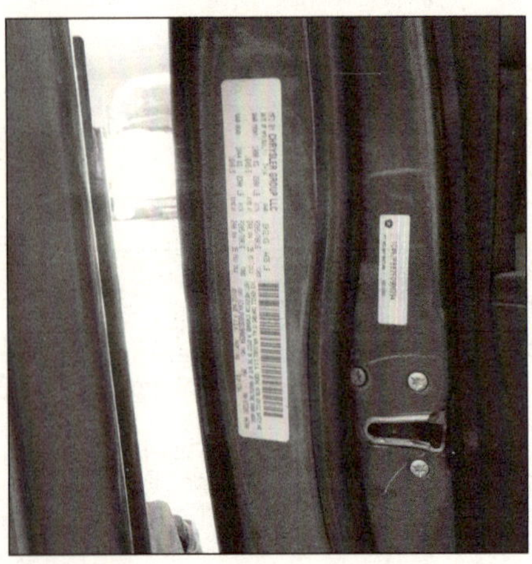

3.4 The Vehicle Safety Certification label is affixed to the end of the driver's door

3.5 Engine identification number location

3.6 Automatic transaxle identification number location

Recall information

Vehicle recalls are carried out by the manufacturer in the rare event of a possible safety-related defect. The vehicle's registered owner is contacted at the address on file at the Department of Motor Vehicles and given the details of the recall. Remedial work is carried out free of charge at a dealer service department.

If you are the new owner of a used vehicle which was subject to a recall and you want to be sure that the work has been carried out, it's best to contact a dealer service department and ask about your individual vehicle - you'll need to furnish them your Vehicle Identification Number (VIN).

The table below is based on information provided by the National Highway Traffic Safety Administration (NHTSA), the body which oversees vehicle recalls in the United States. The recall database is updated constantly. For the latest information on vehicle recalls, check the NHTSA website at www.nhtsa.gov, www.safercar.gov, or call the NHTSA hotline at 1-888-327-4236.

Recall date	Recall campaign number	Model(s) affected	Concern
MAY 7, 2007	07V196000	2007 Patriot	On some models equipped with rear disc brakes, the length of the rear wheel hub mounting bolts may prevent actuation of the park brake. This could allow unintended movement of the vehicle under certain conditions and cause a crash.
OCT 09, 2008	08V528000	2009 Patriot, 2009 Comapss	On some models, a new adhesive used in the Powertrain Control Module (PCM) manufacturing process can cause the printed circuit board to break. This can cause the engine to stall and cause a crash.
JUN 08, 2011	11V315000	2011 Patriot, Compass	Some models have been built with a missing or incorrectly installed steering column pivot rivet. A missing or incorrectly installed rivet could compromise the ability of the steering column to support the occupant loads in the event of a frontal crash, decreasing the effectiveness of the frontal impact safety system. As a result, the condition may increase the potential for injury in a frontal crash.

Recall date	Recall campaign number	Model(s) affected	Concern
JUN 04, 2013	13V233000	2010, 2011, 2012, Patriot, Comapss	Some affected models have a software error which may result in a delayed deployment or non-deployment of the seatbelt pre-tensioners and/or side airbags. In the event of a rollover necessitating airbag deployment, the vehicle occupants have an increased risk of injury in a crash.
NOV 06, 2013	13V552000	2014 Patriot, Compass	Some models may have abrasive debris in the balance shaft bearings. This can cause a loss of engine oil pressure, possibly resulting in an engine stall or engine failure. If the engine stalls while driving it may increase the risk of a crash.
DEC 23, 2015	15V878000	2015 Patriot, Compass	On some models, the power steering hose retention clamp may have been installed at an incorrect location, resulting in the detachment of the low pressure return hose. If the power steering fluid return hose detaches, it would leak fluid and increase the risk of a fire.
SEP 15, 2016	16V668000	2010, 2011, 2012, 2013, 2014 Patriot, Compass	Jeep is recalling certain models where the Occupant Restraint Control (OCR) module may short circuit, preventing the frontal airbags, seat belt pretensioners, and side airbags from deploying in the event of a crash, which could cause an increased risk of injury to the vehicles occupants in the event of a vehicle crash.
DEC 16, 2016	16V907000	2016 Patriot, Compass	On some models, the crankshaft or camshaft sensor may only work intermittently, causing the engine to stall. If the engine stalls, there is an increased risk of a crash.

Buying parts

Replacement parts are available from many sources, which generally fall into one of two categories - authorized dealer parts departments and independent retail auto parts stores. Our advice concerning these parts is as follows:

Retail auto parts stores: Good auto parts stores will stock frequently needed components which wear out relatively fast, such as clutch components, exhaust systems, brake parts, tune-up parts, etc. These stores often supply new or reconditioned parts on an exchange basis, which can save a considerable amount of money. Discount auto parts stores are often very good places to buy materials and parts needed for general vehicle maintenance such as oil, grease, filters, spark plugs, belts, touch-up paint, bulbs, etc. They also usually sell tools and general accessories, have convenient hours, charge lower prices and can often be found not far from home.

Authorized dealer parts department: This is the best source for parts which are unique to the vehicle and not generally available elsewhere (such as major engine parts, transmission parts, trim pieces, etc.).

Warranty information: If the vehicle is still covered under warranty, be sure that any replacement parts purchased - regardless of the source - do not invalidate the warranty!

To be sure of obtaining the correct parts, have engine and chassis numbers available and, if possible, take the old parts along for positive identification.

Maintenance techniques, tools and working facilities

Maintenance techniques

There are a number of techniques involved in maintenance and repair that will be referred to throughout this manual. Application of these techniques will enable the home mechanic to be more efficient, better organized and capable of performing the various tasks properly, which will ensure that the repair job is thorough and complete.

Fasteners

Fasteners are nuts, bolts, studs and screws used to hold two or more parts together. There are a few things to keep in mind when working with fasteners. Almost all of them use a locking device of some type, either a lockwasher, locknut, locking tab or thread adhesive. All threaded fasteners should be clean and straight, with undamaged threads and undamaged corners on the hex head where the wrench fits. Develop the habit of replacing all damaged nuts and bolts with new ones. Special locknuts with nylon or fiber inserts can only be used once. If they are removed, they lose their locking ability and must be replaced with new ones.

Rusted nuts and bolts should be treated with a penetrating fluid to ease removal and prevent breakage. Some mechanics use turpentine in a spout-type oil can, which works quite well. After applying the rust penetrant, let it work for a few minutes before trying to loosen the nut or bolt. Badly rusted fasteners may have to be chiseled or sawed off or removed with a special nut breaker, available at tool stores.

If a bolt or stud breaks off in an assembly, it can be drilled and removed with a special tool commonly available for this purpose. Most automotive machine shops can perform this task, as well as other repair procedures, such as the repair of threaded holes that have been stripped out.

Flat washers and lockwashers, when removed from an assembly, should always be replaced exactly as removed. Replace any damaged washers with new ones. Never use a lockwasher on any soft metal surface (such as aluminum), thin sheet metal or plastic.

Fastener sizes

For a number of reasons, automobile manufacturers are making wider and wider use of metric fasteners. Therefore, it is important to be able to tell the difference between standard (sometimes called U.S. or SAE) and metric hardware, since they cannot be interchanged.

All bolts, whether standard or metric, are sized according to diameter, thread pitch and length. For example, a standard 1/2 - 13 x 1 bolt is 1/2 inch in diameter, has 13 threads per inch and is 1 inch long. An M12 - 1.75 x 25 metric bolt is 12 mm in diameter, has a thread pitch of 1.75 mm (the distance between threads) and is 25 mm long. The two bolts are nearly identical, and easily confused, but they are not interchangeable.

In addition to the differences in diameter, thread pitch and length, metric and standard bolts can also be distinguished by examining the bolt heads. To begin with, the distance across the flats on a standard bolt head is measured in inches, while the same dimension on a metric bolt is sized in millimeters (the same is true for nuts). As a result, a standard wrench should not be used on a metric bolt and a metric wrench should not be used on a standard bolt. Also, most standard bolts have slashes radiating out from the center of the head to denote the grade or strength of the bolt, which is an indication of the amount of torque that can be applied to it. The greater the number of slashes, the greater the strength of the bolt. Grades 0 through 5 are commonly used on automobiles. Metric bolts have a property class (grade) number, rather than a slash, molded into their heads to indicate bolt strength. In this case, the higher the number, the stronger the bolt. Property class numbers 8.8, 9.8 and 10.9 are commonly used on automobiles.

Strength markings can also be used to distinguish standard hex nuts from metric hex nuts. Many standard nuts have dots stamped into one side, while metric nuts are marked with a number. The greater the number of dots, or the higher the number, the greater the strength of the nut.

Metric studs are also marked on their ends according to property class (grade). Larger studs are numbered (the same as metric bolts), while smaller studs carry a geometric code to denote grade.

It should be noted that many fasteners, especially Grades 0 through 2, have no distinguishing marks on them. When such is the case, the only way to determine whether it is standard or metric is to measure the thread pitch or compare it to a known fastener of the same size.

Standard fasteners are often referred to as SAE, as opposed to metric. However, it should be noted that SAE technically refers to a non-metric fine thread fastener only. Coarse thread non-metric fasteners are referred to as USS sizes.

Since fasteners of the same size (both standard and metric) may have different strength ratings, be sure to reinstall any bolts, studs or nuts removed from your vehicle in their original locations. Also, when replacing a fastener with a new one, make sure that the new one has a strength rating equal to or greater than the original.

Tightening sequences and procedures

Most threaded fasteners should be tightened to a specific torque value (torque is the twisting force applied to a threaded component such as a nut or bolt). Overtightening the fastener can weaken it and cause it to break, while undertightening can cause it to eventually come loose. Bolts, screws and studs, depending on the material they are made of and their thread diameters, have specific torque values, many of which are noted in the Specifications at the beginning of each Chapter. Be sure to follow the torque recommen-

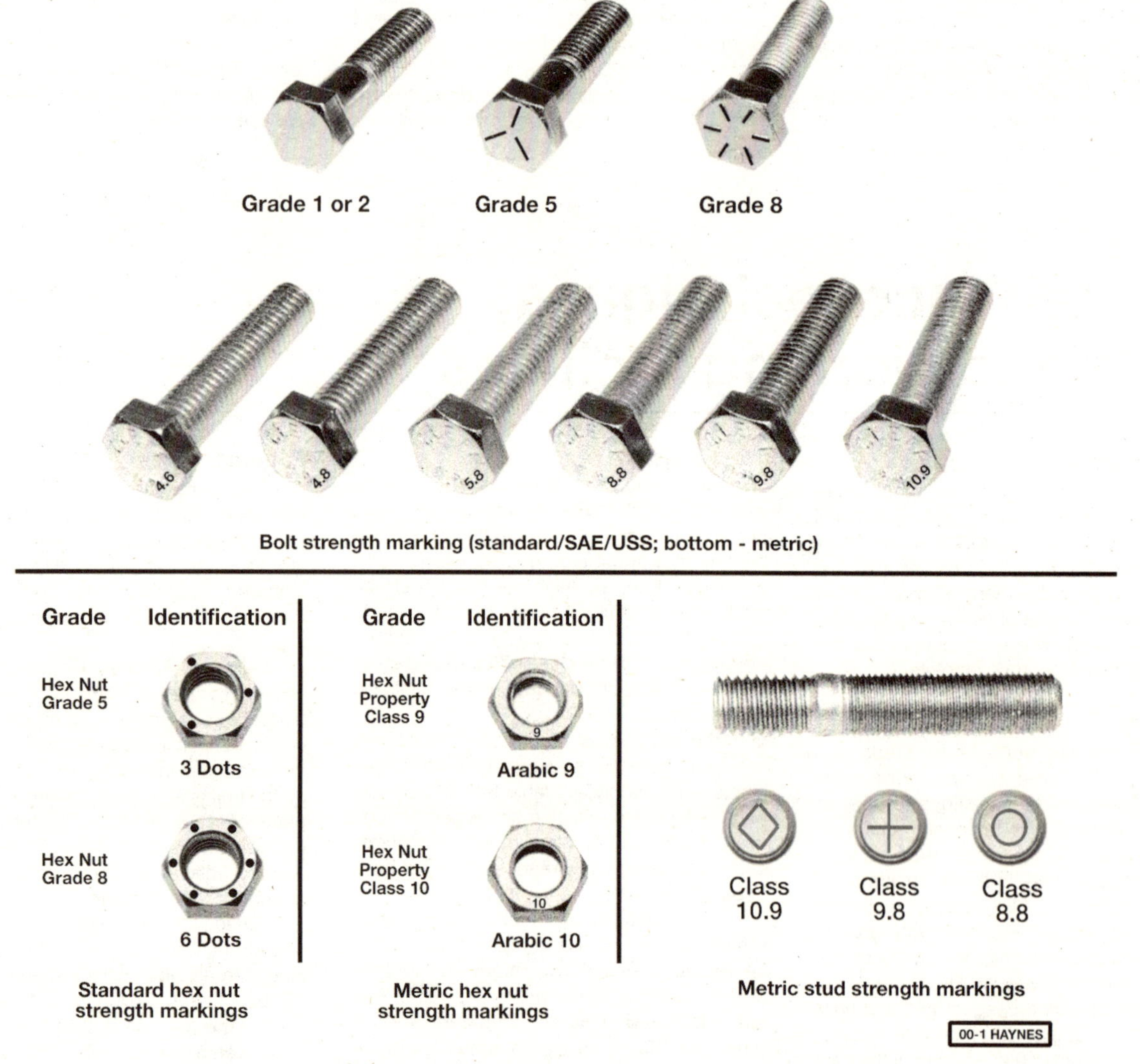

dations closely. For fasteners not assigned a specific torque, a general torque value chart is presented here as a guide. These torque values are for dry (unlubricated) fasteners threaded into steel or cast iron (not aluminum). As was previously mentioned, the size and grade of a fastener determine the amount of torque that can safely be applied to it. The figures listed here are approximate for Grade 2 and Grade 3 fasteners. Higher grades can tolerate higher torque values.

Fasteners laid out in a pattern, such as cylinder head bolts, oil pan bolts, differential cover bolts, etc., must be loosened or tightened in sequence to avoid warping the component. This sequence will normally be shown in the appropriate Chapter. If a specific pattern is not given, the following procedures can be used to prevent warping.

Initially, the bolts or nuts should be assembled finger-tight only. Next, they should be tightened one full turn each, in a crisscross or diagonal pattern. After each one has been tightened one full turn, return to the first one and tighten them all one-half turn, following the same pattern. Finally, tighten each of them one-quarter turn at a time until each fastener has been tightened to the proper torque. To loosen and remove the fasteners, the procedure would be reversed.

Metric thread sizes

	Ft-lbs	Nm
M-6	6 to 9	9 to 12
M-8	14 to 21	19 to 28
M-10	28 to 40	38 to 54
M-12	50 to 71	68 to 96
M-14	80 to 140	109 to 154

Pipe thread sizes

1/8	5 to 8	7 to 10
1/4	12 to 18	17 to 24
3/8	22 to 33	30 to 44
1/2	25 to 35	34 to 47

U.S. thread sizes

1/4 - 20	6 to 9	9 to 12
5/16 - 18	12 to 18	17 to 24
5/16 - 24	14 to 20	19 to 27
3/8 - 16	22 to 32	30 to 43
3/8 - 24	27 to 38	37 to 51
7/16 - 14	40 to 55	55 to 74
7/16 - 20	40 to 60	55 to 81
1/2 - 13	55 to 80	75 to 108

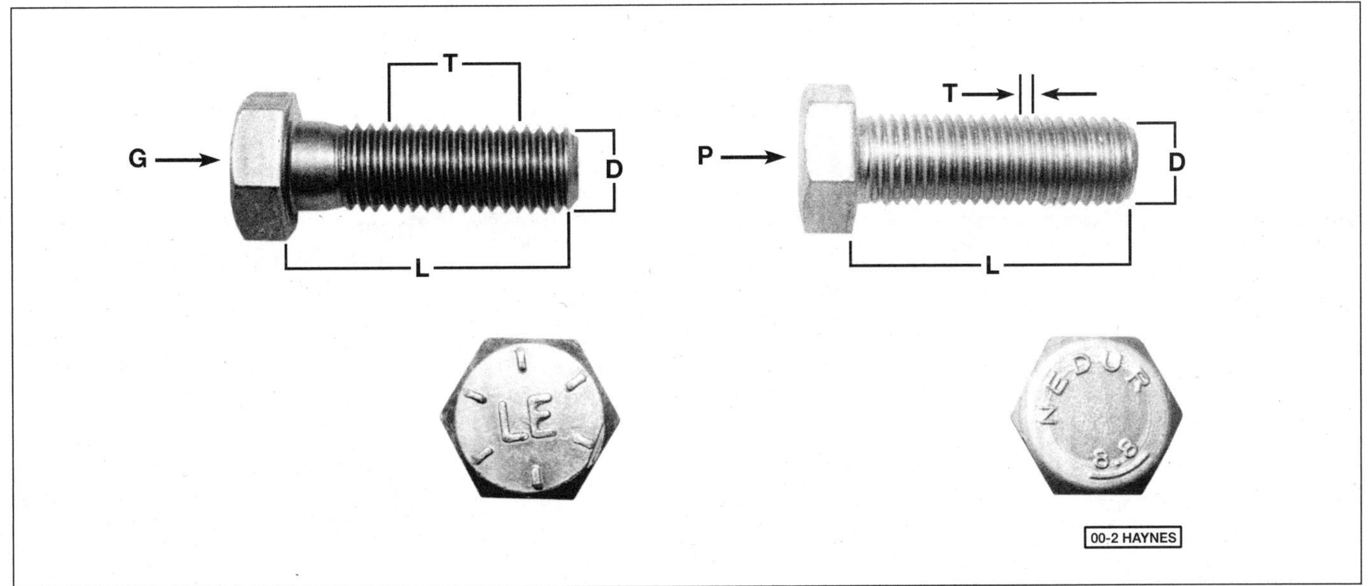

Standard (SAE and USS) bolt dimensions/grade marks

G   Grade marks (bolt strength)
L   Length (in inches)
T   Thread pitch (number of threads per inch)
D   Nominal diameter (in inches)

Metric bolt dimensions/grade marks

P   Property class (bolt strength)
L   Length (in millimeters)
T   Thread pitch (distance between threads in millimeters)
D   Diameter

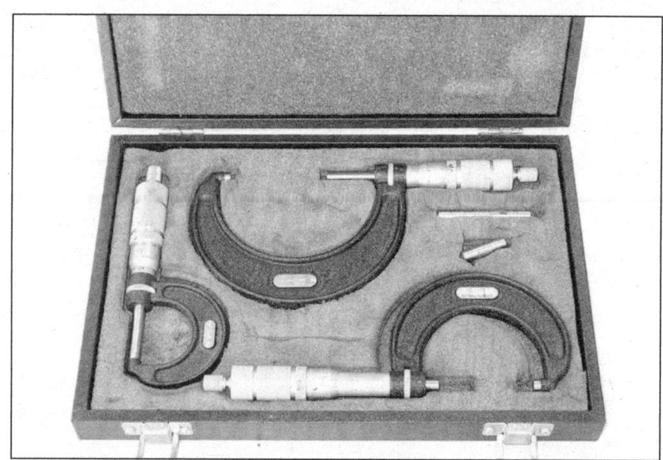

Micrometer set

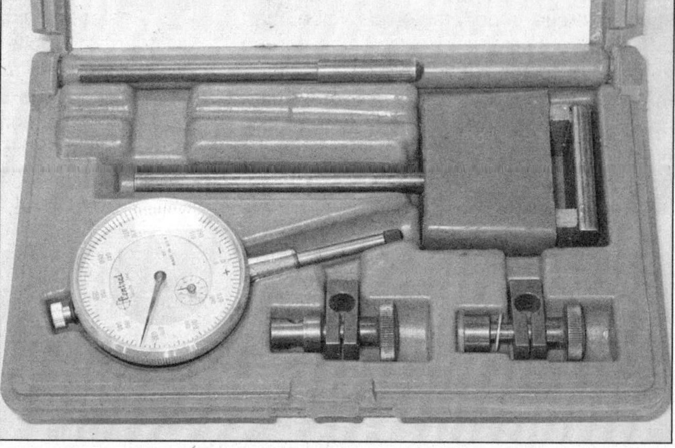

Dial indicator set

Component disassembly

Component disassembly should be done with care and purpose to help ensure that the parts go back together properly. Always keep track of the sequence in which parts are removed. Make note of special characteristics or marks on parts that can be installed more than one way, such as a grooved thrust washer on a shaft. It is a good idea to lay the disassembled parts out on a clean surface in the order that they were removed. It may also be helpful to make sketches or take instant photos of components before removal.

When removing fasteners from a component, keep track of their locations. Sometimes threading a bolt back in a part, or putting the washers and nut back on a stud, can prevent mix-ups later. If nuts and bolts cannot be returned to their original locations, they should be kept in a compartmented box or a series of small boxes. A cupcake or muffin tin is ideal for this purpose, since each cavity can hold the bolts and nuts from a particular area (i.e. oil pan bolts, valve cover bolts, engine mount bolts, etc.). A pan of this type is especially helpful when working on assemblies with very small parts, such as the carburetor, alternator, valve train or interior dash and trim pieces. The cavities can be marked with paint or tape to identify the contents.

Whenever wiring looms, harnesses or connectors are separated, it is a good idea to identify the two halves with numbered pieces of masking tape so they can be easily reconnected.

Gasket sealing surfaces

Throughout any vehicle, gaskets are used to seal the mating surfaces between two parts and keep lubricants, fluids, vacuum or pressure contained in an assembly.

Many times these gaskets are coated with a liquid or paste-type gasket sealing compound before assembly. Age, heat and pressure can sometimes cause the two parts to stick together so tightly that they are very difficult to separate. Often, the assembly can be loosened by striking it with a soft-face hammer near the mating surfaces. A regular hammer can be used if a block of wood is placed between the hammer and the part. Do not hammer on cast parts or parts that could be easily damaged. With any particularly stubborn part, always recheck to make sure that every fastener has been removed.

Avoid using a screwdriver or bar to pry apart an assembly, as they can easily mar the gasket sealing surfaces of the parts, which must remain smooth. If prying is absolutely necessary, use an old broom handle, but keep in mind that extra clean up will be necessary if the wood splinters.

After the parts are separated, the old gasket must be carefully scraped off and the gasket surfaces cleaned. Stubborn gasket material can be soaked with rust penetrant or treated with a special chemical to soften it so it can be easily scraped off. **Caution:** *Never use gasket removal solutions or caustic chemicals on plastic or other composite components.* A scraper can be fashioned from a piece of copper tubing by flattening and sharpening one end. Copper is recommended because it is usually softer than the surfaces to be scraped, which reduces the chance of gouging the part. Some gaskets can be removed with a wire brush, but regardless of the method used, the mating surfaces must be left clean and smooth. If for some reason the gasket surface is gouged, then a gasket sealer thick enough to fill scratches will have to be used during reassembly of the components. For most applications, a non-drying (or semi-drying) gasket sealer should be used.

Hose removal tips

Warning: *If the vehicle is equipped with air conditioning, do not disconnect any of the A/C hoses without first having the system depressurized by a dealer service department or a service station.*

Hose removal precautions closely parallel gasket removal precautions. Avoid scratching or gouging the surface that the hose mates against or the connection may leak. This is especially true for radiator hoses. Because of various chemical reactions, the rubber in hoses can bond itself to the metal spigot that the hose fits over. To remove a hose, first loosen the hose clamps that secure it to the spigot. Then, with slip-joint pliers, grab the hose at the clamp and rotate it around the spigot. Work it back and forth until it is completely free, then pull it off. Silicone or other lubricants will ease removal if they can be applied between the hose and the outside of the spigot. Apply the same lubricant to the inside of the hose and the outside of the spigot to simplify installation.

As a last resort (and if the hose is to be replaced with a new one anyway), the rubber can be slit with a knife and the hose peeled from the spigot. If this must be done, be careful that the metal connection is not damaged.

If a hose clamp is broken or damaged, do not reuse it. Wire-type clamps usually weaken with age, so it is a good idea to replace them with screw-type clamps whenever a hose is removed.

Tools

A selection of good tools is a basic requirement for anyone who plans to maintain and repair his or her own vehicle. For the owner who has few tools, the initial investment might seem high, but when compared to the spiraling costs of professional auto maintenance and repair, it is a wise one.

To help the owner decide which tools are needed to perform the tasks detailed in this manual, the following tool lists are offered: *Maintenance and minor repair, Repair/overhaul* and *Special.*

The newcomer to practical mechanics should start off with the *maintenance and minor repair* tool kit, which is adequate for the simpler jobs performed on a vehicle. Then, as confidence and experience grow, the owner can tackle more difficult tasks, buying additional tools as they are needed. Eventually the basic kit will be expanded into the *repair and overhaul* tool set. Over a period of time, the

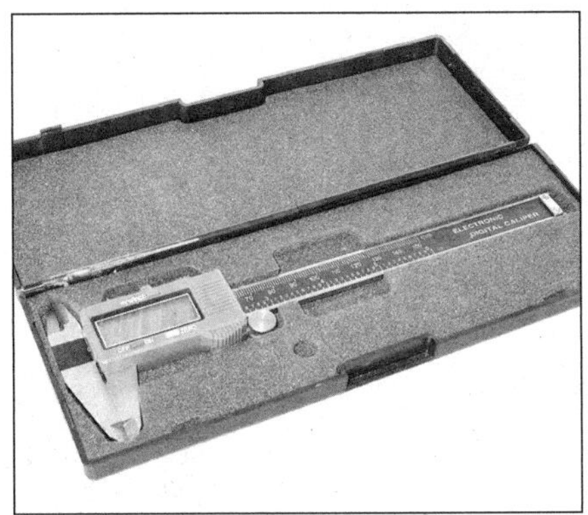

Dial caliper

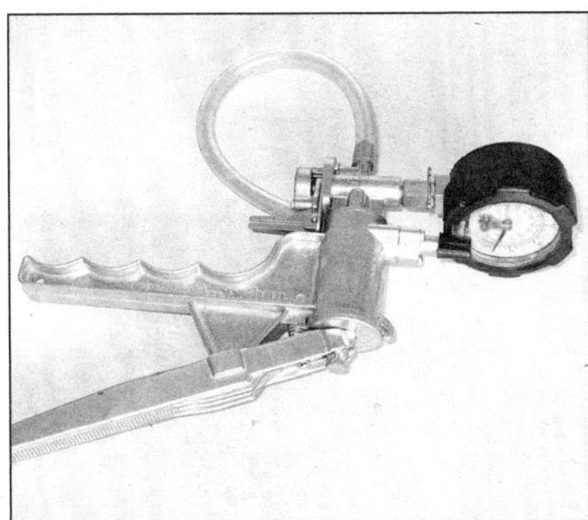

Hand-operated vacuum pump

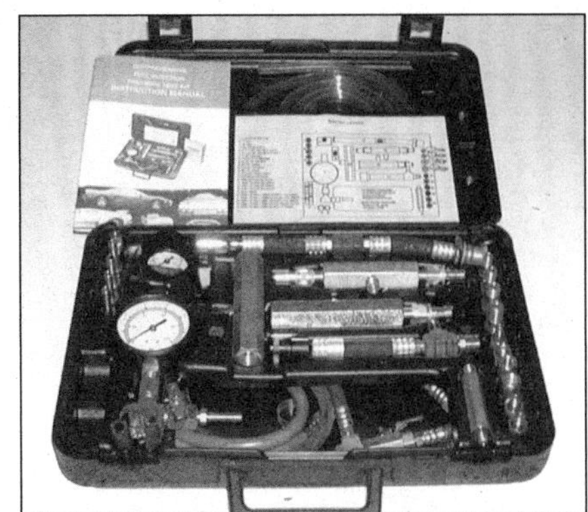

Fuel pressure gauge set

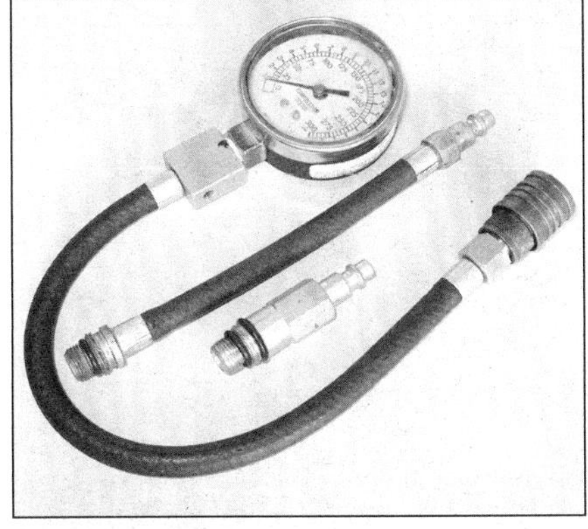

Compression gauge with spark plug hole adapter

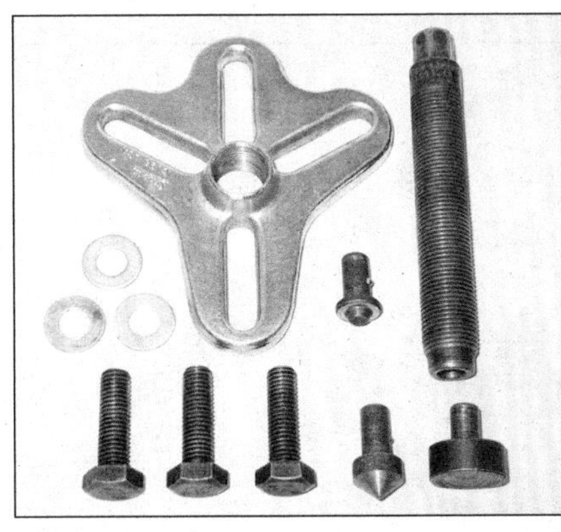

Damper/steering wheel puller

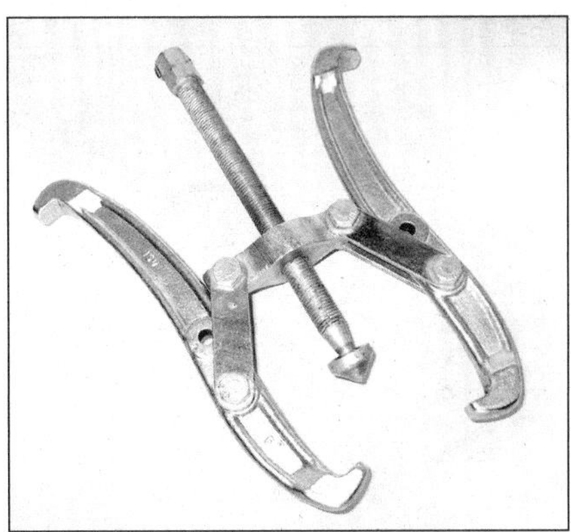

General purpose puller

Hydraulic lifter removal tool

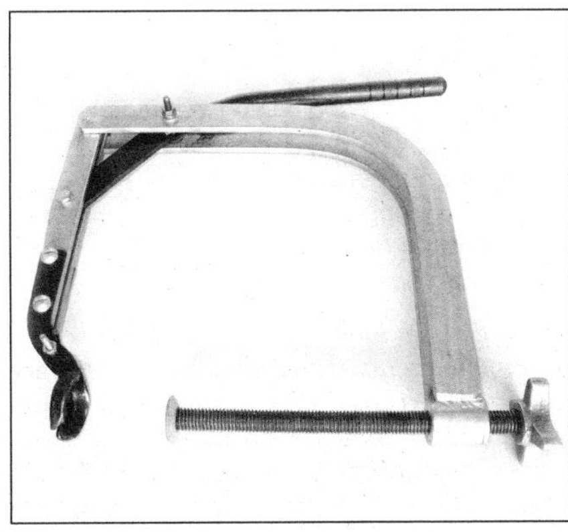

Valve spring compressor

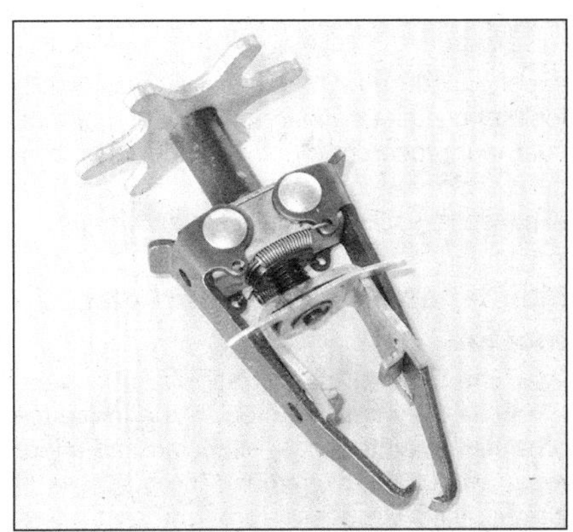

Valve spring compressor

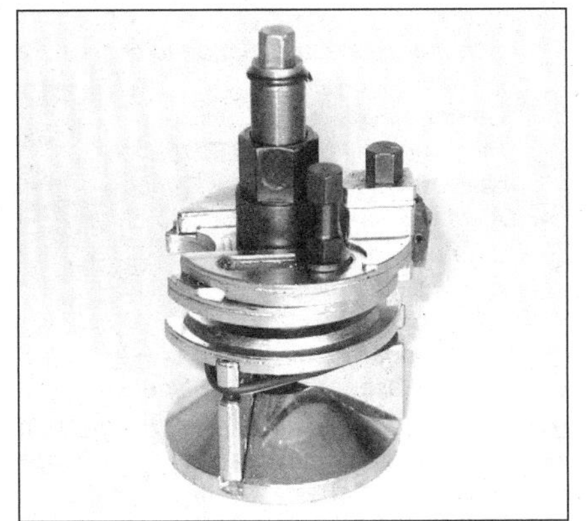

Ridge reamer

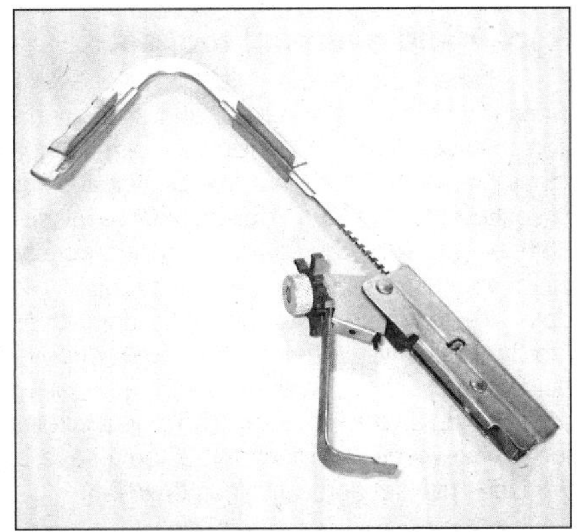

Piston ring groove cleaning tool

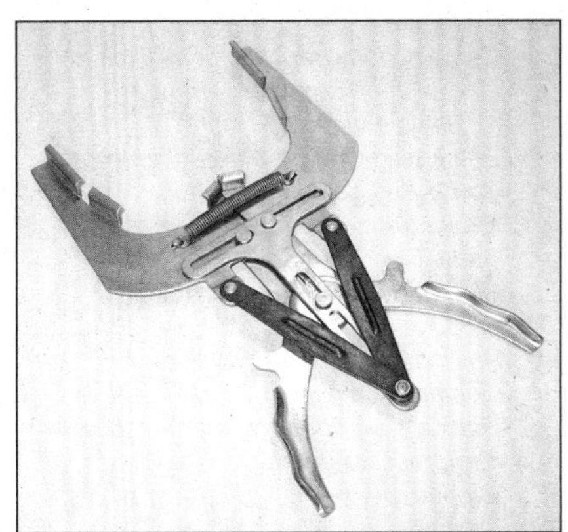

Ring removal/installation tool

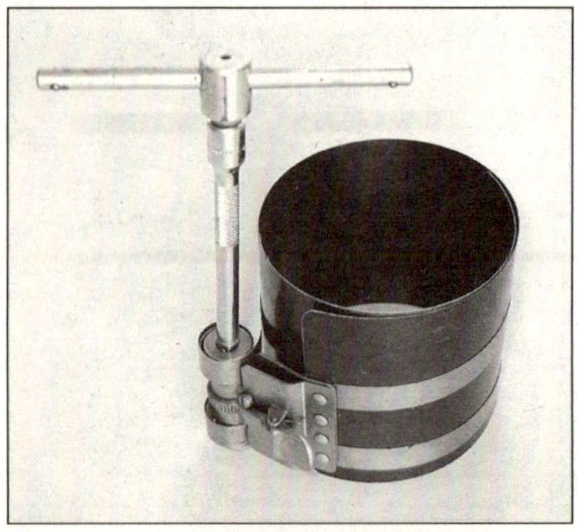

Ring compressor

Cylinder hone

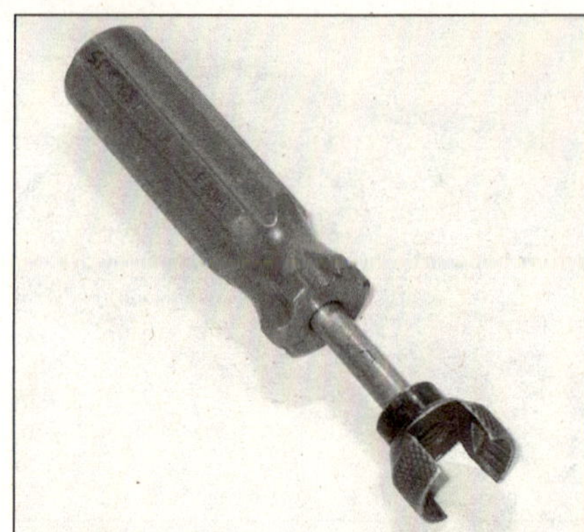

Brake hold-down spring tool

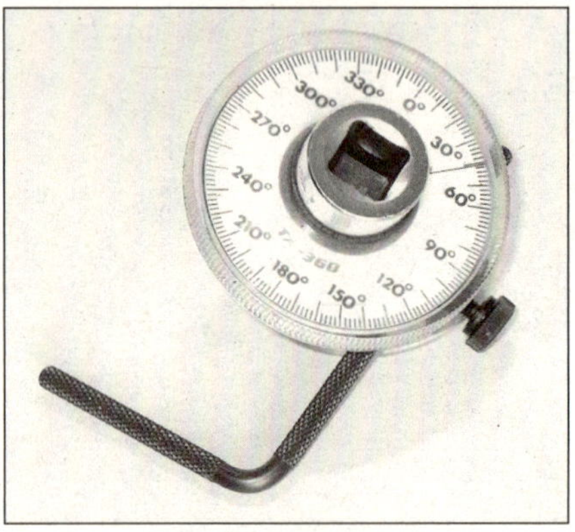

Torque angle gauge

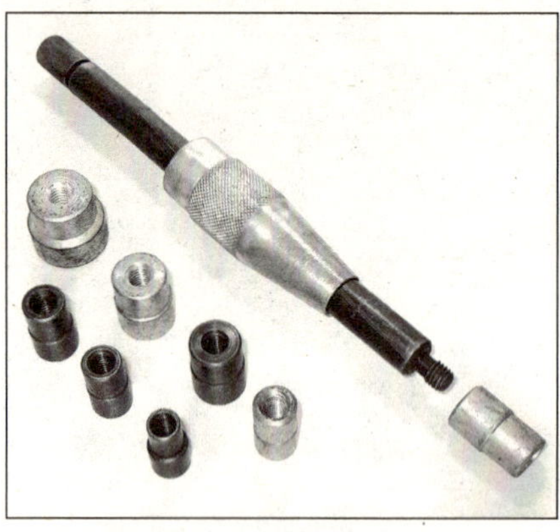

Clutch plate alignment tool

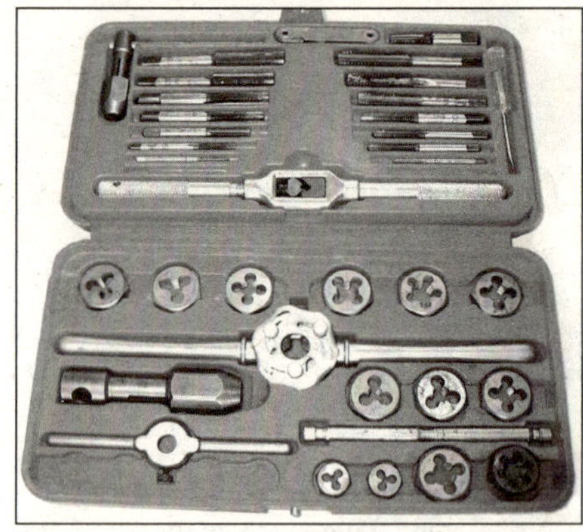

Tap and die set

experienced do-it-yourselfer will assemble a tool set complete enough for most repair and overhaul procedures and will add tools from the special category when it is felt that the expense is justified by the frequency of use.

Maintenance and minor repair tool kit

The tools in this list should be considered the minimum required for performance of routine maintenance, servicing and minor repair work. We recommend the purchase of combination wrenches (box-end and open-end combined in one wrench). While more expensive than open end wrenches, they offer the advantages of both types of wrench.

Combination wrench set (1/4-inch to 1 inch or 6 mm to 19 mm)
Adjustable wrench, 8 inch
Spark plug wrench with rubber insert
Spark plug gap adjusting tool
Feeler gauge set
Brake bleeder wrench
Standard screwdriver (5/16-inch x 6 inch)
Phillips screwdriver (No. 2 x 6 inch)
Combination pliers - 6 inch
Hacksaw and assortment of blades
Tire pressure gauge
Grease gun
Oil can
Fine emery cloth

Wire brush
Battery post and cable cleaning tool
Oil filter wrench
Funnel (medium size)
Safety goggles
Jackstands (2)
Drain pan

Note: *If basic tune-ups are going to be part of routine maintenance, it will be necessary to purchase a good quality stroboscopic timing light and combination tachometer/dwell meter. Although they are included in the list of special tools, it is mentioned here because they are absolutely necessary for tuning most vehicles properly.*

Repair and overhaul tool set

These tools are essential for anyone who plans to perform major repairs and are in addition to those in the maintenance and minor repair tool kit. Included is a comprehensive set of sockets which, though expensive, are invaluable because of their versatility, especially when various extensions and drives are available. We recommend the 1/2-inch drive over the 3/8-inch drive. Although the larger drive is bulky and more expensive, it has the capacity of accepting a very wide range of large sockets. Ideally, however, the mechanic should have a 3/8-inch drive set and a 1/2-inch drive set.

Socket set(s)
Reversible ratchet

Extension - 10 inch
Universal joint
Torque wrench (same size drive as sockets)
Ball peen hammer - 8 ounce
Soft-face hammer (plastic/rubber)
Standard screwdriver (1/4-inch x 6 inch)
Standard screwdriver (stubby - 5/16-inch)
Phillips screwdriver (No. 3 x 8 inch)
Phillips screwdriver (stubby - No. 2)
Pliers - vise grip
Pliers - lineman's
Pliers - needle nose
Pliers - snap-ring (internal and external)
Cold chisel - 1/2-inch
Scribe
Scraper (made from flattened copper tubing)
Centerpunch
Pin punches (1/16, 1/8, 3/16-inch)
Steel rule/straightedge - 12 inch
Allen wrench set (1/8 to 3/8-inch or 4 mm to 10 mm)
A selection of files
Wire brush (large)
Jackstands (second set)
Jack (scissor or hydraulic type)

Note: *Another tool which is often useful is an electric drill with a chuck capacity of 3/8-inch and a set of good quality drill bits.*

Special tools

The tools in this list include those which are not used regularly, are expensive to buy, or which need to be used in accordance with their manufacturer's instructions. Unless these tools will be used frequently, it is not very economical to purchase many of them. A consideration would be to split the cost and use between yourself and a friend or friends. In addition, most of these tools can be obtained from a tool rental shop on a temporary basis.

This list primarily contains only those tools and instruments widely available to the public, and not those special tools produced by the vehicle manufacturer for distribution to dealer service departments. Occasionally, references to the manufacturer's special tools are included in the text of this manual. Generally, an alternative method of doing the job without the special tool is offered. However, sometimes there is no alternative to their use. Where this is the case, and the tool cannot be purchased or borrowed, the work should be turned over to the dealer service department or an automotive repair shop.

Valve spring compressor
Piston ring groove cleaning tool
Piston ring compressor
Piston ring installation tool
Cylinder compression gauge
Cylinder ridge reamer
Cylinder surfacing hone
Cylinder bore gauge
Micrometers and/or dial calipers
Hydraulic lifter removal tool
Balljoint separator
Universal-type puller
Impact screwdriver
Dial indicator set
Stroboscopic timing light (inductive
　pick-up)
Hand operated vacuum/pressure pump
Tachometer/dwell meter
Universal electrical multimeter
Cable hoist
Brake spring removal and installation
　tools
Floor jack

Buying tools

For the do-it-yourselfer who is just starting to get involved in vehicle maintenance and repair, there are a number of options available when purchasing tools. If maintenance and minor repair is the extent of the work to be done, the purchase of individual tools is satisfactory. If, on the other hand, extensive work is planned, it would be a good idea to purchase a modest tool set from one of the large retail chain stores. A set can usually be bought at a substantial savings over the individual tool prices, and they often come with a tool box. As additional tools are needed, add-on sets, individual tools and a larger tool box can be purchased to expand the tool selection. Building a tool set gradually allows the cost of the

tools to be spread over a longer period of time and gives the mechanic the freedom to choose only those tools that will actually be used.

Tool stores will often be the only source of some of the special tools that are needed, but regardless of where tools are bought, try to avoid cheap ones, especially when buying screwdrivers and sockets, because they won't last very long. The expense involved in replacing cheap tools will eventually be greater than the initial cost of quality tools.

Care and maintenance of tools

Good tools are expensive, so it makes sense to treat them with respect. Keep them clean and in usable condition and store them properly when not in use. Always wipe off any dirt, grease or metal chips before putting them away. Never leave tools lying around in the work area. Upon completion of a job, always check closely under the hood for tools that may have been left there so they won't get lost during a test drive.

Some tools, such as screwdrivers, pliers, wrenches and sockets, can be hung on a panel mounted on the garage or workshop wall, while others should be kept in a tool box or tray. Measuring instruments, gauges, meters, etc. must be carefully stored where they cannot be damaged by weather or impact from other tools.

When tools are used with care and stored properly, they will last a very long time. Even with the best of care, though, tools will wear out if used frequently. When a tool is damaged or worn out, replace it. Subsequent jobs will be safer and more enjoyable if you do.

How to repair damaged threads

Sometimes, the internal threads of a nut or bolt hole can become stripped, usually from overtightening. Stripping threads is an all-too-common occurrence, especially when working with aluminum parts, because aluminum is so soft that it easily strips out.

Usually, external or internal threads are only partially stripped. After they've been cleaned up with a tap or die, they'll still work. Sometimes, however, threads are badly damaged. When this happens, you've got three choices:

1) *Drill and tap the hole to the next suitable oversize and install a larger diameter bolt, screw or stud.*
2) *Drill and tap the hole to accept a threaded plug, then drill and tap the plug to the original screw size. You can also buy a plug already threaded to the original size. Then you simply drill a hole to the specified size, then run the threaded plug into the hole with a bolt and jam nut. Once the plug is fully seated, remove the jam nut and bolt.*

3) *The third method uses a patented thread repair kit like Heli-Coil or Slimsert. These easy-to-use kits are designed to repair damaged threads in straight-through holes and blind holes. Both are available as kits which can handle a variety of sizes and thread patterns. Drill the hole, then tap it with the special included tap. Install the Heli-Coil and the hole is back to its original diameter and thread pitch.*

Regardless of which method you use, be sure to proceed calmly and carefully. A little impatience or carelessness during one of these relatively simple procedures can ruin your whole day's work and cost you a bundle if you wreck an expensive part.

Working facilities

Not to be overlooked when discussing tools is the workshop. If anything more than routine maintenance is to be carried out, some sort of suitable work area is essential.

It is understood, and appreciated, that many home mechanics do not have a good workshop or garage available, and end up removing an engine or doing major repairs outside. It is recommended, however, that the overhaul or repair be completed under the cover of a roof.

A clean, flat workbench or table of comfortable working height is an absolute necessity. The workbench should be equipped with a vise that has a jaw opening of at least four inches.

As mentioned previously, some clean, dry storage space is also required for tools, as well as the lubricants, fluids, cleaning solvents, etc. which soon become necessary.

Sometimes waste oil and fluids, drained from the engine or cooling system during normal maintenance or repairs, present a disposal problem. To avoid pouring them on the ground or into a sewage system, pour the used fluids into large containers, seal them with caps and take them to an authorized disposal site or recycling center. Plastic jugs, such as old antifreeze containers, are ideal for this purpose.

Always keep a supply of old newspapers and clean rags available. Old towels are excellent for mopping up spills. Many mechanics use rolls of paper towels for most work because they are readily available and disposable. To help keep the area under the vehicle clean, a large cardboard box can be cut open and flattened to protect the garage or shop floor.

Whenever working over a painted surface, such as when leaning over a fender to service something under the hood, always cover it with an old blanket or bedspread to protect the finish. Vinyl covered pads, made especially for this purpose, are available at auto parts stores.

Booster battery (jump) starting

1   Observe these precautions when using a booster battery to start a vehicle:

a) *Before connecting the booster battery, make sure the ignition switch is in the Off position.*

b) *Turn off the lights, heater and other electrical loads.*

c) *Your eyes should be shielded. Safety goggles are a good idea.*

d) *Make sure the booster battery is the same voltage as the dead one in the vehicle.*

e) *The two vehicles MUST NOT TOUCH each other!*

f) *Make sure the transaxle is in Neutral (manual) or Park (automatic).*

g) *If the booster battery is not a maintenance-free type, remove the vent caps and lay a cloth over the vent holes.*

2   Connect the red jumper cable to the positive (+) terminals of each battery (see illustration).

3   Connect one end of the black jumper cable to the negative (-) terminal of the booster battery. The other end of this cable should be connected to a good ground on the vehicle to be started, such as a bolt or bracket on the body.

4   Start the engine using the booster battery, then, with the engine running at idle speed, disconnect the jumper cables in the reverse order of connection. The vehicle with the dead battery may have to be driven for 20 minutes or more to sufficiently recharge the battery for independent starting.

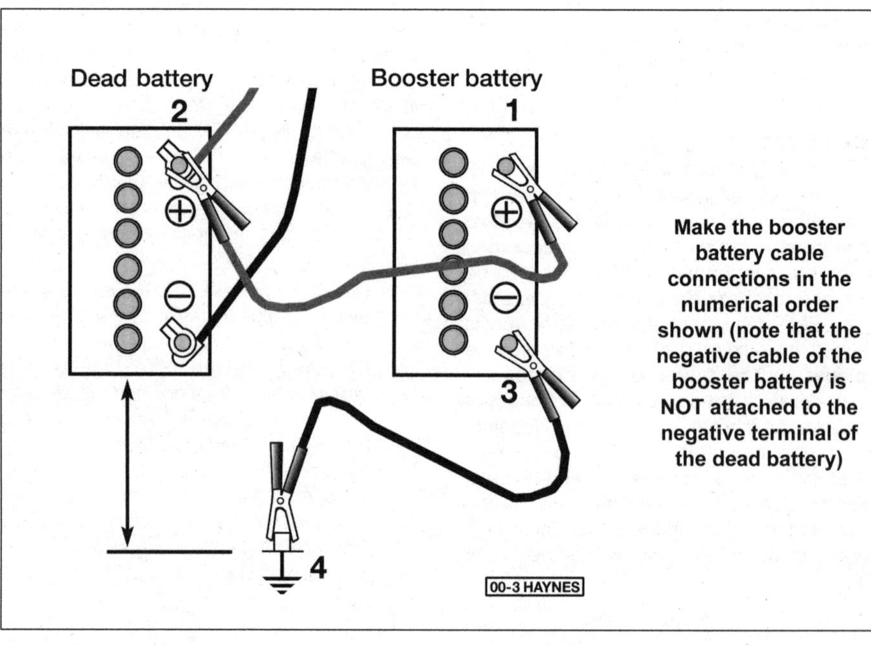

Make the booster battery cable connections in the numerical order shown (note that the negative cable of the booster battery is NOT attached to the negative terminal of the dead battery)

Jacking and towing

Jacking

1   The jack supplied with the vehicle should only be used for raising the vehicle for changing a tire or placing jackstands under the frame.

Warning: *Never crawl under the vehicle or start the engine when the jack is being used as the only means of support.*

2   All vehicles are supplied with a scissors-type jack. When jacking the vehicle, it should be engaged with the relief area in the rocker panel flange (see illustration).

3   The vehicle should be on level ground with the wheels blocked and the transmission in Park. Pry off the hub cap (if equipped) using the tapered end of the lug wrench. Loosen the lug nuts one-half turn and leave them in place until the wheel is raised off the ground.

4   Place the jack under the side of the vehicle in the indicated position. Use the supplied wrench to turn the jackscrew clockwise until the wheel is raised off the ground. Remove the lug nuts, pull off the wheel and install the spare.

5   With the beveled side in, install the lug nuts and tighten them until snug. Lower the vehicle by turning the jackscrew counterclockwise. Remove the jack and tighten the nuts in a diagonal pattern to the torque listed in the Chapter 1 Specifications. If a torque wrench is not available, have the torque checked by a service station as soon as possible. Install the hubcap by placing it in position and using the heel of your hand or a rubber mallet to seat it.

Towing

Front-wheel drive models

6   As a general rule, the vehicle should be towed with the front (drive) wheels off the ground or, preferably, on a flat bed car carrier. If the front wheels can't be raised or a carrier isn't available, place them on a dolly. The ignition key must be in the ACC position, since the steering lock mechanism isn't strong enough to hold the front wheels straight while towing.

7   Towing equipment specifically designed for this purpose should be used and should be attached to the main structural members of the vehicle, not the bumper or brackets.

8   Safety is a major consideration when towing and all applicable state and local laws must be obeyed. A safety chain system must be used for all towing.

9   While towing, the parking brake must be released and the transmission must be in Neutral. The steering must be unlocked (ignition switch in the Off position). Remember that power steering and power brakes will not work with the engine off.

Models with CVT transaxles and All-Wheel Drive

10   A flatbed car carrier must be used to transport these vehicles.

The jack fits over the rocker panel flange (there are two jacking points on each side of the vehicle)

Automotive chemicals and lubricants

A number of automotive chemicals and lubricants are available for use during vehicle maintenance and repair. They include a wide variety of products ranging from cleaning solvents and degreasers to lubricants and protective sprays for rubber, plastic and vinyl.

Cleaners

Carburetor cleaner and choke cleaner is a strong solvent for gum, varnish and carbon. Most carburetor cleaners leave a dry-type lubricant film which will not harden or gum up. Because of this film it is not recommended for use on electrical components.

Brake system cleaner is used to remove brake dust, grease and brake fluid from the brake system, where clean surfaces are absolutely necessary. It leaves no residue and often eliminates brake squeal caused by contaminants.

Electrical cleaner removes oxidation, corrosion and carbon deposits from electrical contacts, restoring full current flow. It can also be used to clean spark plugs, carburetor jets, voltage regulators and other parts where an oil-free surface is desired.

Demoisturants remove water and moisture from electrical components such as alternators, voltage regulators, electrical connectors and fuse blocks. They are non-conductive and non-corrosive.

Degreasers are heavy-duty solvents used to remove grease from the outside of the engine and from chassis components. They can be sprayed or brushed on and, depending on the type, are rinsed off either with water or solvent.

Lubricants

Motor oil is the lubricant formulated for use in engines. It normally contains a wide variety of additives to prevent corrosion and reduce foaming and wear. Motor oil comes in various weights (viscosity ratings) from 0 to 50. The recommended weight of the oil depends on the season, temperature and the demands on the engine. Light oil is used in cold climates and under light load conditions. Heavy oil is used in hot climates and where high loads are encountered. Multi-viscosity oils are designed to have characteristics of both light and heavy oils and are available in a number of weights from 0W-20 to 20W-50.

Gear oil is designed to be used in differentials, manual transmissions and other areas where high-temperature lubrication is required.

Chassis and wheel bearing grease is a heavy grease used where increased loads and friction are encountered, such as for wheel bearings, balljoints, tie-rod ends and universal joints.

High-temperature wheel bearing grease is designed to withstand the extreme temperatures encountered by wheel bearings in disc brake equipped vehicles. It usually contains molybdenum disulfide (moly), which is a dry-type lubricant.

White grease is a heavy grease for metal-to-metal applications where water is a problem. White grease stays soft under both low and high temperatures (usually from -100 to +190-degrees F), and will not wash off or dilute in the presence of water.

Assembly lube is a special extreme pressure lubricant, usually containing moly, used to lubricate high-load parts (such as main and rod bearings and cam lobes) for initial start-up of a new engine. The assembly lube lubricates the parts without being squeezed out or washed away until the engine oiling system begins to function.

Silicone lubricants are used to protect rubber, plastic, vinyl and nylon parts.

Graphite lubricants are used where oils cannot be used due to contamination problems, such as in locks. The dry graphite will lubricate metal parts while remaining uncontaminated by dirt, water, oil or acids. It is electrically conductive and will not foul electrical contacts in locks such as the ignition switch.

Moly penetrants loosen and lubricate frozen, rusted and corroded fasteners and prevent future rusting or freezing.

Heat-sink grease is a special electrically non-conductive grease that is used for mounting electronic ignition modules where it is essential that heat is transferred away from the module.

Sealants

RTV sealant is one of the most widely used gasket compounds. Made from silicone, RTV is air curing, it seals, bonds, waterproofs, fills surface irregularities, remains flexible, doesn't shrink, is relatively easy to remove, and is used as a supplementary sealer with almost all low and medium temperature gaskets.

Anaerobic sealant is much like RTV in that it can be used either to seal gaskets or to form gaskets by itself. It remains flexible, is solvent resistant and fills surface imperfections. The difference between an anaerobic sealant and an RTV-type sealant is in the curing. RTV cures when exposed to air, while an anaerobic sealant cures only in the absence of air. This means that an anaerobic sealant cures only after the assembly of parts, sealing them together.

Thread and pipe sealant is used for sealing hydraulic and pneumatic fittings and vacuum lines. It is usually made from a Teflon compound, and comes in a spray, a paint-on liquid and as a wrap-around tape.

Chemicals

Anti-seize compound prevents seizing, galling, cold welding, rust and corrosion in fasteners. High-temperature anti-seize, usually made with copper and graphite lubricants, is used for exhaust system and exhaust manifold bolts.

Anaerobic locking compounds are used to keep fasteners from vibrating or working loose and cure only after installation, in the absence of air. Medium strength locking compound is used for small nuts, bolts and screws that may be removed later. High-strength locking compound is for large nuts, bolts and studs which aren't removed on a regular basis.

Oil additives range from viscosity index improvers to chemical treatments that claim to reduce internal engine friction. It should be noted that most oil manufacturers caution against using additives with their oils.

Gas additives perform several functions, depending on their chemical makeup. They usually contain solvents that help dissolve gum and varnish that build up on carburetor, fuel injection and intake parts. They also serve to break down carbon deposits that form on the inside surfaces of the combustion chambers. Some additives contain upper cylinder lubricants for valves and piston rings, and others contain chemicals to remove condensation from the gas tank.

Miscellaneous

Brake fluid is specially formulated hydraulic fluid that can withstand the heat and pressure encountered in brake systems. Care must be taken so this fluid does not come in contact with painted surfaces or plastics. An opened container should always be resealed to prevent contamination by water or dirt.

Weatherstrip adhesive is used to bond weatherstripping around doors, windows and trunk lids. It is sometimes used to attach trim pieces.

Undercoating is a petroleum-based, tar-like substance that is designed to protect metal surfaces on the underside of the vehicle from corrosion. It also acts as a sound-deadening agent by insulating the bottom of the vehicle.

Waxes and polishes are used to help protect painted and plated surfaces from the weather. Different types of paint may require the use of different types of wax and polish. Some polishes utilize a chemical or abrasive cleaner to help remove the top layer of oxidized (dull) paint on older vehicles. In recent years many non-wax polishes that contain a wide variety of chemicals such as polymers and silicones have been introduced. These non-wax polishes are usually easier to apply and last longer than conventional waxes and polishes.

Conversion factors

Length (distance)

Inches (in)	X 25.4	= Millimeters (mm)	X 0.0394	= Inches (in)	
Feet (ft)	X 0.305	= Meters (m)	X 3.281	= Feet (ft)	
Miles	X 1.609	= Kilometers (km)	X 0.621	= Miles	

Volume (capacity)

Cubic inches (cu in; in³)	X 16.387	= Cubic centimeters (cc; cm³)	X 0.061	= Cubic inches (cu in; in³)	
Imperial pints (Imp pt)	X 0.568	= Liters (l)	X 1.76	= Imperial pints (Imp pt)	
Imperial quarts (Imp qt)	X 1.137	= Liters (l)	X 0.88	= Imperial quarts (Imp qt)	
Imperial quarts (Imp qt)	X 1.201	= US quarts (US qt)	X 0.833	= Imperial quarts (Imp qt)	
US quarts (US qt)	X 0.946	= Liters (l)	X 1.057	= US quarts (US qt)	
Imperial gallons (Imp gal)	X 4.546	= Liters (l)	X 0.22	= Imperial gallons (Imp gal)	
Imperial gallons (Imp gal)	X 1.201	= US gallons (US gal)	X 0.833	= Imperial gallons (Imp gal)	
US gallons (US gal)	X 3.785	= Liters (l)	X 0.264	= US gallons (US gal)	

Mass (weight)

Ounces (oz)	X 28.35	= Grams (g)	X 0.035	= Ounces (oz)
Pounds (lb)	X 0.454	= Kilograms (kg)	X 2.205	= Pounds (lb)

Force

Ounces-force (ozf; oz)	X 0.278	= Newtons (N)	X 3.6	= Ounces-force (ozf; oz)
Pounds-force (lbf; lb)	X 4.448	= Newtons (N)	X 0.225	= Pounds-force (lbf; lb)
Newtons (N)	X 0.1	= Kilograms-force (kgf; kg)	X 9.81	= Newtons (N)

Pressure

Pounds-force per square inch (psi; lbf/in²; lb/in²)	X 0.070	= Kilograms-force per square centimeter (kgf/cm²; kg/cm²)	X 14.223	= Pounds-force per square inch (psi; lbf/in²; lb/in²)
Pounds-force per square inch (psi; lbf/in²; lb/in²)	X 0.068	= Atmospheres (atm)	X 14.696	= Pounds-force per square inch (psi; lbf/in²; lb/in²)
Pounds-force per square inch (psi; lbf/in²; lb/in²)	X 0.069	= Bars	X 14.5	= Pounds-force per square inch (psi; lbf/in²; lb/in²)
Pounds-force per square inch (psi; lbf/in²; lb/in²)	X 6.895	= Kilopascals (kPa)	X 0.145	= Pounds-force per square inch (psi; lbf/in²; lb/in²)
Kilopascals (kPa)	X 0.01	= Kilograms-force per square centimeter (kgf/cm²; kg/cm²)	X 98.1	= Kilopascals (kPa)

Torque (moment of force)

Pounds-force inches (lbf in; lb in)	X 1.152	= Kilograms-force centimeter (kgf cm; kg cm)	X 0.868	= Pounds-force inches (lbf in; lb in)
Pounds-force inches (lbf in; lb in)	X 0.113	= Newton meters (Nm)	X 8.85	= Pounds-force inches (lbf in; lb in)
Pounds-force inches (lbf in; lb in)	X 0.083	= Pounds-force feet (lbf ft; lb ft)	X 12	= Pounds-force inches (lbf in; lb in)
Pounds-force feet (lbf ft; lb ft)	X 0.138	= Kilograms-force meters (kgf m; kg m)	X 7.233	= Pounds-force feet (lbf ft; lb ft)
Pounds-force feet (lbf ft; lb ft)	X 1.356	= Newton meters (Nm)	X 0.738	= Pounds-force feet (lbf ft; lb ft)
Newton meters (Nm)	X 0.102	= Kilograms-force meters (kgf m; kg m)	X 9.804	= Newton meters (Nm)

Vacuum

Inches mercury (in. Hg)	X 3.377	= Kilopascals (kPa)	X 0.2961	= Inches mercury
Inches mercury (in. Hg)	X 25.4	= Millimeters mercury (mm Hg)	X 0.0394	= Inches mercury

Power

Horsepower (hp)	X 745.7	= Watts (W)	X 0.0013	= Horsepower (hp)

Velocity (speed)

Miles per hour (miles/hr; mph)	X 1.609	= Kilometers per hour (km/hr; kph)	X 0.621	= Miles per hour (miles/hr; mph)

Fuel consumption*

Miles per gallon, Imperial (mpg)	X 0.354	= Kilometers per liter (km/l)	X 2.825	= Miles per gallon, Imperial (mpg)
Miles per gallon, US (mpg)	X 0.425	= Kilometers per liter (km/l)	X 2.352	= Miles per gallon, US (mpg)

Temperature

Degrees Fahrenheit = (°C x 1.8) + 32   Degrees Celsius (Degrees Centigrade; °C) = (°F - 32) x 0.56

*It is common practice to convert from miles per gallon (mpg) to liters/100 kilometers (l/100km), where mpg (Imperial) x l/100 km = 282 and mpg (US) x l/100 km = 235

DECIMALS to MILLIMETERS

Decimal	mm	Decimal	mm
0.001	0.0254	0.500	12.7000
0.002	0.0508	0.510	12.9540
0.003	0.0762	0.520	13.2080
0.004	0.1016	0.530	13.4620
0.005	0.1270	0.540	13.7160
0.006	0.1524	0.550	13.9700
0.007	0.1778	0.560	14.2240
0.008	0.2032	0.570	14.4780
0.009	0.2286	0.580	14.7320
		0.590	14.9860
0.010	0.2540		
0.020	0.5080		
0.030	0.7620		
0.040	1.0160	0.600	15.2400
0.050	1.2700	0.610	15.4940
0.060	1.5240	0.620	15.7480
0.070	1.7780	0.630	16.0020
0.080	2.0320	0.640	16.2560
0.090	2.2860	0.650	16.5100
		0.660	16.7640
0.100	2.5400	0.670	17.0180
0.110	2.7940	0.680	17.2720
0.120	3.0480	0.690	17.5260
0.130	3.3020		
0.140	3.5560		
0.150	3.8100		
0.160	4.0640	0.700	17.7800
0.170	4.3180	0.710	18.0340
0.180	4.5720	0.720	18.2880
0.190	4.8260	0.730	18.5420
		0.740	18.7960
0.200	5.0800	0.750	19.0500
0.210	5.3340	0.760	19.3040
0.220	5.5880	0.770	19.5580
0.230	5.8420	0.780	19.8120
0.240	6.0960	0.790	20.0660
0.250	6.3500		
0.260	6.6040		
0.270	6.8580	0.800	20.3200
0.280	7.1120	0.810	20.5740
0.290	7.3660	0.820	21.8280
		0.830	21.0820
0.300	7.6200	0.840	21.3360
0.310	7.8740	0.850	21.5900
0.320	8.1280	0.860	21.8440
0.330	8.3820	0.870	22.0980
0.340	8.6360	0.880	22.3520
0.350	8.8900	0.890	22.6060
0.360	9.1440		
0.370	9.3980		
0.380	9.6520		
0.390	9.9060	0.900	22.8600
0.400	10.1600	0.910	23.1140
0.410	10.4140	0.920	23.3680
0.420	10.6680	0.930	23.6220
0.430	10.9220	0.940	23.8760
0.440	11.1760	0.950	24.1300
0.450	11.4300	0.960	24.3840
0.460	11.6840	0.970	24.6380
0.470	11.9380	0.980	24.8920
0.480	12.1920	0.990	25.1460
0.490	12.4460	1.000	25.4000

FRACTIONS to DECIMALS to MILLIMETERS

Fraction	Decimal	mm	Fraction	Decimal	mm
1/64	0.0156	0.3969	33/64	0.5156	13.0969
1/32	0.0312	0.7938	17/32	0.5312	13.4938
3/64	0.0469	1.1906	35/64	0.5469	13.8906
1/16	0.0625	1.5875	9/16	0.5625	14.2875
5/64	0.0781	1.9844	37/64	0.5781	14.6844
3/32	0.0938	2.3812	19/32	0.5938	15.0812
7/64	0.1094	2.7781	39/64	0.6094	15.4781
1/8	0.1250	3.1750	5/8	0.6250	15.8750
9/64	0.1406	3.5719	41/64	0.6406	16.2719
5/32	0.1562	3.9688	21/32	0.6562	16.6688
11/64	0.1719	4.3656	43/64	0.6719	17.0656
3/16	0.1875	4.7625	11/16	0.6875	17.4625
13/64	0.2031	5.1594	45/64	0.7031	17.8594
7/32	0.2188	5.5562	23/32	0.7188	18.2562
15/64	0.2344	5.9531	47/64	0.7344	18.6531
1/4	0.2500	6.3500	3/4	0.7500	19.0500
17/64	0.2656	6.7469	49/64	0.7656	19.4469
9/32	0.2812	7.1438	25/32	0.7812	19.8438
19/64	0.2969	7.5406	51/64	0.7969	20.2406
5/16	0.3125	7.9375	13/16	0.8125	20.6375
21/64	0.3281	8.3344	53/64	0.8281	21.0344
11/32	0.3438	8.7312	27/32	0.8438	21.4312
23/64	0.3594	9.1281	55/64	0.8594	21.8281
3/8	0.3750	9.5250	7/8	0.8750	22.2250
25/64	0.3906	9.9219	57/64	0.8906	22.6219
13/32	0.4062	10.3188	29/32	0.9062	23.0188
27/64	0.4219	10.7156	59/64	0.9219	23.4156
7/16	0.4375	11.1125	15/16	0.9375	23.8125
29/64	0.4531	11.5094	61/64	0.9531	24.2094
15/32	0.4688	11.9062	31/32	0.9688	24.6062
31/64	0.4844	12.3031	63/64	0.9844	25.0031
1/2	0.5000	12.7000	1	1.0000	25.4000

Safety first!

Regardless of how enthusiastic you may be about getting on with the job at hand, take the time to ensure that your safety is not jeopardized. A moment's lack of attention can result in an accident, as can failure to observe certain simple safety precautions. The possibility of an accident will always exist, and the following points should not be considered a comprehensive list of all dangers. Rather, they are intended to make you aware of the risks and to encourage a safety conscious approach to all work you carry out on your vehicle.

Essential DOs and DON'Ts

DON'T rely on a jack when working under the vehicle. Always use approved jackstands to support the weight of the vehicle and place them under the recommended lift or support points.

DON'T attempt to loosen extremely tight fasteners (i.e. wheel lug nuts) while the vehicle is on a jack - it may fall.

DON'T start the engine without first making sure that the transmission is in Neutral (or Park where applicable) and the parking brake is set.

DON'T remove the radiator cap from a hot cooling system - let it cool or cover it with a cloth and release the pressure gradually.

DON'T attempt to drain the engine oil until you are sure it has cooled to the point that it will not burn you.

DON'T touch any part of the engine or exhaust system until it has cooled sufficiently to avoid burns.

DON'T siphon toxic liquids such as gasoline, antifreeze and brake fluid by mouth, or allow them to remain on your skin.

DON'T inhale brake lining dust - it is potentially hazardous (see *Asbestos* below).

DON'T allow spilled oil or grease to remain on the floor - wipe it up before someone slips on it.

DON'T use loose fitting wrenches or other tools which may slip and cause injury.

DON'T push on wrenches when loosening or tightening nuts or bolts. Always try to pull the wrench toward you. If the situation calls for pushing the wrench away, push with an open hand to avoid scraped knuckles if the wrench should slip.

DON'T attempt to lift a heavy component alone - get someone to help you.

DON'T rush or take unsafe shortcuts to finish a job.

DON'T allow children or animals in or around the vehicle while you are working on it.

DO wear eye protection when using power tools such as a drill, sander, bench grinder, etc. and when working under a vehicle.

DO keep loose clothing and long hair well out of the way of moving parts.

DO make sure that any hoist used has a safe working load rating adequate for the job.

DO get someone to check on you periodically when working alone on a vehicle.

DO carry out work in a logical sequence and make sure that everything is correctly assembled and tightened.

DO keep chemicals and fluids tightly capped and out of the reach of children and pets.

DO remember that your vehicle's safety affects that of yourself and others. If in doubt on any point, get professional advice.

Steering, suspension and brakes

These systems are essential to driving safety, so make sure you have a qualified shop or individual check your work. Also, compressed suspension springs can cause injury if released suddenly - be sure to use a spring compressor.

Airbags

Airbags are explosive devices that can **CAUSE** injury if they deploy while you're working on the vehicle. Follow the manufacturer's instructions to disable the airbag whenever you're working in the vicinity of airbag components.

Asbestos

Certain friction, insulating, sealing, and other products - such as brake linings, brake bands, clutch linings, torque converters, gaskets, etc. - may contain asbestos or other hazardous friction material. Extreme care must be taken to avoid inhalation of dust from such products, since it is hazardous to health. If in doubt, assume that they do contain asbestos.

Fire

Remember at all times that gasoline is highly flammable. Never smoke or have any kind of open flame around when working on a vehicle. But the risk does not end there. A spark caused by an electrical short circuit, by two metal surfaces contacting each other, or even by static electricity built up in your body under certain conditions, can ignite gasoline vapors, which in a confined space are highly explosive. Do not, under any circumstances, use gasoline for cleaning parts. Use an approved safety solvent.

Always disconnect the battery ground (-) cable at the battery before working on any part of the fuel system or electrical system. Never risk spilling fuel on a hot engine or exhaust component. It is strongly recommended that a fire extinguisher suitable for use on fuel and electrical fires be kept handy in the garage or workshop at all times. Never try to extinguish a fuel or electrical fire with water.

Fumes

Certain fumes are highly toxic and can quickly cause unconsciousness and even death if inhaled to any extent. Gasoline vapor falls into this category, as do the vapors from some cleaning solvents. Any draining or pouring of such volatile fluids should be done in a well ventilated area.

When using cleaning fluids and solvents, read the instructions on the container carefully. Never use materials from unmarked containers.

Never run the engine in an enclosed space, such as a garage. Exhaust fumes contain carbon monoxide, which is extremely poisonous. If you need to run the engine, always do so in the open air, or at least have the rear of the vehicle outside the work area.

The battery

Never create a spark or allow a bare light bulb near a battery. They normally give off a certain amount of hydrogen gas, which is highly explosive.

Always disconnect the battery ground (-) cable at the battery before working on the fuel or electrical systems.

If possible, loosen the filler caps or cover when charging the battery from an external source (this does not apply to sealed or maintenance-free batteries). Do not charge at an excessive rate or the battery may burst.

Take care when adding water to a non maintenance-free battery and when carrying a battery. The electrolyte, even when diluted, is very corrosive and should not be allowed to contact clothing or skin.

Always wear eye protection when cleaning the battery to prevent the caustic deposits from entering your eyes.

Household current

When using an electric power tool, inspection light, etc., which operates on household current, always make sure that the tool is correctly connected to its plug and that, where necessary, it is properly grounded. Do not use such items in damp conditions and, again, do not create a spark or apply excessive heat in the vicinity of fuel or fuel vapor.

Secondary ignition system voltage

A severe electric shock can result from touching certain parts of the ignition system (such as the spark plug wires) when the engine is running or being cranked, particularly if components are damp or the insulation is defective. In the case of an electronic ignition system, the secondary system voltage is much higher and could prove fatal.

Hydrofluoric acid

This extremely corrosive acid is formed when certain types of synthetic rubber, found in some O-rings, oil seals, fuel hoses, etc. are exposed to temperatures above 750-degrees F (400-degrees C). The rubber changes into a charred or sticky substance containing the acid. *Once formed, the acid remains dangerous for years. If it gets onto the skin, it may be necessary to amputate the limb concerned.*

When dealing with a vehicle which has suffered a fire, or with components salvaged from such a vehicle, wear protective gloves and discard them after use.

Troubleshooting

Contents

This section provides an easy reference guide to the more common problems which may occur during the operation of your vehicle. These problems and their possible causes are grouped under headings denoting various components or systems, such as Engine, Cooling system, etc. They also refer you to the chapter and/or section which deals with the problem.

Remember that successful troubleshooting is not a mysterious black art practiced only by professional mechanics. It is simply the result of the right knowledge combined with an intelligent, systematic approach to the problem. Always work by a process of elimination, starting with the simplest solution and working through to the most complex - and never overlook the obvious. Anyone can run the gas tank dry or leave the lights on overnight, so don't assume that you are exempt from such oversights.

Finally, always establish a clear idea of why a problem has occurred and take steps to ensure that it doesn't happen again. If the electrical system fails because of a poor connection, check the other connections in the system to make sure that they don't fail as well. If a particular fuse continues to blow, find out why - don't just replace one fuse after another. Remember, failure of a small component can often be indicative of potential failure or incorrect functioning of a more important component or system.

Engine and performance

1 Engine will not rotate when attempting to start

1 Battery terminal connections loose or corroded (Chapter 1).
2 Battery discharged or faulty (Chapter 1).
3 Automatic transaxle not completely engaged in Park (Chapter 7B).
4 Broken, loose or disconnected wiring in the starting circuit (Chapters 5 and 12).
5 Starter motor pinion jammed in flywheel ring gear (Chapter 5).
6 Starter solenoid faulty (Chapter 5).
7 Starter motor faulty (Chapter 5).
8 Ignition switch faulty (Chapter 12).
9 Transmission Range (TR) sensor faulty (Chapter 6).
10 Starter pinion or driveplate teeth worn or broken (Chapter 5).

2 Engine rotates but will not start

1 Fuel tank empty.
2 Battery discharged (engine rotates slowly) (Chapter 5).
3 Battery terminal connections loose or corroded (Chapter 1).
4 Leaking fuel injector(s), fuel pump, pressure regulator, etc. (Chapter 4).
5 Fuel not reaching fuel injection system (Chapter 4).
6 Broken timing belt or chain (Chapter 2A).
7 Ignition system problem (Chapter 5).
8 Defective crankshaft sensor or camshaft sensor (Chapter 6).

3 Engine hard to start when cold

1 Battery discharged or low (Chapter 1).
2 Fuel system malfunctioning (Chapter 4).
3 Emissions or engine control system malfunctioning (Chapter 6).

4 Engine hard to start when hot

1 Air filter clogged (Chapter 1).
2 Fuel not reaching the fuel injection system (Chapter 4).

3 Corroded battery connections, especially ground (Chapter 1).
4 Emissions or engine control system malfunctioning (Chapter 6).

5 Starter motor noisy or excessively rough in engagement

1 Pinion or driveplate gear teeth worn or broken (Chapter 5).
2 Starter motor mounting bolts loose or missing (Chapter 5).

6 Engine starts but stops immediately

1 Insufficient fuel reaching the fuel injectors (Chapter 4).
2 Vacuum leak at the gasket between the intake manifold/plenum and throttle body (Chapters 1 and 4).
3 Restricted exhaust system (most likely the catalytic converter) (Chapters 4 and 6).

7 Oil puddle under engine

1 Oil pan gasket and/or oil pan drain bolt seal leaking (Chapters 1 or 2A).
2 Oil pressure sending unit leaking (Chapter 2B).
3 Rocker arm cover gaskets leaking (Chapter 2A).
4 Engine oil seals leaking (Chapter 2A).

8 Engine lopes while idling or idles erratically

1 Vacuum leakage (Chapter 4).
2 Leaking EGR valve or plugged PCV valve (Chapter 6).
3 Air filter clogged (Chapter 1).
4 Fuel pump not delivering sufficient fuel to the fuel injection system (Chapter 4).
5 Leaking head gasket (Chapter 2A).
6 Camshaft lobes worn (Chapter 2A).

9 Engine misses at idle speed

1 Spark plugs worn or not gapped properly (Chapter 1).
2 Faulty coil(s) (Chapter 5).
3 Vacuum leaks (Chapters 1 and 4).
4 Uneven or low compression (Chapter 2B).

10 Engine misses throughout driving speed range

1 Fuel filter clogged and/or impurities in the fuel system (Chapter 4).
2 Low fuel pressure (Chapter 4).
3 Faulty or incorrectly gapped spark plugs (Chapter 1).
4 Faulty emission system components (Chapter 6).
5 Low or uneven cylinder compression pressures (Chapter 2B).
6 Weak or faulty ignition system (Chapter 5).
7 Vacuum leak (Chapter 2B).

11 Engine stumbles on acceleration

1 Spark plugs fouled (Chapter 1).
2 Fuel injection system problem (Chapter 4).
3 Fuel filter clogged (Chapter 4).
4 Intake manifold air leak (Chapter 4).
5 Problem with emissions/engine control system (Chapter 6).

12 Engine surges while holding accelerator steady

1 Intake air leak (Chapter 4).
2 Fuel pump faulty (Chapter 4).
3 Problem with the fuel injection system (Chapter 4).
4 Problem with the emission or engine control system (Chapter 6).

13 Engine stalls

1 Fuel filter clogged and/or water and impurities in the fuel system (Chapter 4).
2 Faulty emissions or engine control system components (Chapter 6).
3 Faulty or incorrectly gapped spark plugs (Chapter 1).
4 Vacuum leak (Chapter 2B).

14 Engine lacks power

1   Faulty or incorrectly gapped spark plugs (Chapter 1).
2   Restricted exhaust system (most likely the catalytic converter) (Chapters 4 and 6).
3   Fuel injection system malfunctioning (Chapter 4).
4   Faulty coil(s) (Chapter 5).
5   Brakes binding (Chapter 9).
6   Automatic transaxle fluid level incorrect (Chapter 1).
7   Fuel filter clogged and/or impurities in the fuel system (Chapter 1).
8   Emission control system not functioning properly (Chapter 6).
9   Low or uneven cylinder compression pressures (Chapter 2B).

15 Engine backfires

1   Emissions system not functioning properly (Chapter 6).
2   Fuel injection system malfunctioning (Chapter 4).
3   Vacuum leak at fuel injectors, intake manifold or vacuum hoses (Chapter 4).
4   Valves sticking (Chapter 2A).
5   Timing chain worn (Chapter 2A).

16 Pinging or knocking engine sounds during acceleration or uphill

1   Incorrect grade of fuel.
2   Fuel injection system malfunctioning (Chapter 4).
3   Improper or damaged spark plugs (Chapter 1).
4   Worn or damaged ignition components (Chapter 5).
5   Faulty emissions or engine control system (Chapter 6).
6   Vacuum leak (Chapter 2B).

17 Engine runs with oil pressure light on

1   Low oil level (Chapter 1).
2   Short in wiring circuit (Chapter 12).
3   Faulty oil pressure sender (Chapter 2B).
4   Oil viscosity too low or oil diluted.
5   Worn engine bearings and/or oil pump (Chapter 2B).

18 Engine continues to run after switching off

1   Excessive engine operating temperature (Chapter 3).

2   Excessive carbon deposits on valves and pistons.
3   Leaking fuel injector(s).

Engine electrical system

19 Battery will not hold a charge

1   Drivebelt or tensioner defective (Chapter 1).
2   Battery terminals loose or corroded (Chapter 1).
3   Alternator not charging properly (Chapter 5).
4   Loose, broken or faulty wiring in the charging circuit (Chapter 5).
5   Internally defective battery (Chapters 1 and 5).

20 Voltage warning light fails to go out

1   Faulty alternator or charging circuit (Chapter 5).
2   Drivebelt or tensioner defective (Chapter 1).
3   Alternator voltage regulator inoperative (Chapter 5).

21 Voltage warning light fails to come on when key is turned on

1   Warning light bulb defective (Chapter 12).
2   Fault in the printed circuit, dash wiring or bulb holder (Chapter 12).

Fuel system

22 Excessive fuel consumption

1   Dirty or clogged air filter element (Chapter 1).
2   Emissions or engine control system not functioning properly (Chapter 6).
3   Fuel injection system malfunctioning (Chapter 4).
4   Low tire pressure or incorrect tire size (Chapter 1).

23 Fuel leakage and/or fuel odor

1   Leak in a fuel feed or vent line (Chapter 4).
2   Tank overfilled.
3   Evaporative emissions control canister defective (Chapter 6).
4   Fuel injector seals faulty (Chapter 4).

Cooling system

24 Overheating

1   Insufficient coolant in system (Chapter 1).
2   Drivebelt or tensioner defective (Chapter 1).
3   Radiator core blocked or grille restricted (Chapter 3).
4   Thermostat faulty (Chapter 3).
5   Electric cooling fan blades broken or cracked (Chapter 3).
6   Radiator cap not maintaining proper pressure (Chapter 3).
7   Faulty water pump (Chapter 3).

25 Overcooling

Incorrect (opening temperature too low) or faulty thermostat (Chapter 3).

26 External coolant leakage

1   Deteriorated/damaged hoses or loose clamps (Chapters 1 and 3).
2   Water pump seal defective (Chapter 3).
3   Leakage from radiator core (Chapter 3).
4   Engine drain or water jacket core plugs leaking (Chapter 2B).

27 Internal coolant leakage

1   Leaking cylinder head gasket (Chapter 2A).
2   Cracked cylinder bore or cylinder head (Chapter 2B).

28 Coolant loss

1   Too much coolant in system (Chapter 1).
2   Coolant boiling away because of overheating (Chapter 3).
3   Internal or external leakage (Chapter 3).
4   Faulty radiator cap (Chapter 3).

29 Poor coolant circulation

1   Inoperative water pump (Chapter 3).
2   Restriction in cooling system (Chapters 1 and 3).
3   Drivebelt or tensioner defective or out of adjustment (Chapter 1).
4   Thermostat sticking (Chapter 3).

Clutch

30 Pedal travels to floor - no pressure or very little resistance

Broken release bearing or fork (Chapter 8).

31 Unable to select gears

1 Faulty transaxle (Chapter 7A).
2 Faulty clutch disc or pressure plate (Chapter 8).
3 Faulty release bearing (Chapter 8).
4 Faulty shift lever assembly or cable (Chapter 7A).

32 Clutch slips (engine speed increases with no increase in vehicle speed)

1 Clutch plate worn (Chapter 8).
2 Clutch plate is oil soaked by leaking rear main seal or transaxle input shaft seal (Chapter 8).
3 Clutch plate not seated (Chapter 8).
4 Warped pressure plate or flywheel (Chapter 8).
5 Weak diaphragm springs (Chapter 8).
6 Clutch plate overheated. Allow to cool.

33 Grabbing (chattering) as clutch is engaged

1 Oil on clutch plate lining, burned or glazed facings (Chapter 2A).
2 Worn or loose engine or transaxle mounts (Chapter 2A and 7A).
3 Worn splines on clutch plate hub (Chapter 8).
4 Warped pressure plate or flywheel (Chapter 2A or 8).
5 Burned or smeared resin on flywheel or pressure plate (Chapter 2A or 8).

34 Transaxle rattling (clicking)

1 Release fork loose (Chapter 8).
2 Low engine idle speed (Chapter 6).

35 Noise in clutch area

Faulty release bearing (Chapter 8).

36 Clutch pedal stays on floor

1 Broken release bearing or fork (Chapter 8).
2 Broken or disconnected clutch cable (Chapter 7A or 8).

37 High pedal effort

1 Binding clutch cable (Chapter 7A).
2 Pressure plate faulty (Chapter 8).

Manual transaxle

38 Knocking noise at low speeds

1 Worn driveaxle constant velocity (CV) joints (Chapter 8).
2 Worn side gear shaft counterbore in differential case (Chapter 8).*

39 Noise most pronounced when turning

Differential gear noise (Chapter 8).*

40 Clunk on acceleration or deceleration

1 Loose engine or transaxle mounts (Chapters 2A and 7A).
2 Worn differential pinion shaft in case.*
3 Worn side gear shaft counterbore in differential case (Chapter 8).*
4 Worn or damaged driveaxle inboard CV joints (Chapter 8).

41 Clicking noise in turns

Worn or damaged outboard CV joint (Chapter 8).

42 Vibration

1 Rough wheel bearing (Chapters 1 and 10).
2 Damaged driveaxle (Chapter 8).
3 Out of round tires (Chapter 10).
4 Tire out of balance (Chapters 1 and 10).
5 Worn CV joint (Chapter 8).

43 Noisy in neutral with engine running

1 Damaged input gear bearing (Chapter 7A).*
2 Damaged clutch release bearing (Chapter 8).

44 Noisy in one particular gear

1 Damaged or worn constant mesh gears (Chapter 7A).*

2 Damaged or worn synchronizers (Chapter 7A).*
3 Bent reverse fork (Chapter 7A).*
4 Damaged fourth speed gear or output gear (Chapter 7A).*
5 Worn or damaged reverse idler gear or idler bushing (Chapter 7A).*

45 Noisy in all gears

1 Insufficient lubricant (Chapter 1).
2 Damaged or worn bearings (Chapter 7A).*
3 Worn or damaged input gear shaft and/or output gear shaft (Chapter 7A).*

46 Slips out of gear

1 Worn or improperly adjusted linkage (Chapter 7A).
2 Shift linkage does not work freely, binds (Chapter 7A).
3 Input gear bearing retainer broken or loose.*
4 Worn shift fork (Chapter 7A).*

47 Leaks lubricant

1 Driveshaft seals worn (Chapter 8).
2 Excessive amount of lubricant in transaxle (Chapters 1 and 7A).
3 Loose or broken input gear shaft bearing retainer (Chapter 7A).*
4 Input gear bearing retainer O-ring and/or lip seal damaged (Chapter 7A).*
5 Vehicle speed sensor O-ring leaking (Chapter 7A).

48 Hard to shift

1 Shift linkage loose or worn (Chapter 7A).

Note: * *Although the corrective action necessary to remedy the symptoms described is beyond the scope of this manual, the above information should be helpful in isolating the cause of the condition so that the owner can communicate clearly with a professional mechanic.*

Automatic transaxle

49 Fluid leakage

1 Automatic transmission fluid is a deep red color. Fluid leaks should not be confused with engine oil, which can easily be blown by airflow to the transaxle.
2 To pinpoint a leak, first remove all built-up dirt and grime from the transaxle housing with degreasing agents and/or steam cleaning. Drive the vehicle at low speeds so air flow will

not blow the leak far from its source. Raise the vehicle and determine where the leak is coming from. Common areas of leakage are:

a) *Fluid pan (Chapter 1)*
b) *Fluid cooler lines*
c) *Vehicle Speed Sensor (Chapter 6)*

50   Transaxle fluid brown or has a burned smell

Transaxle overheated. Change fluid (Chapter 1).

51   General shift mechanism problems

1   Chapter 7B deals with checking and adjusting the shift cable on automatic transaxles. Common problems which may be attributed to a poorly adjusted cable are:

a) *Engine starting in gears other than Park or Neutral.*
b) *Indicator on shifter pointing to a gear other than the one actually being used.*
c) *Vehicle moves when in Park.*

52   Engine will start in gears other than Park or Neutral

Transmission Range (TR) sensor malfunctioning (Chapter 6).

53   Transaxle slips, shifts roughly, is noisy or has no drive in forward or reverse gears

1   There are many probable causes for the above problems, but the home mechanic should be concerned with only one possibility - fluid level. Before taking the vehicle to a repair shop, check the level and condition of the fluid as described in Chapter 1 .

2   Correct the fluid level as necessary or change the fluid and filter if needed. If the problem persists, have a professional diagnose the probable cause.

Driveaxles

54   Clicking noise in turns

Worn or damaged outer CV joint. Check for cut or damaged boots (Chapter 1). Repair as necessary (Chapter 8).

55   Knock or clunk when accelerating after coasting

Worn or damaged CV joint. Check for cut or damaged boots (Chapter 1). Repair as necessary (Chapter 8).

56   Shudder or vibration during acceleration

1   Worn or damaged CV joints. Repair or replace as necessary (Chapter 8).

2   Sticking inner joint assembly. Correct or replace as necessary (Chapter 8).

Brakes

57   Vehicle pulls to one side during braking

1   Incorrect tire pressures (Chapter 1).

2   Front end out of alignment (have the front end aligned).

3   Unmatched tires on same axle.

4   Restricted brake lines or hoses (Chapter 9).

5   Sticking caliper or wheel cylinder piston (Chapter 9).

6   Loose suspension parts (Chapter 10).

7   Contaminated brake pad material (Chapter 9).

58   Noise (grinding or high-pitched squeal) when the brakes are applied

Disc brake pads worn out. Replace pads with new ones immediately (Chapter 9).

59   Brake roughness or chatter (pedal pulsates)

1   Excessive brake disc lateral runout.

2   Parallelism of disc not within specifications (Chapter 9).

3   Defective brake disc (Chapter 9).

60   Excessive pedal effort required to stop vehicle

1   Malfunctioning power brake booster (Chapter 9).

2   Partial system failure (Chapter 9).

3   Excessively worn pads (Chapter 9).

4   One or more caliper or wheel cylinder pistons seized or sticking (Chapter 9).

5   Brake pads contaminated with oil or grease (Chapter 9).

6   New pads or shoes installed and not yet seated. It will take a while for the new material to seat.

61   Excessive brake pedal travel

1   Partial brake system failure (Chapter 9).

2   Insufficient fluid in master cylinder (Chapters 1 and 9).

3   Air trapped in system (Chapter 9).

4   Faulty master cylinder (Chapter 9).

62   Dragging brakes

1   Master cylinder pistons not returning correctly (Chapter 9).

2   Restricted brake lines or hoses (Chapters 1 and 9).

3   Incorrect parking brake adjustment (Chapter 9).

4   Defective brake calipers (Chapter 9).

63   Grabbing or uneven braking action

Contaminated brake pads (Chapter 9).

64   Brake pedal feels spongy when depressed

1   Air in hydraulic lines (Chapter 9).

2   Master cylinder mounting bolts loose (Chapter 9).

3   Master cylinder defective (Chapter 9).

65   Brake pedal travels to the floor with little resistance

Little or no fluid in the master cylinder reservoir caused by leaking caliper, or loose, damaged or disconnected brake lines (Chapter 9).

66   Parking brake does not hold

Parking brake cables improperly adjusted (Chapter 9).

Suspension and steering systems

67   Vehicle pulls to one side

1   Mismatched or uneven tires (Chapter 10).

2   Broken or sagging coil springs (Chapter 10).

3   Wheel alignment incorrect.

4   Front brakes dragging (Chapter 9).

68   Abnormal or excessive tire wear

1   Front wheel alignment incorrect.
2   Sagging or broken springs (Chapter 10).
3   Tire out-of-balance (Chapter 10).
4   Worn strut or shock absorber (Chapter 10).
5   Overloaded vehicle.
6   Tires not rotated regularly.

69   Wheel makes a thumping noise

1   Blister or bump on tire (Chapter 1).
2   Improper strut or shock absorber action (Chapter 10).

70   Shimmy, shake or vibration

1   Tire or wheel out-of-balance or out-of-round (Chapter 10).
2   Worn wheel bearings (Chapter 10).
3   Worn tie-rod ends (Chapter 10).
4   Worn balljoints (Chapter 10).
5   Excessive wheel runout (Chapter 10).
6   Blister or bump on tire (Chapter 1).

71   Hard steering

1   Balljoints, tie-rod ends or steering gear worn (Chapter 10).
2   Front wheel alignment incorrect.
3   Low tire pressure (Chapter 1).

72   Steering wheel does not return to center position correctly

1   Balljoints or tie-rod ends worn (Chapters 1 and 10).
2   Defective rack-and-pinion assembly (Chapter 10).
3   Front wheel alignment problem.

73   Abnormal noise at the front end

1   Balljoints or tie-rod ends worn (Chapter 1).
2   Loose upper strut mount (Chapter 10).
3   Worn tie-rod ends (Chapter 10).
4   Loose stabilizer bar (Chapter 10).
5   Loose wheel lug nuts (Chapter 1).
6   Loose suspension bolts (Chapter 10).

74   Wander or poor steering stability

1   Mismatched or uneven tires (Chapter 10).
2   Balljoints or tie-rod ends worn (Chapters 1 and 10).
3   Worn struts or shock absorbers (Chapter 10).
4   Broken or sagging springs (Chapter 10).
5   Front wheel alignment incorrect.
6   Worn steering gear clamp bushing (Chapter 10).

75   Erratic steering when braking

1   Wheel bearings worn (Chapter 10).
2   Broken or sagging springs (Chapter 10).
3   Leaking caliper (Chapter 9).
4   Warped brake discs (Chapter 9).
5   Worn steering gear clamp bushing (Chapter 10).
6   Wheel alignment incorrect.

76   Excessive pitching and/or rolling around corners or during braking

1   Loose stabilizer bar (Chapter 10).
2   Worn struts/shock absorbers or mounts (Chapter 10).
3   Broken or sagging coil springs (Chapter 10).
4   Overloaded vehicle.

77   Suspension bottoms

1   Overloaded vehicle.
2   Worn struts or shock absorbers (Chapter 10).
3   Incorrect, broken or sagging springs (Chapter 10).

78   Cupped tires

1   Front wheel alignment incorrect.
2   Worn struts or shock absorbers (Chapter 10).
3   Wheel bearings worn (Chapter 10).
4   Excessive tire or wheel runout (Chapter 10).
5   Worn balljoints (Chapter 10).

79   Excessive tire wear on outside edge

1   Inflation pressures incorrect (Chapter 1).
2   Excessive speed in turns.
3   Wheel alignment incorrect (excessive toe-in or positive camber). Have professionally aligned.
4   Suspension arm bent (Chapter 10).

80   Excessive tire wear on inside edge

1   Inflation pressures incorrect (Chapter 1).
2   Wheel alignment incorrect (toe-out or excessive negative camber). Have professionally aligned.
3   Loose or damaged steering components (Chapter 10).

81   Tire tread worn in one place

1   Tires out-of-balance.
2   Damaged wheel.
3   Defective tire (Chapter 1).

82   Excessive play or looseness in steering system

1   Wheel bearings worn (Chapter 10).
2   Tie-rod end loose or worn (Chapter 10).
3   Steering gear loose (Chapter 10).

83   Rattling or clicking noise in steering gear

1   Steering gear mounting bolts loose (Chapter 10).
2   Steering gear defective (Chapter 10).

Notes

Chapter 1
Tune-up and routine maintenance

Contents

Specifications

Recommended lubricants and fluids

Engine oil
    Type .... API "Certified for gasoline engines"
    Viscosity .... SAE 5W-20
Automatic transaxle fluid
    6-speed transaxle .... SK Energy ATF SP-4 Transmission Fluid or equivalent
    Continuously Variable Transaxle (CVT) .... Mopar® CVTF +4 Automatic Transmission Fluid or equivalent
Manual transaxle fluid .... Mopar® ATF +4 AutomaticTransmission Fluid or equivalent
Power steering fluid .... Mopar® ATF +4 AutomaticTransmission Fluid or equivalent
Rear differential .... Mopar® SAE 80W-90 API GL 5 Gear and Axle Lubricant or equivalent (non-synthetic).
Transfer case (PTU) .... Mopar® SAE 80W-90 API GL 5 Gear and Axle Lubricant or equivalent (non-synthetic).
Brake fluid .... DOT 3 brake fluid
Engine coolant
    2012 and earlier models .... 50/50 mixture of Mopar® 5 year/100,000 mile, antifreeze/coolant with HOAT (Hybrid Organic Additive Technology) and water*
    2013 and later models .... 50/50 mixture of Mopar® 10 year/150,000 mile, antifreeze/coolant with OAT (Organic Additive Technology) and water*
Door and liftgate latches .... Multi-purpose grease
Fuel filler door remote control latch mechanism .... Multi-purpose grease
Hood, door and liftgate hinge lubricant .... Engine oil
Key lock cylinder lubricant .... Graphite spray
Parking brake mechanism grease .... Mopar Spray White Lube or equivalent

*2012 and earlier vehicles are filled with a 50/50 mixture of Mopar 5 year/100,000 mile (HOAT) coolant and 2013 and later models are filled with 50/50 mixture of Mopar 10 year/150,000 mile (OAT) coolant. These coolants shouldn't be mixed with each other. Refer to the coolant reservoir label under the hood to determine what type coolant you have. Always refill with the correct coolant.

Capacities*

Engine oil (including filter)	4.5 quarts
Automatic transaxle**	
Drain and fill	
CVT models	7.4 quarts
6-speed models	5.0 quarts
Dry fill	
CVT models	8.55 quarts
6-speed models	7.5 quarts
Manual transaxle	
NV T355	2.5 to 2.8 quarts
AISIN BG6	2.1 quarts
Transfer case/power Transfer Unit (PTU)	18.2 ounces
Rear differential	16.2 ounces
Cooling system***	7.2 quarts

*All capacities approximate. Add as necessary to bring to appropriate level.

**The best way to determine the amount of fluid to add during a routine fluid change is to measure the amount drained. It's important to not overfill the transaxle.

***Includes heater and coolant reservoir.

Brakes

Disc brake pad wear limit (minimum)	1/16 inch
Drum brake shoe wear limit	1/16 inch

Ignition system

Spark plug type and gap	
Type	NGK - ZFR5F-11
Gap	0.043 inch
Firing order	1-3-4-2

Four cylinder location diagram

Torque specifications

Ft-lbs (unless otherwise indicated)   **Nm**

Note: *One foot-pound (ft-lb) of torque is equivalent to 12 inch-pounds (in-lbs) of torque. Torque values below approximately 15 ft-lbs are expressed in inch-pounds, because most foot-pound torque wrenches are not accurate at these smaller values.*

Automatic transaxle fluid pan bolts (CVT models)	70 in-lbs
Automatic transaxle oil strainer bolts (CVT models)	70 in-lbs
Automatic transaxle fluid drain plug (6-speed)	30
Automatic transaxle fluid fill/check plug	97 in-lbs
Manual transaxle fluid drain plug	120 in-lbs
Transfer case/Power Transfer Unit drain and fill plugs	24
Drivebelt tensioner mounting bolt	18
Engine oil drain plug	30
Spark plugs	20
Wheel lug nuts	100

2.2a Typical engine compartment layout – 2.4L engine shown, other models similar

1 Brake fluid reservoir	5 Battery (under air inlet duct)	9 Coolant reservoir
2 Air filter housing	6 Cooling system pressure cap	10 Windshield washer fluid reservoir
3 Underhood fuse/relay block	7 Engine oil dipstick	11 Power steering fluid reservoir
4 Remote negative battery terminal	8 Engine oil filler cap	

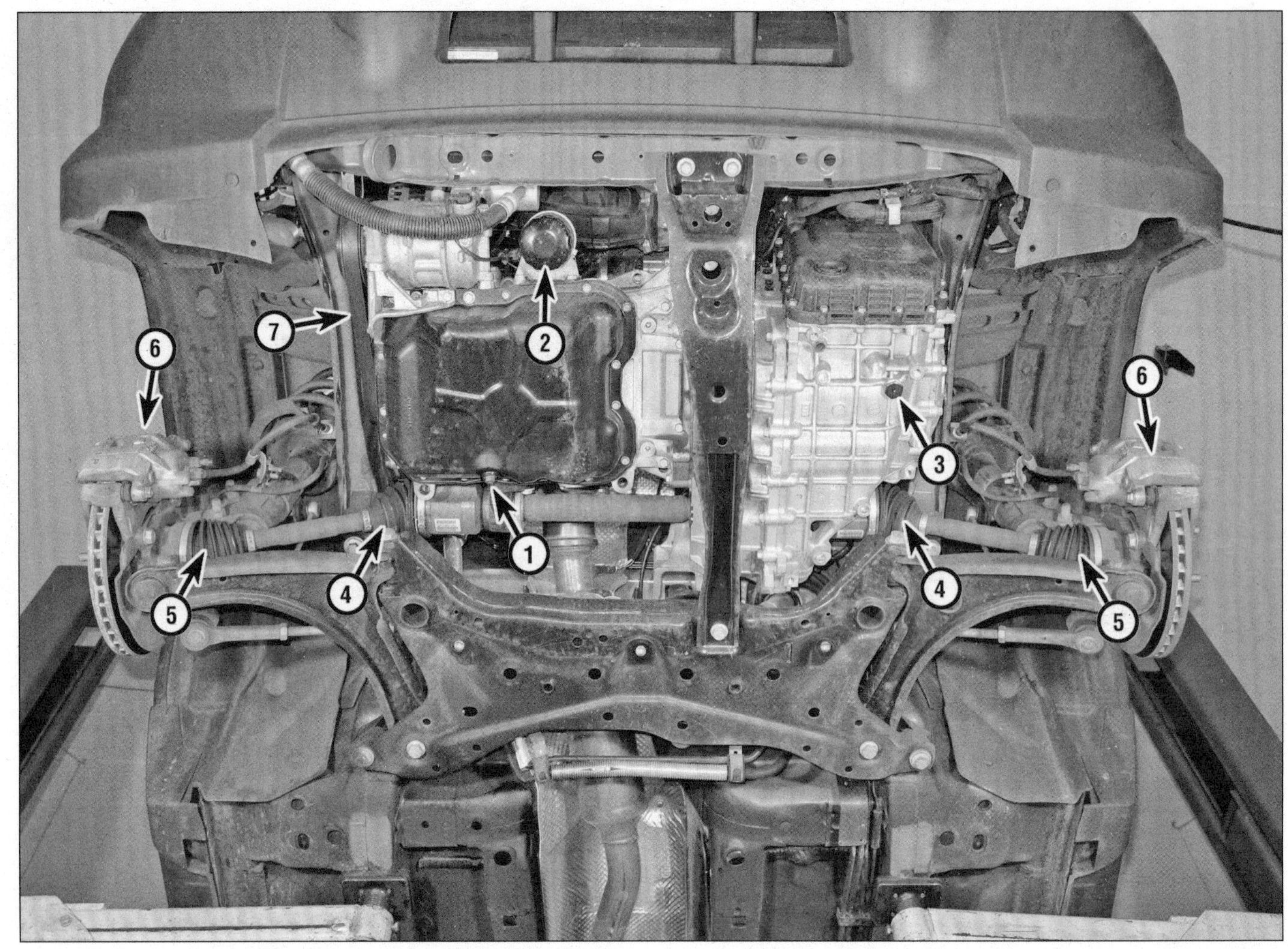

2.2b Typical engine compartment underside components - 2.4L 2WD model shown, other models similar

1   Engine oil drain plug
2   Oil filter
3   Automatic transaxle fluid drain plug
     (6-speed transaxle)
4   Inner driveaxle boots
5   Outer driveaxle boots
6   Brake calipers
7   Drivebelt

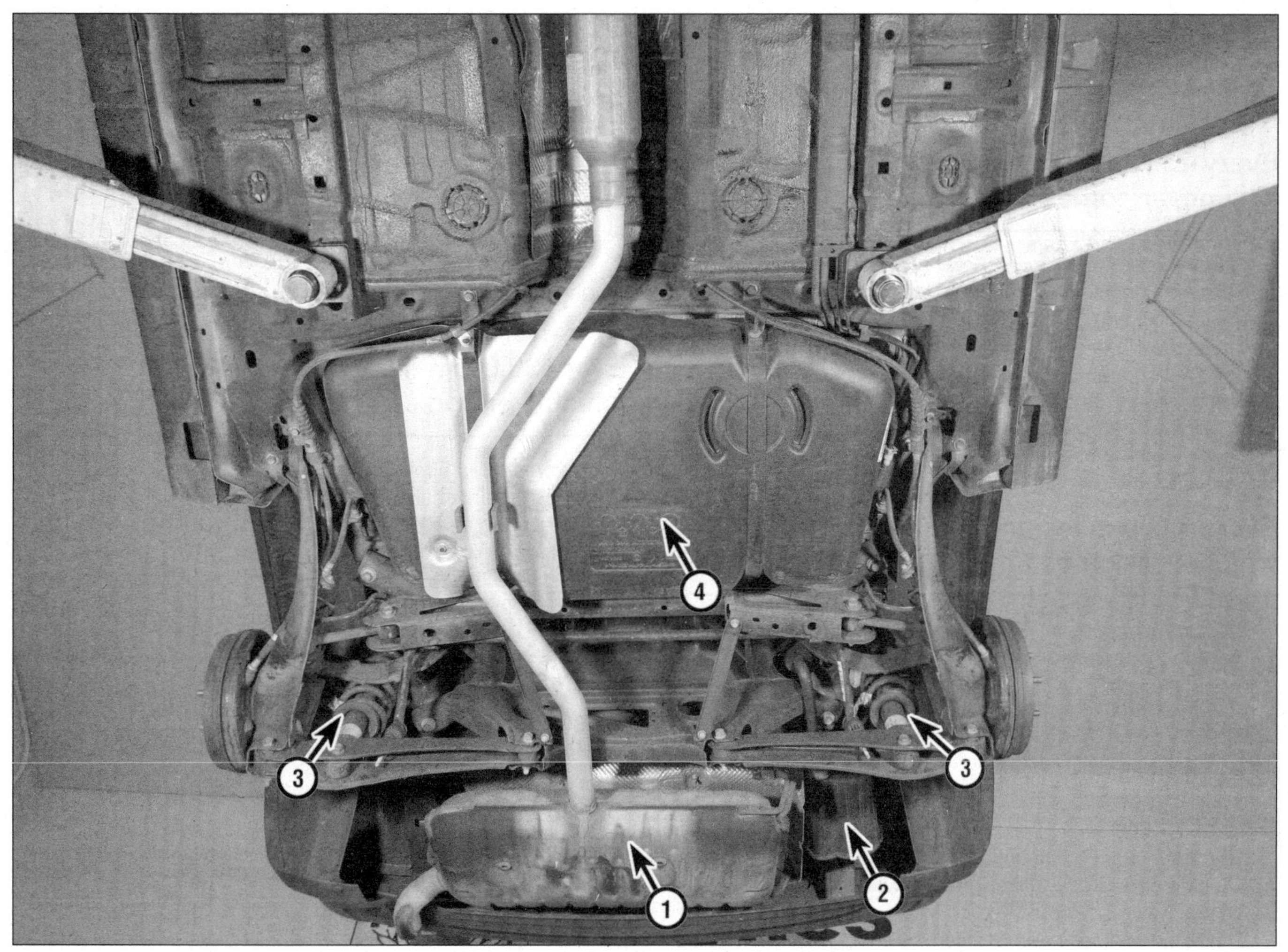

2.2c Typical rear underside components

1	Muffler	3	Rear shock absorber/coil spring assemblies
2	EVAP canister	4	Fuel tank

1 Maintenance schedule

1   The following maintenance intervals are based on the assumption that the vehicle owner will be doing the maintenance or service work, as opposed to having a dealer service department do the work. Although the time/mileage intervals are loosely based on factory recommendations, most have been shortened to ensure, for example, that such items as lubricants and fluids are checked/changed at intervals that promote maximum engine/driveline service life. Also, subject to the preference of the individual owner interested in keeping his or her vehicle in peak condition at all times, and with the vehicle's ultimate resale in mind, many of the maintenance procedures may be performed more often than recommended in the following schedule. We encourage such owner initiative.

2   When the vehicle is new it should be serviced initially by a factory authorized dealer service department to protect the factory warranty. In many cases the initial maintenance check is done at no cost to the owner (check with your dealer service department for more information).

Every 250 miles or weekly, whichever comes first

Check the engine oil level (Section 4)
Check the engine coolant level (Section 4)
Check the windshield washer fluid level (Section 4)
Check the brake fluid level (Section 4)
Check the power steering fluid level (Section 4)
Check the tires and tire pressures (Section 5)
Check the operation of all lights
Check the horn operation

Every 3,000 miles or 3 months, whichever comes first

All items listed above, plus:
Change the engine oil and filter (Section 6)

Every 6,000 miles or 6 months, whichever comes first

All items listed above, plus:
Check the wiper blade condition (Section 7)
Check and clean the battery and terminals (Section 8)
Rotate the tires (Section 9)
Check the seatbelts (Section 10)
Check the condition of all underhood hoses and connections (Section 11)
Check the cooling system hoses and connections for leaks and damage (Section 12)
Check and replace, if necessary, the air filter element (Section 13)

Every 12,000 miles or 12 months, whichever comes first

All items listed above, plus:
Check the automatic transaxle fluid level (Section 4)
Check the manual transaxle lubricant level (Section 16)
Check the brake system (Section 14)

Check the suspension components and driveaxle boots (Section 18)
Check the exhaust pipes and hangers (Section 19)
Check the fuel system hoses and connections for leaks and damage (Section 20)
Replace the cabin air filter (Section 21)

Every 30,000 miles or 30 months, whichever comes first

All items listed above, plus:
Check the drivebelts (Section 22)
Replace the air filter element (Section 13)*
Replace the brake fluid (Section 23)

Every 50,000 miles

Replace the transfer case lubricant (AWD models) (Section 28)
Replace the manual transaxle lubricant (Section 29)
Replace the rear differential lubricant (AWD models) (Section 30)

Every 60,000 miles or 60 months, whichever comes first

All items listed above, plus:
Check and replace, if necessary, the PCV valve (Section 25)*

** This item is affected by severe operating conditions as described below. If the vehicle in question is operated under severe conditions, perform all maintenance procedures marked with an asterisk (*) at the intervals specified by the mileage headings below. Consider the conditions severe if most driving is done . . .*

a) *In dusty areas*
b) *Towing a trailer*
c) *Idling for extended periods and/or low-speed operation*
d) *When outside temperatures remain below freezing and most trips are less than four miles*
e) *In heavy city traffic where outside temperatures regularly reach 90-degrees F or higher*

Every 60 months (regardless of mileage)

Service the cooling system (drain, flush and refill) (Section 26)

Every 100,000 miles

Replace the spark plugs (Section 24)
Change the automatic transaxle fluid and filter (Section 27)*

** This item is affected by severe operating conditions as described below. If the vehicle in question is operated under severe conditions, perform all maintenance procedures marked with an asterisk (*) at the intervals specified by the mileage headings below. Consider the conditions severe if most driving is done . . .*

　a)　*In dusty areas*
　b)　*Towing a trailer*
　c)　*Idling for extended periods and/or low-speed operation*
　d)　*When outside temperatures remain below freezing and most trips are less than four miles*
　e)　*In heavy city traffic where outside temperatures regularly reach 90-degrees F or higher*

Every 3,000 miles

Check and replace, if necessary, the air filter element (Section 13)

Every 60,000 miles

Check and replace, if necessary, the PCV valve (Section 25)
Change the automatic transaxle fluid and filter (Section 27)

2　Introduction

1　This Chapter is designed to help the home mechanic maintain the Jeep Patriot and Compass with the goals of maximum performance, economy, safety and reliability in mind.

2　Included is a master maintenance schedule, followed by procedures dealing specifically with each item on the schedule. Visual checks, adjustments, component replacement and other helpful items are included. Refer to the accompanying illustrations of the engine compartment and the underside of the vehicle for the locations of various components.

3　Adhering to the mileage/time maintenance schedule and following the step-by-step procedures, which is simply a preventive maintenance program, will result in maximum reliability and vehicle service life. Keep in mind that it's not possible for this comprehensive program to produce the same results if you maintain some items at the specified intervals but not others.

4　As you service the vehicle, you'll discover that many of the procedures can - and should - be grouped together because of the nature of the particular procedure you're performing or because of the close proximity of two otherwise unrelated components to one another.

5　For example, if the vehicle is raised, you should inspect the exhaust, suspension, steering and fuel systems while you're under the vehicle. When you're rotating the tires, it makes good sense to check the brakes, since the wheels are already removed. Finally, let's suppose you have to borrow or rent a torque wrench. Even if you only need it to tighten the spark plugs, you might as well check the torque of as many critical fasteners as time allows.

6　The first step in this maintenance program is to prepare before the actual work begins. Read through all the procedures you're planning, then gather together all the parts and tools needed. If it looks like you might run into problems during a particular job, seek advice from a mechanic or an experienced do-it-yourselfer.

Owner's manual and VECI label information

7　Your vehicle owner's manual was written for your year and model and contains very specific information on component locations, specifications, fuse ratings, part numbers, etc. The owner's manual is an important resource for the do-it-yourselfer to have; if one was not supplied with your vehicle, it can generally be ordered from a dealer parts department.

8　Among other important information, the Vehicle Emissions Control Information (VECI) label contains specifications and procedures for applicable tune-up adjustments and, in some instances, spark plugs (see Chapter 6 for more information on the VECI label). The information on this label is the exact maintenance data recommended by the manufacturer. This data often varies by intended operating altitude, local emissions regulations, month of manufacture, etc.

9　This Chapter contains procedural details, safety information and more ambitious maintenance intervals than you might find in manufacturer's literature. However, you may also find procedures or specifications in your owner's manual or VECI label that differ with what's printed here. In these cases, the owner's manual or VECI label can be considered correct, since it is specific to your particular vehicle.

3　Tune-up general information

1　The term tune-up is used in this manual to represent a combination of individual operations rather than one specific procedure.

2　The engine will be kept in relatively good running condition and the need for additional work will be minimized if the routine maintenance schedule is followed closely and frequent checks are made of fluid levels and high wear items, as suggested throughout this manual from the time the vehicle is new.

3　More likely than not, however, there will be times when the engine is running poorly due to lack of regular maintenance. This is even more likely if a used vehicle, which hasn't received regular and frequent maintenance checks, is purchased. In such cases, an engine tune-up will be needed outside of the regular routine maintenance intervals.

4　The first step in any tune-up or diagnostic procedure to help correct a poor running engine is a cylinder compression check. A compression check (see Chapter 2B) will help determine the condition of internal engine components and should be used as a guide for tune-up and repair procedures. For instance, if a compression check indicates serious internal engine wear, a conventional tune-up will not improve the performance of the engine and would be a waste of time and money. Because of its importance, someone with the right equipment and the knowledge to use it properly should do the compression check.

5　The following procedures are those most often needed to bring a generally poor running engine back into a proper state of tune:

Minor tune-up

*Check all engine related fluids
(see Section 4)
Clean and inspect the battery
(see Section 8)
Check all underhood hoses
(see Section 11)
Check and adjust the drivebelts
(see Section 22)
Check the air filter (see Section 13)
Check the PCV valve (see Section 25)*

Major tune-up

Note: *All items listed under Minor tune-up plus...*
*Check the fuel system (see Section 20)
the air filter (see Section 13)
Replace the drivebelt (see Section 22)
the charging system (see Chapter 5)
Replace the spark plugs (see Section 24)
Service the cooling system
(see Section 26)*

4.2 The engine oil dipstick is located at the front of the engine and is clearly marked

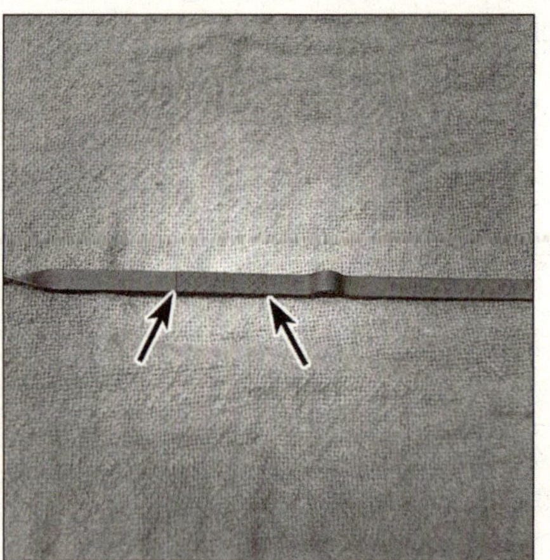

4.4 The oil level should be between the MIN and MAX marks, near the top of the cross-hatched area on the dipstick - if it isn't, add enough oil to bring the level up to or near the upper mark (do not overfill)

4.5 Turn the oil filler cap counterclockwise to remove it

4.9 Maintain the coolant level between the ADD and FULL HOT marks on the reservoir

4   Fluid level checks (see Maintenance Schedule for service intervals)

Note: *The following are fluid level checks to be done on a 250 mile or weekly basis. Additional fluid level checks can be found in specific maintenance procedures that follow. Regardless of the intervals, develop the habit of checking under the vehicle periodically for evidence of fluid leaks.*

1   Fluids are an essential part of the lubrication, cooling, brake and window washer systems. Because the fluids gradually become depleted and/or contaminated during normal operation of the vehicle, they must be replenished periodically. See *Recommended lubricants and fluids* in this Chapter's Specifications before adding fluid to any of the following components.

Note: *The vehicle must be on level ground when fluid levels are checked.*

Engine oil

2   Engine oil level is checked with a dipstick that is located on the side of the engine facing the front of the vehicle (see illustration). The dipstick extends through a tube and into the oil pan at the bottom of the engine.

3   The oil level should be checked before the vehicle has been driven, or about 5 minutes after the engine has been shut off. If the oil is checked immediately after driving the vehicle, some of the oil will remain in the upper engine components, resulting in an inaccurate reading on the dipstick.

4   Pull the dipstick out of the tube and wipe all the oil off the end with a clean rag or paper towel. Insert the clean dipstick all the way back into the tube, then pull it out again. Note the oil level at the end of the dipstick. Add oil as necessary to bring the oil level to the top of the cross-hatched area, or MAX mark (see illustration).

5   Oil is added to the engine after removing a cap located on the valve cover (see illustration). Use a funnel to prevent spills as the oil is added.

6   Don't allow the level to drop below the MIN mark on the dipstick or engine damage may occur. On the other hand, don't overfill the engine by adding too much oil - it may result in oil aeration and loss of oil pressure and also could result in oil fouled spark plugs, oil leaks or seal failures.

7   Checking the oil level is an important preventive maintenance step. A consistently low oil level indicates oil leakage through damaged seals, defective gaskets or past worn rings or valve guides. If the oil looks milky in color or has water droplets in it, the block or head may be cracked and leaking coolant is entering the crankcase. The engine should be checked immediately. The condition of the oil should also be checked. Each time you check the oil level, slide your thumb and index finger up the dipstick before wiping off the oil. If you

see small dirt or metal particles clinging to the dipstick, the oil should be changed (see Section 6).

Engine coolant

Warning: *Do not allow antifreeze to come in contact with your skin or painted surfaces of the vehicle. Flush contaminated areas immediately with plenty of water. Don't store new coolant or leave old coolant lying around where it's accessible to children or pets – they're attracted by its sweet smell. Ingestion of even a small amount of coolant can be fatal! Wipe up garage floor and drip pan spills immediately. Keep antifreeze containers covered and repair cooling system leaks as soon as they're noticed.*

8   All vehicles covered by this manual are equipped with a coolant recovery system. A white plastic coolant reservoir is located at the right side of the engine compartment and is connected by a hose to the cooling system filler neck. If the coolant heats up sufficiently during operation, in excess of the pressure cap rating, it can escape past the cap and into the reservoir. As the engine cools, the coolant is drawn back into the cooling system to maintain the correct level.

Warning: *Do not remove the cooling system pressure cap to check the coolant level when the engine is warm!*

9   The coolant level in the reservoir should be checked regularly. The level in the reservoir varies with the temperature of the engine. When the engine is cold, the coolant level should be mid-way between the ADD and FULL HOT marks on the reservoir. Once the engine has warmed up, the level should be at or near the FULL HOT mark. If it isn't, allow the engine to cool, then remove the cap from the tank and add a 50/50 mixture of ethylene glycol based antifreeze and water (see illustration).

10   Drive the vehicle and recheck the cool-

4.14 The windshield washer fluid reservoir is located in the right (passenger's) side of the engine compartment

4.17 Brake fluid level, indicated on the translucent white plastic brake fluid reservoir, should be kept between the lower ADD and upper (FULL) mark

ant level. If only a small amount of coolant is required to bring the system up to the proper level, water can be used. However, repeated additions of water will dilute the antifreeze and water solution. In order to maintain the proper ratio of antifreeze and water, always top up the coolant level with the correct mixture. Don't use rust inhibitors or additives. An empty plastic milk jug or bleach bottle makes an excellent container for mixing coolant.

11   If the coolant level drops consistently, there may be a leak in the system. Inspect the radiator, hoses, filler cap, drain plugs and water pump (see Section 12). If no leaks are noted, have the pressure cap pressure tested by a service station.

12   If you have to remove the radiator cap, wait until the engine has cooled completely, then wrap a thick cloth around the cap and turn it to the first stop. If coolant or steam escapes, or if you hear a hissing noise, let the engine cool down longer, then remove the cap.

13   Check the condition of the coolant as well. It should be relatively clear. If it's brown or rust colored, the system should be drained, flushed and refilled. Even if the coolant appears to be normal, the corrosion inhibitors wear out, so it must be replaced at the specified intervals.

Windshield and rear window washer fluid

14   The fluid for the windshield and rear window washer system is stored in a plastic reservoir located at the right front corner of the engine compartment (see illustration). The reservoir level should be maintained about one inch (25 mm) below the filler cap.

15   In milder climates, plain water can be used in the reservoir, but it should be kept no more than two-thirds full to allow for expansion if the water freezes. In colder climates, use windshield washer system antifreeze, available at any auto parts store, to lower the freezing point of the fluid. Mix the antifreeze

with water in accordance with the manufacturer's directions on the container.

Caution: *DO NOT use cooling system antifreeze - it will damage the vehicle's paint. To help prevent icing in cold weather, warm the windshield with the defroster before using the washer.*

Brake fluid

16   The brake fluid reservoir is located on top of the brake master cylinder on the driver's side of the engine compartment near the firewall.

17   The fluid level should be maintained between the lower ADD mark and the upper (FULL or MAX) mark on reservoir (see illustration).

18   If additional fluid is necessary to bring the level up, use a rag to clean all dirt off the top of the reservoir to prevent contamination of the system. Also, make sure all painted surfaces around the reservoir are covered, since brake fluid will ruin paint. Carefully pour new, clean brake fluid obtained from a sealed container into the reservoir. Be sure the specified fluid is used; mixing different types of brake fluid can cause damage to the system. See *Recommended lubricants and fluids* in this Chapter's Specifications or your owner's manual.

19   At this time the fluid and the master cylinder should be inspected for contamination. Normally the brake hydraulic system won't need periodic draining and refilling, but if rust deposits, dirt particles or water droplets are observed in the fluid, the system should be dismantled, cleaned and refilled with fresh fluid. Over time brake fluid will absorb moisture from the air. Moisture in the fluid lowers the fluid boiling point; if the fluid boils, the brakes will become ineffective. Normal brake fluid is clear in color. If the brake fluid is dark brown in color, it's a good idea to replace it (see Chapter 9).

20   Reinstall the fluid reservoir cap.

21   The brake fluid in the master cylinder will

4.24 Location of the power steering fluid reservoir

drop slightly as the brake lining material at each wheel wears down during normal operation. If the master cylinder requires repeated replenishing to maintain the correct level, there is a leak in the brake system that should be corrected immediately. Check all brake lines and connections, along with the calipers and power brake booster (see Section 14 and Chapter 9 for more information).

22   If you discover that the reservoir is empty or nearly empty, the system should be thoroughly inspected, refilled and then bled (see Chapter 9 for brake system bleeding).

Power steering fluid

23   Check the power steering fluid level periodically to avoid steering system problems, such as damage to the pump.

Caution: *DO NOT hold the steering wheel against either stop (extreme left or right turn) for more than five seconds. If you do, the power steering pump could be damaged.*

24   The power steering fluid reservoir is located in the right side of the engine compartment (see illustration).

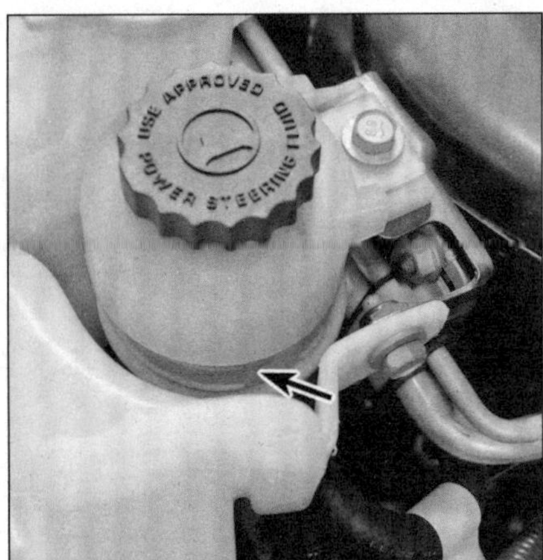

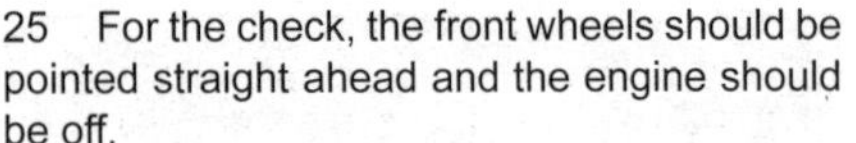

4.26 At normal operating temperature, the power steering fluid level should be between the FILL RANGE marks

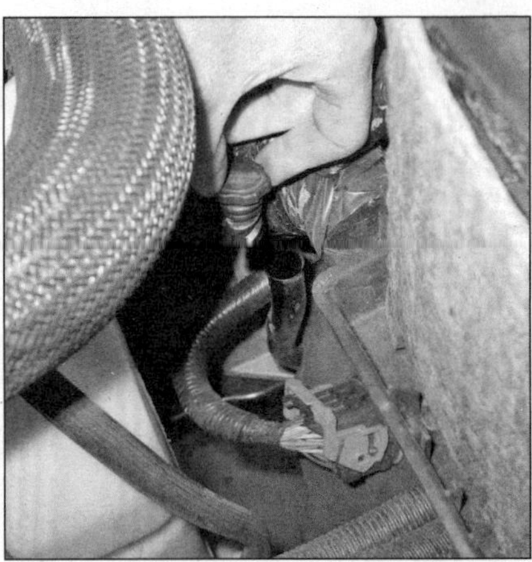

4.32 Locate the dipstick tube at the front of the transaxle and remove the cap

25   For the check, the front wheels should be pointed straight ahead and the engine should be off.

26   The reservoir has ADD and FILL RANGE fluid level marks on the side. The fluid level can be seen without removing the reservoir cap (see illustration).

27   If additional fluid is required, pour the specified type directly into the reservoir, using a funnel to prevent spills.

28   If the reservoir requires frequent fluid additions, all power steering hoses, hose connections, steering gear and the power steering pump should be carefully checked for leaks.

Automatic transaxle

Note: *It isn't necessary to check the transaxle fluid weekly; every 12,000 miles or 12 months will be adequate (unless a fluid leak is noticed).*

CVT transaxle

Note: *The CVT transaxle requires the use of a scan tool to check transaxle fluid temperature and special tool #9336A (or a homemade equivalent) to measure the fluid level. If you do not have both tools to make the proper temperature-to-fluid level comparisons, we do not recommend attempting this procedure.*

29   Make sure the vehicle is parked on a level area.

Warning: *Be sure to set the parking brake and block the front wheels to prevent the vehicle from moving when the engine is running.*

30   Apply the parking brake, start the engine and allow it to idle for a minute, then move the shift lever through each gear position, ending in Park or Neutral.

31   Special oil dipstick tool no. 9336A will be required to check the fluid level. An alternative to this tool can be fabricated from a straightened-out coat hanger long enough to

be inserted into the dipstick tube opening and contact the fluid pan.

32   Allow the transaxle to warm up, waiting at least two minutes, then remove the dipstick tube cap (see illustration).

33   With the engine warmed up and running, check the transaxle oil temperature with a scan tool.

34   Insert the tool into the transaxle fill tube until the tip of the tool contacts the fluid pan. Then pull it out and measure the fluid level. It may be necessary to repeat this several times to get an accurate reading.

35   Compare the reading on the dipstick tool with the transaxle fluid temperature reading on the scan tool.

36   Match the two readings with the transaxle fluid level chart (see illustration) to make sure the transaxle oil level is correct

37   Add or remove transaxle fluid as necessary, then recheck the fluid level and install the dipstick tube cap.

6F24 6-speed transaxle

Note: *There is no service interval recommended for the 6F24 6-speed automatic transaxle when it is operated under normal conditions. These transaxles come pre-filled from the factory, and do not require fluid checking unless there has been a fluid change, repair or a leak.*

Note: *The 6-speed transaxle requires the use of a scan tool to check transaxle fluid temperature and special tool #10323A (or a homemade equivalent) to measure the fluid level. If you do not have both tools to make the proper temperature-to-fluid level comparisons, we do not recommend attempting this procedure.*

Note: *The transaxle fluid must be between 122 and 194-degrees F for this check.*

38   If you do not have access to the special tool, fabricate a dipstick from a coat hanger (see illustration).

39   Make sure the vehicle is parked on a

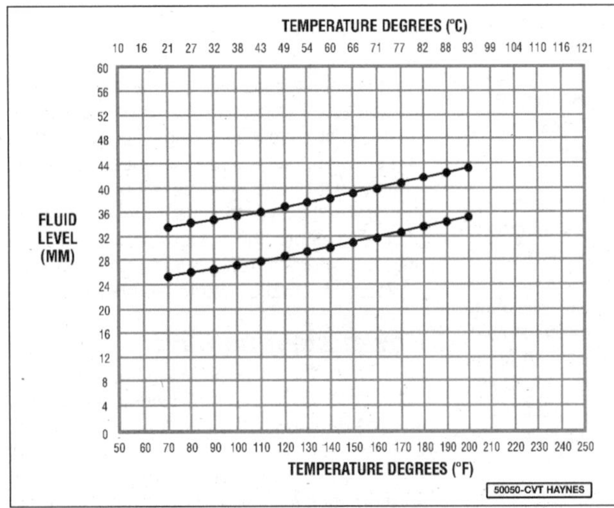

4.36 CVT transaxle fluid level-to-temperature indexing chart

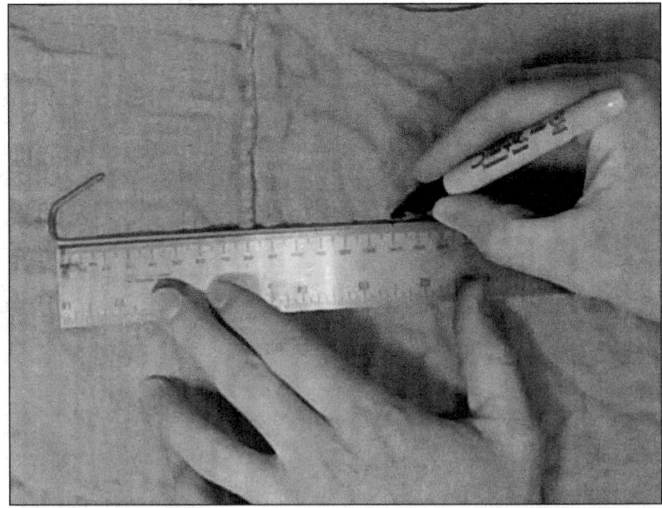

4.38 The dipstick must measure 140 mm from the bend where it will rest on top of the check plug opening. Cut the coat hanger at this point

level area.

40 Remove the check plug from the rear of the transaxle case (see illustration).

Warning: *Be sure to set the parking brake and block the front wheels to prevent the vehicle from moving when the engine is running.*

41 Apply the parking brake, start the engine and allow it to idle for a minute, then move the shift lever through each gear position, ending in Park. Pause for two seconds in each position.

42 Connect a scan tool to the diagnostic connector (see Chapter 6) and locate the temperature display on the scan tool.

43 Insert the tool into the fluid level check hole, then pull it out and measure the level of fluid (from the bottom of the dipstick). It may be necessary to repeat this several times to get an accurate reading.

Note: *Be careful not to burn yourself on the hot exhaust manifold.*

44 Compare the reading on the dipstick tool with the transaxle fluid temperature reading on the scan tool.

45 Match the two readings with the transaxle fluid level chart (see illustration) to make sure the transaxle oil level is correct.

46 Add or remove transaxle fluid as necessary, through the check plug hole, then recheck the fluid level and install the check plug, tightening it to the torque listed in this Chapter's Specifications. If too much fluid is added, loosen the drain plug and allow some fluid to drain until the level is correct, or remove it through the check/fill plug hole with a suction gun.

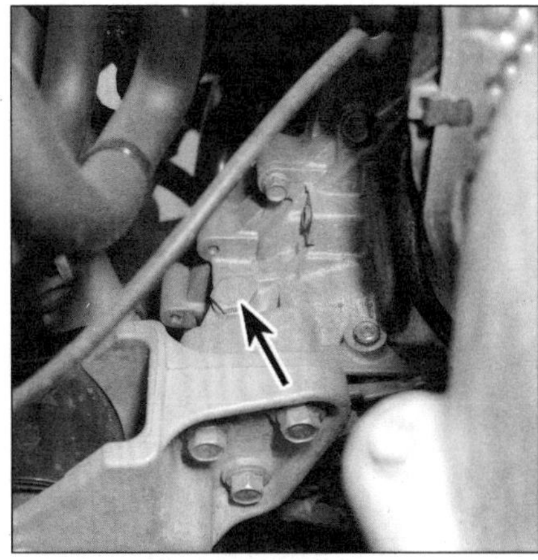

4.40 The transaxle fluid check plug is located on the rear of the transaxle case, near the rear transaxle mount

Fluid temperaure (degrees Fahrenheit)	Minimum level (mm)	Desired level (mm)	Maximum level (mm)
122	21	26	31.5
131	23	27.5	33
140	25	30	34
149	27	31	35.5
158	28.5	33	36.5
167	30	35	38
176	31.5	36	39
185	32.5	37	40
194	34	38	41

4.45 Transaxle fluid level chart

5 Tire and tire pressure checks (every 250 miles or weekly)

1 Periodic inspection of the tires may spare you the inconvenience of being stranded with a flat tire. It can also provide you with vital information regarding possible problems in the steering and suspension systems before major damage occurs.

2 The original tires on this vehicle are equipped with 1/2-inch wide bands that will appear when tread depth reaches 1/16-inch, at which point they can be considered worn out. Tread wear can be monitored with a simple, inexpensive device known as a tread depth indicator (see illustration).

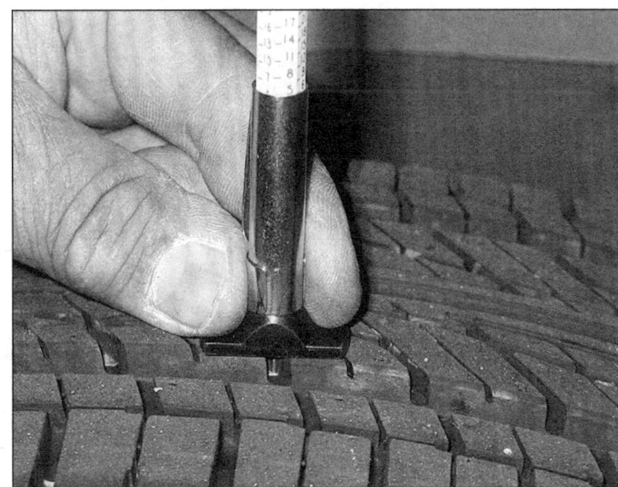

5.2 A tire tread depth indicator should be used to monitor tire wear - they are available at auto parts stores and service stations and cost very little

Cupping may be caused by:
- Underinflation and/or mechanical irregularities such as out-of-balance condition of wheel and/or tire, and bent or damaged wheel.
- Loose or worn steering tie-rod or steering idler arm.
- Loose, damaged or worn front suspension parts.

5.3 This chart will help you determine the condition of your tires, the probable cause(s) of abnormal wear and the corrective action necessary

3   Note any abnormal tread wear (see illustration). Tread pattern irregularities such as cupping, flat spots and more wear on one side than the other are indications of front end alignment and/or balance problems. If any of these conditions are noted, take the vehicle to a tire shop or service station to correct the problem.

4   Look closely for cuts, punctures and embedded nails or tacks. Sometimes a tire will hold air pressure for a short time or leak down very slowly after a nail has embedded itself in the tread. If a slow leak persists, check the valve stem core to make sure it is tight (see illustration). Examine the tread for an object that may have embedded itself in the tire or for a plug that may have begun to leak (radial tire punctures are repaired with a plug that is installed in a puncture). If a puncture is suspected, it can be easily verified by spraying a solution of soapy water onto the puncture area (see illustration). The soapy solution will bubble if there is a leak. Unless the puncture is unusually large, a tire shop or service station can usually repair the tire.

5   Carefully inspect the inner sidewall of each tire for evidence of brake fluid leakage. If you see any, inspect the brakes immediately.

6   Correct air pressure adds miles to the life span of the tires, improves mileage and enhances overall ride quality. Tire pressure cannot be accurately estimated by looking at a tire, especially if it's a radial. A tire pressure gauge is essential. Keep an accurate gauge in the glove compartment. The pressure gauges attached to the nozzles of air hoses at gas stations are often inaccurate.

7   Always check tire pressure when the tires are cold. Cold, in this case, means the vehicle has not been driven over a mile in the three hours preceding a tire pressure check. A pressure rise of four to eight pounds is not

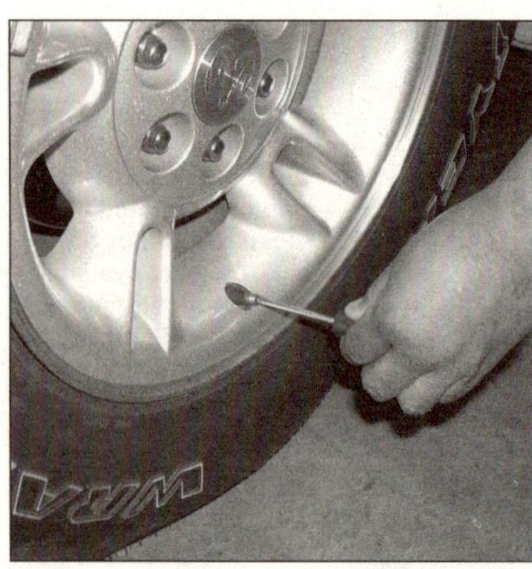

5.4a If a tire loses air on a steady basis, check the valve core first to make sure it's snug (special inexpensive wrenches are commonly available at auto parts stores)

5.4b If the valve core is tight, raise the corner of the vehicle with the low tire and spray a soapy water solution onto the tread as the tire is turned slowly - slow leaks will cause small bubbles to appear

uncommon once the tires are warm.

8   Unscrew the valve cap protruding from the wheel or hubcap and push the gauge firmly onto the valve stem (see illustration). Note the reading on the gauge and compare the figure to the recommended tire pressure shown on the tire placard on the driver's side door. Be sure to reinstall the valve cap to keep dirt and moisture out of the valve stem mechanism. Check all four tires and, if necessary, add enough air to bring them up to the recommended pressure.

9   Don't forget to keep the spare tire inflated to the specified pressure (refer to the pressure molded into the tire sidewall).

6   Engine oil and filter change (every 3000 miles or 3 months)

1   Frequent oil changes are the best preventive maintenance the home mechanic can give the engine, because aging oil becomes diluted and contaminated, which leads to premature engine wear.

2   Make sure you have all the necessary tools before you begin this procedure (see illustration). You should also have plenty of rags or newspapers handy for mopping up any spills.

3   Access to the underside of the vehicle is greatly improved if the vehicle can be lifted on a hoist, driven onto ramps or supported by jackstands.

Warning: *Do not work under a vehicle which is supported only by a bumper, hydraulic or scissors-type jack.*

4   If this is your first oil change, get under the vehicle and familiarize yourself with the locations of the oil drain plug and the oil filter. The engine and exhaust components will be warm during the actual work, so try to anticipate any potential problems before the engine and accessories are hot.

5   Park the vehicle on a level spot. Start the engine and allow it to reach its normal operating temperature. Warm oil and sludge will flow out more easily. Turn off the engine when it's warmed up. Remove the filler cap from the valve cover.

6   Raise the vehicle and support it securely on jackstands.

Warning: *Never get beneath the vehicle when it is supported only by a jack. The jack provided with your vehicle is designed solely for raising the vehicle to remove and replace the wheels. Always use jackstands to support the vehicle when it becomes necessary to place your body underneath the vehicle.*

7   Being careful not to touch the hot exhaust components, place the drain pan under the drain plug in the bottom of the pan and remove the plug (see illustration). You may want to wear gloves while unscrewing the plug the final few turns if the engine is hot.

8   Allow the old oil to drain into the pan. It may be necessary to move the pan farther under the engine as the oil flow slows to a

5.8 To extend the life of your tires, check the air pressure at least once a week with an accurate gauge (don't forget the spare!)

trickle. Inspect the old oil for the presence of metal shavings and chips.

9   After all the oil has drained, wipe off the drain plug with a clean rag. Even minute metal particles clinging to the plug would immediately contaminate the new oil.

10   Clean the area around the drain plug opening, reinstall the plug and tighten it to the torque listed in this Chapter's Specifications.

11   Move the drain pan into position under the oil filter.

12   Loosen the oil filter by turning it counterclockwise with an oil filter wrench (see illustration). Once the filter is loose, use your hands to unscrew it from the block. Keep the open end pointing up to prevent the oil inside the filter from spilling out.

Warning: *The exhaust system may still be hot, so be careful.*

13   With a clean rag, wipe off the mounting surface on the block. If a residue of old oil

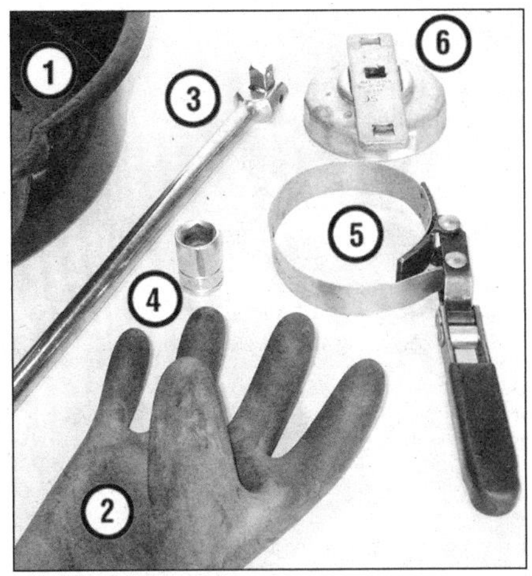

6.2 These tools are required when changing the engine oil and filter

1   ***Drain pan*** - *It should be fairly shallow in depth, but wide to prevent spills*

2   ***Rubber gloves*** - *When removing the drain plug and filter, you will get oil on your hands (the gloves will prevent burns)*

3   ***Breaker bar*** - *Sometimes the oil drain plug is tight, and a long breaker bar is needed to loosen it*

4   ***Socket*** – *To be used with the breaker bar or a ratchet (must be the correct size to fit the drain plug - six-point preferred)*

5   ***Filter wrench*** - *This is a metal band-type wrench, which requires clearance around the filter to be effective*

6   ***Filter wrench*** - *This type fits on the bottom of the filter and can be turned with a ratchet or breaker bar (different-size wrenches are available for different types of filters)*

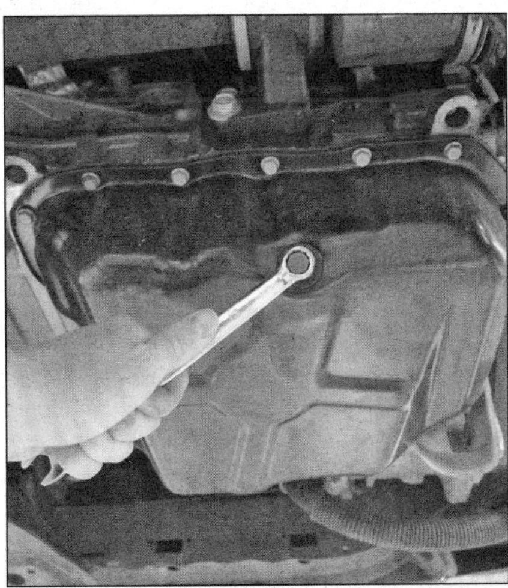

6.7 Use a proper size box-end wrench or socket to remove the oil drain plug and avoid rounding it off

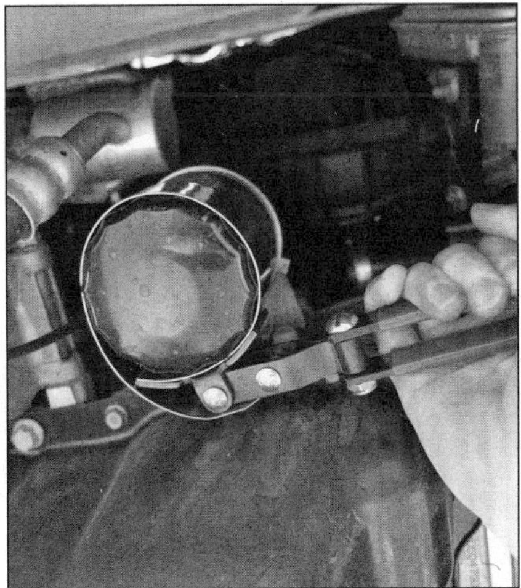

6.12 Use an oil filter wrench to remove the filter

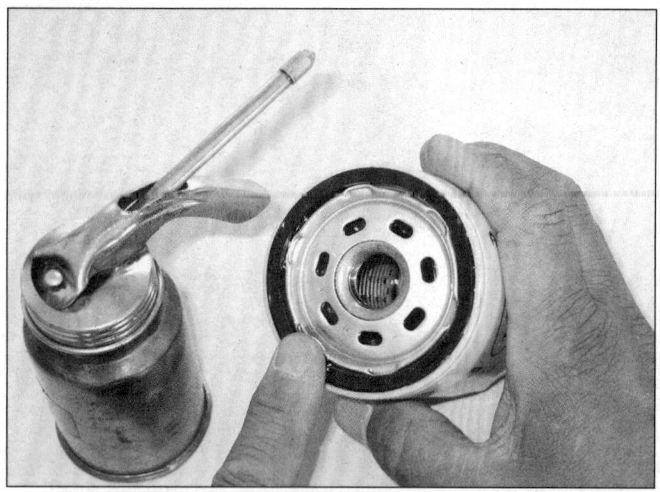

6.14 Lubricate the oil filter gasket with clean engine oil before installing the filter on the engine

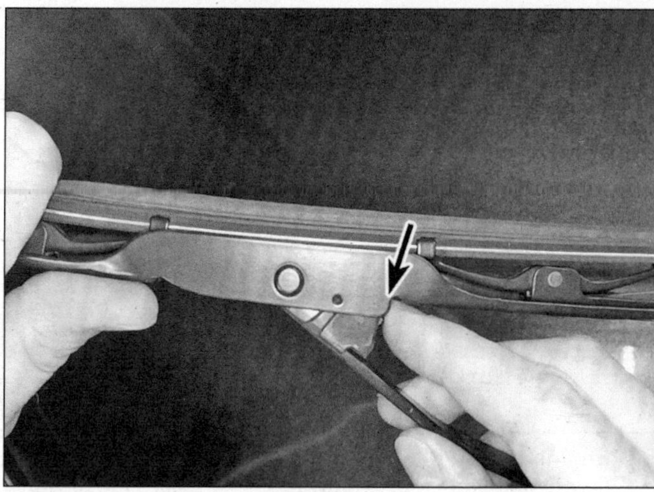

7.5a Depress the locking tab on the pivot block…

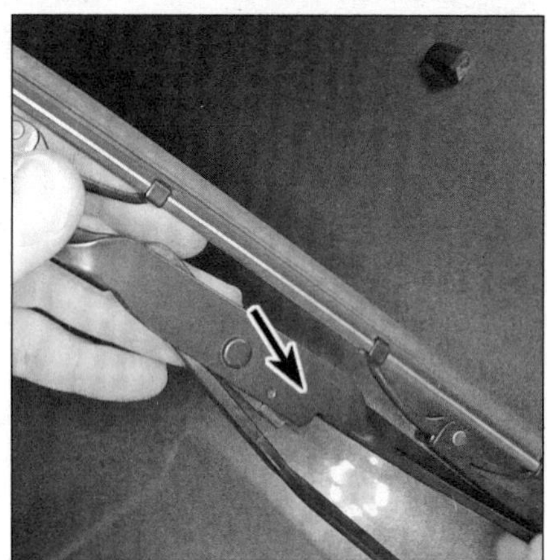

7.5b . . . then slide the wiper blade in the direction of the arrow to separate it from the arm

is allowed to remain, it will smoke when the block is heated up. Also make sure that none of the old gasket remains stuck to the mounting surface. It can be removed with a scraper if necessary.

14　Compare the old filter with the new one to make sure they are the same type. Smear some clean engine oil on the rubber gasket of the new filter (see illustration).

15　Attach the new filter to the engine, following the tightening directions printed on the filter canister or packing box. Most filter manufacturers recommend against using a filter wrench due to the possibility of overtightening and damaging the seal.

16　Remove all tools, rags, etc., from under the vehicle, being careful not to spill the oil in the drain pan, then lower the vehicle.

17　Add new oil to the engine through the oil filler cap in the valve cover. Use a funnel, if necessary, to prevent oil from spilling onto the top of the engine. Pour four quarts of fresh oil into the engine. Wait a few minutes to allow

the oil to drain into the pan, then check the level on the oil dipstick (see Section 4). If the oil level is at or near the FULL mark on the dipstick, install the filler cap, start the engine and allow the new oil to circulate.

18　Allow the engine to run for about a minute. While the engine is running, look under the vehicle and check for leaks at the oil pan drain plug and around the oil filter. If either is leaking, stop the engine and tighten the plug or filter.

19　Wait a few minutes to allow the oil to trickle down into the pan, recheck the level on the dipstick and, if necessary, add enough oil to bring the level to the FULL mark.

20　During the first few trips after an oil change, make it a point to check frequently for leaks and proper oil level.

21　The old oil drained from the engine cannot be reused in its present state and should be disposed of. Check with your local auto parts store, disposal facility or environmental agency to see if they will accept the oil for recycling. After the oil has cooled it can be drained into a container (capped plastic jugs, topped bottles, milk cartons, etc.) for transport to one of these disposal sites. Don't dispose of the oil by pouring it on the ground or down a drain!

Oil change indicator resetting

Note: *It is possible that, driving under the best possible conditions, the oil life monitoring system may not indicate the oil needs to be changed. The manufacturer states that the oil and filter must be changed at least once every year and the oil life monitor reset.*

Note: *If the "Oil Change Required" message comes on when the vehicle is immediately restarted, the oil life monitor was not reset and the reset procedure must be done again.*

Note: *If the message is not reset, it will continue to show up each time you turn the ignition switch On or start the vehicle. It is possible to*

temporarily turn off the message by pressing and releasing the "Menu" button.

22　Turn the ignition key to the On position but DO NOT start the engine.

23　Slowly depress the accelerator pedal all the way to the floor, three times within 10 seconds.

24　Turn the ignition key to the Off or Lock position, then start the vehicle.

7　Wiper blade inspection and replacement (every 6,000 miles or 6 months)

1　The wiper and blade assemblies should be inspected periodically for damage, loose components and cracked or worn blade elements.

2　Road film can build up on the wiper blades and affect their efficiency, so they should be washed regularly with a mild detergent solution.

3　The action of the wiping mechanism can loosen bolts, nuts and fasteners, so they should be checked and tightened, as necessary, at the same time the wiper blades are checked.

4　If the wiper blade elements are cracked, worn or warped, or no longer clean adequately, they should be replaced with new ones.

Windshield wiper blades

5　Lift the arm assembly away from the windshield for clearance. Depress the locking tab on the pivot block, then slide the wiper blade assembly out of the hook at the end of the arm (see illustrations).

Caution: *Do not allow the wiper arm to snap back against the windshield without the wiper blade installed or the arm could damage the window.*

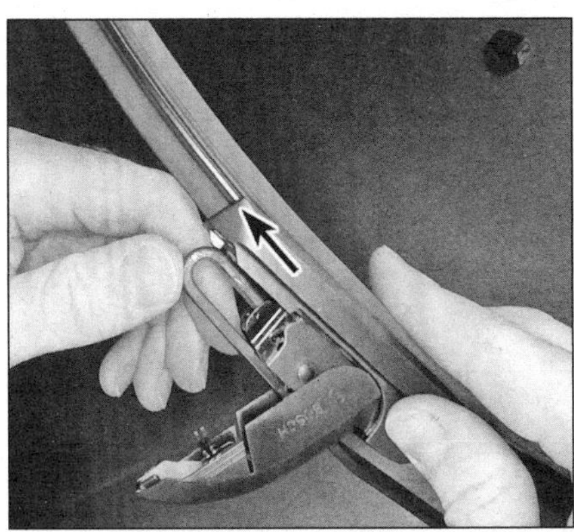

7.6a Attach the new wiper to the arm until it clicks into place…

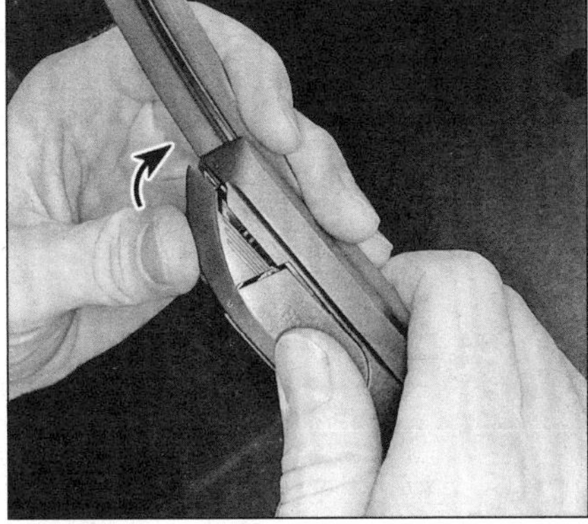

7.6b … then snap the cover down into the locked position.

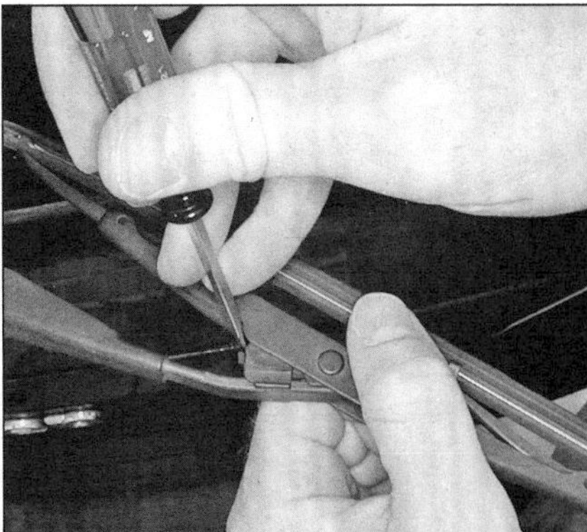

7.7a Depress the locking tab on the pivot block…

6   Attach the new wiper to the arm (see illustration). The connection can be confirmed by an audible click. Then snap the cover down and into the locked position (see illustration).

Rear wiper blade

7   Lift the arm away from the glass for clearance. Depress the locking tab on the pivot block, then slide the wiper blade assembly out of the hook at the end of the arm (see illustrations).
Caution: *Do not allow the wiper arm to snap back against the glass without the wiper blade installed or the arm could damage the window.*
8   Attach the new wiper to the arm; the connection can be confirmed by an audible click.

---

8   Battery check, maintenance and charging (every 6,000 miles or 6 months)

Note: *The battery on these vehicles is located at the left front corner of the vehicle, behind the radiator. Refer to Chapter 5 for the access procedure.*
Warning: *Certain precautions must be followed when checking and servicing the battery. Hydrogen gas, which is highly flammable, is always present in the battery cells, so keep lighted tobacco and all other open flames and sparks away from the battery. The electrolyte inside the battery is actually diluted sulfuric acid, which will cause injury if splashed on your skin or in your eyes. It will also ruin clothes and painted surfaces. When removing the battery cables, always detach the negative cable first and hook it up last!*

1   A routine preventive maintenance program for the battery in your vehicle is the only way to ensure quick and reliable starts. But before performing any battery maintenance, make sure that you have the proper equipment necessary to work safely around the battery (see illustration).
2   There are also several precautions that should be taken whenever battery

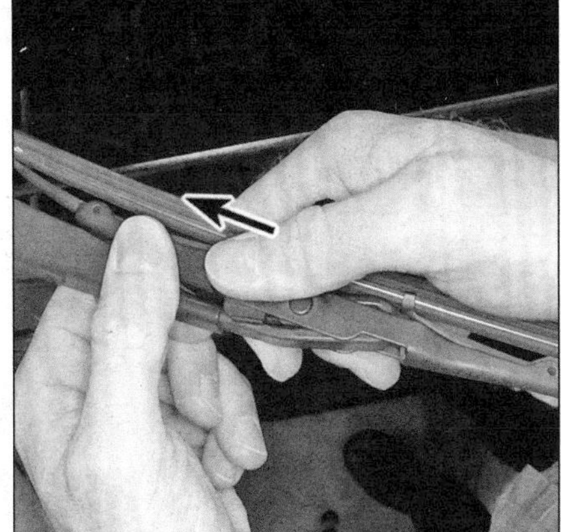

7.7b . . . then slide the wiper blade in the direction of the arrow to separate it from the arm

maintenance is performed. Before servicing the battery, always turn the engine and all accessories off and disconnect the cable from the negative terminal of the battery (see Chapter 5).
3   The battery produces hydrogen gas, which is both flammable and explosive. Never create a spark, smoke or light a match around the battery. Always charge the battery in a ventilated area.
4   Electrolyte contains poisonous and corrosive sulfuric acid. Do not allow it to get in your eyes, on your skin on your clothes. Never ingest it. Wear protective safety glasses when working near the battery. Keep children away from the battery.
5   Note the external condition of the battery. If the positive terminal and cable clamp on your vehicle's battery is equipped with a rubber protector, make sure that it's not torn or damaged. It should completely cover the terminal. Look for any corroded or loose connections, cracks in the case or cover or loose hold-down clamps. Also check the entire length of each cable for cracks and frayed conductors.

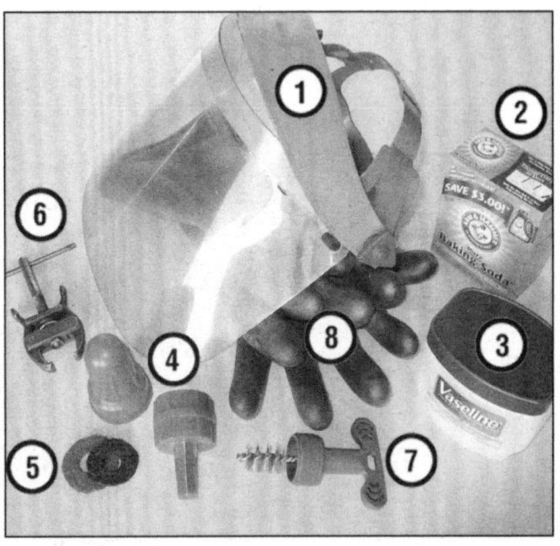

8.1 Tools and materials required for battery maintenance

1   ***Face shield/safety goggles*** *- When removing corrosion with a brush, the acidic particles can easily fly up into your eyes*
2   ***Baking soda*** *- A solution of baking soda and water can be used to neutralize corrosion*
3   ***Petroleum jelly*** *- A layer of this on the battery posts will help prevent corrosion*
4   ***Battery post/cable cleaner*** *- This wire brush cleaning tool will remove all traces of corrosion from the battery posts and cable clamps*
5   ***Treated felt washers*** *- Placing one of these on each post, directly under the cable clamps, will help prevent corrosion*
6   ***Puller*** *- Sometimes the cable clamps are very difficult to pull off the posts, even after the nut/bolt has been completely loosened. This tool pulls the clamp straight up and off the post without damage*
7   ***Battery post/cable cleaner*** *- Here is another cleaning tool which is a slightly different version of Number 4 above, but it does the same thing*
8   ***Rubber gloves*** *- Another safety item to consider when servicing the battery; remember that's acid inside the battery!*

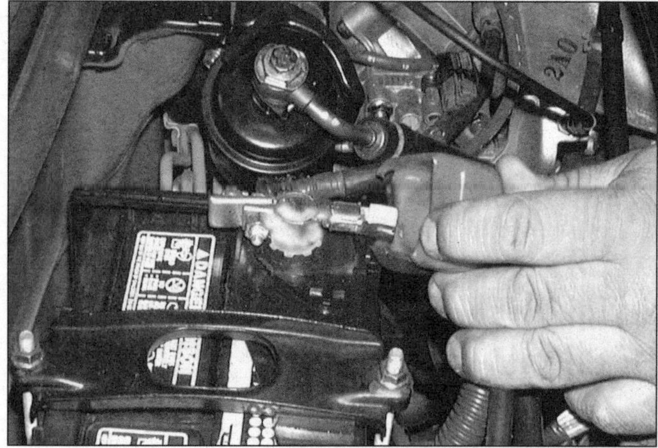

8.6a Battery terminal corrosion usually appears as light, fluffy powder

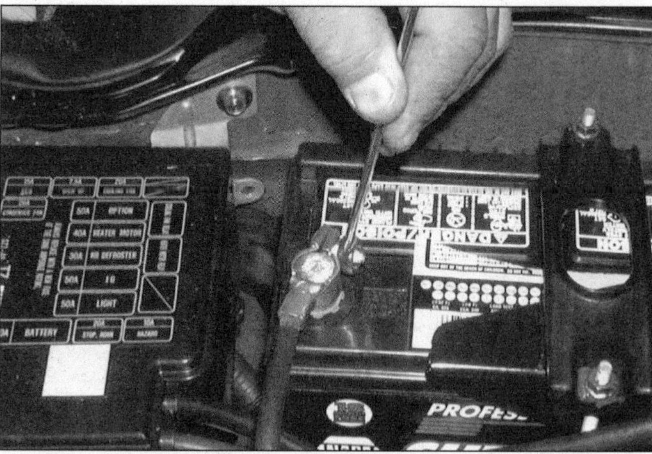

8.6b Removing a cable from the battery post with a wrench - sometimes a pair of special battery pliers are required for this procedure if corrosion has caused deterioration of the nut hex (always remove the ground (-) cable first and hook it up last!)

8.7a When cleaning the cable clamps, all corrosion must be removed

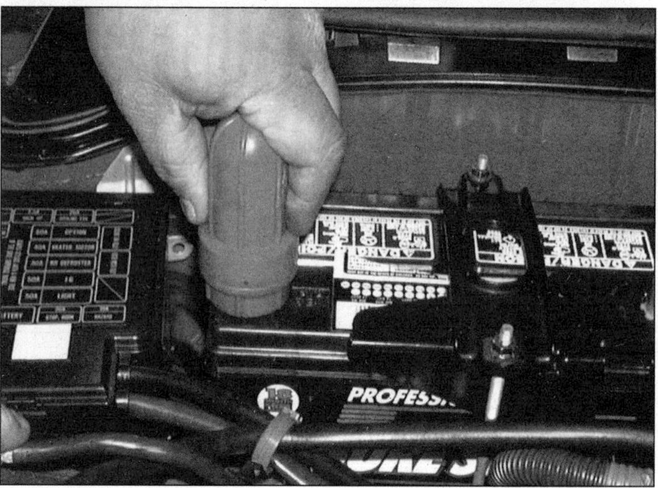

8.7b Regardless of the type of tool used to clean the battery posts, a clean, shiny surface should be the result

6   If corrosion, which looks like white, fluffy deposits (see illustration) is evident, particularly around the terminals, the battery should be removed for cleaning. Loosen the cable clamp bolts with a wrench, being careful to remove the ground cable first, and slide them off the terminals (see illustration). Then disconnect the hold-down clamp bolt and nut, remove the clamp and lift the battery from the engine compartment.

7   Clean the cable clamps thoroughly with a battery brush or a terminal cleaner and a solution of warm water and baking soda (see illustration). Wash the terminals and the top of the battery case with the same solution but make sure that the solution doesn't get into the battery. When cleaning the cables, terminals and battery top, wear safety goggles and rubber gloves to prevent any solution from coming in contact with your eyes or hands. Wear old clothes too - even diluted, sulfuric acid splashed onto clothes will burn holes in them. If the terminals have been extensively corroded, clean them up with a terminal cleaner (see illustration). Thoroughly wash all cleaned areas with plain water.

8   Make sure that the battery tray is in good condition and the hold-down clamp fasteners are tight. If the battery is removed from the tray, make sure no parts remain in the bottom of the tray when the battery is reinstalled. When reinstalling the hold-down clamp bolts, do not overtighten them.

9   Information on removing and installing the battery can be found in Chapter 5. If you disconnected the cable(s) from the negative and/or positive battery terminals, see Chapter 5. Information on jump starting can be found at the front of this manual. For more detailed battery checking procedures, refer to the *Haynes Automotive Electrical Manual*.

Cleaning

10   Corrosion on the hold-down components, battery case and surrounding areas can be removed with a solution of water and baking soda. Thoroughly rinse all cleaned areas with plain water.

11   Any metal parts of the vehicle damaged by corrosion should be covered with a zinc-based primer, then painted.

Charging

Warning: *When batteries are being charged, hydrogen gas, which is very explosive and flammable, is produced. Do not smoke or allow open flames near a charging or a recently charged battery. Wear eye protection when near the battery during charging. Also, make sure the charger is unplugged before connecting or disconnecting the battery from the charger.*

12   Slow-rate charging is the best way to restore a battery that's discharged to the point where it will not start the engine. It's also a good way to maintain the battery charge in a vehicle that's only driven a few miles between

starts. Maintaining the battery charge is particularly important in the winter when the battery must work harder to start the engine and electrical accessories that drain the battery are in greater use.

13　It's best to use a one or two-amp battery charger (sometimes called a trickle charger). They are the safest and put the least strain on the battery. They are also the least expensive. For a faster charge, you can use a higher amperage charger, but don't use one rated more than 1/10th the amp/hour rating of the battery. Rapid boost charges that claim to restore the power of the battery in one to two hours are hardest on the battery and can damage batteries not in good condition. This type of charging should only be used in emergency situations.

14　The average time necessary to charge a battery should be listed in the instructions that come with the charger. As a general rule, a trickle charger will charge a battery in 12 to 16 hours.

9　Tire rotation (every 6,000 miles or 6 months)

Caution: *Some models may have high-performance tires, which have a directional tread pattern installed on them. These tires must be installed on the same sides so that they rotate in the correct direction. This is indicated by arrows located on the tire sidewalls.*

1　The tires should be rotated at the specified intervals and whenever uneven wear is noticed.

2　Refer to the accompanying illustration for the preferred tire rotation pattern.

3　Refer to the information in *Jacking and towing* at the front of this manual for the proper procedures to follow when raising the vehicle and changing a tire. If the brakes are to be checked, don't apply the parking brake as stated. Make sure the tires are blocked to prevent the vehicle from rolling as it's raised.

4　Preferably, the entire vehicle should be raised at the same time. This can be done on a hoist or by jacking up each corner and then lowering the vehicle onto jackstands placed under the frame rails. Always use four jackstands and make sure the vehicle is safely supported.

5　After rotation, check and adjust the tire pressures as necessary. Tighten the lug nuts to the torque listed in this Chapter's Specifications.

10　Seat belt check (every 6,000 miles or 6 months)

1　Check the seat belts, buckles, latch plates and guide loops for obvious damage and signs of wear.

2　Where the seat belt receptacle bolts to the floor of the vehicle, check that the bolts are secure.

3　See if the seat belt reminder light comes on when the key is turned to the Run or Start position.

11　Underhood hose check and replacement (every 6,000 miles or 6 months)

General

Caution: *Never remove air conditioning components or hoses until the system has been depressurized by a licensed air conditioning technician.*

1　High temperatures in the engine compartment can cause the deterioration of the rubber and plastic hoses used for engine, accessory and emission systems operation. Periodic inspection should be made for cracks, loose clamps, material hardening and leaks. Information specific to the cooling system hoses can be found in Section 12.

2　Some, but not all, hoses are secured to their fittings with clamps. Where clamps are used, check to be sure they haven't lost their tension, allowing the hose to leak. If clamps aren't used, make sure the hose has not expanded and/or hardened where it slips over the fitting, allowing it to leak.

Vacuum hoses

3　It's quite common for vacuum hoses, especially those in the emissions system, to be color-coded or identified by colored stripes molded into them. Various systems require hoses with different wall thickness, collapse resistance and temperature resistance. When replacing hoses, be sure the new ones are made of the same material.

4　Often the only effective way to check a hose is to remove it completely from the vehicle. If more than one hose is removed, be sure to label the hoses and fittings to ensure correct installation.

5　When checking vacuum hoses, be sure to include any plastic T-fittings in the check. Inspect the fittings for cracks and the hose where it fits over the fitting for distortion, which could cause leakage.

6　A small piece of vacuum hose (1/4-inch inside diameter) can be used as a stethoscope to detect vacuum leaks. Hold one end of the hose to your ear and probe around vacuum hoses and fittings, listening for the hissing sound characteristic of a vacuum leak. **Warning:** *When probing with the vacuum hose stethoscope, be very careful not to come into contact with moving engine components such as the drivebelt, cooling fan, etc.*

Fuel hose

Warning: *There are certain precautions that must be taken when inspecting or servicing fuel system components. Work in a well-ventilated area and do not allow open flames (cigarettes, appliances, etc.) or bare light*

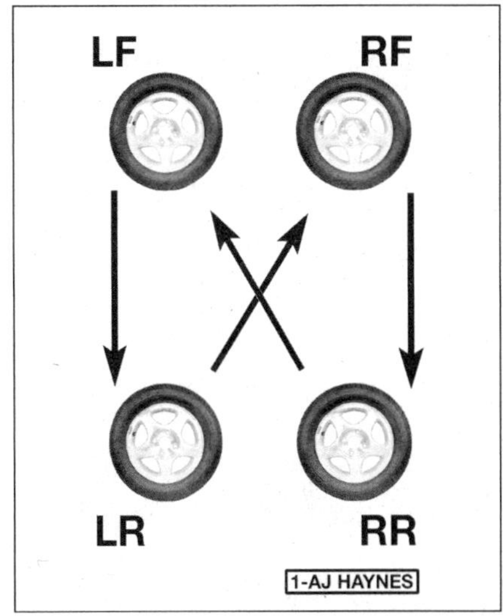

9.2 The recommended four-tire rotation pattern

bulbs near the work area. Mop up any spills immediately and do not store fuel soaked rags where they could ignite. The fuel system is under high pressure, so if any fuel lines are to be disconnected, the pressure in the system must be relieved first (see Chapter 4 for more information).

7　Check all rubber fuel lines for deterioration and chafing. Check especially for cracks in areas where the hose bends and just before fittings, such as where a hose attaches to the fuel filter.

8　High quality fuel line, made specifically for high-pressure fuel injection systems, must be used for fuel line replacement. Never, under any circumstances, use unreinforced vacuum line, clear plastic tubing or water hose for fuel lines.

9　Spring-type clamps are commonly used on fuel lines. These clamps often lose their tension over a period of time, and can be "sprung" during removal. Replace all spring-type clamps with screw clamps whenever a hose is replaced.

Metal lines

10　Sections of metal line are routed along the frame, between the fuel tank and the engine. Check carefully to be sure the line has not been bent or crimped and that cracks have not started in the line.

11　If a section of metal fuel line must be replaced, only seamless steel tubing should be used, since copper and aluminum tubing don't have the strength necessary to withstand normal engine vibration.

12　Check the metal brake lines where they enter the master cylinder and brake proportioning unit for cracks in the lines or loose fittings. Any sign of brake fluid leakage calls for an immediate and thorough inspection of the brake system.

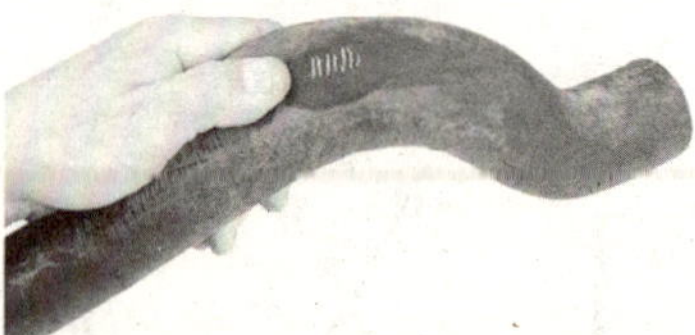

Check for a chafed area that could fail prematurely.

Check for a soft area indicating the hose has deteriorated inside.

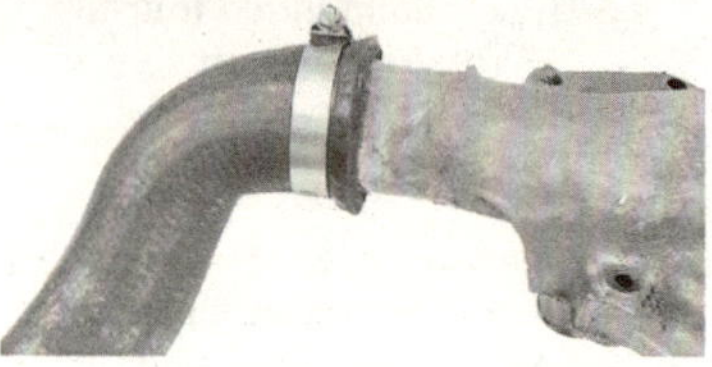

Overtightening the clamp on a hardened hose will damage the hose and cause a leak.

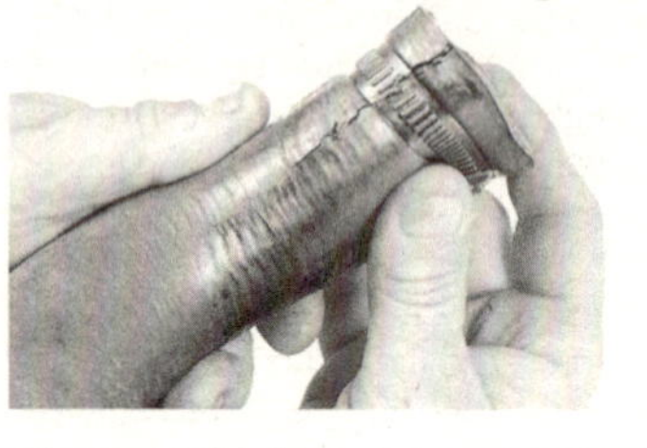

Check each hose for swelling and oil-soaked ends. Cracks and breaks can be located by squeezing the hose.

12.4 Hoses, like drivebelts, have a habit of failing at the worst possible time - to prevent the inconvenience of a blown radiator or heater hose, inspect them carefully as shown here

13.2a Rotate the fresh air inlet duct retainers…

13.3 Remove the support bracket fasteners and bracket

13.2b … then lift the duct up and pull it out from the housing

13.4 Air filter cover screw locations

12 Cooling system check (every 6,000 miles or 6 months)

1   Many major engine failures can be attributed to a faulty cooling system. Since the vehicle is equipped with an automatic transaxle, the cooling system also cools the transaxle fluid and thus plays an important role in prolonging transaxle life.

2   The cooling system should be checked with the engine cold. Do this before the vehicle is driven for the day or after it has been shut off for at least three hours.

3   Remove the cooling system pressure cap and thoroughly clean the cap, inside and out, with clean water. Also clean the filler neck. All traces of corrosion should be removed. The coolant in the system should be relatively transparent. If it is rust-colored, the system should be drained, flushed and refilled (see Section 26). If the coolant level is not up to the top, add additional antifreeze/coolant mixture (see Section 4).

4   Carefully check the large upper and lower radiator hoses along with the smaller diameter heater hoses that run from the engine to the firewall. Inspect each hose along its entire length, replacing any hose that is cracked, swollen or shows signs of deterioration. Cracks may become more apparent if the hose is squeezed (see illustration). Regardless of condition, it's a good idea to replace hoses with new ones every two years.

5   Make sure all hose connections are tight. A leak in the cooling system will usually show up as white or rust-colored deposits on the areas adjoining the leak. If wire-type clamps are used at the ends of the hoses, it may be a good idea to replace them with more secure screw-type clamps.

6   Use compressed air or a soft brush to remove bugs, leaves, etc., from the front of the radiator or air conditioning condenser. Be careful not to damage the delicate cooling fins or cut yourself on them.

7   Every other inspection, or at the first indication of cooling system problems, have the cap and system pressure tested. If you don't have a pressure tester, most repair shops will do this for a minimal charge.

13 Air filter check and replacement (every 6,000 miles or 6 months)

1   The air filter is located inside a housing at the left (driver's) side of the engine compartment.

2   Unlock the retainers for the fresh air inlet duct then remove the fresh air inlet duct from air filter housing (see illustrations).

3   Remove the filter housing support bracket fasteners and bracket (see illustration).

4   Remove the cover-to-air filter housing screws (see illustration).

5   To remove the air filter, separate the cover halves and remove the air filter element (see illustrations).

Caution: *Do not unplug the electrical connectors to the Powertrain Control Module (PCM). A possible voltage spike can occur and erase or damage the PCM (see Chapter 6).*

13.5a Once the screws have been removed lift the cover up...

13.5b ... then remove the air filter element

14.6 With the wheel off, check the thickness of the pads through the inspection hole

6   Inspect the outer surface of the filter element. If it is dirty, replace it. If it is only moderately dusty, it can be reused by blowing it clean from the back to the front surface with compressed air. Because it is a pleated paper type filter, it cannot be washed or oiled. If it cannot be cleaned satisfactorily with compressed air, discard and replace it. While the cover is off, be careful not to drop anything down into the housing.

7   Wipe out the inside of the air filter housing.

8   Place the new filter into the air filter housing, making sure it seats properly.

9   Reinstall the cover, making sure the cover fasteners are tightened securely.

14.13 If the lining is bonded to the brake shoe, measure the lining thickness from the outer surface to the metal shoe; if the lining is riveted to the shoe, measure from the lining outer surface to the rivet head

---

14   Brake system check (every 12,000 miles or 12 months)

Warning: *The dust created by the brake system is harmful to your health. Never blow it out with compressed air and don't inhale any of it. An approved filtering mask should be worn when working on the brakes. Do not, under any circumstances, use petroleum-based solvents to clean brake parts. Use brake system cleaner only!*

Note: *For detailed photographs of the brake system, refer to Chapter 9.*

1   In addition to the specified intervals, the brakes should be inspected every time the wheels are removed or whenever a defect is suspected.

2   Any of the following symptoms could indicate a potential brake system defect: The vehicle pulls to one side when the brake pedal is depressed; the brakes make squealing or dragging noises when applied; brake pedal travel is excessive; the pedal pulsates; or brake fluid leaks, usually onto the inside of the tire or wheel.

3   Disc brakes can be visually checked without removing any parts except the wheels. To check drum brakes, the rear wheels and brake drums will have to be removed. Remove the hub caps (if applicable) and loosen the wheel lug nuts a quarter turn each.

4   Loosen the wheel lug nuts, then raise the vehicle and place it securely on jackstands.

Warning: *Never work under a vehicle that is supported only by a jack!*

Disc brakes

5   Remove the wheels. Now visible is the disc brake caliper which contains the pads. There is an outer brake pad and an inner pad. Both must be checked for wear.

6   Measure the thickness of the pads through the inspection hole in the caliper body (see illustration). Compare the measurement with the limit given in this Chapter's Specifications; if any brake pad thickness is less than specified, then all brake pads must be replaced (see Chapter 9).

7   If you're in doubt as to the exact pad thickness or quality, remove them for measurement and further inspection (see Chapter 9).

8   Check the disc for score marks, wear and burned spots. If any of these conditions exist, the disc should be removed for servicing or replacement (see Chapter 9).

9   Before installing the wheels, check all the brake lines and hoses for damage, wear, deformation, cracks, corrosion, leakage, bends and twists, particularly in the vicinity of the rubber hoses and calipers.

10   Install the wheels, lower the vehicle and tighten the wheel lug nuts to the torque given in this Chapter's Specifications.

Drum brakes

11   Remove the brake drum (see Chapter 9).

12   With the drum removed, carefully clean off any accumulations of dirt and dust using brake system cleaner.

13   Measure the thickness of the lining material on both leading and trailing brake shoes (see illustration). Compare the measurement with the limit given in this Chapter's Specifications. if any brake shoe thickness is less than specified, then all brake shoes must be replaced (see Chapter 9).

14   Inspect the brake shoes for uneven wear patterns, cracks, glazing and delamination and replace if necessary. If the shoes have been saturated with brake fluid, oil or grease, this also necessitates replacement (see Chapter 9).

15   Make sure all the brake assembly springs are connected and in good condition.
16   Check the brake wheel cylinder for signs of fluid leakage. Carefully pry back the rubber dust boots on the wheel cylinder (see illustration). Any leakage here is an indication that the wheel cylinders must be overhauled immediately (see Chapter 9). Also, check all hoses and connections for signs of leakage.
17   Clean the inside of the drum with brake system cleaner. Again, be careful not to breathe the dust.
18   Inspect the inside of the drum for cracks, score marks, deep scratches and hard spots which will appear as small discolored areas. If imperfections cannot be removed with fine emery cloth, the drum must be taken to an automotive machine shop for resurfacing.
19   Repeat the procedure for the remaining wheel.
20   Install the wheels, lower the vehicle and tighten the wheel lug nuts to the torque given in this Chapter's Specifications.

Brake booster check

21   Sit in the driver's seat and perform the following sequence of tests.
22   With the brake fully depressed, start the engine - the pedal should move down a little when the engine starts.
23   With the engine running, depress the brake pedal several times - the travel distance should not change.
24   Depress the brake, stop the engine and hold the pedal in for about 30 seconds - the pedal should neither sink nor rise.
25   Restart the engine, run it for about a minute and turn it off. Then firmly depress the brake several times - the pedal travel should decrease with each application.
26   If your brakes do not operate as described, the brake booster has failed. Refer to Chapter 9 for the replacement procedure.

---

15   Transfer case/Power Transfer Unit (PTU) lubricant level check (AWD/4WD models) (every 12,000 miles or 12 months)

Note: *Make sure the vehicle is on level ground for the check.*
1   The lubricant level is checked by removing a plug from the side of the case. If the vehicle is raised to gain access to the plug, be sure to support it safely on jackstands - DO NOT crawl under the vehicle when it's supported only by a jack!
2   With the engine and transfer case cold, remove the check/fill plug. If lubricant immediately starts leaking out, thread the plug back into the case - the level is correct. If it doesn't, completely remove the plug and reach inside the hole with your finger. The level should be even with the bottom of the plug hole.
3   If more lubricant is needed, use a syringe or small pump to add it through the opening.
4   Thread the plug back into the case and

14.16 Pull the boot away from the cylinder and check for fluid leakage

tighten it securely. Drive the vehicle, then check for leaks around the plug.

---

16   Manual transaxle lubricant level check (every 12,000 miles or 12 months)

Note: *Make sure the vehicle is on level ground for the check.*
1   The lubricant level is checked by removing the check/fill plug from the side of the case. If the vehicle is raised to gain access to the plug, be sure to support it safely on jackstands - DO NOT crawl under the vehicle when it's supported only by a jack!
Note: *The transaxle check/fill plug is located on the left side of the transaxle differential.*
2   With the engine and transfer case cold, remove the check/fill plug. If lubricant immediately starts leaking out, thread the plug back into the case - the level is correct. If it doesn't, completely remove the plug and reach inside the hole with your finger. The level should be even with the bottom of the plug hole.
3   If more lubricant is needed, use a syringe or small pump to add it through the opening.
4   Thread the plug back into the case and tighten it securely. Drive the vehicle, then check for leaks around the plug.

---

17   Differential lubricant level check (AWD/4WD models) (every 12,000 miles or 12 months)

Note: *Make sure the vehicle is on level ground for the check.*
1   The differential has a check/fill plug which must be removed to check the lubricant level. If the vehicle is raised to gain access to the plug, be sure to support it safely on jackstands - DO NOT crawl under the vehicle when it's supported only by the jack!
2   Remove the check/fill plug from the rear

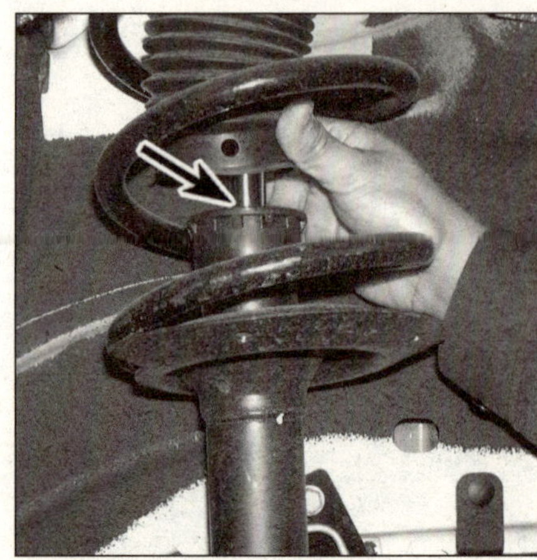

18.4 Check the struts and shocks for leakage at the indicated area

cover of the differential.
3   Use your finger as a dipstick to make sure the lubricant level is even with the bottom of the plug hole. If not, use a syringe to add the recommended lubricant until it just starts to run out of the opening.
4   Install the plug and tighten it securely.

---

18   Steering, suspension and driveaxle boot check (every 12,000 miles or 12 months)

Note: *For detailed illustrations of the steering and suspension components, refer to Chapter 10.*

With the wheels on the ground

1   With the vehicle stopped and the front wheels pointed straight ahead, rock the steering wheel gently back and forth. If freeplay is excessive, a front wheel bearing, steering shaft universal joint, lower arm balljoint or steering gear is worn. Refer to Chapter 10 for the appropriate repair procedure.
2   Other symptoms, such as excessive vehicle body movement over rough roads, swaying (leaning) around corners and binding as the steering wheel is turned, may indicate faulty steering and/or suspension components.
3   Check the struts/shock absorbers by pushing down and releasing the vehicle several times at each corner. If the vehicle does not come back to a level position within one or two bounces, the shocks/struts are worn and must be replaced. When bouncing the vehicle up and down, listen for squeaks and noises from the suspension components.
4   Check the struts and shock absorbers for evidence of fluid leakage (see illustration). A light film of fluid is no cause for concern. Make sure that any fluid noted is from the struts/shocks and not from some other source. If leakage is noted, replace the struts/shocks as a set.

18.10a To check the balljoint for wear, try to pry the control arm up...

18.10b ... and down to make sure there is no play in the balljoint (if there is, replace it)

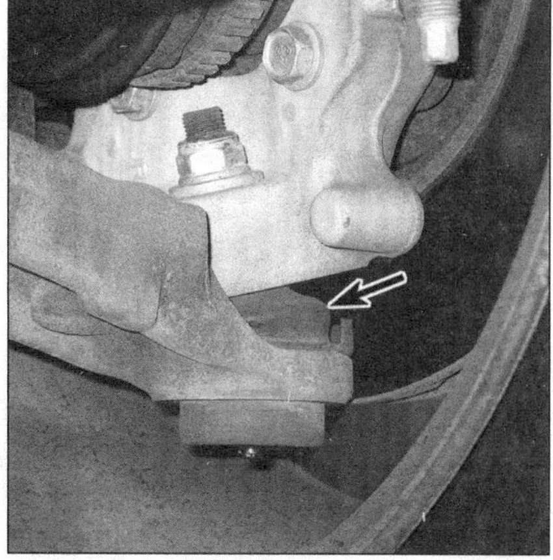

18.11 Check the balljoint boot for damage

5   Check the struts and shocks to be sure they are securely mounted and undamaged. Check the upper mounts for damage and wear. If damage or wear is noted, replace the shocks as a set (front and rear).

6   If the struts or shocks must be replaced, refer to Chapter 10 for the procedure.

Under the vehicle

7   Raise the vehicle and support it securely on jackstands.

8   Check the tires for irregular wear patterns and proper inflation. See Section 5 in this Chapter for information regarding tire wear and Chapter 10 for information on wheel bearing replacement.

9   Inspect the universal joint between the steering shaft and the steering gear housing. Check the steering gear housing for lubricant leakage. Make sure that the dust seals and boots are not damaged and that the boot clamps are not loose. Check the steering linkage for looseness or damage. Check the tie-rod ends for excessive play. Look for loose bolts, broken or disconnected parts and deteriorated rubber bushings on all suspension and steering components. While an assistant turns the steering wheel from side to side, check the steering components for free movement, chafing and binding. If the steering components do not seem to be reacting with the movement of the steering wheel, try to determine where the slack is located.

10   Check the balljoints for wear by trying to move each control arm up and down with a prybar (see illustrations) to ensure that its balljoint has no play. If any balljoint does have play, replace it. See Chapter 10 for the balljoint replacement procedure.

11   Inspect the balljoint boots for damage and leaking grease (see illustration). Replace the balljoints with new ones if they are damaged (see Chapter 10).

12   At the rear of the vehicle, inspect the suspension arm bushings for deterioration. Additional information on suspension components can be found in Chapter 10.

Driveaxle boot check

Note: *For detailed illustrations of the driveaxles, refer to Chapter 8.*

13   The driveaxle boots are very important because they prevent dirt, water and foreign material from entering and damaging the constant velocity (CV) joints. Oil and grease can cause the boot material to deteriorate prematurely, so it's a good idea to wash the boots with soap and water. Because it constantly pivots back and forth following the steering action of the front hub, the outer CV boot wears out sooner and should be inspected regularly.

14   Inspect the boots for tears and cracks as well as loose clamps (see illustration). If there is any evidence of cracks or leaking lubricant, they must be replaced as described in Chapter 8.

19   Exhaust system check (every 12,000 miles or 12 months)

1   With the engine cold (at least three hours after the vehicle has been driven), check the complete exhaust system from the engine to the end of the tailpipe. Ideally, the inspection should be done with the vehicle on a hoist to permit unrestricted access. If a hoist isn't available, raise the vehicle and support it securely on jackstands.

2   Check the exhaust pipes and connections for evidence of leaks, severe corrosion and damage. Make sure that all brackets and hangers are in good condition and tight (see illustration).

3   At the same time, inspect the underside of the body for holes, corrosion, open seams, etc., which may allow exhaust gases to enter the passenger compartment. Seal all body openings with silicone or body putty.

4   Rattles and other noises can often be traced to the exhaust system, especially the mounts and hangers. Try to move the pipes, muffler and catalytic converter. If the compo-

18.14 Flex the driveaxle boots by hand to check for cracks and leaking grease

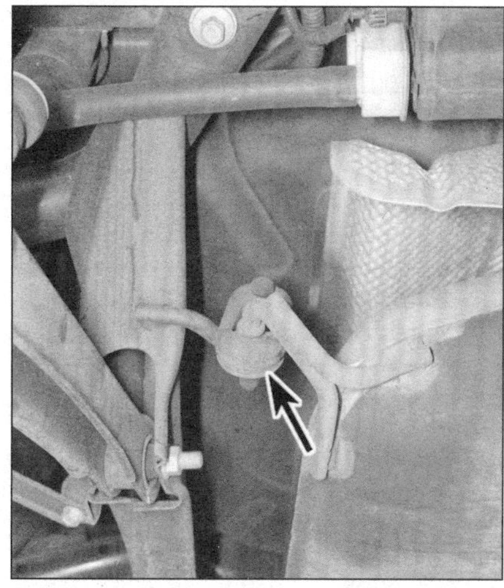

19.2 Check the exhaust system for rust, damage, or broken rubber hangers

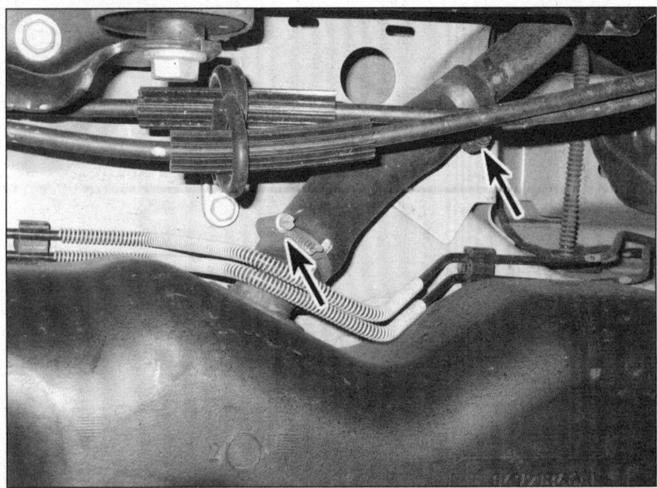

20.6 Check the fuel system hoses and clamps for damage and deterioration

21.2 Press the tabs toward each other to disengage the clips

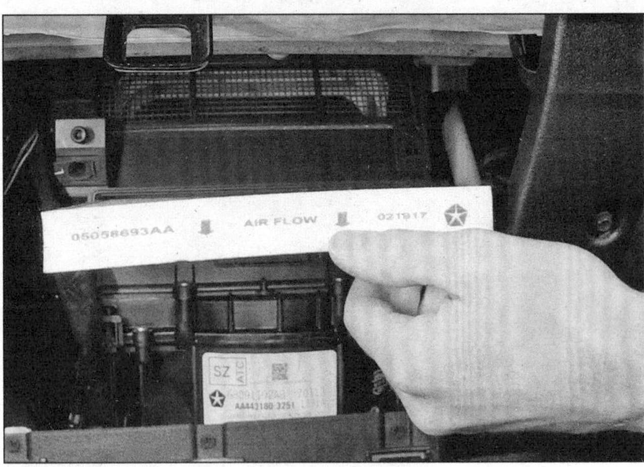

21.3 Remove the filter from the housing, noting the position of the filter as it is removed

nents can come in contact with the body or suspension parts, secure the exhaust system with new mounts.

5   Check the running condition of the engine by inspecting inside the end of the tail-pipe. The exhaust deposits here are an indication of engine state-of-tune. If the pipe is black and sooty or coated with white deposits, the engine may need a tune-up, including a thorough fuel system inspection and adjustment.

20   Fuel system check (every 12,000 miles or 12 months)

Warning: *Gasoline is flammable, so take extra precautions when you work on any part of the fuel system. Don't smoke or allow open flames or bare light bulbs near the work area, and don't work in a garage where a gas-type appliance (such as a water heater or clothes dryer) is present. Since fuel is carcinogenic, wear fuel-resistant gloves when there's a possibility of being exposed to fuel, and, if you spill any fuel on your skin, rinse it off immediately with soap and water. Mop up any spills*

immediately and do not store fuel-soaked rags where they could ignite. When you perform any kind of work on the fuel system, wear safety glasses and have a Class B type fire extinguisher on hand. The fuel system is under constant pressure, so, before any lines are disconnected, the fuel system pressure must be relieved (see Chapter 4).

1   If you smell gasoline while driving or after the vehicle has been sitting in the sun, inspect the fuel system immediately.

2   Remove the fuel filler cap and inspect it for damage and corrosion. The gasket should have an unbroken sealing imprint. If the gasket is damaged or corroded, install a new cap.

3   Inspect the fuel feed line for cracks. Make sure that the connections between the fuel lines and the fuel injection system are tight.

Warning: *Your vehicle is fuel injected, so you must relieve the fuel system pressure before servicing fuel system components. The fuel system pressure relief procedure is outlined in Chapter 4.*

4   Since some components of the fuel system - the fuel tank and the fuel lines, for

example - are underneath the vehicle, they can be inspected more easily with the vehicle raised on a hoist. If that's not possible, raise the vehicle and support it on jackstands.

5   With the vehicle raised and safely supported, inspect the gas tank and filler neck for punctures, cracks and other damage. The connection between the filler neck and the tank is particularly critical. Sometimes a rubber filler neck will leak because of loose clamps or deteriorated rubber. Inspect all fuel tank mounting brackets and straps to be sure that the tank is securely attached to the vehicle.

Warning: *Do not, under any circumstances, try to repair a fuel tank (except rubber components).*

6   Carefully check all hoses and lines leading away from the fuel tank. Check for loose connections, deteriorated hoses, crimped lines and other damage (see illustration). Repair or replace damaged sections as necessary (see Chapter 4).

21   Cabin air filter replacement (every 12,000 miles or 12 months)

Warning: *The models covered by this manual are equipped with a Supplemental Restraint System (SRS), more commonly known as airbags. Always disable the airbag system before working in the vicinity of any airbag system component to avoid the possibility of accidental deployment of the airbag, which could cause personal injury (see Chapter 12).*

1   Disengage the clips on each side of the glove box. Pull the sides inwards until the stops are clear, then lower the glove box (see Chapter 11).

2   Disengage the two clips at the ends of the cover (see illustration) and remove the cover.

3   Remove the filter from the housing (see illustration).

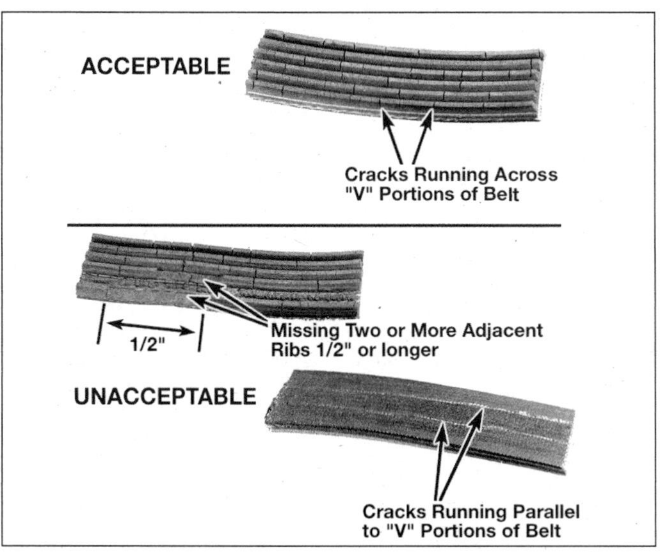

22.3 Here are some of the more common problems associated with drivebelts (check the belts very carefully to prevent an untimely breakdown)

22.5 Remove the drivebelt splash shield fasteners and shield

4   Install the filter, making sure the arrow on the filter is pointing toward the floor.

Note: *The cabin air filter is labeled with an arrow and the word "Airflow" on it. The filter should be installed with the arrow pointing toward the floor.*

5   Installation is the reverse of removal.

22   Drivebelt check and replacement/ tensioner replacement (every 30,000 miles or 30 months)

1   The drivebelt is located at the right end of the engine and plays an important role in the operation of the vehicle and its components. Due to its function and material makeup, the belt is prone to failure after a period of time, and should be inspected and adjusted periodically to prevent major damage.

2   All models covered in this manual use a single serpentine belt to drive all the components.

Check

3   With the engine off, open the hood and use your fingers (and a flashlight, if necessary) to move along the belt checking for cracks and separation of the belt plies. Also check for fraying and glazing, which gives the belt a shiny appearance. Also check the ribs on the underside of the belt. They should all be the same depth, with none of the surface uneven (see illustration).

4   The serpentine belt tension is adjusted by an automatic tensioner.

Replacement

5   Apply the parking brake, loosen the right-front wheel lug nuts, then raise the front of the vehicle and support it securely on jackstands. Remove the wheel, then remove the drivebelt

22.6 Place a wrench on the tensioner pulley center bolt and rotate it counterclockwise - 2.4L engine shown

splash shield (see illustration).

6   The automatic tensioner must be released to allow drivebelt replacement. Place a wrench on the tensioner pulley center bolt and rotate it counterclockwise until the belt can be removed (see illustration). Remove the belt and slowly release the tensioner.

Warning: *Damage to the tensioner or possible injury can occur if the tensioner snaps or springs back without the belt in place.*

7   Installation is the reverse of removal. When installing the belt, make sure the belt is centered on the pulleys.

8   Install the drivebelt splash shield, wheel and lug nuts. Lower the vehicle and tighten the lug nuts to the torque listed in this Chapter's Specifications.

Automatic tensioner replacement

9   Remove the wheel, then remove the drivebelt splash shield (see illustration 22.5)

10   Remove the drivebelt (see Step 6).

11   Unscrew the tensioner mounting bolt and

remove the tensioner.

12   Installation is the reverse of removal. Tighten the mounting bolt to the torque listed in this Chapter's Specifications. Lower the vehicle and tighten the lug nuts to the torque listed in this Chapter's Specifications.

23   Brake fluid change (every 30,000 miles or 30 months)

Warning: *Brake fluid can harm your eyes and damage painted surfaces, so use extreme caution when handling or pouring it. Do not use brake fluid that has been standing open or is more than one year old. Brake fluid absorbs moisture from the air. Excess moisture can cause a dangerous loss of braking effectiveness.*

1   At the specified intervals, the brake fluid should be drained and replaced. Since the brake fluid may drip or splash when pouring it, place plenty of rags around the master cylinder to protect any surrounding painted surfaces.

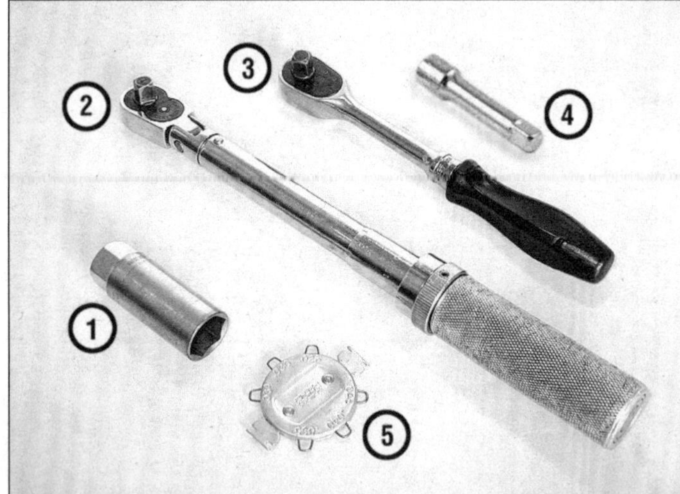

24.2 Tools required for changing spark plugs

1   **Spark plug socket** - *This will have special padding inside to protect the spark plug's porcelain insulator*
2   **Torque wrench** - *Although not mandatory, using this tool is the best way to ensure the plugs are tightened properly*
3   **Ratchet** - *Standard hand tool to fit the spark plug socket*
4   **Extension** - *Depending on model and accessories, you may need special extensions and universal joints to reach one or more of the plugs*
5   **Spark plug gap gauge** - *This gauge for checking the gap comes in a variety of styles. Make sure the gap for your engine is included*

24.5 Spark plug manufacturers recommend using a wire-type gauge when checking the gap - the wire should slide between the electrodes with a slight drag

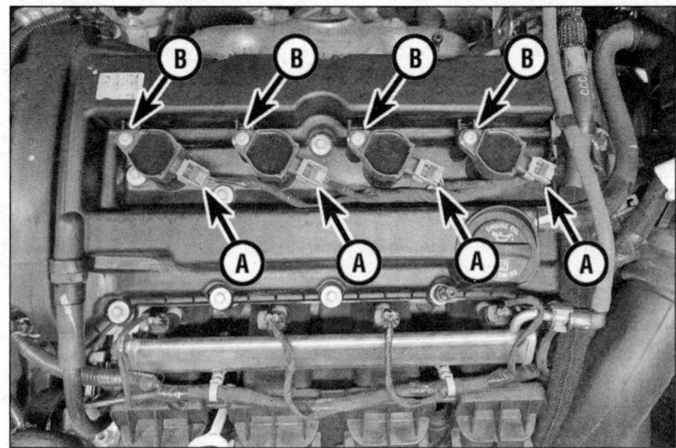

24.7a To remove an ignition coil(s), depress the tab (A), disconnect the electrical connector, remove the coil retaining bolt (B)...

2   Before beginning work, purchase the specified brake fluid (see *Recommended lubricants and fluids* in this Chapter's Specifications).

3   Remove the cap from the master cylinder reservoir.

4   Using a hand suction pump or similar device, withdraw the fluid from the master cylinder reservoir.

5   Add new fluid to the master cylinder until it rises to the base of the filler neck.

6   Bleed the brake system at all four brakes until new and uncontaminated fluid is expelled from the bleeder screw (see Chapter 9). Be sure to maintain the fluid level in the master cylinder as you perform the bleeding process. If you allow the master cylinder to run dry, air will enter the system.

7   Refill the master cylinder with fluid and check the operation of the brakes. The pedal should feel solid when depressed, with no sponginess.

Warning: *Do not operate the vehicle if you are in doubt about the effectiveness of the brake system.*

24   Spark plug check and replacement (every 100,000 miles)

1   The spark plugs are located in the center of the valve cover(s).

2   In most cases the tools necessary for spark plug replacement include a spark plug socket which fits onto a ratchet (this special socket is padded inside to protect the porcelain insulators on the new plugs and hold them in place), various extensions and a feeler gauge to check and adjust the spark plug gap (see illustration). Since these engines are equipped with aluminum cylinder heads, a torque wrench should be used when tightening the spark plugs.

3   The best approach when replacing the spark plugs is to purchase the new spark plugs beforehand, adjust them to the proper gap and then replace each plug one at a time. When buying the new spark plugs, be sure to obtain the correct plug for your specific engine. This information can be found in this Chapter's Specifications or in your owner's manual.

4   Allow the engine to cool completely before attempting to remove any of the plugs. During this cooling-off time, each of the new spark plugs can be inspected for defects and the gaps can be checked.

5   The gap is checked by inserting the proper thickness gauge between the electrodes at the tip of the plug (see illustration). The gap between the electrodes should be as listed in this Chapter's Specifications or in your owner's manual. The wire should touch each of the electrodes. Also, at this time check for cracks in the spark plug body (if any are found, the plug must not be used).

Caution: *The manufacturer recommends against checking the gap on platinum-tipped spark plugs; the platinum coating could be scraped off.*

6   Cover the fender to prevent damage to the paint. Fender covers are available from auto parts stores but an old blanket will work just fine.

7   Pull the engine cover upward to disengage the cover from the ballstuds and remove the cover to gain access to the ignition coils (see illustrations).

8   If compressed air is available, use it to

24.7b ... then pull the coil straight up

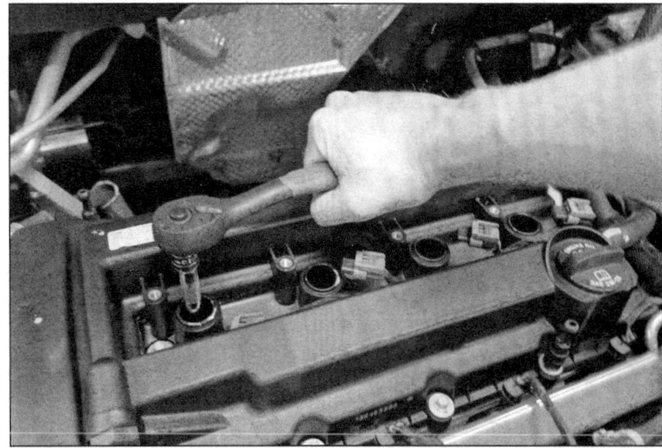

24.9 Use a ratchet, socket and long extension to remove the spark plugs

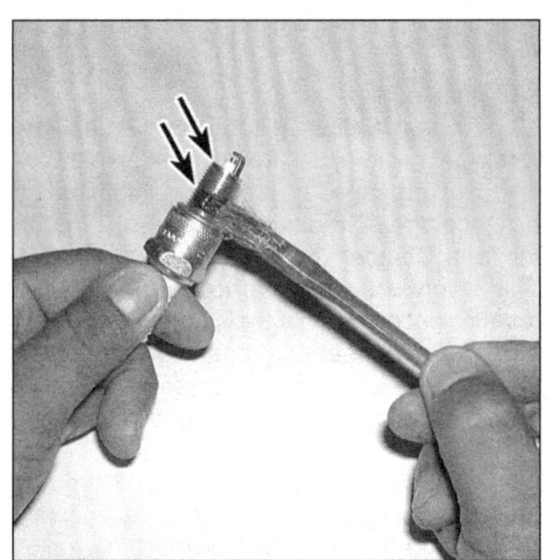

24.11 Apply a thin coat of anti-seize compound to the spark plug threads, but be careful not to get any of it near the electrodes

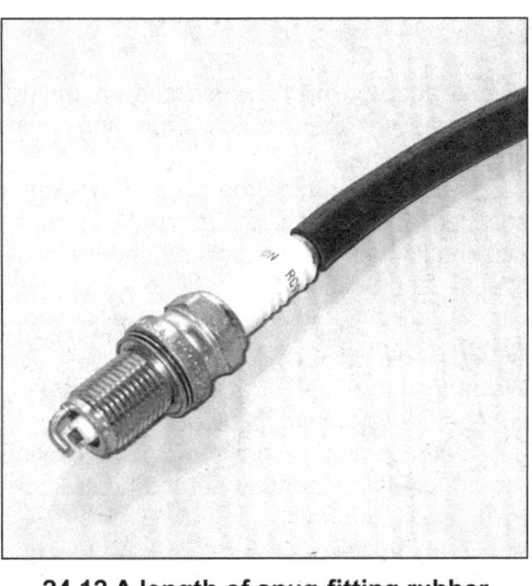

24.12 A length of snug-fitting rubber hose will save time and prevent damaged threads when installing the spark plugs

25.2a Disconnect the PCV hose . . .

blow any dirt or foreign material away from the spark plug area.

Warning: *Wear eye protection!*

9   Place the spark plug socket over the plug and remove it from the engine by turning it in a counterclockwise direction (see illustration).

10   Compare each old spark plug to those shown on the inside of the back cover to get an indication of the general running condition of the engine.

11   It's a good idea to lightly coat the threads of the spark plugs with an anti-seize compound (see illustration) to insure that the spark plugs do not seize in the aluminum cylinder head.

12   It's often difficult to insert spark plugs into their holes without cross-threading them. To avoid this possibility, fit a piece of rubber hose over the end of the spark plug (see illustration). The flexible hose acts as a universal joint to help align the plug with the plug hole. Should the plug begin to cross-thread, the hose will slip on the spark plug, preventing thread damage. Install the spark plug and

tighten it to the torque listed in this Chapter's Specifications.

13   Using a slight twisting motion, install the ignition coils.

14   Follow the above procedure for the remaining spark plugs, replacing them one at a time.

---

25 Positive Crankcase Ventilation (PCV) valve check and replacement (every 60,000 miles or 60 months)

Warning: *Do not attempt to clean the PCV valve.*

Note: If replacing the valve, compare the old and new valves to make sure they're identical. The PCV valve is located at the right front corner of the valve cover.

1   Lift the engine cover up and off of the ballstuds and remove the cover.

2   Detach the PCV hose and remove the valve (see illustrations).

25.2b . . . then use a wrench to unscrew the PCV valve from the valve cover

26.7 The drain fitting is located at the right end of the radiator

26.8a This block drain plug is located on the rear side of the cylinder block, below the exhaust manifold

26.8b This block drain plug is located on the front side of the cylinder block, above the oil filter housing

3   Install the PCV valve and tighten the valve securely.
4   Shake the valve. The valve should rattle freely - if it doesn't, replace it.
5   Replace the PCV valve with the correct one for your specific vehicle and engine size and tighten the mounting screws securely.
6   Installation is the reverse of removal.

26 Cooling system servicing (draining, flushing and refilling) (every 60 months)

Warning: *Do not allow antifreeze to come in contact with your skin or painted surfaces of the vehicle. Flush contaminated areas immediately with plenty of water. Do not store new coolant or leave old coolant lying around where it's accessible to children or pets - they're attracted by its sweet smell. Ingestion of even a small amount of coolant can be fatal! Wipe up garage floor and drip pan spills immediately. Keep antifreeze containers covered and repair cooling system leaks as soon as they're noticed. Check with local authorities about the disposal of used antifreeze. Many communities have collection centers which will see that antifreeze is disposed of properly.*
Warning: *The electric cooling fan(s) on these models can activate at any time when the ignition switch is in the ON position. Make sure the ignition is OFF when working in the vicinity of the fan(s). As an added precaution, disconnect the negative battery cable from the remote ground terminal (see Chapter 5).*
Note: *These vehicles are originally filled with Mopar 5 year/100,000 mile coolant that shouldn't be mixed with other coolants. Always refill with the correct coolant.*
1   Periodically, the cooling system should be drained, flushed and refilled to replenish the antifreeze mixture and prevent formation of rust and corrosion, which can impair the performance of the cooling system and cause engine damage.
2   At the same time the cooling system is serviced, all hoses and the radiator (pressure) cap should be inspected, tested and replaced if faulty (see Section 12).

Draining

Warning: *Wait until the engine is completely cool before beginning this procedure.*
3   With the engine cold, remove the cooling system pressure cap and set the heater control to maximum heat.
4   Loosen the right-front wheel lug nuts, then raise the vehicle and support it securely on jackstands.
5   Remove the right-front wheel, then remove the splash shield (see Chapter 11).
6   Move a large container under the radiator drain fitting to catch the coolant as it's drained.
7   Open the radiator drain fitting by turning it counterclockwise (see illustration) and allow the coolant to completely drain out.
8   After the coolant stops flowing out of the radiator, move the container under the engine block drain plugs and allow the coolant in the block to drain (see illustrations).
9   While the coolant is draining, check the condition of the radiator hoses, heater hoses and clamps. Replace any damaged clamps or hoses (see Section 12).

Flushing

10   Close the radiator and engine block drain plugs. Fill the cooling system with clean water, following the *Refilling* procedure (see Step 17).
11   Start the engine and allow it to reach normal operating temperature, then rev up the engine a few times.
12   Turn the engine off and allow it to cool completely, then drain the system as described earlier.
13   Repeat Steps 10 through 12 until the water being drained is free of contaminants.
14   Severe cases of radiator contamination or clogging will require removing the radiator (see Chapter 3) and reverse flushing it. This involves inserting a hose in the bottom radiator outlet to allow the clean water to run against the normal flow, draining out through the top. A radiator repair shop should be consulted if further cleaning or repair is necessary.
15   When the coolant is regularly drained and the system refilled with the correct coolant mixture, there should be no need to employ chemical cleaners or descalers.
16   Disconnect the coolant reservoir hose, remove the reservoir from the vehicle and flush it with clean water (see Chapter 3). Inspect it for damage and replace if necessary.

Refilling

17   Install the coolant reservoir, reconnect the hose and close the radiator drain fitting.
18   Remove the cooling system pressure cap. Add the correct mixture of the proper type of antifreeze/coolant and water, in the ratio specified on the antifreeze container or in this Chapter's Specifications, through the filler neck until it reaches the radiator cap seat.
19   Add the same coolant mixture to the reservoir until the level is between the FULL HOT and ADD marks. Install the radiator cap.
20   Run the engine until normal operating temperature is reached (the fans will cycle on, then off), then allow the engine to cool. With the engine cold, add coolant as necessary to bring it up to the correct level.
21   Keep a close watch on the coolant level and the various cooling system hoses during the first few miles of driving and check for any coolant leaks. Tighten the hose clamps and add more coolant mixture as necessary.

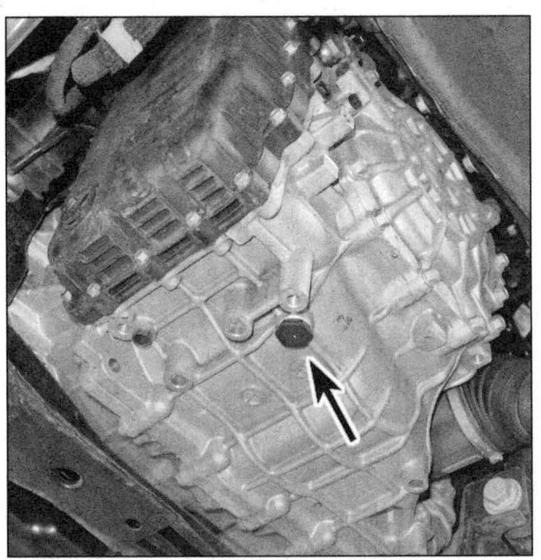

27.11 6-speed (6F24) transaxle drain
plug location

27.13 Location of the fill plug

27.15 Add fluid to the transaxle through
the vent pod hole

27 Automatic transaxle fluid and filter change (every 100,000 miles)

1   The automatic transaxle fluid and filter should be changed and the magnet cleaned at the recommended intervals.
2   Raise the front of the vehicle, support it securely on jackstands, and apply the parking brake.
3   Remove the under-vehicle splash shield.

CVT transaxle

Note: *The CVT transaxles require the use of a scan tool to check transaxle fluid temperature and special tool #9336A (or a homemade equivalent) to measure the fluid level. If you do not have both tools to make the proper temperature-to-fluid level comparisons, we do not recommend attempting this procedure.*

4   Place a container under the transaxle pan and loosen the pan bolts. Completely remove all of the the bolts except the ones along the rear of the pan. Tap the corner of the pan to break the seal and allow the fluid to drain into the container (the remaining bolts will prevent the pan from separating from the transaxle). Remove the remaining bolts and pan.
5   Remove pan gasket, then remove the oil strainer retaining bolts and strainer.
6   Install a new strainer O-ring and strainer then tighten the fasteners to the torque listed in this Chapter's Specifications.
7   Clean the pan and transaxle body (don't nick or gouge the sealing surfaces) and clean the pan magnet with a clean, lint-free cloth.
8   Install a new transaxle oil pan gasket and pan to the transaxle. Install the bolts and tighten them to the torque in this Chapter's Specifications using a criss-cross pattern. Work up to the final torque in three or four steps.

9   Lower the vehicle and add four quarts of the specified transaxle fluid (see Recommended lubricants and fluids in this Chapter's Specifications). Start the engine and allow it to idle for a minute, then move the shift lever through each gear position, ending in Park.
10   Check the fluid level using the fluid level check procedure (see Section 4).

6F24 6-speed transaxle

Note: *The 6-speed transaxle requires the use of a scan tool to check transaxle fluid temperature and special tool #10323A (or a homemade equivalent) to measure the fluid level. If you do not have both tools to make the proper temperature-to-fluid level comparisons, we do not recommend attempting this procedure.*
Note: *The fluid filter in the 6F24 6-speed automatic transaxle is not periodically serviced. To replace the fluid filter the transaxle must be removed and disassembled.*

11   Place a container under the transaxle and remove the drain plug (see illustration). Allow the fluid to drain into the container.
12   Once the fluid is done draining, install the drain plug and tighten it to torque listed in this Chapter's Specifications.
13   Remove the battery and battery tray (see Chapter 5), then remove the fill plug from the vent pod at upper front of the transaxle (see illustration).
14   Remove the check plug from the rear of the transaxle case (see Section 4).
15   Using a long funnel, add 4.3 quarts of the specified transaxle fluid (see *Recommended lubricants and fluids* in this Chapter's Specifications) through the vent pod hole (see illustration).
16   Install the fill plug into the vent pod and tighten it securely.
17   Install the battery and tray. Leave the fresh air inlet duct off for now.
18   Remove the vent cap from the hose that leads out from the base of the vent pod

27.18 Location of the vent cap (twist and
pull it out of the hose)

(see illustration) - this will allow the transaxle to keep venting while the remaining fluid is added.
19   Start the engine and allow it to idle for a minute, then slowly shift through each gear position, pausing for a couple seconds in each range, ending in the Park position. Do this two times.
20   With the engine still running, add one more quart of ATF to the transaxle - but this time, through the check plug hole at the rear of the transaxle case (see Section 4). Be careful not to burn yourself on the exhaust manifold.
21   Check the fluid level as described in Section 4, adding or removing fluid as necessary.
22   Once the fluid level is correct, turn off the engine and install the vent cap into the hose, then reinstall the fresh air inlet duct. Install the check plug and tighten it to the torque listed in this Chapter's Specifications.

28   Transfer case lubricant change (4WD/AWD models) (every 50,000 miles)

1   Drive the vehicle for at least 15 minutes to warm the lubricant in the case. Perform this warm-up procedure with 4WD engaged, if possible.
2   Raise the vehicle and support it securely on jackstands.
3   Remove the filler plug from the side of the case.
4   Remove the drain plug from the lower part of the case and allow the old lubricant to drain completely.
5   After the lubricant has drained completely, clean the plug and the plug opening, apply thread sealant to the plug, then reinstall the plug and tighten it securely.
6   Fill the case with the specified lubricant until it is level with the lower edge of the filler hole.
7   Clean the filler plug and the plug opening, apply thread sealant to the plug, then reinstall the plug and tighten it securely.
8   Drive the vehicle for a short distance, then check the drain and fill plugs for leakage.

29   Manual transaxle lubricant change (every 50,000 miles)

1   Drive the vehicle for at least 15 minutes to warm the lubricant in the case.
2   Raise the vehicle and support it securely on jackstands.
3   Remove the check/fill plug from the side of the left case.
4   Remove the drain plug from the lower part of the case on the left side of the differential area and allow the old lubricant to drain completely.
5   After the lubricant has drained completely, clean the plug and the plug opening. Apply thread sealant to the plug, then reinstall the plug and tighten it securely.
6   Fill the case with the specified lubricant until it is level with the lower edge of the filler hole.
7   Clean the check/fill plug and the plug opening. Apply thread sealant to the plug, then reinstall the plug and tighten it securely.
8   Drive the vehicle for a short distance, then check the drain and fill plugs for leakage.

30   Differential lubricant change (every 50,000 miles)

1   This procedure should be performed after the vehicle has been driven so the lubricant will be warm and therefore flow out of the differential more easily.
2   Raise the vehicle and support it securely on jackstands.
3   Remove the filler plug from the rear cover; it's a few inches above the drain plug.
4   Remove the drain plug from the lower part of the rear cover and allow the old lubricant to drain completely.
5   After the lubricant has drained completely, clean the plug and the plug opening. Apply thread sealant to the plug, then reinstall the plug and tighten it securely.
6   Fill the differential with the specified lubricant until it is level with the lower edge of the filler hole.
7   Clean the filler plug and the plug opening, apply thread sealant to the plug, then reinstall the plug and tighten it securely.
8   Drive the vehicle for a short distance, then check the drain and fill plugs for leakage.

Notes

Notes

Chapter 2 Part A
Engines

Contents

Specifications

General

Bore
2.0 L engine	3.386 inches
2.4L engine	3.465 inches

Stroke
2.0 L engine	3.386 inches
2.4 L engine	3.819 inches

Compression ratio ... 10.5:1

Displacement
2.0 liter	122 cubic inches
2.4 liter	146.5 cubic inches

Firing order ... 1-3-4-2

Camshaft

Bearing bore
Front intake	1.1810 to 1.1819 inches
Front exhaust	1.5747 to 1.5756 inches
Remaining bores	0.9448 to 0.9457 inch

Camshaft journal diameter
Front intake	1.1797 to 1.1803 inches
Front exhaust	1.4166 to 1.4173 inches
Remaining journals	0.943 to 0.944 inch

Bearing clearance
Front intake	0.0008 to 0.0022 inch
Front exhaust	0.0007 to 0.0020 inch
Remaining journals	0.0008 to 0.0026 inch

Endplay ... 0.004 to 0.009 inch

Lobe lift
Intake @ 0.007 inch lash	0.362 inch
Exhaust @ 0.011 inch lash	0.331 inch

Valve clearance
Intake	0.006 to 0.009 inch
Exhaust	0.010 to 0.012 inch

Cylinder head

Head gasket surface warpage limit	0.004 inch maximum
Exhaust manifold mounting surface warpage limit	0.006 inch maximum

Intake and exhaust manifolds

Warpage limit	0.006 inch maximum

Torque specifications

Ft-lbs (unless otherwise indicated)

Note: *One foot-pound (ft-lb) of torque is equivalent to 12 inch-pounds (in-lbs) of torque. Torque values below approximately 15 ft-lbs are expressed in inch-pounds, because most foot-pound torque wrenches are not accurate at these smaller values.*

Alternator drivebelt idler pulley bolt	35
Camshaft bearing cap bolts (in sequence - see illustration 10.34)	
M6 bolts	
2010 and earlier models	106 in-lbs
2011 and later models	97 in-lbs
M8 bolts	22
Phaser-to-camshaft bolt	55
Crankshaft pulley bolt	155
Cylinder head bolts (in sequence - see illustration 11.28)	
Short head (5/16-inch) bolts	
Step 1	25
Step 2	45
Step 3	45
Step 4	Tighten an additional 1/4-turn (90-degrees)
Long head (1/2-inch) bolts	
Step 1	25
Step 2	54
Step 3	54
Step 4	Tighten an additional 1/4-turn (90-degrees)
Driveplate-to-crankshaft bolts	
Step 1	22
Step 2	Tighten an additional 51-degrees
Engine (and transaxle) mounts	
Right mount	
Mount insulator-to-chassis bolts	55
Mount bracket-to-engine bolts	50
Through-bolt	65
Left (transaxle) mount)	
Mount bracket-to-transaxle bolts	Not available
Mount insulator-to-chassis bolts	55
Through-bolt	74
Front mount	
Mount-to-crossmember bolts	35
Through-bolt	74
Rear mount	
Mount bolts	37
Through-bolt	35
Exhaust manifold-to-cylinder head bolts	25
Exhaust manifold-to-exhaust pipe bolts	21
Intake manifold bolts	18
Oil pan bolts	
M6 bolts	80 in-lbs
M8 bolts	18
Balance shaft module	
New bolts - 180 mm	
Step 1	132 in-lbs
Step 2	24
Step 3	Tighten an additional 1/4-turn (90-degrees)
New bolts - 185 mm	
Step 1	132 in-lbs
Step 2	22
Step 3	Tighten an additional 1/4-turn (90-degrees)
Timing chain cover bolts	
M6 bolts	80 in-lbs
M8 bolts	19
Timing chain tensioner assembly bolts	89 in-lbs
Timing chain guide bolts	106 in-lbs
Valve cover bolts	
Step 1	44 in-lbs
Step 2	90 in-lbs

1 General information

1   This Part of Chapter 2 is devoted to in-vehicle engine repair procedures. Information concerning engine removal and installation can be found in Chapter 2B.

2   These engines utilize an aluminum in-line four cylinder block. The double overhead camshaft aluminum cylinder head is heat treated and is equipped with replaceable valve guides, seats, mechanical lifters and four valves per cylinder.

3   The in-line four cylinder 2.0L DOHC and 2.4L DOHC engines incorporate a balance shaft module. The oil pump is integrated into the module and is serviced as a unit with the balance shaft that is installed below the crankshaft. These engines are not free-wheeling engines; if the timing chain fails, the pistons will contact the valves.

4   The following repair procedures are based on the assumption that the engine is installed in the vehicle. If the engine has been removed from the vehicle and mounted on a stand, many of the steps outlined in this Part of Chapter 2 will not apply.

5   The Specifications included in this Part of Chapter 2 apply only to the procedures contained in this Part.

2 Repair operations possible with the engine in the vehicle

1   Many major repair operations can be accomplished without removing the engine from the vehicle.

2   Clean the engine compartment and the exterior of the engine with some type of degreaser before any work is done. It will make the job easier and help keep dirt out of the internal areas of the engine.

3   Depending on the components involved, it may be helpful to remove the hood to improve access to the engine as repairs are performed (refer to Chapter 11 if necessary). Cover the fenders to prevent damage to the paint. Special pads are available, but an old bedspread or blanket will also work.

4   If vacuum, exhaust, oil or coolant leaks develop, indicating a need for gasket or seal replacement, the repairs can generally be made with the engine in the vehicle. The intake and exhaust manifold gaskets, oil pan gasket, camshaft and crankshaft oil seals and cylinder head gasket are all accessible with the engine in place.

5   Exterior engine components, such as the intake and exhaust manifolds, the oil pan, the oil pump, the water pump, the starter motor, the alternator, the distributor and the fuel system components can be removed for repair with the engine in place.

6   Since the camshaft(s) and cylinder head can be removed without pulling the engine, valve component servicing can also be accomplished with the engine in the vehicle. Replacement of the timing belt and sprockets is also possible with the engine in the vehicle.

7   In extreme cases caused by a lack of necessary equipment, repair or replacement of piston rings, pistons, connecting rods and rod bearings is possible with the engine in the vehicle. However, this practice is not recommended because of the cleaning and preparation work that must be done to the components involved.

3 Top Dead Center (TDC) for number one piston - locating

1   Top Dead Center (TDC) is the highest point in the cylinder that each piston reaches as it travels up-and-down when the crankshaft turns. Each piston reaches TDC on the compression stroke and again on the exhaust stroke, but TDC generally refers to piston position on the compression stroke. When the notched timing mark on the crankshaft pulley is aligned with the "T" mark of the indicator on the timing chain cover, number one piston is at TDC (see illustration 3.6).

2   Positioning a specific piston at TDC is an essential part of certain procedures such as camshaft(s) removal, and timing chain and sprocket replacement.

3   Remove all of the spark plugs, as this will make it easier to rotate the engine by hand (see Chapter 1).

4   Insert a compression gauge (screw-in type with a hose) in the number 1 spark plug hole. Place the gauge dial where you can see it while turning the crankshaft pulley bolt.

Note: *The number one cylinder is located at the front (timing chain end) of the engine.*

5   Loosen the right-front wheel lug nuts, raise the front of the vehicle and support it securely on jackstands, then remove the wheel. Remove the drivebelt splash shield for access to the crankshaft pulley (see Chapter 1, Section 22).

6   Turn the crankshaft clockwise with a socket and large breaker bar until you see compression building up on the gauge, indi-cating that you are on the compression stroke for that cylinder. If you did not see compression build up, continue with one more complete revolution to achieve TDC for the number one cylinder.

7   Continue turning the crankshaft until the notch in the crankshaft pulley is aligned with the "T" mark on the timing chain cover indicator (see illustration). This is TDC compression for cylinder number one.

8   After the number one piston has been positioned at TDC on the compression stroke, TDC for any of the remaining cylinders can be located by turning the crankshaft 180-degrees (1/2-turn) at a time and following the firing order (see this Chapter's Specifications).

4 Valve cover - removal and installation

Removal

1   Disconnect the cable from the negative terminal of the battery (see Chapter 5).

2   Remove the engine cover by pulling it up and off of the ballstuds.

3   Remove the ignition coils (see Chapter 5).

4   Clearly label then disconnect any electrical wiring harnesses which connect to, or cross over, the valve cover.

5   Disconnect the PCV valve hose and breather hose from the valve cover.

6   Remove the ballstuds for the engine cover from the valve cover stud bolts (see illustration). Remove the valve cover bolts in the reverse order of the tightening sequence (see illustration 4.9), clean any debris from the cover, then lift off the cover. If the cover sticks to the cylinder head, tap on it with a soft-face hammer or place a wood block against the cover and tap on the wood with a hammer.

Caution: *If you have to pry between the valve cover and the cylinder head, be extremely careful not to gouge or nick the gasket surfaces of either part. A leak could develop after reassembly.*

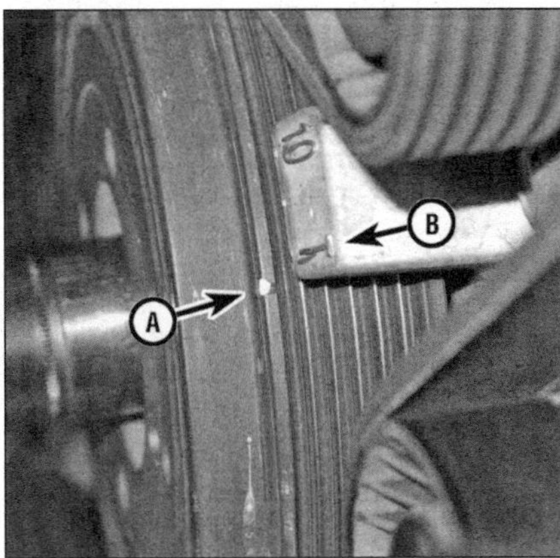

3.7 The notched timing mark on the crankshaft pulley (A) aligns with the "T" mark of the indicator on the timing cover (B) when TDC for number one piston is reached

4.6 Remove the ballstuds from the valve cover stud bolts

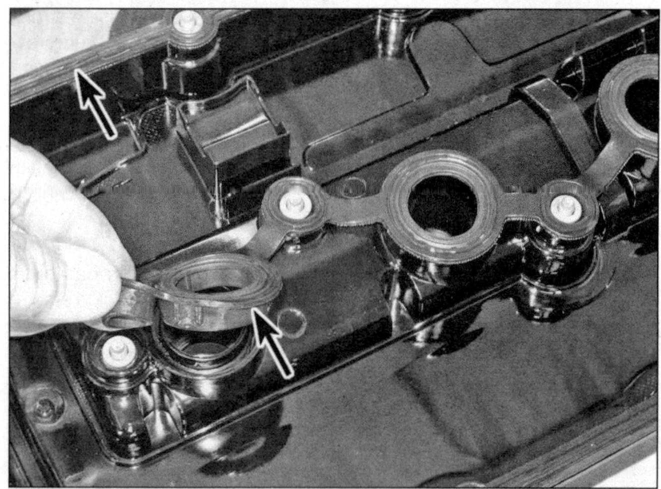

4.8 Install new inner and outer gaskets on the valve cover

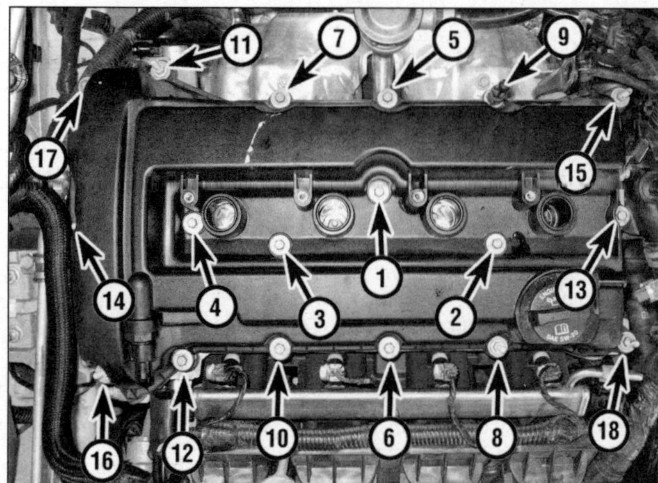

4.9 Valve cover bolt tightening sequence

5.9 Disconnect the wiring harness retainer from the intake manifold

5.10 Disconnect the vacuum line from the manifold

7   Remove the valve cover perimeter rubber seal and spark plug tube seal. Thoroughly clean the valve cover and cylinder head mating surfaces. After cleaning the surfaces, degrease them with a rag soaked in brake system cleaner.

Installation

8   Install new gaskets into the channels on the cover (see illustration). Place the cover on the engine and install the cover bolts.

9   Tighten the bolts, in the proper sequence (see illustration), to the torque listed in this Chapter's Specifications.

10   The remainder of installation is the reverse of removal. Run the engine and check for oil leaks.

5   Intake manifold - removal and installation

Removal

1   Relieve the fuel system pressure (see Chapter 4), then disconnect the cable from the negative terminal of the battery (see Chapter 5).

2   Remove the engine cover by pulling it up and off of the ballstuds.

3   Remove the fresh air inlet duct and the air intake duct between the air filter housing and the throttle body (see Chapter 4).

4   Remove the ignition coils (see Chapter 5).

5   Remove the fuel rail and fuel injectors as a single assembly (see Chapter 4).

6   Disconnect the oil temperature sensor (see Chapter 6).

7   Unplug the electrical connectors from the Variable Valve Timing (VVT) solenoid, the Manifold Absolute Pressure (MAP) sensor and the intake Camshaft Position (CMP) sensor (see Chapter 6), and move the electrical harness out of the way.

8   Disconnect the electrical connector from the throttle body. Remove the fasteners from the transaxle-to-throttle body support bracket at the throttle body end of the bracket, and loosen - but don't remove - the fastener at the transaxle end of the bracket.

9   Remove the wiring harness retainer from the intake manifold (see illustration) and move the harness out of the way.

10   Label, then disconnect the vacuum line(s) from the manifold (see illustration).

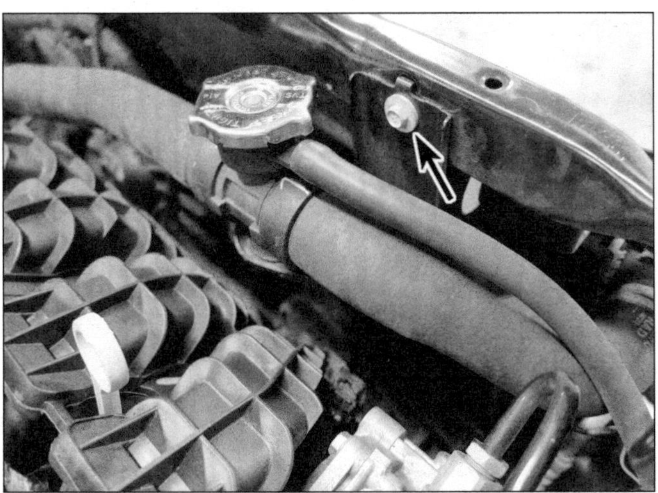

5.11 Remove the upper radiator hose bracket fastener

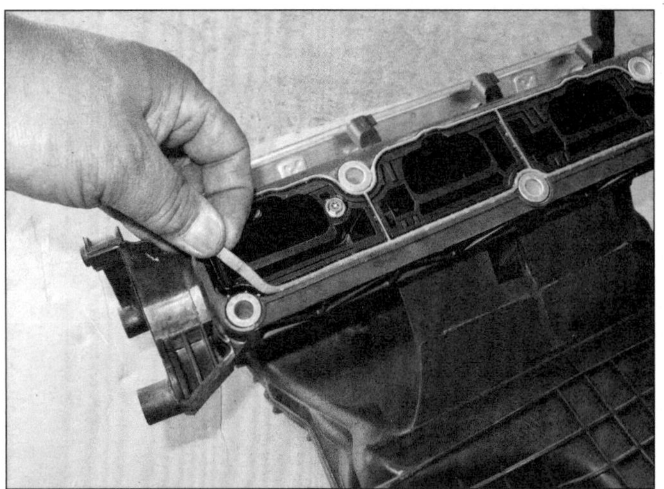

5.13 Remove the intake manifold gasket from the manifold

5.15 Slide the manifold onto the studs

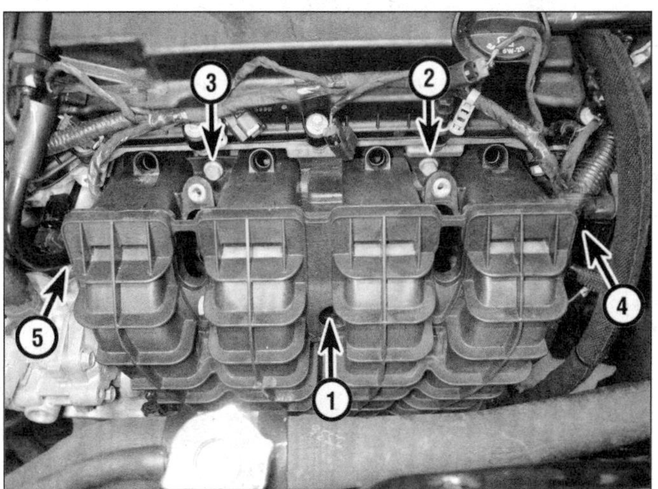

5.16 Intake manifold fastener tightening sequence

11   Remove the upper radiator hose retaining bracket fastener (see illustration) and secure the hose out of the way.

12   If you're planning to replace or service the intake manifold, remove the throttle body (see Chapter 4).

Note: *If you're simply removing the intake manifold to remove or service the cylinder head, it's not necessary to remove the throttle body from the intake manifold.*

13   Remove the intake manifold fasteners and washers (see illustration 5.16), then remove the intake manifold and the manifold gasket (see illustration).

Inspection

14   Using a straightedge and feeler gauge, check the intake manifold mating surface for warpage. Check the intake manifold surface on the cylinder head also. If the warpage on either surface exceeds the limit listed in this Chapter's Specifications, the intake manifold and/or the cylinder head must be resurfaced at an automotive machine shop or, if the warpage is too excessive for resurfacing, replaced.

Installation

15   Clean the mating surfaces of the manifold and cylinder head with brake system cleaner. Using a new manifold gasket, install the intake manifold onto the manifold studs (see illustration).

16   Tighten the intake manifold fasteners gradually and evenly, in the indicated sequence (see illustration), to the torque listed in this Chapter's Specifications.

17   The remainder of installation is the reverse of removal.

6   Exhaust manifold - removal, inspection and installation

Warning: *Allow the engine to cool completely before beginning this procedure.*

Note: *On AWD models, the exhaust manifold and catalytic converter has been combined into a single unit, called a "maniverter".*

Removal

1   Raise the vehicle and support it securely on jackstands.

2   Disconnect the exhaust pipe from the exhaust manifold (see Chapter 6).

Note: *On some models, it might be necessary to remove the exhaust system to create sufficient clearance to remove the manifold.*

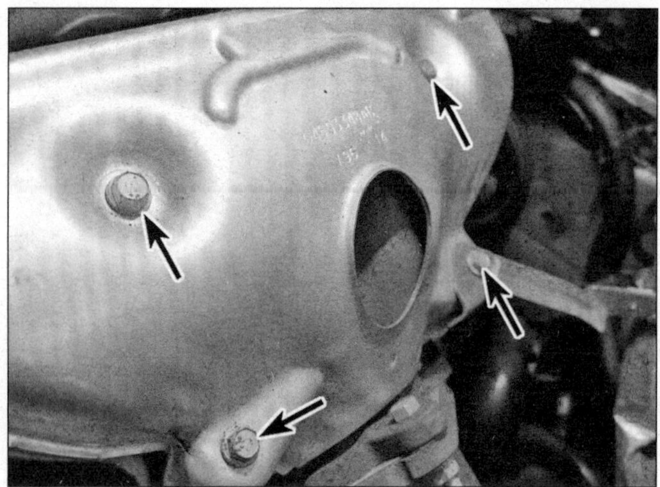

6.3 Exhaust manifold heat shield fasteners

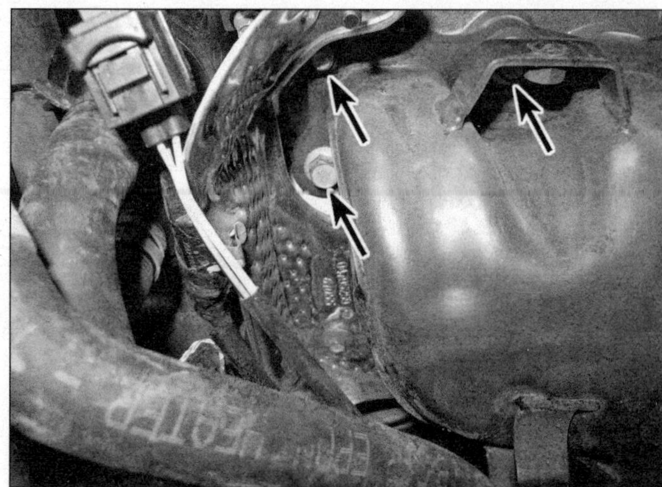

6.5a To detach the exhaust manifold, remove these fasteners from the left end . . .

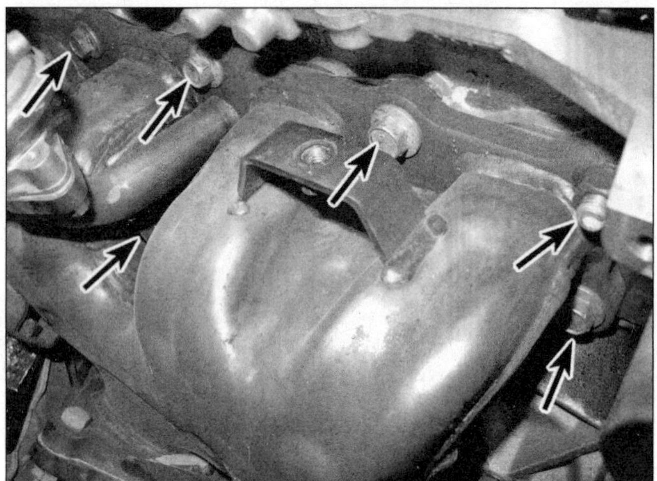

6.5b . . . and these fasteners from the center and the right-end

7.5 Use a special holding tool to prevent the crankshaft from turning while loosening the bolt

3   Remove the exhaust manifold heat shield (see illustration). Also remove the manifold brace.

4   Unplug the electrical connector for the oxygen sensor, then remove the oxygen sensor from the exhaust manifold (see Chapter 6).

5   Unscrew the mounting bolts (see illustrations) and remove the exhaust manifold and the old manifold gasket.

Inspection

6   Inspect the exhaust manifold for cracks and any other obvious damage. If the manifold is cracked or damaged in any way, replace it.

7   Using a wire brush, clean up the threads of the exhaust manifold bolts and inspect the threads for damage. Replace any bolts that have thread damage.

8   Using a scraper, remove all traces of gasket material from the mating surfaces and inspect them for wear and cracks.

Caution: *When removing gasket material from any surface, especially aluminum, be very careful not to scratch or gouge the gasket surface. Any damage to the surface may result in a leak after reassembly. Gasket removal solvents are available from auto parts stores and may prove helpful.*

9   Using a straightedge and feeler gauge, inspect the exhaust manifold mating surface for warpage. Check the exhaust manifold surface on the cylinder head also. If the warpage on any surface exceeds the limits listed in this Chapter's Specifications, the exhaust manifold and/or cylinder head must be replaced or resurfaced at an automotive machine shop.

Installation

10   Using a new exhaust manifold gasket (and NO sealant), install the exhaust manifold and tighten the mounting bolts, a little at a time and working from the center outward, to the torque listed in this Chapter's Specifications.

11   The remainder of installation is the reverse of removal.

7   Crankshaft pulley - removal and installation

Removal

1   Disconnect the cable from the negative terminal of the battery (see Chapter 5).

2   Loosen the right-front wheel lug nuts, then raise the vehicle and support it securely on jackstands.

3   Remove the right-front wheel.

4   Remove the drivebelt (see Chapter 1).

5   The crankshaft pulley bolt is incredibly tight; using a breaker bar, socket and special tool #9707 or equivalent (see illustration), hold the pulley from turning while loosening the bolt.

7.6 Slide the pulley from the end of the crankshaft; a puller shouldn't be required

8.2 Use a hook tool and pry the seal from the timing cover

8.3 Another way of removing an old oil seal is to screw a self-tapping screw partially into the seal, then use pliers as a lever to pull it from the engine

6   Pull the crankshaft pulley off the crankshaft (see illustration).

Installation

7   Apply clean engine oil or multi-purpose grease to the seal contact surface of the pulley hub (if it isn't lubricated, the seal lip could be damaged and oil leakage would result).

8   Install the crankshaft pulley, aligning the keyway on the crankshaft with the slot in the pulley hub. Install the bolt and tighten it by hand.

9   Prevent the engine from rotating (see Step 5) then tighten the bolt to the torque listed in this Chapter's Specifications.

10   The remainder of installation is the reverse of removal.

8   Crankshaft front oil seal - replacement

1   Remove the crankshaft pulley (see Section 7).

2   Use a screwdriver or hook tool to carefully pry out the seal (see illustration).

Note: *Be careful not to damage the oil pump cover bore where the seal is seated or the nose and sealing surface of the crankshaft.*

3   Another procedure for removing the seal is to drill a small hole on each side of the seal and place a self-tapping screw in each hole (see illustration). Use these screws as a means of pulling the seal out without having to pry on it.

4   If the seal is being replaced when the timing chain cover is removed, support the cover on top of two blocks of wood and drive the seal out from the backside with a hammer and punch.

Caution: *Be careful not to scratch, gouge or distort the area that the seal fits into or a leak will develop.*

5   Apply clean engine oil or multi-purpose grease to the outer edge of the new seal, then install it in the cover with the lip (spring side) facing IN. Drive the seal into place with a seal driver or large socket and a hammer (see illustration). Make sure the seal enters the bore squarely and stop when the front face is at the proper depth.

6   Check the surface on the crankshaft pulley hub that the oil seal rides on. If the surface has been grooved from long-time contact with the seal, the pulley will have to be replaced.

7   Lubricate the pulley hub with clean engine oil, then install the crankshaft pulley (see Section 7).

8   The remainder of installation is the reverse of the removal.

9   Timing chain cover, chain and sprockets - removal, inspection and installation

Warning: *Wait until the engine is completely cool before beginning this procedure.*

Caution: *The timing system is complex, and severe engine damage will occur if you make any mistakes. Do not attempt this procedure unless you are highly experienced with this type of repair. If you are at all unsure of your abilities, be sure to consult an expert. Double-check all your work and be sure everything is correct before you attempt to start the engine.*

Caution: *Do not rotate the crankshaft or camshafts separately during this procedure (with the timing chains removed), as damage to the valves may occur.*

Removal

Timing chain cover

1   Relieve the fuel system pressure (see Chapter 4), then disconnect the cable from the negative terminal of the battery (see Chapter 4).

2   Remove the engine cover by pulling the cover up and off of the ballstuds.

3   Loosen the right-front wheel lug nuts,

8.5 Drive the seal squarely into the cover using a seal driver or socket and hammer

then raise the front of the vehicle and support it securely on jackstands.

4   Drain the engine coolant (see Chapter 1).

5   Drain the engine oil (see Chapter 1).

6   Remove the right-front wheel and drivebelt splash shield (see Chapter 1).

7   Remove the drivebelt, drivebelt tensioner and idler pulleys (see Chapter 1).

8   Position the number one piston at Top Dead Center on the compression stroke (see Section 3).

9   Remove the power steering reservoir (see Chapter 10) without disconnecting the lines and secure it out of the way.

10   Remove the power steering hose bracket bolt from the front engine mount. Remove the power steering pump mounting bolts and secure the pump out of the way without disconnecting the hoses (see Chapter 10).

11   Remove the crankshaft pulley (see Section 7).

12   Remove the ignition coils (see Chapter 5).

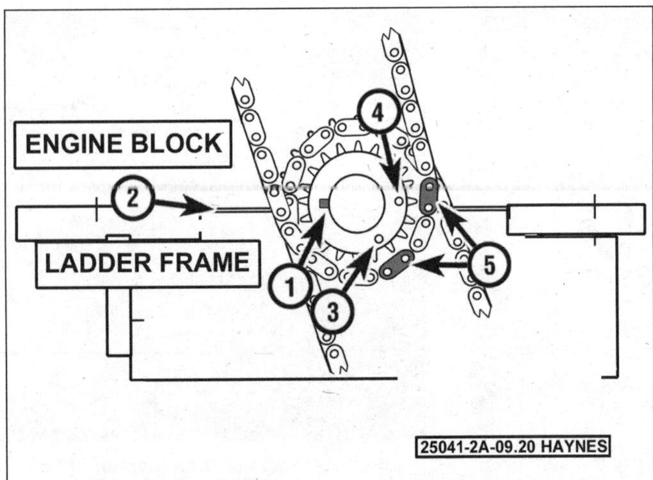

9.20 Align the keyway of the crankshaft to the 9 o'clock position; at this position, the keyway will be pointing to the line made where the engine block and ladder frame meet

1 *Crankshaft keyway at the 9 o'clock position*
2 *Line made between the engine block and ladder frame*
3 *Early production timing mark*
4 *Late production timing mark*
5 *Timing chain plated link - there will only be one plated link on the chain - illustration shows both approximate link locations*

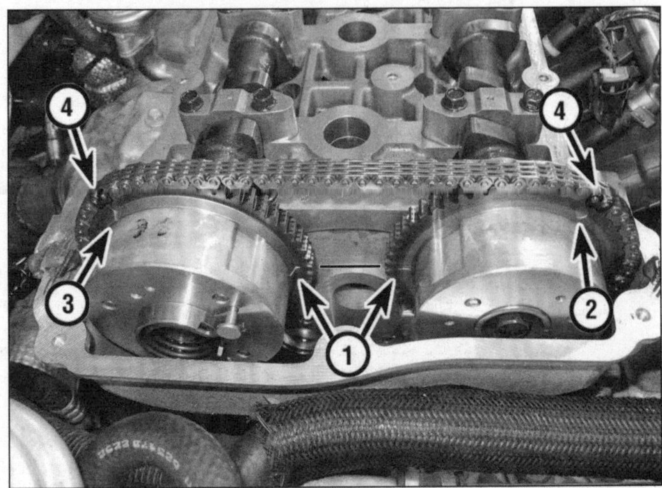

9.21 Camshaft phaser timing mark locations

1 *Timing marks on the camshaft sprockets facing each other and parallel with the cylinder head mating surface*
2 *Intake camshaft phaser timing mark*
3 *Exhaust camshaft phaser timing mark*
4 *Plated timing chain links*

13   Remove the valve cover (see Section 4). **Caution:** *Once the valve cover is removed, the magnetic timing wheels are exposed. The magnetic timing wheels on the camshafts must not come in contact with any type of magnet or magnetic field. If contact is made, the timing wheels will have to be replaced.*

14   Remove the water pump pulley, and the air conditioning compressor and bracket (see Chapter 3). Just unbolt the compressor and reposition it - don't disconnect the refrigerant lines. **Caution:** *Support the air conditioning compressor with a length of wire or rope - don't let it hang by the refrigerant lines.*

15   Support the engine with a floor jack and wooden block placed between on the jackhead. Slightly raise the engine, then remove the right engine mount (see Section 17).

16   Remove the right engine mount bracket from the timing chain cover.

17   Remove the oil pan-to-timing chain cover bolts from the bottom of the timing chain cover. **Note:** *It is not necessary to remove the oil pan to remove the timing chain cover.*

18   Remove the timing chain cover mounting bolts. Note the locations of the mounting bolts; there are several different types of bolts used that must be installed in their original locations. There are seven indented prying points, one on top and three on each side; carefully pry the cover free of the engine block and cylinder head and remove the cover from the bottom of the vehicle. If it still sticks, slip a putty knife between the engine block and cover to break the bond (but be careful not to scratch the surfaces).

19   Once the cover is removed, RTV gasket material must be thoroughly cleaned from the cylinder head, engine block and back side of the timing chain cover.

Timing chain

Warning: *When the timing chains are removed, do not rotate the camshafts or crankshaft; the valves and pistons can be damaged if contact is made.*

20   If the engine has moved from TDC, temporarily install the crankshaft pulley bolt. Turn the crankshaft with the bolt to TDC number 1 to align the timing marks on the crankshaft and camshaft sprockets. Rotate the engine clockwise only, until the crankshaft keyway aligns with the line made where the engine block and ladder frame meets (see illustration). **Note:** *On these engines, there are early and late production runs that have different timing marks on the crankshaft sprocket. On the early production run, the crankshaft sprocket timing mark is between the 5 and 6 o'clock positions. On the later run, the sprocket timing mark is closer to the 3 o'clock position. On both production runs, the crankshaft keyway will always be aligned at the 9 o'clock position, pointing to the line made where the engine block and ladder frame meet.* **Note:** *If the timing chain plated links are faded or can no longer be seen, mark the links to the corresponding timing marks before removing the chain (if you plan to reuse the old chain).*

21   The timing chain plated links should be aligned with the camshaft phaser timing marks. On the intake (front) side camshaft phaser, the plated link should be aligned with the machined dot, which should be facing away from the opposite camshaft phaser dot - about the 1 o'clock position. The machined scribe line should be pointing toward the other camshaft phasers machined line, in a parallel line with the gasket surface of the cylinder head - about the 9 o'clock position. On the exhaust (rear) side camshaft phaser, the timing chain plated link should be aligned with the machined dot, which should be facing away from each other phaser mark - about the 11 o'clock position. The machined scribe line should be pointing toward the phaser scribe line, in a parallel line with the gasket surface of the cylinder head - at the 3 o'clock position (see illustration). **Note:** *Each of the camshaft phasers have two timing marks - a machined dot and machined scribe line. When they are properly timed to No.1 cylinder (TDC) the dots are facing away from each other and the lines are pointing toward each other in a parallel line.*

22   Verify the phaser marks are aligned with the plated links (see illustration 9.21); if the plated links cannot be distinguished but the camshaft phaser marks are in the proper positions, mark the plated links to the corresponding camshaft phaser timing marks before removing the chain or the chain will need to be replaced with a new one that has the identifying plated links. **Note:** *Use paint or a permanent marker to mark the direction of rotation on all chains before removing them so they can be installed in the same direction.*

23   Remove the timing chain tensioner mounting bolts and remove the tensioner and guide from the left side of the timing chain;

the tensioner will not come apart when it is removed.

24   Remove the timing chain from the camshaft phasers and crankshaft sprocket.

25   If necessary, remove the oil pump/balance shaft chain (see Section 14), then remove the crankshaft gear (see Section 8).

26   If necessary, remove the chain guide fasteners and guide.

Inspection

27   Inspect the timing chain dampener (guide) for cracks and wear and replace it, if necessary.

28   Clean the timing chain and sprockets with solvent and dry them with compressed air (if available).

Warning: *Wear eye protection when using compressed air.*

29   Inspect the components for wear and damage. Look for teeth that are deformed, chipped, pitted, and cracked.

30   The timing chain and sprockets should be replaced with new ones if the engine has high mileage, the chain has visible damage, or total freeplay midway between the sprockets exceeds one inch. Failure to replace a worn timing chain and sprockets may result in erratic engine performance, loss of power, and decreased fuel mileage. Loose chains can jump timing. In the worst case, chain jumping or breakage will result in severe engine damage.

Installation

Caution: *Before starting the engine, carefully rotate the crankshaft by hand through at least two full revolutions (use a socket and breaker bar on the crankshaft pulley center bolt). If you feel any resistance, STOP! There is something wrong - most likely, valves are contacting the pistons. You must find the problem before proceeding.*

31   Use a plastic gasket scraper to remove all traces of old gasket material and sealant from the cover, engine block and cylinder heads. The components are all made of aluminum, so be careful not to nick or gouge them. Only clean the gasket sealing surfaces with rubbing alcohol (isopropyl) - do not use any oil based fluids.

32   If removed, install the crankshaft sprocket and oil pump/balance shaft module chain (see Section 14).

33   If removed, install the right side chain guide.

34   Make sure the keyway is installed on the crankshaft and is at TDC, with the keyway pointing toward the 9 o'clock position in line with the line made where the engine block and ladder frame meet (see illustration 9.20).

35   Verify the camshaft phasers are at TDC (see illustration 9.21).

36   Using clean engine oil, coat the sprockets and chain. Place the chain on the crankshaft sprockets, with the plated links aligned with the machined dots on the phasers.

37   Loop the chain down and around the crankshaft sprocket, aligning the plated link with the timing mark on the crankshaft sprocket (see illustration 9.20). Check the alignment of the marks of the plate links and camshaft sprockets (see illustration 9.21). Make sure the slack in the chain is all on the tensioner side.

38   While holding the timing chain tensioner with light pressure against the plunger, use a pick to lift up on the plunger ratchet through the front hole until the plunger can be pressed in and special tool #8514 or a 3 mm Allen wrench can be inserted through the rear hole of the tensioner body, holding the plunger in the compressed position.

39   Install the chain guide and tensioner, then tighten the fasteners to the torque listed in this Chapter's Specifications. Remove the special tool from the tensioner plunger.

40   Temporarily reinstall the crankshaft pulley and rotate the engine two complete turns, with the line made where the engine block and ladder frame meet as the reference point. Verify all the marks line up (see illustrations 9.20 and 9.21); if the marks are off, rotate the engine two more complete turns and check again.

41   Once the timing marks are correct, apply a continuous, 1/8-inch wide by 1/16-inch high bead of RTV sealant to the sealing surfaces of the cylinder block and cylinder head.

42   Apply a 1/8-inch wide by 1/16-inch high bead of RTV sealant to the sealing surface of the oil pan, making sure to make a complete circle around each bolt hole on the pan, including the corners where the timing cover meets the oil pan and cylinder block.

43   Working from under the vehicle, install the pan from the bottom toward the top.

44   Install the timing cover bolts and tighten them in a criss-cross pattern, in three steps, to the torque listed in this Chapter's Specifications.

45   The remainder of installation is the reverse of removal.

46   Add oil and coolant (see Chapter 1), start the engine and check for leaks.

10   Camshaft(s) and lifters – removal, inspection and installation

Warning: *Wait until the engine is completely cool before beginning this procedure.*

Caution: *The timing system is complex, and severe engine damage will occur if you make any mistakes. Do not attempt this procedure unless you are highly experienced with this type of repair. If you are at all unsure of your abilities, be sure to consult an expert. Double-check all your work and be sure everything is correct before you attempt to start the engine.*

Note: *The camshafts can only be removed, leaving the timing chain cover and timing chain in place, by using the tools outlined in this Section. If the tools are not available, the timing chain cover will have to be removed before the camshafts can be removed (see Section 9).*

Removal

1   Remove the engine cover by pulling the cover up and off of the ballstuds.

2   Disconnect the cable from the negative terminal of the battery (see Chapter 5).

3   Loosen the right-front wheel lug nuts, then raise the front of the vehicle and support it securely on jackstands. Remove the right front wheel and the drivebelt splash shield.

4   Drain the engine oil and coolant, then remove the drivebelt (see Chapter 1).

5   Remove the ignition coils (see Chapter 5) and the spark plugs (see Chapter 1).

6   Remove the valve cover (see Section 4).

7   Rotate the crankshaft clockwise and place the no. 1 piston at TDC on the compression stroke (see Section 3).

8   Verify the timing marks are in alignment (see Section 9), then use a permanent marker or paint to mark the camshaft phasers to the timing chains for reinstallation.

9   Locate, then remove the timing chain tensioner plug from the timing chain cover (when looking straight at the crankshaft pulley, the plug is located at approximately the 10 o'clock position.

10   With the plug removed you should be able to see tensioner. Working through the small hole in the side of the tensioner, use a pick to lift up on the plunger ratchet through the front hole then insert special tool #8514 or a 3 mm Allen wrench through the rear hole of the tensioner body, holding the plunger in this position for the reminder of the repair.

11   Insert the special chain holding tool #9701 (wedge) between the two camshaft phasers, then lightly tap the tool down until it won't go any further.

Caution: *The chain holding tool must remain in place while the phasers are removed or the timing chain becomes disengaged with the crankshaft sprocket.*

Note: *The camshaft bearing caps should have marks with a number and letter code; " 1I " is for the number one intake camshaft bearing cap. The notch or arrow on the caps should always be installed toward the front. If the caps are not marked, use a paint marker or permanent ink to mark the cap locations and installation direction.*

Caution: *Don't use a punch or number stamp to mark the caps.*

12   Loosen the camshaft bearing cap bolts in the reverse order of the tightening sequence (see illustration 10.33).

13   Remove the front (or joined) camshaft bearing cap and upper half of the bearing insert from the exhaust side of the cap first, then carefully remove the remaining camshaft bearing caps.

Note: *Only the front (or joined) bearing cap has bearing inserts on the exhaust side of the cap.*

14   Carefully remove the intake camshaft first by lifting the rear of the intake camshaft upward from the journals while slightly rotating the camshaft clockwise, then lift the chain off of the phaser sprocket.

15   Once the intake camshaft is removed,

10.20 Use a micrometer to measure cam lobe height

10.31 Location of the exhaust bearing insert number location (A) and installation direction (B) of the front cap

10.32a Install the exhaust camshaft bearing caps in the correct order (A) and directions (B), then . . .

10.32b . . . install the intake camshaft bearing caps in the correct order (A) and directions (B)

lift the chain up and remove the exhaust camshaft, then secure the chain from falling into the timing chain cover.

16   Remove the lower half of the bearing from the exhaust camshaft journal.

17   Using a large wrench on the camshaft flats and a socket and ratchet on the phaser sprocket bolt, loosen, then remove the bolt and phaser from the end of the camshaft. **Caution:** *Do not remove the phaser lock or try to disassemble the phasers.*

18   Mark the lifters so they can be installed in the same locations, then remove them from the cylinder head.

Inspection

19   Check the camshaft bearing surfaces for pitting, score marks, galling, and abnormal wear. If the bearing surfaces are damaged, the cylinder head will have to be replaced.

20   Compare the camshaft lobe height by measuring each lobe with a micrometer (see illustration). Measure each of the intake lobes and record the measurements and relative positions. Then measure each of the exhaust

lobes and record the measurements and relative positions also. This will let you compare all of the intake lobes to one another and all of the exhaust lobes to one another. If the difference between the lobes exceeds 0.005 inch, the camshaft should be replaced. Do not compare intake lobe heights to exhaust lobe heights as lobe lift may be different. Only compare intake lobes to intake lobes and exhaust lobes to exhaust lobes for this comparison.

21   Check the lifters for abnormal wear, pits, galling, score marks, and rough spots. Replace defective parts.

Installation

Caution: *Before starting the engine, carefully rotate the crankshaft by hand through at least two full revolutions (use a socket and breaker bar on the crankshaft pulley center bolt). If you feel any resistance, STOP! There is something wrong - most likely, valves are contacting the pistons. You must find the problem before proceeding.*

22   Carefully slide the intake or exhaust phaser onto the camshaft and verify the

marks are aligned. Install the bolt, then tighten the bolt to the torque listed in this Chapter's Specifications.

23   Be sure to prevent the camshafts from turning by holding the camshaft with a large wrench on the camshaft flats.

24   Dip the lifters in clean engine oil and install them into their original locations.

25   Lubricate the camshaft bearing journals and lobes with moly-base grease or engine assembly lube.

26   The front (or joined) cap has a number stamped into the cap. The stamped numbers 1, 2 or 3 correspond to the exhaust bearing insert needed to be used. If replacing the bearing select the proper bearing and insert the lower bearing insert into the cylinder head.

27   Starting with the exhaust camshaft, set the timing chain over the exhaust phaser sprocket making sure the plate link or mark is aligned with the dot on the phaser sprocket.

28   Set the exhaust camshaft onto the cylinder head making sure to the machined scribe line on the phaser is in a parallel line with the gasket surface of the cylinder head at the 3 o'clock position (see illustration 9.21).

29   Install the intake camshaft at an angle with the rear of the camshaft upward then roll the sprocket into the timing chain making sure the plate link or mark is aligned with the dot on the phaser sprocket.

30   Set the intake camshaft onto the cylinder head making sure the machined scribe line on the phaser is in a parallel line with the gasket surface of the cylinder head at the 9 o'clock position (see illustration 9.21).

31   The front (or joined) cap has a number stamped into the cap (see illustration). The stamped numbers 1, 2 or 3 correspond to the exhaust bearing insert required. If replacing the bearing, select the proper bearing and install the lower bearing insert into the cylinder head before the camshafts are installed.

32   Install the camshaft bearing caps (see illustrations) and front cap, then install the mounting bolts and finger-tighten them.

33   Tighten bearing cap bolts 1 through 16

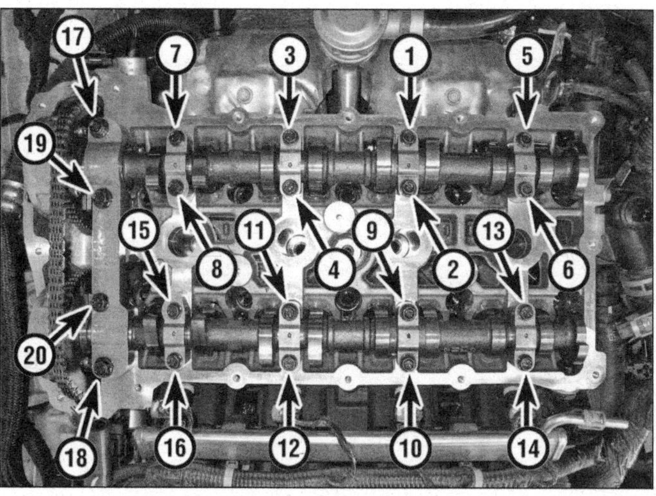

10.33 Camshaft bearing cap tightening sequence - bolts 1 through 16 first, then bolts 17 through 20

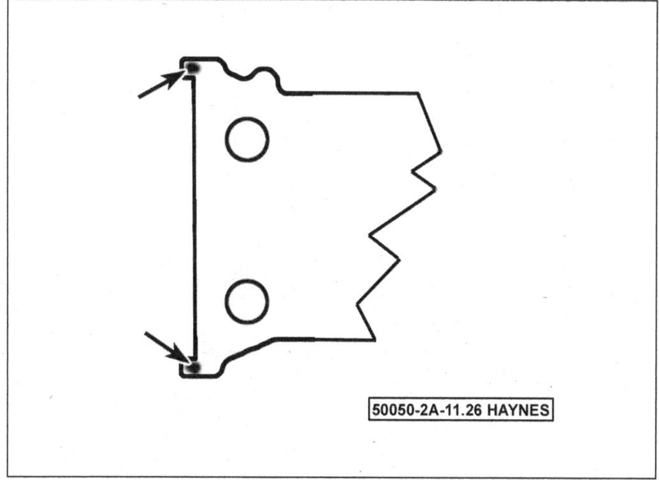

11.26 Sealant bead application area

in sequence first, then bolts 17 through 20 in sequence (see illustration) to the torque listed in this Chapter's Specifications.

Caution: *Prevent the camshafts from turning by holding the camshaft with a large wrench on the camshaft flats.*

34 Verify all the timing marks are aligned (see illustrations 9.20 and 9.21).

35 Remove the Allen wrench from the timing chain tensioner.

36 Remove the chain holding tool.

37 Slowly rotate the engine two complete turns (720-degrees) and verify that the camshaft alignment marks are correct when the crankshaft keyway is aligned with the mating surface of the engine block and the ladder frame (see illustrations 9.20 and 9.21).

38 Check the valve adjustment (see Chapter 1).

39 Coat the timing chain tensioner plug with thread sealant then install the plug and tighten it securely.

40 The remainder of installation is the reverse of removal.

11 Cylinder head - removal and installation

Warning: *Allow the engine to cool completely before beginning this procedure.*

Caution: *It is recommended that new cylinder head bolts be installed upon reassembly.*

Removal

1 Loosen the right-front wheel lug nuts, then raise the front of the vehicle and support it securely on jackstands.

2 Remove the right-front wheel, then remove the under-vehicle splash shield, the drivebelt splash shield and the inner fender liner (see Chapter 11).

3 Position the number one piston at Top Dead Center (see Section 3).

4 Disconnect the cable from the negative ter-

minal of the battery (see Chapter 5).

5 Remove the engine cover by pulling it up and off of the ballstuds.

6 Drain the cooling system and remove the spark plugs (see Chapter 1).

7 Remove the air filter housing (see Chapter 4).

8 Remove the coolant reservoir (see Chapter 3).

9 Remove the power steering reservoir without disconnecting the lines and secure it out of the way.

10 Remove the drivebelt (see Chapter 1).

11 Remove the intake manifold (see Section 5). Cover the intake ports with duct tape to keep out debris.

12 Remove the power steering hose bracket bolt from the front mount. Remove the power steering pump mounting bolts and secure the pump out of the way without disconnecting the hoses (see Chapter 10).

13 Remove the exhaust manifold (see Section 6).

14 Remove the ignition coils (see Chapter 5) and spark plugs (see Chapter 1).

15 Remove the valve cover (see Section 4).

16 Remove the water pump pulley, the air conditioning compressor and bracket (see Chapter 3).

17 Remove the timing chain cover and timing chain (see Section 9).

18 Remove the camshaft bearing caps, camshafts and lifters from the bores in the cylinder head (see Section 10). Store the lifters so they can be reinstalled in their original locations.

Caution: *The lifters must be reinstalled in their original locations or the valve adjustment will be incorrect.*

19 Loosen the cylinder head bolts, 1/4-turn at a time, in the reverse of the tightening sequence (see illustration 11.28) until they can be removed by hand from the cylinder head.

Note: *The cylinder head bolt washers are "captured washers," meaning they will stay on*

the bolts after the bolts have been removed, except for the two nearest the timing chain end of the head. The first two bolts have removable washers; one side is flat and the other side is beveled.

20 Carefully lift the cylinder head straight up and place the head on wood blocks to prevent damage to the sealing surfaces. If the head sticks to the engine block, dislodge it by placing a wood block against the head casting and tapping the wood with a hammer, or by prying the head with a prybar placed carefully on a casting protrusion.

Caution: *The cylinder head is aluminum, so you must be very careful not to gouge the sealing surfaces.*

Note: *It's a good idea to have the head checked for warpage, even if you're just replacing the gasket.*

21 Once the cylinder head is removed, use a pair of needle nose pliers to remove the VVT filter from the engine block.

Note: *The VVT filter is located at the right front corner of the cylinder head.*

22 Remove all traces of old gasket material from the block and head. Special gasket removal solvents that soften gaskets and make removal much easier are available at auto parts stores. Do not allow anything to fall into the engine. Clean and inspect all threaded fasteners and be sure the threaded holes in the block are clean and dry.

Installation

23 Install a new VVT filter into the hole in the right front corner of the cylinder block.

24 Apply clean engine oil to the cylinder head bolt threads prior to installation.

25 Place the washers, beveled side up, on the first two head bolts.

26 Apply two small beads of RTV sealant at the timing chain end of the cylinder block face (see illustration).

Note: *The cylinder head must be installed within 10 minutes after the RTV has been applied.*

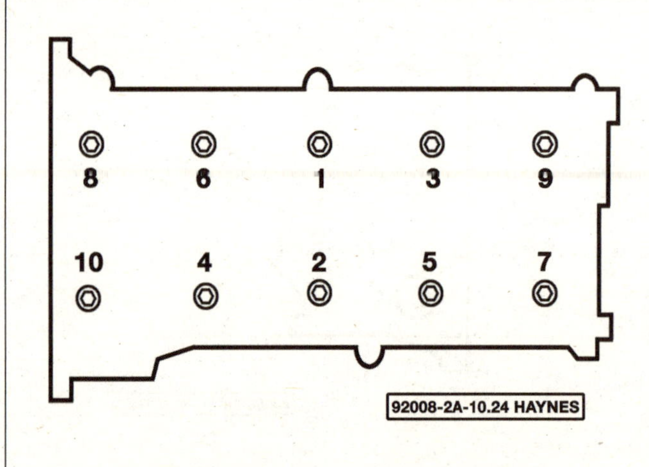

11.28 Cylinder head bolt TIGHTENING sequence

12.6 Check the clearance of each valve with a feeler gauge of the specified thickness - if the clearance is correct, you should feel a slight drag on the gauge as you pull it out

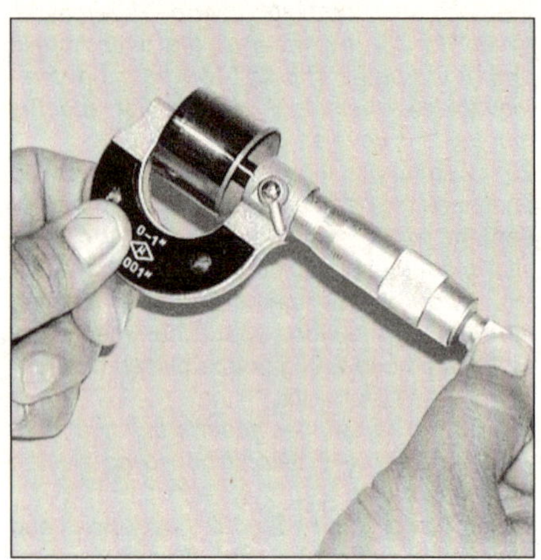

12.9 Measure the thickness of each lifter head with a micrometer

27   Place a new gasket and the cylinder head in position on the engine block.

Caution: *Two different types of cylinder head bolts have been used on these engines - you must determine which ones your engine has in order to tighten them properly. One style has a short head (5/16-inch from the washer to the top of the bolt head). The other style has a long bolt head (1/2-inch from the washer to the top of the bolt head).*

28   Install the head bolts and tighten them in several stages, in the recommended sequence (see illustration), to the torque listed in this Chapter's Specifications.

Note: *The final step in the tightening procedure requires you to tighten the bolts a specific number of degrees. An angle-torque gauge is available at most auto parts stores and is highly recommended for this procedure. If the tool is not available, paint marks on the bolt heads and tighten them in sequence until the mark is the specified number of degrees from the starting point.*

29   Reinstall the timing chain and cover (see Section 9).

30   The remainder of installation is the reverse of removal.

31   Refill the cooling system and change the engine oil and filter (see Chapter 1). Rotate the crankshaft clockwise slowly by hand through six complete revolutions. Recheck the camshaft timing marks (see Section 9).

32   Start the engine and run it until normal operating temperature is reached. Check for leaks and proper operation.

12   Valve clearance check and adjustment

1   Position the number 1 piston at TDC on the compression stroke (see Section 3).

2   Remove the engine cover by pulling it up and off of the ballstuds.

3   Disconnect the cable from the negative terminal of the battery (see Chapter 5).

4   Blow out the recessed area around the spark plug openings with compressed air, if available, to remove any debris that might fall into the cylinders, then remove the spark plugs (see Chapter 1).

5   Remove the valve cover (see Section 4).

Check

6   The lobes must be measured one set at a time. Rotate the camshaft(s) until two lobes on any one cylinder are pointing straight up and measure the clearances of those valves with feeler gauges (see illustration). Record any measurements that don't fall within this Chapter's Specifications. These measurements will be used later to determine the required replacement lifters.

7   Rotate the camshaft(s) until all the lobes have been checked.

Adjustment

8   Remove the camshaft(s) for the valve(s) that you intend to adjust (see Section 10).

9   Remove and measure each lifter (whose clearance is not correct) with a micrometer (see illustration). Put each lifter back into its bore in the cylinder head before moving on to the next lifter. Record the measurement for each lifter.

10   To calculate the correct thickness of a replacement lifter that will put the valve clearance within the specified range, use the following formula:

S - C = change, where:

S = specified valve clearance (see this Chapter's Specifications)

C = measured valve clearance

11   Remove the lifter and read the size from the bottom of the lifter then reduce the lifter by subtracting the specified valve clearance from the measured valve clearance or as close as possible to the calculated size.

12   Install the camshaft(s) (see Section 10).

13   Check the valve clearances again to verify that they're now within the range listed in this Chapter's Specifications.

14   The remainder of installation is the reverse of removal.

13   Oil pan - removal and installation

Removal

1   Disconnect the cable from the negative terminal of the battery (see Chapter 5).

2   Raise the vehicle and support it securely on jackstands.

3   Drain the engine oil (see Chapter 1).

4   Remove the drivebelt splash shield.

5   Remove the air conditioning compressor (see Chapter 3) and support it out of the way with a length of wire or rope, then remove the compressor bracket.

Warning: *Don't disconnect the refrigerant lines from the compressor.*

6   Remove the oil pan bolts, then carefully separate the oil pan from the block. Use

a putty knife or gasket scraper to loosen the seal around the pan, but don't pry between the block and the pan or damage to the sealing surfaces could occur and oil leaks may develop.

7   Thoroughly clean the oil pan and sealing surfaces on the block and pan. Use a scraper to remove all traces of old gasket material. Gasket removal solvents are available at auto parts stores and may prove helpful. Check the oil pan sealing surface for distortion. Straighten or replace as necessary, then wipe the gasket surfaces of the pan and block with a rag soaked in brake system cleaner.

Installation

8   Apply a 1/8-inch bead of RTV sealant at the cylinder block-to-front cover joint at the oil pan flange.

9   Apply a 1/8-inch wide by 1/16-inch high bead of RTV sealant to the sealing surface of the pan. Install the pan and the bolts, then tighten the bolts finger-tight.

Note: *The oil pan must be installed and tightened within 10 minutes of applying the RTV sealant.*

10   Working side-to-side from the center out, tighten the oil pan bolts to the torque listed in this Chapter's Specifications.

11   The remainder of installation is the reverse of removal.

12   Refill the crankcase with the correct quantity and grade of oil, run the engine and check for leaks.

13   Road test the vehicle and check for leaks again.

14   Oil pump/Balance Shaft Module (BSM) and chain - removal, inspection and installation

Note: *The oil pump is an integral component of the balance shaft module and can't be removed or disassembled from the module. If there is a problem with the oil pump, the balance shaft module must be replaced.*

Removal

1   Relieve the fuel system pressure (see Chapter 4), then disconnect the cable from the negative terminal of the battery (see Chapter 5).

2   Rotate the engine to Top Dead Center (TDC) for #1 cylinder on the compression stroke (see Section 3).

3   Loosen the right-front wheel lug nuts, then raise the front of the vehicle and support it securely on jackstands.

4   Remove the right-front wheel, then remove the splash shield and inner fender splash shield (see Chapter 11).

5   Remove the valve cover (see Section 4).

6   Remove the oil pan (see Section 13).

7   Remove the timing chain cover, timing chain and crankshaft sprocket (see Section 9).

8   Align the drive chain plated links with the timing marks on the crankshaft sprocket and

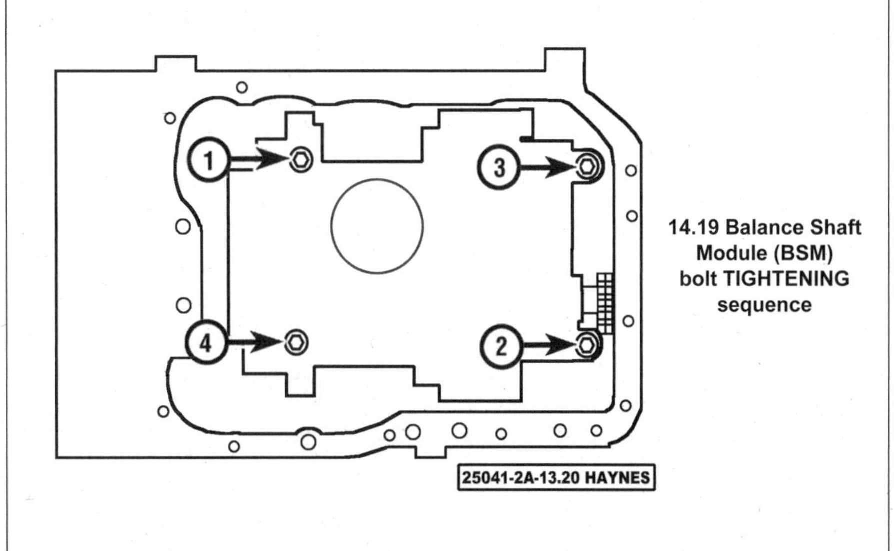

14.19 Balance Shaft Module (BSM) bolt TIGHTENING sequence

the Balance Shaft Module (BCM) drive gear.

Note: *If the marks or plated links can't be found, mark the oil pump/Balance Shaft Module (BSM) drive chain to the BSM drive sprocket and to the crankshaft gear, so the chain can be installed in the same position.*

9   Press the oil pump/BSM tensioner piston back into the tensioner body. While holding the piston in, insert special tool #9703 or a 3 mm drill bit into the hole in the side of the tensioner to retain the piston in the locked position.

Caution: *Do not remove the oil pump/BSM drive sprocket.*

10   Remove the BSM mounting bolts, in the reverse of the tightening sequence (see illustration 14.19), in several steps. There are two different length bolts that can be used.

11   Lower the rear of the balance shaft module, remove the timing chain from the sprocket, then remove the BSM.

12   Remove the chain from the crankshaft sprocket.

Inspection

13   Two different lengths of mounting bolts can be used on the BSM: 180 mm and 185 mm length bolts. The 180 mm bolts must be discarded and replaced with new bolts. Measure the BSM mounting bolts and replace the bolts as needed.

14   Place a straightedge or ruler against the threads of each 185 mm mounting bolt; if there is a gap or space between the edges of the threads and the ruler, the mounting bolt(s) must be replaced. Apply clean engine oil to the mounting bolt threads prior to installation.

Installation

15   Clean the bolt holes for the BSM mounting bolts.

16   Place the timing chain over the crankshaft sprocket and align the plated link with the timing mark on the gear, or marks made prior to removal (see Step 8).

17   Lift up the BSM and place the drive sprocket into the timing chain, aligning the plated link with the timing mark on the drive gear, or marks made prior to removal (see Step 8). Pivot the BSM up into place against the ladder frame on the engine block.

18   While holding the BSM in place, insert the mounting bolts and tighten by hand in several even stages.

19   Tighten the bolts in several stages, in the recommended sequence (see illustration), to the torque listed in this Chapter's Specifications.

Note: *The final step in the tightening procedure requires you to tighten the bolts a specific number of degrees. An angle-torque gauge is available at most auto parts stores and is highly recommended for this procedure. If the tool is not available, paint marks on the bolt heads and tighten them in sequence until the mark is the specified number of degrees from the starting point.*

20   Remove the pin from the tensioner and release the piston, then verify that the timing marks are aligned.

21   Install the timing chain and timing cover (see Section 9).

22   Install the oil pan (see Section 13).

23   Install the valve cover (see Section 4).

24   The remainder of installation is the reverse of removal.

25   Install a new oil filter and engine oil (see Chapter 1).

26   Start the engine and check for oil pressure and leaks.

27   Recheck the engine oil level.

15   Driveplate - removal and installation

Removal

1   Remove the transaxle (see Chapter 7B).

2   To ensure correct alignment during reinstallation, mark the position of the driveplate

15.2 Mark the relative position of the driveplate to the crankshaft . . .

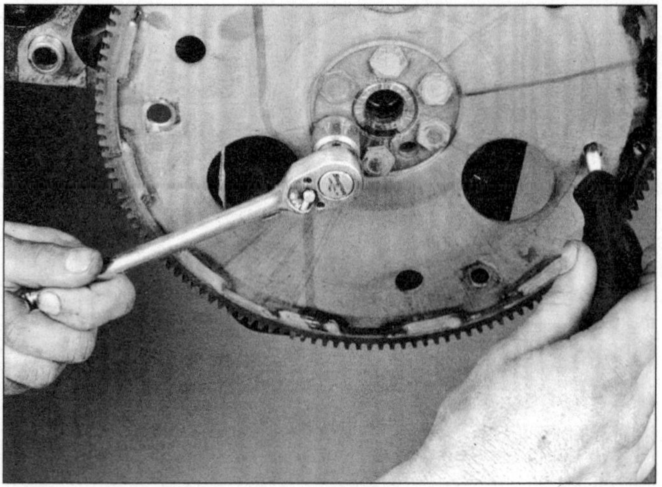

15.3 . . . and, using an appropriate tool to hold the driveplate, remove the bolts

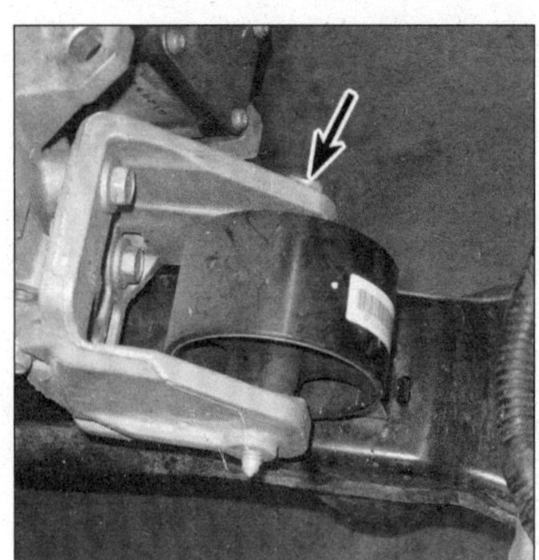

17.9 Front mount through-bolt

to the crankshaft before removal (see illustration).

3   Remove the bolts that secure the driveplate to the crankshaft (see illustration). A tool is available at most auto parts stores to hold the driveplate while loosening the bolts. If the tool is not available, wedge a screwdriver in the ring gear teeth to jam the driveplate.

4   Remove the driveplate from the crankshaft.

5   Clean and inspect the mating surfaces of the driveplate and the crankshaft. If the crankshaft rear main seal is leaking, replace it before reinstalling the driveplate (see Section 16).

Installation

6   Position the driveplate against the crankshaft. Align the previously applied match marks. Before installing the bolts, apply thread locking compound to the threads.

7   Hold the driveplate with the holding tool, or wedge a screwdriver in the ring gear teeth to keep the driveplate from turning as you

tighten the bolts to the torque listed in this Chapter's Specifications.

8   The remainder of installation is the reverse of removal.

---

16   Rear main oil seal - replacement

1   Remove the driveplate (see Section 15).

2   Use a screwdriver wrapped with tape to pry out the seal, being careful not to gouge or nick the housing.

3   Lubricate the crankshaft seal journal and the lip of the new seal with multi-purpose grease.

4   Install the seal with the seal lip toward the engine and the dust seal toward the transaxle.

5   Tap the seal into place using a seal driver to make sure that it doesn't become tilted.

6   Install the seal so that its rear edge is flush with the face of the engine block, or up to 0.020 inch recessed.

7   The remainder of installation is the reverse of removal.

---

17   Engine mounts - check and replacement

1   There are four powertrain mounts: the front mount attaches the transaxle to the crossmember; the left mount attaches the driver's side of the engine to the subframe; the right engine mount attaches the engine block to the passenger's side of the subframe; and a rear mount attaches the engine block to the subframe.

Check

2   During the check, the engine must be raised slightly to remove the weight from the mounts.

3   Raise the vehicle and support it securely

on jackstands. Remove the front wheels and tires. Position two jacks, one under the crankshaft pulley and the other under the transaxle bellhousing. Place a block of wood between a floor jack head and the crankshaft pulley or bellhousing, then carefully raise the engine/transaxle just enough to take the weight off the mounts.

Warning: *DO NOT place any part of your body under the engine when it's supported only by a jack!*

4   Check the mounts to see if the rubber is cracked, hardened or separated from the metal sleeve in the center of the mount.

5   Check for relative movement between the mount bracket and the engine, subframe or chassis (use a large screwdriver or prybar to attempt to move the mounts). If movement is noted, lower the engine and tighten the mount fasteners.

Replacement

Front mount

6   Raise the vehicle and support it securely on jackstands.

7   Remove the splash shield fasteners and remove the shield.

8   Place a block of wood between the floor jack head and the oil pan and support the engine.

9   Remove the front mount through-bolt (see illustration).

10   Remove the crossmember-to-mount bolts from under the crossmember.

11   Remove the mount from the crossmember. If the mount bracket needs to be replaced, remove the bracket-to-block bolts and the bracket.

12   Installation is the reverse of removal. Tighten the fasteners to the torque values listed in this Chapter's Specifications.

Left mount

13   Disconnect the cable from the negative terminal of the battery (see Chapter 5), then

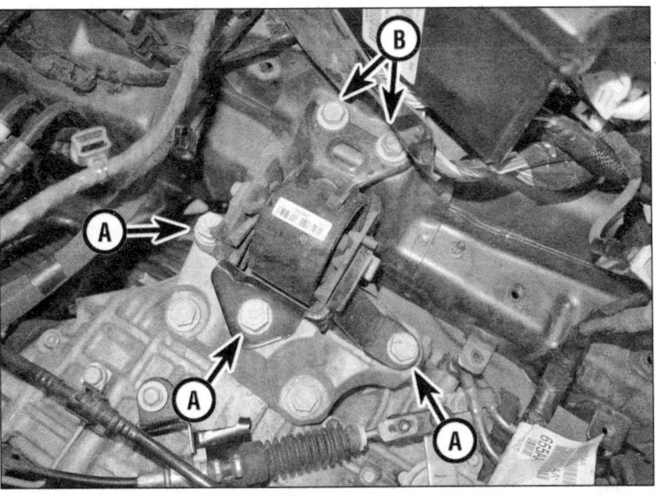

17.17 Remove the mount-to-transaxle bolts (A) and the mount-to-body bolts (B)

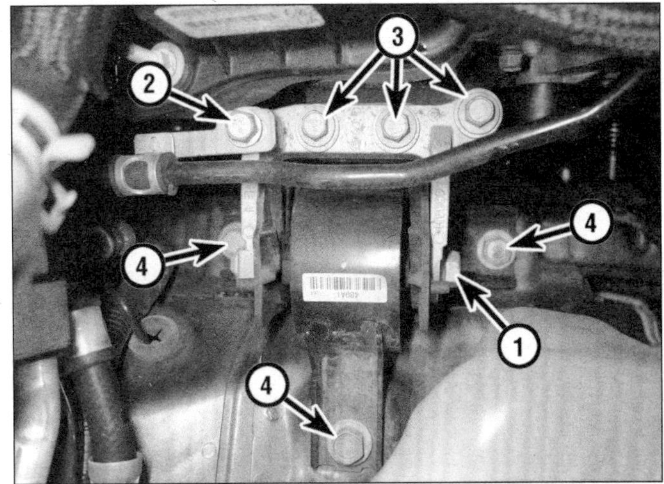

17.23 Right-side engine mount details

1   *Through-bolt*
2   *Power steering line bracket bolt*
3   *Mount bracket-to-engine bolts*
4   *Mount insulator-to-chassis bolts*

raise the vehicle and support it securely on jackstands.

14   Remove the air filter housing (see Chapter 4).

15   Support the transaxle with a floor jack and wooden block placed between the jack and the transaxle.

16   Raise the transaxle enough to take the weight off of the mount.

17   Remove the mount through-bolt and the mount-to-chassis bolts and remove the mount (see illustration).

18   Installation is the reverse of removal. Tighten the fasteners to the torque values listed in this Chapter's Specifications.

Right mount

19   Remove the coolant reservoir (see Chapter 3) and set it out of the way.

20   Remove the power steering fluid reservoir (see Chapter 10) and line bracket fastener from the engine mount bracket. Also detach the ground strap.

21   Remove the windshield washer fluid reservoir fastener and move the reservoir out of the way.

22   Support the engine with a floor jack and wooden block placed between the jack and the engine.

23   Remove the engine mount through-bolt (see illustration).

24   Remove the power steering line support bracket bolt and the three engine mount bracket bolts and remove the mount bracket.

25   Remove the engine mount insulator-to-chassis bolts and remove the mount.

26   Installation is the reverse of removal.

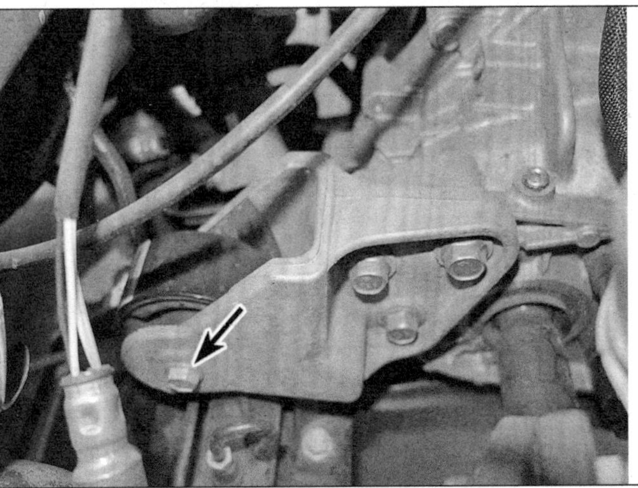

17.32 Remove the rear mount through-bolt (mount-to-crossmember bolts not visible in this photo)

Tighten the mounting bolts to the torque listed in this Chapter's Specifications, in the following order:

> *Mount insulator-to-chassis bolts*
> *Mount bracket-to-engine bolts*
> *Mount through-bolt*

27   The remainder of installation is the reverse of removal.

Rear mount

28   Raise the vehicle and support it securely on jackstands.

29   Remove the engine splash shield.

30   Remove the downstream oxygen sensor (see Chapter 6).

31   Support the engine with a floor jack and wooden block placed between the jack and the engine.

32   Remove the rear mount through-bolt (see illustration).

33   Remove the mount-to-crossmember bolts and remove the mount.

34   Install the new mount into the bracket, then install the through-bolt, but don't tighten it yet.

35   Align the mount on the crossmember, then install and tighten the bolts to the torque listed in this Chapter's Specifications.

36   Tighten the through-bolt to the torque listed in this Chapter's Specifications.

37   The remainder of installation is the reverse of removal.

Notes

Chapter 2 Part B
General engine overhaul procedures

Contents

Specifications

General

Displacement
2.0L	122 cubic inches
2.4L	146.5 cubic inches

Bore
2.0L	3.386 inches
2.4L	3.465 inches

Stroke
2.0L	3.386 inches
2.4L	3.819 inches

Compression ratio
2.0L	10.5:1
2.4L	10.5: 1

Compression pressure .... 100 psi minimum and no more than 25% variance between cylinders

Oil pressure*
At idle speed	4 psi (minimum)
At 3000 rpm	25 to 80 psi

*If the idle oil pressure test result was zero, don't perform the 3000 rpm or higher test

Torque specifications

Ft-lbs (unless otherwise indicated)

Note: *One foot-pound (ft-lb) of torque is equivalent to 12 inch-pounds (in-lbs) of torque. Torque values below approximately 15 ft-lbs are expressed in inch-pounds, because most foot-pound torque wrenches are not accurate at these smaller values.*

Connecting rod bearing cap bolts*
    Step 1 15
    Step 2 .... Tighten an additional 1/4 turn (90-degrees)
Crankshaft target wheel bolts .... 110 in-lbs
Driveplate-to-crankshaft bolts 70
Driveplate-to-torque converter bolts 65
Main bearing cap bolts* (in sequence, see illustration 10.31)
    With main bolt markings b or 6
        Step 1 .... 132 in-lbs
        Step 2 20
        Step 3 .... Tighten an additional 1/8 turn (45-degrees)
    With main bolt markings M
        Step 1 .... 132 in-lbs
        Step 2 33
        Step 3 .... Tighten an additional 1/8 turn (45-degrees)
Ladder frame bolts
    Step 1 .... 89 in-lbs
    Step 2 19

Use new bolts

1.9a An engine block being bored. An engine rebuilder will use special machinery to recondition the cylinder bores

1.9b If the cylinders are bored, the machine shop will normally hone the engine on a machine like this

1 General information - engine overhaul

1 Included in this Part of Chapter 2 are general information and diagnostic testing procedures for determining the overall mechanical condition of your engine.

2 The information ranges from advice concerning preparation for an overhaul and the purchase of replacement parts and/or components to detailed, step-by-step procedures covering removal and installation.

3 The following Sections have been written to help you determine whether your engine needs to be overhauled and how to remove and install it once you've determined it needs to be rebuilt. For information concerning in-vehicle engine repair, see Chapter 2A .

4 It's not always easy to determine when, or if, an engine should be completely overhauled, because a number of factors must be considered.

5 High mileage is not necessarily an indication that an overhaul is needed, while low mileage doesn't preclude the need for an overhaul. Frequency of servicing is probably the most important consideration. An engine that's had regular and frequent oil and filter changes, as well as other required maintenance, will most likely give many thousands of miles of reliable service. Conversely, a neglected engine may require an overhaul very early in its service life.

6 Excessive oil consumption is an indication that piston rings, valve seals and/or valve guides are in need of attention. Make sure that oil leaks aren't responsible before deciding that the rings and/or guides are bad. Perform a cylinder compression check to determine the extent of the work required (see Section 3). Also check the vacuum readings under various conditions (see Section 4).

7 Check the oil pressure with a gauge installed in place of the oil pressure sending unit and compare it to this Chapter's Specifications (see Section 2). If it's extremely low, the bearings and/or oil pump are probably worn out.

8 Loss of power, rough running, knocking or metallic engine noises, excessive valve train noise and high fuel consumption rates may also point to the need for an overhaul, especially if they're all present at the same time. If a complete tune-up doesn't remedy the situation, major mechanical work is the only solution.

9 An engine overhaul involves restoring the internal parts to the specifications of a new engine. During an overhaul, the piston rings are replaced and the cylinder walls are reconditioned (rebored and/or honed) (see illustrations). If a rebore is done by an automotive machine shop, new oversize pistons will also be installed. The main bearings, connecting rod bearings and camshaft bearings are generally replaced with new ones and, if necessary, the crankshaft may be reground to restore the journals (see illustration). Generally, the valves are serviced as well, since they're usually in less-than-perfect condition at this point. While the engine is being overhauled, other components, such as the starter and alternator, can be rebuilt as well. The end result should be similar to a new engine that will give many trouble free miles.

Note: *Critical cooling system components such as the hoses, drivebelts, thermostat and water pump should be replaced with new parts when an engine is overhauled. The radiator should be checked carefully to ensure that it isn't clogged or leaking (see Chapter 3). If you purchase a rebuilt engine or short block, some rebuilders will not warranty their engines unless the radiator has been professionally flushed. Also, we don't recommend overhauling the oil pump - always install a new one when an engine is rebuilt.*

10 Overhauling the internal components on today's engines is a difficult and time-consuming task which requires a significant amount of specialty tools and is best left to a professional engine rebuilder (see illustrations). A competent engine rebuilder will handle the inspection of your old parts and offer advice concerning the reconditioning or replacement of the original engine. Never purchase parts or have machine work done on other components until the block has been thoroughly inspected by a professional machine shop. As a general rule, time is the primary cost of an overhaul, especially since the vehicle

1.9c A crankshaft having a main bearing journal ground

1.10a A machinist checks for a bent connecting rod, using specialized equipment

may be tied up for a minimum of two weeks or more. Be aware that some engine builders only have the capability to rebuild the engine you bring them while other rebuilders have a large inventory of rebuilt exchange engines in stock. Also be aware that many machine shops could take as much as two weeks time to completely rebuild your engine depending on shop workload. Sometimes it makes more sense to simply exchange your engine for another engine that's already rebuilt to save time.

2   Oil pressure check

1   Low engine oil pressure can be a sign of an engine in need of rebuilding. A low oil pressure indicator (often called an idiot light) is not a test of the oiling system. Such indicators only come on when the oil pressure is dangerously low. Even a factory oil pressure gauge in the instrument panel is only a relative indication, although much better for driver information than a warning light. A better test is with a mechanical (not electrical) oil pressure gauge.
2   Locate the oil pressure indicator sending unit on the engine block.
3   The oil pressure switch is threaded into the engine block, behind the intake manifold, between the alternator and the starter (see illustration). To access the switch, unbolt and reposition the air conditioning compressor (without disconnecting the refrigerant lines) (see Chapter 3).
4   Unscrew and remove the oil pressure sending unit, screw in the hose for your oil pressure gauge, then reinstall the air conditioning compressor and the drivebelt. If necessary, install an adapter fitting. Use Teflon tape or thread sealant on the threads of the adapter and/or the fitting on the end of your gauge's hose.
5   Connect an accurate tachometer to the engine, according to the tachometer manufacturer's instructions.
6   Check the oil pressure with the engine

1.10b A bore gauge being used to check a cylinder bore

running (normal operating temperature) at the specified engine speed, and compare it to this Chapter's Specifications. If it's extremely low, the bearings and/or oil pump are probably worn out.

3   Cylinder compression check

1   A compression check will tell you what mechanical condition the upper end of your engine (pistons, rings, valves, head gaskets) is in. Specifically, it can tell you if the compression is down due to leakage caused by worn piston rings, defective valves and seats or a blown head gasket.
Note: *The engine must be at normal operating temperature and the battery must be fully charged for this check.*
2   Begin by cleaning the area around the ignition coils before you remove them (compressed air should be used, if available). The idea is to prevent dirt from getting into the cylinders as the compression check is being done.
3   Remove all of the spark plugs from the engine (see Chapter 1).
4   Remove the rear seat cushion and dis-

1.10c Uneven piston wear like this indicates a bent connecting rod

able the fuel system by unplugging the fuel pump module electrical connector (see Chapter 4).
5   Install a compression gauge in the spark plug hole (see illustration).
6   Have an assistant depress the accelerator pedal and crank the engine over at least seven compression strokes while you watch the gauge. The compression should build up quickly in a healthy engine. Low compression on the first stroke, followed by gradually increasing pressure on successive strokes, indicates worn piston rings. A low compression reading on the first stroke, which doesn't build up during successive strokes, indicates leaking valves or a blown head gasket (a cracked head could also be the cause). Deposits on the undersides of the valve heads can also cause low compression. Record the highest gauge reading obtained.
7   Repeat the procedure for the remaining cylinders and compare the results to this Chapter's Specifications .
8   Add some engine oil (about three squirts from a plunger-type oil can) to each cylinder, through the spark plug hole, and repeat the test.
9   If the compression increases after the oil is added, the piston rings are definitely worn.

2.3 Location of the oil pressure sending unit

3.5 A compression gauge with a threaded fitting for the spark plug hole is preferred over the type that requires hand pressure to maintain the seal

4.4 A simple vacuum gauge can be handy in diagnosing engine condition and performance

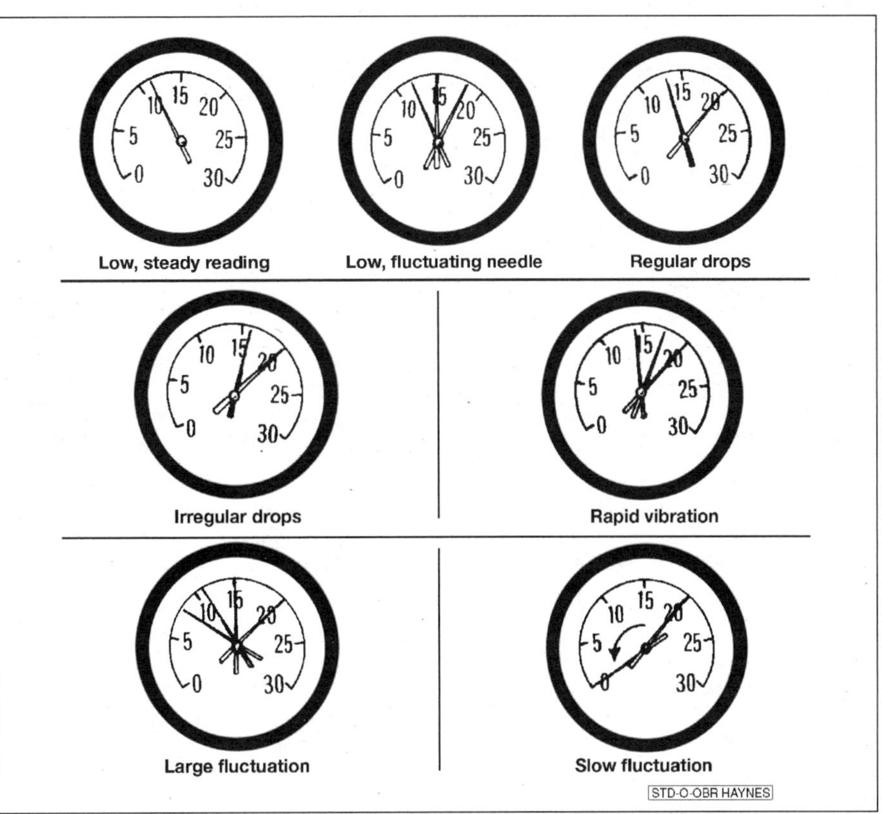

4.6 Typical vacuum gauge readings

If the compression doesn't increase significantly, the leakage is occurring at the valves or head gasket. Leakage past the valves may be caused by burned valve seats and/or faces or warped, cracked or bent valves.

10   If two adjacent cylinders have equally low compression, there's a strong possibility that the head gasket between them is blown. The appearance of coolant in the combustion chambers or the crankcase would verify this condition.

11   If one cylinder is slightly lower than the others, and the engine has a slightly rough idle, a worn lobe on the camshaft could be the cause.

12   If the compression is unusually high, the combustion chambers are probably coated with carbon deposits. If that's the case, the cylinder head(s) should be removed and decarbonized.

13   If compression is way down or varies greatly between cylinders, it would be a good idea to have a leak-down test performed by an automotive repair shop. This test will pinpoint exactly where the leakage is occurring and how severe it is.

4   Vacuum gauge diagnostic checks

1   A vacuum gauge provides inexpensive but valuable information about what is going on in the engine. You can check for worn rings or cylinder walls, leaking head or intake manifold gaskets, restricted exhaust, stuck or burned valves, weak valve springs, improper ignition or valve timing and ignition problems.

2   Unfortunately, vacuum gauge readings are easy to misinterpret, so they should be used in conjunction with other tests to confirm the diagnosis.

3   Both the absolute readings and the rate of needle movement are important for accurate interpretation. Most gauges measure vacuum in inches of mercury (in-Hg). The following references to vacuum assume the diagnosis is being performed at sea level. As

elevation increases (or atmospheric pressure decreases), the reading will decrease. For every 1,000 foot increase in elevation above approximately 2,000 feet, the gauge readings will decrease about one inch of mercury.

4   Connect the vacuum gauge directly to the intake manifold vacuum, not to ported (throttle body) vacuum (see illustration). Be sure no hoses are left disconnected during the test or false readings will result.

5   Before you begin the test, allow the engine to warm up completely. Block the wheels and set the parking brake. With the transaxle in Park, start the engine and allow it to run at normal idle speed.

Warning: *Keep your hands and the vacuum gauge clear of the fans.*

6   Read the vacuum gauge; an average, healthy engine should normally produce about 17 to 22 in-Hg with a fairly steady needle (see illustration) . Refer to the following vacuum gauge readings and what they indicate about the engine's condition.

7   A low, steady reading usually indicates a leaking gasket between the intake manifold and cylinder head(s) or throttle body, a leaky vacuum hose, late ignition timing or incorrect camshaft timing. Check ignition timing with a timing light and eliminate all other possible causes, utilizing the tests provided in this Chapter before you remove the timing chain cover to check the timing marks.

8   If the reading is three to eight inches below normal and it fluctuates at that low reading, suspect an intake manifold gasket

leak at an intake port or a faulty fuel injector.

9   If the needle has regular drops of about two-to-four inches at a steady rate, the valves are probably leaking. Perform a compression check or leak-down test to confirm this.

10   An irregular drop or down-flick of the needle can be caused by a sticking valve or an ignition misfire. Perform a compression check or leak-down test and read the spark plugs.

11   A rapid vibration of about four in-Hg vibration at idle combined with exhaust smoke indicates worn valve guides. Perform a leak-down test to confirm this. If the rapid vibration occurs with an increase in engine speed, check for a leaking intake manifold gasket or head gasket, weak valve springs, burned valves or ignition misfire.

12   A slight fluctuation, say one inch up and down, may mean ignition problems. Check all the usual tune-up items and, if necessary, run the engine on an ignition analyzer.

13   If there is a large fluctuation, perform a compression or leak-down test to look for a weak or dead cylinder or a blown head gasket.

14   If the needle moves slowly through a wide range, check for a clogged PCV system, incorrect idle fuel mixture, throttle body or intake manifold gasket leaks.

15   Check for a slow return after revving the engine by quickly snapping the throttle open until the engine reaches about 2,500 rpm and let it shut. Normally the reading should drop to near zero, rise above normal idle reading (about 5 in-Hg over) and then return to the

6.3a After tightly wrapping water-vulnerable components, use a spray cleaner on everything, with particular concentration on the greasiest areas, usually around the valve cover and lower edges of the block. If one section dries out, apply more cleaner

6.3b Depending on how dirty the engine is, let the cleaner soak in according to the directions and then hose off the grime and cleaner. Get the rinse water down into every area you can get at, then dry important components with compressed air, a hair dryer or paper towels

previous idle reading. If the vacuum returns slowly and doesn't peak when the throttle is snapped shut, the rings may be worn. If there is a long delay, look for a restricted exhaust system (often the muffler or catalytic converter). An easy way to check this is to temporarily disconnect the exhaust ahead of the suspected part and redo the test.

5   Engine rebuilding alternatives

1   The do-it-yourselfer is faced with a number of options when purchasing a rebuilt engine. The major considerations are cost, warranty, parts availability and the time required for the rebuilder to complete the project. The decision to replace the engine block, piston/connecting rod assemblies and crankshaft depends on the final inspection results of your engine. Only then can you make a cost effective decision whether to have your

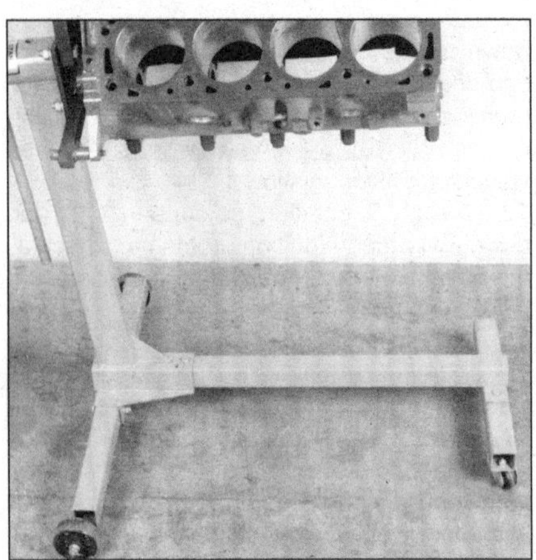

6.6 Get an engine stand sturdy enough to firmly support the engine while you're working on it. Stay away from three-wheeled models: they have a tendency to tip over more easily, so get a four-wheeled unit

engine overhauled or simply purchase an exchange engine for your vehicle.

2   Some of the rebuilding alternatives include:

a) *Individual parts - If the inspection procedures reveal that the engine block and most engine components are in reusable condition, purchasing individual parts and having a rebuilder rebuild your engine may be the most economical alternative. The block, crankshaft and piston/connecting rod assemblies should all be inspected carefully by a machine shop first.*

b) *Short block - A short block consists of an engine block with a crankshaft and piston/connecting rod assemblies already installed. All new bearings are incorporated and all clearances will be correct. The existing camshafts, valve train components, cylinder head and external parts can be bolted to the short block with little or no machine shop work necessary.*

c) *Long block - A long block consists of a short block plus an oil pump, oil pan, cylinder head, valve cover, camshaft and valve train components, timing sprockets and chain or gears and timing cover. All components are installed with new bearings, seals and gaskets incorporated throughout. The installation of manifolds and external parts is all that's necessary.*

d) *Low mileage used engines - Some companies now offer low mileage used engines which is a very cost effective way to get your vehicle up and running again. These engines often come from vehicles which have been in totaled in accidents or come from other countries which have a higher vehicle turnover rate. A low mileage used engine also usually has a similar warranty like the newly remanufactured engines.*

3   Give careful thought to which alternative is best for you and discuss the situation with

local automotive machine shops, auto parts dealers and experienced rebuilders before ordering or purchasing replacement parts.

6   Engine removal - methods and precautions

1   If you've decided that an engine must be removed for overhaul or major repair work, several preliminary steps should be taken. Read all removal and installation procedures carefully prior to committing to this job.

2   Locating a suitable place to work is extremely important. Adequate work space, along with storage space for the vehicle, will be needed. If a shop or garage isn't available, at the very least a flat, level, clean work surface made of concrete or asphalt is required.

3   Cleaning the engine compartment and engine before beginning the removal procedure will help keep tools clean and organized (see illustrations).

4   An engine hoist will also be necessary. Make sure the hoist is rated in excess of the combined weight of the engine and transaxle. Safety is of primary importance, considering the potential hazards involved in removing the engine from the vehicle.

5   If you're a novice at engine removal, get at least one helper. One person cannot easily do all the things you need to do to remove a big heavy engine and transaxle assembly from the engine compartment. Also helpful is to seek advice and assistance from someone who's experienced in engine removal.

6   Plan the operation ahead of time. Arrange for or obtain all of the tools and equipment you'll need prior to beginning the job (see illustration). Some of the equipment necessary to perform engine removal and installation safely and with relative ease are (in addition to a vehicle hoist and an engine hoist) a heavy duty floor jack (preferably fitted with a transmission jack head adapter),

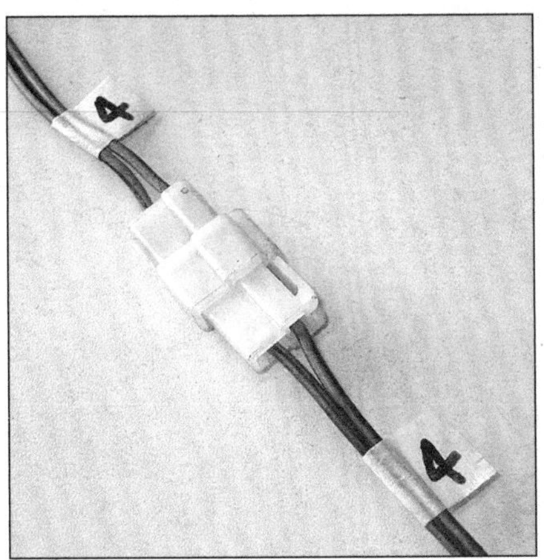

7.8 Label each wire before unplugging the connector

7.26a Connect the hoist chain to the lift hook at the left rear of the cylinder head...

7.26b ... and to the right front of the cylinder head at this threaded hole. Attach the chain using the proper-size bolt and a washer and tighten the bolt securely

complete sets of wrenches and sockets as described in the front of this manual, wooden blocks, plenty of rags and cleaning solvent for mopping up spilled oil, coolant and gasoline.

7   Plan for the vehicle to be out of use for quite a while. A machine shop can do the work that is beyond the scope of the home mechanic. Machine shops often have a busy schedule, so before removing the engine, consult the shop for an estimate of how long it will take to rebuild or repair the components that may need work.

7   Engine - removal and installation

Warning: *Gasoline is extremely flammable, so take extra precautions when you work on any part of the fuel system. Don't smoke or allow open flames or bare light bulbs near the work area, and don't work in a garage where a gas-type appliance (such as a water heater or clothes dryer) is present. Since gasoline is carcinogenic, wear fuel-resistant gloves when there's a possibility of being exposed to fuel, and, if you spill any fuel on your skin, rinse it off immediately with soap and water. Mop up any spills immediately and do not store fuel-soaked rags where they could ignite. The fuel system is under constant pressure, so, if any fuel lines are to be disconnected, the fuel pressure in the system must be relieved first (see Chapter 4 for more information). When you perform any kind of work on the fuel system, wear safety glasses and have a Class B type fire extinguisher on hand.*
Warning: *The engine must be completely cool before beginning this procedure.*
Warning: *The air conditioning system is under high pressure. Do not loosen any hose fittings or remove any components until after the system has been discharged. Air conditioning refrigerant must be properly discharged into an EPA-approved recovery/recycling unit at*

a dealer service department or an automotive air conditioning repair facility. Always wear eye protection when disconnecting air conditioning system fittings.
Note: *The engine can be separated from the transaxle and removed from above using a conventional engine hoist.*
Note: *Read through the entire Section before beginning this procedure.*

Removal

1   Have the air conditioning system discharged by an automotive air conditioning technician.
2   Remove the engine cover (see Chapter 1).
3   Relieve the fuel system pressure (see Chapter 4).
4   Remove the battery and battery tray (see Chapter 5).
5   Place protective covers on the fenders and cowl and remove the hood (see Chapter 11).
6   Remove the Powertrain Control Module (PCM) (see Chapter 6).
7   Remove the air filter housing (see Chapter 4).
8   Clearly label and disconnect all vacuum lines, emissions hoses, wiring harness connectors, ground straps and fuel lines. Once all the harness connectors have been disconnected, move the engine harness out of the way. Masking tape and/or a touch up paint applicator work well for marking items (see illustration). Take instant photos or sketch the locations of components and brackets.
9   Loosen the right-front wheel lug nuts.
10   Raise the front of the vehicle and support it securely on jackstands. Remove the wheel and the under-vehicle splash shield.
Note: *Keep in mind that during this procedure you'll have to adjust the height of the vehicle to perform certain operations.*
11   Drain the cooling system and engine oil and remove the drivebelt (see Chapter 1).

12   Remove the coolant reservoir (see Chapter 3).
13   Remove the engine oil dipstick.
14   Remove the intake manifold (see Chapter 2A).
15   Remove the power steering fluid reservoir and set it off to the side without disconnecting the fluid lines (see Chapter 10).
16   Detach the heater hoses at the firewall.
17   Detach the radiator hoses from the thermostat housing (see Chapter 3).
18   Unbolt the upper hose bracket at the center of the radiator support (near the pressure cap).
19   Remove the power steering hose support bracket from the front engine mount.
20   Remove the air conditioning compressor (see Chapter 3).
21   Remove the alternator (see Chapter 5).
Note: *The alternator removal procedure in Chapter 5 describes removing the alternator from below. Since the intake manifold has been removed, access from the top is easier.*
22   Remove the power steering pump and support it out of the way (see Chapter 10).
23   Remove the upper idler pulley.
24   Detach the exhaust pipe from the exhaust manifold (see Chapter 2A).
Note: *On AWD models, the exhaust manifold and catalytic converters are combined and are referred to as "maniverters."*
25   Remove the torque converter inspection cover and remove the torque converter bolts (see Chapter 7B).
26   Connect a lifting chain strong enough to support the full weight of the engine (see illustrations). Using an engine hoist connected to the chain, slightly raise the engine and remove the front mount (see Chapter 2A).
Warning: *Make sure the bolt is able to be tightened-up against the chain. If necessary (depending on the length of the bolt), several washers can be used. If the this is not done, the bolt could break.*
27   Remove the transaxle-to-engine mounting bolts.

28   Carefully separate the engine from the transaxle and remove the engine from the vehicle. Place the engine on an engine stand and disconnect the hoist and chain.

Installation

29   Installation is the reverse of removal, noting the following points:

a) *Check the engine mount. If it's worn or damaged, replace it.*
b) *Inspect the torque converter seal and bushing.*
c) *Add coolant, oil, power steering and transmission fluids as needed (see Chapter 1).*
d) *Run the engine and check for proper operation and leaks. Shut off the engine and recheck fluid levels.*
e) *Have the air conditioning system recharged by the shop that discharged it.*

8   Engine overhaul - disassembly sequence

1   It's much easier to remove the external components if it's mounted on a portable engine stand. A stand can often be rented quite cheaply from an equipment rental yard. Before the engine is mounted on a stand, the driveplate should be removed from the engine.

2   If a stand isn't available, it's possible to remove the external engine components with it blocked up on the floor. Be extra careful not to tip or drop the engine when working without a stand.

3   If you're going to obtain a rebuilt engine, all external components must come off first, to be transferred to the replacement engine. These components include:

Driveplate
Ignition system components
Emissions-related components
Engine mounts and mount brackets
Engine rear cover (spacer plate between driveplate and engine block)
Intake/exhaust manifolds
Fuel injection components
Oil filter
Thermostat and housing assembly
Water pump

Note: *When removing the external components from the engine, pay close attention to details that may be helpful or important during installation. Note the installed position of gaskets, seals, spacers, pins, brackets, washers, bolts and other small items.*

4   If you're going to obtain a short block (assembled engine block, crankshaft, pistons and connecting rods), then remove the timing belt/timing chain, cylinder head, oil pan, oil pump pick-up tube, oil pump and water pump from your engine so that you can turn in your old short block to the rebuilder as a core. See Section 5 for additional information regarding the different possibilities to be considered.

9.1 Before you try to remove the pistons, use a ridge reamer to remove the raised material (ridge) from the top of the cylinders

9   Pistons and connecting rods - removal and installation

Removal

Note: *Prior to removing the piston/connecting rod assemblies, remove the cylinder head, oil pan, and the timing chain cover (see Chapter 2A).*

1   Use your fingernail to feel if a ridge has formed at the upper limit of ring travel (about 1/4-inch down from the top of each cylinder). If carbon deposits or cylinder wear have produced ridges, they must be completely removed with a special tool (see illustration). Follow the manufacturer's instructions provided with the tool. Failure to remove the ridges before attempting to remove the piston/connecting rod assemblies may result in piston breakage.

2   After the cylinder ridges have been removed, turn the engine so the crankshaft is facing up. Remove the balance shaft module (see Chapter 2A) then remove the ladder frame mounting bolts and remove the ladder frame from the engine block.

3   Before the main bearing caps and connecting rods are removed, check the connecting rod endplay with feeler gauges. Slide them between the first connecting rod and the crankshaft throw until the play is removed (see illustration). Repeat this procedure for each connecting rod. The endplay is equal to the thickness of the feeler gauge(s). Check with an automotive machine shop for the endplay service limit (a typical endplay limit should measure between 0.005 to 0.015 inch [0.127 to 0.396 mm]). If the play exceeds the service limit, new connecting rods will be required. If new rods (or a new crankshaft) are installed, the endplay may fall under the minimum allowable. If it does, the rods will have to be machined to restore it. If necessary, consult an automotive machine shop for advice.

4   Check the connecting rods and caps for identification marks. If they aren't plainly

9.3 Checking the connecting rod endplay (side clearance)

9.4 If the connecting rods or caps are not marked, use permanent ink or paint to mark the caps to the rods by cylinder number (for example, this would be number 4 cylinder connecting rod)

marked, use paint or a marker to clearly identify each rod and cap (1, 2, 3, etc., depending on the cylinder they're associated with) (see illustration).

Caution: *Do not use a punch and hammer to mark the connecting rods or they may be damaged.*

5   Loosen each of the connecting rod cap bolts 1/2-turn at a time until they can be removed by hand.

Note: *New connecting rod cap bolts must be used when reassembling the engine, but save the old bolts for use when checking the connecting rod bearing oil clearance.*

6   Remove the number one connecting rod cap and bearing insert. Don't drop the bearing insert out of the cap.

7   Remove the bearing insert and push the connecting rod/piston assembly out through the top of the engine. Use a wooden or plastic hammer handle to push on the upper bearing surface in the connecting rod. If resistance is felt, double-check to make sure that all of the ridge was removed from the cylinder.

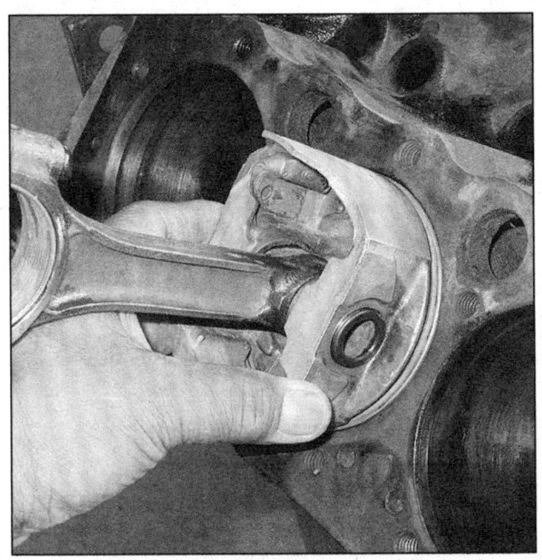

9.13 Install the piston ring into the cylinder then push it down into position using a piston so the ring will be square in the cylinder

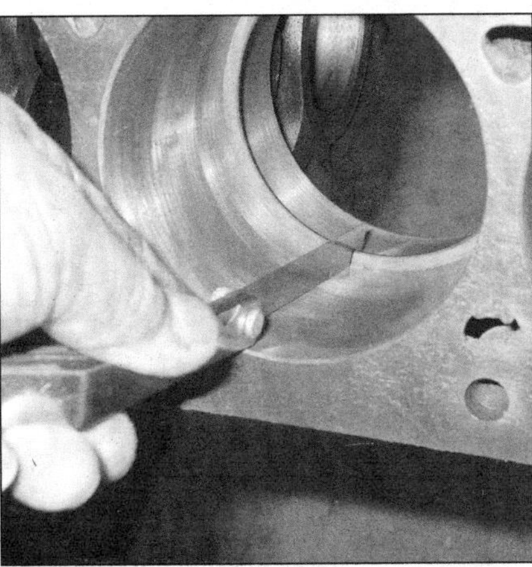

9.14 With the ring square in the cylinder, measure the ring end gap with a feeler gauge

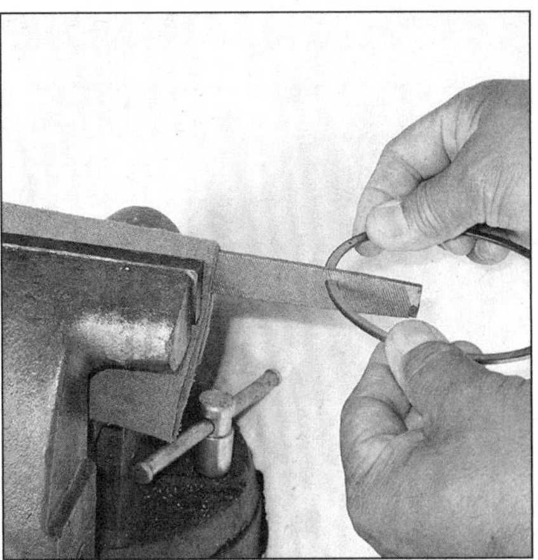

9.15 If the ring end gap is too small, clamp a file in a vise as shown and file the piston ring ends - be sure to remove all raised material

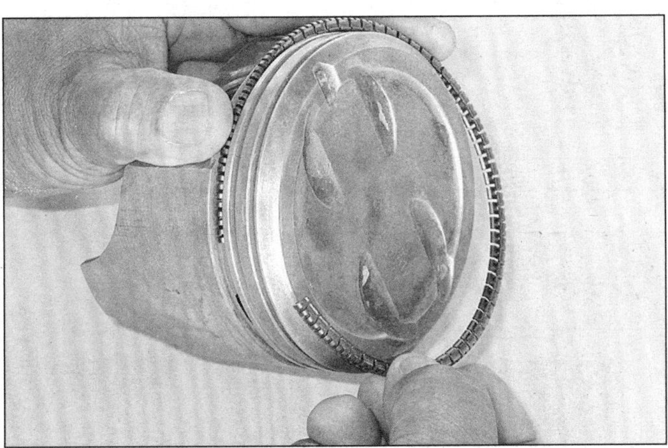

9.19a Installing the spacer/expander in the oil ring groove

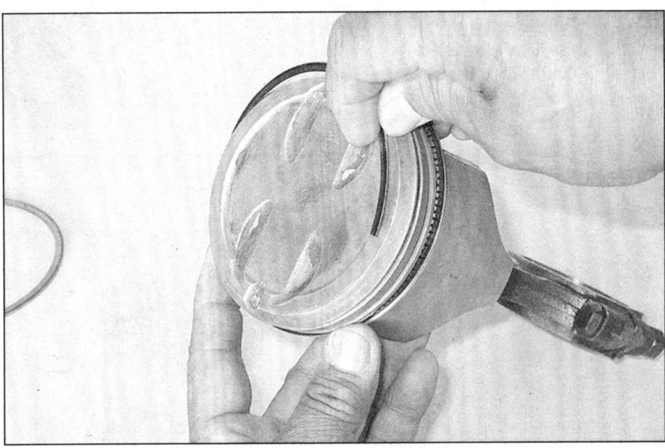

9.19b DO NOT use a piston ring installation tool when installing the oil control side rails

8   Repeat the procedure for the remaining cylinders.

9   After removal, reassemble the connecting rod caps and bearing inserts in their respective connecting rods and install the cap bolts finger-tight. Leaving the old bearing inserts in place until reassembly will help prevent the connecting rod bearing surfaces from being accidentally nicked or gouged.

10   The pistons and connecting rods are now ready for inspection and overhaul at an automotive machine shop.

Piston ring installation

11   Before installing the new piston rings, the ring end gaps must be checked. It's assumed that the piston ring side clearance has been checked and verified correct.

12   Lay out the piston/connecting rod assemblies and the new ring sets so the ring sets will be matched with the same piston and cylinder during the end gap measurement and engine assembly.

13   Insert the top (number one) ring into the first cylinder and square it up with the cylinder walls by pushing it in with the top of the piston

(see illustration). The ring should be near the bottom of the cylinder, at the lower limit of ring travel.

14   To measure the end gap, slip feeler gauges between the ends of the ring until a gauge equal to the gap width is found (see illustration). The feeler gauge should slide between the ring ends with a slight amount of drag. A typical ring gap should fall between 0.010 and 0.020 inch [0.25 to 0.50 mm] for compression rings and up to 0.030 inch [0.76 mm] for the oil ring steel rails. If the gap is larger or smaller than specified, double-check to make sure you have the correct rings before proceeding.

15   If the gap is too small, it must be enlarged or the ring ends may come in contact with each other during engine operation, which can cause serious damage to the engine. If necessary, increase the end gaps by filing the ring ends very carefully with a fine file. Mount the file in a vise equipped with soft jaws, slip the ring over the file with the ends contacting the file face and slowly move the ring to remove material from the ends. When performing this operation, file only by pushing

the ring from the outside end of the file toward the vise (see illustration).

16   Excess end gap isn't critical unless it's greater than 0.040 inch (1.01 mm). Again, double-check to make sure you have the correct ring type.

17   Repeat the procedure for each ring that will be installed in the first cylinder and for each ring in the remaining cylinders. Remember to keep rings, pistons and cylinders matched up.

18   Once the ring end gaps have been checked/corrected, the rings can be installed on the pistons.

19   The oil control ring (lowest one on the piston) is usually installed first. It's composed of three separate components. Slip the spacer/expander into the groove (see illustration). If an anti-rotation tang is used, make sure it's inserted into the drilled hole in the ring groove. Next, install the upper side rail in the same manner (see illustration). Don't use a piston ring installation tool on the oil ring side rails, as they may be damaged. Instead, place one end of the side rail into the groove between the spacer/expander and the ring

ENGINE BEARING ANALYSIS

Debris

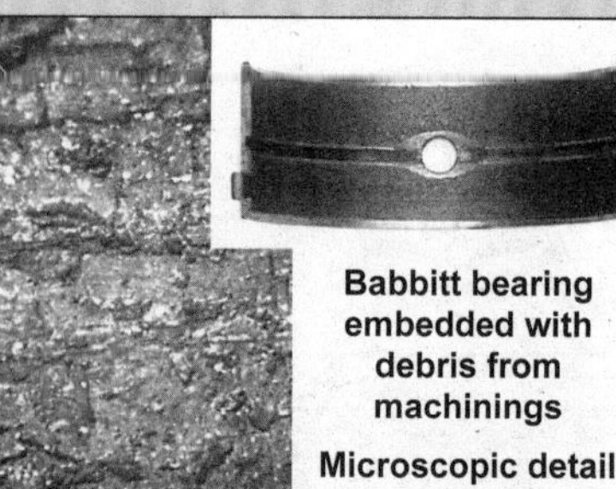

Babbitt bearing embedded with debris from machinings

Microscopic detail of debris

Microscopic detail of gouges

Overplated copper alloy bearing gouged by cast iron debris

Aluminum bearing embedded with glass beads

Microscopic detail of glass beads

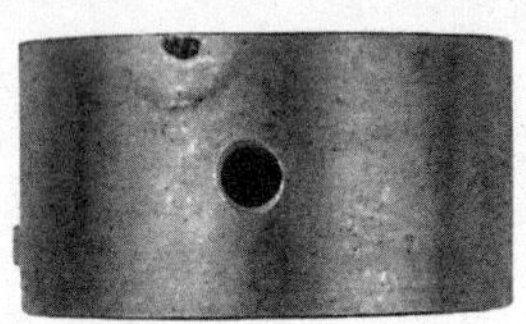

Damaged lining caused by dirt left on the bearing back

Misassembly

Result of a lower half assembled as an upper - blocking the oil flow

Excessive oil clearance is indicated by a short contact arc

Polished and oil-stained backs are a result of a poor fit in the housing bore

Result of a wrong, reversed, or shifted cap

Overloading

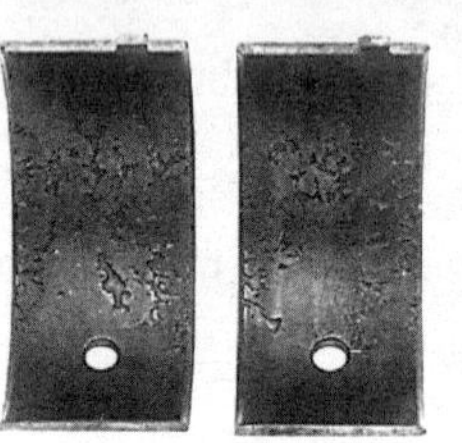

Damage from excessive idling which resulted in an oil film unable to support the load imposed

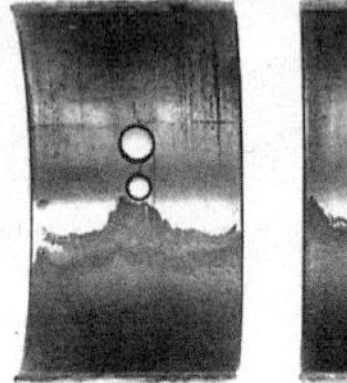

Damaged upper connecting rod bearings caused by engine lugging; the lower main bearings (not shown) were similarly affected

The damage shown in these upper and lower connecting rod bearings was caused by engine operation at a higher-than-rated speed under load

Misalignment

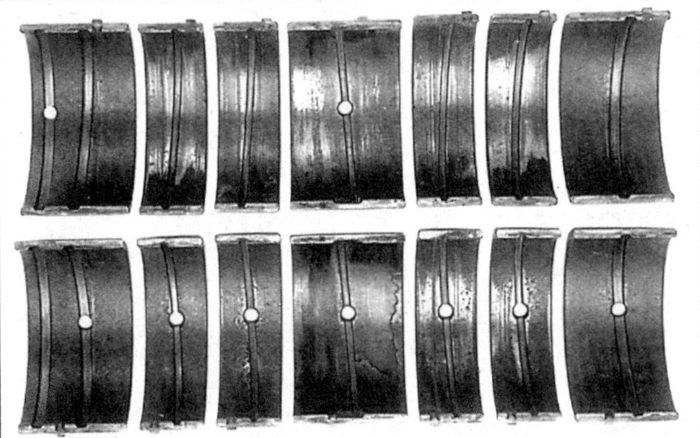

A warped crankshaft caused this pattern of severe wear in the center, diminishing toward the ends

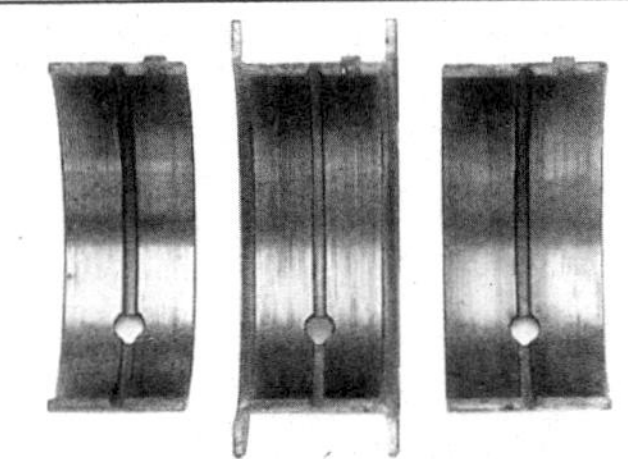

A poorly finished crankshaft caused the equally spaced scoring shown

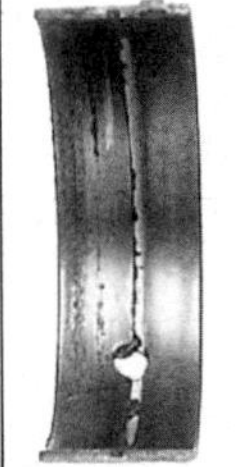

A tapered housing bore caused the damage along one edge of this pair

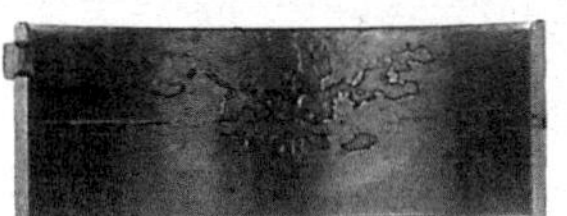

A bent connecting rod led to the damage in the "V" pattern

Lubrication

Result of dry start: The bearings on the left, farthest from the oil pump, show more damage

Result of a low oil supply or oil starvation

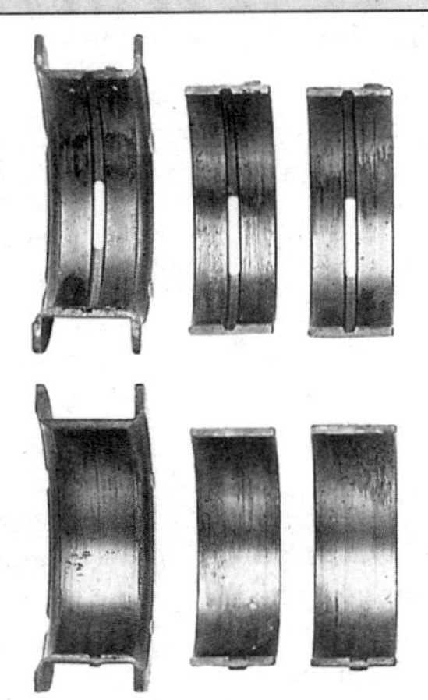

Severe wear as a result of inadequate oil clearance

Corrosion

Microscopic detail of corrosion

Corrosion is an acid attack on the bearing lining generally caused by inadequate maintenance, extremely hot or cold operation, or inferior oils or fuels

Microscopic detail of cavitation

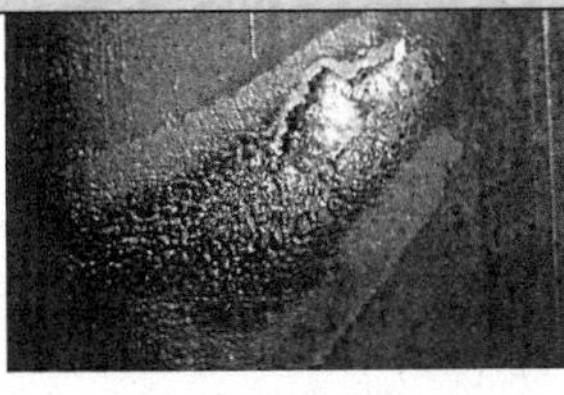

Example of cavitation - a surface erosion caused by pressure changes in the oil film

Damage from excessive thrust or insufficient axial clearance

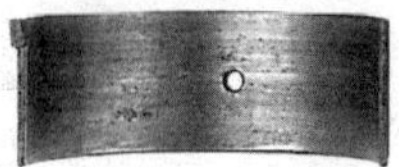

Bearing affected by oil dilution caused by excessive blow-by or a rich mixture

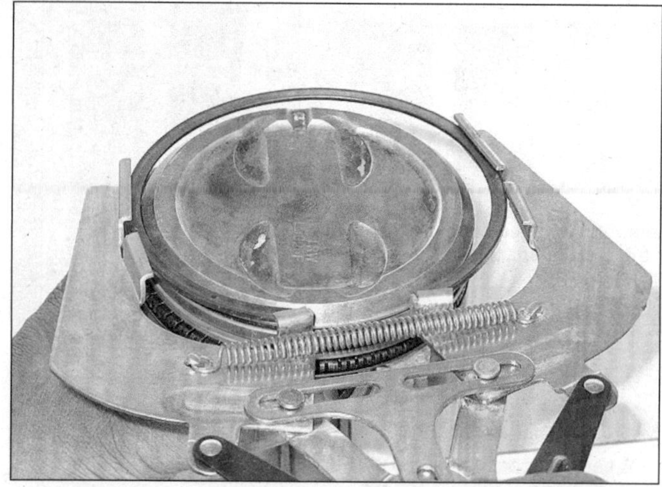

9.22 Use a piston ring installation tool to install the number 2 and the number 1 (top) rings - be sure the directional mark on the piston ring(s) is facing toward the top of the piston

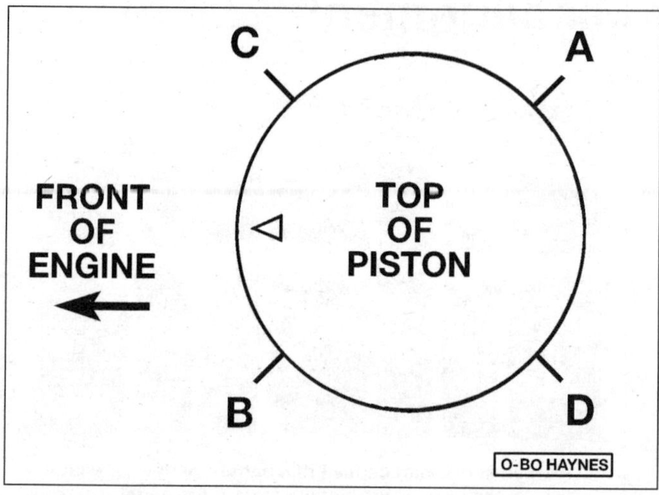

9.30 Position the piston ring end gaps as shown here before installing the piston/connecting rod assemblies into the engine

A   *Top compression ring gap*
B   *Second compression ring and oil ring spacer gap*
C   *Upper oil ring gap*
D   *Lower oil ring gap*

land, hold it firmly in place and slide a finger around the piston while pushing the rail into the groove. Finally, install the lower side rail.

20   After the three oil ring components have been installed, check to make sure that both the upper and lower side rails can be rotated smoothly inside the ring grooves.

21   The number two (middle) ring is installed next. It's usually stamped with a mark which must face up, toward the top of the piston. Do not mix up the top and middle rings, as they have different cross-sections.

Note: *Always follow the instructions printed on the ring package or box - different manufacturers may require different approaches.*

22   Use a piston ring installation tool and make sure the identification mark is facing the top of the piston, then slip the ring into the middle groove on the piston (see illustration). Don't expand the ring any more than necessary to slide it over the piston.

23   Install the number one (top) ring in the same manner. Make sure the mark is facing up. Be careful not to confuse the number one and number two rings.

24   Repeat the procedure for the remaining pistons and rings.

Installation

25   Before installing the piston/connecting rod assemblies, the cylinder walls must be perfectly clean, the top edge of each cylinder bore must be chamfered, and the crankshaft must be in place.

26   Remove the cap from the end of the number one connecting rod (refer to the marks made during removal). Remove the original bearing inserts and wipe the bearing surfaces of the connecting rod and cap with a clean, lint-free cloth. They must be kept spotlessly clean.

Connecting rod bearing oil clearance check

27   Clean the back side of the new upper bearing insert, then lay it in place in the connecting rod.

28   Make sure the tab on the bearing fits into the recess in the rod. Don't hammer the bearing insert into place and be very careful not to nick or gouge the bearing face. Don't lubricate the bearing at this time.

29   Clean the back side of the other bearing insert and install it in the rod cap. Again, make sure the tab on the bearing fits into the recess in the cap, and don't apply any lubricant. It's critically important that the mating surfaces of the bearing and connecting rod are perfectly clean and oil free when they're assembled.

30   Position the piston ring gaps at 90-degree intervals around the piston as shown (see illustration).

31   Lubricate the piston and rings with clean engine oil and attach a piston ring compressor to the piston. Leave the skirt protruding about 1/4-inch to guide the piston into the cylinder. The rings must be compressed until they're flush with the piston.

32   Rotate the crankshaft until the number one connecting rod journal is at BDC (bottom dead center) and apply a liberal coat of engine oil to the cylinder walls.

33   With the directional stamp (arrow) on top of the piston facing the front (timing belt/timing chain end) of the engine, gently insert the piston/connecting rod assembly into the number one cylinder bore and rest the bottom edge of the ring compressor on the engine block. Install the pistons with the (arrow) mark facing toward the timing belt/timing chain end.

34   Tap the top edge of the ring compressor to make sure it's contacting the block around its entire circumference.

35   Gently tap on the top of the piston with the end of a wooden or plastic hammer handle (see illustration) while guiding the end of the connecting rod into place on the crankshaft journal. The piston rings may try to pop out of

9.35 Use a plastic or wooden hammer handle to push the piston into the cylinder

9.37 Place Plastigage on each connecting rod bearing journal parallel to the crankshaft centerline

9.41 Use the scale on the Plastigage package to determine the bearing oil clearance - be sure to measure the widest part of the Plastigage and use the correct scale; it comes with both standard and metric scales

the ring compressor just before entering the cylinder bore, so keep some downward pressure on the ring compressor. Work slowly, and if any resistance is felt as the piston enters the cylinder, stop immediately. Find out what's hanging up and fix it before proceeding. Do not force the piston into the cylinder - you might break a ring and/or the piston.

36   Once the piston/connecting rod assembly is installed, the connecting rod bearing oil clearance must be checked before the rod cap is permanently installed.

37   Cut a piece of the appropriate size Plastigage slightly shorter than the width of the connecting rod bearing and lay it in place on the number one connecting rod journal, parallel with the journal axis (see illustration).

38   Clean the connecting rod cap bearing face and install the rod cap. Make sure the mating mark on the cap is on the same side as the mark on the connecting rod (see illustration 9.4).

39   Install the old rod bolts, at this time, and tighten them to the torque listed in this Chapter's Specifications.

Note: *Use a thin-wall socket to avoid erroneous torque readings that can result if the socket is wedged between the rod cap and the bolt. If the socket tends to wedge itself between the bolt and the cap, lift up on it slightly until it no longer contacts the cap. DO NOT rotate the crankshaft at any time during this operation.*

40   Remove the bolts and detach the rod cap, being very careful not to disturb the Plastigage. Discard the cap bolts at this time as they cannot be reused.

Note: *You MUST use new connecting rod bolts.*

41   Compare the width of the crushed Plastigage to the scale printed on the Plastigage envelope to obtain the oil clearance (see illustration). The connecting rod oil clearance is usually about 0.001 to 0.002 inch. Consult an automotive machine shop for the clearance specified for the rod bearings on your engine.

42   If the clearance is not as specified, the bearing inserts may be the wrong size (which means different ones will be required). Before deciding that different inserts are needed, make sure that no dirt or oil was between the bearing inserts and the connecting rod or cap when the clearance was measured. Also, recheck the journal diameter. If the Plastigage was wider at one end than the other, the journal may be tapered. If the clearance still exceeds the limit specified, the bearing will have to be replaced with an undersize bearing.

Caution: *When installing a new crankshaft, always use a standard size bearing.*

Final installation

43   Carefully scrape all traces of the Plastigage material off the rod journal and/or bearing face. Be very careful not to scratch the bearing - use your fingernail or the edge of a plastic card.

44   Make sure the bearing faces are perfectly clean, then apply a uniform layer of clean moly-base grease or engine assembly lube to both of them. You'll have to push the piston into the cylinder to expose the face of the bearing insert in the connecting rod.

Caution: *Install new connecting rod cap bolts. Do NOT reuse old bolts - they have stretched and cannot be reused.*

45   Slide the connecting rod back into place on the journal, install the rod cap, install the new bolts and tighten them to the torque listed in this Chapter's Specifications. Again, work up to the torque in three steps.

46   Repeat the entire procedure for the remaining pistons/connecting rods.

47   The important points to remember are:

a) *Keep the back sides of the bearing inserts and the insides of the connecting rods and caps perfectly clean when assembling them.*

b) *Make sure you have the correct piston/rod assembly for each cylinder.*

c) *The mark on the piston must face the front (timing belt/chain end) of the engine.*

d) *Lubricate the cylinder walls liberally with clean oil.*

e) *Apply a 1/8-inch bead of RTV engine sealant to the block, then place the ladder frame onto the block and tighten the bolts in a circular pattern, starting from the center and working outward, in two steps, to the torque listed in this Chapter's Specifications.*

48   After all the piston/connecting rod assemblies have been correctly installed, rotate the crankshaft a number of times by hand to check for any obvious binding.

49   As a final step, check the connecting rod endplay again.

50   Compare the measured endplay to the tolerance listed in this Chapter's Specifications to make sure it's acceptable. If it was correct before disassembly and the original crankshaft and rods were reinstalled, it should still be correct. If new rods or a new crankshaft were installed, the endplay may be inadequate. If so, the rods will have to be removed and taken to an automotive machine shop for resizing.

10   Crankshaft - removal and installation

Removal

Note: *The crankshaft can be removed only after the engine has been removed from the vehicle. It's assumed that the driveplate, crankshaft pulley, timing belt/timing chain, oil pan, oil pump body, oil filter, oil pump pick-up tube, windage tray and piston/connecting rod assemblies have already been removed. The rear main oil seal retainer must be unbolted and separated from the block before proceeding with crankshaft removal.*

10.1 Checking crankshaft endplay with a dial indicator

10.3 Checking crankshaft endplay with feeler gauges at the thrust bearing journal

1   Before the crankshaft is removed, measure the endplay. Mount a dial indicator with the indicator in line with the crankshaft and just touching the end of the crankshaft as shown (see illustration).

2   Pry the crankshaft all the way to the rear and zero the dial indicator. Next, pry the crankshaft to the front as far as possible and check the reading on the dial indicator. The distance traveled is the endplay. A typical crankshaft endplay will fall between 0.003 to 0.010 inch (0.076 to 0.254 mm). If it is greater than that, check the crankshaft thrust surfaces for wear after it's removed. If no wear is evident, new main bearings should correct the endplay.

3   If a dial indicator isn't available, feeler gauges can be used. Gently pry the crankshaft all the way to the front of the engine. Slip feeler gauges between the crankshaft and the front face of the thrust bearing or washer to determine the clearance (see illustration).

4   Remove the ladder frame bolts and carefully separate the ladder frame from the engine block.

5   Loosen the main bearing cap bolts 1/4-turn at a time each, until they can be removed by hand, then gently tap the main bearing cap with a soft-face hammer around the perimeter

of the assembly. Pull the main bearing cap straight up and off the cylinder block. Try not to drop the bearing inserts if they come out with the assembly.

Note: *New main bearing cap bolts must be used when reassembling the engine, but save the old bolts for use when checking the main bearing oil clearance.*

6   Carefully lift the crankshaft out of the engine. It may be a good idea to have an assistant available, since the crankshaft is quite heavy and awkward to handle. With the bearing inserts in place inside the engine block and main bearing caps, reinstall the bedplate/main bearing caps onto the engine block and tighten the bolts finger-tight. Make sure you install the bedplate/main bearing caps with the arrow facing the front end of the engine.

Installation

7   Crankshaft installation is the first step in engine reassembly. It's assumed at this point that the engine block and crankshaft have been cleaned, inspected and repaired or reconditioned. Install the target wheel to the crankshaft and tighten the new bolts to the torque listed in this Chapter's Specifications, if removed.

8   Position the engine block with the bottom facing up.

9   Remove the mounting bolts and lift off the main bearing caps.

10   If they're still in place, remove the original bearing inserts from the block main bearing caps. Wipe the bearing surfaces of the block and bedplate with a clean, lint-free cloth. They must be kept spotlessly clean. This is critical for determining the correct bearing oil clearance.

Main bearing oil clearance check

11   Without mixing them up, clean the back sides of the new upper main bearing inserts (with grooves and oil holes) and lay one in each main bearing saddle in the block (see illustration). Each upper bearing has an oil groove and oil hole in it.

Caution: *The oil holes in the block must line up with the oil holes in the upper bearing inserts.*

12   The thrust washers or thrust bearing inserts must be installed in the number 3 crankshaft journal. Clean the back sides of the lower main bearing inserts and lay them in the corresponding location in the main bearing caps. Make sure the tab on the bearing insert fits into the recess in the block or bedplate or main bearing caps. The upper bearings with the oil holes are installed into the engine block, while the lower bearings without the oil holes are installed in the main bearing caps.

Caution: *Do not hammer the bearing insert into place and don't nick or gouge the bearing faces. DO NOT apply any lubrication at this time.*

13   Clean the faces of the bearing inserts in the block and the crankshaft main bearing journals with a clean, lint-free cloth.

14   Check or clean the oil holes in the crankshaft, as any dirt here can go only one way - straight through the new bearings.

15   Once you're certain the crankshaft is clean, carefully lay it in position in the cylinder block.

16   Before the crankshaft can be permanently installed, the main bearing oil clearance must be checked.

17   Cut several strips of the appropriate size of Plastigage. They must be slightly shorter than the width of the main bearing journal.

18   Place one piece on each crankshaft main bearing journal, parallel with the journal axis as shown (see illustration).

19   Clean the faces of the bearing inserts in the main bearing caps. Hold the bearing inserts in place and install the assembly onto the crankshaft and cylinder block. DO NOT disturb the Plastigage. Make sure you install the main bearing caps with the arrow facing the front (timing belt/timing chain end) of the engine.

Caution: *The number 3 main bearing cap must be centered over the inner bolt holes of the block. If the bearing cap is not centered*

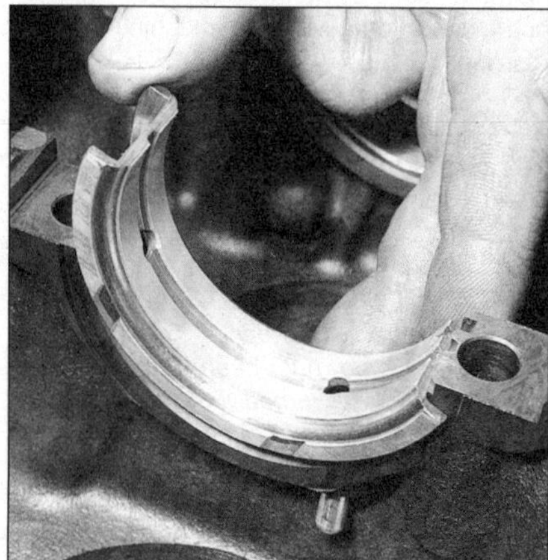

10.11 Installing a crankshaft main bearing onto the engine block main bearing saddle

10.18 Place the Plastigage onto the crankshaft bearing journal as shown

the crankshaft counterweights can contact the main bearing cap and cause severe engine damage.

Caution: *The manufacturer used three different head bolts. The bolts have different torque values and are not interchangeable. The bolts have an identifying mark on top of the bolt head - the letter "b," the letter "M," or the number "6" - the correct bolts must be reinstalled to prevent incorrect tightening torque.*

20   Apply clean engine oil to all bolt threads prior to installation, then install the old bolts finger-tight; do not install the side bolts at this time. Tighten all the bolts in the sequences shown (see illustration 10.31) progressing in steps, to the torque listed in this Chapter's Specifications.

21   Remove the bolts in the reverse order of the tightening sequence and carefully lift the caps straight up and off the block. Do not disturb the Plastigage or rotate the crankshaft. If the cap(s) is difficult to remove, tap it gently from side-to-side with a soft-face hammer to loosen it.

22   Compare the width of the crushed Plastigage on each journal to the scale printed on the Plastigage envelope to determine the main bearing oil clearance (see illustration). Check with an automotive machine shop for the crankshaft main bearing oil clearance limits.

23   If the clearance is not as specified, the bearing inserts may be the wrong size (which means different ones will be required). Before deciding if different inserts are needed, make sure that no dirt or oil was between the bearing inserts and the cap assembly or block when the clearance was measured. If the Plastigage was wider at one end than the other, the crankshaft journal may be tapered. If the clearance still exceeds the limit specified, the bearing insert(s) will have to be replaced with an undersize bearing insert(s).

Caution: *When installing a new crankshaft, always install a standard bearing insert set.*

24   Carefully scrape all traces of the Plastigage material off the main bearing journals and/or the bearing insert faces. Be sure to remove all residue from the oil holes. Use your fingernail or the edge of a plastic card - don't nick or scratch the bearing faces.

Final installation

25   Carefully lift the crankshaft out of the cylinder block.

26   Clean the bearing insert faces in the cylinder block, then apply a thin, uniform layer of moly-base grease or engine assembly lube to each of the bearing surfaces. Coat the thrust faces as well as the journal face of the thrust bearing.

27   Make sure the crankshaft journals are clean, then lay the crankshaft back in place in the cylinder block.

28   Clean the bearing insert faces and then apply the same lubricant to them.

29   Install the main bearing caps onto the designated journals.

30   Prior to installation, apply clean engine oil to the NEW bolt threads, wiping off any excess, then install all bolts finger-tight.

31   Tighten the cap bolts, in sequence (see illustration), to the torque listed in this Chapter's Specifications.

32   Recheck crankshaft endplay with a feeler gauge or a dial indicator. The endplay should be correct if the crankshaft thrust faces aren't worn or damaged and if new bearings have been installed.

33   Rotate the crankshaft a number of times by hand to check for any obvious binding. It should rotate with a running torque of 50 in-lbs or less. If the running torque is too high, correct the problem at this time.

34   Apply a continuous 1/8-inch bead of RTV sealant to the engine block surface then carefully place the ladder frame on to the block. Install the mounting bolts hand-tight. Tighten the bolts in a circular pattern, starting from the center and working outward progressing in steps, to the torque listed in this Chapter's Specifications .

35   Install the new rear main oil seal assembly (see Chapter 2A).

36   Install the oil pump, pick up tube or balance shaft module (see Chapter 2A).

11   Engine overhaul - reassembly sequence

1   Before beginning engine reassembly, make sure you have all the necessary new parts, gaskets and seals as well as the following items on hand:

Common hand tools
A 1/2-inch drive torque wrench
New engine oil
Gasket sealant
Thread locking compound

2   If you obtained a short block, it will be necessary to install the cylinder head, the oil pump and pick-up tube, the oil pan, the water pump, the timing belt/timing chain and timing

10.22 Use the scale on the Plastigage package to determine the bearing oil clearance - be sure to measure the widest part of the Plastigage and use the correct scale; it comes with both standard and metric scales

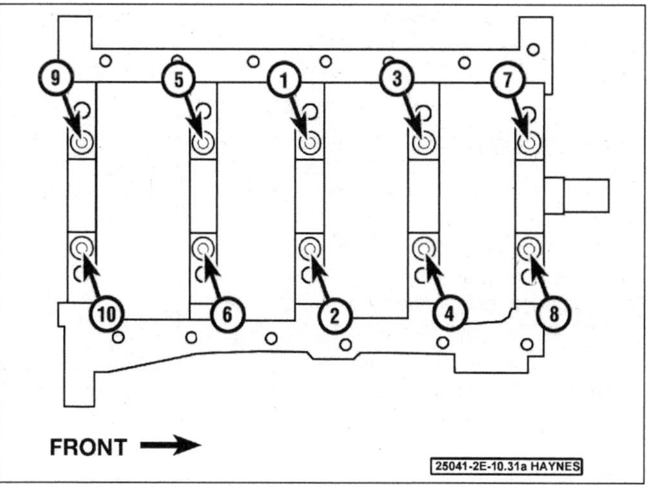

10.31 Main bearing cap bolt and side bolt tightening sequence

COMMON ENGINE OVERHAUL TERMS

B

Backlash - The amount of play between two parts. Usually refers to how much one gear can bo movod back and forth without moving the gear with which it's meshed.

Bearing Caps - The caps held in place by nuts or bolts which, in turn, hold the bearing surface. This space is for lubricating oil to enter.

Bearing clearance - The amount of space left between shaft and bearing surface. This space is for lubricating oil to enter.

Bearing crush - The additional height which is purposely manufactured into each bearing half to ensure complete contact of the bearing back with the housing bore when the engine is assembled.

Bearing knock - The noise created by movement of a part in a loose or worn bearing.

Blueprinting - Dismantling an engine and reassembling it to EXACT specifications.

Bore - An engine cylinder, or any cylindrical hole; also used to describe the process of enlarging or accurately refinishing a hole with a cutting tool, as to bore an engine cylinder. The bore size is the diameter of the hole.

Boring - Renewing the cylinders by cutting them out to a specified size. A boring bar is used to make the cut.

Bottom end - A term which refers collectively to the engine block, crankshaft, main bearings and the big ends of the connecting rods.

Break-in - The period of operation between installation of new or rebuilt parts and time in which parts are worn to the correct fit. Driving at reduced and varying speed for a specified mileage to permit parts to wear to the correct fit.

Bushing - A one-piece sleeve placed in a bore to serve as a bearing surface for shaft, piston pin, etc. Usually replaceable.

C

Camshaft - The shaft in the engine, on which a series of lobes are located for operating the valve mechanisms. The camshaft is driven by gears or sprockets and a timing chain. Usually referred to simply as the cam.

Carbon - Hard, or soft, black deposits found in combustion chamber, on plugs, under rings, on and under valve heads.

Cast iron - An alloy of iron and more than two percent carbon, used for engine blocks and heads because it's relatively inexpensive and easy to mold into complex shapes.

Chamfer - To bevel across (or a bevel on) the sharp edge of an object.

Chase - To repair damaged threads with a tap or die.

Combustion chamber - The space between the piston and the cylinder head, with the piston at top dead center, in which air-fuel mixture is burned.

Compression ratio - The relationship between cylinder volume (clearance volume) when the piston is at top dead center and cylinder volume when the piston is at bottom dead center.

Connecting rod - The rod that connects the crank on the crankshaft with the piston. Sometimes called a con rod.

Connecting rod cap - The part of the connecting rod assembly that attaches the rod to the crankpin.

Core plug - Soft metal plug used to plug the casting holes for the coolant passages in the block.

Crankcase - The lower part of the engine in which the crankshaft rotates; includes the lower section of the cylinder block and the oil pan.

Crank kit - A reground or reconditioned crankshaft and new main and connecting rod bearings.

Crankpin - The part of a crankshaft to which a connecting rod is attached.

Crankshaft - The main rotating member, or shaft, running the length of the crankcase, with offset throws to which the connecting rods are attached; changes the reciprocating motion of the pistons into rotating motion.

Cylinder sleeve - A replaceable sleeve, or liner, pressed into the cylinder block to form the cylinder bore.

D

Deburring - Removing the burrs (rough edges or areas) from a bearing.

Deglazer - A tool, rotated by an electric motor, used to remove glaze from cylinder walls so a new set of rings will seat.

E

Endplay - The amount of lengthwise movement between two parts. As applied to a crankshaft, the distance that the crankshaft can move forward and back in the cylinder block.

F

Face - A machinist's term that refers to removing metal from the end of a shaft or the face of a larger part, such as a flywheel.

Fatigue - A breakdown of material through a large number of loading and unloading cycles. The first signs are cracks followed shortly by breaks.

Feeler gauge - A thin strip of hardened steel, ground to an exact thickness, used to check clearances between parts.

Free height - The unloaded length or height of a spring.

Freeplay - The looseness in a linkage, or an assembly of parts, between the initial application of force and actual movement. Usually perceived as slop or slight delay.

Freeze plug - See Core plug.

G

Gallery - A large passage in the block that forms a reservoir for engine oil pressure.

Glaze - The very smooth, glassy finish that develops on cylinder walls while an engine is in service.

H

Heli-Coil - A rethreading device used when threads are worn or damaged. The device is installed in a retapped hole to reduce the thread size to the original size.

I

Installed height - The spring's measured length or height, as installed on the cylinder head. Installed height is measured from the spring seat to the underside of the spring retainer.

J

Journal - The surface of a rotating shaft which turns in a bearing.

K

Keeper - The split lock that holds the valve spring retainer in position on the valve stem.

Key - A small piece of metal inserted into matching grooves machined into two parts fitted together - such as a gear pressed onto a shaft - which prevents slippage between the two parts.

Knock - The heavy metallic engine sound, produced in the combustion chamber as a result of abnormal combustion - usually detonation. Knock is usually caused by a loose or worn bearing. Also referred to as detonation, pinging and spark knock. Connecting rod or main bearing knocks are created by too much oil clearance or insufficient lubrication.

L

Lands - The portions of metal between the piston ring grooves.

Lapping the valves - Grinding a valve face and its seat together with lapping compound.

Lash - The amount of free motion in a gear train, between gears, or in a mechanical assembly, that occurs before movement can begin. Usually refers to the lash in a valve train.

Lifter - The part that rides against the cam to transfer motion to the rest of the valve train.

M

Machining - The process of using a machine to remove metal from a metal part.

Main bearings - The plain, or babbit, bearings that support the crankshaft.

Main bearing caps - The cast iron caps, bolted to the bottom of the block, that support the main bearings.

O

O.D. - Outside diameter.

Oil gallery - A pipe or drilled passageway in the engine used to carry engine oil from one area to another.

Oil ring - The lower ring, or rings, of a piston; designed to prevent excessive amounts of oil from working up the cylinder walls and into the combustion chamber. Also called an oil-control ring.

Oil seal - A seal which keeps oil from leaking out of a compartment. Usually refers to a dynamic seal around a rotating shaft or other moving part.

O-ring - A type of sealing ring made of a special rubberlike material; in use, the O-ring is compressed into a groove to provide the sealing action.

Overhaul - To completely disassemble a unit, clean and inspect all parts, reassemble it with the original or new parts and make all adjustments necessary for proper operation.

P

Pilot bearing - A small bearing installed in the center of the flywheel (or the rear end of the crankshaft) to support the front end of the input shaft of the transmission.

Pip mark - A little dot or indentation which indicates the top side of a compression ring.

Piston - The cylindrical part, attached to the connecting rod, that moves up and down in the cylinder as the crankshaft rotates. When the fuel charge is fired, the piston transfers the force of the explosion to the connecting rod, then to the crankshaft.

Piston pin (or wrist pin) - The cylindrical and usually hollow steel pin that passes through the piston. The piston pin fastens the piston to the upper end of the connecting rod.

Piston ring - The split ring fitted to the groove in a piston. The ring contacts the sides of the ring groove and also rubs against the cylinder wall, thus sealing space between piston and wall. There are two types of rings: Compression rings seal the compression pressure in the combustion chamber; oil rings scrape excessive oil off the cylinder wall.

Piston ring groove - The slots or grooves cut in piston heads to hold piston rings in position.

Piston skirt - The portion of the piston below the rings and the piston pin hole.

Plastigage - A thin strip of plastic thread, available in different sizes, used for measuring clearances. For example, a strip of plastigage is laid across a bearing journal and mashed as parts are assembled. Then parts are disassembled and the width of the strip is measured to determine clearance between journal and bearing. Commonly used to measure crankshaft main-bearing and connecting rod bearing clearances.

Press-fit - A tight fit between two parts that requires pressure to force the parts together. Also referred to as drive, or force, fit.

Prussian blue - A blue pigment; in solution, useful in determining the area of contact between two surfaces. Prussian blue is commonly used to determine the width and location of the contact area between the valve face and the valve seat.

R

Race (bearing) - The inner or outer ring that provides a contact surface for balls or rollers in bearing.

Ream - To size, enlarge or smooth a hole by using a round cutting tool with fluted edges.

Ring job - The process of reconditioning the cylinders and installing new rings.

Runout - Wobble. The amount a shaft rotates out-of-true.

S

Saddle - The upper main bearing seat.

Scored - Scratched or grooved, as a cylinder wall may be scored by abrasive particles moved up and down by the piston rings.

Scuffing - A type of wear in which there's a transfer of material between parts moving against each other; shows up as pits or grooves in the mating surfaces.

Seat - The surface upon which another part rests or seats. For example, the valve seat is the matched surface upon which the valve face rests. Also used to refer to wearing into a good fit; for example, piston rings seat after a few miles of driving.

Short block - An engine block complete with crankshaft and piston and, usually, camshaft assemblies.

Static balance - The balance of an object while it's stationary.

Step - The wear on the lower portion of a ring land caused by excessive side and back-clearance. The height of the step indicates the ring's extra side clearance and the length of the step projecting from the back wall of the groove represents the ring's back clearance.

Stroke - The distance the piston moves when traveling from top dead center to bottom dead center, or from bottom dead center to top dead center.

Stud - A metal rod with threads on both ends.

T

Tang - A lip on the end of a plain bearing used to align the bearing during assembly.

Tap - To cut threads in a hole. Also refers to the fluted tool used to cut threads.

Taper - A gradual reduction in the width of a shaft or hole; in an engine cylinder, taper usually takes the form of uneven wear, more pronounced at the top than at the bottom.

Throws - The offset portions of the crankshaft to which the connecting rods are affixed.

Thrust bearing - The main bearing that has thrust faces to prevent excessive endplay, or forward and backward movement of the crankshaft.

Thrust washer - A bronze or hardened steel washer placed between two moving parts. The washer prevents longitudinal movement and provides a bearing surface for thrust surfaces of parts.

Tolerance - The amount of variation permitted from an exact size of measurement. Actual amount from smallest acceptable dimension to largest acceptable dimension.

U

Umbrella - An oil deflector placed near the valve tip to throw oil from the valve stem area.

Undercut - A machined groove below the normal surface.

Undersize bearings - Smaller diameter bearings used with re-ground crankshaft journals.

V

Valve grinding - Refacing a valve in a valve-refacing machine.

Valve train - The valve-operating mechanism of an engine; includes all components from the camshaft to the valve.

Vibration damper - A cylindrical weight attached to the front of the crankshaft to minimize torsional vibration (the twist-untwist actions of the crankshaft caused by the cylinder firing impulses). Also called a harmonic balancer.

W

Water jacket - The spaces around the cylinders, between the inner and outer shells of the cylinder block or head, through which coolant circulates.

Web - A supporting structure across a cavity.

Woodruff key - A key with a radiused backside (viewed from the side).

cover, and the valve cover (see Chapter 2A) and balance shaft module on 2.4L models (see Chapter 2A). In order to save time and avoid problems, the external components must be installed in the following general order:

    Thermostat and housing cover
    Water pump
    Intake and exhaust manifolds
    Fuel injection components
    Emissions control components
    Spark plug wires and spark plugs
    Ignition coils
    Oil filter
    Engine mounts and mount brackets
    Driveplate

12   Initial start-up and break-in after overhaul

Warning: *Have a fire extinguisher handy when starting the engine for the first time.*

1   Once the engine has been installed in the vehicle, double-check the engine oil and coolant levels.

2   With the spark plugs out of the engine and the fuel pump disabled (see Section 3, Step 5), crank the engine until oil pressure registers on the gauge or the light goes out.

3   Install the spark plugs, install the coils, and reconnect the electrical connector to the fuel pump module.

4   Start the engine. It may take a few moments for the fuel system to build up pressure, but the engine should start without a great deal of effort.

5   After the engine starts, it should be allowed to warm up to normal operating temperature. While the engine is warming up, make a thorough check for fuel, oil and coolant leaks.

6   Shut the engine off and recheck the engine oil and coolant levels.

7   Drive the vehicle to an area with minimum traffic, accelerate from 30 to 50 mph, then allow the vehicle to slow to 30 mph with the throttle closed. Repeat the procedure 10 or 12 times. This will load the piston rings and cause them to seat properly against the cylinder walls. Check again for oil and coolant leaks.

8   Drive the vehicle gently for the first 500 miles (no sustained high speeds) and keep a constant check on the oil level. It is not unusual for an engine to use oil during the break-in period.

9   At approximately 500 to 600 miles, change the oil and filter.

10   For the next few hundred miles, drive the vehicle normally. Do not pamper it or abuse it.

11   After 2000 miles, change the oil and filter again and consider the engine broken in.

Chapter 3
Cooling, heating and air conditioning systems

Contents

Specifications

General

Refrigerant type..........	R-134a
Radiator cap pressure rating..........	14 to 18 psi
Thermostat rating (opening temperature)	
Starts to open..........	179 degrees F
Fully open..........	203 degrees F
Cooling system capacity..........	See Chapter 1
Refrigerant capacity*	
2010 and earlier models..........	1.25 lb
2011 and later models..........	1.31 lbs

** Check the refrigerant capacity listed on the underhood HVAC label; if the charge capacity listed on the label differs from that shown here, assume the label is correct.*

Torque specifications   Ft-lbs (unless otherwise indicated)

Note: *One foot-pound (ft-lb) of torque is equivalent to 12 inch-pounds (in-lbs) of torque. Torque values below approximately 15 ft-lbs are expressed in inch-pounds, since most foot-pound torque wrenches are not accurate at these smaller values.*

Thermostat housing bolts	
Primary thermostat..........	79 in-lbs
Secondary thermostat..........	159 in-lbs
Water inlet tube bolts..........	17.5
Water pump mounting bolts..........	18
Water pump pulley bolts..........	80 in-lbs

2.2 The cooling system pressure tester is connected in place of the pressure cap, then pumped up to pressurize the system

2.5a The combustion leak detector consists of a bulb, syringe and test fluid

2.5b Place the tester over the cooling system filler neck and use the bulb to draw a sample into the tester

1   General information

Warning: *Do not allow antifreeze to come in contact with your skin or painted surfaces of the vehicle. Rinse off spills immediately with plenty of water. Antifreeze is highly toxic if ingested. Never leave antifreeze lying around in an open container or in puddles on the floor; children and pets are attracted by its sweet smell and may drink it. Check with local authorities about disposing of used antifreeze. Many communities have collection centers which will see that antifreeze is disposed of safely. Never dump used antifreeze on the ground or pour it into drains.*

Engine cooling system

1   All modern vehicles employ a pressurized engine cooling system with thermostatically controlled coolant circulation. The cooling system consists of a radiator, an expansion tank or coolant reservoir, a pressure cap (located on the expansion tank or cooling system filler neck), a thermostat, a cooling fan, and a water pump.

2   The water pump circulates coolant through the engine. The coolant flows around each cylinder and around the intake and exhaust ports, near the spark plug areas and in close proximity to the exhaust valve guides.

3   A thermostat controls engine coolant temperature. During warm up, the closed thermostat prevents coolant from circulating through the radiator. As the engine nears normal operating temperature, the thermostat opens and allows hot coolant to travel through the radiator, where it's cooled before returning to the engine.

Heating system

4   The heating system consists of a blower fan and heater core located in a housing under the dash, the hoses connecting the heater core to the engine cooling system and the heater/air conditioning control head on the dashboard. Hot engine coolant is circulated through the heater core. When the heater mode is activated, a flap door in the housing opens to expose the heater core to the passenger compartment through air ducts. A fan switch on the control head activates the blower motor, which forces air through the core, heating the air.

Air conditioning system

5   The air conditioning system consists of a condenser mounted in front of the radiator, an evaporator mounted adjacent to the heater core, a compressor mounted on the engine, a receiver-drier or accumulator and the plumbing connecting all of the above components.

6   A blower fan forces the warmer air of the passenger compartment through the evaporator core (sort of a radiator-in-reverse), transferring the heat from the air to the refrigerant. The liquid refrigerant boils off into low pressure vapor, taking the heat with it when it leaves the evaporator.

2   Troubleshooting

Coolant leaks

1   A coolant leak can develop anywhere in the cooling system, but the most common causes are:

   a)   *A loose or weak hose clamp*
   b)   *A defective hose*
   c)   *A faulty pressure cap*
   d)   *A damaged radiator*
   e)   *A bad heater core*
   f)   *A faulty water pump*
   g)   *A leaking gasket at any joint that carries coolant*

2   Coolant leaks aren't always easy to find. Sometimes they can only be detected when the cooling system is under pressure. Here's where a cooling system pressure tester comes in handy. After the engine has cooled completely, the tester is attached in place of the pressure cap, then pumped up to the pressure value equal to that of the pressure cap rating (see illustration). Now, leaks that only exist when the engine is fully warmed up will become apparent. The tester can be left connected to locate a nagging slow leak.

Coolant level drops, but no external leaks

3   If you find it necessary to keep adding coolant, but there are no external leaks, the probable causes include:

   a)   *A blown head gasket*
   b)   *A leaking intake manifold gasket (only on engines that have coolant passages in the manifold), or a cracked cylinder head or cylinder block*

4   Any of the above problems will also usually result in contamination of the engine oil, which will cause it to take on a milkshake-like appearance. A bad head gasket or cracked head or block can also result in engine oil contaminating the cooling system.

5   Combustion leak detectors (also known as block testers) are available at most auto parts stores. These work by detecting exhaust gases in the cooling system, which indicates a compression leak from a cylinder into the coolant. The tester consists of a large bulb-type syringe and bottle of test fluid (see illustration). A measured amount of the fluid is added to the syringe. The syringe is placed over the cooling system filler neck and, with the engine running, the bulb is squeezed and a sample of the gases present in the cooling system are drawn up through the test fluid (see illustration). If any combustion gases are present in the sample taken, the test fluid will change color.

6   If the test indicates combustion gas is present in the cooling system, you can be sure that the engine has a blown head gasket or a crack in the cylinder head or block, and will require disassembly to repair.

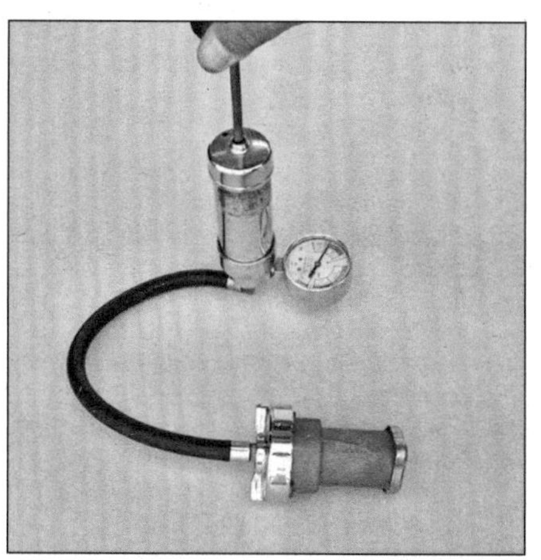

2.8 Checking the cooling system pressure cap with a cooling system pressure tester

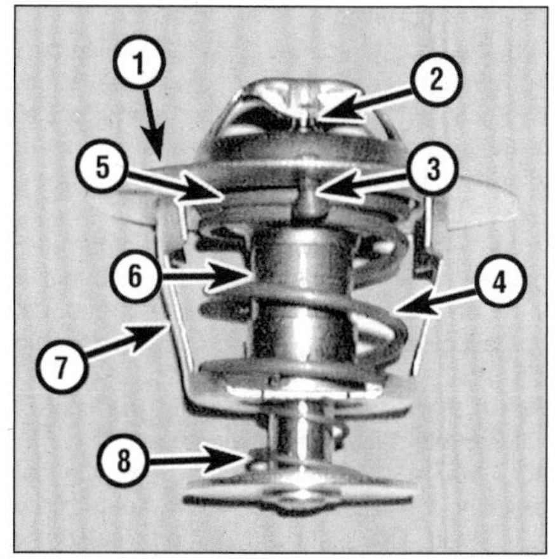

2.10 Typical thermostat

1	*Flange*	5	*Valve seat*
2	*Piston*	6	*Valve*
3	*Jiggle valve*	7	*Frame*
4	*Main coil spring*	8	*Secondary coil spring*

2.28 The water pump weep hole is generally located on the underside of the pump

Pressure cap

Warning: *Wait until the engine is completely cool before beginning this check.*

7   The cooling system is sealed by a spring-loaded cap, which raises the boiling point of the coolant. If the cap's seal or spring are worn out, the coolant can boil and escape past the cap. With the engine completely cool, remove the cap and check the seal; if it's cracked, hardened or deteriorated in any way, replace it with a new one.

8   Even if the seal is good, the spring might not be; this can be checked with a cooling system pressure tester (see illustration). If the cap can't hold a pressure within approximately 1-1/2 lbs of its rated pressure (which is marked on the cap), replace it with a new one.

9   The cap is also equipped with a vacuum relief spring. When the engine cools off, a vacuum is created in the cooling system. The vacuum relief spring allows air back into the system, which will equalize the pressure and prevent damage to the radiator (the radiator tanks could collapse if the vacuum is great enough). If, after turning the engine off and allowing it to cool down you notice any of the cooling system hoses collapsing, replace the pressure cap with a new one.

Thermostat

10   Before assuming the thermostat (see illustration) is responsible for a cooling system problem, check the coolant level (see Chapter 1), drivebelt tension (see Chapter 1) and temperature gauge (or light) operation.

11   If the engine takes a long time to warm up (as indicated by the temperature gauge or heater operation), the thermostat is probably stuck open. Replace the thermostat with a new one.

12   If the engine runs hot or overheats, a thorough test of the thermostat should be performed.

13   Definitive testing of the thermostat can only be made when it is removed from the vehicle. If the thermostat is stuck in the open position at room temperature, it is faulty and must be replaced.

Caution: *Do not drive the vehicle without a thermostat. The computer may stay in open loop and emissions and fuel economy will suffer.*

14   To test a thermostat, suspend the (closed) thermostat on a length of string or wire in a pot of cold water.

15   Heat the water on a stove while observing the thermostat. The thermostat should fully open before the water boils.

16   If the thermostat doesn't open and close as specified, or sticks in any position, replace it.

Cooling fan

Electric cooling fan

17   If the engine is overheating and the cooling fan is not coming on when the engine temperature rises to an excessive level, unplug the fan motor electrical connector(s) and connect the motor directly to the battery with fused jumper wires. If the fan motor doesn't come on, replace the motor.

18   If the radiator fan motor is okay, but it isn't coming on when the engine gets hot, the fan relay might be defective. A relay is used to control a circuit by turning it on and off in response to a control decision by the Powertrain Control Module (PCM). These control circuits are fairly complex, and checking them should be left to a qualified automotive technician. Sometimes, the control system can be fixed by simply identifying and replacing a bad relay.

19   Locate the fan relays in the engine compartment fuse/relay box.

20   Test the relay (see Chapter 12).

21   If the relay is okay, check all wiring and connections to the fan motor. Refer to the wiring diagrams in Chapter 12. If no obvious problems are found, the problem could be the Engine Coolant Temperature (ECT) sensor or the Powertrain Control Module (PCM). Have the cooling fan system and circuit diagnosed by a dealer service department or repair shop with the proper diagnostic equipment.

Belt-driven cooling fan

22   Disconnect the negative battery cable from the remote ground terminal (see Chapter 5) and rock the fan back and forth by hand to check for excessive bearing play.

23   With the engine cold (and not running), turn the fan blades by hand. The fan should turn freely.

24   Visually inspect for substantial fluid leakage from the clutch assembly. If problems are noted, replace the clutch assembly.

25   With the engine completely warmed up, turn off the ignition switch and disconnect the negative battery cable from the remote ground terminal. Turn the fan by hand. Some drag should be evident. If the fan turns easily, replace the fan clutch.

Water pump

26   A failure in the water pump can cause serious engine damage due to overheating.

Drivebelt-driven water pump

27   There are two ways to check the operation of the water pump while it's installed on the engine. If the pump is found to be defective, it should be replaced with a new or rebuilt unit.

28   Water pumps are equipped with weep (or vent) holes (see illustration). If a failure occurs in the pump seal, coolant will leak from the hole.

29   If the water pump shaft bearings fail, there may be a howling sound at the pump

while it's running. Shaft wear can be felt with the drivebelt removed if the water pump pulley is rocked up and down (with the engine off). Don't mistake drivebelt slippage, which causes a squealing sound, for water pump bearing failure.

Timing chain or timing belt-driven water pump

30   Water pumps driven by the timing chain or timing belt are located underneath the timing chain or timing belt cover.

31   Checking the water pump is limited because of where it is located. However, some basic checks can be made before deciding to remove the water pump. If the pump is found to be defective, it should be replaced with a new or rebuilt unit.

32   One sign that the water pump may be failing is that the heater (climate control) may not work well. Warm the engine to normal operating temperature, confirm that the coolant level is correct, then run the heater and check for hot air coming from the ducts.

33   Check for noises coming from the water pump area. If the water pump impeller shaft or bearings are failing, there may be a howling sound at the pump while the engine is running.

Note: *Be careful not to mistake drivebelt noise (squealing) for water pump bearing or shaft failure.*

34   It you suspect water pump failure due to noise, wear can be confirmed by feeling for play at the pump shaft. This can be done by rocking the drive sprocket on the pump shaft up and down. To do this you will need to remove the tension on the timing chain or belt as well as access the water pump.

All water pumps

35   In rare cases or on high-mileage vehicles, another sign of water pump failure may be the presence of coolant in the engine oil. This condition will adversely affect the engine in varying degrees.

Note: *Finding coolant in the engine oil could indicate other serious issues besides a failed water pump, such as a blown head gasket or a cracked cylinder head or block.*

36   Even a pump that exhibits no outward signs of a problem, such as noise or leakage, can still be due for replacement. Removal for close examination is the only sure way to tell. Sometimes the fins on the back of the impeller can corrode to the point that cooling efficiency is diminished significantly.

Heater system

37   Little can go wrong with a heater. If the fan motor will run at all speeds, the electrical part of the system is okay. The three basic heater problems fall into the following general categories:

   a) *Not enough heat*
   b) *Heat all the time*
   c) *No heat*

38   If there's not enough heat, the control valve or door is stuck in a partially open position, the coolant coming from the engine isn't hot enough, or the heater core is restricted. If the coolant isn't hot enough, the thermostat in the engine cooling system is stuck open, allowing coolant to pass through the engine so rapidly that it doesn't heat up quickly enough. If the vehicle is equipped with a temperature gauge instead of a warning light, watch to see if the engine temperature rises to the normal operating range after driving for a reasonable distance.

39   If there's heat all the time, the control valve or the door is stuck wide open.

40   If there's no heat, coolant is probably not reaching the heater core, or the heater core is plugged. The likely cause is a collapsed or plugged hose, core, or a frozen heater control valve. If the heater is the type that flows coolant all the time, the cause is a stuck door or a broken or kinked control cable.

Air conditioning system

41   If the cool air output is inadequate:

   a) *Inspect the condenser coils and fins to make sure they're clear*
   b) *Check the compressor clutch for slippage*
   c) *Check the blower motor for proper operation*
   d) *Inspect the blower discharge passage for obstructions*
   e) *Check the system air intake filter for clogging*

42   If the system provides intermittent cooling air:

   a) *Check the circuit breaker, blower switch and blower motor for a malfunction*
   b) *Make sure the compressor clutch isn't slipping*
   c) *Inspect the plenum door to make sure it's operating properly*
   d) *Inspect the evaporator to make sure it isn't clogged*
   e) *If the unit is icing up, it may be caused by excessive moisture in the system, incorrect super heat switch adjustment, or low thermostat adjustment*

43   If the system provides no cooling air:

   a) *Inspect the compressor drivebelt; make sure it isn't loose or broken*
   b) *Make sure the compressor clutch engages; if it doesn't, check for a blown fuse*
   c) *Inspect the wire harness for broken or disconnected wires*
   d) *If the compressor clutch doesn't engage, bridge the terminals of the AC pressure switch(es) with a jumper wire; if the clutch now engages, and the system is properly charged, the pressure switch is bad*
   e) *Make sure the blower motor is not disconnected or burned out*
   f) *Make sure the compressor isn't partially or completely seized*
   g) *Inspect the refrigerant lines for leaks*
   h) *Check the components for leaks*
   i) *Inspect the receiver-drier/accumulator or expansion valve/tube for clogged screens*

44   If the system is noisy:

   a) *Look for loose panels in the passenger compartment*
   b) *Inspect the compressor drivebelt; it may be loose or worn*
   c) *Check the compressor mounting bolts; they should be tight*
   d) *Listen carefully to the compressor; it may be worn out*
   e) *Listen to the idler pulley and bearing, and the clutch; either may be defective*
   f) *The winding in the compressor clutch coil or solenoid may be defective*
   g) *The compressor oil level may be low*
   h) *The blower motor fan bushing or the motor itself may be worn out*
   i) *If there is an excessive charge in the system, you'll hear a rumbling noise in the high pressure line, a thumping noise in the compressor, or see bubbles or cloudiness in the sight glass*
   j) *If there is a low charge in the system, you might hear hissing in the evaporator case at the expansion valve, or see bubbles or cloudiness in the sight glass*

---

3   Air conditioning and heating system - check and maintenance

---

Air conditioning system

Warning: *The air conditioning system is under high pressure. Do not loosen any hose fittings or remove any components until after the system has been discharged. Air conditioning refrigerant should be properly discharged into an EPA-approved recovery/recycling unit at a dealer service department or an automotive air conditioning repair facility. Always wear eye protection when disconnecting air conditioning system fittings.*

Caution: *All models covered by this manual use environmentally friendly R-134a. This refrigerant (and its appropriate refrigerant oils) are not compatible with R-12 refrigerant system components and must never be mixed or the components will be damaged.*

Caution: *When replacing entire components, additional refrigerant oil should be added equal to the amount that is removed with the component being replaced. Be sure to read the can before adding any oil to the system, to make sure it is compatible with the R-134a system.*

1   The following maintenance checks should be performed on a regular basis to ensure that the air conditioning continues to operate at peak efficiency.

   a) *Inspect the condition of the drivebelt. If it is worn or deteriorated, replace it (see Chapter 1).*
   b) *Check the drivebelt tension (see Chapter 1).*

3.9 Insert a thermometer in the center vent, turn on the air conditioning system and wait for it to cool down; depending on the humidity, the output air should be 35 to 40 degrees cooler than the ambient air temperature

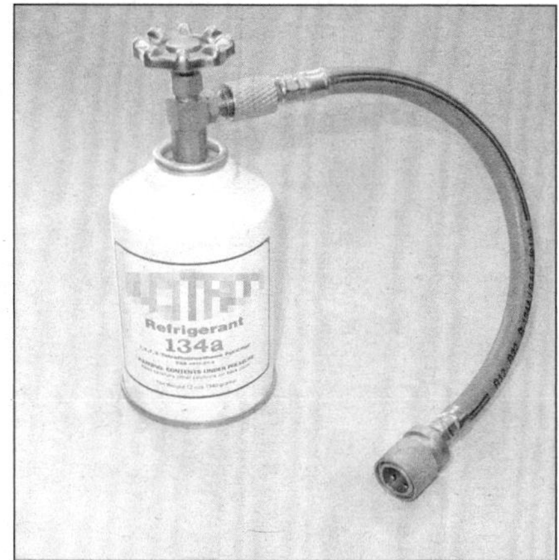

3.11 R-134a automotive air conditioning charging kit

3.13 Low-side charging port (A) and high-side charging port (B, DON'T use) locations

c) *Inspect the system hoses. Look for cracks, bubbles, hardening and deterioration. Inspect the hoses and all fittings for oil bubbles or seepage. If there is any evidence of wear, damage, or leakage, replace the hose(s).*

d) *Inspect the condenser fins for leaves, bugs and any other foreign material that may have embedded itself in the fins. Use a fin comb or compressed air to remove debris from the condenser.*

e) *Make sure the system has the correct refrigerant charge.*

f) *If you hear water sloshing around in the dash area or have water dripping on the carpet, check the evaporator housing drain tube, and insert a piece of wire into the opening to check for blockage.*

Note: *The evaporator housing drain tube exits the floorpan through a grommet in the driver's side footwell.*

2   It's a good idea to operate the system for about ten minutes at least once a month. This is particularly important during the winter months because long term non-use can cause hardening, and subsequent failure, of the seals. Note that using the Defrost function operates the compressor.

3   If the air conditioning system is not working properly, proceed to Step 6 and perform the general checks outlined below.

4   Because of the complexity of the air conditioning system and the special equipment necessary to service it, in-depth troubleshooting and repairs beyond checking the refrigerant charge and the compressor clutch operation are not included in this manual. However, simple checks and component replacement procedures are provided in this Chapter. For more complete information on the air conditioning system, refer to the *Haynes Automotive Heating and Air Conditioning Manual.*

5   The most common cause of poor cooling is simply a low system refrigerant charge. If a noticeable drop in system cooling ability

occurs, one of the following quick checks will help you determine if the refrigerant level is low.

Checking the refrigerant charge

6   Warm the engine up to normal operating temperature.

7   Place the air conditioning temperature selector at the coldest setting and put the blower at the highest setting.

8   After the system reaches operating temperature, feel the larger pipe exiting the evaporator at the firewall. The outlet pipe should be cold (the tubing that leads back to the compressor). If the evaporator outlet pipe is warm, the system probably needs a charge.

9   Insert a thermometer in the center air distribution duct (see illustration) while operating the air conditioning system at its maximum setting - the temperature of the output air should be 35 to 40 degrees F below the ambient air temperature (down to approximately 40 degrees F). If the ambient (outside) air temperature is very high, say 110 degrees F, the duct air temperature may be as high as 60 degrees F, but generally the air conditioning is 35 to 40 degrees F cooler than the ambient air.

10   Further inspection or testing of the system requires special tools and techniques and is beyond the scope of the home mechanic.

Adding refrigerant

Caution: *Make sure any refrigerant, refrigerant oil or replacement component you purchase is designated as compatible with R-134a systems.*

11   Purchase an R-134a automotive charging kit at an auto parts store (see illustration). A charging kit includes a can of refrigerant, a tap valve and a short section of hose that can be attached between the tap valve and the system low side service valve.

Caution: *Never add more than one can of refrigerant to the system. If more refrigerant than that is required, the system should be evacu-*

ated and leak tested.

12   Back off the valve handle on the charging kit and screw the kit onto the refrigerant can, making sure first that the O-ring or rubber seal inside the threaded portion of the kit is in place.

Warning: *Wear protective eyewear when dealing with pressurized refrigerant cans.*

13   Remove the dust cap from the low-side charging port and attach the hose's quick-connect fitting to the port (see illustration).

Warning: *DO NOT attempt to hook the charging kit hose to the system high side! The fittings on the charging kit are designed to fit only on the low side of the system.*

14   Warm up the engine and turn the air conditioning on. Keep the charging kit hose away from the fan and other moving parts.

Note: *The charging process requires the compressor to be running. If the clutch cycles off, you can put the air conditioning switch on High and leave the car doors open to keep the clutch on and compressor working. The compressor can be kept on during the charging by removing the connector from the pressure switch and bridging it with a paper clip or jumper wire during the procedure.*

15   Turn the valve handle on the kit until the stem pierces the can, then back the handle out to release the refrigerant. You should be able to hear the rush of gas. Keep the can upright at all times, but shake it occasionally. Allow stabilization time between each addition.

Note: *The charging process will go faster if you wrap the can with a hot-water-soaked rag to keep the can from freezing up.*

16   If you have an accurate thermometer, you can place it in the center air conditioning duct inside the vehicle and keep track of the output air temperature. A charged system that is working properly should cool down to approximately 40 degrees F. If the ambient (outside) air temperature is very high, say 110 degrees F, the duct air temperature may be as high as 60 degrees F, but generally the air

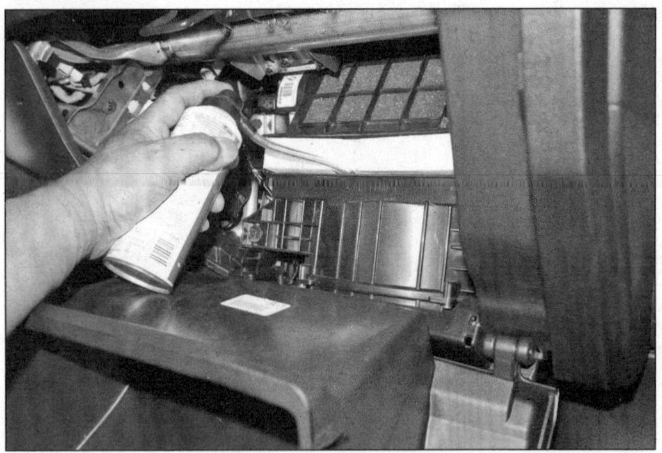

3.24 Insert the nozzle of the disinfectant can into the return-air intake behind the glove box (typical shown)

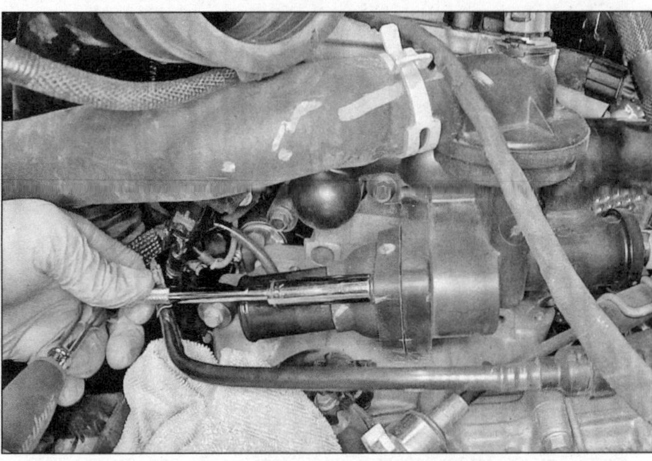

4.4 Remove the thermostat housing cover and mounting bolts

conditioning is 35 to 40 degrees F cooler than the ambient air.

17   When the can is empty, turn the valve handle to the closed position and release the connection from the low-side port. Reinstall the dust cap.

18   Remove the charging kit from the can and store the kit for future use with the piercing valve in the UP position, to prevent inadvertently piercing the can on the next use.

Heating systems

19   If the carpet under the heater core is damp, or if antifreeze vapor or steam is coming through the vents, the heater core is leaking. Remove it (see Section 10) and install a new unit (most radiator shops will not repair a leaking heater core).

20   If the air coming out of the heater vents isn't hot, the problem could stem from any of the following causes:

a) *The thermostat is stuck open, preventing the engine coolant from warming up enough to carry heat to the heater core. Replace the thermostat (see Section 4).*

b) *There is a blockage in the system, preventing the flow of coolant through the heater core. Feel both heater hoses at the firewall. They should be hot. If one of them is cold, there is an obstruction in one of the hoses or in the heater core, or the heater control valve is shut. Detach the hoses and back flush the heater core with a water hose. If the heater core is clear but circulation is impeded, remove the two hoses and flush them out with a water hose.*

c) *If flushing fails to remove the blockage from the heater core, the core must be replaced (see Section 10).*

Eliminating air conditioning odors

21   Unpleasant odors that often develop in air conditioning systems are caused by the growth of a fungus, usually on the surface of the evaporator core. The warm, humid environment there is a perfect breeding ground for mildew to develop.

22   The evaporator core on most vehicles is difficult to access, and factory dealerships have a lengthy, expensive process for eliminating the fungus by opening up the evaporator case and using a powerful disinfectant and rinse on the core until the fungus is gone. You can service your own system at home, but it takes something much stronger than basic household germ-killers or deodorizers.

23   Aerosol disinfectants for automotive air conditioning systems are available in most auto parts stores, but remember when shopping for them that the most effective treatments are also the most expensive. The basic procedure for using these sprays is to start by running the system in the RECIRC mode for ten minutes with the blower on its highest speed. Use the highest heat mode to dry out the system and keep the compressor from engaging by disconnecting the wiring connector at the compressor.

24   The disinfectant can usually comes with a long spray hose. Insert the nozzle into an intake port inside the cabin filter housing (see illustration), and spray according to the manufacturer's recommendations. Try to cover the whole surface of the evaporator core, by aiming the spray up, down and sideways. Follow the manufacturer's recommendations for the length of spray and waiting time between applications.

25   Once the evaporator has been cleaned, the best way to prevent the mildew from coming back again is to make sure your evaporator housing drain tube is clear.

Automatic heating and air conditioning systems

26   Some vehicles are equipped with an optional automatic climate control system. This system has its own computer that receives inputs from various sensors in the heating and air conditioning system. This computer, like the PCM, has self-diagnostic capabilities to help pinpoint problems or faults within the system. Vehicles equipped with automatic heating and air conditioning systems are very complex and considered beyond the scope of the home mechanic. Vehicles equipped with automatic heating and air conditioning systems should be taken to a dealer service department or other qualified facility for repair.

---

4   Thermostat - replacement

Warning: *Wait until the engine is completely cool before beginning this procedure.*

Removal

1   Disconnect the cable from the negative terminal of the battery (see Chapter 5).

2   Drain the cooling system (see Chapter 1). If the coolant is relatively new or in good condition, save it and reuse it. Read the Warning in Section 2.

Primary thermostat

3   Remove the air filter housing (see Chapter 4).

4   Follow the coolant hose to the thermostat housing inlet (see illustration). Detach the hose from the fitting. If it's stuck, grasp it near the engine end with a pair of adjustable pliers and twist it to break the seal, then pull it off. If the hose is old or deteriorated, cut it off and install a new one.

Note: *If the outer surface of the large fitting that mates with the hose is deteriorated (corroded, pitted, etc.), it may be damaged further by hose removal. If it is, the thermostat housing cover will have to be replaced.*

Note: *If the hose has recently been replaced and the fitting is known to be in good condition, the thermostat can be serviced without removing the hose from the housing cover.*

5   Remove thermostat housing fasteners and cover. If the cover is stuck, tap it with a soft-face hammer to jar it loose. Be prepared for some coolant to spill as the seal is broken. Remove the thermostat (see illustration).

4.5 Water inlet removed, use a small screwdriver to free the thermostat from the housing

4.7 Disconnect the radiator hoses (A) and heater hoses (B) from the housing

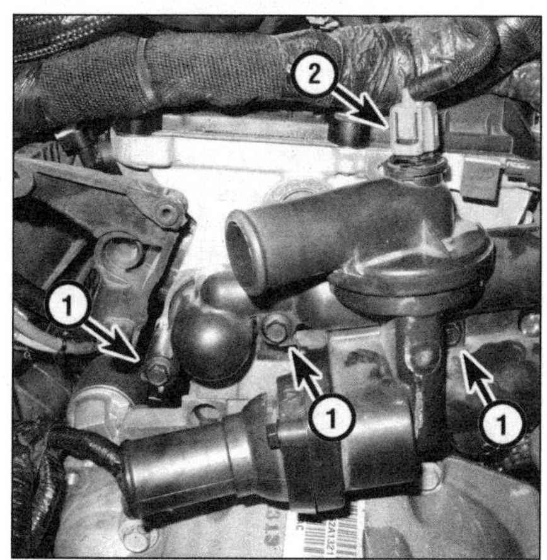

4.8 Secondary thermostat coolant adapter mounting bolts (1) and electrical connector (2)

4.11 Remove the O-ring from the water pipe

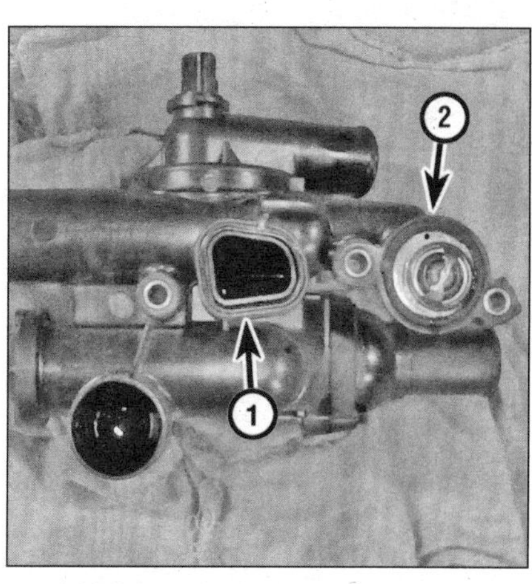

4.12 Secondary thermostat coolant adapter seal (1) and thermostat with gasket (2)

Secondary thermostat

6   Remove the air filter housing (see Chapter 4).

7   Disconnect the radiator hoses and heater hoses from the coolant adapter/thermostat housing (see illustration).

8   Disconnect the electrical connector at the top of the housing (see illustration).

9   Unscrew the mounting bolts from the coolant adapter housing.

10   Carefully remove the coolant adapter and secondary thermostat from the cylinder head and water pump inlet tube.

11   Remove the O-ring from the water pump inlet tube (see illustration). Avoid gouging the metal, or leaks may result.

12   Take note of how the thermostat and gasket or O-ring are installed as well as the coolant adapter housing seal (see illustration). Remove the thermostat from the housing.

13   Remove all traces of the old gasket from the mating surfaces and clean them thoroughly.

14   Install a new gasket to the thermostat, and a new adapter housing seal. Be sure to orient the thermostat with the spring end directed into the housing, with the vent hole in the 12 o'clock position.

Note: *It is standard practice to use a thin layer of RTV sealant when installing flat replacement gaskets. However, if the gasket is designed with a raised crushable sealing surface (not flat), or if it is an O-ring, no RTV sealant is necessary.*

Installation

15   The remainder of installation is the reverse of removal. Make sure that the replacement thermostat is installed in the same direction and position as the one removed. Tighten the fasteners to the torque listed in this Chapter's Specifications.

16   Reattach the hose(s) to the housing cover and fitting(s), then tighten the hose clamp(s) securely.

17   Reconnect the battery (see Chapter 5).

18   Refill the cooling system (see Chapter 1).

19   Start the engine and allow it to reach normal operating temperature, then check for leaks and proper thermostat operation (as described in Section 2).

---

5   Engine cooling fans - removal and installation

Warning: *To avoid possible injury or damage, DO NOT operate the engine with a damaged fan. Do not attempt to repair fan blades - replace a damaged fan with a new one.*

Warning: *The electric fans can start at any time; keep hands, clothes and tools away from the fan until the battery is disconnected to avoid possible injury or damage.*

Warning: *Wait until the engine is completely cool before beginning this procedure.*

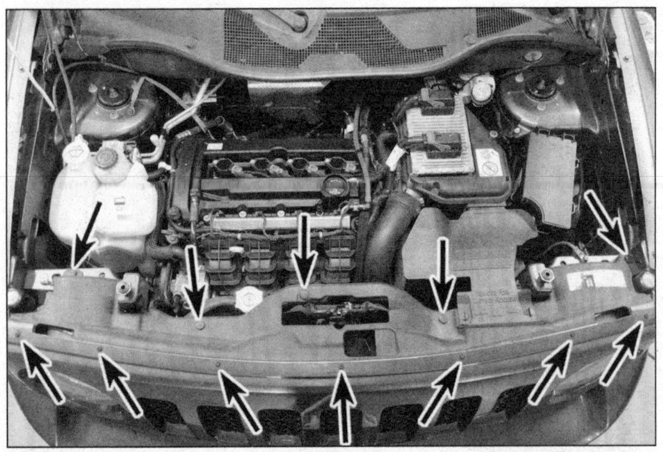

5.5 Locations of the close-out panel fasteners

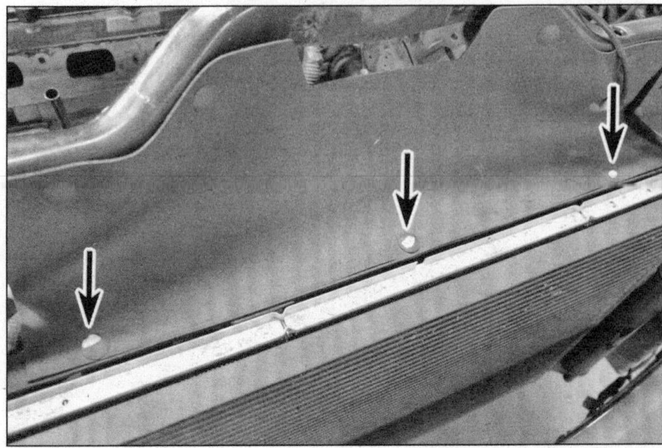

5.7 Air dam lower fastener locations

5.8 Upper radiator hose support bracket fastener location

5.9 Radiator support fastener locations (right side shown, left side identical)

5.10 Disconnect the harness retaining pins and unplug the electrical connectors

1   Disconnect the cable from the negative terminal of the battery (see Chapter 5).
2   Set the parking brake, raise the front of the vehicle and support it securely on jackstands.
3   Drain the cooling system to a level that is just below the upper radiator hose (see Chapter 1).
4   Remove the air intake duct (see Chapter 4).
5   Remove the close-out panel between the grille and the radiator support (see illustration).

6   Remove the hood latch (see Chapter 10).
7   Remove the air dam lower fasteners and release the air dam from the fan shroud (see illustration).
8   Remove the upper radiator hose support bracket fastener (see illustration), then disconnect the hose and position it out of the way.
9   Remove the radiator support fasteners and remove the panel (see illustration).
10   Disconnect the cooling fan electrical connectors and harness retaining pins (see illustration).
11   Move the wiring harness away from the fan shroud (see illustration).
12   Release the upper clips and fasteners holding the fan assembly to the radiator (see illustration).
13   Remove the cooling fan assembly by pulling it straight up and out of the engine compartment.
14   Installation is the reverse of removal. Place the fan assembly back into the retaining clips for the side and bottom.
15   Refill the cooling system (see Chapter 1).

5.11 Detach the wiring harness from the fan shroud

5.12 Release the fan assembly-to-radiator upper clips and fasteners

6.3 Coolant reservoir mounting bolt location

7.6 Transaxle cooler line junction block bolt (6F24 transaxle)

8.5 Loosen the water pump pulley bolts before removing the drivebelt

6   Coolant reservoir - removal and installation

Warning: *Wait until the engine is completely cool before beginning this procedure.*
1   Clamp-off the return hose between the reservoir and the radiator hose tee fitting.
2   Disconnect the return hose from the radiator hose tee.
3   Remove the coolant reservoir mounting bolt from the mounting bracket (see installation).
4   Detach the front of the coolant reservoir from the windshield washer bottle.
5   Lift the reservoir straight up and out.
6   While the reservoir is off the vehicle, it should be cleaned with soapy water and a brush to remove any deposits inside. Inspect it for damage and replace it if necessary.
7   Installation is the reverse of removal. Fill the reservoir with the proper type and amount of coolant (see Chapter 1).

7   Radiator - removal and installation

Warning: *Wait until the engine is completely cool before beginning this procedure.*

Removal

1   Disconnect the cable from the negative terminal of the battery (see Chapter 5).
2   Set the parking brake, raise the front of the vehicle and support it securely on jackstands.
3   Drain the cooling system (see Chapter 1).
4   Remove the engine cooling fans (see Section 5).
5   Disconnect the lower radiator hose from the radiator.
6   On models with a 6-speed automatic transaxle (6F24), remove the bolt that secures the transaxle cooler line junction block to the

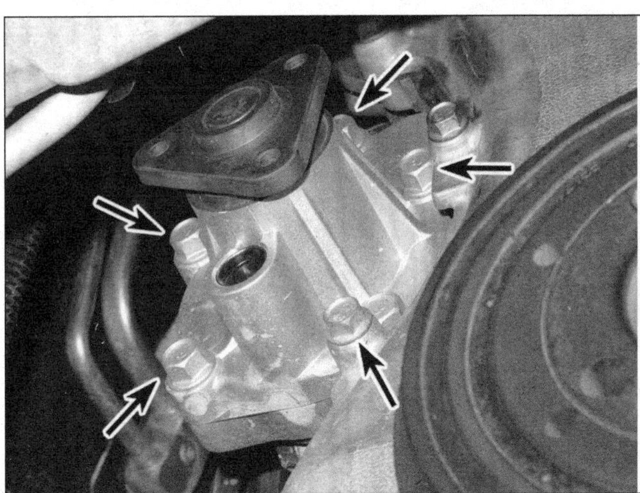

8.8 Water pump mounting bolts

left side of the radiator (see illustration).
7   Remove the condenser-to-radiator fasteners and move the condenser slightly forward (see Section 14).
8   Lift the radiator out of the vehicle.
9   Bugs and dirt can be removed from the radiator by spraying it from the back side with a garden hose. The radiator should be flushed out with a garden hose before reinstallation.
10   Check the radiator rubber mounts for deterioration and replace them if necessary.

Installation

11   Installation is the reverse of removal. Make sure the air conditioning condenser is properly attached to the radiator before seating the radiator into the lower rubber mounts.
Note: *Be sure that the flexible air seals on each side of the radiator are in the correct position while installing the radiator.*
12   After installation, fill the cooling system with the proper mixture of antifreeze and water (see Chapter 1).
13   Start the engine and check for leaks. Allow the engine to reach normal operating temperature, indicated by the upper radiator

hose becoming hot. Recheck the coolant level and add more if required.

8   Water pump - replacement

Warning: *Wait until the engine is completely cool before beginning this procedure.*
1   Disconnect the cable from the negative terminal of the battery (see Chapter 5).
2   Loosen the right-front wheel lug nuts. Set the parking brake, then raise the front of the vehicle and support it securely on jackstands. Remove the wheel.
3   Drain the cooling system (see Chapter 1).
4   Remove the drivebelt splash shield and the inner fender splash shield (see Chapter 11).
5   Loosen the water pump pulley bolts (the drivebelt will prevent the pulley from turning) (see illustration).
6   Remove the drivebelt (see Chapter 1).
7   Remove the water pump pulley bolts and separate the pulley from the pump.
8   Remove the water pump mounting bolts (see illustration).

8.9 Carefully pry the pump to separate it from the housing

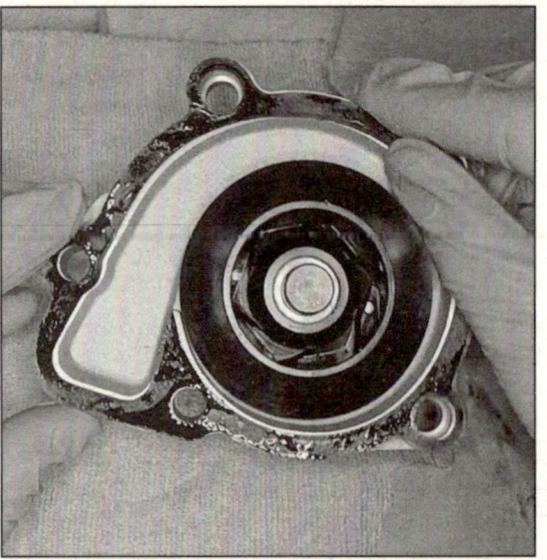

8.11 Install a new gasket to the pump, making sure all the bolt holes are aligned

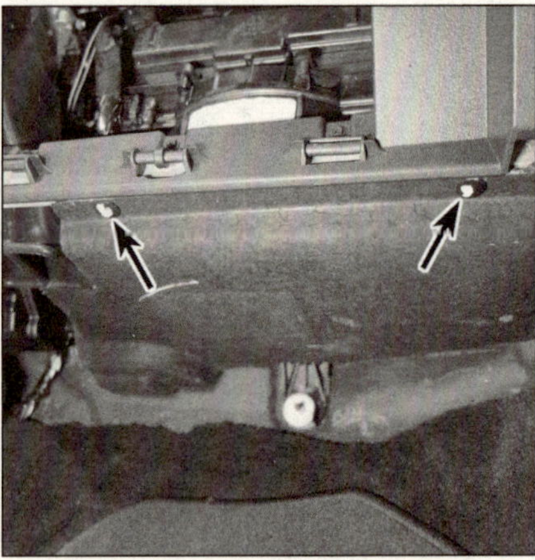

9.2 Remove the insulation panel fasteners and detach the panel

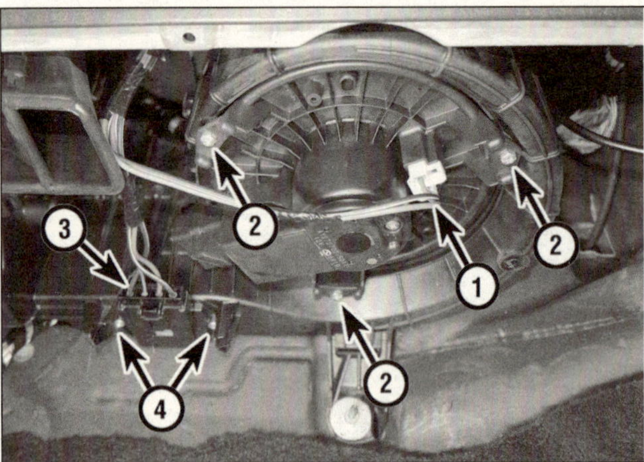

9.4 Blower motor electrical connector (1), blower motor mounting fasteners (2), power module electrical connector (3) and fasteners (4)

9   Use a small prybar to free the pump from the housing (see illustration).

10   Remove all traces of old gasket material from the water pump housing. Clean the mating surface with brake system cleaner.

11   Install a new gasket on the back of the water pump (see illustration), then carefully mate the pump to the engine.

Note: *It's a good idea to use gasket cement on the pump surface to prevent the gasket from shifting as the pump is guided into place.*

12   Install the water pump mounting bolts and tighten them in an alternating pattern to the torque listed in this Chapter's Specifications.

13   The remainder of installation is the reverse of removal. Refill and bleed the cooling system (see Chapter 1). Run the engine and check for leaks and proper operation.

---

9   Blower motor resistor/power module and blower motor assembly - replacement

---

Warning: *The models covered by this manual are equipped with a Supplemental Restraint System (SRS), more commonly known as airbags. Always disable the airbag system before working in the vicinity of any airbag system component to avoid the possibility of accidental deployment of the airbag, which could cause personal injury (see Chapter 12).*

1   Disconnect the cable from the negative terminal of the battery (see Chapter 5).

2   Remove the insulation panel from underneath the glove box (see illustration).

Blower motor assembly

Note: *The blower motor and blower wheel are balanced to each other at the factory and can only be replaced as an assembly.*

3   Disconnect the electrical connector from the blower motor.

4   Remove the three screws holding the blower motor and wire bracket (see illustration). Remove the blower motor from the housing.

5   Installation is the reverse of removal.

Blower motor power module (automatic temperature control systems)

6   Disconnect the electrical connector for the blower motor power module (see illustration 9.4).

7   Remove the screws and detach the power module from the heater/air conditioning housing.

8   Installation is the reverse of removal.

Blower motor resistor (manual temperature control systems)

Warning: *If the vehicle has been recently driven, the blower motor resistors may be hot. In order to avoid personal injury, wait at least five minutes for the blower motor resistor to cool before servicing.*

Caution: *Do not operate the blower motor without the blower motor resistor, it may damage the vehicle.*

Note: *Models with a manually controlled system use a resistor instead of a power module. They are similar in the way they are mounted and connected.*

9   Disconnect the electrical connector from the blower motor resistor.

10   Remove the screws and detach the blower motor resistor from the heater/air conditioning housing.

11   Installation is the reverse of removal.

---

10   Heater core - replacement

Warning: *The air conditioning system is under high pressure. DO NOT loosen any fittings or remove any components until after the system has been discharged. Air conditioning refrigerant must be properly discharged into an EPA-approved container at a dealer service department or an automotive air conditioning repair facility. Always wear eye protection when disconnecting air conditioning system fittings.*

Warning: *Wait until the engine is completely cool before beginning this procedure.*

Warning: *The models covered by this manual are equipped with a Supplemental Restraint System (SRS), more commonly known as airbags. Always disable the airbag system before working in the vicinity of any airbag system component to avoid the possibility of accidental deployment of the airbag, which could cause personal injury (see Chapter 12).*

10.5 Heat shield nut locations

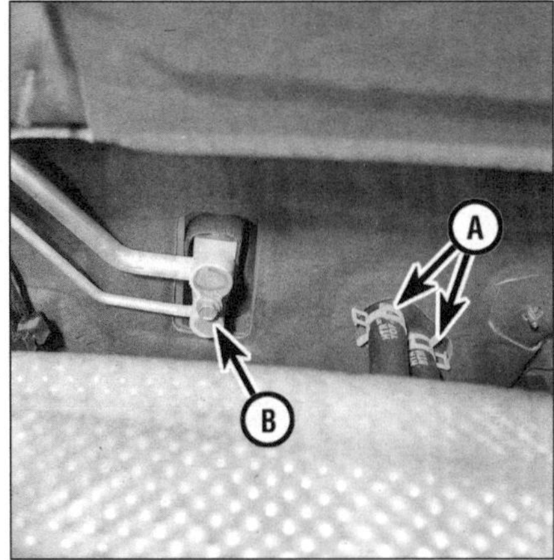

10.6 Detach the heater hoses from the heater core tubes (A) and the refrigerant lines at the evaporator (B)

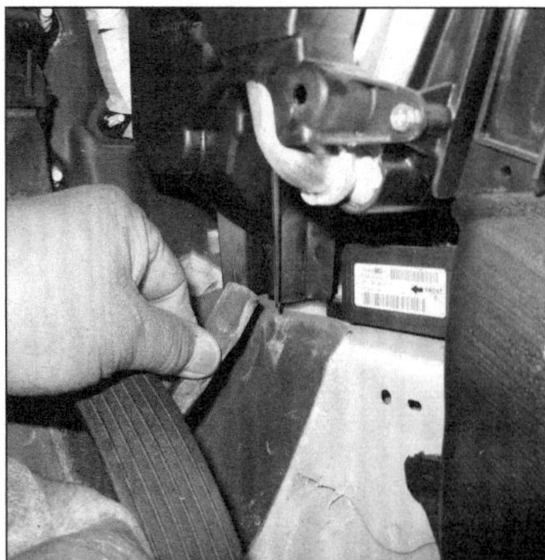

10.13 Disconnect the air conditioner condensation tube

10.14a Disconnect the driver's side rear distribution air duct from the heating/air conditioning housing

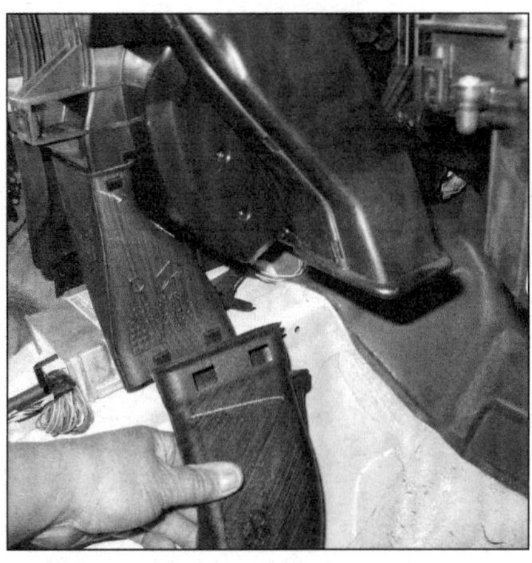

10.14b Disconnect the passenger's side rear distribution air duct from the heating/ air conditioning housing

10.15 Remove the nut holding the heating/air conditioning housing to the passenger's side of the firewall

Note: *Removing interior trim requires the use of special upholstery removal tools used to pry apart fastening clips without damaging them. Be sure to use these tools when removing interior components.*

1   Have the air conditioning system discharged and the refrigerant recovered by an air conditioning technician.

2   Disconnect the cable from the negative terminal of the battery (see Chapter 5).

3   Drain the cooling system (see Chapter 1).

4   Remove the instrument panel (see Chapter 11).

5   Remove the two nuts holding the heat shield to studs on the dash panel (see illustration).

6   Detach the hoses from the heater core tubes at the firewall (see illustration).

7   Remove the bolt securing the refrigerant lines to the air conditioning evaporator. Disconnect the lines and remove the seals.

Note: *To prevent the entry of moisture or debris, place plugs in the lines, or use tape to cover the openings.*

8   Remove the front sill trim on both the passenger's and driver's sides. Remove the front seats (see Chapter 11).

9   If equipped, loosen fasteners and remove the passenger's side amplifier.

10   Pull back the carpet to expose the rear seat ducts.

11   Disconnect the shift interlock cable connected to the floor duct and move it aside.

12   Remove the screws holding the left front floor duct to the heating/air conditioning housing and remove the duct.

13   Remove the air conditioner condensation tube (see illustration).

14   Remove the fasteners holding the left and right rear distribution ducts. Disconnect the ducts from the heating and air conditioning housing (see illustrations).

15   Remove the nut holding the heater/air conditioner housing to the passenger's side of the firewall (see illustration).

16   Pull the heater/air conditioning unit rearward. Remove the heating/air conditioning housing through the passenger compartment (see illustration).

Note: *During removal of the heating/air conditioning housing, ensure that the interior of the car is properly covered with towels to catch any fluids that may come off the housing components.*

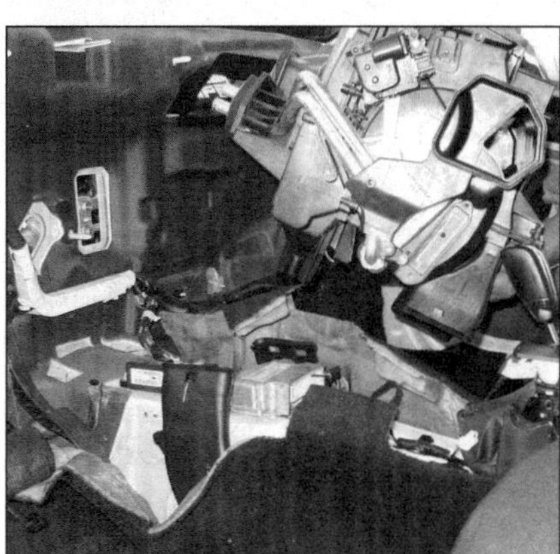

10.16 Remove the heating/air conditioner housing through the passenger side of the vehicle

10.17 Place the heating/air conditioner housing on a work bench

10.19 Unclip the fastener and remove the flange from the heating/air conditioning housing

10.20a Remove the fasteners holding the retaining bracket

10.20b Remove the bracket holding the heater core lines

10.21 Pull the heater core from the heater/air conditioning housing

11.2 Pry the control panel from the instrument panel

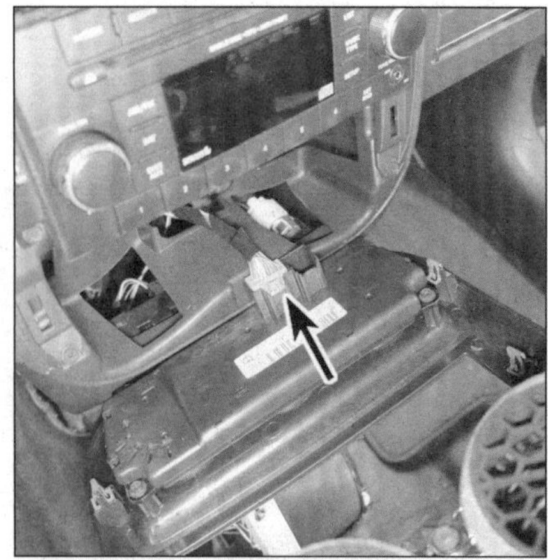

11.3 Disconnect all electrical connectors from the back of the heating/air conditioning control assembly - Automatic heating/air conditioning model shown

17   Place the heater/air conditioning housing on a clean working surface (see illustration).

18   Remove the foam seal from the connection tube flange holding the heater core outlets.

19   Un-clip the fasteners securing the flange and remove the flange from the heating/air conditioning housing (see illustration).

20   Remove the fasteners securing the retaining brackets. Remove the heater core line retaining brackets (see illustrations).

21   Remove the heater core from the heater/air conditioning housing (see illustration).

22   Installation is the reverse of removal. Use new seals for the heater core fittings and refill the cooling system (see Chapter 1).

Note: *If a new heater core is being installed, the cooling system must be flushed (see Chapter 1).*

11   Heater/air conditioner control assembly - removal and installation

Warning: *The models covered by this manual are equipped with a Supplemental Restraint System (SRS), more commonly known as airbags. Always disable the airbag system before working in the vicinity of any airbag system component to avoid the possibility of accidental deployment of the airbag, which could cause personal injury (see Chapter 12).*

1   Disconnect the cable from the negative terminal of the battery (see Chapter 5).

2   Carefully pry the heater/air conditioning control bezel assembly from the instrument panel (see illustration).

3   Disconnect all electrical connectors from the back of the heater/air conditioning control assembly (see illustration). On models with

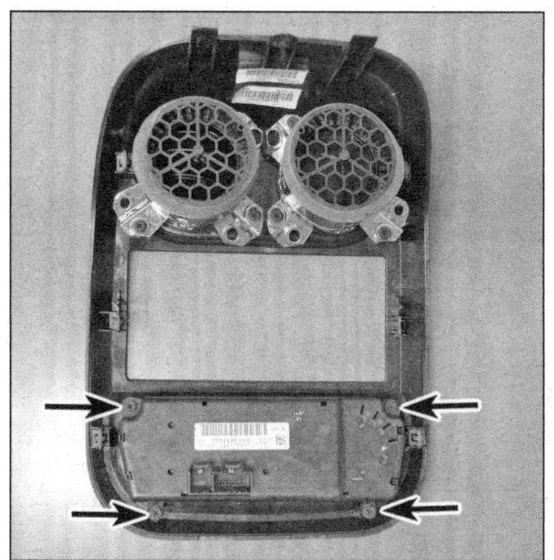

11.4 Remove these fasteners to separate the control assembly from the bezel

12.6 Disconnect the air conditioning compressor electrical connector

12.8a Remove the rear mounting bolt...

manual heating and air conditioning, disconnect the control cables from the back of the heater/air conditioning control assembly.

4   Remove the mounting fasteners at each corner (see illustration), then remove the control assembly from the bezel.

5   Installation is the reverse of removal. If the heater/air conditioning control assembly is being replaced, calibration/diagnostic tests will be necessary. This will require a specialized scan tool; take the vehicle to a dealer service department or other qualified repair shop to have this service performed.

12   Air conditioning compressor - removal and installation

Warning: *The air conditioning system is under high pressure. DO NOT loosen any fittings or remove any components until after the system has been discharged. Air conditioning refrigerant must be properly discharged into an EPA-approved container at a dealer service department or an automotive air conditioning repair facility. Always wear eye protection when disconnecting air conditioning system fittings.*

Caution: *When replacing entire components, additional refrigerant oil must be added equal to the amount that is removed with the component being replaced. Read the label on the oil container to verify that it is compatible with the R-134a system before adding any of it to the system.*

Note: *The receiver-drier should always be replaced when the compressor is replaced (see Section 13).*

Removal

1   Have the system discharged and the refrigerant recovered by an air conditioning technician.

2   Disconnect the cable from the negative terminal of the battery (see Chapter 5).

3   Loosen the right-front wheel lug nuts, then raise the front of the vehicle and support

it securely on jackstands.

4   Remove the wheel and the inner-fender splash shields (see Chapter 11)

5   Remove the drivebelt (see Chapter 1).

6   Disconnect the wire harness connected to the air conditioning compressor (see illustration).

7   Remove the fasteners securing the refrigerant lines to the compressor and detach the refrigerant lines. Plug all open fittings to prevent entry of dirt and moisture.

8   Remove the compressor mounting fasteners (see illustrations) and lower the compressor from the vehicle.

9   If a new compressor is being installed, remove the drain plug and drain 1.7 ounces (50 ml) of oil into a graduated container (genuine Denso replacement compressors are filled with 3.4 ounces [100 ml] of oil). Also follow any directions included with the new compressor.

Installation

Caution: *On clutch type compressors, ensure the clutch coil wiring is not damaged during installation. Be careful not to damage the contact surface of the pulley.*

10   Installation is the reverse of removal. Install new O-rings onto the line fittings and lightly coat them with the correct refrigerant oil.

Note: *Only use O-rings that are designed specifically for A/C system applications.*

11   Have the system evacuated, recharged and leak tested by the shop that discharged it.

13   Air conditioning receiver-drier - removal and installation

Warning: *The air conditioning system is under high pressure. DO NOT loosen any fittings or remove any components until after the system has been discharged. Air conditioning refrigerant must be properly discharged into an EPA-*

12.8b ... and the two front mounting bolts, then lower the compressor

approved container at a dealer service department or an automotive air conditioning repair facility. Always wear eye protection when disconnecting air conditioning system fittings.

Caution: *When replacing entire components, additional refrigerant oil must be added equal to the amount that is removed with the component being replaced. Read the label on the oil container to verify that it is compatible with the R-134a system before adding any of it to the system.*

Note: *On 2014 late-build models and all later models, the receiver-drier is not separately serviceable from the condenser. If there is a problem with the receiver-drier the condenser must be replaced.*

Removal

1   Have the system discharged and the refrigerant recovered by an air conditioning technician.

2   Loosen the right-front wheel lug nuts. Set the parking brake, raise the front of the vehicle and support it securely on jackstands.

3   Remove the right front wheel.

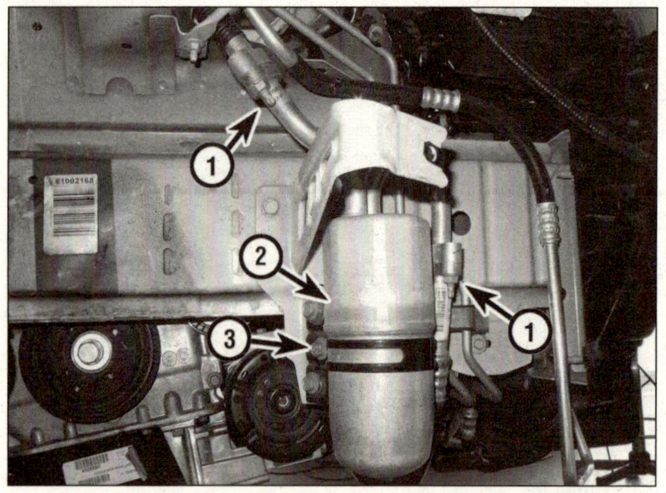

13.5 Receiver-drier details (early-build 2014 and earlier models only)

1   Refrigerant line fitting nuts
2   Receiver-drier
3   Receiver-drier clamp bolt

14.5 Transmission cooler line connections (models with a 6-speed transaxle)

14.6 Disconnect the refrigerant lines - later models shown, earlier models similar

4   Remove the inner fender splash shield retainers and pull out the splash shield far enough to gain access to the receiver-drier.
Note: *The front bumper cover (see Chapter 11) and windshield washer reservoir (see Section 6) may be removed for more access to the receiver-drier.*
5   Remove both line fittings from the receiver-drier (see illustration).
Note: *Plug all openings immediately to prevent contamination.*
6   Remove the mounting fastener retaining the receiver-drier to the mounting bracket.
7   Loosen the mounting strap and remove the receiver-drier.

Installation

8   Installation is the reverse of removal. Install new O-rings onto the line fittings and lightly coat them with the correct refrigerant oil.

Note: *Only use O-rings that are designed specifically for A/C system applications.*
9   If you are replacing the receiver-drier with a new unit, add 0.7-ounce (20 ml) of refrigerant oil to the replacement.
10   Have the system evacuated, recharged and leak tested by the shop that discharged it.

14   Air conditioning condenser - removal and installation

Warning: *The air conditioning system is under high pressure. DO NOT loosen any fittings or remove any components until after the system has been discharged. Air conditioning refrigerant must be properly discharged into an EPA-approved container at a dealer service department or an automotive air conditioning repair facility. Always wear eye protection when disconnecting air conditioning system fittings.*

Caution: *When replacing entire components, additional refrigerant oil must be added equal to the amount that is removed with the component being replaced. Read the label on the oil container to verify that it is compatible with the R-134a system before adding any of it to the system.*
Note: *If the condenser is being replaced because of damage (cracked or punctured), the receiver-drier should also be replaced (see Section 13) (early-build 2014 and earlier models only; on all other models the receiver-drier is built into the condenser).*

Removal

1   Have the system discharged and the refrigerant recovered by an air conditioning technician.
2   Disconnect the cable from the negative terminal of the battery (see Chapter 5).
3   Remove the bumper cover (see Chapter 11).
4   On models equipped with a 6-speed automatic transaxle (6F24), remove the bolt retaining the transmission cooler line block to the left of the radiator (see Section 7, illustration 7.6).
5   Also on models equipped with a 6-speed automatic transaxle (6F24), disconnect the transmission cooler lines from the condenser (see illustration).
Note: *Special Tool 8875A (or equivalent) will be required for this step).*
6   Remove the retaining bolts and disconnect the refrigerant lines (see illustration). Plug all open fittings to prevent entry of dirt and moisture.
7   Remove the condenser upper mounting brackets (see illustration).
8   Remove the condenser lower mounting bolts (see illustration).

14.7 Condenser upper mounting bracket bolts

14.8 Condenser lower mounting bolts

9   Carefully pull straight up to release the condenser from the lower clips, then remove the condenser from the vehicle.

Installation

10   If you are replacing the condenser with a new unit, add 0.3-ounce (10 ml) of refrigerant oil to the replacement.

11   Installation is the reverse of removal. Make certain to fully seat the condenser into the mounting clips and retainers. Install new O-rings onto the line fittings and lightly coat them with the proper refrigerant oil.

Note: *Only use O-rings that are designed specifically for A/C system applications.*

12   Have the system evacuated, recharged and leak tested by the shop that discharged it.

Notes

Chapter 4
Fuel and exhaust systems

Contents

Specifications

Fuel system

Fuel system pressure (all models).. 58 psi +/- 5 psi

Torque specifications   Ft-lbs (unless otherwise indicated)

Note: *One foot-pound (ft-lb) of torque is equivalent to 12 inch-pounds (in-lbs) of torque. Torque values below approximately 15 ft-lbs are expressed in inch-pounds, since most foot-pound torque wrenches are not accurate at these smaller values.*

Fuel rail bolts 20
Throttle body mounting bolts
     2007 models.. 79.5 in-lbs
     2008 through 2010 models .... 65 in-lbs
     2011 and later models... 80 in-lbs

1 General information and precautions

Fuel system warnings

Note: *Gasoline is extremely flammable and repairing fuel system components can be dangerous. Consider your automotive repair knowledge and experience before attempting repairs which may be better suited for a professional mechanic.*

a) *Don't smoke or allow open flames or bare light bulbs near the work area*

b) *Don't work in a garage with a gas-type appliance (water heater, clothes dryer)*

c) *Use fuel-resistant gloves. If any fuel spills on your skin, wash it off immediately with soap and water*

d) *Clean up spills immediately*

e) *Do not store fuel-soaked rags where they could ignite*

f) *Prior to disconnecting any fuel line, you must relieve the fuel pressure (see Section 3)*

g) *Wear safety glasses*

h) *Have a proper fire extinguisher on hand*

Fuel system

1   The fuel system consists of the fuel tank, electric fuel pump/fuel level sending unit (located in the fuel tank), fuel rail and fuel injectors. The fuel injection system is a multi-port system; multi-port fuel injection uses timed impulses to inject the fuel directly into the intake port of each cylinder. The Powertrain Control Module (PCM) controls the injectors. The PCM monitors various engine parameters and delivers the exact amount of fuel required into the intake ports.

2   Fuel is circulated from the fuel pump to the fuel rail through fuel lines running along the underside of the vehicle. Various sections of the fuel line are either rigid metal or nylon, or flexible fuel hose. The various sections of the fuel hose are connected either by quick-connect fittings or threaded metal fittings.

Exhaust system

3   The exhaust system consists of the exhaust manifold(s), catalytic converter(s), muffler(s), tailpipe and all connecting pipes, flanges and clamps. The catalytic converters are an emission control device added to the exhaust system to reduce pollutants.

2 Troubleshooting

Fuel pump

1   The fuel pump is located inside the fuel tank. Sit inside the vehicle with the windows closed, turn the ignition key to ON (not START) and listen for the sound of the fuel pump as it's briefly activated. You will only hear the sound for a second or two, but that sound tells you that the pump is working. Alternatively, have an assistant listen at the fuel filler cap.

2   If the pump does not come on, check all of the fuses in the underhood fuse block (see illustration).

Note: *There is no replaceable fuel pump relay; it is actually just a circuit incorporated into the Totally Integrated Power Module, which is part of the underhood fuse/relay block.*

3   If the fuses are okay, check the wiring back to the fuel pump. If the wiring is okay, the fuel pump module or Totally Integrated Power Module is probably defective. If the pump runs continuously with the ignition key in the ON position, the Totally Integrated Power Module or Powertrain Control Module (PCM) is probably defective. Have the circuit checked by a professional mechanic.

Fuel injection system

Note: *The following procedure is based on the assumption that the fuel pump is working and the fuel pressure is adequate (see Section 4).*

4   Check all electrical connectors that are related to the system. Check the ground wire connections for tightness.

5   Verify that the battery is fully charged (see Chapter 5).

6   Inspect the air filter element (see Chapter 1).

7   Check all fuses related to the fuel system (see Chapter 12).

8   Check the air induction system between the throttle body and the intake manifold for air leaks. Also inspect the condition of all vacuum hoses connected to the intake manifold and to the throttle body.

9   Remove the air intake duct from the throttle body and look for dirt, carbon, varnish, or other residue in the throttle body, particularly around the throttle plate. If it's dirty, clean it with carb cleaner, a toothbrush and a clean shop towel.

10   With the engine running, place an automotive stethoscope against each injector, one at a time, and listen for a clicking sound that indicates operation (see illustration).

Warning: *Stay clear of the drivebelt and any rotating or hot components.*

11   If you can hear the injectors operating, but the engine is misfiring, the electrical circuits are functioning correctly, but the injectors might be dirty or clogged. Try a commercial injector cleaning product (available at auto parts stores). If cleaning the injectors doesn't help, replace the injectors.

12   If an injector is not operating (it makes no sound), disconnect the injector electrical connector and measure the resistance across the injector terminals with an ohmmeter. Compare this measurement to the other injectors. If the resistance of the non-operational injector is quite different from the other injectors, replace it.

13   If the injector is not operating, but the resistance reading is within the range of resistance of the other injectors, the PCM or the circuit between the PCM and the injector might be faulty.

2.2 The underhood fuse block is located at the left side of the engine compartment

2.10 An automotive stethoscope is used to listen to the fuel injectors in operation

3.3 Pull off this cover for access to the fuel pump module

3.4 To relieve the pressure in the fuel system, disable the electric fuel pump by unplugging the electrical connector

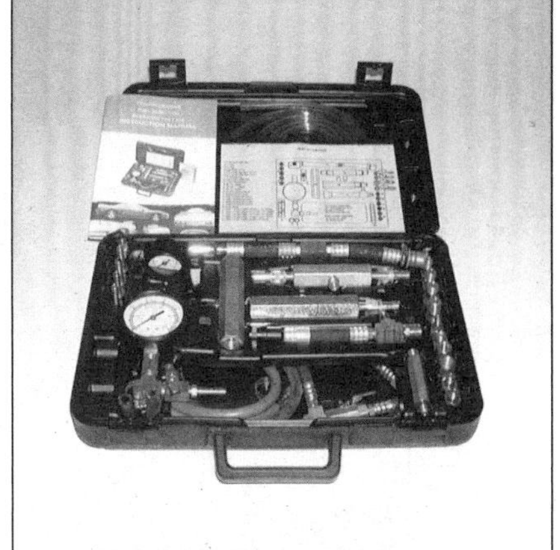

4.2 This typical fuel pressure testing kit contains all the necessary fittings and adapters, along with the fuel pressure gauge, to test most automotive fuel systems

3   Fuel pressure relief procedure

Warning: *Gasoline is extremely flammable. See* Fuel system warnings *in Section 1.*

1   Remove the fuel filler cap to relieve any pressure built up in the fuel tank.

2   Remove the lower rear seat cushion.

3   Remove the fuel pump module cover (see illustration).

4   Unplug the electrical connector from the fuel pump module (see illustration).

5   Start the engine; it should run momentarily then stall. Crank the engine several more times to ensure the fuel system has been completely relieved. Disconnect the cable from the negative terminal of the battery (see Chapter 5) before working on the fuel system.

6   It's a good idea to cover any fuel connection to be disassembled with rags to absorb the residual fuel that may leak out. Properly dispose of the rags.

7   After servicing the fuel system, diagnostic trouble codes may have been stored in the PCM's memory due to disconnecting the fuel pump circuit (see Chapter 6).

4   Fuel pressure - check

Warning: *Gasoline is extremely flammable. See* Fuel system warnings *in Section 1.*

Note: *The following procedure assumes that the fuel pump is receiving voltage and runs.*

1   Relieve the fuel system pressure (see Section 3).

2   In addition to a fuel pressure gauge capable of reading fuel pressure up to 70 psi, you'll need a hose and an adapter suitable for tee-ing into the fuel system at the quick-connect fitting between the fuel delivery hose and the fuel rail (see illustration).

3   Disconnect the quick-connect fitting at the connection between the fuel feed line and the fuel rail (if you're unfamiliar with quick-connect fittings, refer to Section 5).

4   Tee-in the fuel pressure gauge between the fuel delivery hose and the fuel rail (see illustration).

5   Start the engine and allow it to idle. Note the gauge reading as soon as the pressure stabilizes, and compare it with the pressure listed in this Chapter's Specifications.

6   If the fuel pressure is not within specifications, check the following:

If the pressure is lower than specified, check for a restriction in the fuel system (kinked fuel line, plugged fuel pump inlet strainer or clogged fuel filter). If no restrictions are found, replace the fuel pump module (see Section 8). If the fuel pressure is higher than specified, replace the fuel pump module (see Section 8).

7   Turn off the engine. Fuel pressure should not fall more than 8 psi over five minutes. If it does, the problem could be a leaky fuel injector, fuel line leak, or faulty fuel pump module.

8   Relieve the fuel system pressure, then disconnect the fuel pressure gauge. Reconnect the fuel line and wipe up any spilled gasoline.

5   Fuel lines and fittings - general information and disconnection

Warning: *Gasoline is extremely flammable. See* Fuel system warnings *in Section 1.*

1   Relieve the fuel pressure before servicing fuel lines or fittings (see Section 3), then disconnect the cable from the negative battery terminal (see Chapter 5) before proceeding.

2   The fuel supply line connects the fuel pump in the fuel tank to the fuel rail on the engine. The Evaporative Emission (EVAP) system lines connect the fuel tank to the EVAP canister and connect the canister to the

4.4 Fuel gauge connection details

1   *Fuel feed line*
2   *Tee fitting*
3   *Quick-connect fitting attached to fuel rail*

intake manifold.

3   Whenever you're working under the vehicle, be sure to inspect all fuel and evaporative emission lines for leaks, kinks, dents and other damage. Always replace a damaged fuel or EVAP line immediately.

4   If you find signs of dirt in the lines during disassembly, disconnect all lines and blow them out with compressed air. Inspect the fuel strainer on the fuel pump pick-up unit for damage and deterioration.

Steel tubing

5   It is critical that the fuel lines be replaced with lines of equivalent type and specification.

6   Some steel fuel lines have threaded fittings. When loosening these fittings, hold the stationary fitting with a wrench while turning the tube nut.

Disconnecting Fuel Line Fittings

Two-tab type fitting; depress both tabs with your fingers, then pull the fuel line and the fitting apart

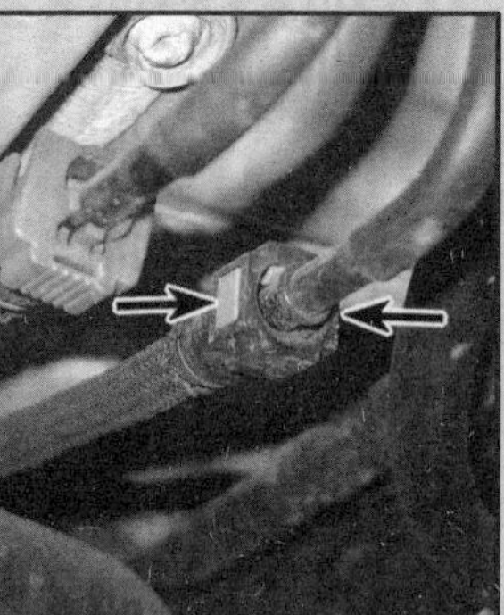

On this type of fitting, depress the two buttons on opposite sides of the fitting, then pull it off the fuel line

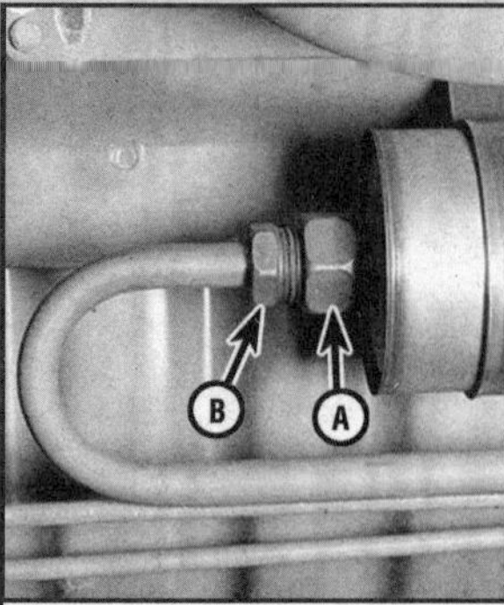

Threaded fuel line fitting; hold the stationary portion of the line or component (A) while loosening the tube nut (B) with a flare-nut wrench

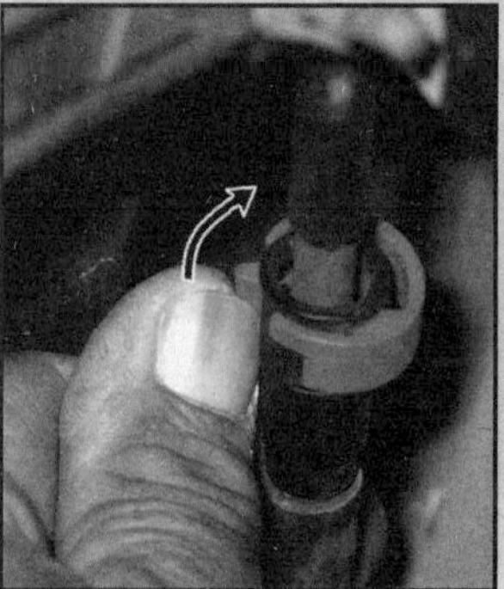

Plastic collar-type fitting; rotate the outer part of the fitting

Metal collar quick-connect fitting; pull the end of the retainer off the fuel line and disengage the other end from the female side of the fitting . . .

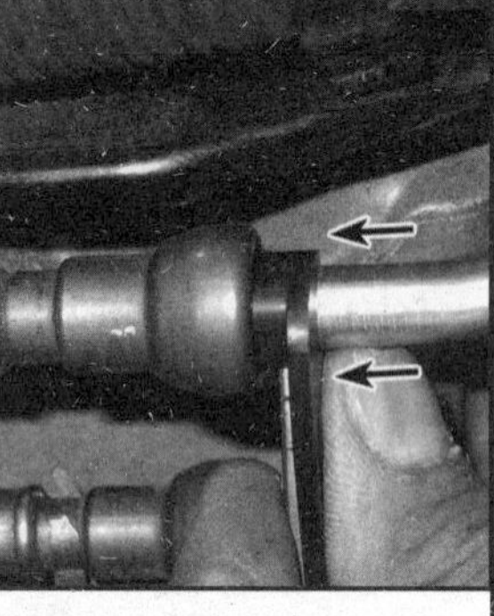

. . . insert a fuel line separator tool into the female side of the fitting, push it into the fitting and pull the fuel line off the pipe

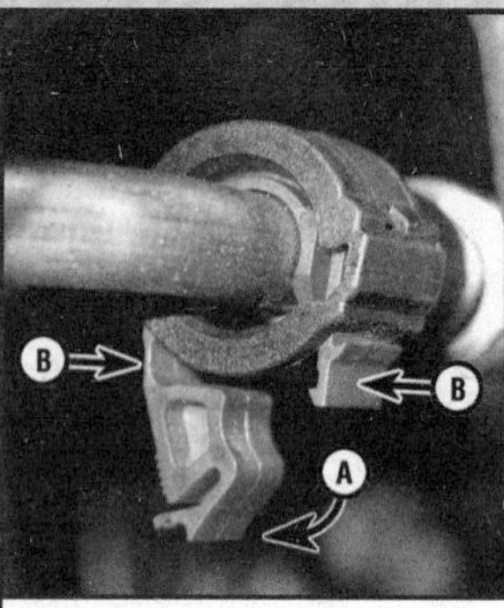

Some fittings are secured by lock tabs. Release the lock tab (A) and rotate it to the fully-opened position, squeeze the two smaller lock tabs (B) . . .

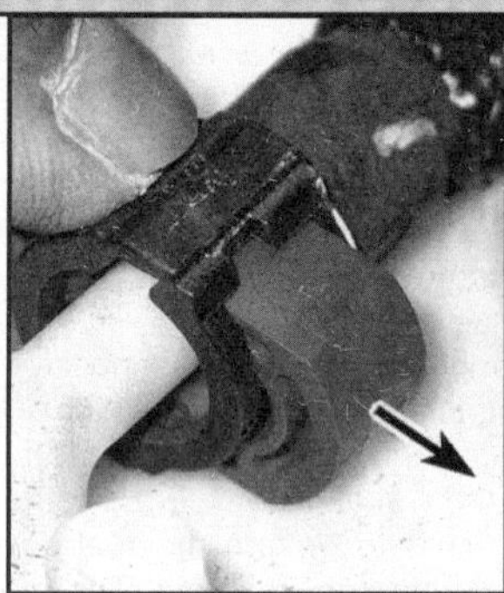

. . . then push the retainer out and pull the fuel line off the pipe

Spring-lock coupling; remove the safety cover, install a coupling release tool and close the tool around the coupling . . .

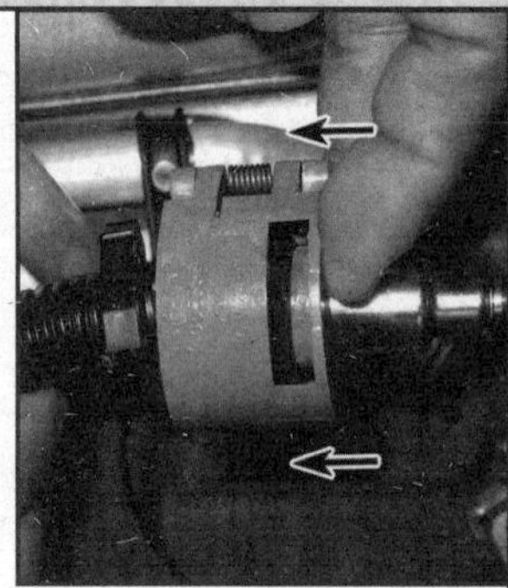

. . . push the tool into the fitting, then pull the two lines apart

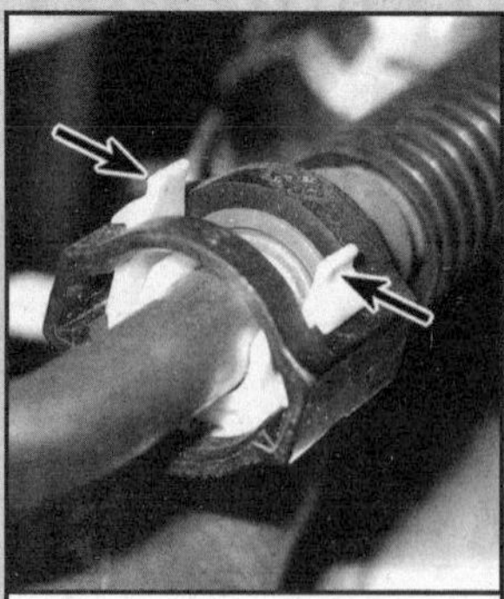

Hairpin clip type fitting: push the legs of the retainer clip together, then push the clip down all the way until it stops and pull the fuel line off the pipe

6.1 Inspect the exhaust system rubber hangers for damage. This is a typical exhaust hanger for the intermediate exhaust pipe and muffler.

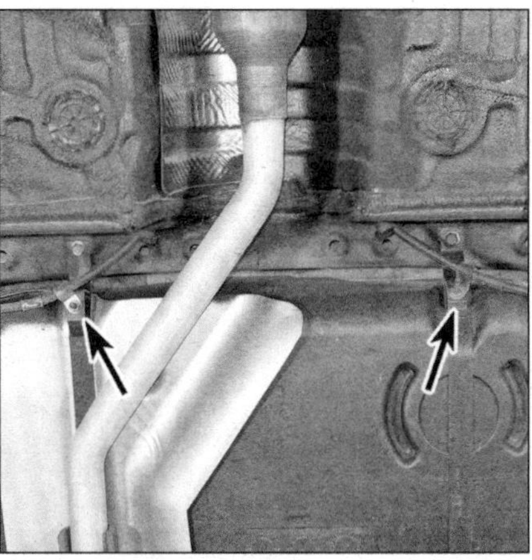

7.6 Parking brake cable mounting strap nut locations

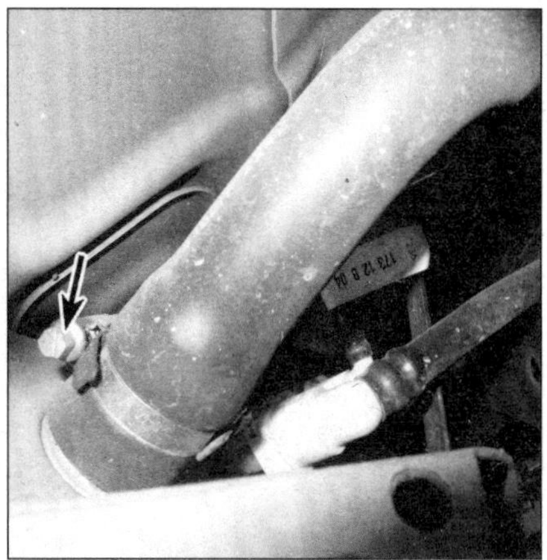

7.12 Loosen the clamp and detach the filler hose from the fuel tank

Plastic tubing

Warning: *When removing or installing plastic fuel line tubing, be careful not to bend or twist it too much, which can damage it. Also, plastic fuel tubing is NOT heat resistant, so keep it away from excessive heat.*

7   When replacing fuel system plastic tubing, use only original equipment replacement plastic tubing.

Flexible hoses

8   When replacing fuel system flexible hoses, use only original equipment replacements.

9   Don't route fuel hoses (or metal lines) within four inches of the exhaust system or within ten inches of the catalytic converter. Make sure that no rubber hoses are installed directly against the vehicle, particularly in places where there is any vibration. If allowed to touch some vibrating part of the vehicle, a hose can easily become chafed and it might start leaking. A good rule of thumb is to maintain a minimum of 1/4-inch clearance around a hose (or metal line) to prevent contact with the vehicle underbody.

6   Exhaust system servicing - general information

Warning: *Allow exhaust system components to cool before inspection or repair. Also, when working under the vehicle, make sure it is securely supported on jackstands.*

1   The exhaust system consists of the exhaust manifolds, catalytic converter, muffler, tailpipe and all connecting pipes, flanges and clamps. The exhaust system is isolated from the vehicle body and from chassis components by a series of rubber hangers. Periodically inspect these hangers for cracks or other signs of deterioration, replacing them as necessary (see illustration).

2   Conduct regular inspections of the exhaust system to keep it safe and quiet. Look for any damaged or bent parts, open seams, holes, loose connections, excessive corrosion or other defects which could allow exhaust fumes to enter the vehicle. Do not repair deteriorated exhaust system components; replace them with new parts.

3   If the exhaust system components are extremely corroded, or rusted together, a cutting torch is the most convenient tool for removal. Consult a properly-equipped repair shop. If a cutting torch is not available, you can use a hacksaw, or if you have compressed air, there are special pneumatic cutting chisels that can also be used. Wear safety goggles to protect your eyes from metal chips and wear work gloves to protect your hands.

4   Here are some simple guidelines to follow when repairing the exhaust system:

a) *Work from the back to the front when removing exhaust system components.*

b) *Apply penetrating oil to the exhaust system component fasteners to make them easier to remove.*

c) *Use new gaskets, hangers and clamps.*

d) *Apply anti-seize compound to the threads of all exhaust system fasteners during reassembly.*

e) *Be sure to allow sufficient clearance between newly installed parts and all points on the underbody to avoid overheating the floor pan and possibly damaging the interior carpet and insulation. Pay particularly close attention to the catalytic converter and heat shield.*

7   Fuel tank - removal and installation

Warning: *Gasoline is extremely flammable. See* Fuel system warnings *in Section 1.*

Note: *The following procedure is much easier to perform if the fuel tank is empty. If the fuel tank isn't empty or nearly empty, you can siphon fuel from the tank with a siphon kit, available at most auto parts stores.*

Warning: *NEVER start the siphoning action with your mouth!*

1   Relieve the fuel system pressure (see Section 3).

2   Disconnect the cable from the negative terminal of the battery (see Chapter 5).

3   Raise the rear of the vehicle and support it securely on jackstands.

4   Remove the fuel pump module and, on AWD models, the auxiliary module (see Section 8).

5   Remove the fuel tank skid plate(s), if equipped.

6   Detach the parking brake cable mounting straps from the fuel tank strap studs (see illustration).

7   Remove the exhaust pipe and muffler from below the fuel tank (see Section 6).

AWD models

8   Remove the rear differential support bracket fasteners and brackets.

9   Remove the driveshaft and the rear differential electronically controlled clutch (see Chapter 8).

10   Remove the rear differential (see Chapter 8).

All models

11   Remove the left and right stay brackets between the rear crossmember and the chassis, if equipped. Also remove the splash shields from each side at the front of the tank, if equipped.

12   Loosen the hose clamp and disconnect the fuel filler hose from the fuel tank (see illustration).

13   Disconnect the fuel line and EVAP line quick-connect fittings, both of which are

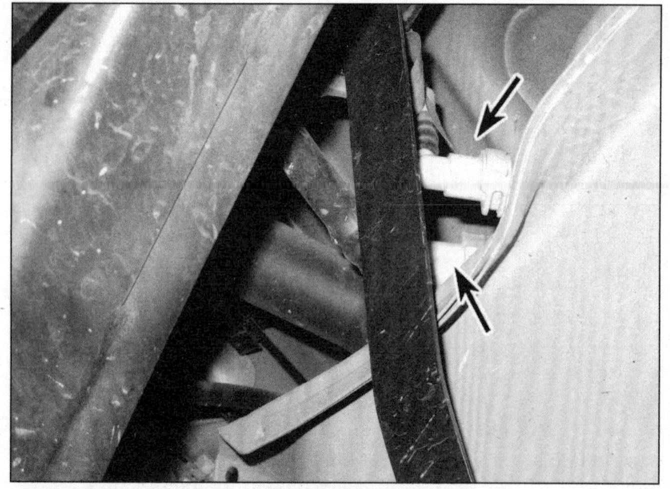

7.13a Disconnect the fuel delivery quick disconnect line and EVAP line

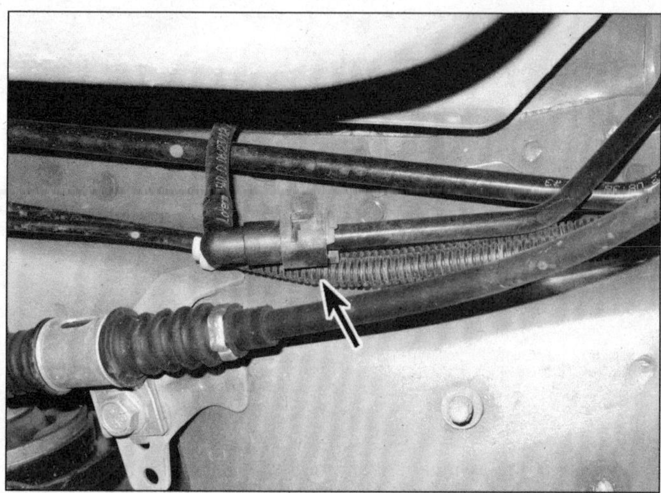

7.13b Disconnect the quick connect fitting from the fuel supply line

7.15 Fuel tank strap bolts

8.3 Fuel pump module electrical connector and fuel line quick-connect fitting

located at the front of the fuel tank (see illustrations). If you're unfamiliar with fuel line quick-connect fittings, refer to Section 5.

14   Support the fuel tank with a transmission jack or with a floor jack. If you're using a floor jack, put a piece of plywood between the jack head and the tank to protect the tank.

15   Remove the fuel tank support strap bolts and carefully lower the fuel tank from the vehicle, making sure no hoses or wiring harnesses are still attached (see illustration).

16   Installation is the reverse of removal. Tighten the fuel tank strap bolts securely.

17   Start the engine and check for leaks at any fuel line connectors that were disconnected.

8   Fuel pump module - removal and installation

Warning: *Gasoline is extremely flammable. See* Fuel system warnings *in Section 1.*

Note: *All wheel drive (AWD) models have a saddle-type fuel tank configuration with a primary and secondary fuel pump module. Front wheel drive (FWD) models have only one primary module. Each module has a sending unit. The primary fuel pump module has an electric fuel pump, venturi jet pump (AWD models only), fuel pump reservoir, strainer, fuel pressure regulator, fuel sending unit and fuel filter. The secondary fuel pump module (AWD only) contains the fuel pick-up line connection and fuel level sending unit. The only serviceable component is the fuel level sending unit on the primary fuel pump module. If there is a problem with any of the other components the module must be replaced.*

1   Relieve the fuel system pressure (see Section 3).

2   Disconnect the cable from the negative terminal of the battery (see Chapter 5).

3   Disconnect the electrical connector and the fuel delivery line quick-connect fitting from the primary fuel pump module (see Section 5) (see illustration).

4   Before removing the primary fuel pump module, cap the module fuel line fitting then make alignment marks on the assembly and the fuel tank (if marks don't already exist),

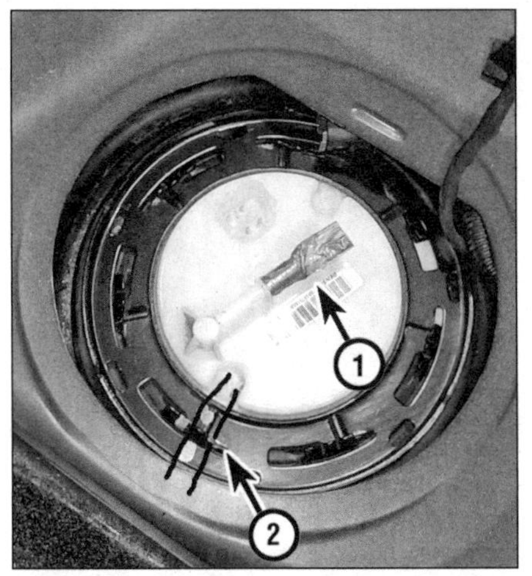

8.4 Cap the fuel line fitting (1) and make marks on the fuel pump module and fuel tank that will help you install the assembly in the correct orientation (2)

8.5 Loosen the fuel pump module lock ring using a brass drift (only) - the ring must be turned counterclockwise

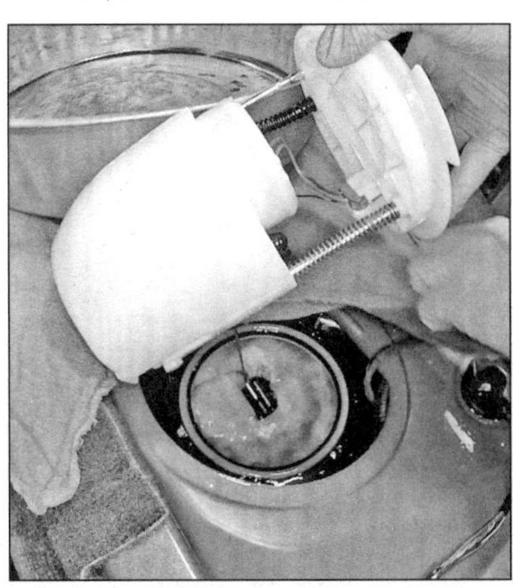

8.6 The fuel pump module is a tight fit and must be removed carefully to avoid damaging the sending unit float arm.

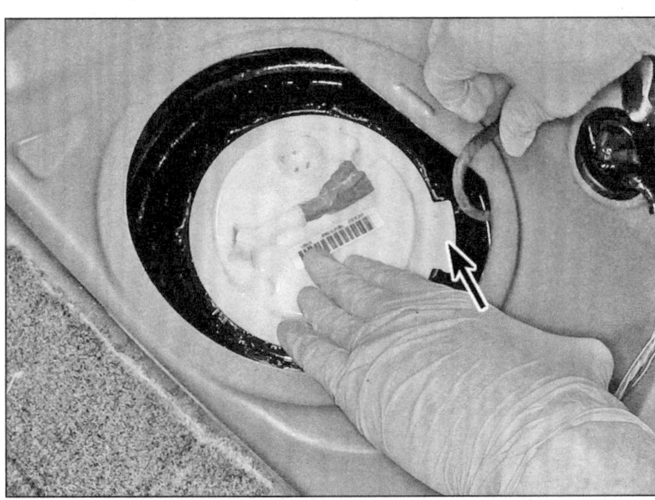

8.10 The module should be in the proper position in the tank with the locating lug fully seated

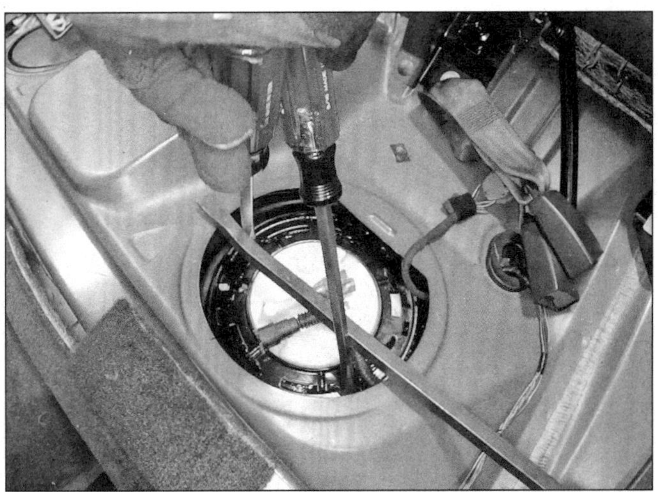

8.11 If special tool #9340 (or equivalent) is not available, use two screwdrivers and a prybar to lock the ring into place

to ensure the assembly will be correctly realigned when it's installed again (see illustration).

5   Using special service tool #9340 or equivalent, loosen the lock ring that secures the fuel pump module. If the service tool is not available, use a brass drift to carefully tap the locking ring counterclockwise until it is free (see illustration).

Warning: *Don't use a steel punch - it could produce sparks.*

6   Carefully lift the fuel pump/fuel pressure regulator/fuel level sending unit assembly from the fuel tank (see illustration). Angle the module so that you don't bend the float arm of the fuel level sending unit or damage the fuel pump inlet strainer.

Caution: *When you're removing the primary*

fuel pump module, the reservoir does not empty out when the tank is drained. The fuel in the reservoir will spill out when the module is removed. Have a small container and lots of rags ready to catch any fuel once the module is pulled up from the tank.

Note: *If you're removing the primary or secondary fuel pump module on an AWD models, raise the fuel pump module and disconnect the internal fuel line at the bottom of the module.*

7   While the pump is removed, inspect the pump inlet strainer. Make sure that it's not clogged or damaged. If the inlet strainer is dirty, try washing it in clean solvent.

8   Clean groove out for the rubber O-ring. Check the O-ring for cuts or damage and replace it as necessary, then install the O-ring into the groove on the tank.

9   On AWD models, connect the internal fuel line to the bottom of the module.

10   Carefully install the module into the tank, making sure the module is in the proper position on the tank with the locating lug seated (see illustration).

11   Installation is the reverse of removal. Line up the marks, and tighten the fuel pump module lock ring securely (see illustration).

9   Fuel level sending unit - replacement

1   Gasoline is extremely flammable. See *Fuel system warnings* in Section 1.

2   Remove the fuel pump module (see Section 8).

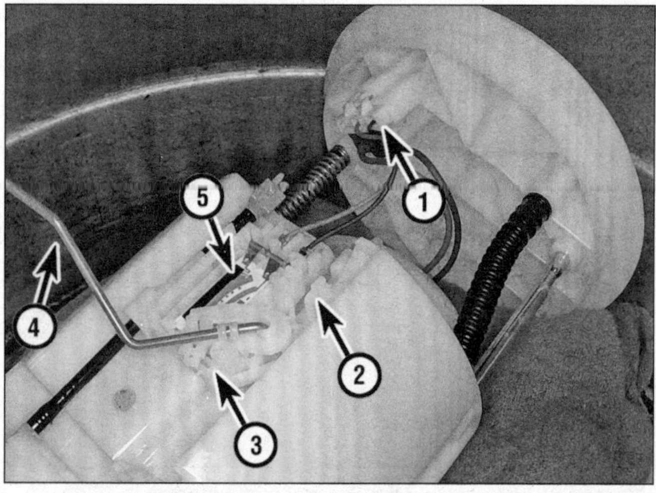

9.3a Fuel level sending unit details

1   *Fuel level sending unit electrical connector*
2   *Fuel level sending unit snap tab*
3   *Fuel level sending unit*
4   *Fuel level sending unit arm*
5   *Resistor card and terminals*

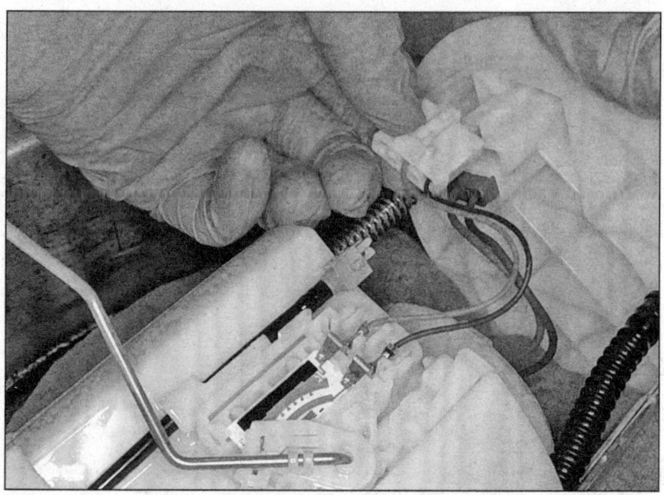

9.3b Depress the tab and disconnect the electrical connector from the underside of the fuel pump module

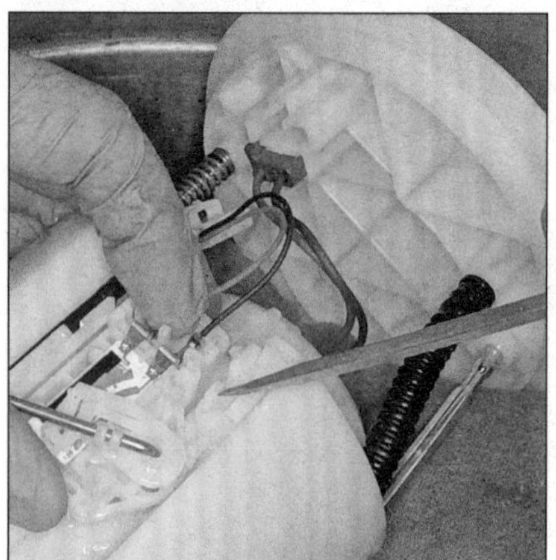

9.4 Release the snap tab and slide the sending unit off the fuel pump module

10.1a Rotate the fresh air inlet duct retainers…

10.1b … then lift the duct up and pull it out from the housing

10.2 Disconnect the electrical connector from the IAT sensor

3   Disconnect the fuel level sending unit electrical connector (see illustrations).
Caution: *Do not touch the terminals or the sending unit resistor card. Do not pull the sending unit by the wires or float arm.*
4   Press the fuel level sending unit snap tab to the left while gently pushing up on the bottom of the sending unit to remove it (see illustration).
5   Using a narrow electrical connector terminal tool, dislodge the sending unit terminals from the connector body, then install the terminals of the new sending unit into the correct positions in the connector.
6   The remainder of installation is the reverse of removal.

10   Air filter housing - removal and installation

1   Unlock the retainers for the fresh air inlet duct then remove the fresh air inlet duct from air cleaner housing (see illustrations).

Air intake duct

2   Disconnect the electrical connector from the Intake Air Temperature sensor (see illustration).
3   Loosen the clamp and detach the air intake hose from the air filter housing.
4   Loosen the clamp retaining the duct to

10.4 Loosen the clamp at the throttle body (1) and disconnect the harness retainer (2) from the duct

10.8 Remove the support bracket fasteners and bracket

10.10 Pull up to disengage the pins from the grommets

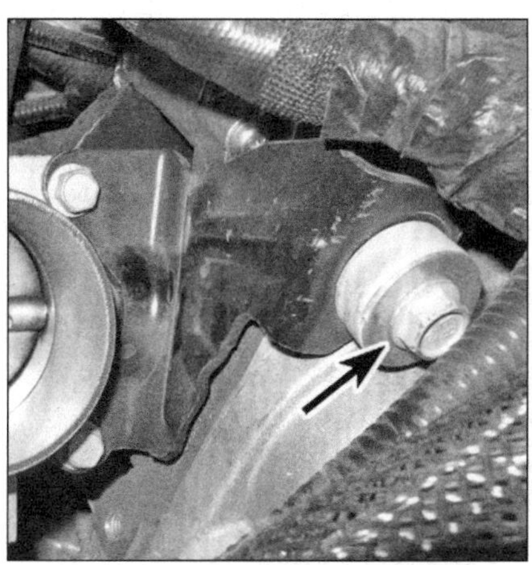

11.4 Throttle body support bracket mounting bolt location

11.6 Throttle body gasket location

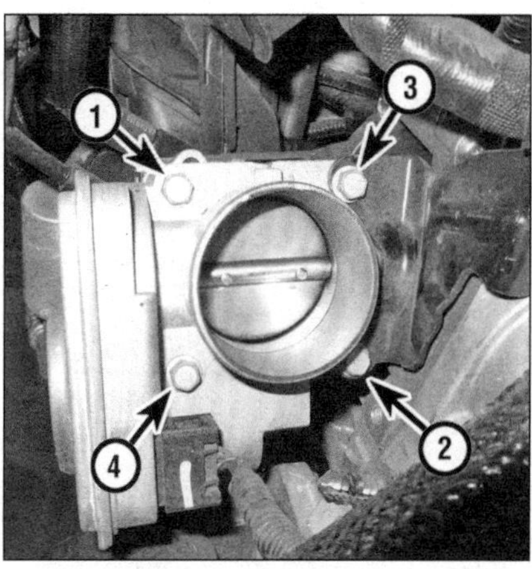

11.8 Throttle body mounting bolt tightening sequence

the throttle body (see illustration), then disconnect the harness plastic retainer and remove the duct.

5   Installation is the reverse of removal.

Air filter housing

6   Disconnect the cable from the negative terminal of the battery (see Chapter 5).

7   Remove the PCM from the top of the filter housing (see Chapter 6).

Note: *If you are just removing the air filter housing for access to other components, the PCM can remain attached to the filter housing cover. Separate the cover from the housing as you would do when replacing the air filter element (see Chapter 1).*

8   Remove the filter housing support bracket fasteners and bracket (see illustration).

9   Disconnect the by-pass hose from the air filter housing.

10   Pull the housing upwards to disengage the pins from the grommets (see illustration).

11   Inspect the rubber mounting grommets on the underside of the air filter housing. If the grommets are cracked, dried out, torn or otherwise damaged, replace them.

12   Installation is the reverse of removal.

11   Throttle body - removal and installation

Warning: *Wait until the engine is completely cool before beginning this procedure.*

1   Disconnect the cable from the negative terminal of the battery (see Chapter 5). Remove the engine cover.

2   Detach the air intake duct or resonator, as applicable, from the throttle body.

3   Disconnect the throttle body electrical connector.

4   Remove the throttle body support bracket mounting bolt (see illustration).

5   Remove the throttle body mounting fasteners in reverse order of the tightening sequence (see illustration 11.8) and detach the throttle body from the intake manifold.

6   Remove the throttle body gasket (see illustration) and inspect it for cracks, tears and deterioration. If it isn't in perfect condition, replace it.

7   Make sure that the gasket mating surfaces of the throttle body and the intake manifold are clean.

8   Installation is the reverse of removal. Tighten the throttle body bolts in sequence (see illustration) to the torque listed in this Chapter's Specifications.

Caution: *Do not overtighten the bolts - it can cause damage to the throttle body, the gaskets, the bolts and/or the intake manifold.*

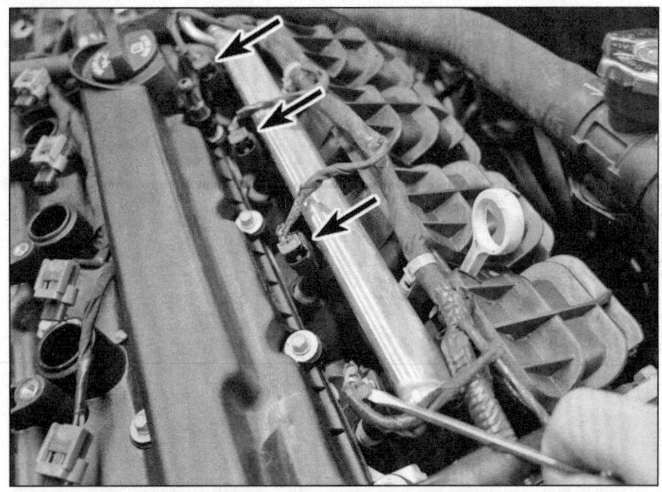

12.5 Slide the connector lock up and disconnect the electrical connector from the fuel injector

12.6 Detach the injector wiring harness mounting clips from the studs

12.7 Fuel rail mounting bolts

12.8a Carefully pull up on the fuel rail and disengage the injectors from the intake manifold

12 Fuel rail and injectors - removal and installation

Warning: *Gasoline is extremely flammable. See* Fuel system warnings *in Section 1.*

Warning: *Wait until the engine is completely cool before beginning this procedure.*

1   Remove the engine cover.

2   Relieve the fuel system pressure (see Section 3).

3   Disconnect the cable from the negative terminal of the battery (see Chapter 5).

4   Disconnect the fuel delivery line quick-connect fitting from the fuel rail (if you're unfamiliar with quick-connect fittings, see Section 5).

5   Disconnect the fuel injector electrical connectors (see illustration). Detach the injector wiring harness clips from the fuel rail (if equipped) and set the harness aside.

6   Remove the harness retainers from the fuel rail bolt studs (see illustration).

7   Remove the fuel rail mounting bolts (see illustration).

8   Carefully pull up on the fuel rail to disengage the injectors from their respective bores in the intake manifold, then remove the fuel rail and injectors as a single assembly (see illustrations). The injectors might initially stick in their bores, but they'll pull free when sufficient force is applied.

9   Remove the O-rings from each injector (see illustration) and discard them. Install new O-rings and coat them with some clean engine oil to facilitate installation of the injectors.

10   Make sure that the injector is square to the bore of the mounting pipe and push it down into the mounting pipe until it's fully seated (see illustration).

11   Installation is the reverse of removal. Tighten the fuel rail retaining bolts to the torque listed in this Chapter's Specifications.

12   Start the engine and check for leaks at the quick-connect fitting that connects the fuel supply hose to the fuel rail. Also look for leaks at the upper end of each injector, where it's installed into the fuel rail.

12.8b Using a screwdriver or pliers, remove the injector retaining clip . . .

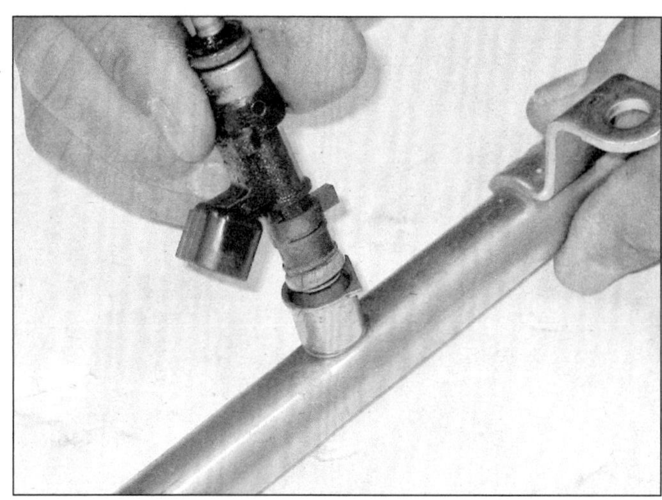

12.8c . . . and withdraw the injector from the fuel rail

12.9 Carefully remove the O-rings from the injectors

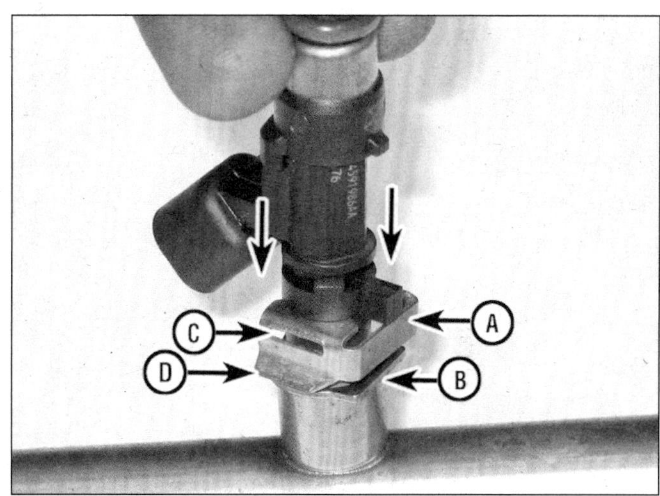

12.10 Fuel injector installation details: align the flat on the retainer (A) with the flat on the flange (B), and engage the slots in the retainer (C) with the semi-circular flanges (D) when the injector is pushed into fuel rail pipe - (typical injector shown)

Notes

Chapter 5
Engine electrical systems

Contents

Specifications

Charging system

Charging voltage	13.5 to 14.5 volts

Torque specifications   Ft-lbs

Note: *One foot-pound (ft-lb) of torque is equivalent to 12 inch-pounds (in-lbs) of torque. Torque values below approximately 15 ft-lbs are expressed in inch-pounds, because most foot-pound torque wrenches are not accurate at these smaller values.*

	Ft-lbs
Alternator mounting bolts	40
Drivebelt idler pulley bolt	35
Starter mounting bolts	40

1   General information and precautions

General information

Ignition system

1   The electronic ignition system consists of the Crankshaft Position (CKP) sensor, the Camshaft Position (CMP) sensor, the Knock Sensor (KS), the Powertrain Control Module (PCM), the ignition switch, the battery, the individual ignition coils, and the spark plugs. For more information on the CKP, CMP and KS sensors, as well as the PCM, refer to Chapter 6.

Charging system

2   The charging system includes the alternator, the Powertrain Control Module (PCM), which incorporates the Electronic Voltage Regulator (EVR), the Body Control Module (BCM), a charge indicator light on the dash, the battery, a fuse or fusible link and the wiring connecting all of these components. The charging system supplies electrical power for the ignition system, the lights, the radio, etc. The alternator is driven by the drivebelt.

Starting system

3   The starting system consists of the battery, the ignition switch, the starter relay, the Powertrain Control Module (PCM), the Body Control Module (BCM), the clutch start switch (manual transaxle models), the Transmission Range (TR) switch, the starter motor and solenoid assembly, and the wiring connecting all of the components.

Precautions

4   Always observe the following precautions when working on the electrical system:

a) *Be extremely careful when servicing engine electrical components. They are easily damaged if checked, connected or handled improperly.*
b) *Never leave the ignition switched on for long periods of time when the engine is not running.*
c) *Never disconnect the battery cables while the engine is running.*
d) *Maintain correct polarity when connecting battery cables from another vehicle during jump starting - see* Booster battery (jump) starting *at the front of this manual.*
e) *Always disconnect the cable from the negative battery terminal before working on the electrical system, but read the battery disconnection procedure first (see Section 3).*

5   It's also a good idea to review the safety-related information regarding the engine electrical systems in *Safety first!* at the front of this manual before beginning any operation included in this Chapter.

2   Troubleshooting

Ignition system

1   If a malfunction occurs in the ignition system, do not immediately assume that any particular part is causing the problem. First, check the following items:

a) *Make sure that the cable clamps at the battery terminals are clean and tight.*
b) *Test the condition of the battery (see Steps 14 through 18). If it doesn't pass all the tests, replace it.*
c) *Check the ignition coil or coil pack connections.*
d) *Check any relevant fuses in the engine compartment fuse and relay box (see Chapter 12). If they're burned, determine the cause and repair the circuit.*

Check

Warning: *Because of the high voltage generated by the ignition system, use extreme care when performing a procedure involving ignition components.*

Note: *The ignition system components on these vehicles are difficult to diagnose. In the event of ignition system failure that you can't diagnose, have the vehicle tested at a dealer service department or other qualified auto repair facility.*

Note: *You'll need a spark tester for the following test. Spark testers are available at most auto supply stores.*

2   If the engine turns over but won't start, verify that there is sufficient ignition voltage to fire the spark plugs as follows.
3   On models with a coil-over-plug type ignition system, remove a coil and install the tester between the boot at the lower end of the coil and the spark plug (see illustration).
4   Crank the engine and note whether or not the tester flashes.
Caution: *Do NOT crank the engine or allow it to run for more than five seconds; running the engine for more than five seconds may set a Diagnostic Trouble Code (DTC) for a cylinder misfire.*
5   If the tester flashes during cranking, the coil is delivering sufficient voltage to the spark plug to fire it. Repeat this test for each cylinder to verify that the other coils are OK.
6   If the tester doesn't flash, remove a coil from another cylinder and swap it for the one being tested. If the tester now flashes, you know that the original coil is bad. If the tester still doesn't flash, the PCM or wiring harness is probably defective. Have the PCM checked out by a dealer service department or other qualified repair shop (testing the PCM is beyond the scope of the do-it-yourselfer because it requires expensive special tools).
7   If the tester flashes during cranking but a misfire code (related to the cylinder being tested) has been stored, the spark plug could be fouled or defective.

Charging system

8   If a malfunction occurs in the charging system, do not automatically assume the alternator is causing the problem. First check the following items:

a) *Check the drivebelt tension and condition, as described in Chapter 1. Replace it if it's worn or deteriorated.*
b) *Make sure the alternator mounting bolts are tight.*
c) *Inspect the alternator wiring harness and the connectors at the alternator and voltage regulator. They must be in good condition, tight and have no corrosion.*
d) *Check the fusible link (if equipped) or main fuse in the underhood fuse/relay box. If it is burned, determine the cause, repair the circuit and replace the link or fuse (the vehicle will not start and/or the accessories will not work if the fusible link or main fuse is blown).*
e) *Start the engine and check the alternator for abnormal noises (a shrieking or squealing sound indicates a bad bearing).*
f) *Check the battery. Make sure it's fully charged and in good condition (one bad cell in a battery can cause overcharging by the alternator).*
g) *Disconnect the battery cables (negative first, then positive). Inspect the battery posts and the cable clamps for corrosion. Clean them thoroughly if necessary (see Chapter 1). Reconnect the cables (positive first, negative last).*

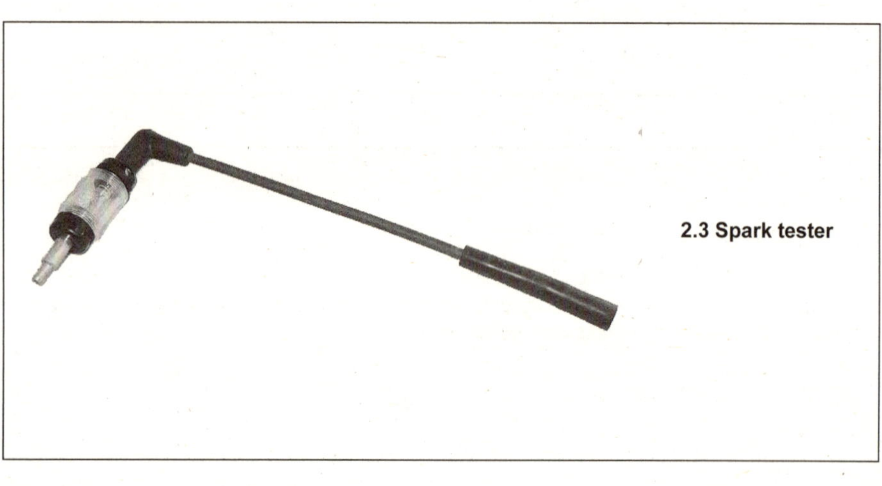

2.3 Spark tester

2.15 To test the open circuit voltage of the battery, connect the black probe of the voltmeter to the negative terminal and the red probe to the positive terminal of the battery; a fully charged battery should be at least 12.6 volts

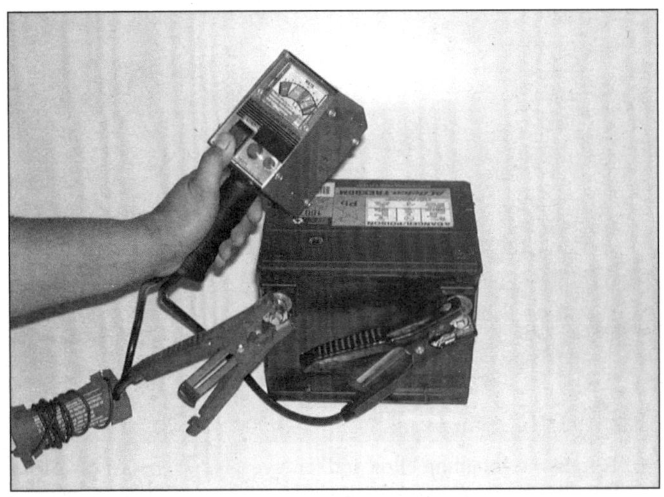

2.17 Connect a battery load tester to the battery and check the battery condition under load following the tool manufacturer's instructions

Alternator - check

9   Use a voltmeter to check the battery voltage with the engine off. It should be at least 12.6 volts (see illustration 2.15).

10   Start the engine and check the battery voltage again. It should now be approximately 13.5 to 15 volts.

11   If the voltage reading is more or less than the specified charging voltage, the alternator might be defective, the Electronic Voltage Regulator (EVR) within the Powertrain Control Module (PCM) might be defective, or there might be a problem in the circuitry between the alternator, PCM or battery. Check for the presence of trouble codes related to the system (see Chapter 6). If no codes are found, remove the alternator and have it bench tested (most auto parts stores will do this for you); if it checks out ok, inspect all connectors and wiring in the circuit. If no problems are found, have the PCM checked by a dealer service department or other qualified repair shop.

12   The charging system (battery) light on the instrument cluster lights up when the ignition key is turned to On, but it should go out when the engine starts.

13   If the charging system light stays on after the engine has been started, there is a problem with the charging system.

Battery - check

14   Check the battery state of charge. Visually inspect the indicator eye on the top of the battery (if equipped with one); if the indicator eye is black in color, charge the battery as described in Chapter 1. Next perform an open circuit voltage test using a digital voltmeter.

Note: *The battery's surface charge must be removed before accurate voltage measurements can be made. Turn on the high beams for ten seconds, then turn them off and let the vehicle stand for two minutes.*

15   With the engine and all accessories Off, touch the negative probe of the voltmeter to the negative terminal of the battery and the positive probe to the positive terminal of battery (see illustration). The battery voltage should be 12.6 volts or slightly above. If the battery is less than the specified voltage, charge the battery before proceeding to the next test. Do not proceed with the battery load test unless the battery charge is correct.

16   Disconnect the negative battery cable, then the positive cable from the battery.

17   Perform a battery load test. An accurate check of the battery condition can only be performed with a load tester (see illustration). This test evaluates the ability of the battery to operate the starter and other accessories during periods of high current draw. Connect the load tester to the battery terminals. Load test the battery according to the tool manufacturer's instructions. This tool increases the load demand (current draw) on the battery.

18   Maintain the load on the battery for 15 seconds and observe that the battery voltage does not drop below 9.6 volts. If the battery condition is weak or defective, the tool will indicate this condition immediately.

Note: *Cold temperatures will cause the minimum voltage reading to drop slightly. Follow the chart given in the manufacturer's instructions to compensate for cold climates. Minimum load voltage for freezing temperatures (32 degrees F) should be approximately 9.1 volts.*

Starting system

The starter rotates, but the engine doesn't

19   Remove the starter (see Section 8). Check the overrunning clutch and bench test the starter to make sure the drive mechanism extends fully for proper engagement with the flywheel ring gear. If it doesn't, replace the starter.

20   Check the flywheel ring gear for missing teeth and other damage. With the ignition turned off, rotate the flywheel so you can check the entire ring gear.

The starter is noisy

21   If the solenoid is making a chattering noise, first check the battery (see Steps 14 through 18). If the battery is okay, check the cables and connections.

22   If you hear a grinding, crashing metallic sound when you turn the key to Start, check for loose starter mounting bolts. If they're tight, remove the starter and inspect the teeth on the starter pinion gear and flywheel ring gear. Look for missing or damaged teeth.

23   If the starter sounds fine when you first turn the key to Start, but then stops rotating the engine and emits a zinging sound, the problem is probably a defective starter drive that's not staying engaged with the ring gear. Replace the starter.

The starter rotates slowly

24   Check the battery (see Steps 14 through 18).

25   If the battery is okay, verify all connections (at the battery, the starter solenoid and motor) are clean, corrosion-free and tight. Make sure the cables aren't frayed or damaged.

26   Check that the starter mounting bolts are tight so it grounds properly. Also check the pinion gear and flywheel ring gear for evidence of a mechanical bind (galling, deformed gear teeth or other damage).

The starter does not rotate at all

27   Check the battery (see Steps 14 through 18).

28   If the battery is okay, verify all connections (at the battery, the starter solenoid and motor) are clean, corrosion-free and tight. Make sure the cables aren't frayed or damaged.

4.2 Rotate the retaining clips and remove the duct from between the air filter housing and the fan shroud

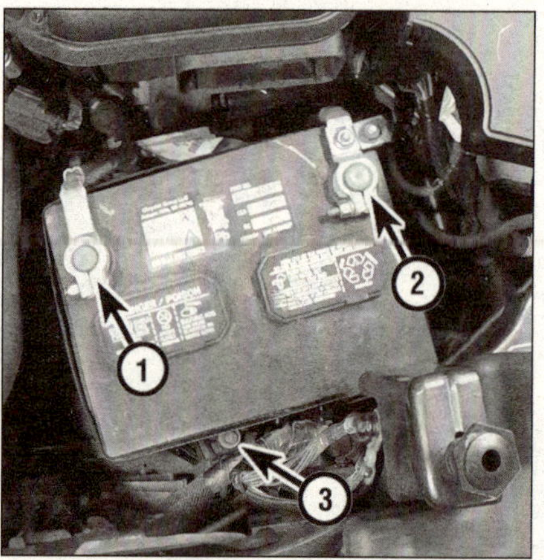

4.3 Battery details:

1   *Negative battery cable*
2   *Positive battery cable*
3   *Hold-down clamp*

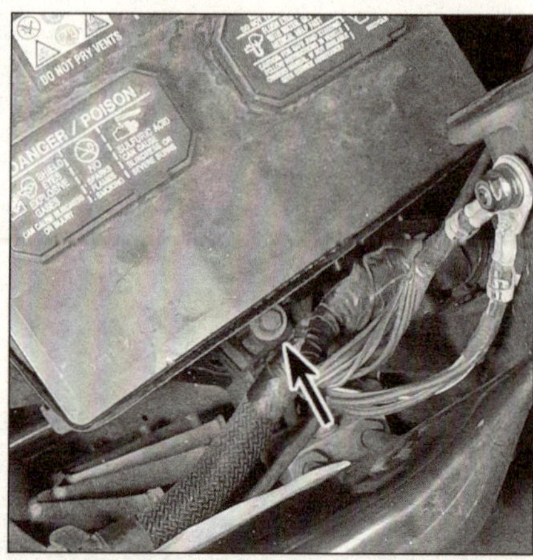

4.4a Remove the battery hold-down clamp bolt from the battery base...

29   Check all of the fuses in the underhood fuse/relay box.
30   Check that the starter mounting bolts are tight so it grounds properly.
31   Check for voltage at the starter solenoid "S" terminal when the ignition key is turned to the start position. If voltage is present, replace the starter/solenoid assembly. If no voltage is present, the problem could be the starter relay, the Transmission Range (TR) switch (see Chapter 6), or with an electrical connector somewhere in the circuit (see the wiring diagrams - Chapter). Also, on many modern vehicles, the Powertrain Control Module (PCM) and the Body Control Module (BCM) control the voltage signal to the starter solenoid; on such vehicles a special scan tool is required for diagnosis.

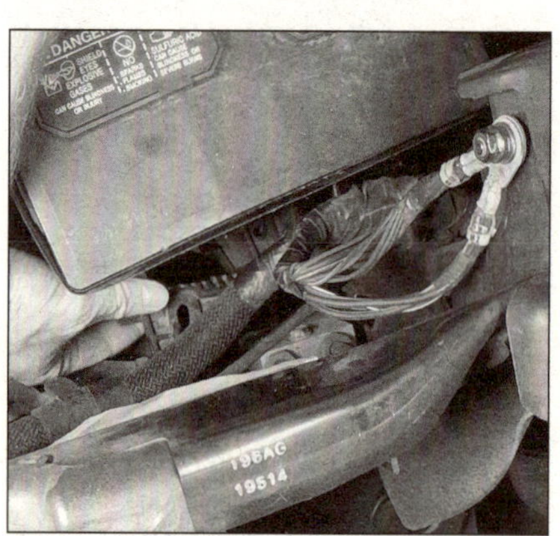

4.4b ... then slide the retaining clamp out

3   Battery - disconnection

Warning: *Always disconnect the cable from the negative battery terminal FIRST and hook it up LAST or the battery may be shorted by the tool being used to loosen the cable clamps.*
Warning: *Hydrogen gas is produced by the battery, so keep open flames and lighted cigarettes away from it at all times. Always wear eye protection when working around the battery. Rinse off spilled electrolyte immediately with large amounts of water.*

1   Some systems on the vehicle require battery power to be available at all times, either to maintain continuous operation (alarm system, power door locks, etc.), or to maintain control unit memory (radio station presets, Powertrain Control Module and other control units). When the battery is disconnected, the power that maintains these systems is cut. So, before you disconnect the battery, please note that on a vehicle with power door locks, it's a wise precaution to remove the key from

the ignition and to keep it with you, so that it does not get locked inside if the power door locks should engage accidentally when the battery is reconnected!
2   Devices known as "memory-savers" can be used to avoid some of these problems. Precise details vary according to the device used. The typical memory saver is plugged into the cigarette lighter and is connected to a spare battery. Then the vehicle battery can be disconnected from the electrical system. The memory saver will provide sufficient current to maintain audio unit security codes, PCM memory, etc., and will provide power to always hot circuits such as the clock and radio memory circuits.
Warning: *Some memory savers deliver a considerable amount of current in order to keep vehicle systems operational after the main battery is disconnected. If you're using a memory saver, make sure that the circuit concerned is actually open before servicing it.*
Warning: *If you're going to work near any of the airbag system components, the battery MUST be disconnected and a memory saver*

must NOT be used. If a memory saver is used, power will be supplied to the airbag, which means that it could accidentally deploy and cause serious personal injury.
3   To disconnect the battery for service procedures requiring power to be cut from the vehicle, loosen the cable clamp nut and disconnect the cable from the negative battery terminal (see Section 4). Isolate the cable end to prevent it from coming into accidental contact with the battery terminal.

4   Battery and battery tray - removal and installation

Battery

1   Install a memory saver device to avoid having to reprogram several of the vehicle's systems (see Section 3).
2   Remove the air filter housing fresh air duct by rotating the retaining clips and removing the duct (see illustration).
3   Disconnect the negative battery cable, then the positive battery cable, from the battery (see illustration).
Warning: *Always disconnect the negative cable first and hook it up last or the battery may be shorted by the tool being used to loosen the cable clamps.*
4   Unscrew the bolt and remove the hold-down clamp from the bottom edge of the battery (see illustrations).
5   Lift out the battery. Special battery removal and installation tools are available at auto parts stores; lifting and moving the battery is much easier if you use one.
6   Installation is the reverse of removal. If equipped, and if you're replacing the battery, transfer the battery insulator to the new battery. Connect the positive cable first, then the negative cable.

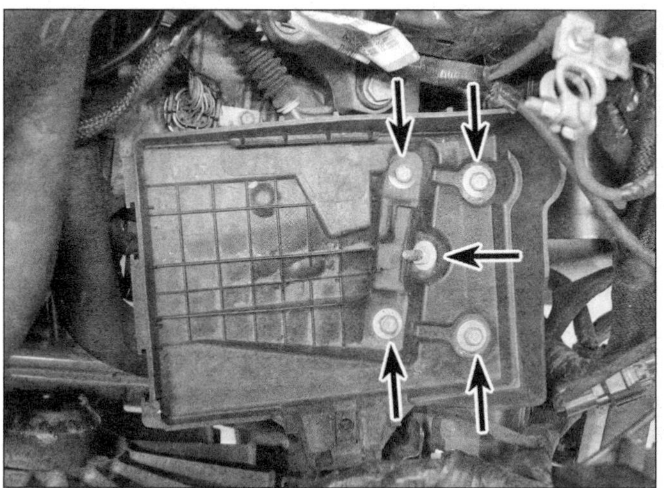

4.9 Battery tray fastener locations

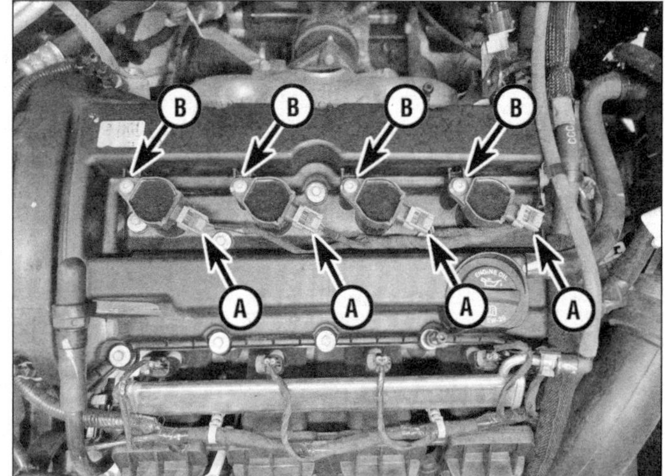

6.4 To remove an ignition coil, depress the tab (A), disconnect the electrical connector, remove the coil retaining bolt (B)

Battery tray

7   Remove the battery (see Steps 1 through 5).

8   Remove the battery tray liner, if equipped.

9   Remove the battery tray fasteners (see illustration) and lift the tray out.

10   Installation is the reverse of removal.

---

5   Battery cables - replacement

1   When removing the cables, always disconnect the cable from the battery negative terminal first and hook it up last, or you might accidentally short out the battery with the tool you're using to loosen the cable clamps. Even if you're only replacing the cable for the positive terminal, aways disconnect the negative cable from the battery first.

2   Disconnect the old cables from the battery, then trace each of them to their opposite ends and disconnect them. Be sure to note the routing of each cable before disconnecting it to ensure correct installation.

3   If you are replacing any of the old cables, take them with you when buying new cables. It is vitally important that you replace the cables with identical parts.

4   Clean the threads of the solenoid or ground connection with a wire brush to remove rust and corrosion. Apply a light coat of battery terminal corrosion inhibitor or petroleum jelly to the threads to prevent future corrosion.

5   Attach the cable to the solenoid or ground connection and tighten the mounting nut/bolt securely.

6   Before connecting a new cable to the battery, make sure that it reaches the battery post without having to be stretched.

7   Connect the cable to the positive battery

6.6 Pull the coil(s) off the spark plug using a twisting motion

terminal first, then connect the ground cable to the negative battery terminal.

6   Ignition coils - removal and installation

1   If available, spray compressed air around the tops of the coils to ensure debris will not fall into the spark plug tube upon removal.

Warning: *Wear eye protection when using compressed air.*

2   Remove the engine cover.

3   Disconnect the cable from the negative terminal of the battery (see Section 3).

4   Disconnect the electrical connector from the ignition coil (see illustration).

5   Remove the bolt attaching the ignition coil to the valve cover.

6   Grasp the ignition coil firmly and pull off

the spark plug using a twisting motion (see illustration).

7   Installation is the reverse of removal.

---

7   Alternator - removal and installation

1   Remove the air filter fresh air duct by rotating the retaining clips and pulling the duct from the air filter housing (see illustration 4.2).

2   Disconnect the cable from the negative terminal of the battery (see Section 3).

3   Loosen the right front wheel lug nuts, raise the front of the vehicle and support it securely on jackstands, then remove the wheel.

4   Remove the under-vehicle splash shield. Also, remove the fasteners from the front of the inner fender liner and pull the liner back to

7.7a Carefully lower the air conditioning compressor…

7.7b … then secure the compressor with a length of wire or rope

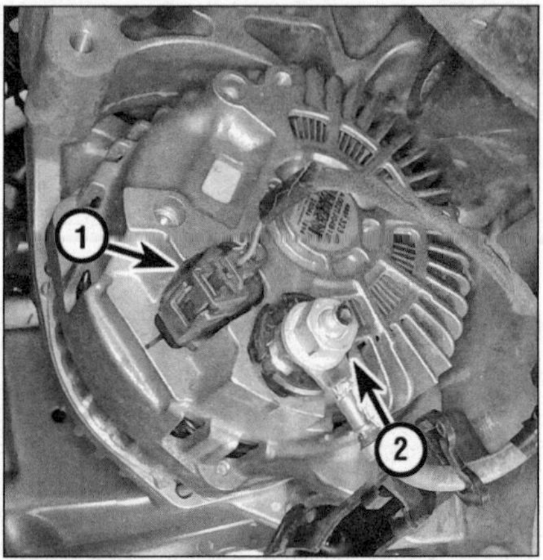

7.8 Unplug the field connector (1) from the alternator then remove the nut (2) that secures the B+ wire terminal to the stud on the back of the alternator

7.9 Remove the alternator upper bolt (1), then the lower mounting bolt (2)

8.4 Remove the starter mounting bolts

8.5 Position the starter nose-down so the electrical connectors can be removed

provide working room (see Chapter 11, Section 11).

5   Remove the drivebelt (see Chapter 1).

6   Remove the drivebelt idler pulley.

7   Unplug the air conditioning compressor clutch electrical connector, then unbolt and relocate the compressor out of the way (see Chapter 3) without disconnecting the lines, enough to allow the alternator to be removed (see illustrations).

Warning: *Do not disconnect the refrigerant lines.*

Caution: *Secure the compressor with bailing wire or similar. DO NOT let the compressor hang by the refrigerant lines or electrical harness to prevent damage to the lines or wiring.*

8   Unplug the field connector from the alternator, then remove the nut that secures the B+ wire terminal to the stud on the back of the alternator (see illustration).

9   Remove the upper and lower alternator mounting bolts (see illustration).

10   Detach the alternator from its mounting bracket, then maneuver the alternator out from the bottom of the vehicle.

11   Installation is the reverse of removal. Tighten the alternator bolts to the torque listed in this Chapter's Specifications. Tighten the air conditioning compressor bolts to the torque listed in the Chapter 3 Specifications. Tighten the drivebelt idler pulley to the torque listed in this Chapter's Specifications.

12   Install the wheel and lug nuts, then lower the vehicle and tighten the lug nuts to the torque listed in the Chapter 1 Specifications.

8   Starter motor - removal and installation

1   Disconnect the cable from the negative terminal of the battery (see Section 3).

2   Remove the air filter housing and intake duct (see Chapter 4).

3   Remove the throttle body (see Chapter 4).

4   Remove starter mounting bolts (see illustration).

5   Push the starter under the intake manifold, position the starter to face the nose downward, then pull the starter up and out enough to access the electrical connections (see illustration).

6   Disconnect the starter wiring and remove the starter.

7   Installation is the reverse of removal. Tighten the starter mounting bolts to the torque listed in this Chapter's Specifications.

Notes

Notes

Chapter 6
Emissions and engine control systems

Contents

Torque specifications

Ft-lbs (unless otherwise indicated)

Note: *One foot-pound (ft-lb) of torque is equivalent to 12 inch-pounds (in-lbs) of torque. Torque values below approximately 15 ft-lbs are expressed in inch-pounds, since most foot-pound torque wrenches are not accurate at these smaller values.*

Accelerator Pedal Position (APP) sensor	21
Air injection system check valve bolts	105 in-lbs
Positive Crankcase Ventilation (PCV) valve	72 in-lbs
Camshaft/Crankshaft Position (CMP/CKP) sensor mounting bolt	80 in-lbs
Oil temperature sensor	160 in-lbs
Oxygen sensors	30
Knock sensor bolt	177 in-lbs
Manifold Absolute Pressure (MAP) sensor mounting bolt	71 in-lbs

---

1 General information

1 To prevent pollution of the atmosphere from incompletely burned and evaporating gases, and to maintain good driveability and fuel economy, a number of emission control systems are incorporated. They include the:

Catalytic converter

2 A catalytic converter is an emission control device in the exhaust system that reduces certain pollutants in the exhaust gas stream. There are two types of converters: oxidation converters and reduction converters.

3 Oxidation converters contain a monolithic substrate (a ceramic honeycomb) coated with the semi-precious metals platinum and palladium. An oxidation catalyst reduces unburned hydrocarbons (HC) and carbon monoxide (CO) by adding oxygen to the exhaust stream as it passes through the substrate, which, in the presence of high temperature and the catalyst materials, converts the HC and CO to water vapor (H_2O) and carbon dioxide (CO_2).

4 Reduction converters contain a monolithic substrate coated with platinum and rhodium. A reduction catalyst reduces oxides of nitrogen (NOx) by removing oxygen, which in the presence of high temperature and the catalyst material produces nitrogen (N) and carbon dioxide (CO_2).

5 Catalytic converters that combine both types of catalysts in one assembly are known as "three-way catalysts" or TWCs. A TWC can reduce all three pollutants.

Evaporative Emissions Control (EVAP) system

6 The Evaporative Emissions Control (EVAP) system prevents fuel system vapors

(which contain unburned hydrocarbons) from escaping into the atmosphere. On warm days, vapors trapped inside the fuel tank expand until the pressure reaches a certain threshold. Then the fuel vapors are routed from the fuel tank through the fuel vapor vent valve and the fuel vapor control valve to the EVAP canister, where they're stored temporarily until the next time the vehicle is operated. When the conditions are right (engine warmed up, vehicle up to speed, moderate or heavy load on the engine, etc.) the PCM opens the canister purge valve, which allows fuel vapors to be drawn from the canister into the intake manifold. Once in the intake manifold, the fuel vapors mix with incoming air before being drawn through the intake ports into the combustion chambers where they're burned up with the rest of the air/fuel mixture. The EVAP system is complex and virtually impossible to troubleshoot without the right tools and training.

Exhaust Gas Recirculation (EGR) system

7   The EGR system reduces oxides of nitrogen by recirculating exhaust gases from the exhaust manifold, through the EGR valve and intake manifold, then back to the combustion chambers, where it mixes with the incoming air/fuel mixture before being consumed. These recirculated exhaust gases dilute the incoming air/fuel mixture, which cools the combustion chambers, thereby reducing NOx emissions.

8   The EGR system consists of the Powertrain Control Module (PCM), the EGR valve, the EGR valve position sensor and various other information sensors that the PCM uses to determine when to open the EGR valve. The degree to which the EGR valve is opened is referred to as "EGR valve lift." The PCM is programmed to produce the ideal EGR valve lift for varying operating conditions. The EGR valve position sensor, which is an integral part of the EGR valve, detects the amount of EGR valve lift and sends this information to the PCM. The PCM then compares it with the appropriate EGR valve lift for the operating conditions. The PCM increases current flow

to the EGR valve to increase valve lift and reduces the current to reduce the amount of lift. If EGR flow is inappropriate to the operating conditions (idle, cold engine, etc.) the PCM simply cuts the current to the EGR valve and the valve closes.

Secondary Air Injection (AIR) system

9   Some models are equipped with a secondary air injection (AIR) system. The secondary air injection system is used to reduce tailpipe emissions on initial engine start-up. The system uses an electric motor/pump assembly, relay, vacuum valve/solenoid, air shut-off valve, check valves and tubing to inject fresh air directly into the exhaust manifolds. The fresh air (oxygen) reacts with the exhaust gas in the catalytic converter to reduce HC and CO levels. The air pump and solenoid are controlled by the PCM through the AIR relay. During initial start-up, the PCM energizes the AIR relay, the relay supplies battery voltage to the air pump and the vacuum valve/solenoid, engine vacuum is applied to the air shut-off valve which opens and allows air to flow through the tubing into the exhaust manifolds. The PCM will operate the air pump until closed loop operation is reached (approximately four minutes). During normal operation, the check valves prevent exhaust backflow into the system.

Powertrain Control Module (PCM)

10   The Powertrain Control Module (PCM) is the brain of the engine management system. It also controls a wide variety of other vehicle systems. In order to program the new PCM, the dealer needs the vehicle as well as the new PCM. If you're planning to replace the PCM with a new one, there is no point in trying to do so at home because you won't be able to program it yourself.

Positive Crankcase Ventilation (PCV) system

11   The Positive Crankcase Ventilation (PCV) system reduces hydrocarbon emis-

sions by scavenging crankcase vapors, which are rich in unburned hydrocarbons. A PCV valve or orifice regulates the flow of gases into the intake manifold in proportion to the amount of intake vacuum available.

12   The PCV system generally consists of the fresh air inlet hose, the PCV valve or orifice and the crankcase ventilation hose (or PCV hose). The fresh air inlet hose connects the air intake duct to a pipe on the valve cover. The crankcase ventilation hose (or PCV hose) connects the PCV valve or orifice in the valve cover to the intake manifold.

Vehicle Emission Control Information (VECI) label

13   This label (see illustration), located on the underside of the hood, indicates what emission control systems the vehicle is equipped with and for what market the vehicle is certified (California, Federal, etc.), as well as any tune-up specifications and adjustments that may be needed.

Information Sensors

14   Typical information sensors:

---

2   On Board Diagnosis (OBD) system

General description

1   All models are equipped with the second generation OBD-II system. This system consists of an on-board computer known as the Powertrain Control Module (PCM), and information sensors, which monitor various functions of the engine and send data to the PCM. This system incorporates a series of diagnostic monitors that detect and identify fuel injection and emissions control system faults and store the information in the computer memory. This system also tests sensors and output actuators, diagnoses drive cycles, freezes data and clears codes.

2   The PCM is the brain of the electronically controlled fuel and emissions system. It receives data from a number of sensors and other electronic components (switches, relays, etc.). Based on the information it receives, the PCM generates output signals to control various relays, solenoids (fuel injectors) and other actuators. The PCM is specifically calibrated to optimize the emissions, fuel economy and driveability of the vehicle.

3   It isn't a good idea to attempt diagnosis or replacement of the PCM or emission control components at home while the vehicle is under warranty. Because of a federally-mandated warranty which covers the emissions system components and because any owner-induced damage to the PCM, the sensors and/or the control devices may void this warranty, take the vehicle to a dealer service department if the PCM or a system component malfunctions.

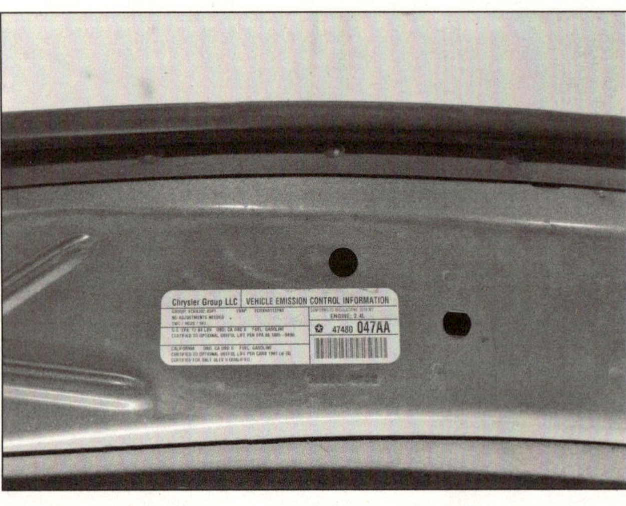

1.13 The Vehicle Emission Control Information (VECI) label is affixed to the underside of the hood

Information Sensors

Accelerator Pedal Position (APP) sensor - as you press the accelerator pedal, the APP sensor alters its voltage signal to the PCM in proportion to the angle of the pedal, and the PCM commands a motor inside the throttle body to open or close the throttle plate accordingly

Camshaft Position (CMP) sensor - produces a signal that the PCM uses to identify the number 1 cylinder and to time the firing sequence of the fuel injectors

Crankshaft Position (CKP) sensor - produces a signal that the PCM uses to calculate engine speed and crankshaft position, which enables it to synchronize ignition timing with fuel injector timing, and to detect misfires

Engine Coolant Temperature (ECT) sensor - a thermistor (temperature-sensitive variable resistor) that sends a voltage signal to the PCM, which uses this data to determine the temperature of the engine coolant

Fuel tank pressure sensor - measures the fuel tank pressure and controls fuel tank pressure by signaling the EVAP system to purge the fuel tank vapors when the pressure becomes excessive

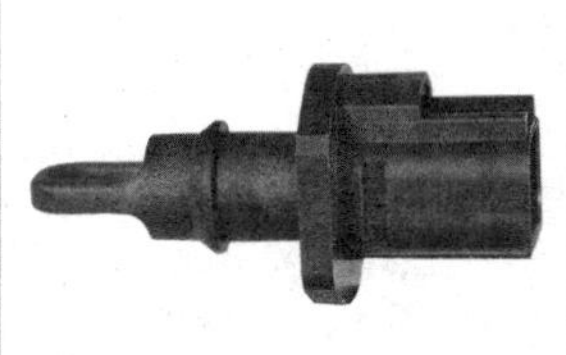

Intake Air Temperature (IAT) sensor - monitors the temperature of the air entering the engine and sends a signal to the PCM to determine injector pulse-width (the duration of each injector's on-time) and to adjust spark timing (to prevent spark knock)

Knock sensor - a piezoelectric crystal that oscillates in proportion to engine vibration which produces a voltage output that is monitored by the PCM. This retards the ignition timing when the oscillation exceeds a certain threshold

Manifold Absolute Pressure (MAP) sensor - monitors the pressure or vacuum inside the intake manifold. The PCM uses this data to determine engine load so that it can alter the ignition advance and fuel enrichment

Mass Air Flow (MAF) sensor - measures the amount of intake air drawn into the engine. It uses a hot-wire sensing element to measure the amount of air entering the engine

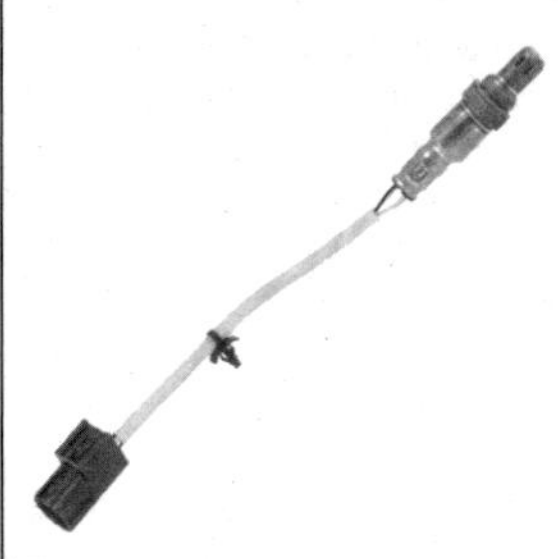

Oxygen sensors - generates a small variable voltage signal in proportion to the difference between the oxygen content in the exhaust stream and the oxygen content in the ambient air. The PCM uses this information to maintain the proper air/fuel ratio. A second oxygen sensor monitors the efficiency of the catalytic converter

Throttle Position (TP) sensor - a potentiometer that generates a voltage signal that varies in relation to the opening angle of the throttle plate inside the throttle body. Works with the PCM and other sensors to calculate injector pulse width (the duration of each injector's on-time)

Photos courtesy of Wells Manufacturing, except APP and MAF sensors.

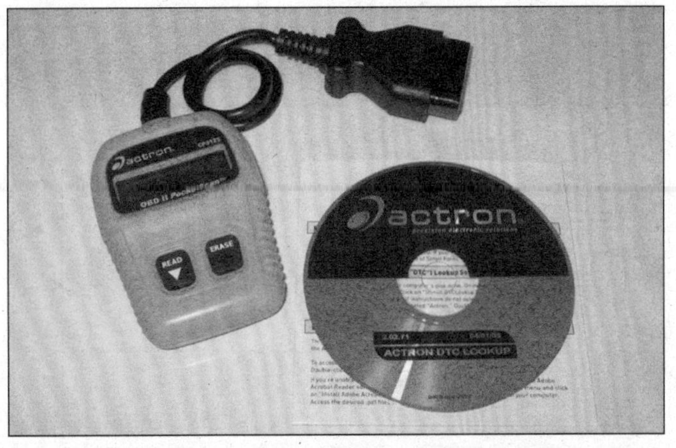

2.4a Simple code readers are an economical way to extract trouble codes when the CHECK ENGINE light comes on

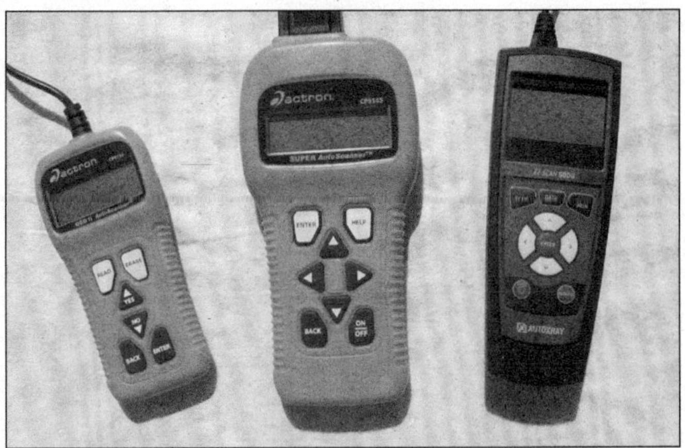

2.4b Hand-held scan tools like these can extract computer codes and also perform diagnostics

Scan tool information

4　Because extracting the Diagnostic Trouble Codes (DTCs) from an engine management system is now the first step in troubleshooting many computer-controlled systems and components, a code reader, at the very least, will be required (see illustration). More powerful scan tools can also perform many of the diagnostics once associated with expensive factory scan tools (see illustration). If you're planning to obtain a generic scan tool for your vehicle, make sure that it's compatible with OBD-II systems. If you don't plan to purchase a code reader or scan tool and don't have access to one, you can have the codes extracted by a dealer service department or an independent repair shop.

Note: *Some auto parts stores even provide this service.*

3.3 The 16-pin Data Link Connector (DLC) is located under the left side of the dash

---

3　Obtaining and clearing Diagnostic Trouble Codes (DTCs)

1　All models covered by this manual are equipped with on-board diagnostics. When the PCM recognizes a malfunction in a monitored emission or engine control system, component or circuit, it turns on the Malfunction Indicator Light (MIL) on the dash. The PCM will continue to display the MIL until the problem is fixed and the Diagnostic Trouble Code (DTC) is cleared from the PCM's memory. You'll need a scan tool to access any DTCs stored in the PCM.

2　Before outputting any DTCs stored in the PCM, thoroughly inspect ALL electrical connectors and hoses. Make sure that all electrical connections are tight, clean and free of corrosion. And make sure that all hoses are correctly connected, fit tightly and are in good condition (no cracks or tears).

Accessing the DTCs

3　The Diagnostic Trouble Codes (DTCs) can only be accessed with a code reader or scan tool. Professional scan tools are expensive, but relatively inexpensive generic code readers or scan tools (see illustrations 2.4a and 2.4b) are available at most auto parts stores. Simply plug the connector of the scan tool into the diagnostic connector (see illustration). Then follow the instructions included with the scan tool to extract the DTCs.

4　Once you have outputted all of the stored DTCs, look them up on the accompanying DTC chart.

5　After troubleshooting the source of each DTC, make any necessary repairs or replace the defective component(s).

Clearing the DTCs

6　Clear the DTCs with the code reader or scan tool in accordance with the instructions provided by the tool's manufacturer.

Diagnostic Trouble Codes

7　The accompanying tables are a list of the Diagnostic Trouble Codes (DTCs) that can be accessed by a do-it-yourselfer working at home (there are many, many more DTCs available to professional mechanics with proprietary scan tools and software, but those codes cannot be accessed by a generic scan tool). If, after you have checked and repaired the connectors, wire harness and vacuum hoses (if applicable) for an emission-related system, component or circuit, the problem persists, have the vehicle checked by a dealer service department or other qualified repair shop.

OBD-II trouble codes

Note: *Not all trouble codes apply to all models.*

Code	Probable cause
P000A	Camshaft 1 position, (bank no.1), slow response
P000B	Camshaft 2 position, (bank no.1), slow response
P0010	Camshaft 1 position, (bank no.1), actuator circuit open
P0013	Camshaft 2 position, (bank no.1), actuator circuit open
P0016	Crankshaft/camshaft timing (bank no.1. sensor no.1) misalignment
P0017	Crankshaft/camshaft timing (bank no.1. sensor no.2) misalignment
P0031	Upstream oxygen sensor (cylinder bank no. 1), heater circuit low voltage
P0032	Upstream oxygen sensor heater (cylinder bank no. 1), heater circuit high voltage
P0037	Downstream oxygen sensor (cylinder bank no. 1), heater circuit low voltage
P0038	Downstream oxygen sensor (cylinder bank no. 1), heater circuit high voltage
P0068	Manifold pressure/throttle position correlation - high-flow/vacuum leak
P0070	Ambient temperature sensor stuck
P0071	Ambient temperature sensor performance
P0072	Ambient temperature sensor, low voltage
P0073	Ambient temperature sensor, high voltage
P0107	Manifold Absolute Pressure (MAP) sensor, low voltage
P0108	Manifold Absolute Pressure (MAP) sensor, high voltage
P0110	Intake Air Temperature (IAT) sensor, stuck
P0111	Intake Air Temperature (IAT) sensor performance
P0112	Intake Air Temperature (IAT) sensor, low voltage
P0113	Intake Air Temperature (IAT) sensor, high voltage
P0116	Engine Coolant Temperature (ECT) sensor performance
P0117	Engine Coolant Temperature (ECT) sensor, low voltage
P0118	Engine Coolant Temperature (ECT) sensor, high voltage
P0121	Throttle Position (TP) sensor performance
P0122	Throttle Position (TP) sensor, low voltage
P0123	Throttle Position (TP) sensor, high voltage
P0125	Insufficient coolant temperature for closed-loop control; closed-loop temperature not reached
P0128	Thermostat rationality

OBD-II trouble codes (continued)

Note: *Not all trouble codes apply to all models.*

Code	Probable cause
P0129	Barometric pressure out-of-range (low)
P0131	Upstream oxygen sensor (cylinder bank no. 1), low voltage or shorted to ground
P0132	Upstream oxygen sensor (cylinder bank no. 1), high voltage or shorted to voltage
P0133	Upstream oxygen sensor (cylinder bank no. 1), slow response
P0134	Upstream oxygen sensor (cylinder bank no. 1), sensor remains at center (not switching)
P0135	Upstream oxygen sensor (cylinder bank no. 1), heater failure
P0137	Downstream oxygen sensor (cylinder bank no. 1), low voltage or shorted to ground
P0138	Downstream oxygen sensor (cylinder bank no. 1), high voltage or shorted to voltage
P0139	Downstream oxygen sensor (cylinder bank no. 1), slow response
P0140	Downstream oxygen sensor (cylinder bank no. 1), sensor remains at center (not switching)
P0141	Downstream oxygen sensor (cylinder bank no. 1), heater failure
P0171	Fuel control system too lean (cylinder bank no. 1)
P0172	Fuel control system too rich (cylinder bank no. 1)
P0201	Injector circuit malfunction - cylinder no. 1
P0202	Injector circuit malfunction - cylinder no. 2
P0203	Injector circuit malfunction - cylinder no. 3
P0204	Injector circuit malfunction - cylinder no. 4
P0300	Multiple cylinder misfire detected
P0301	Cylinder no. 1 misfire detected
P0302	Cylinder no. 2 misfire detected
P0303	Cylinder no. 3 misfire detected
P0304	Cylinder no. 4 misfire detected
P0315	No crank sensor learned
P0320	No crankshaft reference signal at Powertrain Control Module (PCM)
P0325	Knock sensor circuit malfunction
P0335	Crankshaft Position (CKP) sensor circuit
P0339	Crankshaft Position (CKP) sensor intermittent
P0340	Camshaft Position (CMP) sensor circuit
P0344	Camshaft Position (CMP) sensor intermittent

Code	Probable cause
P0351	Ignition coil no. 1, primary circuit
P0352	Ignition coil no. 2, primary circuit
P0353	Ignition coil no. 3, primary circuit
P0354	Ignition coil no. 4, primary circuit
P0365	Camshaft Position (CMP) sensor circuit (bank no.1. sensor no.2)
P0369	Camshaft Position (CMP) sensor intermittent (bank no.1. sensor no.2)
P0440	General Evaporative Emission Control (EVAP) system failure
P0441	Evaporative Emission Control (EVAP) system, incorrect purge flow
P0442	Evaporative Emission Control (EVAP) system, medium leak (0.040-inch) detected
P0443	Evaporative Emission Control (EVAP) system, purge solenoid circuit malfunction
P0452	Natural Vacuum Leak Detector (NVLD) pressure sensor circuit, low voltage
P0453	Natural Vacuum Leak Detector (NVLD) pressure sensor circuit, high input
P0455	Evaporative Emission Control (EVAP) system, large leak detected
P0456	Evaporative Emission Control (EVAP) system, small leak (0.020-inch) detected
P0460	Fuel level sending unit, no change as vehicle is operated
P0461	Fuel level sensor circuit, range or performance problem
P0462	Fuel level sending unit or sensor circuit, low voltage
P0463	Fuel level sending unit or sensor circuit, high voltage
P0480	Low-speed fan control relay circuit malfunction
P0498	Natural Vacuum Leak Detector (NVLD) canister vent valve solenoid circuit, low voltage
P0499	Natural Vacuum Leak Detector (NVLD) canister vent valve solenoid circuit, high voltage
P0500	No vehicle speed signal (four-speed automatic transaxles)
P0501	Vehicle speed sensor, range or performance problem
P0503	Vehicle speed sensor 1, erratic
P0506	Idle speed control system, rpm lower than expected
P0507	Idle speed control system, rpm higher than expected
P0508	Idle Air Control (IAC) valve circuit, low voltage
P0509	Idle Air Control (IAC) valve circuit, high voltage
P0513	Invalid SKIM key (engine immobilizer problem)
P0516	Battery temperature sensor, low voltage
P0517	Battery temperature sensor, high voltage

OBD-II trouble codes (continued)

Note: *Not all trouble codes apply to all models.*

P0519	Idle speed performance
P0522	Engine oil pressure sensor/switch circuit, low voltage
P0532	Air conditioning refrigerant pressure sensor, low voltage
P0533	Air conditioning refrigerant pressure sensor, high voltage
P0551	Power Steering Pressure (PSP) switch circuit, range or performance problem
P0562	Battery voltage low
P0563	Battery voltage high
P0579	Speed control switch circuit, range or performance problem
P0580	Speed control switch circuit, low voltage
P0581	Speed control switch circuit, high voltage
P0582	Speed control vacuum solenoid circuit
P0858	Speed control switch 1/2 correlation
P0586	Speed control vent solenoid circuit
P0591	Speed control switch 2 circuit, performance problem
P0592	Speed control switch 2 circuit, low voltage
P0593	Speed control switch circuit 2, high voltage
P0594	Speed control servo power circuit
P0600	Serial communication link malfunction
P0601	Powertrain Control Module (PCM), internal controller failure
P0622	Alternator field control circuit malfunction or field not switching correctly
P0627	Fuel pump relay circuit
P0630	Vehicle Identification Number (VIN) not programmed in Powertrain Control Module (PCM)
P0632	Odometer not programmed in Powertrain Control Module (PCM)
P0633	SKIM key not programmed in Powertrain Control Module (PCM)
P0642	Sensor reference voltage 2 circuit, low voltage
P0643	Sensor reference voltage 2 circuit, high voltage
P0645	Air conditioning clutch relay circuit
P0685	Automatic Shutdown (ASD) relay control circuit
P0688	Automatic Shutdown (ASD) relay sense circuit, low voltage
P0700	Electronic Automatic Transaxle (EATX) control system malfunction or DTC present

Code	Probable cause
P0703	Brake switch circuit malfunction
P0833	Clutch released switch circuit
P0850	Park/Neutral switch malfunction
P0856	Traction control torque request circuit

4   Accelerator Pedal Position (APP) sensor - replacement

1   Disconnect the cable from the negative terminal of the battery (see Chapter 5).
2   Disconnect the electrical connector from the upper end of the APP sensor (see illustration).
3   Remove the accelerator pedal/APP sensor assembly mounting nuts and remove the assembly.
4   Installation is the reverse of removal. Tighten the mounting fasteners to the torque listed in this Chapter's Specifications.

5   Camshaft Position (CMP) sensor - replacement

Caution: *After the sensor has been removed, do not insert any magnetic tools into the hole in the valve cover. Doing so could damage the magnetic timing wheels on the ends of the camshafts.*

Note: *On these engines there are two CMP sensors, located at the left end of the cylinder head, at the front (intake) and rear (exhaust), just below the valve cover.*

1   Disconnect the cable from the negative terminal of the battery (see Chapter 5).

Remove the engine cover.
2   If you're removing the intake CMP sensor, remove the intake duct between the air filter housing and the throttle body (see Chapter 4).
3   Disconnect the electrical connector from the sensor.
4   Unscrew the sensor mounting bolt and pull the sensor from the cylinder head (see illustrations).
5   If you're going to reinstall the same sensor, check the O-ring for damage. If it's OK, it can be reused.
6   Apply a film of clean engine oil to the O-ring, then insert the sensor into the valve cover and install the mounting bolt, tightening it securely.
7   Installation is the reverse of removal.

6   Crankshaft Position (CKP) sensor - replacement

Note: *The CKP sensor is located at the rear of the cylinder block, near the transmission.*
1   Disconnect the cable from the negative terminal of the battery (see Chapter 5).
2   Raise the vehicle and support it securely on jackstands.
3   Remove the heat shield (if equipped) from over the sensor.
4   Disconnect the electrical connector from

the sensor (see illustration).
5   Remove the sensor mounting bolt and pull the sensor from the engine block.
6   If you're going to reinstall the same sensor, check the O-ring for damage.
7   Apply a film of clean engine oil to the O-ring and insert the sensor into the cylinder block.
8   Install the mounting bolt and tighten it to the torque listed in this Chapter's Specifications.

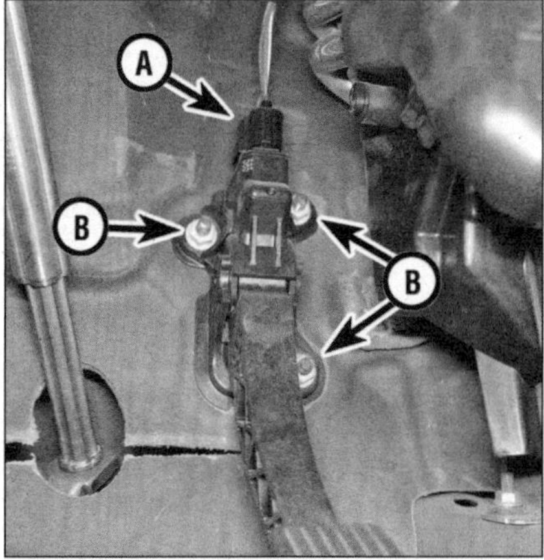

4.2 APP sensor electrical connector (A) and mounting fasteners (B)

5.4a The intake CMP sensor (no. 2) is located at the left front end of the cylinder head

5.4b The exhaust CMP sensor (no. 1) is located at the left rear end of the cylinder head

6.4 Location of the CKP sensor

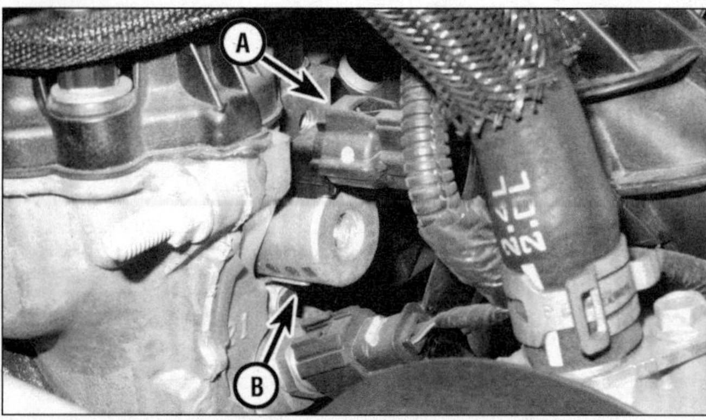

7.6 Variable valve timing solenoid connector (A) and mounting bolt (B) - (front/intake)

7.10 Variable valve timing solenoid - (rear/exhaust)

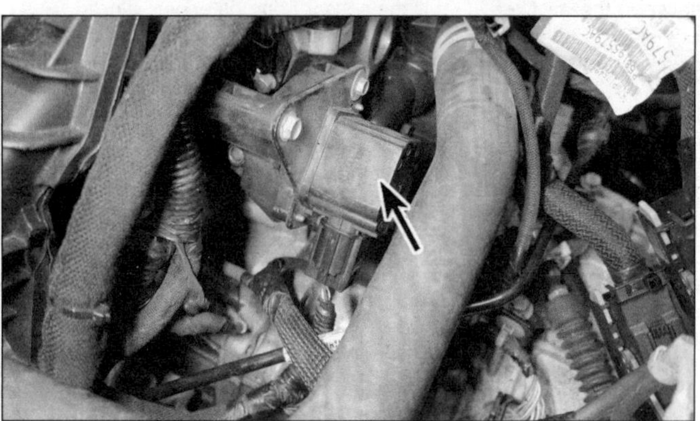

8.4 Manifold flow valve location

9.4 Wrap the threads of the ECT sensor with Teflon tape to prevent coolant from leaking past the threads

7   Variable valve timing solenoids - removal and installation

Note: *The variable valve timing solenoids are located at the front and rear end of the right end cylinder head.*

1   Disconnect the cable from the negative terminal of the battery (see Chapter 5).
2   Remove the engine cover.

Front (intake) solenoid

3   Use a pair of pliers and rotate the hose clamp until it's out of the way.
4   Remove the oil pressure sending unit (see Chapter 2B).
5   Disconnect the solenoid valve electrical connector.
6   Unscrew the mounting bolt and remove the variable valve timing solenoid (see illustration).
7   Inspect the O-ring for damage. If it's cracked, torn or otherwise deteriorated, replace it.
8   Lubricate the sensor O-ring with clean engine oil. Installation is the reverse of removal.

Rear (exhaust) solenoid

9   Disconnect the solenoid valve electrical connector.

10   Unscrew the mounting bolt and remove the variable valve timing solenoid (see illustration).
11   Inspect the O-ring for damage. If it's cracked, torn or otherwise deteriorated, replace it.
12   Lubricate the sensor O-ring with clean engine oil. Installation is the reverse of removal.

8   Manifold flow valve - removal and installation

Warning: *Wait until the engine has cooled completely before beginning this procedure.*

1   Disconnect the cable from the negative terminal of the battery (see Chapter 5).
2   Remove the engine cover.
3   Remove the intake air duct between the air filter housing and the throttle body (see Chapter 4).
4   Disconnect the electrical connector from the flow valve (see illustration).
5   Unscrew the mounting bolts and remove the manifold flow valve.
6   Remove the old O-ring from the manifold flow valve and discard it. Install a new O-ring to the valve.
7   Installation is the reverse of removal.

9   Engine Coolant Temperature (ECT) sensor - replacement

Warning: *Wait until the engine has cooled completely before beginning this procedure.*
Caution: *Handle the Engine Coolant Temperature (ECT) sensor with care. Damage to the ECT sensor will affect the operation of the entire fuel injection system.*
Note: *2010 and earlier engines have two ECT sensors: Sensor 1 is located at the left end of the engine on the coolant adapter housing; Sensor 2 is located on the right front side of the engine block, near the knock sensor. 2011 and later models only have one ECT sensor, located at the left end of the engine on the coolant adapter housing.*

1   Disconnect the cable from the negative terminal of the battery (see Chapter 5).
2   Drain the engine coolant to a point lower than that of the sensor (see Chapter 1).

Engine block ECT sensor 2 (2010 and earlier models)

3   Disconnect the electrical connector from the sensor, then unscrew the sensor from the engine block.
4   Before installing a threaded ECT sensor, wrap the threads of the sensor with Teflon tape to prevent coolant leakage (see illustration).

9.6a Depress the tab and disconnect the electrical connector from the sensor...

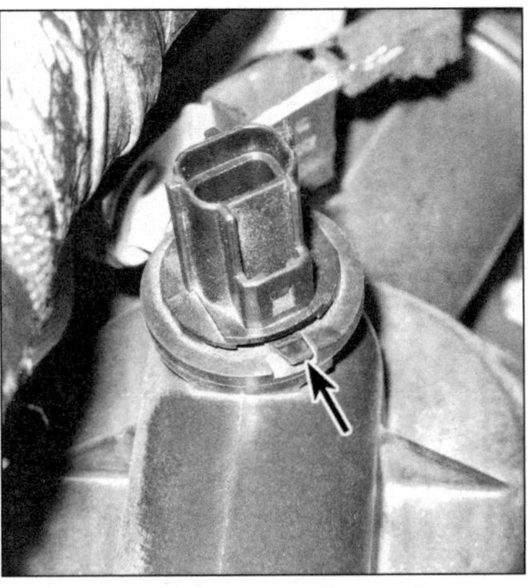

9.6b ... then pry up the locking tab, rotate the sensor counterclockwise and pull it out of the coolant adapter housing

10.1a Rotate the fresh air inlet duct retainers...

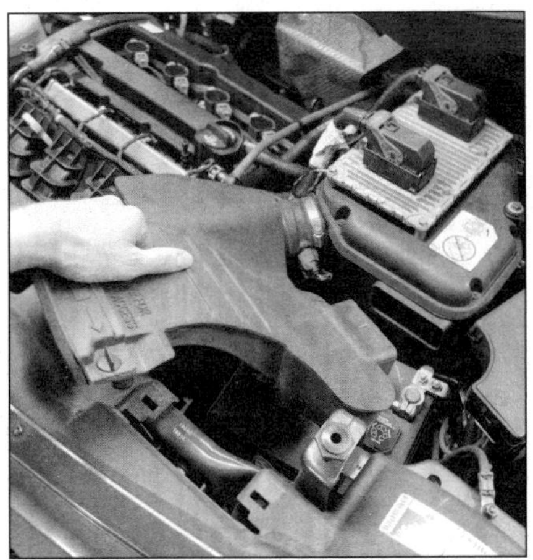

10.1b ... then lift the duct up and pull it out from the housing

10.2 The IAT sensor is located in the air inlet duct. To remove it, twist it counterclockwise and pull it from the duct

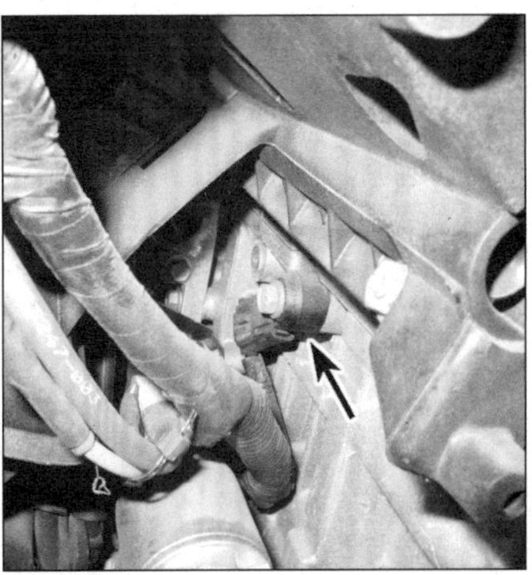

11.3 The knock sensor is located on the side of the cylinder block in front of the starter

5   Installation is otherwise the reverse of removal. Tighten threaded ECT sensors to the torque listed in this Chapter's Specifications.

Coolant adapter ECT sensor 1 (2011 and later models)

6   Disconnect the electrical connector from the sensor, then unscrew the sensor (see illustrations).

7   Installation is otherwise the reverse of removal, making sure the sensor is locked in place.

All models

8   Refill the cooling system (see Chapter 1).

10   Intake Air Temperature (IAT) sensor - replacement

Caution: *The IAT sensor must be installed with the correct orientation to the air duct in order to function properly.*
Note: *The IAT sensor is located on the air inlet ducting.*

1   Unlock the retainers for the fresh air inlet duct then remove the fresh air inlet duct from air filter housing (see illustrations).

2   Disconnect the electrical connector from the IAT sensor (see illustration).

3   Remove the sensor by turning it 1/4-turn counterclockwise and pulling it out.

4   Inspect the condition of the sensor O-ring. If it is cracked, torn or otherwise deteriorated, replace it.

5   Installation is the reverse of removal.

11   Knock sensor - replacement

Warning: *Wait for the engine to cool completely before performing this procedure.*
Note: *The knock sensor is located on the side of the engine block, in front of the starter, under the intake manifold.*

1   Disconnect the cable from the negative terminal of the battery (see Chapter 5).

2   Remove the engine cover.

3   Disconnect the electrical connector(s) from the knock sensor(s) (see illustration).

4   Remove the mounting bolt and detach the sensor from the engine block.

5   Installation is the reverse of removal. Tighten the knock sensor bolt to the torque listed in this Chapter's Specifications.

12 Manifold Absolute Pressure (MAP) sensor - replacement

Note: *The MAP sensor is located on the front of the intake manifold.*

1   Remove the engine cover by pulling it up off the ballstuds.

2   Disconnect the electrical connector from the MAP sensor (see illustration), remove the screw and pull the sensor from the manifold.

3   Inspect the MAP sensor O-ring for cracks, tears and deterioration; if it's damaged, replace it.

4   Installation is the reverse of removal.

13 Oxygen sensors - general information and replacement

1   Be particularly careful when servicing an oxygen sensor:

a) *Oxygen sensors have a permanently attached pigtail and an electrical connector that cannot be removed. Damaging or removing the pigtail or electrical connector will render the sensor useless.*

b) *Keep grease, dirt and other contaminants away from the electrical connector and the louvered end of the sensor.*

c) *Do not use cleaning solvents of any kind on an oxygen sensor.*

d) *Oxygen sensors are extremely delicate. Do not drop a sensor or handle it roughly.*

e) *Make sure that the silicone boot on the sensor is installed in the correct position. Otherwise, the boot might melt and it might prevent the sensor from operating correctly.*

Note: *Because it is installed in the exhaust manifold, catalytic converter or pipe, all of which contract when cool, an oxygen sensor might be very difficult to loosen when the en-*

12.2 The MAP sensor is located on the front of the intake manifold, just above the alternator, and is retained by a screw

gine is cold. Rather than risk damage to the sensor, start and run the engine for a minute or two, then shut it off. Be careful not to burn yourself during the following procedure.

Note: *Use an oxygen sensor socket, if available, for removal and installation of oxygen sensors.*

Note: *The downstream sensor is located on the side of each catalytic converter.*

2   Disconnect the negative battery cable from the remote ground terminal (see Chapter 5).

Upstream oxygen sensor

Note: The upstream sensor is located near the exhaust manifold.

3   Remove the engine cover.

4   Disconnect the oxygen sensor wire harness mounting clips from the engine or body, if equipped.

5   Disconnect the oxygen sensor connector from the engine wiring harness (see illustration).

6   Remove the oxygen sensor from the exhaust pipe.

7   Installation is otherwise the reverse of removal.

Downstream oxygen sensor

Note: *The downstream sensor is located on the side of each catalytic converter.*

8   Disconnect the oxygen sensor connector mounting clips from the engine or body, if equipped.

9   Raise the vehicle and support it securely on jackstands.

10   Disconnect the oxygen sensor connector from the engine wiring harness (see illustration).

11   Remove the oxygen sensor from the catalytic converter.

12   Installation is the reverse of removal.

14 Throttle Position (TP) sensor - replacement

1   The TP sensor is an integral component of the electronic throttle body, and is not separately serviceable. If you need to replace the TP sensor, you must replace the throttle body (see Chapter 4).

13.5 Disconnect the upstream oxygen sensor connector (A) from the engine wiring harness, then unscrew the sensor (B)

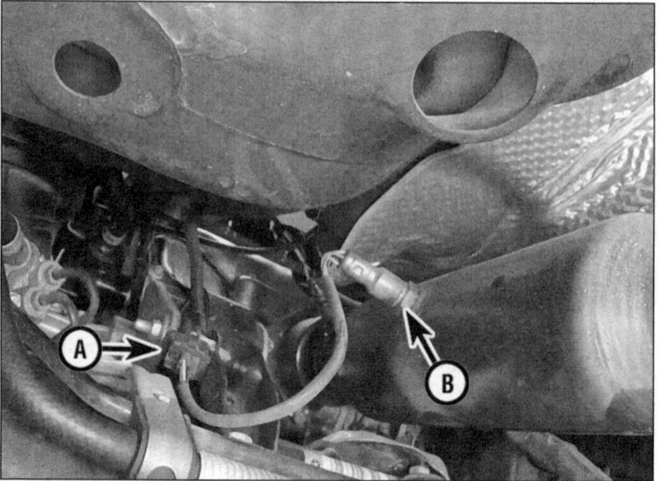

13.10 Downstream oxygen sensor connector (A) and downstream oxygen sensor (B)

15 Transmission Range (TR) and transmission temperature sensors - replacement

1   The TR sensor and transmission temperature sensor (which is an integral part of the TR sensor) are located on the automatic transaxle valve body. In order to replace the TR sensor/transmission temperature sensor, you must remove the valve body, which is beyond the scope of the home mechanic.

16 Transaxle speed sensors - replacement

1   Transaxle speed sensors are located in the valve body and/or below the valve body internally in the transaxle. In order to replace the speed sensors, you must remove the valve body, which is beyond the scope of the home mechanic.

17 Powertrain Control Module (PCM) - replacement

Caution: *To avoid electrostatic discharge damage to the PCM, handle the PCM only by its case. Do not touch the electrical terminals during removal and installation. If available, ground yourself to the vehicle with an anti-static ground strap, available at computer supply stores.*
Note: *This procedure applies only to disconnecting, removing and installing the PCM that is already installed in your vehicle. If, however, you need to replace the PCM, it must be programmed with new software and calibrations, and information from the old PCM must be transferred to the new one. This will require the use of a special scan tool, so you will not*

be able to replace the PCM at home.
Note: *The PCM is located in the left-rear corner of the engine compartment on top of the air filter housing.*
1   Disconnect the cable from the negative terminal of the battery (see Chapter 5).
2   Unlock the electrical connectors and disconnect them from the PCM (see illustration).
3   Unscrew the mounting bolts and remove the PCM.
4   Installation is the reverse of removal.

18 Catalytic converter - replacement

Warning: *Wait until the engine has cooled completely before beginning this procedure.*
Note: *On 2.4L (AWD) models, there are two catalytic converters used, one that combines the exhaust manifold and catalytic converter into a single unit called a "maniverter" and an under-floor converter. To replace the maniverter see Chapter 2A.*
1   Raise the vehicle and place it securely on jackstands.
2   Before trying to loosen the nuts and bolts at the flange(s) and the clamp bolt and nut behind the converter (on models so equipped), spray them with penetrating oil and wait the specified amount of time (see the instructions on the can) for the penetrant to loosen things up.
3   Remove the oxygen sensor from the converter (see Section 13).
4   Remove the rear portion of the exhaust system.
5   Remove the flange nuts at the exhaust manifold and detach the converter from the exhaust manifold (see illustration).
6   Before installing the converter, coat the threads of the exhaust manifold flange nuts and bolts, and the clamp bolt with anti-seize compound. Tighten the fasteners securely.
7   Installation is otherwise the reverse of removal.

19 Evaporative Emissions Control (EVAP) system - component replacement

EVAP canister purge solenoid

Note: *The EVAP canister purge solenoid is located on the left side of the firewall, below the power brake booster.*
1   Remove the air filter housing (see Chapter 4).
2   Clearly label the EVAP hoses to ensure correct reassembly (see illustration), then disconnect them from the solenoid.
3   Slide out the red lock, depress the tab and disconnect the electrical connector from the EVAP canister purge solenoid.
4   Depress the retaining tab and detach the purge solenoid from the mounting bracket.
5   Installation is the reverse of removal.

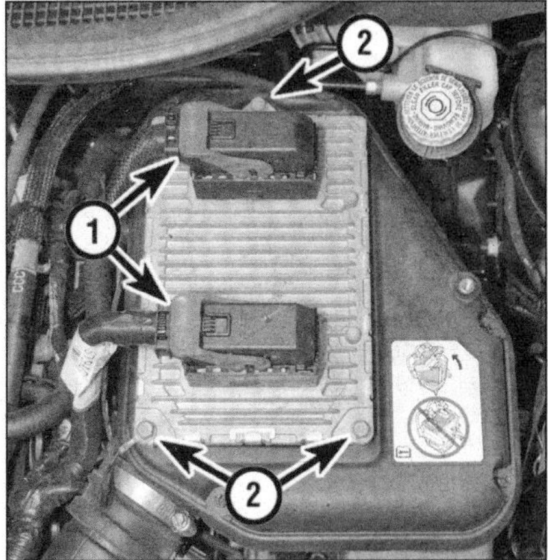

17.2 PCM mounting details

1   *Connector latches (flip up to release connectors)*
2   *Mounting bolts*

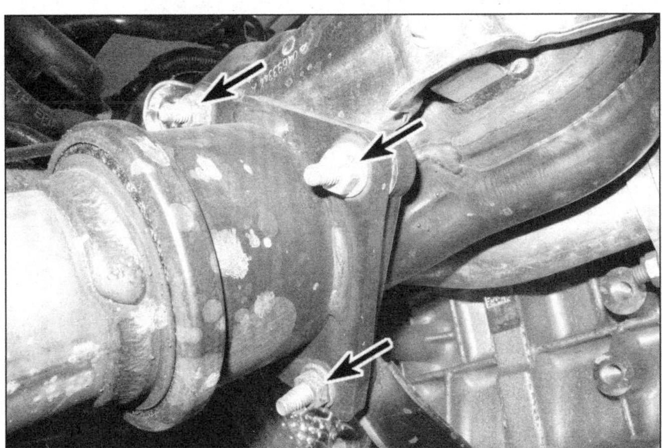

18.5 Catalytic converter-to-exhaust manifold flange nuts

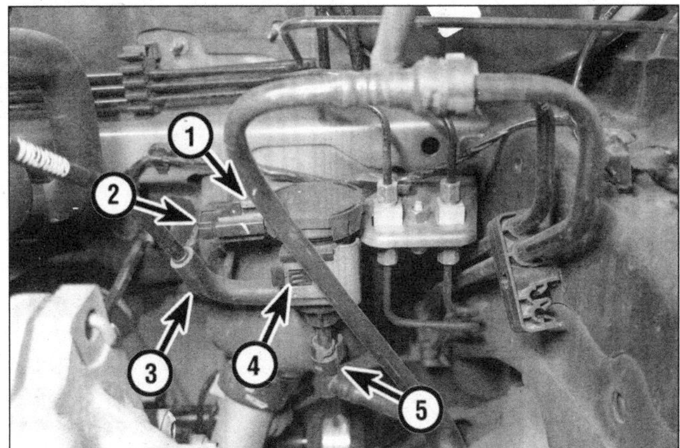

19.2 Canister purge solenoid details

1   *Electrical connector lock*
2   *Electrical connector release tab*
3   *Purge hose*
4   *Solenoid retaining tab*
5   *Fuel tank vapor hose*

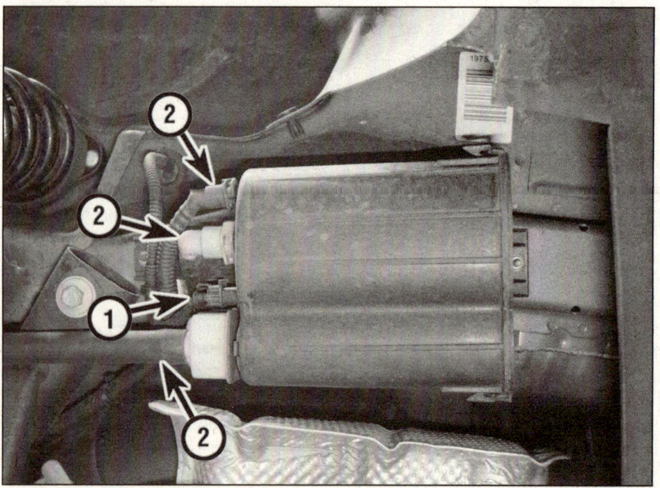

19.8 Disconnect the electrical connector (1) then remove all the hoses (2) from the EVAP canister taking care not to damage the plastic fittings

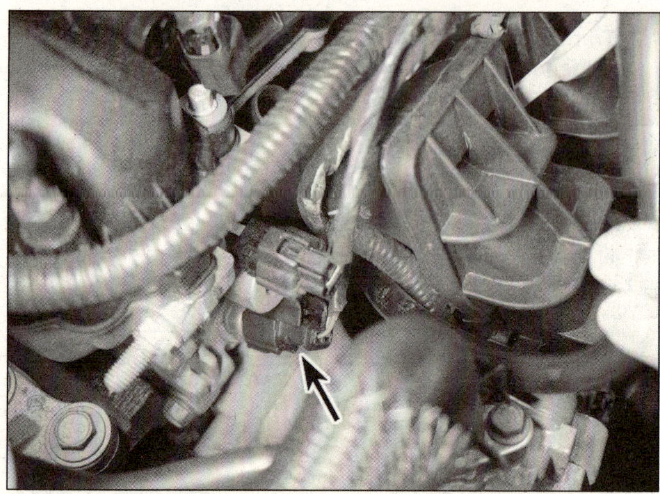

21.2 Location of the oil temperature sensor

EVAP canister

Note: *The EVAP canister is located behind the left rear wheel opening.*

6   Raise the vehicle and place it securely on jackstands.

7   Disconnect the electrical connector from the EVAP canister.

8   Disconnect the hoses from the EVAP canister (see illustration).

9   Remove the mounting fasteners from the mounting bracket and remove the EVAP canister assembly.

10   Installation is the reverse of removal.

20 Positive Crankcase Ventilation (PCV) system

1   The Positive Crankcase Ventilation (PCV) system reduces hydrocarbon emissions by scavenging crankcase vapors. It does this by circulating fresh air from the air filter housing through the crankcase, where it mixes with blow-by gases, before being drawn through a PCV valve into the intake manifold.

2   The PCV system consists of the PCV valve and two hoses. The fresh air inlet hose connects the air filter housing to the valve cover. The crankcase ventilation hose (or PCV hose) connects the valve cover to the intake manifold. The PCV valve is located at the right front corner of the valve cover.

3   To maintain idle quality, the PCV valve restricts the flow when the intake manifold vacuum is high. If abnormal operating conditions (such as piston ring problems) arise, the system is designed to allow excessive amounts of blow-by gases to flow back through the crankcase vent tube into the air cleaner to be consumed by normal combustion.

4   Checking and replacement of the PCV valve is covered in Chapter 1.

21 Oil temperature sensor - removal and installation

Note: *The oil temperature sensor is located at the left front corner of the cylinder head, behind the power steering pump.*

1   Remove the engine cover.

2   Depress the tab and disconnect the electrical connector from the sensor (see illustration).

3   Unscrew the sensor from the cylinder head.

4   If necessary for clearance, remove the drivebelt (see Chapter 1), loosen the power steering pump mounting bolts (see Chapter 10) and pivot the pump forward to provide extra room.

5   Before installing the new sensor, wrap the threads with Teflon sealing tape or coat the threads with thread sealant.

6   Thread the sensor into the cylinder head, then tighten it to the torque listed in this Chapter's Specifications. Reconnect the electrical connector.

Notes

Notes

Chapter 7 Part A
Manual transaxle

Contents

Specifications

General

Lubricant type and capacity.. See Chapter 1

Torque specifications   Ft-lbs

Transaxle-to-engine bolts 35
Transaxle mount bolts .... See Chapter 2A
Check/fill and drain plugs .... See Chapter 1

1   General information

1   The vehicles covered in this manual are equipped with either a 5-speed manual transaxle, a 6-speed automatic transaxle, or a continuously variable-ratio (CVT) transaxle. Information on the manual transaxle is included in this Part of Chapter 7A. Service procedures for the automatic (and CVT) transaxles are contained in Chapter 7B.

2   The T355 manual transaxle is a compact, two-piece, lightweight aluminum alloy housing containing both the transmission and differential assemblies.

3   Because of the complexity, unavailability of replacement parts and special tools necessary, internal repair procedures for the manual transaxle are beyond the scope of this manual. The bulk of information in this Chapter is devoted to removal and installation procedures.

2   Shift cables - replacement, installation and adjustment

Warning: *These vehicles are equipped with airbags. Always disable the airbag system before working in the vicinity of any airbag system components to avoid the possibility of accidental deployment of the airbag(s), which could cause personal injury (see Chapter 12).*

Removal

1   Disconnect the cable from the negative terminal of the battery (see Chapter 5).

2   Remove the center console (see Chapter 11).

3   Remove the shift lever assembly (see Section 3).

4   Remove the clip securing the selector cable and shift cable to the shift lever bracket and slide the cable off of the lever (see Section 3).

5   Pull the carpet back and disconnect the wiring to the occupant restraint control module then remove the module fasteners and module.

6   Remove the grommet plate-to-floorpan fasteners.

7   Remove the air filter housing (see Chapter 4).

8   Remove the battery and battery tray (see Chapter 5).

9   Use two flat blade screwdrivers and carefully pry the shift and selector cables from the shifter lever at the transaxle.

10   Remove both cable retaining clips and remove the cables from the bracket.

11   Raise the vehicle and place it securely on jackstands.

12   Installation is the reverse of removal, noting the following points:

    a) Install new cable retaining clips.

    b) Use a rubber mallet and strike the knob to engage it to the lever.

3   Shift lever - removal and installation

Warning: *These vehicles are equipped with airbags. Always disable the airbag system before working in the vicinity of any airbag system components to avoid the possibility of accidental deployment of the airbag(s), which could cause personal injury (see Chapter 12).*

1   On 2009 and earlier models, firmly pull up on the gearshift knob and remove it from the lever.

2   Detach the shifter lever boot from the center console.

3   Remove the center console (see Chapter 11).

4   Pull the shift cable out of the shift lever grommet, then disconnect the cable by removing the retaining clip at the base of the shift lever and slide the cable off of the lever.

5   Unbolt the four shift lever riser bolts and remove the shift lever assembly from the vehicle.

6   Installation is the reverse of removal. Carefully tap on the knob with a rubber mallet to seat it.

4   Back-up light switch - replacement

Note: *The back-up light switch is located on the bottom front side of the transaxle.*

1   Raise the vehicle and support it securely on jackstands.

2   Disconnect the electrical connector from the back-up light switch.

3   Unscrew the switch from the case.

4   Wrap the threads of the new switch with Teflon tape, or equivalent.

5   Screw in the new switch and tighten it securely.

6   Connect the electrical connector.

7   Check the operation of the back-up lights.

5   Transaxle mounts - check and replacement

1   Refer to Chapter 2A, Section 17 for the mount check and replacement procedure.

6   Manual transaxle - removal and installation

Removal

1   Open the hood and place protective covers on the front fenders and cowl. Special fender covers are available, but an old bedspread or blankets will also work.

2   Remove the battery and battery tray (see Chapter 5).

Caution: *Always disconnect the negative cable first and hook it up last or the battery may be shorted by the tool being used to loosen the cable clamps.*

3   Remove the air filter housing assembly (see Chapter 4).

4   Remove the throttle body (see Chapter 4).

5   Disconnect the shift cables from the transaxle (see Section 2).

6   Disconnect the harness connectors from the vehicle speed sensor and back-up light switch.

7   Disconnect the master cylinder hydraulic line from the quick connect fitting at the bracket (see Chapter 8).

8   Remove the transaxle-to-engine upper bolts.

9   Loosen the driveaxle/hub nuts (see Chapter 8) and front wheel lug nuts. Raise the vehicle and place it securely on jackstands. Remove both front wheels.

Note: *Depending on the type of wheels installed on the vehicle and the thickness of the socket you are using, you may have to loosen the driveaxle/hub nuts after the wheels have been removed.*

10   Support the engine from above with a hoist, or place a floor jack under the oil pan. Place a wood block on the jack head to spread the load on the oil pan.

11   Drain the transaxle lubricant (see Chapter 1).

12   Remove the driveaxles (see Chapter 8).

13   Remove the transfer case, if equipped (see Chapter 7C).

14   Remove the starter (see Chapter 5).

15   Remove the lower inspection cover.

16   If the modular clutch assembly is to be reinstalled, match-mark the clutch assembly to the driveplate at the slotted tolerance hole, and remove the four modular clutch assembly-to-driveplate bolts (see illustration). To gain access to each bolt, rotate the engine from the drivebelt end of the engine using the crankshaft damper/pulley bolt. Remove all four bolts and discard them. Use a screwdriver placed in the ring gear of the driveplate to keep the crankshaft from turning during removal of the bolts.

17   Support the transaxle with a transmission jack, if available, or use a floor jack. Secure the transaxle to the jack using straps or chains so it doesn't fall off during removal.

18   Remove the transaxle crossmember mounting bolts and mount through-bolts (see Chapter 2A, Section 17).

19   Remove the lower transaxle clutch housing-to-engine bolts. Make sure all clutch housing-to-engine bolts are removed.

20   Make a final check that all wires, hoses and brackets have been disconnected from the transaxle, then with the engine properly supported, carefully lower the transaxle and remove it from under the vehicle. Make sure you keep the transaxle level as you maneuver it out or the modular clutch assembly may fall out.

Note: *If necessary have someone help with the removal procedure.*

Installation

21   With the transaxle secured to the hoist/floor jack as on removal, raise it into position, and then carefully slide it onto the engine.

22   Once the transaxle is successfully mated to the engine, insert as many of the mounting bolts as possible, and tighten them progressively, to draw the transaxle fully onto the locating dowels.

23   Install the remaining transaxle-to-engine bolts, and tighten all of them to the specified torque.

24   Install the driveplate-to-clutch module bolts.

25   Once the transaxle mount has been reinstalled, the engine hoist or supporting jack can be removed.

26   The remainder of installation is a reversal of removal, noting the following points:

   a) *Install the starter motor as described in Chapter 5.*

   b) *Install the driveaxles as described in Chapter 8.*

   c) *Fill the transaxle with the specified lubricant (see Chapter 1).*

   d) *Road test the vehicle and check for proper transaxle operation and check for fluid leaks.*

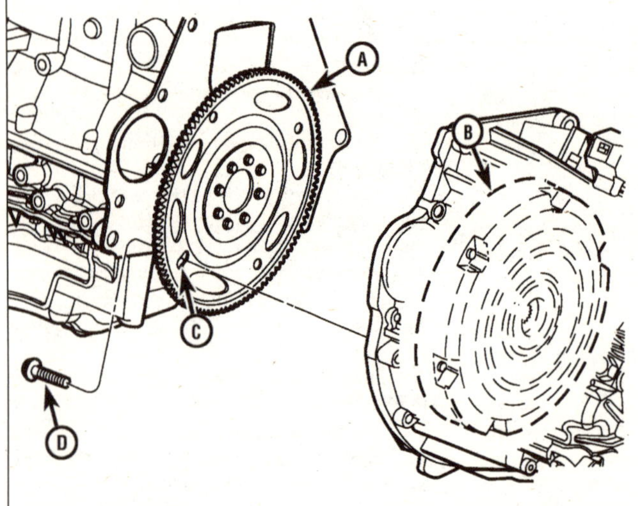

6.16 Modular clutch-to-driveplate bolts

A   Driveplate
B   Modular clutch assembly
C   Tolerance hole
D   Bolt

7 Manual transaxle overhaul - general information

1 Overhauling a manual transaxle unit is a difficult and involved job for the home mechanic. In addition to assembling and reassembling many small parts, clearances must be precisely measured and, if necessary, changed by selecting shims and spacers. Internal transaxle components are also often difficult to obtain and in many instances, extremely expensive. Because of this, if the transaxle develops a fault or becomes noisy, the best course of action is to have the unit overhauled by a transmission specialist or to obtain an exchange reconditioned unit.

2 Nevertheless, it is not impossible for the more experienced mechanic to overhaul the transaxle if the special tools are available and the job is carried out in a deliberate step-by-step manner, to ensure that nothing is overlooked.

3 The tools necessary for an overhaul include internal and external snap-ring pliers, bearing pullers, a slide hammer, a set of pin punches, a dial test indicator and possibly a hydraulic press. In addition, a large, sturdy workbench and a vise will be required.

4 During dismantling of the transaxle, make careful notes of how each component is fitted to make reassembly easier and accurate.

5 Before disassembling the transaxle, it will help if you have some idea of where the problem lies. Certain problems can be closely related to specific areas in the transaxle which can make component examination and replacement easier. Refer to the *Troubleshooting* section in this manual for more information.

Notes

Chapter 7 Part B
Automatic transaxle

Contents

Specifications

General

Lubricant type and capacity... See Chapter 1

Torque specifications
Ft-lbs (unless otherwise indicated)

Note: *One foot-pound (ft-lb) of torque is equivalent to 12 inch-pounds (in-lbs) of torque. Torque values below approximately 15 ft-lbs are expressed in inch-pounds, since most foot-pound torque wrenches are not accurate at these smaller values.*

CVT transaxle
Shift cable adjustment bolt	120 in-lbs
Torque converter-to-driveplate bolts	35
Transaxle-to-engine bolts	35
Transaxle crossmember bolts	55
Oil cooler mounting bolts	37 in-lbs

6F24 transaxle
Shift cable adjustment lever bolt	71 in-lbs
Stamped transaxle mounting brace-to-crossmember bolts	70
Torque converter-to-driveplate bolts	27
Transaxle-to-engine bolts	
M12 x 1.25 x 65.00 bolt	69
M10 x 1.25 x 45.00 bolt	37
M12 x 1.25 x 80.0 bolt	70
M12 x 1.25 x 50.00 bolt	69

1   General information

1   These models are equipped with the Continuously Variable Transmission (CVT) or the 6F24 (6-speed) automatic transaxle. The automatic transaxle and the differential are housed in a compact, lightweight, two-piece aluminum alloy housing.

2   These models are equipped with a Transmission Control Module (TCM) which is the brain of the transaxle. The TCM monitors engine and transaxle operating parameters through numerous sensors, then generates output signals to various relays and solenoids to regulate hydraulic pressures, optimize drivability, provide efficient torque management and maintain maximum fuel economy. All models incorporate the TCM into the PCM. The TCM is part of the On-Board Diagnostic system (OBD-II). For more information, see Chapter 6.

3   Because of the complexity of the automatic transaxles and the specialized equipment necessary to perform most service operations, this Chapter contains only those procedures related to general diagnosis, adjustment and removal and installation procedures.

4   If the transaxle requires major repair work, it should be left to a dealer service department or an automotive or transmission repair shop. Once properly diagnosed you can, however, remove and install the transaxle yourself and save the expense, even if the repair work is done by a transmission shop.

2 Diagnosis - general

1 Automatic transaxle malfunctions may be caused by five general conditions:

 a) *Poor engine performance*
 b) *Improper adjustment*
 c) *Hydraulic malfunctions*
 d) *Mechanical malfunctions*
 e) *Malfunctions in the computer or its signal network*

2 Diagnosis of these problems should always begin with a check of the easily repaired items: fluid level and condition (see Chapter 1), shift cable adjustment and shift lever installation. Next, perform a road test to determine if the problem has been corrected or if more diagnosis is necessary. If the problem persists after the preliminary tests and corrections are completed, additional diagnosis should be performed by a dealer service department or other qualified transmission repair shop. Refer to *Troubleshooting* at the front of this manual for information on symptoms of transaxle problems.

Preliminary checks

3 Drive the vehicle to warm the transaxle to normal operating temperature.
4 Check the fluid level as described in Chapter 1:

 a) *If the fluid level is unusually low, add enough fluid to bring the level within the designated area of the dipstick, then check for external leaks (see following).*
 b) *If the fluid level is abnormally high, drain off the excess, then check the drained fluid for contamination by coolant. The presence of engine coolant in the automatic transaxle fluid indicates that a failure has occurred in the internal radiator oil cooler walls that separate the coolant from the transaxle fluid (see Chapter 3).*
 c) *If the fluid is foaming, drain it and refill the transaxle, then check for coolant in the fluid, or a high fluid level.*

5 Check the engine idle speed.
Note: *If the engine is malfunctioning, do not proceed with the preliminary checks until it has been repaired and runs normally.*

6 Check and adjust the shift cable, if necessary (see Section 4).
7 If hard shifting is experienced, inspect the shift cable under the center console and at the manual lever on the transaxle (see Section 4).

Fluid leak diagnosis

8 Most fluid leaks are easy to locate visually. Repair usually consists of replacing a seal or gasket. If a leak is difficult to find, the following procedure may help.
9 Identify the fluid. Make sure it's transaxle fluid and not engine oil or brake fluid.
10 Try to pinpoint the source of the leak. Drive the vehicle several miles, then park it over a large sheet of cardboard. After a minute or two, you should be able to locate the leak by determining the source of the fluid dripping onto the cardboard.
11 Make a careful visual inspection of the suspected component and the area immediately around it. Pay particular attention to gasket mating surfaces. A mirror is often helpful for finding leaks in areas that are hard to see.
12 If the leak still cannot be found, clean the suspected area thoroughly with a degreaser or solvent, then dry it thoroughly.
13 Drive the vehicle for several miles at normal operating temperature and varying speeds. After driving the vehicle, visually inspect the suspected component again.
14 Once the leak has been located, the cause must be determined before it can be properly repaired. If a gasket is replaced but the sealing flange is bent, the new gasket will not stop the leak. The bent flange must be straightened.
15 Before attempting to repair a leak, check to make sure that the following conditions are corrected or they may cause another leak.
Note: *Some of the following conditions cannot be fixed without highly specialized tools and expertise. Such problems must be referred to a qualified transmission shop or a dealer service department.*

Gasket leaks

16 Check the pan periodically. Make sure the bolts are tight, no bolts are missing, the gasket is in good condition and the pan is flat (dents in the pan may indicate damage to the valve body inside).
17 If the pan gasket is leaking, the fluid level or the fluid pressure may be too high, the vent may be plugged, the pan bolts may be too tight, the pan sealing flange may be warped, the sealing surface of the transaxle housing may be damaged, the gasket may be damaged or the transaxle casting may be cracked or porous. If sealant instead of gasket material has been used to form a seal between the pan and the transaxle housing, it may be the wrong type of sealant.

Seal leaks

18 If a transaxle seal is leaking, the fluid level may be too high, the vent may be plugged, the seal bore may be damaged, the seal itself may be damaged or improperly installed, the surface of the shaft protruding through the seal may be damaged or a loose bearing may be causing excessive shaft movement.
19 Make sure the dipstick tube seal is in good condition and the tube is properly seated. Periodically check the area around the sensors for leakage. If transaxle fluid is evident, check the seals for damage.

Case leaks

20 If the case itself appears to be leaking, the casting is porous and will have to be repaired or replaced.
21 Make sure the oil cooler hose fittings are tight and in good condition.

Fluid comes out vent pipe or fill tube

22 If this condition occurs, the possible causes are: the transaxle is overfilled; there is coolant in the fluid; the dipstick is incorrect; the vent is plugged or the drain-back holes are plugged.

3 Driveaxle oil seals - replacement

Note: *On AWD models, the right-side driveaxle oil seal replacement procedure is covered in Chapter 7C.*
1 The driveaxle oil seals are located on the sides of the transaxle, where the inner ends of the driveaxles are splined into the differential side gears. If you suspect that a driveaxle oil seal is leaking, raise the vehicle and support it securely on jackstands. If the seal is leaking, you'll see lubricant on the side of the transaxle, below the seal.
2 Remove the driveaxle or driveaxle/intermediate shaft (see Chapter 8).
3 Using a screwdriver or prybar, carefully pry the oil seal out of the transaxle bore (see illustration).
4 If the oil seal cannot be removed with a screwdriver or prybar, a special oil seal removal tool (available at auto parts stores) will be required.

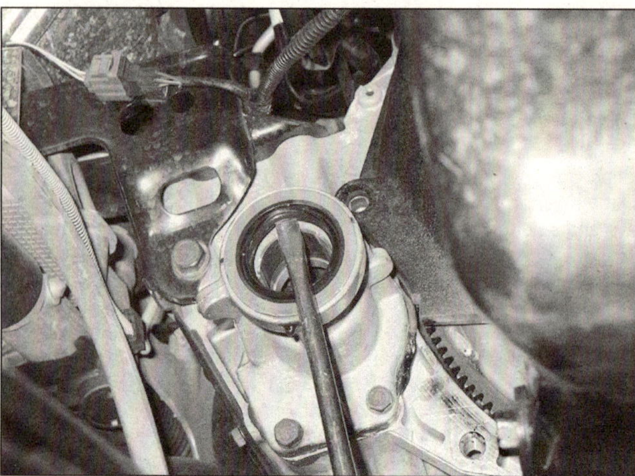

3.3 Using a large screwdriver or prybar, carefully pry the oil seal out of the transaxle

3.5 Using a seal installer, large section of pipe or a large deep socket as a drift, drive the new seal squarely into the bore and make sure that it's completely seated; lubricate the lip of the new seal with multi-purpose grease

4.4 Pry the shift cable from the manual lever using a trim panel tool or flat-bladed screwdriver

4.5a Use pliers to squeeze the retaining clip, then pull the shift cable up off the bracket on the transaxle

4.5b Pull the cable and insulator out and up to release it from the wire mount

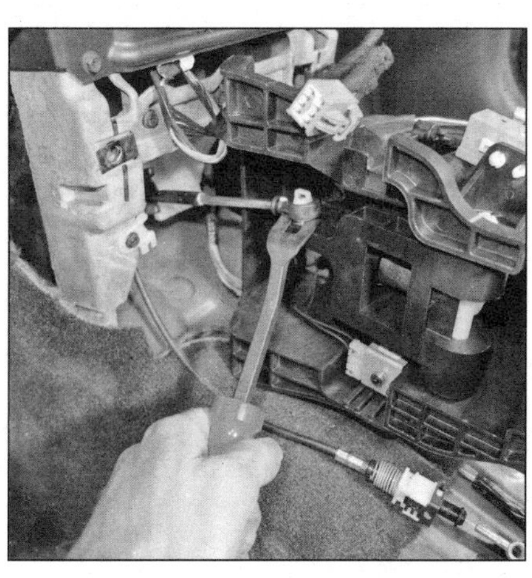

4.7a Pry the shift cable from the shifter lever using a trim panel tool or flat-bladed screwdriver

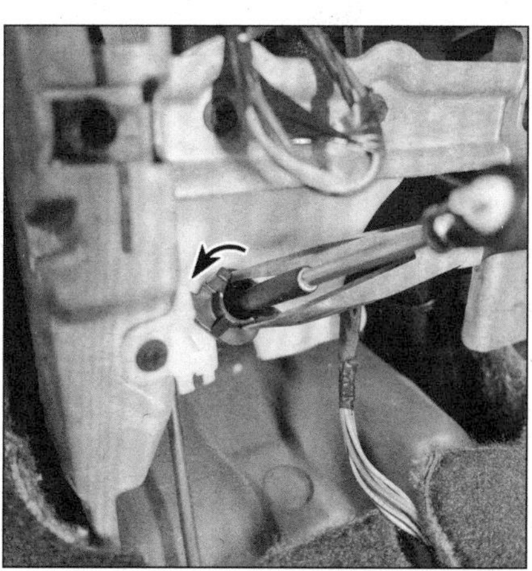

4.7b Using needle-nose pliers, unscrew the cable fastener…

5   Using a seal installer, install the new oil seal. Drive it into the bore squarely until it bottoms (see illustration).

6   Install the driveaxle or intermediate shaft/driveaxle (see Chapter 8).

7   Check the fluid level (see Chapter 1) and adjust as necessary.

---

4   Shift cable - removal, installation and adjustment

Warning: *The models covered by this manual are equipped with a Supplemental Restraint System (SRS), more commonly known as airbags. Always disarm the airbag system before working in the vicinity of any airbag system component to avoid the possibility of accidental deployment of the airbag, which could cause personal injury (see Chapter 12). Do not use a memory saving device to preserve*

the PCM's memory when working on or near airbag system components.
Warning: *Do not attempt this procedure until the vehicle has cooled completely. The exhaust system components must be cold to avoid physical harm.*

Removal and installation

1   Shift the vehicle into Park.

2   Remove the battery and battery tray (see Chapter 5).

3   Remove the air filter housing (see Chapter 4).

4   Disconnect the shift cable from the shift lever (see illustration).

5   Disconnect the shift cable from the bracket (see illustrations).

6   Remove the center console (see Chapter 11).

7   Disconnect the shift cable from the shifter assembly (see illustrations).

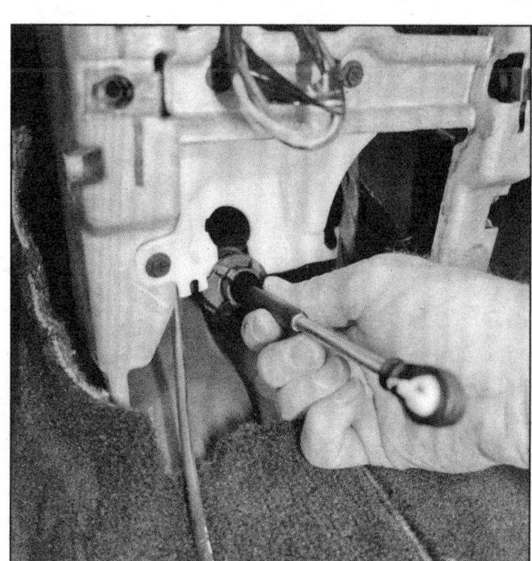

4.7c … then remove the cable from the bracket

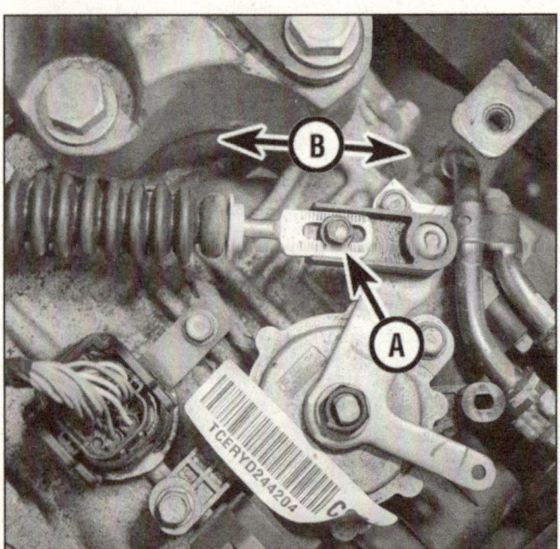

4.15 Loosen the shift cable adjustment bolt (A) and slide the cable (B) to adjust

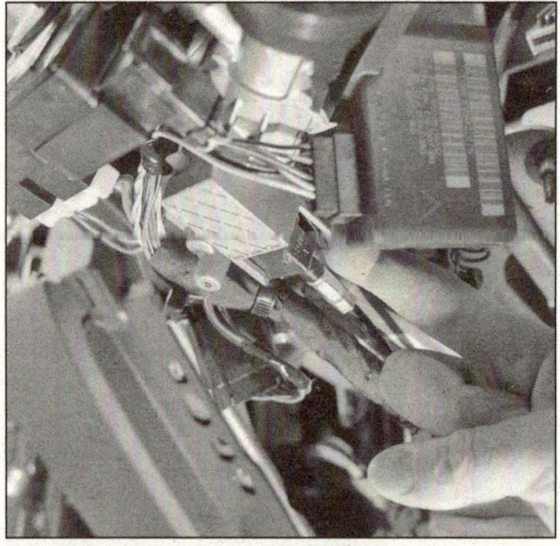

5.12a Depress the retaining tab…

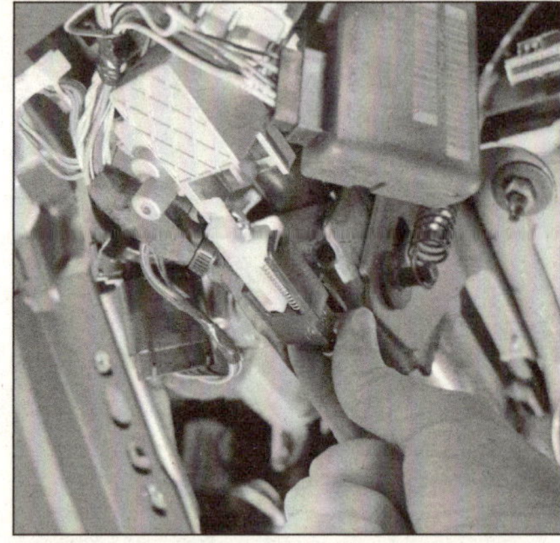

5.12b … then disconnect the BTSI cable from the lock cylinder housing

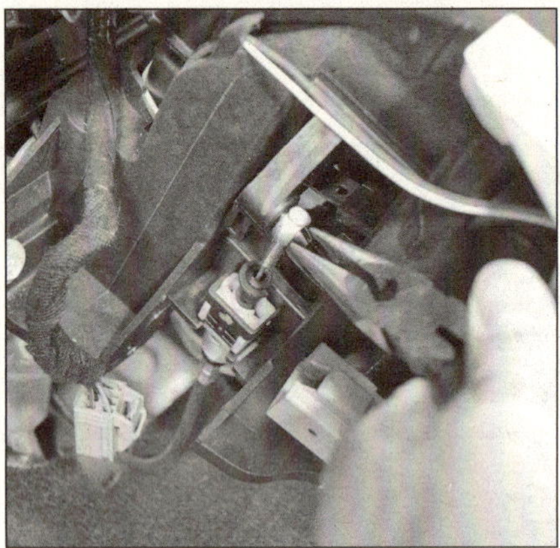

5.15 Use a pair of pliers to squeeze the retaining tab closed and slide the BTSI cable end off of the tab

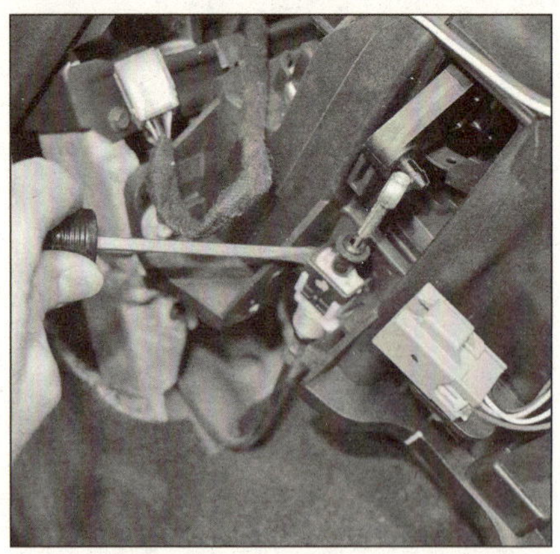

5.16 Disconnect the cable from the shifter base

8   Raise the vehicle and support it securely on jackstands.

9   Working under the vehicle, remove the grommet from the floorpan and pull shift cable out of opening.

10   Carefully unfasten the cable from the retainers under the vehicle.

11   Remove the cable from the vehicle.

12   Installation is the reverse of removal. Feed the shift cable into the passenger compartment and ensure the grommet is installed properly. Lubricate the grommet if necessary to ensure proper installation.

Adjustment

13   Park the vehicle on a flat surface and set the parking brake.

14   Place the shift lever in the Park position. Remove the key from the ignition.

15   Loosen the shift cable adjustment bolt at the transaxle shift lever (see illustration).

16   Make sure the shift lever at the transaxle is in the Park position by pulling it forward all the way. The parking pawl must be engaged when adjusting the cable. If applied, release the parking brake, then rock the vehicle back and forth to ensure that the parking pawl is

fully engaged.

17   Tighten the shift cable adjustment bolt to the torque listed in this Chapter's Specifications.

18   Check the shift lever for proper operation. It should operate smoothly without binding. The engine should start only in the Park or Neutral positions.

19   Shift the transaxle into all gear positions to make sure the cable is functioning properly. Readjust if necessary.

---

5   Brake Transmission Shift Interlock (BTSI) system - description, check, replacement and adjustment

---

Description

1   The Brake Transmission Shift Interlock (BTSI) system prevents the shift lever from being moved out of Park unless the brake pedal is depressed. The BTSI system also prevents the ignition key from being turned to the Lock or Accessory position unless the shift lever is fully locked into the Park position.

Check

2   Verify that the ignition key can be removed only when the shift lever is in the Park position.

3   When the shift lever is in the Park position, you should be able to rotate the ignition key from Off to Lock. But when the shift lever is in any gear position other than Park (including Neutral), you should not be able to rotate the ignition key to the Lock position.

4   You should be able to move the shift lever out of the Park position when the ignition key is turned to the Off position.

5   You should not be able to move the shift lever out of the PARK position when the ignition key is turned to the Run or Start position until you depress the brake pedal.

6   With the shifter in any gear selection other than Park, you should not be able to turn the key back to the ACC or Lock position.

7   Once in gear, with the ignition key in the Run position, you should be able to move the shift lever between gears, or put it into Neutral or Park, without depressing the brake pedal.

8   If the BTSI system doesn't operate as described, the cable requires adjustment as outlined below.

Component replacement

BTSI cable

9   Insert the key into the ignition switch and turn it to the ACC position.

10   Disconnect the cable from the negative terminal of the battery (see Chapter 5).

11   Remove the driver's side knee bolster and hush panel (see Chapter 11).

12   Detach the BTSI cable from the ignition lock cylinder housing (see illustrations).

13   Remove the center floor console (see Chapter 11).

14   Remove the HVAC ducts as necessary to allow removal of the cable.

15   Release the BTSI cable from the lever (see illustration).

16   Disconnect the BTSI cable from the shifter assembly (see illustration).

17   Remove the cable from the vehicle.

5.27 Remove the BTSI solenoid mounting screws from the housing

5.28 Disconnect the BTSI solenoid connector and remove the solenoid from the shifter base

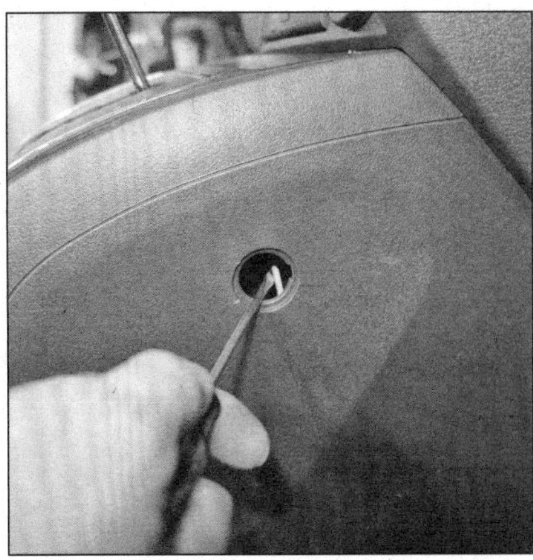

5.36 Move the BTSI solenoid bypass lever forward as you shift the gear select lever out of park

18   Installation is reverse of removal. Adjust the BTSI cable (see Steps 19 through 24).

BTSI cable adjustment

19   Remove center floor console (see Chapter 11).
20   Place the shifter assembly in the Park position.
21   Insert the key into the ignition and turn it to the Lock position. Remove the key from the ignition switch.
22   NEW CABLE: Remove the lock pin and the cable will adjust automatically. Once adjusted, push the cable locking clip down to secure the adjustment.
23   USED/EXISTING CABLE: Pull up on the cable locking clipand the cable will adjust automatically. Once adjusted, push the clip down to secure the adjustment.
24   Verify correct operation as outlined above and readjust as necessary.

BTSI solenoid

25   Disconnect the negative battery cable from the remote ground terminal (see Chapter 5).
26   Remove the center floor console (see Chapter 11).
27   Working on the passenger's side of the shifter assembly, remove the BTSI solenoid fasteners (see illustration).
28   Rotate the shifter housing and disconnect the BTSI solenoid electrical connector then remove the solenoid from the shifter assembly (see illustration).
Note: *Disconnect the BTSI cable from the shifter assembly if necessary (see Steps 15 and 16).*
29   Installation is the reverse of removal.
30   Verify correct operation as outlined above and adjust BTSI cable if necessary (see Steps 19 through 24).

Steering column BTSI mechanism

31   Remove the upper and lower steering column covers (see Chapter 11).

32   Disconnect the BTSI cable from the steering column BTSI mechanism (see Step 12).
33   Remove the two screws attaching the steering column BTSI mechanism.
34   Remove the steering column BTSI mechanism.
35   Installation is reverse of removal. Adjust the BTSI cable as necessary (see Steps 19 through 24).

Bypassing BTSI solenoid

Note: *In the event that the vehicle needs to be placed into Neutral and moved while deep into a repair, and the transaxle won't come out of gear, there is a simple workaround for this without the need to install the battery. Make sure the vehicle is on level ground and/or can be safely stopped when doing this.*
Note: *This also serves as a temporary fix if the BTSI components aren't functioning properly and the transaxle needs to be placed in whichever gear necessary to drive the vehicle. Make absolutely sure that the transaxle can be shifted safely while the vehicle is driven, and diagnose and fix the problems related to*

the BTSI components as soon as possible (see previous Steps).
36   On the passenger side of the shift housing you'll find a small round cover that can be pried out. There should be a flat plastic lever visible in the hole. Using a screwdriver or your finger, move the lever forward (toward the front of the vehicle) to allow the transmission shift select lever to be placed into Neutral (see illustration).

---

6   Shift lever - removal and installation

---

1   Disconnect the negative battery cable from the remote ground terminal (see Chapter 5).
2   Remove the center floor console (see Chapter 11).
3   Detach the shift cable (see Section 4) and the BTSI cable (see Section 5) from the shift lever.
4   Remove the shifter asssembly mounting bolts and detach the shifter from the floor (see illustration).

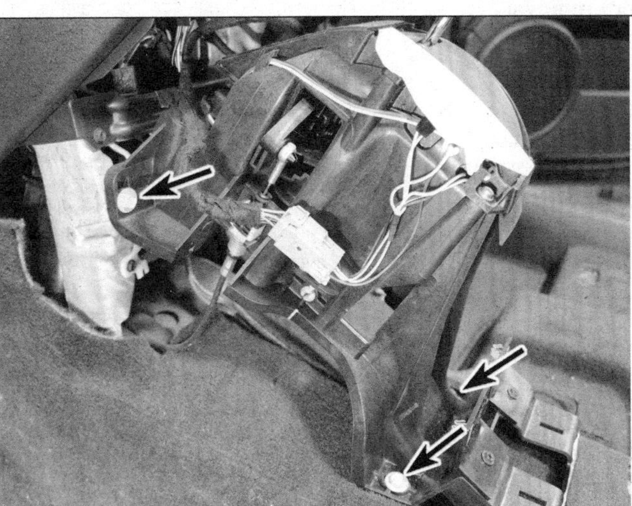

6.4 Shift lever mounting bolts - 3 of 4 shown

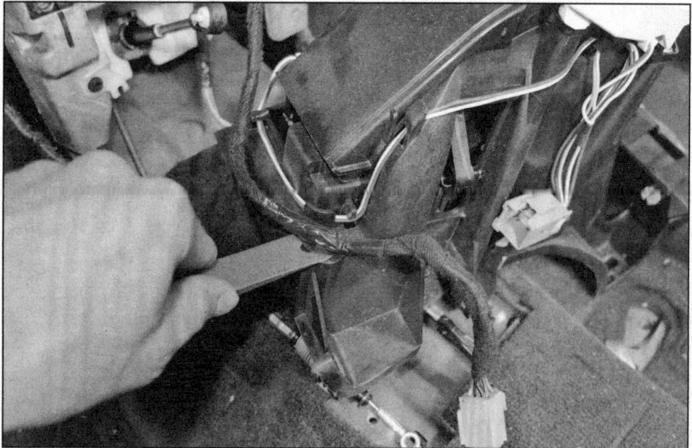

6.5 Use a trim tool to remove the wiring harness retainers

8.5a Disconnect the wiring harness retainers…

8.5b … then remove the air filter housing bracket fasteners

8.8 Unplug the transaxle electrical connectors

5   Disconnect the electrical connectors and harness retainers (see illustration) to the shifter.
6   Installation is the reverse of removal.
7   Adjust the BTSI cable, if necessary (see Section 5) and the shift cable (see Section 4).

7   Transaxle oil cooler - removal and installation

6F24 (6-speed) models

1   The transaxle oil cooler and air conditioning condenser are serviced as an assembly. See Chapter 3 for the condenser removal and installation procedure.

CVT transaxles

2   Loosen the left-front wheel lug nuts, then raise the vehicle and support it securely on jackstands. Remove the left-front wheel.
3   Remove the left-front inner fender splash shield (see Chapter 11).
4   Drain the engine coolant (see Chapter 1).
5   Disconnect and cap the coolant lines to the cooler, then remove the transaxle cooler lines and cap all the ends.

6   Disconnect and cap the transaxle cooler lines and ends of the cooler.
7   Remove the transaxle cooler mounting bolts and remove the cooler from the side of the transaxle.
8   Remove the cooler fluid filter and discard the sealing ring from the cooler.
Note: *Not all models are equipped with a fluid filter.*
9   Install a new filter into the transaxle, if equipped.
10   Install a new O-ring onto the cooler, then place the cooler onto the transaxle. Install the mounting bolts and tighten the bolts to the torque listed in this Chapter's Specifications.
11   Installation is the reverse of removal.
12   Refill the cooling system and check the transaxle fluid level (see Chapter 1).

8   Automatic transaxle - removal and installation

Removal

1   Disconnect the negative battery cable from the battery (see Chapter 5).

2   Loosen the front wheel lug nuts and the driveaxle/hub nuts.
Note: *Depending on the type of wheels installed on the vehicle and the thickness of the socket you are using, you may have to loosen the driveaxle/hub nuts after the wheels have been removed (see Chapter 8).*
3   Remove the air filter housing and air inlet tube from the vehicle (see Chapter 4).
4   Remove the battery and battery tray (see Chapter 5).
5   Remove the air filter housing mounting bracket fasteners, then disconnect the harness clips (see illustrations) and remove the bracket.

6F24 (six-speed) models

6   Disconnect the shift cable from the shift lever and the bracket (see Section 4).
7   Drain the transaxle fluid (see Chapter 1).
8   Unplug the electrical connectors from the transaxle solenoid and transaxle range sensor (see illustration).
9   Remove the vent tube bracket bolt and move the vent tube and bracket out of the way.
10   Remove the starter motor (see Chap-

8.15 Remove the transaxle mount bolts and mount through-bolt

8.16 Remove the transaxle cooler line clamps

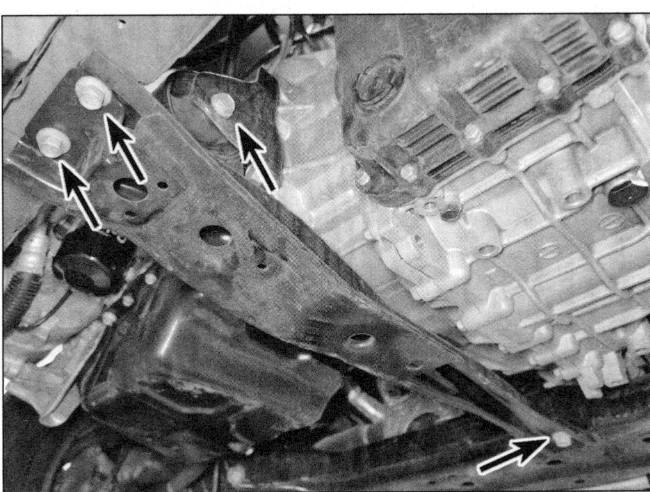

8.20 Longitudinal crossmember mounting bolt locations

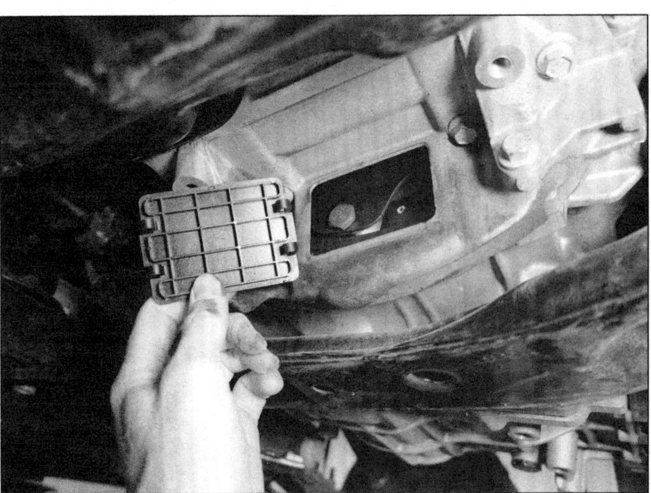

8.22 Torque converter cover removed

ter 5), then remove the ground cable bolt hidden under the thermostat housing/hoses.

11 Raise the vehicle and support it securely on jackstands. Remove the front wheels.

12 Remove the lower splash shields (see Chapter 1).

13 On AWD models, remove the transfer case (see Chapter 7C).

14 Place a floor jack under the transaxle for support, then slightly lift the transaxle to take the weight off of the mount.

15 Remove the bolts attaching the mount and mount bracket to the transaxle case (see illustration).

16 Using pliers, remove the transaxle cooler line clamps (see illustration) then disconnect and plug the cooler lines. Always replace the cooler line clamps with new ones.

17 Remove the front driveaxles (see Chapter 8).

18 Support the engine from above with a hoist or engine support fixture.

19 Remove the front mount through-bolt.

20 Remove the longitudinal crossmember (see illustration).

21 Remove the bolts attaching the front mount support and mount to the engine and the transaxle and remove the mount.

22 Remove the torque converter cover (see illustration).

23 Mark the relationship of the torque converter to the driveplate so they can be installed in the same position.

24 Wedge a screwdriver between the teeth on the driveplate and the opening to prevent the engine from rotating, then remove the torque converter-to-driveplate bolts.

25 After all the bolts are removed, push the torque converter into the bellhousing so it doesn't stay with the engine when the transaxle is removed.

26 If not already done, support the transaxle with a transmission jack, if available, or use a floor jack. Secure the transaxle to the jack using straps or chains so it doesn't fall off during removal.

27 Lower the engine/transaxle slightly and remove the engine-to-transaxle bolts (see illustrations).

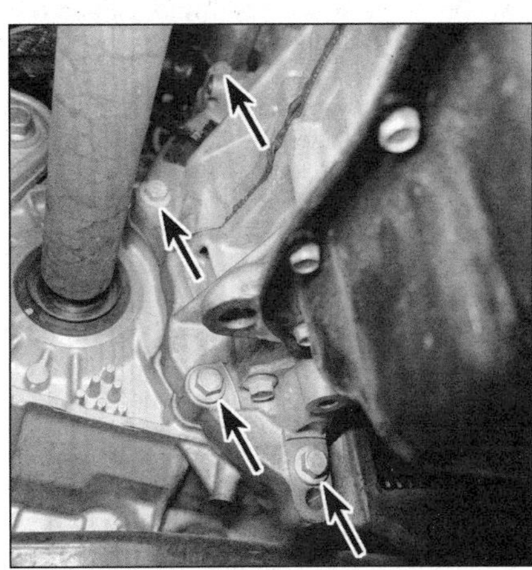

8.27a Rear engine-to-transaxle bolts

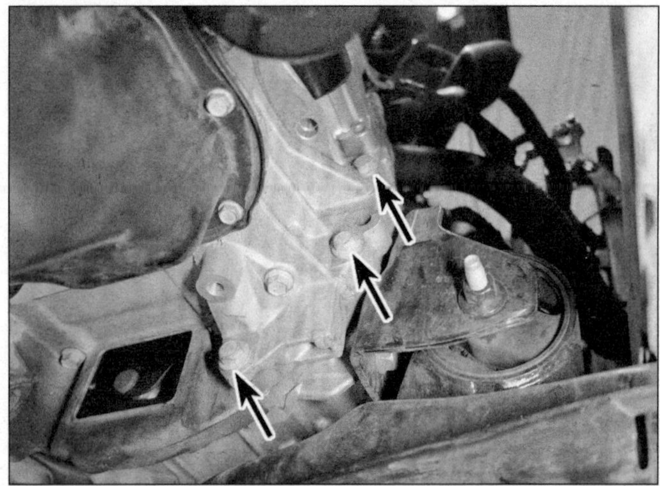

8.27b Front engine-to-transaxle bolts

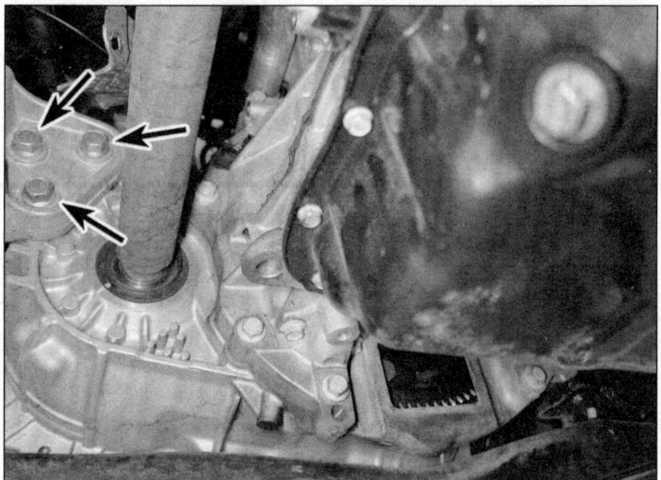

8.28 Rear transaxle mount bolt locations

28　Remove the bolts holding the rear transaxle mount to the transaxle (see illustration).

29　Make a final check that all connectors, harnesses and hoses have been disconnected from the transaxle, then move the transaxle jack toward the side of the vehicle until the transaxle is clear of the engine locating dowels. Make sure you keep the transaxle level as you do this.

CVT transaxle

30　Remove the coolant reservoir (see Chapter 3).

31　Remove the heater hose bracket bolts and move the hoses back. Clearly label, and unplug, all electrical connectors from the transaxle.

32　Disconnect the shift cable from the manual lever and bracket (see Section 4).

33　On models equipped with a transaxle mounted fluid cooler, disconnect and cap the coolant lines to the cooler then remove the transaxle cooler lines and cap all the ends.

34　On models, equipped with a transaxle cooler bypass valve, disconnect lines to the valves.

35　Drain the transaxle fluid (see Chapter 1).

36　Disconnect the speed sensors and the range sensor at the transaxle (see Chapter 6).

37　Remove the throttle body and throttle body support bracket (see Chapter 4).

38　Remove the bolts attaching the stamped transaxle mounting brace.

39　Remove the starter motor (see Chapter 5).

40　Remove the upper transaxle-to-engine bolts.

41　Support the engine from above with a hoist or engine support fixture, or place a jack and a block of wood under the transaxle.

42　Remove the left transaxle mount and bracket and disconnect the ground cable (if equipped).

43　Remove the three bolts attaching the left mount to the bracket.

44　Remove the lower splash shields.

45　Remove both driveaxles (see Chapter 8).

46　Unbolt the lower transaxle mount from the subframe and bracket and remove.

47　Remove the four bolts attaching the lower transaxle mount bracket to the engine and remove the bracket.

48　Remove the torque converter cover.

49　Mark the relationship of the torque converter to the driveplate so they can be installed in the same position.

50　Remove the torque converter-to-driveplate bolts. After all the bolts are removed, push the torque converter into the bellhousing so it doesn't stay with the engine when the transaxle is removed.

51　Disconnect the oxygen sensor connector located near the differential of the transaxle.

52　Support the transaxle with a transmission jack, if available, or use a floor jack. Secure the transaxle to the jack using straps or chains so it doesn't fall off during removal.

53　Remove the transaxle upper mount-to-bracket bolts (see Chapter 2A). Remove the upper transaxle-to-engine bolts.

54　Remove the front transaxle/engine bracket and the rear engine mount and bracket (see Chapter 2A).

55　Remove the lower transaxle-to-engine bolts.

56　Make a final check that all connectors, harnesses and hoses have been disconnected from the transaxle, then move the transaxle jack toward the side of the vehicle until the transaxle is clear of the engine locating dowels. Make sure you keep the transaxle level as you do this.

Installation

57　Installation is the reverse of removal, noting the following points:

Note: *Wedge a screwdriver between the teeth on the driveplate and the opening to prevent the engine from rotating while tightening the torque converter bolts.*

a)　*As the torque converter is reinstalled, ensure that the drive tangs at the center of the torque converter hub engage with the recesses in the automatic transaxle fluid pump inner gear. This can be confirmed by turning the torque converter while pushing it toward the transaxle. If it isn't fully engaged, it will clunk into place.*

b)　*When installing the transaxle, make sure the match marks you made on the torque converter and driveplate line up.*

c)　*Install all of the driveplate-to-torque converter bolts before tightening any of them.*

d)　*Tighten the driveplate-to-converter bolts to the torque listed in this Chapter's Specifications.*

e)　*Tighten the transaxle mounting bolts to the torque listed in this Chapter's Specifications.*

f)　*Tighten the driveaxle/hub nuts to the torque listed in the Chapter 8 Specifications.*

g)　*Tighten the wheel lug nuts to the torque listed in the Chapter 1 Specifications.*

h)　*Fill the transaxle with the correct type and amount of fluid (see Chapter 1).*

i)　*Adjust the shift cable (see Section 4).*

9　Transaxle mounts - check and replacement

1　Refer to Chapter 2A, Section 17 for the mount check and replacement procedure.

10 Automatic transaxle overhaul - general information

1   In the event of a problem occurring, it will be necessary to establish whether the fault is electrical, mechanical or hydraulic in nature, before repair work can be contemplated. Diagnosis requires detailed knowledge of the transaxle's operation and construction, as well as access to specialized test equipment, and so is deemed to be beyond the scope of this manual. It is therefore essential that problems with the automatic transaxle are referred to a dealer service department or other qualified repair facility for assessment.

2   Note that a faulty transaxle should not be removed before the vehicle has been diagnosed by a knowledgeable technician equipped with the proper tools, as trouble-shooting must be performed with the transaxle installed in the vehicle.

Notes

Chapter 7 Part C
Transfer case

Contents

Specifications

Transfer case fluid type .... See Chapter 1

Torque specifications   Ft-lbs (unless otherwise indicated)

Note: *One foot-pound (ft-lb) of torque is equivalent to 12 inch-pounds (in-lbs) of torque. Torque values below approximately 15 foot-pounds are expressed in inch-pounds, because most foot-pound torque wrenches are not accurate at these smaller values.*

Drain/fill plugs	See Chapter 1
Vent shield bolt	17
Transmission bracket bolts	40
Transfer case-to-transaxle bolts	43

1   General information

1   Due to the complexity of the transfer case covered in this manual and the need for specialized equipment to perform most service operations, this Chapter contains only removal and Installation procedures.
2   If the transfer case requires major repair work, it should be taken to a dealer service department or an automotive or transmission repair shop. You can, however, remove and install the transfer case yourself and save the expense of that labor, even if the repair work is done by a transmission shop.

2   Output shaft seal - replacement

1   Raise the vehicle and support it securely on jackstands.
2   Remove the driveshaft (see Chapter 8).
3   Use a flatblade screwdriver to pry the seal out. Use care not to damage the sealing surfaces inside the transfer case.
4   Lubricate the lip of the new seal with multi-purpose grease.
5   Using a seal installer or a large deep socket as a drift, install the new oil seal. Drive it into the bore squarely and make sure it's completely seated.
6   Installation is the reverse of removal. Check the transfer case and transaxle fluid levels and fill as necessary (see Chapter 1).

3   Driveaxle oil seal (right side) - replacement

1   Loosen the right front wheel driveaxle/hub nut and wheel lug nuts. Raise the vehicle and support it securely on jackstands. Remove the wheel.
2   Remove the right side driveaxle and intermediate shaft (if equipped) (see Chapter 8).
3   Carefully pry out the driveaxle oil seal with a seal removal tool or a large screwdriver. Be careful not to damage or scratch the seal bore.
4   Using a seal installer or a large deep socket as a drift, install the new oil seal. Drive it into the bore squarely and make sure it's completely seated.
5   Lubricate the lip of the new seal with multi-purpose grease.
6   Install the right side driveaxle and inter-

mediate shaft (if equipped).
7   Check the transfer case fluid level and add some if necessary, to bring it to the appropriate level (see Chapter 1).

4   Extension housing dust shield - replacement

1   Loosen the right front wheel driveaxle/hub nut and the front wheel lug nuts. Raise the vehicle and support it securely on jackstands. Remove the wheels.
2   Remove the driveshaft (see Chapter 8).
3   Remove the extension housing bolts then pull the extension housing off and inspect the housing O-ring. If the O-ring has not been damaged it can be reused.
4   Drill holes in the input shaft seal and use screws and a slide hammer to remove the seal. Use care not to get metal shavings inside the transfer case.
5   Place the extension housing in a vice, then use a hammer and chisle, drive the dust shield off the end of the housing.
6   Lightly lubricate the new dust shield, then center the shield on the end of the extension housing.
7   Place a block of wood against the end of the dust shield and use a hammer to install the dust shield onto the extension housing. Drive it onto the housing squarely and make sure it's completely seated.
8   Installation is the reverse of removal.

5   Transfer case - removal and installation

Removal

1   Loosen the right front wheel driveaxle/hub nut and the front wheel lug nuts. Raise the vehicle and support it securely on jackstands. Remove the wheels.
2   Open the hood and remove the engine cover, then remove the air cleaner housing (see Chapter 4).
3   Remove the engine undercover, if equipped.
4   Drain the transfer case lubricant (see Chapter 1).
5   Remove the driveshaft (see Chapter 8).
Caution: *DO NOT allow the driveshaft to hang from the front, rear or center support bearing - always suppport the driveshaft. Damage to*

the joints, boots and or center support bearing may occur, resulting in vibration.
6   Remove the right driveaxle (see Chapter 8).
7   Remove the exhaust manifold or maniverter (see Chapter 2A), slide the manifold upwards and to the right and secure it in place using balling wire, or equivalent.
8   Remove the front mount through bolt for the front-to-rear crossmember.
9   Remove the front-to-rear crossmember to subframe bolts and lower the crossmember down.
10   Support the engine from above with a hoist or engine support fixture, or place a jack and a block of wood under the transaxle or engine oil pan.
11   Support the transfer case with a jack, jackstand or equivelent. Secure the transfer case so it does not fall and get damaged.
12   Disconnect any electrical connectors or vent hoses.
13   Remove the three upper transfer case mounting bolts.
14   Remove the three lower transfer case mounting bolts.
15   Raise the front of the engine slightly until the rear mount can be removed.
16   Carfully rotate the transfer case forward and down to remove it.

Installation

17   Installation is the reverse of removal, noting the following points:

a) *Install a new O-ring seal between the transfer case and transaxle.*
b) *Tighten the exhaust system fasteners to the torque listed in the Chapter 4 Specifications.*
c) *Tighten the driveshaft fasteners to the torque listed in the Chapter 8 Specifications.*
d) *Tighten the transfer case mounting bolts to the torque listed in this Chapter's Specifications.*
e) *Refill the transfer case and transaxle with the proper type and amount of lubricant (see Chapter 1).*
f) *Tighten the driveaxle/hub nut to the torque listed in the Chapter 8 Specifications.*
g) *Tighten the wheel lug nuts to the torque listed in the Chapter 1 Specifications.*

Chapter 8
Clutch and driveline

Contents

Specifications

Torque specifications
Ft-lbs

Note: *One foot-pound (ft-lb) of torque is equivalent to 12 inch-pounds (in-lbs) of torque. Torque values below approximately 15 foot-pounds are expressed in inch-pounds, because most foot-pound torque wrenches are not accurate at these smaller values.*

Clutch components
Clutch release cylinder bolts
Step 1	18 in-lbs
Step 2	44 in-lbs
Step 3	74 in-lbs
Clutch pressure plate bolts	23

Driveaxles
Driveaxle/hub nut (front or rear)*	180
Intermediate shaft bearing bracket fasteners	35
Wheel lug nuts	See Chapter 1

Driveshaft (AWD models)
Center support bearing mounting nuts	30
Center support bearing heat shield nuts	15
Driveshaft-to-rear differential bolts	43

Rear differential assembly (AWD models)
Differential drain/fill plugs	15
Differential-to-crossmember front bolts	75
Differential-to-crossmember rear bolt	75
Electronic controlled clutch (ECC) bolts	50
Pinion flange nut*	100

** Nut must be replaced*

1   General information

1   The information in this Chapter deals with the components from the rear of the engine to the wheels, except for the transaxle, which is dealt with in Chapter 7A and Chapter 7B, and the transfer case on AWD models, which is covered in Chapter 7C.

2   Since nearly all the procedures covered in this Chapter involve working under the vehicle, make sure it's securely supported on sturdy jackstands or a hoist where the vehicle can be easily raised and lowered.

2 Clutch - description and check

1 All vehicles with a manual transaxle use a single dry plate, diaphragm spring type clutch also referred to as a modular clutch assembly. The clutch disc has a splined hub which allows it to slide along the splines of the transaxle input shaft. The clutch and pressure plate are held in contact by spring pressure exerted by the diaphragm in the pressure plate. All models use a modular clutch assembly that includes a clutch assembly where the clutch pressure plate and friction disc are an integral unit and incorporates a self-adjusting design.

2 The clutch release system is operated by hydraulic pressure. The system consists of the clutch pedal, a master cylinder, the hydraulic line, the release cylinder and release bearing. The release cylinder and bearing are integral parts of a single assembly which is installed concentric to the input shaft and is bolted to the transaxle.

3 Terminology can be a problem regarding the clutch components because common names have in some cases changed from that used by the manufacturer. For example, the driven plate is also called the clutch plate or disc. The pressure plate assembly is sometimes referred to as the clutch cover. The clutch release bearing is sometimes called a throw-out bearing, and so on.

4 Other than replacing components that have obvious damage, some preliminary checks should be performed to diagnose a clutch system failure:

a) *The first check should be of the fluid level in the clutch master cylinder. If the fluid level is low, add fluid as necessary and inspect the hydraulic clutch system for leaks. If the master cylinder reservoir has run dry, bleed the system as described in Section 5 and re-test the clutch operation.*

b) *To check clutch spin down time, run the engine at normal idle speed with the transaxle in Neutral (clutch pedal up - engaged). Disengage the clutch (pedal down), wait several seconds and shift the transaxle into Reverse. No grinding noise should be heard. A grinding noise would most likely indicate a problem in the pressure plate or the clutch disc.*

c) *To check for complete clutch release, run the engine (with the parking brake applied to prevent movement) and hold the clutch pedal approximately 1/2-inch from the floor. Shift the transaxle between 1st gear and Reverse several times. If the shift is not smooth, component failure is indicated.*

d) *Visually inspect the clutch pedal bushings at the top of the clutch pedal to make sure there is no sticking or excessive wear.*

3 Clutch master and release cylinders - removal and installation

Caution: *Brake fluid will quickly damage paint. Cover all body parts and be careful not to spill fluid during any of the following procedures. Wipe up any spilled fluid immediately and then flush the area thoroughly with water.*

Master cylinder

Removal

1 Disconnect the cable from the negative battery terminal (see Chapter 5).

2 Remove the air filter housing (see Chapter 4).

3 Remove the clip securing the hydraulic line to the master cylinder and pull the tube out of the master cylinder. Cap or cover the opening to prevent brake fluid from leaking out.

4 Disconnect the supply line at the clutch master cylinder from the brake fluid reservoir and plug the line to prevent fluid loss.

5 Working inside the vehicle, remove the knee bolster (see Chapter 11), then disconnect the master cylinder pushrod from the clutch pedal pin.

6 Rotate the clutch master cylinder assembly 1/4 turn from its installed position and remove it from the engine compartment.

Installation

7 Connect the supply hose from the brake master cylinder to the clutch master cylinder. Fill the brake fluid reservoir with the proper fluid (see Chapter 1), then point the clutch master cylinder down (pushrod pointing down) for a few seconds to allow any trapped air to exit the master cylinder.

8 Place the master cylinder pushrod through the firewall and carefully route the hydraulic line into position. Rotate the master cylinder 1/4 turn to lock it into place.

9 Working inside the vehicle, connect the master cylinder pushrod to the clutch pedal.

10 Connect the hydraulic line to the clutch master cylinder. Install the retainers onto the line connectors and lock the lines in place.

11 The remainder of installation is the reverse of removal. Tighten the mounting fasteners securely.

12 Wash off any spilled brake fluid with water.

Release cylinder

Note: *These models utilize a release cylinder that is integral to the release bearing (see Section 6).*

4 Clutch hydraulic system - bleeding

Note: *Although clutch hydraulic system components are pre-filled at the factory, the clutch hydraulic system may require bleeding after servicing. Follow the preliminary bleeding procedure (see Step 1), and if this does not produce a proper operating clutch pedal, bleed the system.*

1 Make sure the clutch fluid reservoir is full. Actuate the clutch pedal between 10 to 15 times and check the operation of the clutch pedal. If the pedal remains spongy or the clutch does not engage properly, perform the release cylinder bleeding procedure.

Caution: *Do not allow hydraulic fluid to contaminate the clutch bellhousing or any clutch components. Contamination may severely reduce clutch operation.*

2 Verify the clutch fluid reservoir is properly filled but leave the cap off (see Chapter 1).

3 Raise the vehicle and support it securely on jackstands.

4 Remove the protective cover from the bleeder port and install a clear hose. Guide the hose to a small container to catch the fluid during bleeding.

5 Have the assistant press down and hold the clutch pedal until it reaches the floor.

6 Open the bleed port on the clutch slave cylinder enough to allow hydraulic fluid to drain. Any air in the system will escape at this time. Repeat this process approximately 15 times.

7 When no air is present in the escaping fluid, bleeding is complete.

8 Ensure the level in the master cylinder is correct, then replace the cap.

9 Actuate the clutch pedal slowly about 10 times and check the operation of the clutch pedal. Start the engine and confirm proper clutch operation. If the pedal remains spongy or the clutch does not engage properly, perform Steps 4 through 7.

10 Confirm proper clutch operation and repeat the bleeding procedure if necessary.

5 Clutch components - removal and installation

Warning: *Dust produced by clutch wear and deposited on clutch components is hazardous to your health. DO NOT blow it out with compressed air and DO NOT inhale it. DO NOT use gasoline or petroleum-based solvents to remove the dust. Brake system cleaner should be used to flush the dust into a drain pan. After the clutch components are wiped clean with a rag, dispose of the contaminated rags and cleaner in a labeled, covered container.*

Note: *If the clutch pressure plate or flywheel requires replacement, the modular clutch assembly must be replaced as a set. Separate components are not available.*

Removal

Note: *Access to the clutch components is normally accomplished by removing the transaxle, leaving the engine in the vehicle. If, of course, the engine is being removed for major overhaul, then the opportunity should always be* taken to check the clutch for wear and replace worn components as necessary. However, the relatively low cost of the clutch components compared to the time and labor involved in gaining access to them warrants their replacement any time the engine or transaxle is removed, unless they are new or in near-perfect condition. The following procedures assume that the engine will stay in place.

1   Remove the transaxle from the vehicle (see Chapter 7A). Support the engine while the transaxle is out. Preferably, an engine hoist or support fixture should be used to support it from above. However, if a jack is used underneath the engine, make sure a piece of wood is used between the jack and oil pan to spread the load.

Note: *The clutch pressure plate can be unbolted from the flywheel, allowing the clutch disc to be removed.*

2   Remove the modular clutch assembly from the transaxle input shaft.

3   Inspect the clutch release bearing (see Section 6).

Installation

4   Using moly-base grease, lightly lubricate the face of the release bearing where it contacts the fingers of the pressure plate diaphragm spring. Lightly lubricate the splines of the transaxle input shaft.

Caution: *Don't use too much grease.*

5   Slide the modular clutch assembly onto the transaxle input shaft.

6   Install the transaxle (see Chapter 7A) and all components removed previously, tightening all fasteners to the proper torque specifications (where given).

---

6   Clutch release cylinder and bearing - removal, inspection and installation

---

Warning: *Dust produced by clutch wear and deposited on clutch components is hazardous to your health. DO NOT blow it out with compressed air and DO NOT inhale it. DO NOT use gasoline or petroleum-based solvents to remove the dust. Brake system cleaner should be used to flush it into a drain pan. After the clutch components are wiped clean with a rag, dispose of the contaminated rags and cleaner in a labeled, covered container.*

Caution: *Don't allow brake fluid to come into contact with paint as it will damage the finish.*

Removal

1   Disconnect the hydraulic quick-connect fitting from the release cylinder.

2   Remove the transaxle (see Chapter 7A).

3   Remove the modular clutch assembly (see Section 5).

4   Disconnect the clutch hydraulic line from the bleeder, then detach the bleeder from the release cylinder.

5   Remove the bolts securing the release cylinder to the transaxle and slide the release cylinder assembly off the transaxle input shaft.

Inspection

6   Hold the bearing by the outer race and rotate the inner race while applying pressure. If the bearing doesn't turn smoothly or if it's noisy, replace the release cylinder/bearing assembly with a new one. Wipe the bearing with a clean rag and inspect it for damage, wear and cracks.

Installation

7   Installation is the reverse of the removal Steps with the following additions:

a) *Install the release cylinder mounting bolts and tighten them in three steps to the torque listed in this Chapter's Specifications.*

b) *Install the bleeder assembly and the hydraulic line.*

c) *Using moly-base grease, lightly lubricate the face of the release bearing where it contacts the fingers of the pressure plate diaphragm spring. Lightly lubricate the splines of the transaxle input shaft.*

d) *Install the modular clutch assembly (see Section 5).*

e) *Install the transaxle (see Chapter 7A).*

f) *Connect the hydraulic line and check the brake fluid level in the reservoir, adding fluid if necessary, until the level is correct.*

g) *Bleed the clutch hydraulic system (see Section 4).*

---

7   Clutch start switch - check, replacement and adjustment

Check

1   Verify that the engine will not start when the clutch pedal is released.

2   Verify that the engine will start when the clutch pedal is depressed all the way.

3   If the engine won't start with the pedal depressed, or starts with the pedal released, unplug the electrical connector to the switch (located near the top of the clutch pedal) and check continuity between the connector terminals with the clutch pedal depressed.

4   If there's continuity between the terminals with the pedal depressed, the switch is okay; if there's no continuity between the terminals with the pedal depressed, replace the switch. If there's continuity between the terminals when the clutch pedal is released, replace the switch.

Replacement

5   Remove the knee bolster from the instrument panel (see Chapter 11).

6   Unplug the switch electrical connector, if you haven't already done so.

7   Depress the wing tabs on the switch and push the switch out of the mounting bracket.

8   Remove the clip securing the clutch master cylinder pushrod to the pedal pin.

9   Remove the switch and wires out of the slot in the bracket.

10   Installation is the reverse of removal.

Adjustment

11   Loosen the adjustment screw on the clutch master cylinder pushrod.

12   Carefully lift the pedal upward and connect the pushrod to the pedal pin.

13   Tighten the pushrod adjustment screw.

14   Verify the switch operates properly.

---

8   Driveaxle - removal and installation

Front

Removal

1   Set the parking brake. Loosen the wheel lug nuts, then raise the vehicle and support it securely on jackstands. Remove the wheel.

2   Remove the cotter pin, nut lock and spring washer (see illustrations) from the end of the driveaxle.

8.2a Using pliers, remove the cotter pin (always replace it with a new one)...

8.2b ... then the nut lock ...

8.2c ... and the spring washer

8.3a Prevent the brake disc from turning by inserting a long punch into a disc cooling vane, then loosen the driveaxle/hub nut

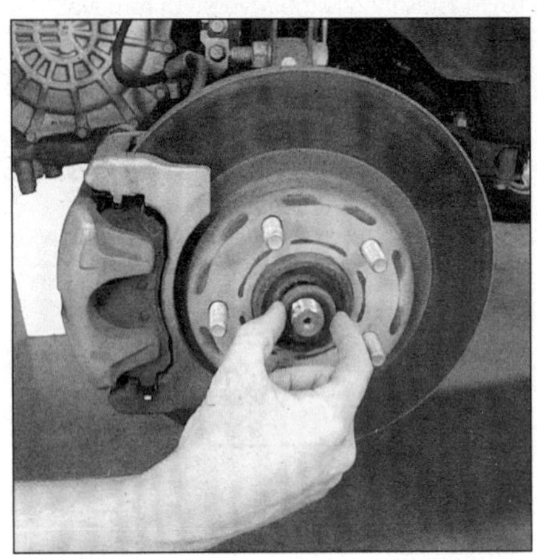

8.3b Remove the nut and the washer

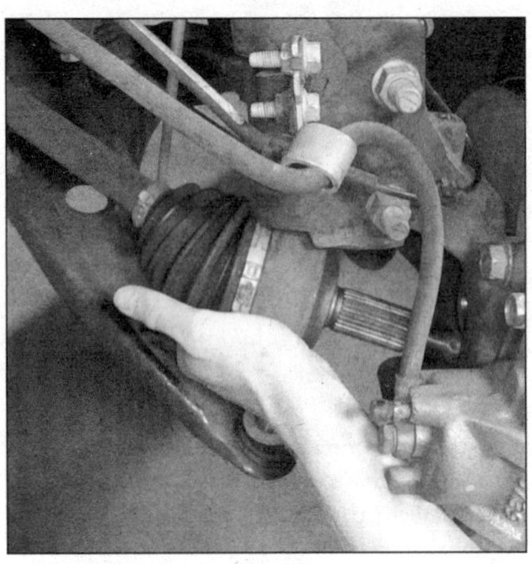

8.6 Pull the steering knuckle away from the outer CV joint

8.7 Intermediate shaft support bracket lower mounting bolt (upper two mounting bolts not visible)

8.8 From under the transaxle, pry the inner CV joint out sharply to disengage the circlip from the differential side gear

3   Prevent the brake disc from turning by inserting a long punch into a disc cooling vane and letting it come to rest against the caliper mounting bracket, or have an assistant apply the brake and remove the driveaxle/hub nut, then the washer (see illustrations).

Caution: *Discard the driveaxle/hub nut and obtain a new one for reassembly.*

4   Remove the ABS wheel speed sensor, if equipped, from the steering wheel (see Chapter 9).

5   Disconnect the control arm from the steering knuckle (see Chapter 10).

6   Pull the steering knuckle out and away from the outer CV joint of the driveaxle (see illustration). Strike the end of the stub shaft with a soft-faced hammer to separate the splines from the hub and bearing assembly, if necessary.

Note: *If the driveaxle is stuck in the hub, push it out with a puller.*

Left side (all models)/right side (AWD models)

7   Remove the intermediate shaft support bracket bolts (see illustration).

All models

8   Support the outer end of the driveaxle and insert a prybar between the inner CV joint and the transaxle case (see illustration). Pry out sharply to disengage the inner CV joint from the transaxle.

9   Carefully withdraw the inner CV joint or intermediate shaft from the transaxle. Do not let the spline or the snap-ring drag across the sealing lip of the driveaxle oil seal.

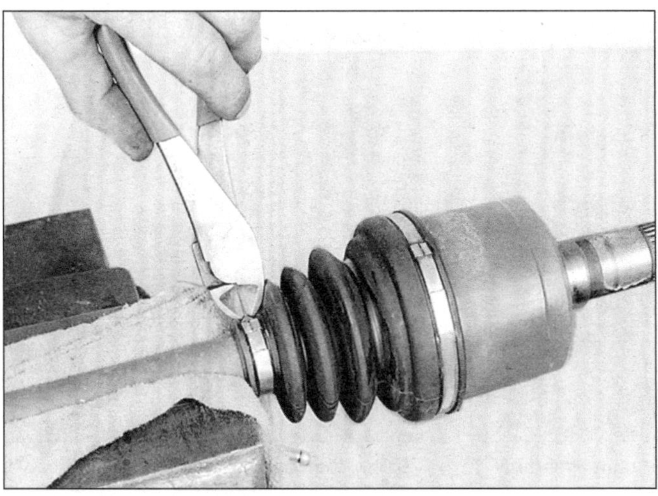

9.3 Cut off the boot clamps and discard them

9.5 Strike the edge of the CV joint housing sharply with a soft-faced hammer to dislodge the CV joint from the shaft

Installation

10   Installation is the reverse of removal, noting the following additional points:

a) *Thoroughly clean the splines and bearing shield on the outer CV joint. This is very important, as the bearing shield protects the wheel bearings from water and contamination. Also clean the wheel bearing area of the steering knuckle. Don't forget to install the washer on the stub shaft.*

b) *Thoroughly clean the splines and oil seal sealing surface on the inner CV joint. Apply an even bead of multi-purpose grease around the oil seal sealing surface of the inner CV joint.*

c) *When installing the driveaxle, push it in sharply to seat the snap-ring on the inner CV joint stub shaft into its groove in the differential gears inside the transaxle. Pull out on the inner CV joint housing to ensure it's seated.*

d) *On models equipped with a passenger's side intermediate shaft, insert the splined shaft assembly into the splined differential gears inside the transaxle, then install the support bearing mounting bolts and tighten the bolts to the torque listed in this Chapter's Specifications.*

e) *Reconnect the control arm balljoint to the steering knuckle (see Chapter 10).*

f) *Tighten the NEW driveaxle/hub nut to the torque listed in this Chapter's Specifications.*

g) *Tighten the lug nuts to the torque listed in the Chapter 1 Specifications.*

Rear

Removal

11   Set the parking brake. Remove the rear wheel cover or hubcap.
12   Loosen, but do not remove, the driveaxle/hub nut.
13   Raise the vehicle and support it securely on jackstands. Place the shift selector lever in Neutral.
14   Remove the rear differential assembly from the vehicle (see Section 15).
15   Remove the driveaxle/hub nut and pull the driveaxle from the hub and bearing assembly toward the center of the vehicle. Strike the end of the stub shaft with a soft-faced hammer to separate the splines from the hub and bearing assembly, if necessary.

Installation

16   Installation is the reverse of removal, noting the following additional points:

a) *Thoroughly clean the splines and bearing shield on the outer CV joint.*

b) *This is very important, as the bearing shield protects the wheel bearings from water and contamination. Also clean the wheel bearing area of the steering knuckle.*

c) *Thoroughly clean the splines and oil seal sealing surface on the inner CV joint. Apply an even bead of multi-purpose grease around the oil seal sealing surface of the inner CV joint.*

d) *When installing the driveaxle, push it in sharply to seat the snap-ring on the inner CV joint stub shaft into its groove in the rear differential gears. Pull out on the inner CV joint housing to ensure it's seated.*

e) *Tighten the driveaxle/hub nut to the torque listed in this Chapter's Specifications.*

f) *Tighten the lug nuts to the torque listed in the Chapter 1 Specifications.*

---

9   Driveaxle boot replacement

Note: *If the CV joints or boots must be replaced, explore all options before beginning the job. Complete, rebuilt driveaxles are available on an exchange basis, eliminating much time and work. Whichever route you choose to take, check on the cost and availability of parts before disassembling the vehicle.*

Front driveaxle

1   Remove the driveaxle (see Section 8).
2   Mount the driveaxle in a vise with wood-lined jaws, to prevent damage to the axleshaft. Check the CV joints for excessive play in the radial direction, which indicates worn parts. Check for smooth operation throughout the full range of motion for each CV joint. If a boot is torn, the recommended procedure is to disassemble the joint, clean the components and inspect for damage due to loss of lubrication and possible contamination by foreign matter. If the CV joint is in good condition, lubricate it with CV joint grease and install a new boot.

Outer CV joint

Disassembly

3   Cut the boot clamps with side-cutters, then remove and discard them (see illustration).
4   Using a screwdriver, pry up on the edge of the boot, pull it off the CV joint housing and slide it down the axleshaft.
5   Strike the edge of the CV joint housing sharply with a soft-faced hammer to dislodge the outer CV joint from the axleshaft (see illustration). Remove and discard the bearing retainer clip from the axleshaft.
6   Remove the large stop-ring from the axleshaft, then slide the boot off the shaft.

Inspection

7   Clean the components with solvent to remove all traces of grease. Inspect the cage and races for pitting, score marks, cracks and other signs of wear and damage. Shiny, polished spots are normal and won't adversely affect CV joint operation.

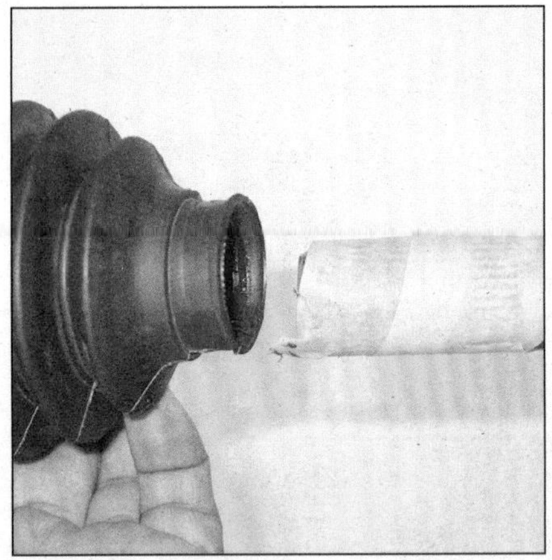

9.8 Wrap the axleshaft splines with tape to prevent damaging the boot as it's slid onto the shaft

9.9a Pack the outer CV joint assembly with grease...

9.9b... then apply grease to the inside of the boot

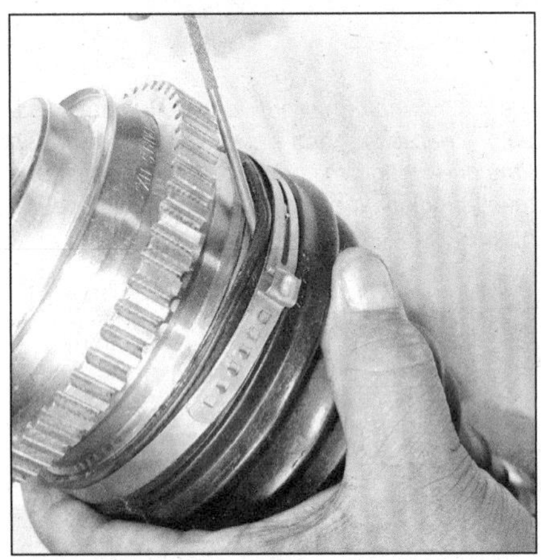

9.12 Equalize the pressure inside the boot by inserting a screwdriver between the boot and the CV joint housing

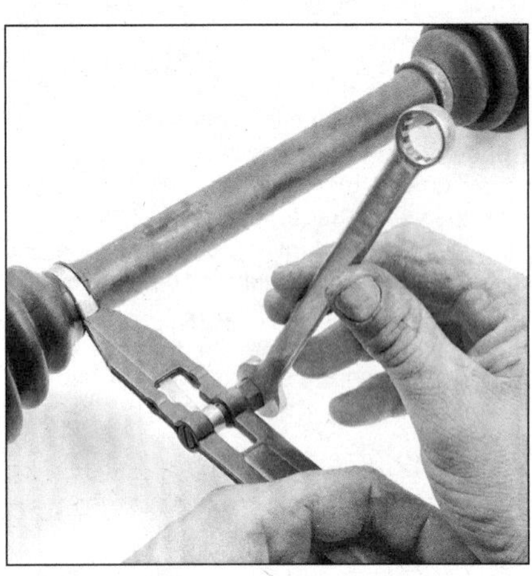

9.14a You'll need a special tightening tool to install "band" type boot clamps: Install the band with its end pointing in the direction of axle rotation and tighten it securely...

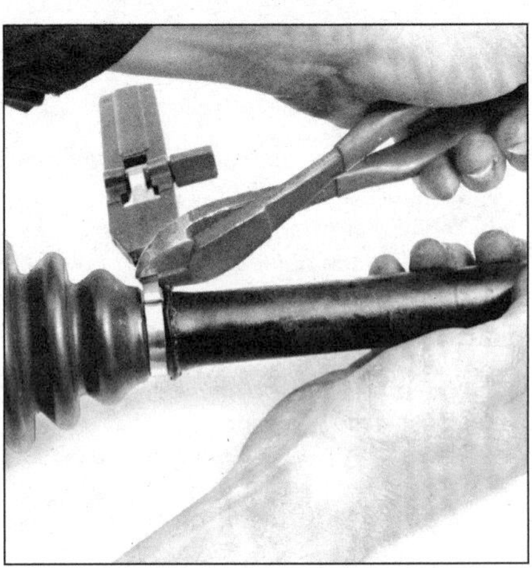

9.14b... then bend down the end of the clamp back and cut off the excess

9.14c If you're installing crimp-type boot clamps, you'll need a pair of special crimping pliers (available at most auto parts stores)

Reassembly

8   Wrap the splines on the inner end of the axleshaft with tape to protect the boots from the sharp edges of the splines, and slide the clamps, then the boot onto the axleshaft (see illustration). Remove the tape and install a NEW stop-ring and circlip on the axleshaft.

9   Place half the grease provided in the sealing boot kit into the outer CV joint assembly housing (see illustration). Put the remaining grease into the sealing boot (see illustration).

10   Align the splines on the axleshaft with the splines on the outer CV joint assembly and gently drive the CV joint onto the axleshaft using a soft-faced hammer until the CV joint is seated to the axleshaft.

11   Slide the boot into place, making sure the raised bead on the inside of the seal boot is positioned in the groove on the interconnecting shaft. If the driveaxle has multiple locating grooves on the shaft, position the boot so only

one of the grooves (the thinnest) is exposed. Position the sealing boot into the groove on the outer CV joint housing.

12   Using a thin screwdriver, equalize the pressure in the boot (see illustration).

13   Make sure each end of the boot is seated properly, and the boot is not distorted.

14   Install the boot clamps. There are three types of clamps you're likely to encounter: the band type, which requires a special tightening tool, the crimp type (which also requires a special tool), or the fold-over type (see illustrations).

15   Install the driveaxle (see Section 8).

Inner CV joint

16   At the time of writing, replacement inner CV joint boots were not available, nor did the manufacturer provide a replacement procedure. If the inner boot becomes torn, the entire driveaxle may have to be replaced. Check with your local auto parts store and

9.14d To install fold-over type boot clamps, bend the tang down...

9.14e... then tap the tabs over to hold it in place

dealer parts department to see if replacement boots have become available.

Rear driveaxle (AWD models)

17   At the time of writing, replacement CV joint boots for the rear driveaxles were not available, nor did the manufacturer provide replacement procedures. If a boot on a rear driveaxle becomes torn, the entire driveaxle may have to be replaced. Check with your local auto parts store and dealer parts department to see if replacement boots have become available.

10   Driveshaft (AWD models) - removal and installation

Caution: *DO NOT allow the driveshaft to hang from the front, rear or center support bearing - always suppport the driveshaft. Damage to the joints, boots and/or center support bearing may occur, resulting in vibration.*
Note: *The manufacturer recommends replacing driveshaft fasteners with new ones when installing the driveshaft.*
1   Raise the vehicle and support it securely on jackstands. Place the shift selector lever in Neutral.
2   Use chalk or a scribe to index the relationship of the driveshaft to the differential pinion yoke and the flange at the transfer case.
3   Remove the four fasteners and disconnect the rear driveshaft rubber coupler from the rear axle flange. Support the rear of the driveshaft.
4   Remove the center support heat shield and remove the bolts attaching the driveshaft center support to the vehicle. Support the center of the driveshaft.
5   With the help of an assistant, if needed, support the entire driveshaft and slide the end of the driveshaft out from the transfer case.
6   Remove the driveshaft from the vehicle.
7   Installation is the reverse of removal,

noting the following points:
   a)   *Make sure the marks you made previously are aligned.*
   b)   *Tighten the fasteners to the torques listed in this Chapter's Specifications.*

11   Driveshaft universal joints (AWD models) - general information and check

1   Universal joints are mechanical couplings which connect two rotating components that meet each other at different angles.
2   These joints are composed of a yoke on each side connected by a crosspiece called a trunnion. Cups at each end of the trunnion contain needle bearings which provide smooth transfer of the torque load. Snap-rings, either inside or outside of the bearing cups, hold the assembly together.
3   Wear in the needle roller bearings is characterized by vibration in the driveline, noise during acceleration, and in extreme cases of lack of lubrication, metallic squeaking and ultimately grating and shrieking sounds as the bearings disintegrate.
4   It is easy to check if the needle bearings are worn with the driveshaft in position, by trying to turn the shaft with one hand, the other hand holding the front yoke or rear differential pinion flange when the rear universal joint is being checked, and the front half coupling when the front universal joint is being checked. Any movement between the driveshaft and the front half couplings, and around the rear half couplings, is indicative of considerable wear. Another method of checking for universal joint wear is to use a prybar inserted into the gap between the universal joint and the driveshaft or flange. Leave the vehicle in gear and try to pry the joint both radially and axially. Any looseness should be apparent with this method. A final test for wear is to attempt to lift the shaft and note any movement between

the yokes of the joints.
5   If any of the above conditions exist, replace the driveshaft.

12   Driveshaft center support bearing (AWD models) - replacement

1   The center support bearing is not replaceable separately; if it is in need of replacement, the entire driveshaft must be replaced.

13   Rear differential driveaxle oil seals (AWD models) - replacement

1   Raise the vehicle and support it securely on jackstands. Place the transaxle in Neutral with the parking brake off.
2   Remove the rear differential (see Section 15).
3   Carefully pry out the driveaxle oil seal with a seal removal tool or a large screwdriver. Be careful not to damage or scratch the seal bore.
4   Using a seal installer or a large deep socket as a drift, install the new oil seal. Drive it into the bore squarely and make sure it's completely seated.
5   Lubricate the lip of the new seals with multi-purpose grease.
6   Install the rear differential (see Section 15).
7   Check the differential lubricant level and add some, if necessary, to bring it to the appropriate level.

14   Rear differential pinion seal (AWD models) - replacement

1   Raise the vehicle and support it securely on jackstands.

2   Use chalk or a scribe to index the relationship of the driveshaft to the differential pinion yoke.
Caution: *DO NOT allow the driveshaft to hang from the front, rear or center support bearing - always support the driveshaft. Damage to the joints, boots and or center support bearing may occur, resulting in vibration.*
3   Remove the fasteners and disconnect the rear driveshaft rubber coupler from the differential pinion yoke. Support the rear of the driveshaft.
4   Remove the rear differential electronic clutch (see Section 16).
5   Remove the RTV material around the sealing area.
6   Remove the wave washer on top of the seal.
7   Carefully pry out the pinion seal with a seal removal tool or a large screwdriver. Be careful not to damage or scratch the seal bore.
8   Using a seal installer or a large deep socket as a drift, install the new oil seal. Drive it into the bore squarely and make sure it's completely seated.
9   Lubricate the lip of the new seal with multi-purpose grease.
10   Installation is the reverse of removal, noting the following points:

a) *Tighten all fasteners to the torque listed in this Chapter's Specifications.*
b) *Check the differential lubricant level and add some, if necessary, to bring it to the appropriate level.*

15   Rear differential assembly (AWD models) - removal and installation

1   Raise the vehicle and support it securely on jackstands.
2   Remove the rear stabilizer bar (see Chapter 10).
3   Remove the left and right stay bracket bolts and bracket from each side of the differential.
4   Remove the center hanger for the exhaust system near the driveshaft center support bearing. Disconnect the rear exhaust hangers.
5   Lower and support the exhaust system using jackstands or appropriate wire, with a minimum of 10 inches of clearance below the vehicle to allow for removal of the rear differential.
6   Drain the differential fluid to prevent spilling when removing.
7   Support the rear differential using a floor jack or similar.
8   Use chalk or a scribe to index the relationship of the driveshaft to the differential pinion yoke and the flange at the transfer case.
Caution: *DO NOT allow the driveshaft to hang from the front, rear or center support bearing - always suppport the driveshaft. Damage to the joints, boots and or center support bearing may occur, resulting in vibration.*
9   Remove the three fasteners and disconnect the rear driveshaft rubber coupler from the rear axle flange. Support the rear of the driveshaft.
10   Disconnect the electronic clutch control module electrical connector and the vent hose.
11   Use a prybar or similar to dislodge the driveaxles part way from the rear differential housing.
12   Remove the three rear differential-to-crossmember mounting bolts.
13   Lower the rear differential partially and remove the driveaxles from the rear differential housing (see Section 8).
14   Carefully lower and remove the differential from the vehicle.
15   Installation is the reverse of removal, noting the following points:

a) *Don't tighten any of the mounting fasteners until all of them have been installed.*
b) *Tighten all fasteners to the torque listed in this Chapter's Specifications.*

16   Rear differential electronic clutch - removal and installation

1   Raise the vehicle and support it securely on jackstands.
2   Use chalk or a scribe to index the relationship of the driveshaft to the differential pinion yoke.
Caution: *DO NOT allow the driveshaft to hang from the front, rear or center support bearing - always support the driveshaft. Damage to the joints, boots and or center support bearing may occur, resulting in vibration.*
3   Remove the four fasteners and disconnect the rear driveshaft rubber coupler from the rear axle flange. Support the rear of the driveshaft.
4   Remove the rear section of the exhaust and secure it out of the way.
5   Remove the (ECC) bracket bolt then disconnect the electronic clutch control (ECC) module electrical connector.
6   Remove the mounting bolts attaching the electronic clutch assembly to the rear differential.
7   Remove the electronic clutch assembly from the vehicle.
8   Installation is the reverse of removal, noting the following points:

a) *Ensure the electronic clutch and rear differential splines engage properly.*
b) *Apply RTV to the sealing surface of the ECC.*
c) *Tighten all fasteners to the torque listed in this Chapter's Specifications.*

Notes

Notes

Chapter 9
Brakes

Contents

Specifications

General

Brake fluid type	See Chapter 1

Disc brakes

Brake pad minimum thickness	See Chapter 1
Disc lateral runout limit	
16-inch wheel	
Front (11.5-inch disc)	0.004 inch
Rear (11.8-inch disc)	0.0016 inch
14-inch wheel (10.3-inch disc)	0.0024
Disc minimum thickness	Cast into disc
Thickness variation (parallelism)	
Front	0.0002 inch
Rear	0.0006 inch

Drum Brakes

Minimum shoe lining thickness	See Chapter 1
Maximum radial runout	0.0024 inch
Maximum drum diameter	Cast into drum

Torque specifications   Ft-lbs (unless otherwise indicated)

Note: *One foot-pound (ft-lb) of torque is equivalent to 12 inch-pounds (in-lbs) of torque. Torque values below approximately 15 ft-lbs are expressed in inch-pounds, since most foot-pound torque wrenches are not accurate at these smaller values.*

Brake booster mounting nuts	17
Brake hose banjo bolt to caliper (front)	18
Brake hose to caliper (rear)	133 in-lbs
Metal brake line to flexible brake hose	150 in-lbs
Caliper mounting (guide pin) bolts	32
Caliper mounting bracket bolts	80
Master cylinder-to-brake booster mounting nuts	18
Wheel speed sensor mounting screw	
Front	108 in-lbs
Rear	89 in-lbs
Wheel cylinder mounting bolts	115 in-lbs
Wheel lug nuts	See Chapter 1

1   General Information

1   The vehicles covered by this manual are equipped with hydraulically operated front and rear brake systems. The front brakes are disc type and the rear brakes are disc or drum type. Both the front and rear brakes are self adjusting. The disc brakes automatically compensate for pad wear, while the drum brakes incorporate an adjustment mechanism that is activated as the parking brake is applied.

Hydraulic system

2   The hydraulic system consists of two separate circuits. The master cylinder has separate reservoir chambers for the two circuits, and, in the event of a leak or failure in one hydraulic circuit, the other circuit will remain operative. A dynamic proportioning valve, integral with the ABS hydraulic unit, provides brake balance to each individual wheel.

Power brake booster and vacuum pump

3   The power brake booster, utilizing engine manifold vacuum, and atmospheric pressure to provide assistance to the hydraulically operated brakes, is mounted on the firewall in the engine compartment. An auxiliary vacuum pump, mounted below the power brake booster in the left side of the engine compartment, provides additional vacuum to the booster under certain operating conditions.

Parking brake

4   The parking brake operates the rear brakes only, through cable actuation. It's activated by a lever mounted in the center console.

Service

5   After completing any operation involving disassembly of any part of the brake system, always test drive the vehicle to check for proper braking performance before resuming normal driving. When testing the brakes, perform the tests on a clean, dry, flat surface. Conditions other than these can lead to inaccurate test results.

6   Test the brakes at various speeds with both light and heavy pedal pressure. The vehicle should stop evenly without pulling to one side or the other. Avoid locking the brakes, because this slides the tires and diminishes braking efficiency and control of the vehicle.

7   Tires, vehicle load and wheel alignment are factors which also affect braking performance.

Precautions

8   There are some general cautions and warnings involving the brake system on this vehicle:

a) *Use only brake fluid conforming to DOT 3 specifications.*

b) *The brake pads and linings contain fibers that are hazardous to your health if inhaled. Whenever you work on brake system components, clean all parts with brake system cleaner. Do not allow the fine dust to become airborne. Also, wear an approved filtering mask.*

c) *Safety should be paramount whenever any servicing of the brake components is performed. Do not use parts or fasteners that are not in perfect condition, and be sure that all clearances and torque specifications are adhered to. If you are at all unsure about a certain procedure, seek professional advice. Upon completion of any brake system work, test the brakes carefully in a controlled area before putting the vehicle into normal service. If a problem is suspected in the brake system, don't drive the vehicle until it's fixed.*

d) *Used brake fluid is considered a hazardous waste and it must be disposed of in accordance with federal, state and local laws. DO NOT pour it down the sink, into septic tanks or storm drains, or on the ground. Clean up any spilled brake fluid immediately and then wash the area with large amounts of water. This is especially true for any finished or painted surfaces.*

2   Troubleshooting

PROBABLE CAUSE	CORRECTIVE ACTION

No brakes - pedal travels to floor

PROBABLE CAUSE	CORRECTIVE ACTION
1 Low fluid level 2 Air in system	1 and 2 Low fluid level and air in the system are symptoms of another problem a leak somewhere in the hydraulic system. Locate and repair the leak
3 Defective seals in master cylinder	3 Replace master cylinder
4 Fluid overheated and vaporized due to heavy braking	4 Bleed hydraulic system (temporary fix). Replace brake fluid (proper fix)

Brake pedal slowly travels to floor under braking or at a stop

PROBABLE CAUSE	CORRECTIVE ACTION
1 Defective seals in master cylinder	1 Replace master cylinder
2 Leak in a hose, line, caliper or wheel cylinder	2 Locate and repair leak
3 Air in hydraulic system	3 Bleed the system, inspect system for a leak

Brake pedal feels spongy when depressed

PROBABLE CAUSE	CORRECTIVE ACTION
1 Air in hydraulic system	1 Bleed the system, inspect system for a leak
2 Master cylinder or power booster loose	2 Tighten fasteners
3 Brake fluid overheated (beginning to boil)	3 Bleed the system (temporary fix). Replace the brake fluid (proper fix)
4 Deteriorated brake hoses (ballooning under pressure)	4 Inspect hoses, replace as necessary (it's a good idea to replace all of them if one hose shows signs of deterioration)

PROBABLE CAUSE	CORRECTIVE ACTION

Brake pedal feels hard when depressed and/or excessive effort required to stop vehicle

PROBABLE CAUSE	CORRECTIVE ACTION
1 Power booster faulty	1 Replace booster
2 Engine not producing sufficient vacuum, or hose to booster clogged, collapsed or cracked	2 Check vacuum to booster with a vacuum gauge. Replace hose if cracked or clogged, repair engine if vacuum is extremely low
3 Brake linings contaminated by grease or brake fluid	3 Locate and repair source of contamination, replace brake pads or shoes
4 Brake linings glazed	4 Replace brake pads or shoes, check discs and drums for glazing, service as necessary
5 Caliper piston(s) or wheel cylinder(s) binding or frozen	5 Replace calipers or wheel cylinders
6 Brakes wet	6 Apply pedal to boil-off water (this should only be a momentary problem)
7 Kinked, clogged or internally split brake hose or line	7 Inspect lines and hoses, replace as necessary

Excessive brake pedal travel (but will pump up)

PROBABLE CAUSE	CORRECTIVE ACTION
1 Drum brakes out of adjustment	1 Adjust brakes
2 Air in hydraulic system	2 Bleed system, inspect system for a leak

Excessive brake pedal travel (but will not pump up)

PROBABLE CAUSE	CORRECTIVE ACTION
1 Master cylinder pushrod misadjusted	1 Adjust pushrod
2 Master cylinder seals defective	2 Replace master cylinder
3 Brake linings worn out	3 Inspect brakes, replace pads and/or shoes
4 Hydraulic system leak	4 Locate and repair leak

Brake pedal doesn't return

PROBABLE CAUSE	CORRECTIVE ACTION
1 Brake pedal binding	1 Inspect pivot bushing and pushrod, repair or lubricate
2 Defective master cylinder	2 Replace master cylinder

Brake pedal pulsates during brake application

PROBABLE CAUSE	CORRECTIVE ACTION
1 Brake drums out-of-round	1 Have drums machined by an automotive machine shop
2 Excessive brake disc runout or disc surfaces out-of-parallel	2 Have discs machined by an automotive machine shop
3 Loose or worn wheel bearings	3 Adjust or replace wheel bearings
4 Loose lug nuts	4 Tighten lug nuts

Brakes slow to release

PROBABLE CAUSE	CORRECTIVE ACTION
1 Malfunctioning power booster	1 Replace booster
2 Pedal linkage binding	2 Inspect pedal pivot bushing and pushrod, repair/lubricate
3 Malfunctioning proportioning valve	3 Replace proportioning valve
4 Sticking caliper or wheel cylinder	4 Repair or replace calipers or wheel cylinders
5 Kinked or internally split brake hose	5 Locate and replace faulty brake hose

Brakes grab (one or more wheels)

PROBABLE CAUSE	CORRECTIVE ACTION
1 Grease or brake fluid on brake lining	1 Locate and repair cause of contamination, replace lining
2 Brake lining glazed	2 Replace lining, deglaze disc or drum

Troubleshooting (continued)

PROBABLE CAUSE	CORRECTIVE ACTION

Vehicle pulls to one side during braking

PROBABLE CAUSE	CORRECTIVE ACTION
1 Grease or brake fluid on brake lining	1 Locate and repair cause of contamination, replace lining
2 Brake lining glazed	2 Deglaze or replace lining, deglaze disc or drum
3 Restricted brake line or hose	3 Repair line or replace hose
4 Tire pressures incorrect	4 Adjust tire pressures
5 Caliper or wheel cylinder sticking	5 Repair or replace calipers or wheel cylinders
6 Wheels out of alignment	6 Have wheels aligned
7 Weak suspension spring	7 Replace springs
8 Weak or broken shock absorber	8 Replace shock absorbers

Brakes drag (indicated by sluggish engine performance or wheels being very hot after driving)

PROBABLE CAUSE	CORRECTIVE ACTION
1 Brake pedal pushrod incorrectly adjusted	1 Adjust pushrod
2 Master cylinder pushrod (between booster and master cylinder)	2 Adjust pushrod incorrectly adjusted
3 Obstructed compensating port in master cylinder	3 Replace master cylinder
4 Master cylinder piston seized in bore	4 Replace master cylinder
5 Contaminated fluid causing swollen seals throughout system	5 Flush system, replace all hydraulic components
6 Clogged brake lines or internally split brake hose(s)	6 Flush hydraulic system, replace defective hose(s)
7 Sticking caliper(s) or wheel cylinder(s)	7 Replace calipers or wheel cylinders
8 Parking brake not releasing	8 Inspect parking brake linkage and parking brake mechanism, repair as required
9 Improper shoe-to-drum clearance	9 Adjust brake shoes
10 Faulty proportioning valve	10 Replace proportioning valve

Brakes fade (due to excessive heat)

PROBABLE CAUSE	CORRECTIVE ACTION
1 Brake linings excessively worn or glazed	1 Deglaze or replace brake pads and/or shoes
2 Excessive use of brakes	2 Downshift into a lower gear, maintain a constant slower speed (going down hills)
3 Vehicle overloaded	3 Reduce load
4 Brake drums or discs worn too thin	4 Measure drum diameter and disc thickness, replace drums or discs as required
5 Contaminated brake fluid	5 Flush system, replace fluid
6 Brakes drag	6 Repair cause of dragging brakes
7 Driver resting left foot on brake pedal	7 Don't ride the brakes

Brakes noisy (high-pitched squeal)

PROBABLE CAUSE	CORRECTIVE ACTION
1 Glazed lining	1 Deglaze or replace lining
2 Contaminated lining (brake fluid, grease, etc.)	2 Repair source of contamination, replace linings
3 Weak or broken brake shoe hold-down or return spring	3 Replace springs
4 Rivets securing lining to shoe or backing plate loose	4 Replace shoes or pads
5 Excessive dust buildup on brake linings	5 Wash brakes off with brake system cleaner
6 Brake drums worn too thin	6 Measure diameter of drums, replace if necessary
7 Wear indicator on disc brake pads contacting disc	7 Replace brake pads
8 Anti-squeal shims missing or installed improperly	8 Install shims correctly

PROBABLE CAUSE	CORRECTIVE ACTION

Brakes noisy (scraping sound)

1 Brake pads or shoes worn out; rivets, backing plate or brake	1 Replace linings, have discs and/or drums machined (or replace) shoe metal contacting disc or drum

Brakes chatter

1 Worn brake lining	1 Inspect brakes, replace shoes or pads as necessary
2 Glazed or scored discs or drums	2 Deglaze discs or drums with sandpaper (if glazing is severe, machining will be required)
3 Drums or discs heat checked	3 Check discs and/or drums for hard spots, heat checking, etc. Have discs/drums machined or replace them
4 Disc runout or drum out-of-round excessive	4 Measure disc runout and/or drum out-of-round, have discs or drums machined or replace them
5 Loose or worn wheel bearings	5 Adjust or replace wheel bearings
6 Loose or bent brake backing plate (drum brakes)	6 Tighten or replace backing plate
7 Grooves worn in discs or drums	7 Have discs or drums machined, if within limits (if not, replace them)
8 Brake linings contaminated (brake fluid, grease, etc.)	8 Locate and repair source of contamination, replace pads or shoes
9 Excessive dust buildup on linings	9 Wash brakes with brake system cleaner
10 Surface finish on discs or drums too rough after machining	10 Have discs or drums properly machined (especially on vehicles with sliding calipers)
11 Brake pads or shoes glazed	11 Deglaze or replace brake pads or shoes

Brake pads or shoes click

1 Shoe support pads on brake backing plate grooved or	1 Replace brake backing plate excessively worn
2 Brake pads loose in caliper	2 Loose pad retainers or anti-rattle clips
3 Also see items listed under Brakes chatter	

Brakes make groaning noise at end of stop

1 Brake pads and/or shoes worn out	1 Replace pads and/or shoes
2 Brake linings contaminated (brake fluid, grease, etc.)	2 Locate and repair cause of contamination, replace brake pads or shoes
3 Brake linings glazed	3 Deglaze or replace brake pads or shoes
4 Excessive dust buildup on linings	4 Wash brakes with brake system cleaner
5 Scored or heat-checked discs or drums	5 Inspect discs/drums, have machined if within limits (if not, replace discs or drums)
6 Broken or missing brake shoe attaching hardware	6 Inspect drum brakes, replace missing hardware

Rear brakes lock up under light brake application

1 Tire pressures too high	1 Adjust tire pressures
2 Tires excessively worn	2 Replace tires
3 Defective proportioning valve	3 Replace proportioning valve

Brake warning light on instrument panel comes on (or stays on)

1 Low fluid level in master cylinder reservoir (reservoirs with fluid level sensor)	1 Add fluid, inspect system for leak, check the thickness of the brake pads and shoes
2 Failure in one half of the hydraulic system	2 Inspect hydraulic system for a leak
3 Piston in pressure differential warning valve not centered	3 Center piston by bleeding one circuit or the other (close bleeder valve as soon as the light goes out)

Troubleshooting (continued)

PROBABLE CAUSE

CORRECTIVE ACTION

Brake warning light on instrument panel comes on (or stays on) (continued)

PROBABLE CAUSE	CORRECTIVE ACTION
4 Defective pressure differential valve or warning switch	4 Replace valve or switch
5 Air in the hydraulic system	5 Bleed the system, check for leaks
6 Brake pads worn out (vehicles with electric wear sensors - small	6 Replace brake pads (and sensors) probes that fit into the brake pads and ground out on the disc when the pads get thin)

Brakes do not self adjust

Disc brakes

PROBABLE CAUSE	CORRECTIVE ACTION
1 Defective caliper piston seals	1 Replace calipers. Also, possible contaminated fluid causing soft or swollen seals (flush system and fill with new fluid if in doubt)
2 Corroded caliper piston(s)	2 Same as above

Drum brakes

PROBABLE CAUSE	CORRECTIVE ACTION
1 Adjuster screw frozen	1 Remove adjuster, disassemble, clean and lubricate with high-temperature grease
2 Adjuster lever does not contact star wheel or is binding	2 Inspect drum brakes, assemble correctly or clean or replace parts as required
3 Adjusters mixed up (installed on wrong wheels after brake job)	3 Reassemble correctly
4 Adjuster cable broken or installed incorrectly (cable-type adjusters)	4 Install new cable or assemble correctly

Rapid brake lining wear

PROBABLE CAUSE	CORRECTIVE ACTION
1 Driver resting left foot on brake pedal	1 Don't ride the brakes
2 Surface finish on discs or drums too rough	2 Have discs or drums properly machined
3 Also see Brakes drag	

---

3   Anti-lock Brake System (ABS) - general information

General information

1   The Anti-lock Brake System is designed to maintain vehicle steerability, directional stability and optimum deceleration under severe braking conditions on most road surfaces. It does so by monitoring the rotational speed of each wheel and controlling the brake line pressure to each wheel during braking. This prevents the wheels from locking up.

2   The ABS system has three main components: the wheel speed sensors, an electronic control unit and a hydraulic unit. Four wheel speed sensors - one at each wheel - send a variable voltage signal to the control unit, which monitors these signals, compares them to its program and determines whether a wheel is about to lock up. When a wheel is about to lock up, the control unit signals the hydraulic unit to reduce hydraulic pressure (or not increase the braking pressure any further) at that wheel's brake caliper. Pressure modulation is handled by electrically-operated solenoid valves within the hydraulic control unit (see illustration).

3   If a problem develops within the system, an ABS warning light will illuminate on the dashboard. Sometimes, a visual inspection of the ABS system can help you locate the problem. Carefully inspect the ABS wiring harness. Pay particularly close attention to the harness and connections near each wheel. Look for signs of chafing and other damage caused by incorrectly routed wires. If a wheel sensor harness is damaged, it must be replaced along with the sensor (if they are assembled together).

Warning: *Do NOT try to repair an ABS wiring harness. The ABS system is sensitive to even the smallest changes in resistance. Repairing the harness could alter resistance values and cause the system to malfunction. If the ABS wiring harness is damaged in any way, it must be replaced.*

Caution: *Make sure the ignition is turned off before unplugging or reattaching any electrical connections.*

3.2 The integrated electronic and hydraulic control unit is located in the right rear corner of the engine compartment

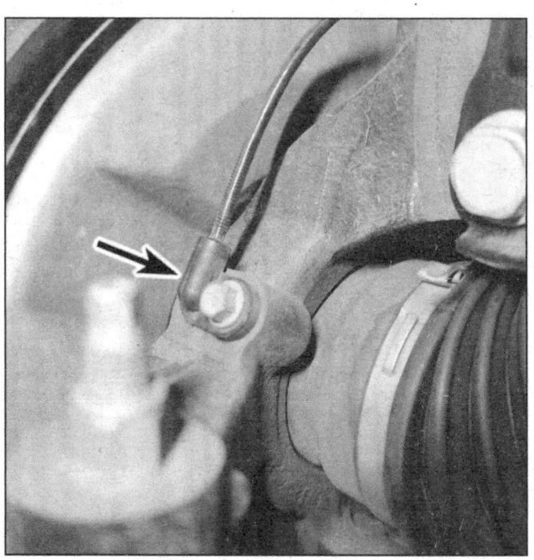

3.9a The front wheel speed sensor is mounted to the steering knuckle

3.9b The rear wheel speed sensor is mounted to the rear hub and bearing assembly. This is a disc brake model...

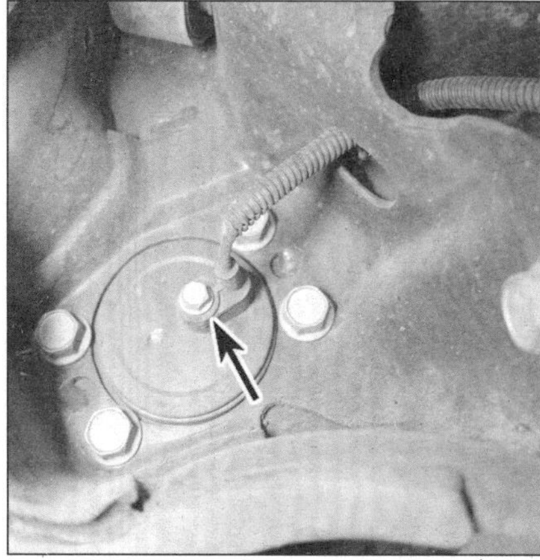

3.9c ... and this is a drum brake model

Diagnosis and repair

4   If the ABS warning light comes on and stays on while the vehicle is in operation, the ABS system requires attention. Although special electronic ABS diagnostic testing tools are necessary to properly diagnose the system, you can perform a few preliminary checks before taking the vehicle to a dealer service department.

a) *Check the brake fluid level in the reservoir.*

b) *Verify that the computer electrical connectors are securely connected.*

c) *Check the electrical connectors at the hydraulic control unit.*

d) *Check the fuses.*

e) *Follow the wiring harness to each wheel and verify that all connections are secure and that the wiring is undamaged.*

5   If the above preliminary checks do not solve the problem, the vehicle should be diagnosed by a dealer service department or other qualified repair shop. Due to the complex nature of the ABS system, all actual repair work must be done by a qualified automotive technician.

Wheel speed sensor - removal and installation

6   Loosen the wheel lug nuts, raise the vehicle and support it securely on jackstands. Remove the wheel.

7   Make sure the ignition key is turned to the Off position.

8   Trace the wiring back from the sensor, detaching all brackets, grommets and clips while noting its correct routing, then disconnect the electrical connector. The front speed sensor electrical connector may be easier to reach on some models from under the hood. To reach the electrical connector for the rear speed sensor(s), remove the cargo floor cover.

9   Remove the mounting fasteners and carefully detach the sensor from the knuckle (front) or hub and bearing assembly (rear) (see illustrations).

4.4 Spray the disc and brake pads with brake cleaner to remove brake dust; DO NOT blow brake dust off with compressed air - collect the contaminated fluid in a suitable container and dispose of it properly!

Note: *The rear sensor on AWD models is held in place by a spring-loaded retainer.*

10   Installation is the reverse of the removal procedure. Tighten the bolt to the torque listed in this Chapter's Specifications.

11   Install the wheel and lug nuts, lower the vehicle and tighten the lug nuts to the Chapter 1 Specifications.

---

4   Disc brake pads - replacement

Warning: *Disc brake pads must be replaced on both front or both rear wheels at the same time; never replace the pads on only one side. Also, the dust created by the brake system is harmful to your health. Never blow it out with compressed air and don't inhale any of it. An approved filtering mask should be worn when working on the brakes. Do not, under any circumstances, use petroleum-based solvents to clean brake parts. Use brake system cleaner only!*

4.5 Use a C-clamp to press the caliper piston into its bore

Caution: *Don't depress the brake pedal with the caliper removed.*

1   Using a syringe or equivalent, remove approximately two-thirds of the fluid from the master cylinder reservoir and discard it.

Caution: *Brake fluid will damage paint. If any fluid is spilled, wash it off immediately with plenty of clean, cold water.*

2   Loosen the wheel lug nuts, raise the end of the vehicle you will be working on and support it securely on jackstands. Block the wheels that remain on the ground.

3   Remove the wheels. Work on one brake assembly at a time, using the assembled brake for reference if necessary.

Front

4   Position a drain pan under the brake assembly and clean the caliper and surrounding area with brake system cleaner (see illustration).

5   Push the piston back into its bore using a C-clamp (see illustration). As the piston is depressed to the bottom of the caliper bore, the fluid in the master cylinder will rise as the brake fluid is displaced. Make sure it doesn't

4.6a Remove the caliper lower mounting bolt (guide pin) . . .

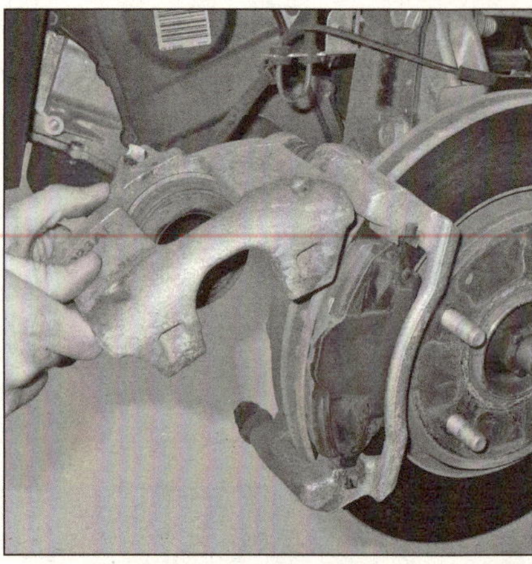

4.6b . . . then rotate the caliper up on the mounting bracket

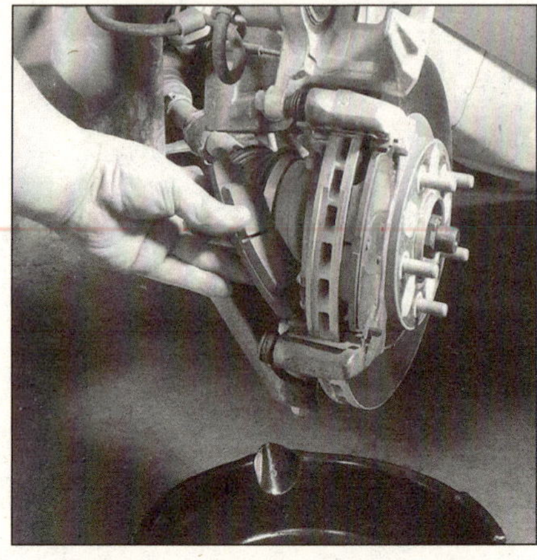

4.6c Remove the inner brake pad

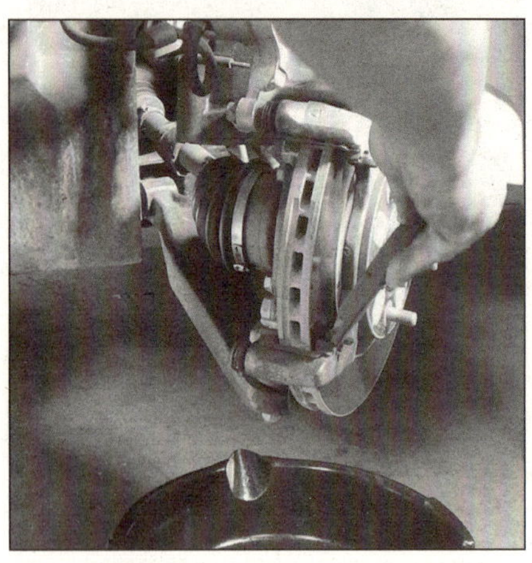

4.6d Remove the outer brake pad

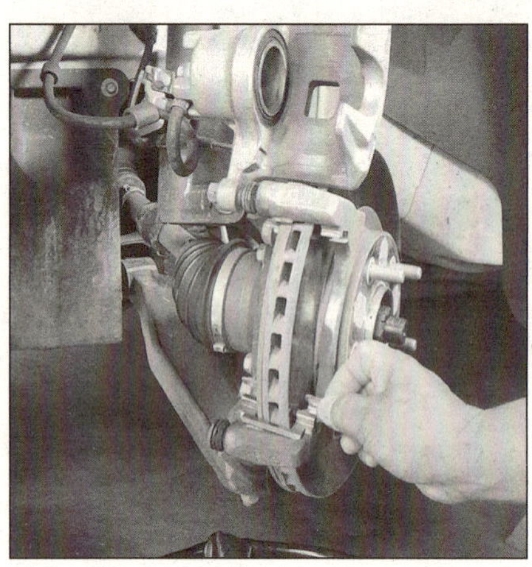

4.6e Remove the brake pad support plates from the caliper bracket

4.6f Slide the guide pin out and remove the caliper from the mounting bracket

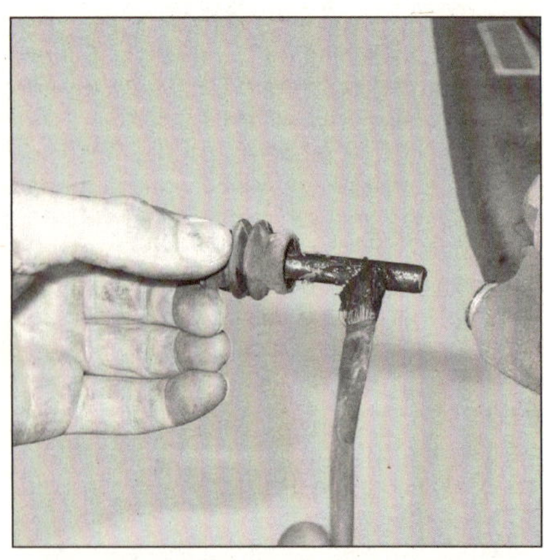

4.6g Pull out the caliper guide pins and clean them, then apply a coat of high-temperature grease to the pins and reinstall the pins in the caliper bracket

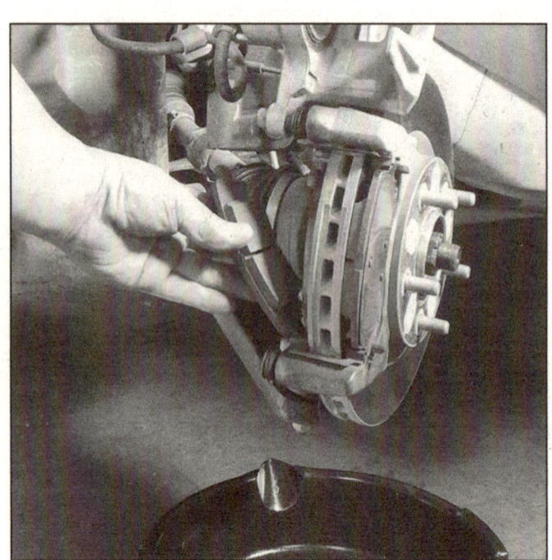

4.6h Clean the support plates, lubricate the wear points with high-temp brake grease and reinstall on the caliper mounting bracket, then place the pads in the caliper mounting bracket

overflow. If necessary, remove more of the fluid.

6   To replace the brake pads, follow the accompanying photos, beginning with illustration 4.6a. Stay in order and read the caption under each illustration.

7   While the pads are removed, inspect the caliper for brake fluid leaks and ruptures of the piston dust boot. Replace the caliper if necessary (see Section 5). Also inspect the brake disc carefully (see Section 6). If machining is necessary, follow the information in that section to remove the disc. Inspect the brake hoses for damage and replace if necessary (see Section 10).

8   Before installing the caliper, clean and inspect the guide pin bolts for corrosion and damage. If they're significantly corroded or damaged, replace them. Also check the guide pin rubber bushings for wear. When installing the caliper, tighten the guide pin bolts to the torque listed in this Chapter's Specifications.

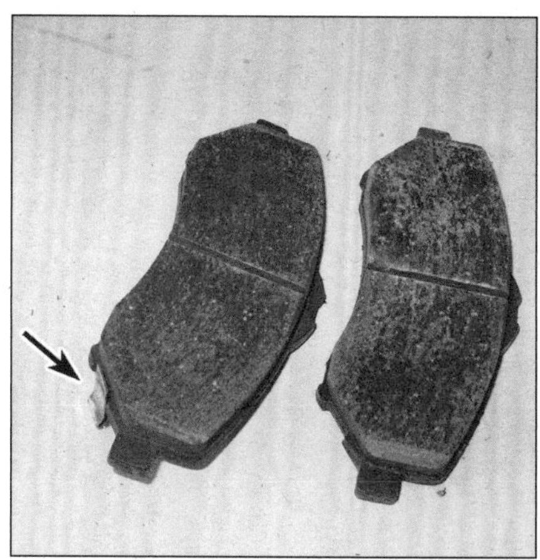

4.6i The inner pad is the one with the wear indicator - when installed, the wear indicator must be positioned at the top

4.6j Install the caliper and tighten the caliper mounting bolts to the torque listed in this Chapter's Specifications

4.14a Use a C-clamp, positioned alternately on each caliper mounting bolt (guide pin) and the caliper bracket, and evenly compress the piston into its bore

4.14b Remove the caliper lower mounting (guide pin) bolt

4.14c Rotate the caliper up and hold it in place with wire or a bungee cord

4.14d Remove the inner pad from the caliper mounting bracket

9   Repeat the procedure on the opposite wheel, then install the wheels and lug nuts, lower the vehicle back to the ground and tighten the lug nuts to the torque listed in the Chapter 1 Specifications.

10   Add the specified type of brake fluid to the reservoir until it's full (see Chapter 1).

11   Pump the brake pedal a few times to bring the pads into contact with the disc. Check the level of the brake fluid, adding some if necessary.

12   Check the operation of the brakes carefully before placing the vehicle into normal service. Try to avoid heavy brake application until the brakes have been applied several times to seat the pads.

Warning: *The first time you apply the brakes, the pedal will fall a great deal further than you are expecting. Be aware of this before you try to move the vehicle. Pump the brakes until the pedal returns to its normal position. Check for any leaks or misaligned components if the pedal does not return to the normal position.*

Rear

13   Position a drain pan under the brake assembly and clean the caliper and surrounding area with brake system cleaner (see illustration 4.4).

14   To replace the brake pads, follow the accompanying photos, beginning with illustration 4.14a. Stay in order and read the caption under each illustration.

15   While the pads are removed, inspect the caliper for brake fluid leaks and ruptures of the piston dust boot. Replace the caliper if necessary (see Section 5). Also inspect the brake disc carefully (see Section 6). If machining is necessary, follow the information in that Section to remove the disc. Inspect the brake hoses for damage and replace if necessary (see Section 10).

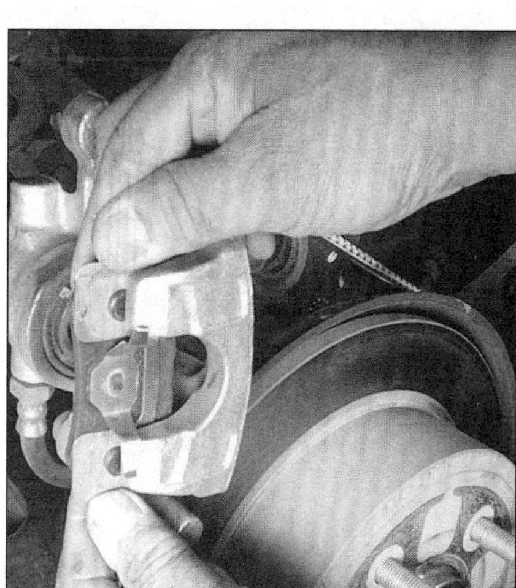

4.14e Remove the outer pad from the caliper

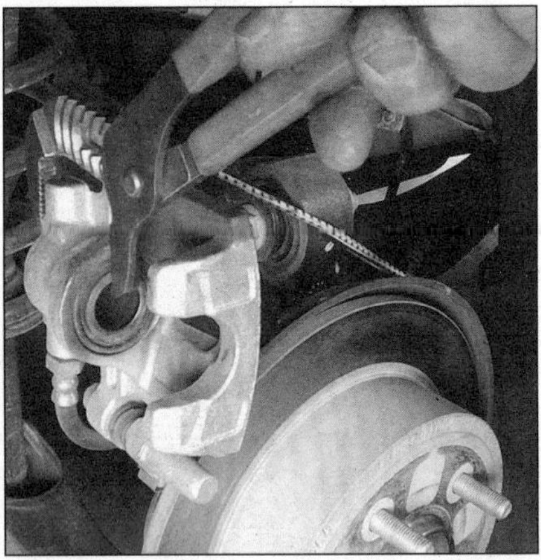

4.14f Compress the piston into its bore to make room for the new pads

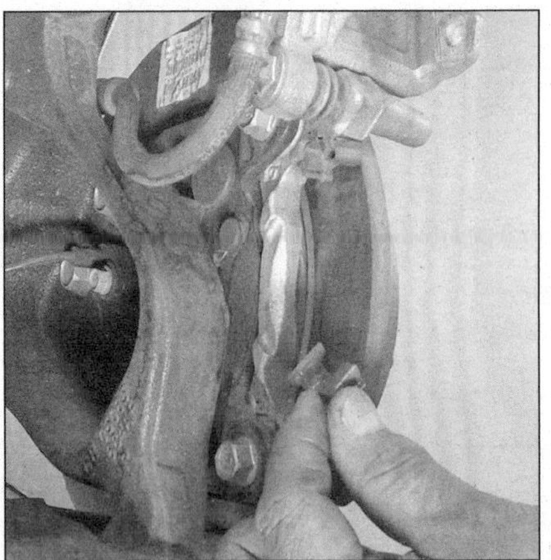

4.14g Remove the pad support plates from the caliper mounting bracket and inspect them. If they are cracked or fit loosely, replace them

4.14h Lubricate the shanks of the caliper mounting bolts (guide pins) with high-temperature brake grease

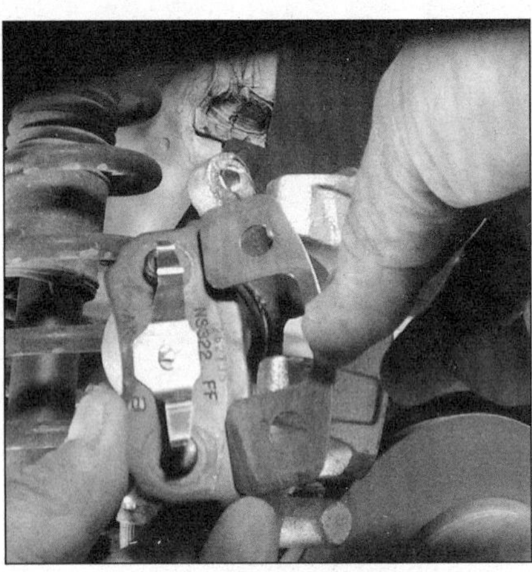

4.14i If equipped, install the shim to the new outer pad…

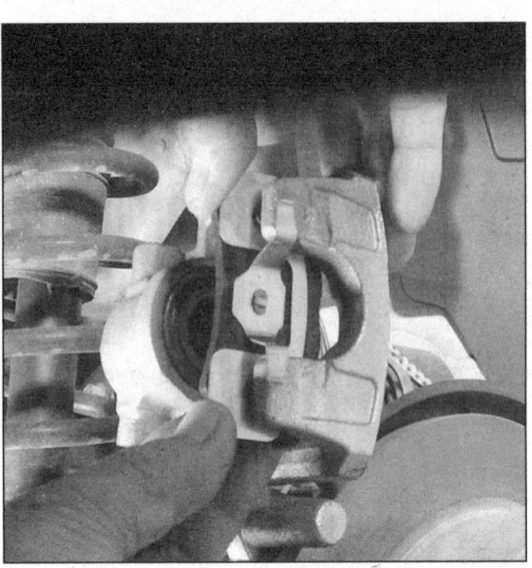

4.14j . . . then install the outer pad and shim to the caliper, making sure the projections on the pad backing plate engage properly with the holes in the caliper frame

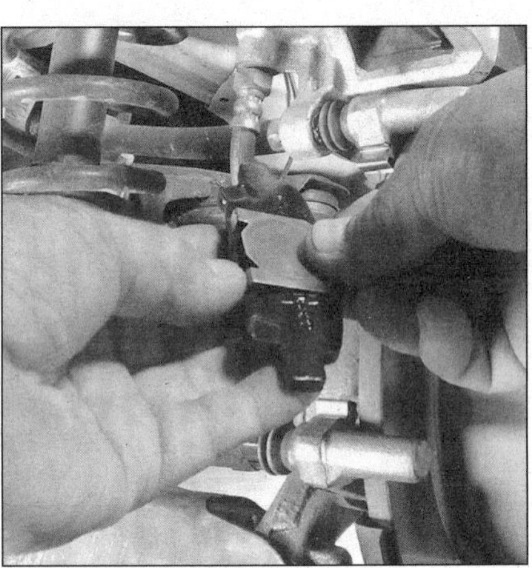

4.14k If equipped, install the shim to the new inner pad…

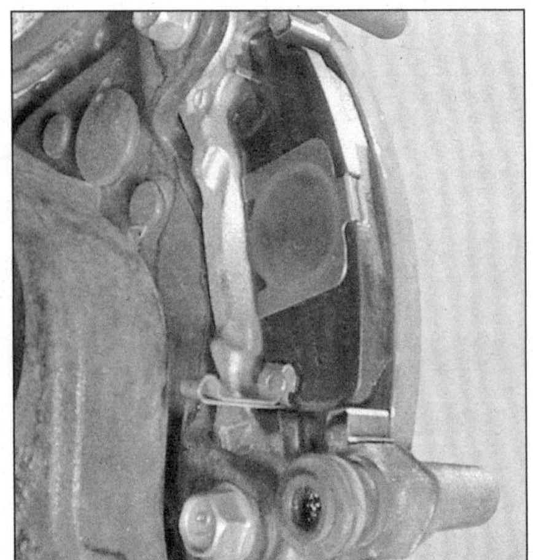

4.14l . . . then install the pad into the caliper mounting bracket

4.14m Rotate the caliper back down into place, install the lower mounting bolt (guide pin) and tighten it to the torque listed in this Chapter's Specifications

16　Before installing the caliper mounting bolts (guide pins), clean and inspect them for corrosion and damage. If they're significantly corroded or damaged, replace them. Also check the guide pin rubber bushings for wear. Tighten them to the torque listed in this Chapter's Specifications.

17　Repeat the procedure on the opposite wheel, then install the wheels and lug nuts, lower the vehicle and tighten the lug nuts to the torque listed in the Chapter 1 Specifications.

18　Add the specified type of brake fluid to the reservoir until it's up to the appropriate level (see Chapter 1).

19　Pump the brake pedal a few times to bring the pads into contact with the disc. Check the level of the brake fluid, adding some if necessary.

20　Check the operation of the brakes carefully before placing the vehicle into normal service. Try to avoid heavy brake application

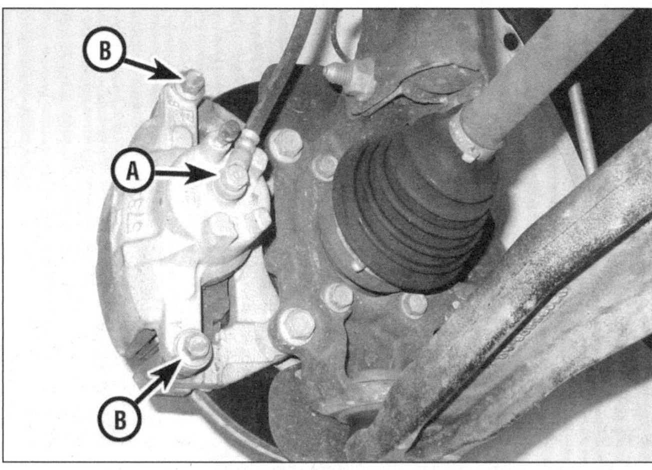

5.2 Remove the banjo bolt (A), then remove the caliper mounting (guide pin) bolts (B)

6.3 The brake pads on this vehicle were obviously neglected - they wore down completely and cut deep grooves into the disc (wear this severe means the disc must be replaced)

until the brakes have been applied several times to seat the pads.

Warning: *The first time you apply the brake, the pedal will fall a great deal further than you are expecting. Be aware of this before you try to move the vehicle. Pump the brakes until the pedal returns to its normal position. Check for any leaks or misaligned components if the pedal does not return to the normal position.*

5 Disc brake caliper - removal and installation

Warning: *Dust created by the brake system is harmful to your health. Never blow it out with compressed air and don't inhale any of it. An approved filtering mask should be worn when working on the brakes. Do not, under any circumstances, use petroleum-based solvents to clean brake parts. Use brake system cleaner only.*

Note: *If replacement is indicated (usually because of fluid leakage), it is recommended that the calipers be replaced, not overhauled. New and factory rebuilt units are available on an exchange basis. Always replace the calipers in pairs - never replace just one of them.*

Removal

1   Loosen the wheel lug nuts, raise the vehicle and support it securely on jackstands. Remove the wheel.

2   If you're removing a front caliper, remove the banjo bolt and disconnect the brake hose from the caliper (see illustration). Plug the brake hose to keep contaminants out of the brake system and to prevent losing any more brake fluid than is necessary. Discard the sealing washers - new ones should be used during installation. If you're removing a rear caliper, remove the brake hose in same manner as the front brake hose (see Section 10)

Note: *If the caliper is being removed for access to other components, don't disconnect*

the hose.

3   Remove the caliper mounting bolts (guide pins).

Installation

4   Install the caliper by reversing the removal procedure. On front calipers, remember to replace the sealing washers at the brake hose-to-caliper connection. Tighten the caliper mounting bolts (guide pins) to the torque listed in this Chapter's Specifications.

5   Bleed the brake circuit (see Section 11). Make sure there are no leaks from the hose connections. Pump the brake pedal several times to bring the pads into contact with the disc.

Warning: *The first time you apply the brake, the pedal will fall a great deal further than you are expecting. Be aware of this before you try to move the vehicle. Pump the brakes until the pedal returns to its normal position. Check for any leaks or misaligned components if the pedal does not return to the normal position.*

6   Test the brakes carefully before returning the vehicle to normal service.

6 Brake disc - inspection, removal and installation

Warning: *Dust created by the brake system is harmful to your health. Never blow it out with compressed air and don't inhale any of it. An approved filtering mask should be worn when working on the brakes. Do not, under any circumstances, use petroleum-based solvents to clean brake parts. Use brake system cleaner only.*

Note: *This procedure applies to both front and rear brake discs.*

Inspection

1   Loosen the wheel lug nuts, raise the vehicle and support it securely on jackstands. Remove the wheel and reinstall the lug nuts

6.4a Use a dial indicator to measure disc runout - if the reading exceeds the maximum allowable runout limit, the disc will have to be machined or replaced

to hold the disc in place (washers may be required). If the rear brake disc is being worked on, release the parking brake.

2   Remove the brake caliper and pads (see Sections 4 and 5). Don't disconnect the brake hose from the caliper, or you'll have to bleed the brakes when everything is reassembled. After removing the caliper, suspend it out of the way with a piece of wire.

3   Visually inspect the disc surface for score marks and other damage. Light scratches and shallow grooves are normal after use and may not always be detrimental to brake operation, but deep scoring requires disc removal and refinishing by an automotive machine shop. Check both sides of the disc (see illustration). If pulsating has been noticed during application of the brakes, suspect excessive disc runout.

4   To check disc runout, place a dial indicator at a point about 1/2-inch from the outer edge of the disc (see illustration). Set the indicator to zero and turn the disc. The indicator

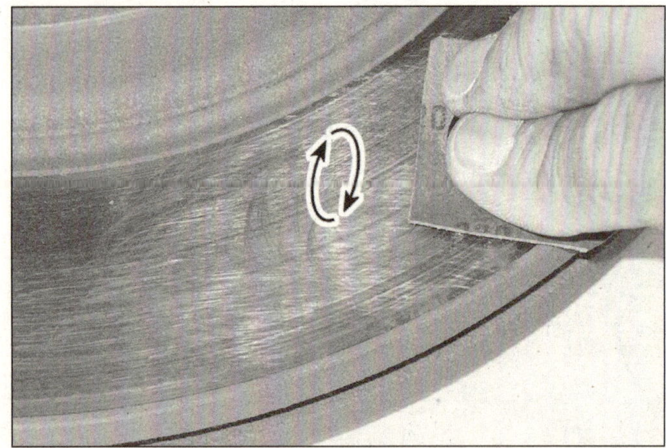

6.4b Using a swirling motion, remove the glaze from the disc surface with sandpaper or emery cloth

6.5a The minimum wear dimension is cast into the back side of the disc (typical)

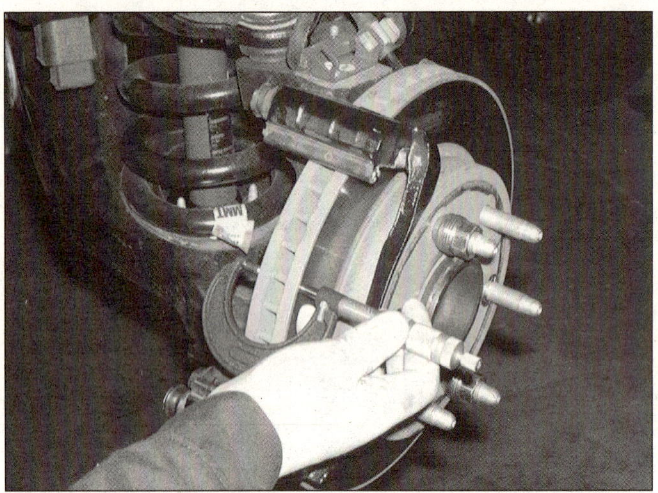

6.5b Use a micrometer to measure disc thickness

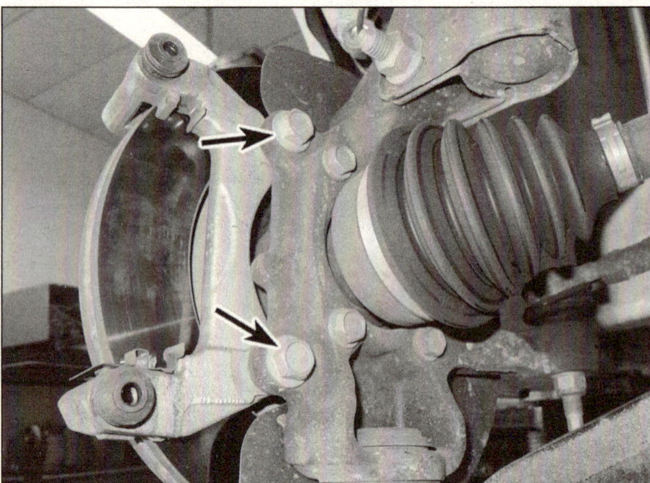

6.6 Remove the caliper mounting bracket bolts and remove the bracket (front caliper shown, rear similar)

reading should not exceed the specified allowable runout limit. If it does, the disc should be refinished by an automotive machine shop.

Note: *The discs should be resurfaced regardless of the dial indicator reading, as this will impart a smooth finish and ensure a perfectly flat surface, eliminating any brake pedal pulsation or other undesirable symptoms related to questionable discs. At the very least, if you elect not to have the discs resurfaced, remove the glaze from the surface with emery cloth using a swirling motion (see illustration).*

5   It's absolutely critical that the disc not be machined to a thickness under the specified minimum allowable thickness. The minimum thickness is cast into the inside of the disc (see illustration). The disc thickness can be checked with a micrometer (see illustration).

Note: *As the pads wear and the disc gets thinner it's not unusual to have lip on the outer edge or rim of the rotor. This is a good indication that the rotor may be too thin to reuse. Check the overall thickness as described. If*

you're having an issue getting a reading because of the lip, place a coin on either side of the rotor and use the coins to measure off of. Once you have taken the measurement, subtract the width of the coins to obtain the actual width of the rotor. Check that measurement against the factory specifications that are stamped into the rotor or in the specification page of this manual.

Removal

6   Remove the caliper mounting bracket bolts (see illustration). Remove the lug nuts which were put on to hold the disc in place and remove the disc from the hub.

Note: *Remove and discard any retaining clips on the wheel studs that hold the disc to the hub. These clips are not necessary for reinstallation of the brake disc.*

Installation

7   Place the disc in position over the wheel studs. Install the mounting bracket, tightening

the bolts to the torque listed in this Chapter's Specifications.

8   Install the brake pads and caliper (see Section 4). Tighten the caliper mounting bolts (guide pins) to the torque listed in this Chapter's Specifications.

9   Install the wheel, lower the vehicle and tighten the lug nuts to the torque listed in the Chapter 1 Specifications.

10   Pump the brake pedal a few times to bring the brake pads into contact with the disc. Bleeding won't be necessary unless the brake hose was disconnected from the caliper. Check the operation of the brakes carefully before driving the vehicle.

Warning: *The first time you apply the brake, the pedal will fall a great deal further than you are expecting. Be aware of this before you try to move the vehicle. Pump the brakes until the pedal returns to its normal position. Check for any leaks or misaligned components if the pedal does not return to the normal position.*

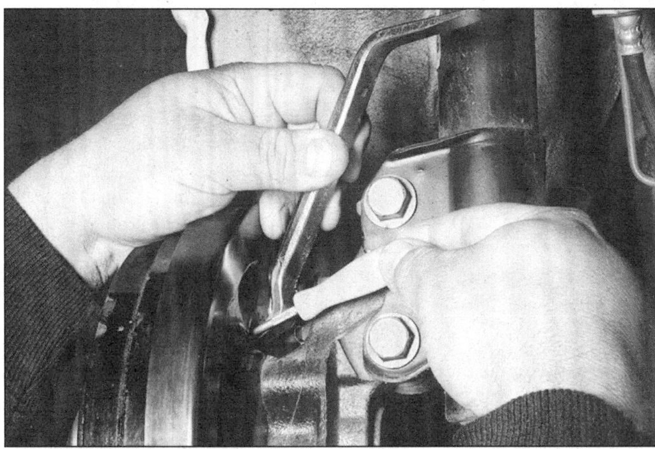

7.2a If the brake drums are hanging up on the brake shoes because of excessive wear, remove the access plug from the backing plate, insert a pair of small screwdrivers (or a screwdriver and a brake adjuster tool, as shown) and retract the shoes

7.2b Lift the adjuster lever off the adjuster wheel with the screwdriver and rotate the adjuster wheel until the shoes are retracted sufficiently to allow drum removal (brake drum removed for clarity)

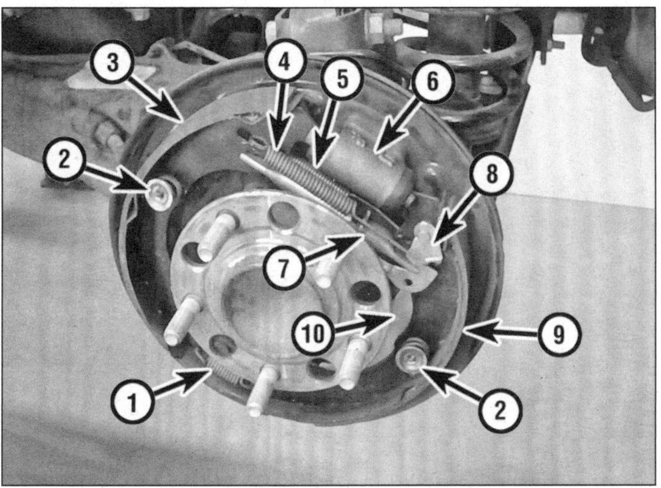

7.3 Drum brake details (left side shown)

1	Lower return spring	6	Wheel cylinder
2	Hold-down spring and retainer	7	Adjuster
3	Leading shoe	8	Adjuster lever
4	Adjuster spring	9	Trailing shoe
5	Upper return spring	10	Parking brake lever

7.4a Before disassembling the brake, wash it thoroughly with brake system cleaner and allow it to dry - position a drain pan under the brake to catch the residue - DO NOT use compressed air to blow the brake dust off!

7 Drum brake shoes - replacement

Warning: *Drum brake shoes must be replaced on both wheels at the same time - never replace the shoes on only one wheel. Also, the dust created by the brake system is harmful to your health. Never blow it out with compressed air and don't inhale any of it. An approved filtering mask should be worn when working on the brakes. Do not, under any circumstances, use petroleum-based solvents to clean brake parts. Use brake system cleaner only!*

Caution: *Whenever the brake shoes are replaced, the return and hold-down springs should also be replaced. Due to the continuous heating/cooling cycle the springs are subjected to, they lose tension over a period of time and may allow the shoes to drag on the drum and wear at a much faster rate than normal.*

1   Loosen the wheel lug nuts, raise the rear of the vehicle and support it securely on jackstands. Block the front wheels to keep vehicle from rolling. Remove the wheels.

Note: *Work on one side at a time and use the opposite side as a pattern for the brake shoes and spring locations. Keeping in mind that the leading shoe and trailing shoes are different. Be sure to have the correct shoe in the correct position. (Use the opposite side to confirm the locations).*

2   Release the parking brake and remove the brake drums. If the brake drum is difficult to remove, try tapping lightly around the outer edge of the drum on one side as you pull on the other. If this doesn't help, then remove the access plug from the backing plate, insert a small screwdriver through the hole, lift the adjuster lever off the adjusting wheel and turn the wheel with another screwdriver to back off the brake shoes (see illustrations). The drum should now come off.

3   All four rear brake shoes must be replaced at the same time, but to avoid mixing up parts, work on only one brake assembly at a time (see illustration).

4   Before disassembling anything, wash off the brake assembly with brake system cleaner (see illustration). Follow the accompanying illustrations for the brake shoe replacement

procedures (see illustrations). Be sure to stay in order and read the caption under each illustration.

5   Before reinstalling the drum, it should be checked for cracks, score marks, deep scratches and hard spots, which will appear as small discolored areas. If the hard spots cannot be removed with fine emery cloth or if any of the other conditions listed above exist, the drum must be taken to an automotive machine shop to have it resurfaced. If there is a lip of material on the outer rim of the drum this will need to be removed by resurfacing the drum.

Caution: *Resurfacing the drums will eliminate the possibility of the drums being out of round and also eliminate glaze and hard spots. If the drums are worn so much that they can't be* *resurfaced without exceeding the maximum allowable diameter, (which is stamped into the drum) then new ones will be required. At the very least, if you elect not to have the drums resurfaced, remove the glaze from the surface with emery cloth using a swirling motion.*

6   Install the brake drum.

7   Normally when installing new shoes the adjuster will need to be turned in to its lowest (smallest) position, then slide the drum over the shoes. It's a good idea to adjust the shoe adjuster star wheel so that a slight grab is felt as you slide the drum over the shoes. Keep adjusting the star wheel until you feel the drag by pulling the drum off and onto the shoes. This will speed up the adjustment process. To make a preliminary adjustment of the brakes, with the drum in place, turn the adjuster star wheel until the brakes just begin to drag on the drum as it is turned, then back-off the star wheel until no dragging can be heard when you rotate the drum. Depress the brake pedal firmly several times, then rotate the drum to ensure that the brakes are not dragging. If they are, back off the star wheel a little more.

8   Mount the wheel, install the lug nuts, then lower the vehicle. Tighten the wheel lug nuts to the torque listed in the Chapter 1 Specifications.

9   Make a number of forward and reverse stops and operate the parking brake to adjust the brakes until satisfactory pedal action is obtained.

10   Check the operation of the brakes carefully before driving the vehicle.

7.4b Unhook and remove the lower return spring

7.4c Remove the retainer and hold-down spring from the trailing shoe

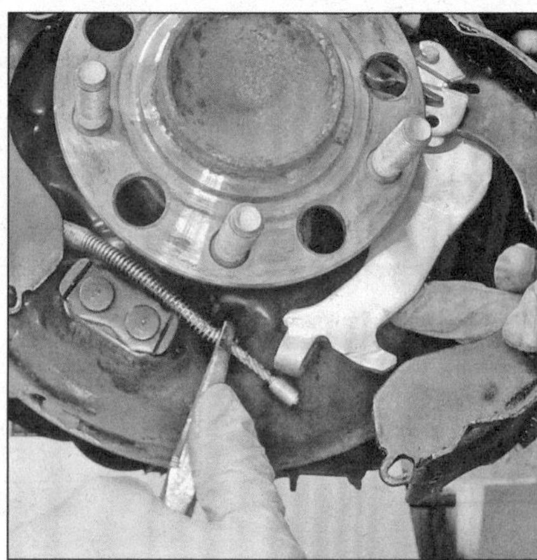

7.4d Pull back the spring and unhook the parking brake cable from the parking brake lever

7.4e Remove the retainer and hold-down spring from the leading shoe

7.4f Remove the brakes shoes and adjuster assembly upward, out from behind the hub flange

7.4g Clean the backing plate with brake system cleaner

7.4h Lubricate the brake shoe contact areas with a thin film of high-temperature brake grease

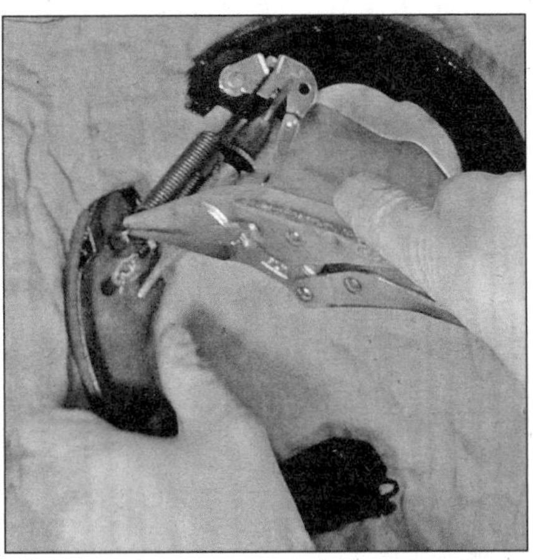

7.4i Unhook and remove the adjuster spring from the leading shoe and adjuster

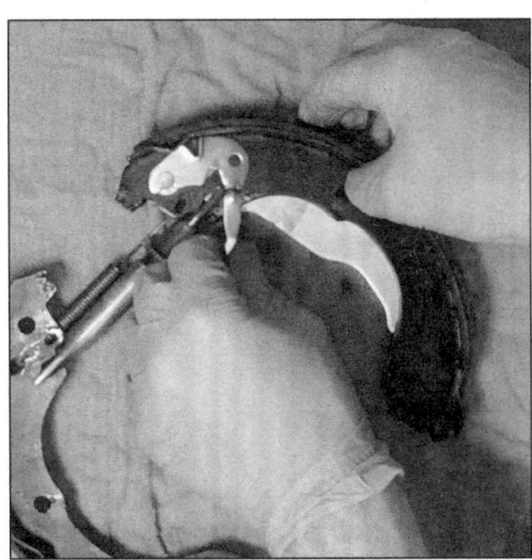

7.4j Remove the adjuster lever from the pin on the trailing shoe

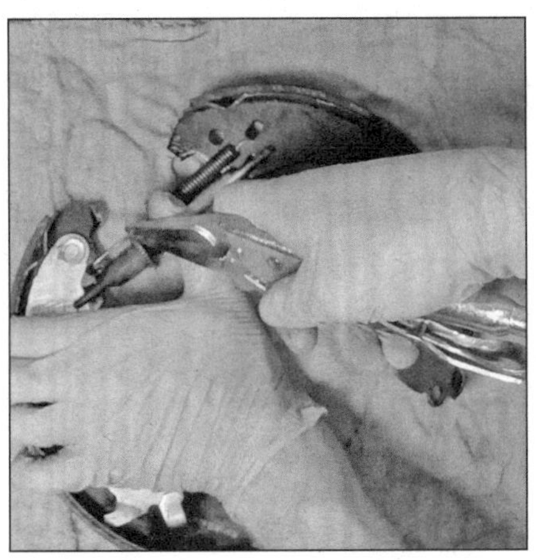

7.4k Unhook and remove the upper return spring

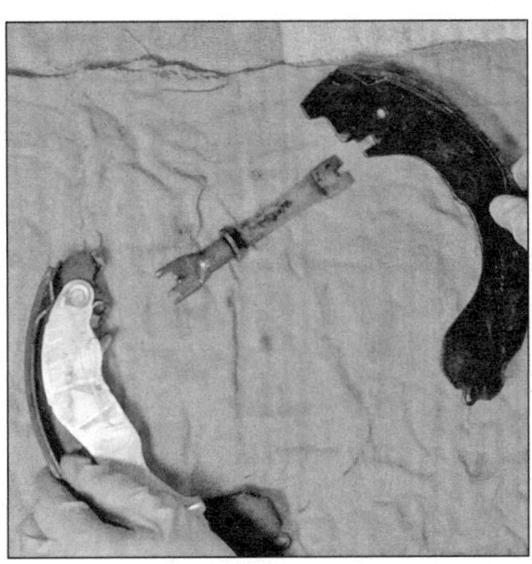

7.4l Separate the shoes and adjuster

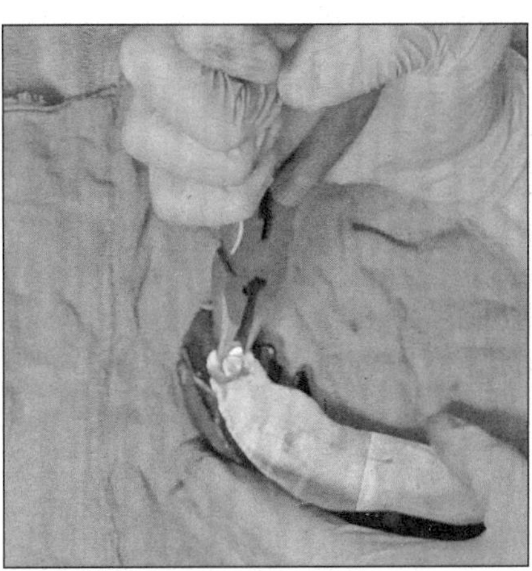

7.4m Spread the bottom of the parking brake lever retaining clip apart, then force the clip off the pin with a pair of pliers

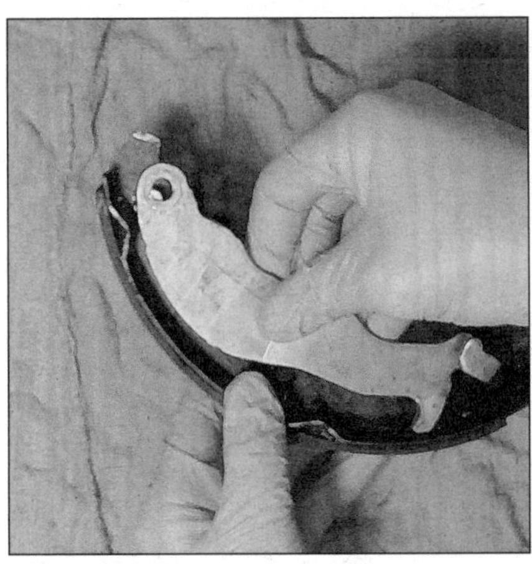

7.4n Transfer the parking brake lever to the new trailing shoe…

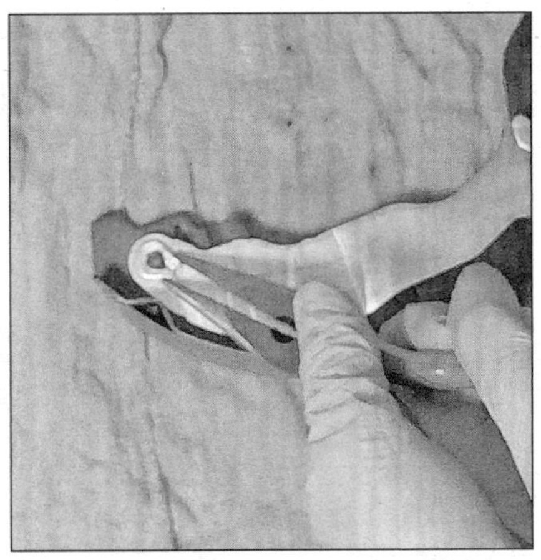

7.4o … then install the retaining clip and crimp it closed around the pin

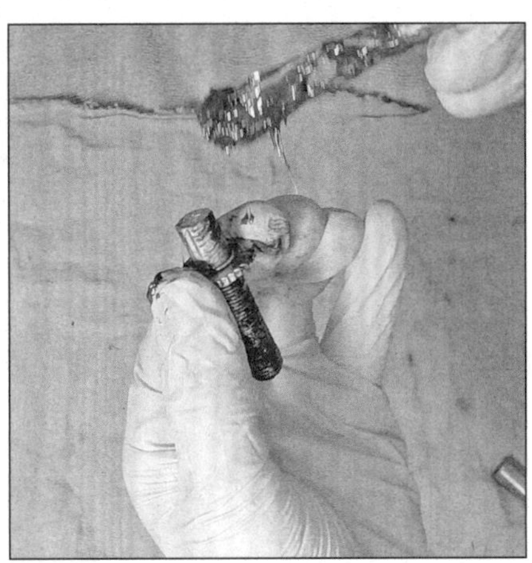

7.4p Disassemble and clean the adjuster, then lubricate the moving parts with high-temperature brake grease

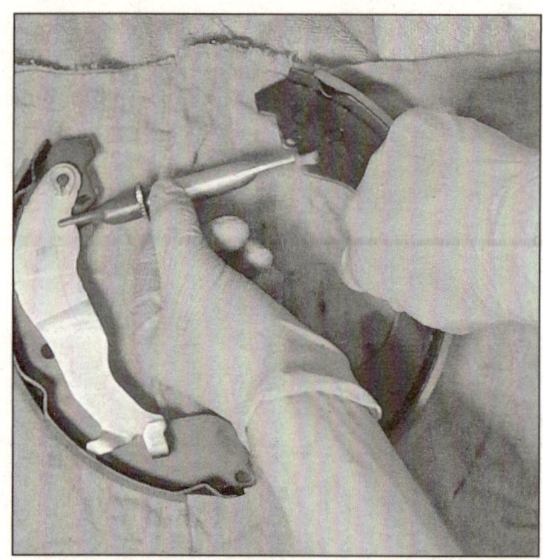

7.4q Install the adjuster between the brake shoes. Note that the end with the adjuster wheel is closest to the parking brake lever

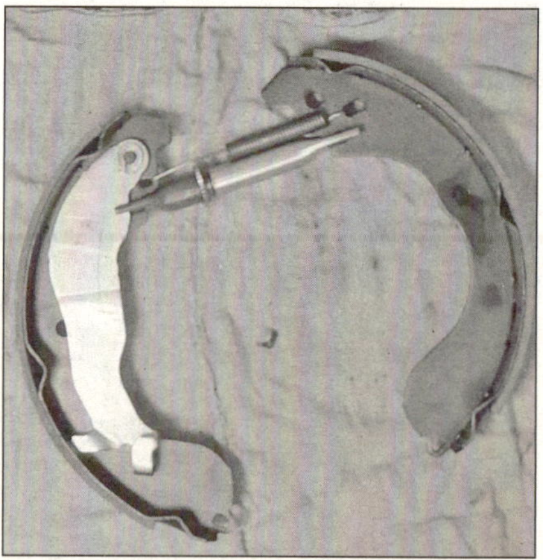

7.4r Install the upper return spring on the backside of the shoes

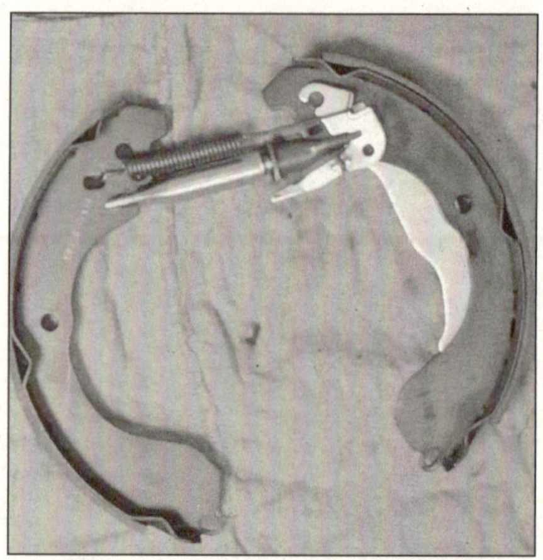

7.4s Turn the shoes over and install the adjuster lever and adjuster spring

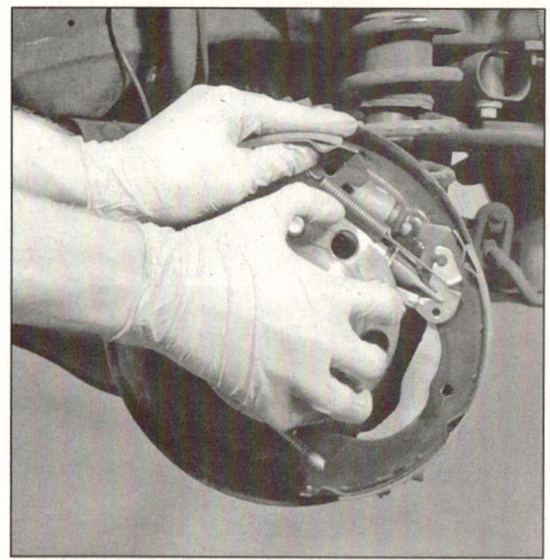

7.4t Guide the shoe assembly into place on the backing plate, making sure the tops of the shoes engage with the wheel cylinder pushrods

7.4u Install the leading shoe hold-down spring and retainer

7.4v Connect the parking brake cable to the lever

7.4w Install the trailing shoe hold-down spring and retainer

7.4x Connect the lower return spring to the bottom of each shoe

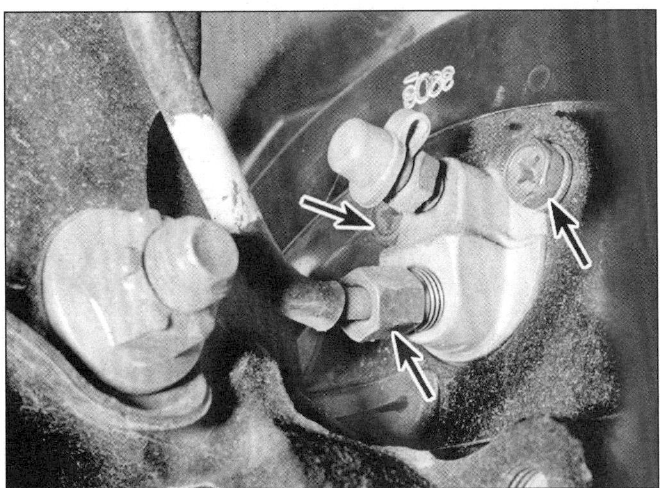

8.2 To detach the wheel cylinder from the brake backing plate, disconnect the brake line fitting, then remove the wheel cylinder bolts

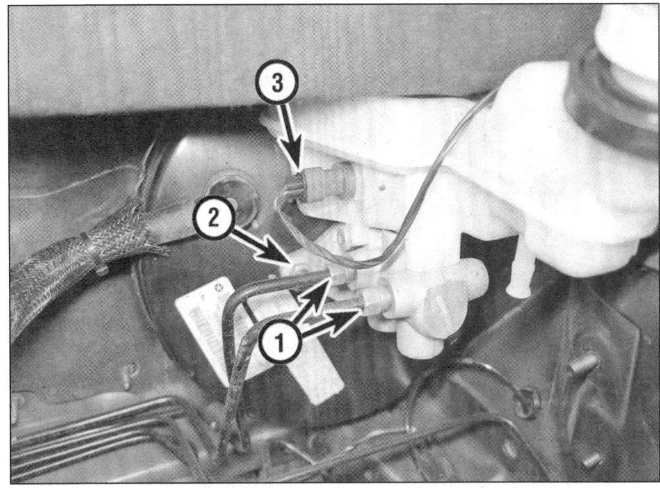

9.6 Master cylinder details:

1   *Brake line fittings*
2   *Mounting nut (other nut not visible)*
3   *Fluid level switch electrical connector*

8   Wheel cylinder - removal and installation

Note: *If replacement is warranted (usually because of fluid leakage or sticky operation) explore all options before beginning the job. New wheel cylinders are available, which makes this job quite easy. Never replace only one wheel cylinder. Always replace both of them at the same time.*

Removal

1   Remove the rear brake shoes (see Section 7).
2   Use a flare-nut wrench to disconnect the brake line fitting from the wheel cylinder (see illustration). Plug the end of the brake line to prevent fluid loss and contamination.
3   Remove the two bolts securing the wheel cylinder to the backing plate and remove the wheel cylinder.

Installation

4   Installation is the reverse of removal. Tighten the wheel cylinder mounting bolts to the torque listed in this Chapter's Specifications. Tighten the line fitting securely.
5   Install the brake shoes and brake drum (see Section 7).
6   Bleed the brakes (see Section 11). Carefully test brake operation before resuming normal operation.

9   Master cylinder - removal and installation

Caution: *Brake fluid will quickly damage paint. Cover all body parts and be careful not to spill fluid during any of the following procedures. Wipe up any spilled fluid immediately and then flush the area thoroughly with water.*

Removal

Note: *The master cylinder is located in the engine compartment, mounted to the power brake booster.*

1   Disconnect the cable from the negative terminal of the battery (see Chapter 5). With the engine off, pump the brake pedal several times to relieve the vacuum reserve inside the power brake booster.
Note: *This step will prevent contaminants from being sucked into the power brake booster when the cylinder is removed.*
2   Remove the air filter housing (see Chapter 4).
3   Using a syringe or equivalent, siphon the brake fluid from the master cylinder reservoir and dispose of it properly.
4   If equipped with a manual transaxle, detach the fluid hose from the bottom of the brake fluid reservoir. Plug the hose to prevent contamination and fluid spillage.
5   Disconnect the brake fluid level switch connector and move the harness out of the way.
6   Place rags under the fluid fittings and prepare caps or plastic bags to cover the ends of the lines once they are disconnected. Loosen the fittings at the ends of the brake lines where they enter the master cylinder (see illustration). Pull the brake lines slightly away from the master cylinder and quickly plug the ends to prevent contamination.
Note: *To prevent rounding off the corners on these nuts, the use of a flare-nut wrench, which wraps around the nut, is preferred.*
7   Thoroughly clean the area where the master cylinder mounts to the power booster. Remove the nuts attaching the master cylinder to the power booster. Pull the master cylinder off the studs and out of the engine compartment. Again, be careful not to spill any fluid as this is done.
8   If necessary, disengage the retaining tabs holding the reservoir and transfer the

9.10 The best way to bleed air from the master cylinder before installing it on the vehicle is with a pair of bleeder tubes that direct brake fluid into the reservoir during bleeding

reservoir to the new master cylinder.
Note: *Install new seals between the master cylinder and reservoir.*

Installation

9   Bench bleed the new master cylinder before installing it. Mount the master cylinder in a vise, with the jaws of the vise clamping on the mounting flange.
10   Attach a pair of master cylinder bleeder tubes to the outlet ports of the master cylinder (see illustration).
11   Fill the reservoir with brake fluid of the recommended type (see Chapter 1).
12   Slowly push the pistons into the master cylinder (a large Phillips screwdriver can be used for this) - air will be expelled from the pressure chambers and into the reservoir. Because the tubes are submerged in fluid, air

10.3 Front brake hose/line details

1   Brake line fitting
2   Brake hose retaining clip
3   Brake hose-to-strut
    bracket
4   Brake line banjo fitting
    at caliper

10.12 Rear brake hose/line details (disc brake model)

1   Brake line fitting
2   Brake hose retaining clip
3   Brake hose
    threaded fitting

can't be drawn back into the master cylinder when you release the pistons.

13   Repeat the procedure until no more air bubbles are present.

14   Remove the bleed tubes, one at a time, and install plugs in the open ports to prevent fluid leakage and air from entering. Install the reservoir cap.

15   Install a new vacuum seal onto the master cylinder where it mates with the power booster.

Warning: *Do not skip this step or a vacuum leak could occur and render the power booster ineffective; this results in greatly increased pedal effort and longer stopping distances.*

16   Install the master cylinder over the studs on the power brake booster and tighten the attaching nuts only finger-tight at this time.

17   Carefully thread the brake line fittings into the master cylinder. Since the master cylinder is still a bit loose, it can be moved slightly in order for the fittings to thread in easily. Do not strip the threads as the fittings are tightened.

18   Fully tighten the mounting nuts, and then the brake line fittings. Tighten the nuts to the torque listed in this Chapter's Specifications.

19   Fill the master cylinder reservoir with fluid, then bleed the master cylinder and the brake system (see Section 11). To bleed the cylinder on the vehicle, have an assistant depress the brake pedal and hold the pedal to the floor. Loosen the fitting to allow air and fluid to escape. Repeat this procedure on both fittings until the fluid is clear of air bubbles.

Caution: *Have plenty of rags on hand to catch the fluid - brake fluid will ruin painted surfaces. After the bleeding procedure is completed, rinse the area under the master cylinder thoroughly with clean water.*

20   Test the operation of the brake system carefully before placing the vehicle into normal service.

Warning: *Do not operate the vehicle if you are in doubt about the effectiveness of the brake system. It is possible for air to become trapped in the anti-lock brake system hydraulic control unit; if the pedal continues to feel spongy after repeated bleedings or the BRAKE or ANTI-LOCK light stays on, have the vehicle towed to a dealer service department or other qualified shop to be bled with the aid of a scan tool.*

10   Brake hoses and lines - inspection and replacement

Brake hose inspection

1   Whenever the vehicle is raised and supported securely on jackstands, the rubber hoses which connect the steel brake lines with the front and rear brake assemblies should be inspected for cracks, chafing of the outer cover, leaks, blisters and other damage. These are important and vulnerable parts of the brake system and inspection should be thorough. A light and mirror will be helpful for a complete check. If a hose exhibits any of the above conditions, replace it immediately.

Flexible hose replacement

Front

2   Clean all dirt away from the hose and line fittings.

3   Using a flare-nut wrench, disconnect the metal brake line from the hose fitting and immediately plug the metal line to prevent excessive leakage and contamination (see illustration). Be careful not to bend the metal line. If the threaded fitting is corroded, spray it with a penetrating oil and allow it to soak in for about 10 minutes, then try again. If you try to break loose a brake tube nut that's stuck, you will kink the metal line, which will then have to

be replaced.

4   Remove the clip retaining the brake hose to the bracket.

5   Remove the bolt retaining the brake hose bracket to the strut.

6   Unscrew the banjo bolt at the caliper and remove the hose, discarding the sealing washers on either side of the fitting.

7   Attach the new brake hose to the caliper.

Note: *When replacing the brake hoses, always use new sealing washers.*

8   Tighten the banjo bolt to the torque listed this Chapter's Specifications.

9   Attach the brake hose bracket to the strut, making sure the hose isn't kinked or twisted. Then connect the hose to the bracket on the chassis and install the retaining clip.

10   Connect the metal line to the hose fitting, tightening the fitting securely.

Rear

11   Clean all dirt away from the hose and line fittings.

Disc brake models

12   Using a flare-nut wrench, disconnect the metal brake line from the hose fitting and immediately plug the metal line to prevent excessive leakage and contamination (see illustration). Be careful not to bend the metal line. If the threaded fitting is corroded, spray it with a penetrating oil and allow it to soak in for about 10 minutes, then try again. If you try to break loose a brake tube nut that's stuck, you will kink the metal line, which will then have to be replaced.

13   Remove the clip retaining the brake hose to the bracket.

14   Unscrew the brake hose from the caliper.

15   Thread the new hose into the caliper and tighten it securely.

11.8 When bleeding the brakes, a hose is connected to the bleed screw at the caliper or wheel cylinder and then submerged in clean brake fluid - air will be seen as bubbles exiting the tube (all air must be expelled before moving to the next wheel)

16   Connect the hose to the bracket, making sure it isn't twisted, then install the retaining clip.

17   Connect the brake line fitting to the hose and tighten it securely.

Drum brake models

18   Using a flare-nut wrench, disconnect the metal brake lines from the hose fittings at each end and immediately plug the metal lines to prevent excessive leakage and contamination. Be careful not to bend the metal lines. If the threaded fitting is corroded, spray it with a penetrating oil and allow it to soak in for about 10 minutes, then try again. If you try to break loose a brake tube nut that's stuck, you will kink the metal line, which will then have to be replaced.

19   Remove the clips retaining the brake hose to the brackets.

20   Reverse the removal procedure to install the new hose. Make sure the hose is not twisted and does not contact any surrounding components.

Front or rear

21   Carefully check to make sure the suspension or steering components don't make contact with the hose. Have an assistant push down on the vehicle while you watch to see whether the hose interferes with suspension operation. If you're replacing a front hose, have your assistant turn the steering wheel lock-to-lock while you make sure the hose doesn't interfere with the steering linkage or the steering knuckle.

22   After installation, check the master cylinder fluid level and add fluid as necessary. Bleed the brakes (see Section 11). Carefully test brake operation before resuming normal operation.

Metal brake line replacement

23   When replacing brake lines, be sure to use the correct parts. Do not use copper tubing for any brake system components. Purchase steel brake lines from a dealer parts department or auto parts store.

24   Prefabricated brake lines, with the tube ends already flared and fittings installed, are available at auto parts stores and dealer parts

departments. These lines can be bent to the proper shapes using a tubing bender.

25   When installing the new line make sure it's well supported in the brackets and has plenty of clearance between moving or hot components. Make sure you tighten the fittings securely.

26   After installation, check the master cylinder fluid level and add fluid as necessary. Bleed the brakes (see Section 11). Carefully test brake operation before resuming normal operation.

---

11 Brake system - bleeding

Warning: *The following procedure is a manual bleeding procedure. This is the only bleeding procedure which can be performed at home without special tools. However, if air has found its way into the hydraulic control unit, the entire system must be bled manually, then with a DRB scan tool (or equivalent), then manually a second time. If the brake pedal feels spongy even after bleeding the brakes, or the ABS light on the instrument panel does not go off, or if you have any doubts whatsoever about the effectiveness of the brake system, have the vehicle towed to a dealer service department or other repair shop equipped with the necessary tools for bleeding the system.*

Warning: *Wear eye protection when bleeding the brake system. If the fluid comes in contact with your eyes, immediately rinse them with water and seek medical attention.*

Note: *Bleeding the hydraulic system is necessary to remove any air that manages to find its way into the system when it's been opened during removal and installation of a hydraulic component.*

1   It will be necessary to bleed the complete system if air has entered the system due to low fluid level, or if the brake lines have been disconnected at the master cylinder.

2   If a brake line was disconnected only at a wheel, then only that caliper or wheel cylinder must be bled.

3   If a brake line is disconnected at a fitting located between the master cylinder and any

of the brakes, that part of the system served by the disconnected line must be bled. The following procedure describes bleeding the entire system, however.

4   Remove any residual vacuum from the brake power booster by applying the brake several times with the engine off.

5   Remove the cap from the master cylinder reservoir and fill the reservoir with brake fluid. Reinstall the cap.

Note: *Check the fluid level often during the bleeding operation and add fluid as necessary to prevent the fluid level from falling low enough to allow air bubbles into the master cylinder.*

6   Have an assistant on hand, as well as a supply of new brake fluid, a clear container partially filled with clean brake fluid, a length of clear tubing to fit over the bleeder valve and a wrench to open and close the bleeder valve.

7   Begin the bleeding process by bleeding the first wheel in the bleeding sequence, loosen the bleeder valve slightly, then tighten it to a point where it is snug but can still be loosened quickly and easily. The bleeding sequence is as follows:

Left rear
Right front
Right rear
Left front

8   Place one end of the hose over the bleeder valve and submerge the other end in brake fluid in the container (see illustration).

9   Have the assistant push the brake pedal slowly to the floor, then hold the pedal firmly depressed.

10   While the pedal is held depressed, open the bleeder valve just enough to allow a flow of fluid to leave the valve. Watch for air bubbles to exit the submerged end of the tube. When the fluid flow slows after a couple of seconds, close the valve and have your assistant release the pedal.

11   Repeat Steps 9 and 10 until no more air is seen leaving the tube, then tighten the bleeder valve and proceed to bleed the other calipers/wheel cylinders, in the proper sequence, using the same procedure. Check the fluid in the master cylinder reservoir frequently.

Note: *Be careful not to over-tighten the bleeder valve.*

12   Never use old brake fluid. It contains moisture which can boil, rendering the brakes inoperative.

13   Refill the master cylinder with fluid at the end of the operation.

14   Check the operation of the brakes. The pedal should feel solid when depressed, with no sponginess. If necessary, repeat the entire process.

Warning: *If, after bleeding the system, you do not have a firm brake pedal, if the ABS light on the instrument panel does not go off, or if you have any doubts whatsoever about the effectiveness of the brake system, have it towed to a dealer service department or other repair shop to have the system bled.*

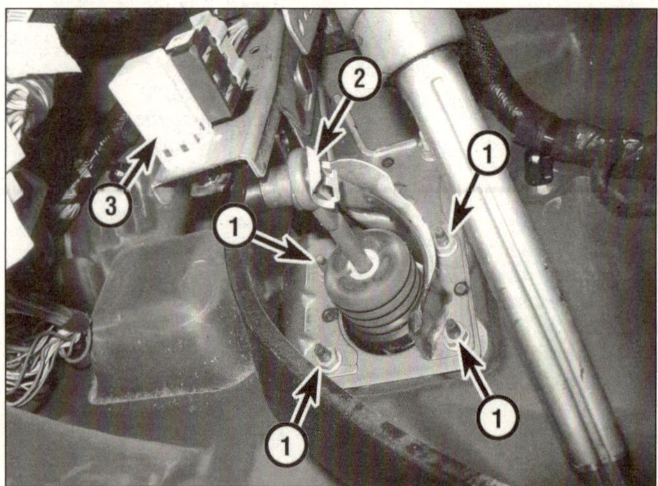

12.12 Power brake booster mounting details:

1 Mounting nuts
2 Pushrod-to-brake pedal retaining clip (DO NOT reuse)
3 Brake light switch

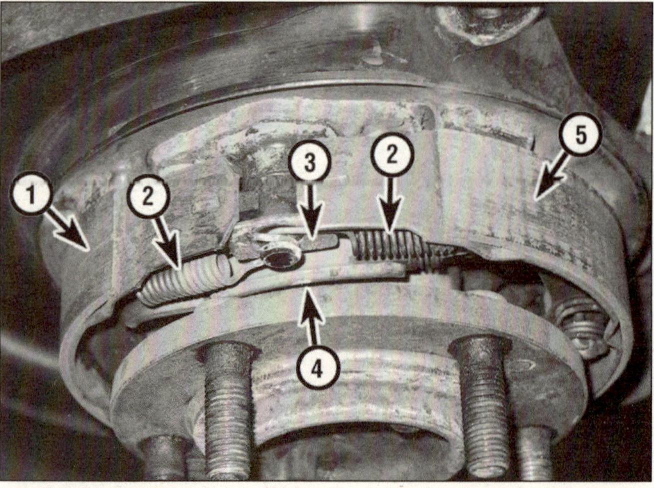

13.4a Parking brake shoe details (right side, viewed from above)

1 Trailing shoe
2 Upper return spring
3 Anchor plate
4 Strut
5 Leading shoe

12 Power brake booster - check, removal and installation

Operating check

1 Depress the pedal and start the engine. If the pedal goes down slightly, operation is normal.
2 Depress the brake pedal several times with the engine running and make sure that there is no change in the pedal reserve distance.

Airtightness check

3 Start the engine and turn it off after one or two minutes. Depress the brake pedal several times slowly. If the pedal goes down farther the first time but gradually rises after the second or third depression, the booster is airtight.
4 Depress the brake pedal while the engine is running, then stop the engine with the pedal depressed. If there is no change in the pedal reserve travel after holding the pedal for 30 seconds, the booster is airtight.

Removal

5 The power brake booster unit requires no special maintenance apart from periodic inspection of the vacuum hoses and the case. The booster should never be disassembled. If a problem develops, it must be replaced with a new one.
6 Remove any vacuum from the booster by pumping the pedal several times with the engine off, until the pedal feels hard to push.
7 Remove the air filter housing (see Chapter 4).
8 Clean the area where the master cylinder attaches to the power brake booster.
9 Remove the master cylinder (see Sec-

tion 9). Also disconnect the brake lines from the junction block below the power brake booster. Plug all open lines.
10 Disconnect the vacuum hose from the check valve that's located on the outside of the brake booster.
Warning: *Do not remove the check valve from the booster.*
11 Working under the dash, remove the knee bolster (see Chapter 11), then disconnect and remove the brake light switch (see Section 15).
12 Disconnect the brake pedal pushrod from the top of the brake pedal by inserting a small screwdriver into the center of the retaining clip and carefully prying the tang back (see illustration). For safety reasons, discard the old pushrod retaining clip and buy a new clip for reassembly.
13 Remove the nuts attaching the booster to the firewall.
14 Working inside the engine compartment, carefully withdraw the brake booster unit from the firewall and out of the engine compartment.

Installation

15 To install the booster, place it into position on the firewall, then tighten the retaining nuts to the torque listed in this Chapter's Specifications. Connect the brake pedal to the brake booster pushrod using a new retaining clip.
Warning: *DO NOT reuse the old booster pushrod retaining clip.*
16 The remainder of installation is the reverse of removal. Install a new vacuum seal on the master cylinder before reinstalling it to the power brake booster.
17 Bleed the brake system (see Section 11).
18 Carefully test the operation of the brakes

before placing the vehicle into normal operation.

13 Parking brake shoes (models with rear disc brakes) - replacement

Warning: *Parking brake shoes must be replaced on both wheels at the same time - never replace the shoes on only one wheel. Also, the dust created by the brake system is harmful to your health. Never blow it out with compressed air and don't inhale any of it. An approved filtering mask should be worn when working on the brakes. Do not, under any circumstances, use petroleum-based solvents to clean brake parts. Use brake system cleaner only!*

1 Loosen the rear wheel lug nuts, raise the rear end of the vehicle and support it securely on jackstands. Block the front wheels to keep the vehicle from rolling. Release the parking brake and remove the rear wheels.
2 Remove the brake caliper and brake disc (see Sections 5 and 6).
3 Once the disc is removed, clean the parking brake assembly with brake system cleaner.
4 Using locking pliers, unhook and remove the springs (see illustrations).
5 Remove the adjuster assembly (noting which end is facing forward) and strut from between the brake shoes.
6 Grasp one of the shoe hold-down cups with pliers and push it toward the brake backing plate to compress the hold-down spring. Twist the cup 1/4-turn to align the slot in the hold-down pin with the cup, then release the spring pressure (the pin will pass through the cup slot) and take off the cup and spring.

13.4b Parking brake shoe details (right side, viewed from below)

1	Hold-down spring and retainer	3	Lower return spring
2	Trailing shoe	4	Adjuster screw assembly
		5	Leading shoe

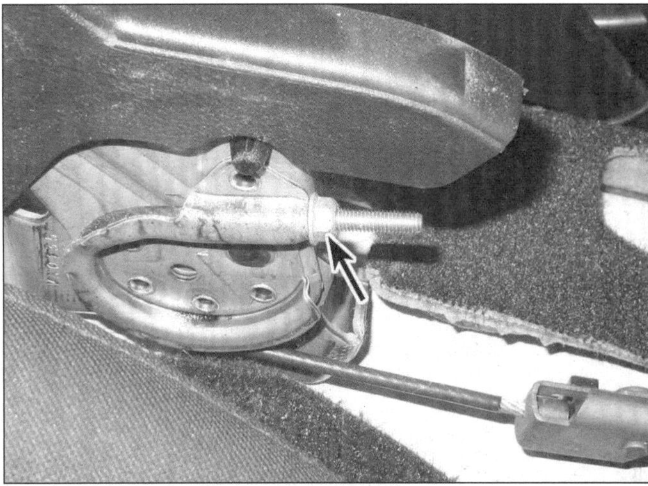

14.4 Parking brake adjustment nut

Repeat this with the cup and spring on the other parking brake shoe.

7   Take the shoes off the backing plate. Disengage the parking brake lever from the cable.

8   Check all parts for wear and damage, paying special attention to metal-to-metal contact points. Replace worn or damaged parts. The parking brake lever is integral with the shoe it's attached to.

Note: *If the vehicle has high mileage, it's a good idea to replace all of the springs as well as any parts that have visible problems.*

9   Check the parking brake drum surface inside the brake disc for score marks, cracks, deep scratches and hard spots, which will appear as small discolored areas. If the hard spots cannot be removed with emery cloth or if any of the other conditions are seen, the drum must be resurfaced by an automotive machine shop.

Note: *If you don't have the drums resurfaced, remove the glazing from the surface with emery cloth or sandpaper using a swirling motion.*

10   Apply a small amount of high-temperature brake grease to the friction points of the backing plate and adjuster screw assembly.

11   Reverse the removal steps to install the brake shoes. The shoe-to-anchor spring with the paint mark is installed with the paint mark toward the rear of the vehicle (for both left and right sides). Expand the shoes, using the automatic adjuster, until the drum will just fit over them.

12   Install the brake disc and caliper. Remove the rubber plug in the hub portion of the disc, then turn the adjuster screw until the disc will not turn. Now turn the adjuster in the opposite direction five notches.

13   Adjust the parking brake (see Section 14).

14   Install the wheel and lug nuts. Lower the vehicle and tighten the lug nuts to the torque listed in the Chapter 1 Specifications.

15   Check the operation of the parking brake.

14   Parking brake - adjustment

1   Loosen the wheel lug nuts. Raise the rear of the vehicle and support it securely on jackstands, then remove the wheels.

2   Adjust the parking brake shoes (models with rear disc brakes; see Section 13) or the brake shoes (models with rear drum brakes; see Section 7).

3   Remove the center console (see Chapter 11).

4   Turn the parking brake cable adjustment nut until the parking brake lever travels 5 to 7 clicks when applied with moderate force (see illustration).

5   Release the parking brake lever and verify that the parking brake shoes (models with rear disc brakes) or brake shoes (models with rear drum brakes) don't drag as the rear discs or drums are turned.

6   Reinstall the console and the wheels. Tighten the wheel lug nuts to the torque listed in the Chapter 1 Specifications.

15   Brake light switch - check, replacement and adjustment

1   The brake light switch is located along the arm of the brake pedal and is attached to a bracket near the power brake booster mount (see illustration). When the brake pedal is applied, the pedal arm moves away from the switch and a spring-loaded plunger closes the

15.1 Brake light switch location

circuit to the brake lights.

2   Models equipped with cruise control use a dual-purpose brake light switch that also deactivates the cruise control system when the brake pedal is depressed.

Check

Caution: *This switch can only be adjusted once and this occurs when the switch is installed. Do not move the small lever on the switch or remove the switch unless you intend on replacing it. Once the switch is removed, it cannot be reused.*

3   Check the brake light fuse (see Chapter 12). If the fuse has blown, replace it. If it blows again, look for a short in the brake light circuit.

4   If the fuse is okay, remove the driver's knee bolster (see Chapter 11) and use a test light or voltmeter to verify that there's voltage to the switch. If there's no voltage to the

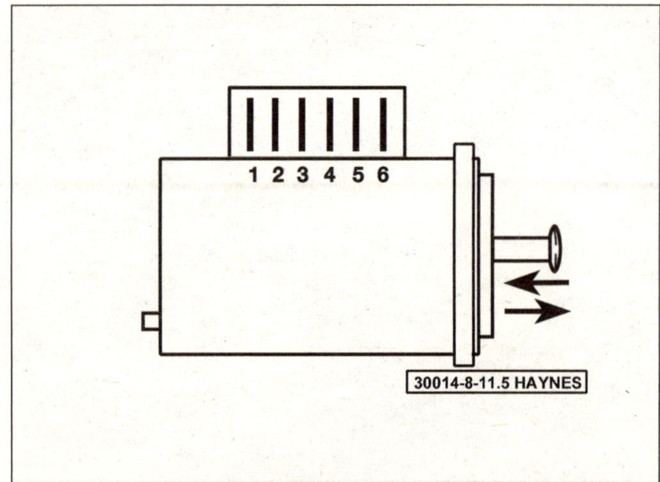

15.5a With the switch closed (plunger extended fully), there should be continuity between terminals 1 and 2 (brake lights will be on). When the pedal is at rest (plunger depressed) there should be continuity between terminals 3 and 4, and 5 and 6 (2007 and early production 2008 models)

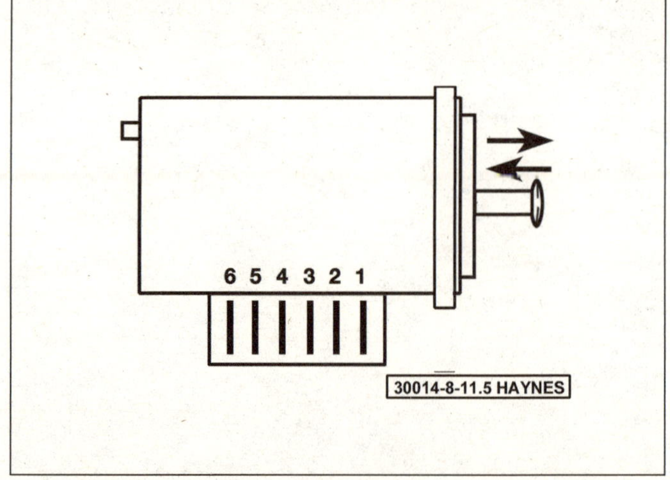

15.5b With the switch closed (plunger extended fully), there should be continuity between terminals 1 and 2 (brake lights will be on). When the pedal is at rest (plunger depressed) there should be continuity between terminals 3 and 4, and 5 and 6 (late-production 2008 models and all 2009 and later models)

switch, look for an open or short in the power wire to the switch. Repair as necessary.

5　If the brake lights still don't come on when the brake pedal is applied, unplug the electrical connector from the brake light switch and, using an ohmmeter, verify that there is continuity between the switch terminals when the brake pedal is applied (the switch is closed and the plunger is extended). If continuity is not detected, replace the switch (see illustrations).

6　If there is continuity between the switch terminals when the brake is applied (plunger fully extended), but the brake lights don't come on, check the following: power at the brake switch on lead no#1 (red lead), with switch installed and brake pedal applied, check for voltage at lead no#2 (green/white tracer lead). If voltage is present, check for power at the brake light bulbs sockets (right side white/violet - left side dark green/red). If no power is present at the bulb sockets, check

wiring from the sockets to the TIPM (Totally Integrated Power Module) (under the hood). If the problem is suspected to be in the TIPM refer to a professional repair shop for further evaluation. (Some TIPM's require programming if replaced.) If voltage is present, check the ground lead (right side black/yellow - left side black/light green). If the voltage AND the ground are present but not at the socket - replace the socket fixture.

Note: *The center high mounted stop lamp is not wired through the TIPM but is wired directly to the center high mounted stop lamp bulb socket from the brake switch. As long as the brake switch, the leads, the sockets, and the bulbs are in working order the center high mounted stop lamp should always work regardless of the two rear stop lamps condition.*

Replacement and adjustment

7　Disconnect the cable from the negative terminal of the battery (see Chapter 5).

8　Depress and hold the brake pedal, then rotate the brake light switch about 30-degrees in a counterclockwise direction and remove it from the mounting bracket.

9　Unplug the electrical connector from the switch, remove the switch from the vehicle and discard it.

10　Pull the plunger out on the new switch, depress the brake pedal and install the switch into the bracket by aligning the slots, inserting the switch and rotating it about 30-degrees clockwise.

Caution: *Do not move the small lever on the switch before it is fully installed.*

11　Release the brake pedal and gently pull it back to make certain that it is seated against the pedal striker. The switch plunger will ratchet backward to the correct position.

12　Plug the electrical connector into the switch.

13　Reconnect the battery and test the brake lights for proper operation.

Notes

Notes

Chapter 10
Suspension and steering

Contents

Specifications

Torque specifications   Ft-lbs (unless otherwise indicated)

Note: *One foot-pound (ft-lb) of torque is equivalent to 12 inch-pounds (in-lbs) of torque. Torque values below approximately 15 ft-lbs are expressed in inch-pounds, since most foot-pound torque wrenches are not accurate at these smaller values.*

Front suspension

Control arm	
Front pivot bolt	
Build date before 8/01/08	100
Build date after 8/01/08	118
Rear pivot bolt nut	135
Driveaxle/hub nut	See Chapter 8
Stabilizer bar	
Stabilizer bar link nuts	43
Stabilizer bar bracket bolts	22
Strut	
Strut-to-steering knuckle bolt/nuts	81
Strut damper shaft nut	44
2010 and earlier models	44
2011 and later models	58
Strut upper mounting nuts	35
Tie-rod end	
Tie-rod end jam nut	55
Tie-rod end-to-steering knuckle nut	97
Balljoint pinch bolt nut	60
Crosmember (main) reinforcement bracket bolts	37
Crossmember (main) mounting bolts	111
Longitudinal crossmember bolts	41
Wheel lug nuts	See Chapter 1

Rear suspension

Hub and bearing mounting bolts	77
Driveaxle/hub nut	See Chapter 8
Lower control arm-to-trailing link bolt/nut	70
Lower control arm-to-crossmember bolt/nut	70
Shock absorber lower mounting bolt/nut	73
Shock absorber upper mounting nuts	35
Stabilizer bar bracket bolts	18
Stabilizer bar link nuts	
Balljoint-style link	37
Insulator style link	25
Toe link-to-trailing link mounting bolt/nut	70
Toe link cam bolt/nut	26
Trailing link-to-body mounting bolts	81
Upper control arm-to-trailing link bolt/nut	70
Upper control arm-to-crossmember bolt nut	70
Crossmember brace bolts	18
Crossmember bolts	111
Wheel lug nuts	See Chapter 1

Steering system

Steering wheel bolt	37
Airbag module bolts	120 in-lbs
Steering column-to-dash nuts and bolts	250 in-lbs
Steering gear mounting bolts	52
Intermediate shaft pinch bolt	31
Reservoir mounting screws	106 in-lbs
Tie-rod end-to-knuckle nut	97
Tie-rod end jam nut	55
Power steering pump mounting bolts	19

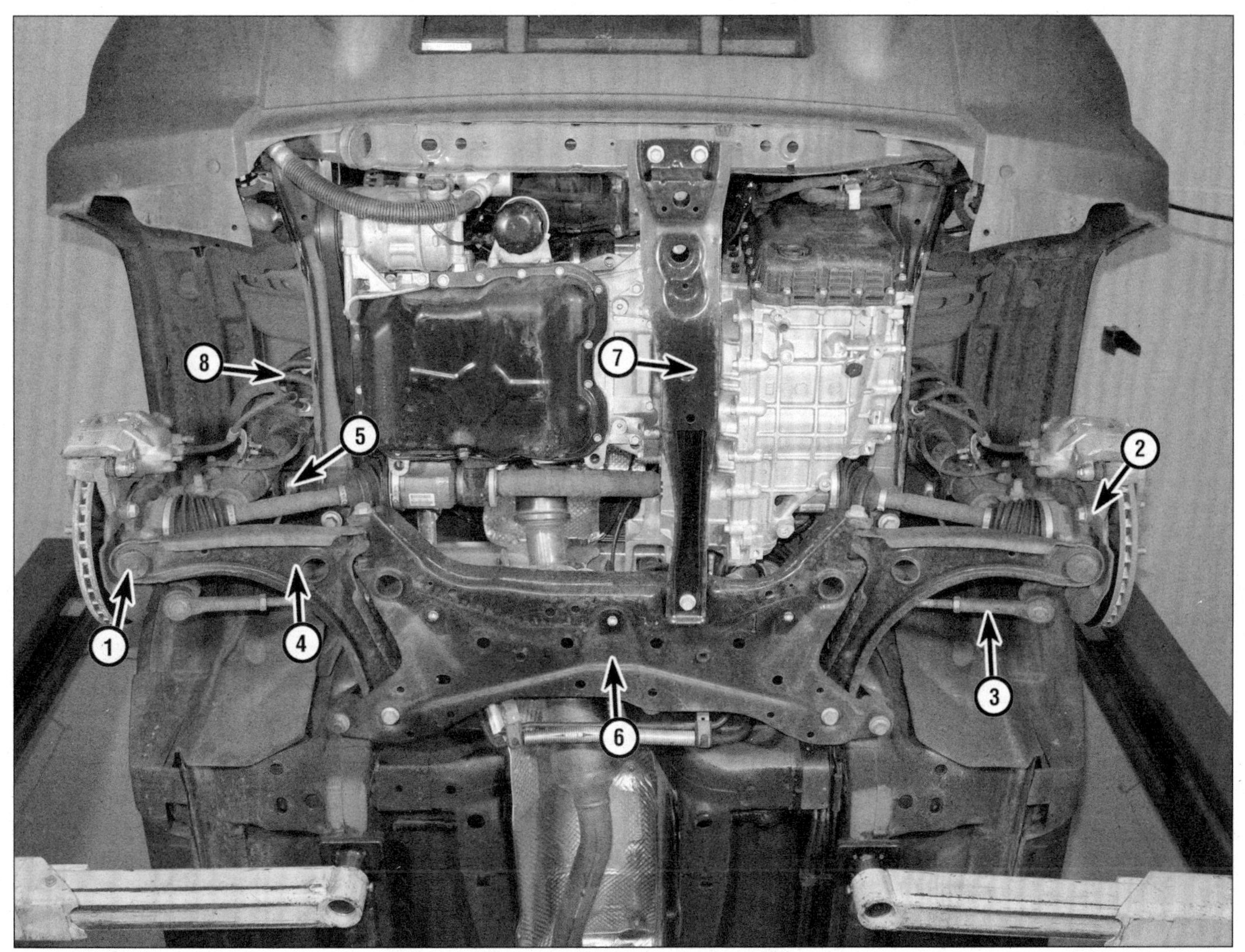

1.1 Front suspension and steering components

1 Control arm balljoint	4 Control arm	7 Longitudinal crossmember
2 Steering knuckle	5 Stabilizer bar	8 Strut/coil spring assembly
3 Tie-rod end	6 Front suspension crossmember	

1.2 Rear suspension components

1	Trailing link	4	Shock absorber/coil spring assembly	6	Stabilizer bar
2	Toe link	5	Lower control arm	7	Crossmember
3	Upper control arm				

1   General information and precautions

Front suspension

1   The front suspension (see illustration) on these vehicles is a MacPherson strut design. The upper end of each strut is attached to the vehicle's body strut support. The lower end of the strut is connected to the upper end of the steering knuckle. The lower end of the steering knuckle is attached by a balljoint mounted to the outer end of the suspension control arm. The control arm is connected to the front suspension crossmember. A stabilizer bar, mounted to the crossmember and connected to the strut, reduces body roll while cornering.

Rear suspension

2   The rear suspension (see illustration) is of a multi-link design, using upper and lower control arms, toe-links, trailing links, coil-over shock absorber assemblies, and a stabilizer bar.

Steering

3   The power-assisted rack-and-pinion steering gear is attached to the front suspension subframe. The steering gear actuates the tie-rods, which are attached to the steering knuckles. The steering column is designed to collapse in the event of an accident.

Precautions

4   Frequently, when working on the suspension or steering system components, you may come across fasteners that seem impossible to loosen. These fasteners on the underside of the vehicle are continually subjected to water, road grime, mud, etc., and can become rusted or frozen, making them extremely difficult to remove. In order to unscrew these stubborn fasteners without damaging them (or other components), Use lots of penetrating oil and allow it to soak in for a while. Using a wire brush to clean exposed threads will also ease removal of the nut or bolt and prevent damage to the threads. Sometimes a sharp blow with a hammer and punch will break the bond between a nut and bolt threads, but care must be taken to prevent the punch from slipping off the fastener and ruining the threads. Heating the stuck fastener and surrounding area with a torch sometimes helps too, but isn't recommended because of the obvious dangers associated with fire. Long breaker bars and extension, or cheater, pipes will increase leverage, but never use an extension pipe on a ratchet - the ratcheting mechanism could be damaged. Sometimes tightening the nut or bolt first will help to break it loose. Fasteners that require drastic measures to remove should always be replaced with new ones.

5   Since most of the procedures dealt with in this Chapter involve jacking up the vehicle and working underneath it, a good pair of jackstands will be needed. A hydraulic floor jack is the preferred type of jack to lift the vehicle, and it can also be used to support certain components during various operations.

Warning: *Never, under any circumstances, rely on a jack to support the vehicle while working on it.*

6   Whenever any of the suspension or steering fasteners are loosened or removed they must be inspected and, if necessary, replaced with new ones of the same part number or of original equipment quality and design. Torque specifications must be followed for proper reassembly and component retention. Never attempt to heat or straighten any suspension or steering components. Instead, replace any bent or damaged part with a new one.

2   Stabilizer bar and bushings (front) - removal and installation

Warning: *The stabilizer bar removal requires the removing of several bulky and somewhat heavy components to gain access. Take the needed safety precautions to prevent personal injury.*

Removal

1   Loosen the front wheel lug nuts, raise the front of the vehicle and support it securely on jackstands. Apply the parking brake and block the rear wheels to keep the vehicle from rolling off the stands. Remove the front wheels.

Note: *There is no need to remove the subframe entirely if you are just replacing the stabilizer bar links.*

2   Familiarize yourself with the components that make up the stabilizer (see illustration).

Note: *To remove the link nut, hold the stud with an Allen wrench while turning the nut with a box-end wrench.*

3   Remove the under-vehicle splash shield.

4   Remove the rear engine mount (see Chapter 2A).

5   Remove the front engine mount through-bolt.

6   Remove the lower stabilizer link nut (see illustration).

Note: *If you are just replacing the stabilizer bar there is no need to disconnect the upper end link nut.*

7   Remove the two screws attaching the power steering hose clamps to the rear of the crossmember.

8   Remove the heat shield.

9   Remove the two bolts that secure the steering gear to the crossmember. Support the steering gear with a rope, bungee cord or wire to hold it in place as the crossmember is lowered.

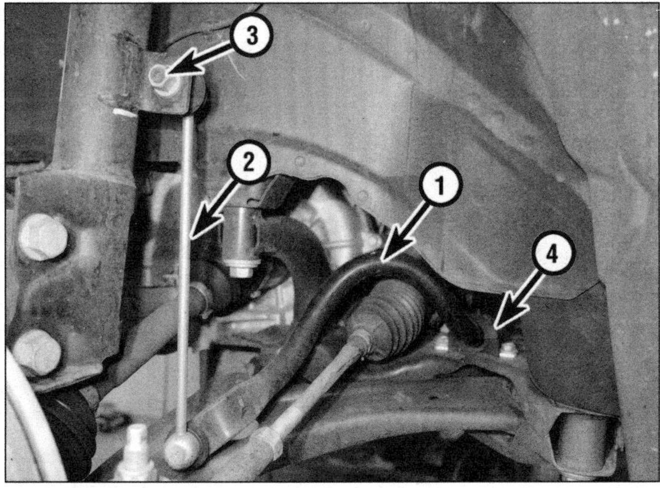

2.2 Stabilizer bar details

1 Stabilizer bar	4 Stabilizer bar
2 Stabilizer bar link	bushing/bracket
3 Link nut	

2.6 Lower link nut connects the end link to the stabilizer bar

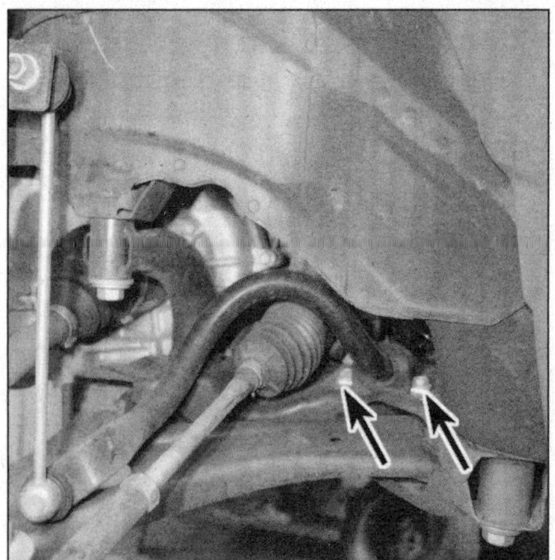

2.10 Stabilizer bar bushing bracket bolts

3.1 Only loosen the three strut upper mounting nuts. Do not loosen the center nut

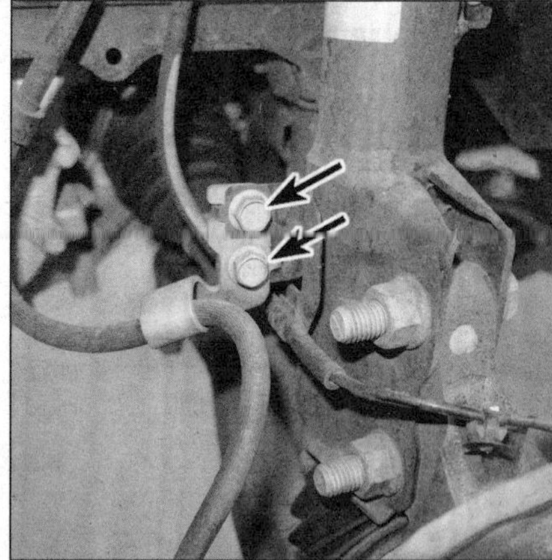

3.4 Remove the bolts securing the brake line and wheel speed sensor to the strut assembly

3.5 Hold the bolts with a wrench while turning the nuts

10   Mark the relationship of the main crossmember to the vehicle. Support the main crossmember with a floor jack, Remove the bolts and lower the crossmember (see Section 24) far enough to allow for the stabilizer bar to be removed. Remove the stabilizer bar bracket bolts and remove the brackets and the bushings (see illustration). Remove the stabilizer bar.

Note: *It is sometimes easier to disconnect the stabilizer bar from the crossmember before you lower the crossmember. Remember to match mark the crossmember location before removing the mounting bolts.*

Installation

11   Install the stabilizer bar, bushings and brackets onto the crossmember, but do not tighten them yet.

12   Center the stabilizer bar on the crossmember. Tighten the bracket bolts to the torque listed in this Chapter's Specifications.

13   Align the crossmember with the marks you made earlier and install the mounting

bolts and screws. Tighten to the torque listed in this Chapter's Specifications.

14   Install the engine mount and power steering line brackets/fasteners.

15   Install the stabilizer links and tighten the nuts to the torque listed in this Chapter's Specifications.

16   Install the wheels and lug nuts. Lower the vehicle and tighten the wheel lug nuts to the torque listed in the Chapter 1 Specifications.

---

3   Strut assembly (front) - removal, inspection and installation

---

Removal

Warning: *Always replace the struts and/or coil springs in pairs - never replace just one strut or one coil spring; this could cause dangerous handling peculiarities.*

Note: *If both strut assemblies are going to be removed, mark the assemblies Right and Left so they will be reinstalled on the correct side.*

1   Open the hood and loosen (but don't remove) the three strut upper mounting nuts (see illustration). Loosen the wheel lug nuts, then raise the vehicle and support it securely on jackstands. Remove the wheel.

2   Disconnect the stabilizer bar link from the strut assembly (see Section 2).

3   Mark the position of the strut to the steering knuckle (this is only necessary if special camber adjusting bolts have been installed in place of the regular strut-to-knuckle bolts).

4   Remove the bolts securing the brake line and wheel speed sensor to the strut assembly (see illustration).

5   Remove the nuts and bolts, then separate the strut from the steering knuckle (see illustration).

Caution: *The bolts are serrated and must not be turned. Hold the bolts with a wrench, then remove the strut-to-knuckle nuts. Knock the bolts out with a brass hammer, noting which*

way the bolt heads face.

6   Secure the steering knuckle safely aside. Remove the assembly from the fenderwell.

Inspection

7   Check the strut body for leaking fluid, dents, cracks and other obvious damage which would warrant repair or replacement.

8   Check the coil spring for chips or cracks in the spring coating (this will cause premature spring failure due to corrosion). Inspect the spring seat for cuts, hardness and general deterioration.

9   If any undesirable conditions exist, proceed to the strut disassembly procedure (see Section 4).

Installation

10   Guide the strut assembly up into the fenderwell and insert the upper mounting studs through the holes in the body. Once the studs protrude, install the nuts so the strut won't fall back through. This is most easily accomplished with the help of an assistant, as the strut is quite heavy and awkward.

11   Tighten the upper mounting nuts to the torque listed in this Chapter's Specifications.

12   Slide the steering knuckle into the strut flange and insert the two bolts. Install the nuts, align the previously made match marks (if applicable) and tighten them to the torque listed in this Chapter's Specifications.

Note: *Make certain that the bolts are installed in their original direction.*

13   Install the brake hose and speed sensor mounting brackets.

14   Connect the stabilizer bar link to the strut. Tighten the nut to the torque listed in this Chapter's Specifications.

15   Install the wheel and lug nuts, then lower the vehicle and tighten the lug nuts to the torque listed in the Chapter 1 Specifications.

16   Have the front end alignment checked, and if necessary, adjusted.

4   Strut/coil spring - replacement

Warning: *Struts and/or coil springs must be replaced in pairs - never replace just one of them.*
Note: *You'll need a spring compressor for this procedure. Spring compressors are available on a daily rental basis at most auto parts stores or equipment rental yards.*

1   If the struts or coil springs exhibit the telltale signs of wear (leaking fluid, loss of damping capability, chipped, sagging or cracked coil springs) explore all options before beginning any work. The strut body is not serviceable and must be replaced if a problem develops. However, complete strut assemblies (with springs) may be available on an exchange basis, which eliminates much time and work. Whichever route you choose to take, check on the cost and availability of parts before disassembling your vehicle.

Warning: *Disassembling a strut assembly is potentially dangerous and utmost attention must be directed to the job, or serious injury may result. Use only a high-quality spring compressor and carefully follow the manufacturer's instructions furnished with the tool. After removing the coil spring from the strut, set it aside in a safe, isolated area.*

Disassembly

2   Remove the strut and spring assembly (see Section 3).
3   Mount the strut clevis bracket portion of the strut assembly in a vise and mark the components for reassembly (see illustration).
Caution: *Do not clamp any other portion of the strut assembly in the vise; it will be dam-*

4.3 The strut assembly is carefully clamped in a vise with necessary components marked for disassembly and with a spring compressor installed

aged. Line the vise jaws with wood or rags to prevent damage to the unit and don't tighten the vise excessively.
4   Following the tool manufacturer's instructions, install the spring compressor on the spring and compress it sufficiently to relieve all pressure from the upper mount. This can be verified by wiggling the spring.
5   While holding the damper shaft from turning, loosen the shaft nut with a socket. A special tool is available to do this, but an offset box-end wrench and an open-end wrench can be used (see illustration).
6   Remove the nut and upper mount (see illustration). Inspect the pivot bearing for smooth operation. If it doesn't turn smoothly, replace it. Remove the upper spring seat and check the upper spring isolator for cracking and general deterioration. Replace any parts

that are damaged or worn.
7   Carefully lift the compressed spring from the assembly.
Warning: *When removing the compressed spring, lift it off very carefully and set it in a safe place. Keep the ends of the spring away from your body.*
8   Remove the dust boot from the damper shaft.
9   Slide the rubber bumper off the damper shaft. Check the lower spring isolator for cracking and hardness; replace it if necessary.

Reassembly

10   Extend the damper rod to its full length and install the rubber bumper.
11   Install the dust boot onto the damper.
12   Carefully place the coil spring onto the

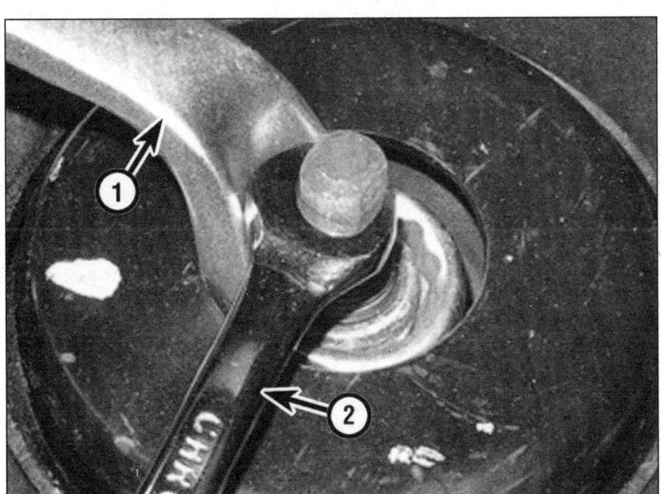

4.5 Here's an example of the setup that can be used to unscrew the damper shaft nut

1   18 mm offset box-end wrench
2   8 mm open-end wrench

4.6 Front strut/coil assembly details

1   Nut
2   Upper mount
3   Pivot bearing
4   Upper spring seat
5   Upper spring isolator
6   Dust boot (rubber bumper underneath - hidden by dust boot)
7   Coil spring (with spring compressor)
8   Lower spring isolator
9   Damper unit

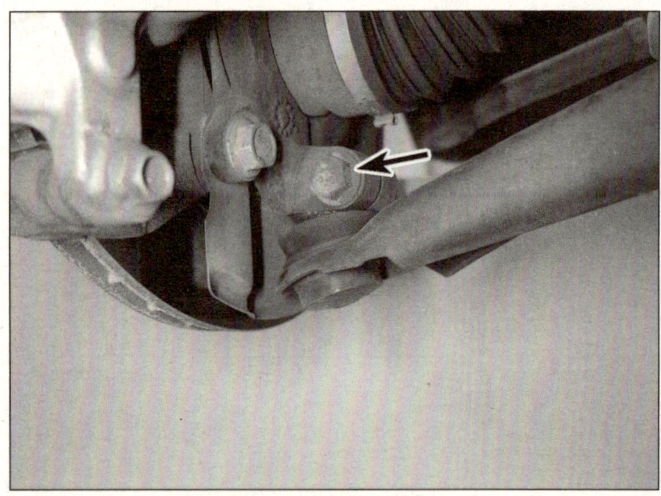

5.2 Balljoint pinch bolt

5.4 Control arm-to-subframe bolts (rear nut not visible in photo)

damper. Align the coil spring on the damper using the reference marks made during disassembly. If a new spring or strut damper unit is being installed, use the marks on the old component to help you orient the spring properly.

Note: *Installing tip: When installing the spring, make sure the end with the ID tag is placed upwards. Be sure to have the bottom of the spring end facing at the 9 o'clock position as viewed looking down from the top with the assembly facing as it would be if it were installed in the car.*

13   Install the upper spring isolator and seat onto the damper shaft, noting reference marks.

14   Install the upper mount to the damper shaft, noting its alignment.

15   Install the nut on the damper shaft and tighten it to the torque listed in this Chapter's Specifications.

16   Loosen the coil spring compressor until the top coil is properly seated against the upper spring seat and upper mount. Relieve all tension from the spring compressor and remove the tool from the coil spring.

17   Install the strut/spring assembly (see Section 3).

---

5   Control arm - removal, inspection and installation

Removal

1   Loosen the lug nuts on both front wheels, raise the front of the vehicle and support it securely on jackstands. Remove the wheels.

2   Remove the nut and balljoint pinch bolt (see illustration).

Warning: *Discard the nut and bolt. Obtain new fasteners for installation.*

3   Pry the control arm down to free the balljoint from the steering knuckle.

Note: *Once the balljoint is separated, do not pull outward on the knuckle; this can lead to separation and damage to the driveaxle inner CV joint.*

4   Remove the control arm-to-subframe fasteners (see illustration) and remove the control arm.

Inspection

5   Make sure the control arm is straight. If it is bent, replace it. Do not attempt to straighten a bent control arm.

6   Inspect all bushings for cracks, distortion, and tears. If a bushing is torn or worn, replace the control arm.

Installation

7   Position the control arm in the subframe and install the NEW rear bolt and nut, but do not tighten the nut yet.

8   Install the control arm front pivot bolt, but don't tighten it yet.

9   Reconnect the balljoint to the control arm and tighten the NEW bolt/nut to the torque listed in this Chapter's Specifications.

Warning: *Install the bolt with the head facing forward.*

10   Tighten the front and rear control arm-to-subframe fasteners to the torque listed in this Chapter's Specifications.

11   Install the wheel and lug nuts, lower the vehicle and tighten the lug nuts to the torque listed in the Chapter 1 Specifications.

12   Have the front wheel alignment checked and, if necessary, adjusted.

---

6   Balljoints - replacement

1   If the balljoint has been diagnosed and has been determined that it needs to be replaced, the entire control arm and balljoint must be replaced as a unit.

---

7   Hub and bearing assembly (front) - replacement

Note: *The hub and bearing assembly is only removed from the steering knuckle by using a press. The steering knuckle must be removed in order to remove the hub and bearing assembly. A special fixture and press adapters are available through the manufacturer's special tool department, but suitable alternative equipment may be available. If you don't have access to a press and the proper adapters, take the steering knuckle to a repair shop or an automotive machine shop to have the bearing pressed out of the steering knuckle and the new one pressed in.*

1   Remove the steering knuckle (see Section 8).

Disassembly

2   Mount the steering knuckle in the press (preferably using the recommended fixture) with the hub flange facing down. Using the proper adapter, press the hub and flange out of the wheel bearing and knuckle.

3   Remove the knuckle from the fixture (if used), then turn the knuckle over and remove the snap-ring.

4   Place the steering knuckle back in the fixture (if used) and press the bearing out towards the outside (the same direction as the hub and flange was removed).

5   The bearing race might have come out with the bearing, but if it stuck to the hub, remove it with a bearing splitter and the press.

6   Thoroughly clean the hub and flange, especially the spindle area where the bearing rides. Also clean the knuckle bore.

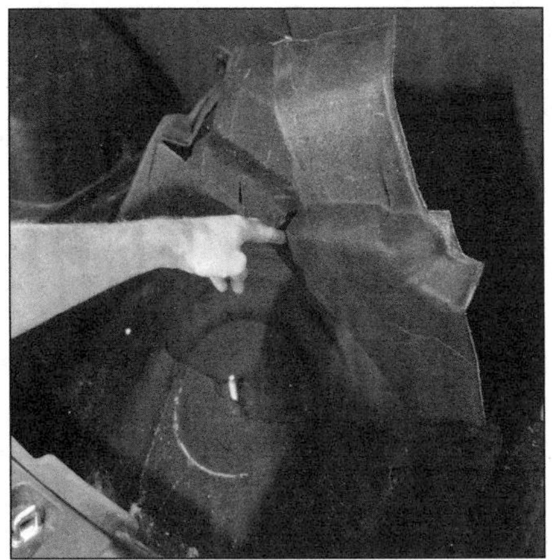

9.1 Remove the side trim panes in the trunk for access to the shock absorber upper mounting fasteners

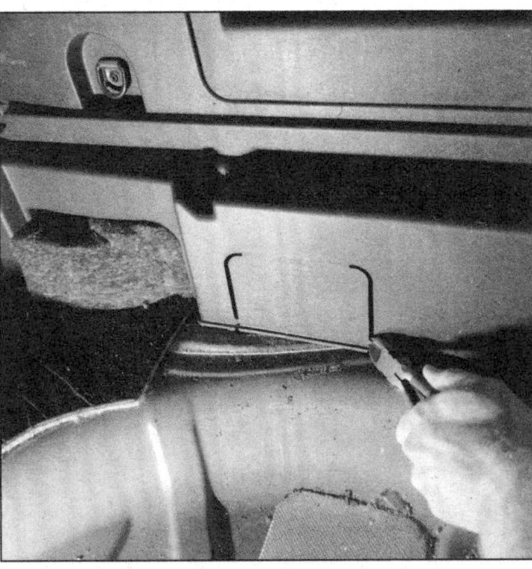

9.3a If this is the first time removing the rear shocks, you'll have to cut the door open. Notice the two small tabs that will need to be cut away

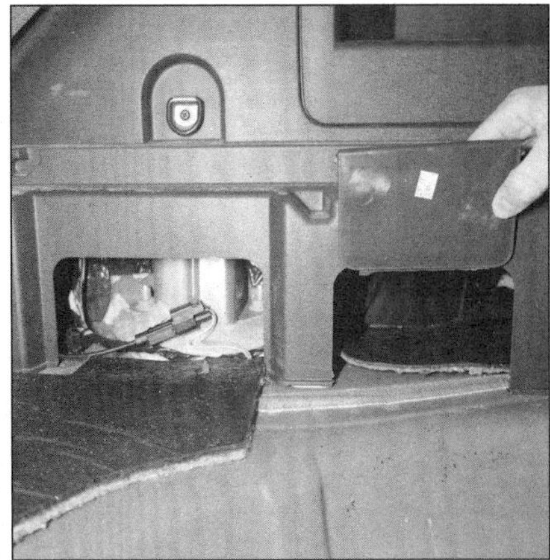

9.3b With the tabs cut away you can gain access to the area where the upper shock nuts are located (opposite side is similar). Use this opening and the opening created when the silencer pad was removed to gain access to both of the upper shock nuts

Reassembly

7　Place the knuckle on the press, with the outer side facing up and resting on a properly sized support cup. Install the new bearing with the magnetic encoder ring inserted into the knuckle bore first. Press the bearing into place with the proper-size adapter (the adapter must only contact the outer race of the bearing).

8　Remove the steering knuckle from the press and install a new snap-ring.

9　Place the knuckle back on the press, outer side facing up, and supported by the properly sized support cup (the inside diameter of the support cup must be large enough to accept the hub spindle).

10　Set the hub spindle squarely into the wheel bearing and, using a driver that contacts the recessed area of the hub flange, press the hub fully into the bearing.

11　Remove the knuckle and hub assembly from the press and check to see that the hub rotates freely.

12　Install the steering knuckle (see Section 8).

8　Steering knuckle - removal and installation

Removal

1　Loosen the wheel lug nuts and the driveaxle/hub nut (see Chapter 8). Raise the vehicle and support it securely on jackstands.

2　Remove the wheel.

3　Remove the driveaxle/hub nut (see Chapter 8, Section 8).

4　Remove the brake disc and the ABS wheel speed sensor (see Chapter 9).

5　Detach the tie-rod end from the steering

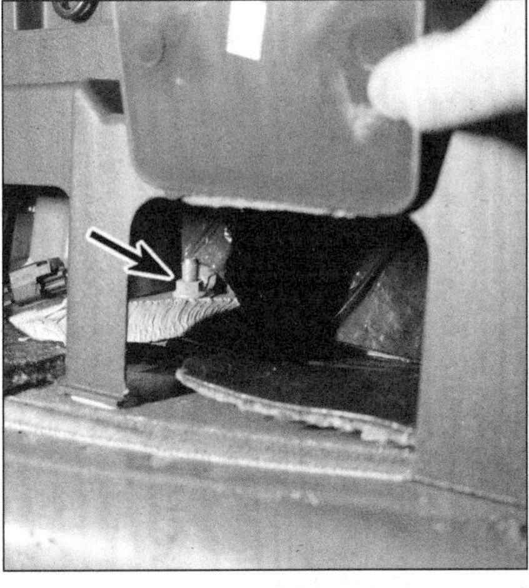

9.3c Upper shock nut (one shown) two per shock

knuckle (see Section 19).

6　Separate the balljoint from the control arm (see Section 5).

7　Remove the two strut-to-steering knuckle bolts, noting their installed direction (see Section 3).

Caution: *The strut-to-steering knuckle bolts are serrated and must not be turned during removal - turn the nuts only.*

Note: *If the strut assembly is attached to the steering knuckle using a cam bolt in the lower slotted hole, mark the relationship of the cam bolt to the strut to preserve the wheel alignment setting on reassembly (see Section 3).*

8　Remove the steering knuckle from the strut, separate the driveaxle from the hub splines and suspend it safely aside.

Caution: *Do not pull out on the inner CV joint during this operation. Do not allow the*

driveshaft to hang by the inner CV joint. If the driveaxle splines stick in the hub, push the driveaxle out with a puller.

Installation

9　Installation is the reverse of removal. Tighten all suspension fasteners to the torque listed in this Chapter's Specifications.

10　Install the wheel, lower the vehicle and tighten the lug nuts to the torque listed in the Chapter 1 Specifications. Tighten the driveaxle/hub nut to the torque listed in the Chapter 8 Specifications.

11　Have the front end alignment checked and, if necessary, adjusted.

9　Shock absorber/coil spring assembly (rear) - removal and installation

Removal

Warning: *Always replace the shock absorbers and/or coil springs in pairs - never replace just one shock absorber or one coil spring; this could cause dangerous handling peculiarities.*

1　Remove the cargo floor covering and rear floor pan silencer covers (see illustration).

Note: *If equipped with a satellite receiver or a factory amplifier, remove these from the floor pan silencer covers and set them aside.*

2　Remove the spare tire.

3　Locate the shock upper nut access door (next to the opening created when you removed the silencer cover). Remove the nuts in the trunk that hold the shock absorber to the vehicle body (see illustrations).

4　Loosen the rear wheel lug nuts. Raise the vehicle and support it securely on jackstands. Remove the rear wheels.

9.5 Shock absorber lower mounting bolt/nut

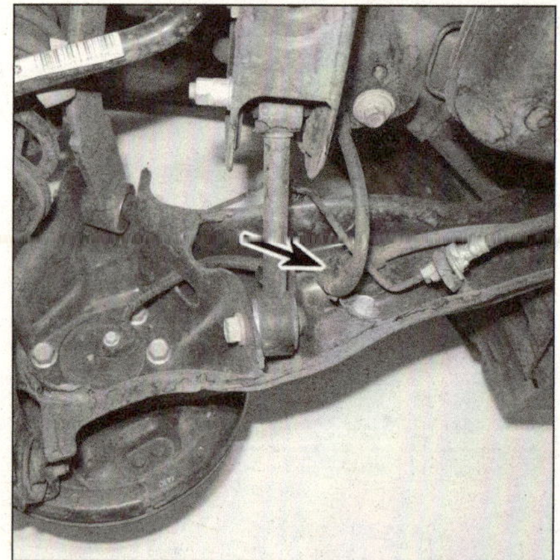

11.2a Brake hose bracket bolts

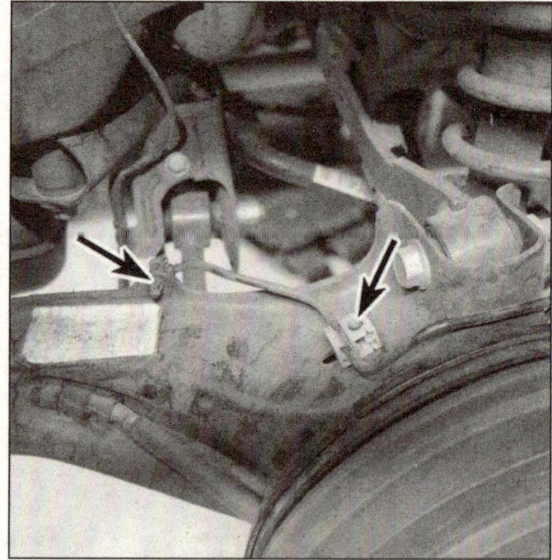

11.2b Push the plastic retainer clip off, then remove the fastener securing the plastic insulator block off of the trailing link

5   Remove the shock absorber lower mounting nut and bolt and remove the shock unit (see illustration).
Note: *It may be necessary to pry the lower control arm down to make room for the shock to be removed.*
6   Installation is the reverse of removal. It is a good idea to grease the lower mount with white lithium grease to facilitate installation and prolong the life of the lower shock bushing. If you plan on removing the springs and overhauling the shock unit, follow the procedures in Section 10.

Installation

Note: *When installed, the side of the upper mount that protrudes more must be facing towards the outside of the vehicle.*
7   Raise the rear suspension with a floor jack positioned under the outer end of the lower control arm to simulate normal ride height, then tighten the lower mounting bolt to the torque listed in this Chapter's Specifications.
8   Install the wheel and lug nuts. Lower the vehicle and tighten the lug nuts to the torque listed in the Chapter 1 Specifications.
9   Tighten the shock absorber upper mounting nuts to the torque listed in this Chapter's Specifications. Reinstall the trim panels in the trunk.

10   Shock absorber/coil spring assembly (rear) - component replacement

Warning: *Always replace the shock absorbers and/or coil springs in pairs - never replace just one shock absorber or one coil spring; this could cause dangerous handling peculiarities.*

Removal

1   Loosen the rear wheel lug nuts. Raise the vehicle and support it securely on jackstands. Remove the rear wheels.

2   Remove the rear shock absorber/coil spring assembly (see Section 9).
Note: *If you plan on servicing both shocks at the same time, mark the parts right and left to ensure proper reassembly.*
3   Compress the coil spring with a spring compressor; read and follow the tool manufacturer's instructions on placement of the hooks and proper usage.
4   Compress the spring until the tension is removed from the upper bracket.
5   After the spring has been compressed, hold the damper shaft with a wrench while you remove the damper shaft nut.
Warning: *Do not use air or power tools on the nut or damper shaft. Damage or severe injury may occur.*
6   While keeping the spring compressed, remove the shock through the bottom of the spring and remove all of the parts from the shock body, inspecting each one for cracks, wear, or other signs of damage. If damage is found, replace that part.

Installation

7   Install the parts on the new shock as follows.

    Lower spring isolator
    Spring
    Upper spring isolator
    Dust shield
    Jounce bumper
    Washer
    Bushing
    Sleeve
    Upper mounting bracket
    Bushing
    Washer
    Nut

Note: *The upper mount must be oriented so that the side that protrudes more faces outward when installed in the vehicle.*
8   Install the washer and damper shaft nut. Hold the damper shaft with a wrench and tighten the nut to the torque listed in this Chapter's Specifications.

9   Once the nut is tight and tools removed, slowly release the tension from the spring by backing off on the spring compressor. Ensure that your spring has settled in the locator holes and ensure the brackets/mounts are not twisted or off center.
10   Install the shock absorber/coil spring assembly (see Section 9).

11   Trailing link - removal and installation

1   Loosen the wheel lug nuts. Raise the vehicle and support it securely on jackstands. Remove the wheels. If you're working on an all-wheel drive model, have an assistant apply the brakes while you remove the driveaxle/hub nut.
2   Remove the bolts that hold the brake hose to the trailing link and the bolt that holds the parking brake cable near the forward end of the trailing arm (see illustrations). Remove the brake line from the clip on the trailing link. Also remove the wheel speed sensor wire from the clips on the trailing arm.
3   If your vehicle is equipped with rear disc brakes, remove the caliper and mounting bracket as an assembly (see Chapter 9). Hang it out of the way using wire, zip-ties, or equivalent. Do not allow the caliper to hang or over-extend the brake line; this can lead to brake failure.
4   Remove the speed sensor routing screws and clips that attach it to the trailing link.
5   If equipped with rear drum brakes, detach the parking brake cable from the parking brake lever on the trailing brake shoe (see Chapter 9, Section 7, illustration 7.4d).
6   Remove the hairpin fastening the parking brake cable to the backing plate (brake support bracket). Slide the parking brake cable out of the backing plate.
7   Unbolt the toe link from the trailing link (see Section 12).

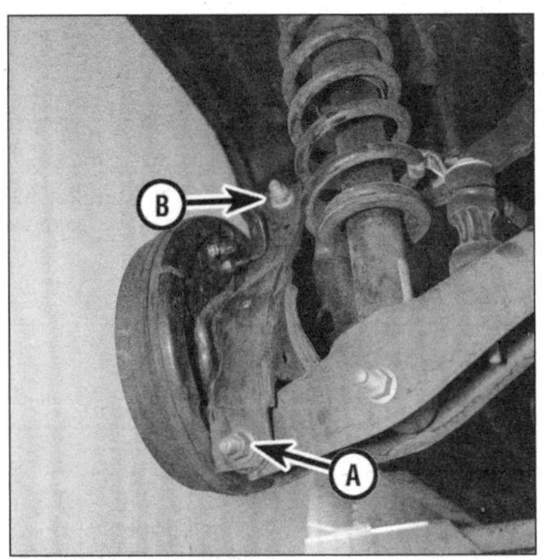

11.8 Lower control arm-to-trailing link nut/ bolt (A) and upper control arm-to-trailing link nut/bolt (B)

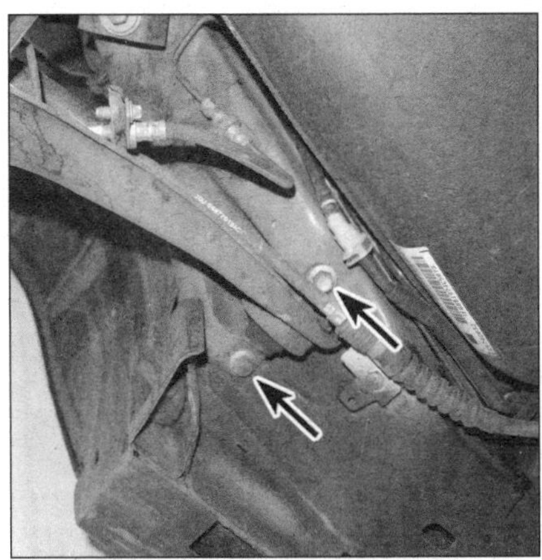

11.9 Trailing link-to-body bolts

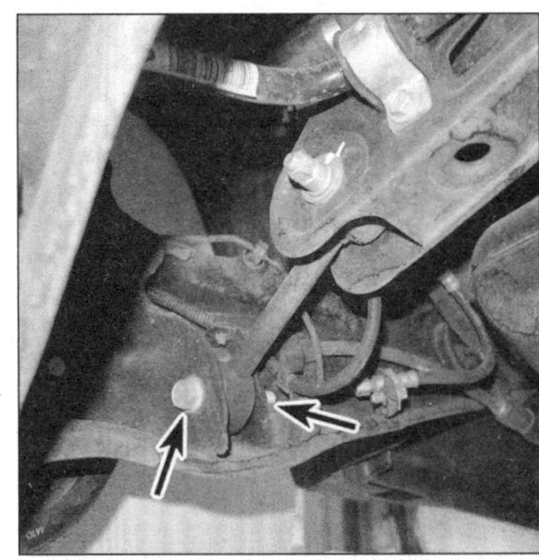

12.2 Toe link-to-trailing arm bolt/nut

12.3 Mark the position of the adjuster cam to the crossmember (do this on the other side of the crossmember, too)

13.2a Detach the stabilizer bar links from the stabilizer bar (balljoint-style link)

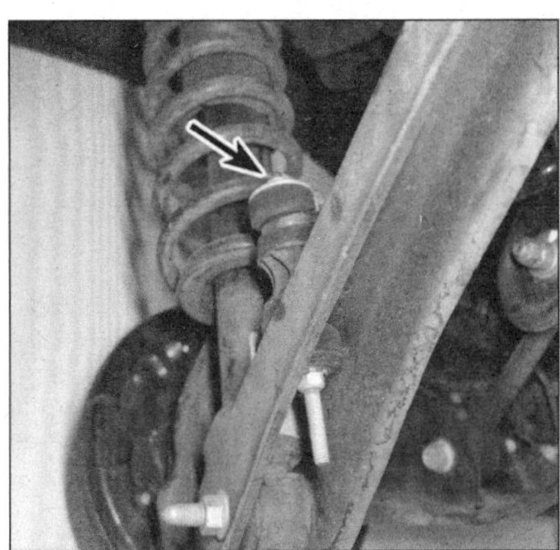

13.2b Remove the nut, bolt and insulators (insulator-style link)

8   Remove the bolts securing the trailing link to the upper and lower control arms (see illustration).

9   Remove the two bolts that attach the trailing link to the vehicle frame (see illustration). Remove the trailing link. On all-wheel drive models, guide the driveaxle out of the hub, being careful not to pull out on the inner CV joint.

Note: *On AWD models, if the driveaxle sticks in the hub splines, push it out with a two-jaw or flange puller.*

10   Install the body side of the trailing link first and tighten the bolts to the torque listed in this Chapter's Specifications.

11   Installation is otherwise the reverse of removal. Tighten the control arm-to-trailing link bolt/nuts and the toe link bolt/nut to the torque listed in this Chapter's Specifications.

Note: *Raise the outer end of the lower control arm with a floor jack to simulate normal ride height before tightening the fasteners.*

12   If you're working on an AWD model, tighten the driveaxle/hub nut to the torque listed in the Chapter 8 Specifications.

13   Install the wheel and lug nuts. Lower the vehicle and tighten the lug nuts to the torque listed in the Chapter 1 Specifications.

12   Toe link - removal and installation

Removal

1   Loosen the wheel lug nuts. Raise the vehicle and support it securely on jackstands. Remove the wheels.

2   Remove the nut and bolt that secures the link to the trailing arm (see illustration).

3   Mark the position of the inner pivot bolt adjuster cam to the crossmember using a marker or crayon (see illustration). Do not scratch the finish of the crossmember to make your mark. Hold the bolt in place and remove the nut.

4   Remove the bolt and detach the toe link from the crossmember.

Installation

5   Install the inner pivot and adjuster cams, lining up the marks you made earlier.

6   Raise the rear suspension with a floor jack placed under the outer end of the lower control arm to simulate normal ride height, then tighten the fasteners to the torque listed in this Chapter's Specifications.

7   Install the wheels and lug nuts, lower the vehicle and tighten the lug nuts to the torque listed in the Chapter 1 Specifications.

8   Have the rear wheel alignment checked and, if necessary, adjusted.

13   Stabilizer bar and bushings (rear) - removal and installation

Removal

1   Loosen the rear wheel lug nuts. Raise the rear of the vehicle and support it securely with jackstands. Remove the rear wheels.

2   On models with balljoint-style stabilizer bar links, remove the link-to stabilizer bar nut and detach the link from the bar (see illustration). If the ballstud turns, hold it with an Allen wrench. On models with insulator-type links, remove the nut, bolt and insulators (see illustration).

13.3 Stabilizer bar bushing bracket bolts

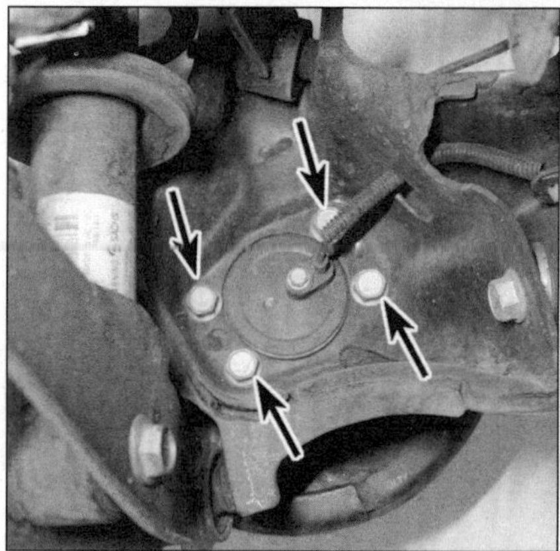

14.4 Rear hub and bearing assembly mounting bolts

3   Remove the stabilizer bar bushing bracket bolts (see illustration).
Note: *On all-wheel drive models, remove the rear differential (drive module) and drive shaft in order to remove the stabilizer bar (see Chapter 8).*
4   Remove the bushing brackets and pull out the stabilizer bar.

Installation

5   Installation is the reverse of removal. Tighten the fasteners to the torque listed in this Chapter's Specifications.
6   Install the wheel and lug nuts. Lower the vehicle and tighten the lug nuts to the torque listed in the Chapter 1 Specifications.

14   Hub and bearing assembly (rear) - replacement

1   Loosen the rear wheel lug nuts, raise the rear of the vehicle, support it securely on jackstands and remove the wheels.
Note: *On all wheel drive models, remove the*

cotter pin, nut and washer, Then, have an assistant depress the brake pedal while you loosen the hub nut. Use a board to tap on the end of the shaft to loosen its bond in the hub assembly.
2   Remove the ABS wheel speed sensor (see Chapter 9).
3   Remove the brake disc (see Chapter 9) and parking brake cable bracket fasteners.
4   Remove the four bolts retaining the hub/bearing assembly to the rear trailing link (see illustration).
5   Remove the hub/bearing assembly.
Note: *On all wheel drive models, slide the driveaxle out of the hub assembly. If the shaft sticks in the hub, push it out with a two-jaw or flange-type puller.*
6   Installation is the reverse of removal. Tighten the mounting bolts to the torque settings listed in this Chapter's Specifications. On all-wheel drive models, tighen the drive-axle/hub nut to the torque listed in the Chapter 8 Specifications.
7   Install the wheel and lug nuts. Lower the vehicle and tighten the lug nuts to the torque listed in the Chapter 1 Specifications.

15   Rear suspension knuckle - removal and installation

Note: *On these vehicles, the rear knuckle is integral with the suspension trailing link. See Section 11 for the trailing link removal and installation procedure.*

16   Upper control arm (rear) - removal and installation

1   Loosen the rear wheel lug nuts. Raise the rear of the vehicle and support it securely with jackstands. Remove the wheel.
2   Remove the upper control arm-to-trailing link fasteners and upper control arm-to-crossmember fasteners (see illustration). Remove the upper control arm.
3   Installation is the reverse of removal.
4   Raise the rear suspension with a floor jack placed under the outer end of the lower control arm to simulate normal ride height, then tighten the mounting fasteners to the torque listed in this Chapter's Specifications.
5   Install the wheel and lug nuts. Lower the vehicle and tighten the lug nuts to the torque listed in the Chapter 1 Specifications.

17   Lower control arm (rear) - removal and installation

1   Raise the rear of the vehicle and support it securely on jackstands.
2   While keeping the stabilizer bar link lower stud stationary, remove the nut.
3   Remove the cover from the lower control arm, if equipped.
4   Remove the lower shock mount bolt and the stabilizer bar link-to-lower control arm nut (see illustration). Separate the link from the arm.
5   Remove the lower control arm-to-knuckle bolt.

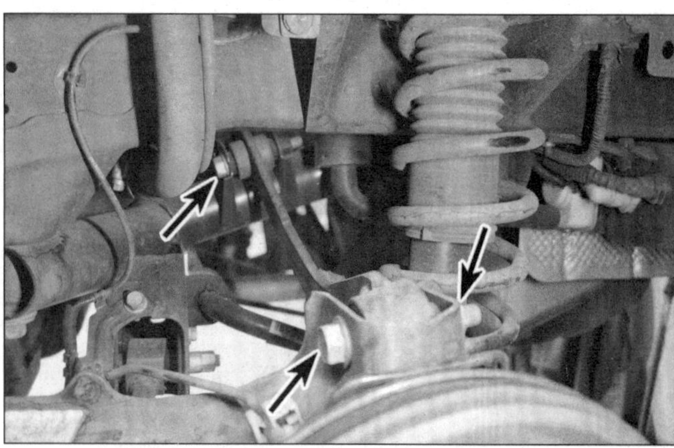

16.2 Upper control arm mounting nuts and bolts

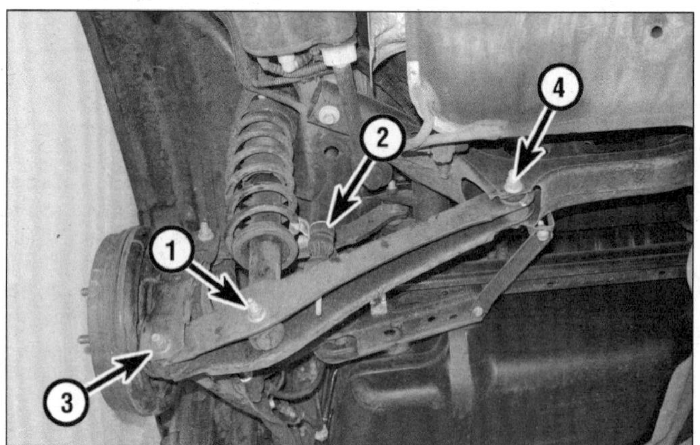

17.4 Lower control arm details

1   *Shock absorber lower mounting nut/bolt*
2   *Stabilizer bar link*
3   *Lower control arm-to-trailing link bolt*
4   *Lower control arm-to-crossmember bolt*

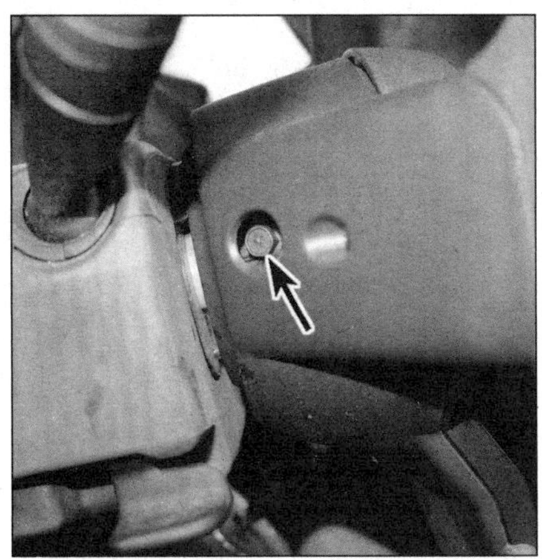

18.2 Work from either side of the steering wheel access holes and remove the two bolts securing the airbag module to the steering wheel (one on each side)

18.3 Squeeze the tabs of the electrical connectors to release them from the airbag. Also disconnect the horn electrical connector

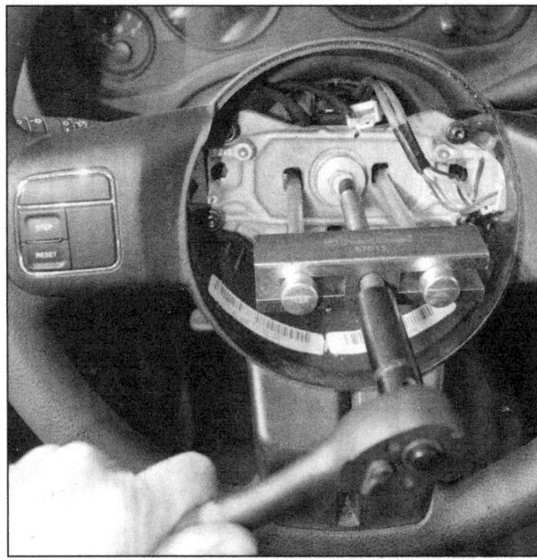

18.6 Use a puller with hooked legs to remove the steering wheel from the steering shaft; ensure that you hold the wheel in the straight ahead position while doing so

6   Remove the lower control arm-to-cross-member fastener and remove the lower control arm.

7   Installation is the reverse of removal. Before tightening any of the fasteners, raise the suspension with a floor jack placed under the outer end of the lower control arm to simulate normal ride height, then tighten the fasteners to the torque listed in this Chapter's Specifications.

18   Steering wheel - removal and installation

Warning: *These models have airbags. Always disarm the airbag system before working in the vicinity of the impact sensors, steering column, or instrument panel to avoid accidental deployment of the airbag, which could cause personal injury (see Chapter 12).*

Warning: *Do not use a memory saving device to preserve the PCM's memory when working on or near airbag system components.*

Removal

1   Park the vehicle with the wheels pointing straight ahead and the steering wheel centered. Disconnect the cable from the negative terminal of the battery (see Chapter 5).

Warning: *Wait at least two minutes before proceeding with the following steps.*

2   Remove the airbag module from the steering wheel by removing the two bolts (see illustration).

3   Disconnect the electrical connectors from the airbag module (see illustration). Set the airbag module in an isolated area, with the trim (upholstered) side of the module facing Up.

4   Disconnect the steering wheel wiring harness connector at the clockspring.

Warning: *When carrying the airbag module, keep the driver's (trim) side facing away from you.*

5   While firmly holding the steering wheel in the straight ahead position, loosen the steering wheel retaining bolt a few turns.

6   Break loose the steering wheel from the shaft using a puller with hooked legs (see illustration). The puller screw must contact the steering wheel bolt. Once the wheel has broken loose, remove the puller and bolt, then mark the position of the steering wheel to the shaft.

Caution: *Do not hammer on the steering shaft or the steering wheel in an attempt to free the steering wheel from the shaft. Also, do not use a slide hammer puller to remove the steering wheel.*

Caution: *While the steering wheel is removed, DO NOT turn the steering shaft. If you do so, the airbag clockspring could be damaged when the vehicle is put back in service.*

7   After the steering wheel has been removed, tape the clockspring so it can't turn (see illustration).

Note: *A locking pin is installed on a replacement clockspring in order to be assured of correct center position installation. When installing a replacement clockspring be sure to have the front wheels straight ahead, fasten the clockspring in place and then pull the tab out of the clockspring.*

Note: *The clockspring is integral with the SCCM (Steering Column Control Module) - For more information on the replacement of the SCCM, refer to the procedure listed in Chapter 12.*

Installation

8   Make sure the clockspring is still centered, the wheels are straight ahead, and the turn signal stalk is in the middle (neutral) position.

9   If the clockspring has become uncentered, turn the clockspring rotor clockwise until it stops (don't apply too much force, though), then turn it counterclockwise approximately 2-1/2 turns. The dowel pin

18.7 Apply a piece of tape over the clockspring so it can't turn and become uncentered

should be at the 6 o'clock position and the wiring should be at the top.

10   Install the wheel on the steering shaft, aligning the wide spline on the shaft with the gap in the steering wheel splines. Push the wheel onto the shaft and ensure the clockspring lines up on the back of the steering wheel.

Note: *Make sure the clockspring wires are routed correctly through the steering wheel.*

11   Install a NEW steering wheel retaining bolt and tighten it to the torque listed in this Chapter's Specifications.

12   Reconnect the clockspring connector.

13   Reconnect the electrical connectors to the airbag module, then install the module to the steering wheel. Tighten the fasteners to the torque listed in this Chapter's Specifications.

14   Connect the cable to the negative battery terminal (see Chapter 5).

15   Turn the ignition key On and verify that

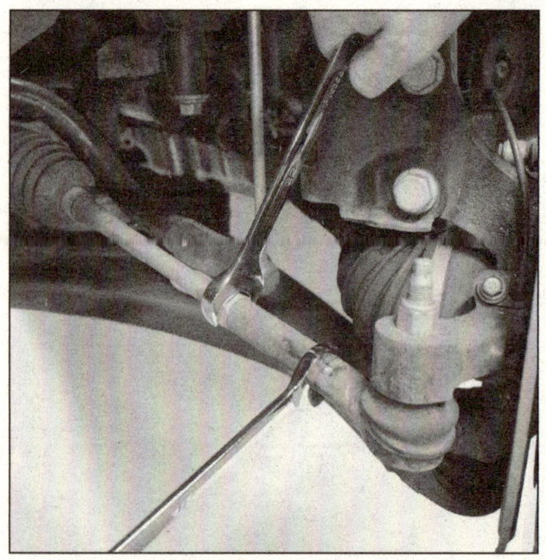

19.2 Hold the tie-rod end while breaking loose the jam nut

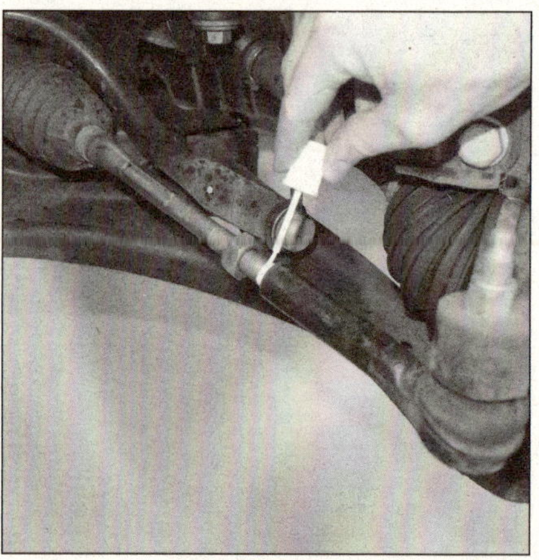

19.3 Back-off the jam nut and mark the exposed threads

19.4a If the tie-rod end stud spins when loosening the nut, hold the stud with a wrench or socket

19.4b Use a puller to break loose the tie-rod end ballstud

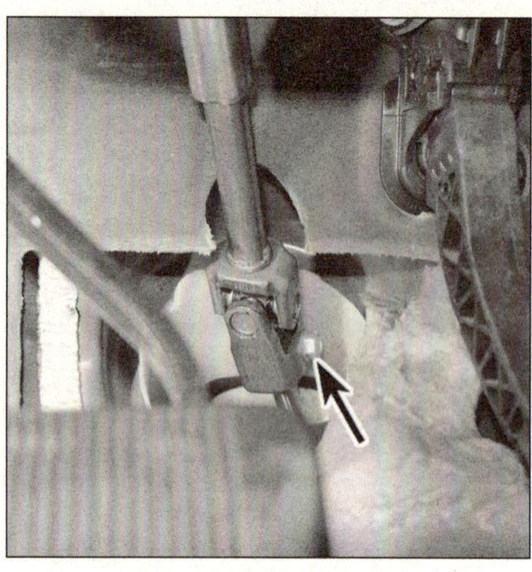

20.2 Rotate the steering shaft to gain access to the pinch bolt

the airbag system is operating properly by watching the airbag warning light in the instrument cluster (see Chapter 12).

Warning: *If the airbag system is not operating properly (as indicated by the airbag warning light), DO NOT drive the vehicle. Have the airbag system repaired at a dealership service department or other qualified repair shop.*

19 Tie-rod ends - removal and installation

Removal

1   Loosen the wheel lug nuts, raise the front of the vehicle and support it securely on jackstands. Apply the parking brake and block the rear wheels to keep the vehicle from rolling off the jackstands. Remove the wheel.

2   Loosen the tie-rod end jam nut (see illustration).

3   Mark the relationship of the tie-rod end to the threaded portion of the tie-rod. This

will ensure the toe-in setting is restored when reassembled (see illustration).

Note: *When marking the tie rod end be sure to use something that isn't going to be easily rubbed off. A back up method is to count the number of turns as you remove the tie rod end.*

4   Loosen the nut on the tie-rod end ballstud a few turns (see illustration). Break loose the tie-rod end ballstud from the steering knuckle arm with a puller (see illustration).

5   Remove the nut and separate the tie-rod end from the steering knuckle, then unscrew the tie-rod end from the tie-rod.

Installation

6   Thread the tie-rod end onto the tie-rod to the marked position and connect the tie-rod end to the steering knuckle arm. Install the nut on the ballstud and tighten it to the torque listed in this Chapter's Specifications.

7   Tighten the jam nut securely and install the wheel. Lower the vehicle and tighten the lug nuts to the torque listed in the Chapter 1 Specifications.

8   Have the front end alignment checked and, if necessary, adjusted.

20 Steering column - removal and installation

Warning: *These models have airbags. Always disarm the airbag system before working in the vicinity of the impact sensors, steering column, or instrument panel to avoid accidental deployment of the airbag, which could cause personal injury (see Chapter 12).*

Warning: *Do not use a memory saving device to preserve the PCM's memory when working on or near airbag system components.*

Removal

1   Park the vehicle with the wheels pointing straight ahead. Disconnect the cable from the negative terminal of the battery (see Chapter 5).

2   Lift the carpeting up to expose the intermediate shaft and steering coupling. Rotate the steering wheel to gain access to the head of the bolt that secures the intermediate shaft to the steering column (see illustration). Remove the bolt, rotate the steering wheel back to the straight forward position, then separate the intermediate shaft and the column.

3   If needed, remove the driver's airbag module (see Section 18).

4   If needed, remove the steering wheel as well (see Section 18).

Warning: *Do not move the steering shaft after the steering wheel has been removed or damage to the clockspring could occur when the vehicle is put back into service. To ensure this doesn't happen, make sure the steering column is locked.*

5   Remove the driver's side knee bolster trim panel (see Chapter 11).

6   Remove the steering column covers (see Chapter 11).

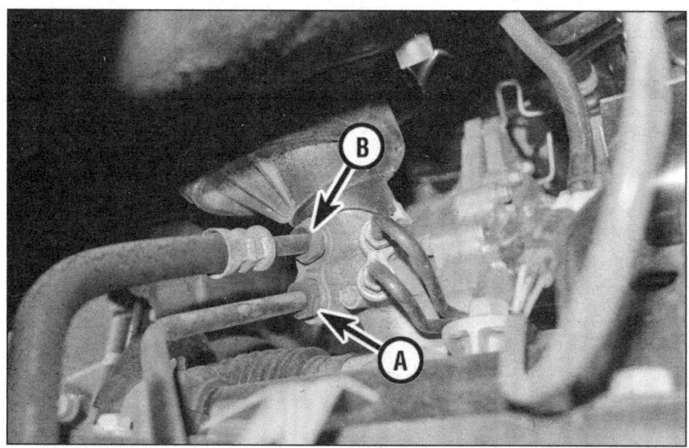

21.9 Power steering pressure (A) and return (B) lines at the steering gear

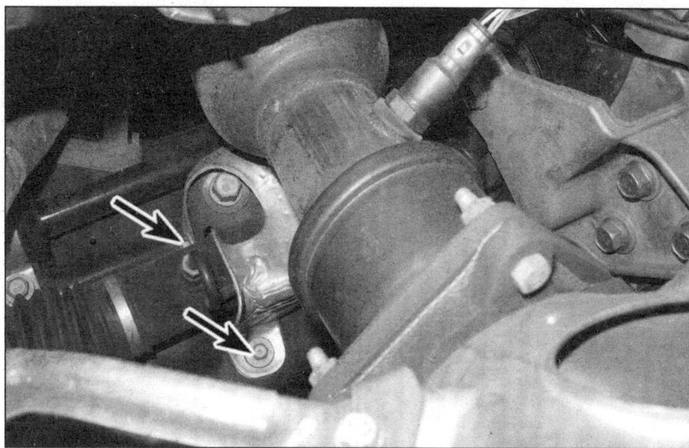

21.10a Heat shield bolts - right side

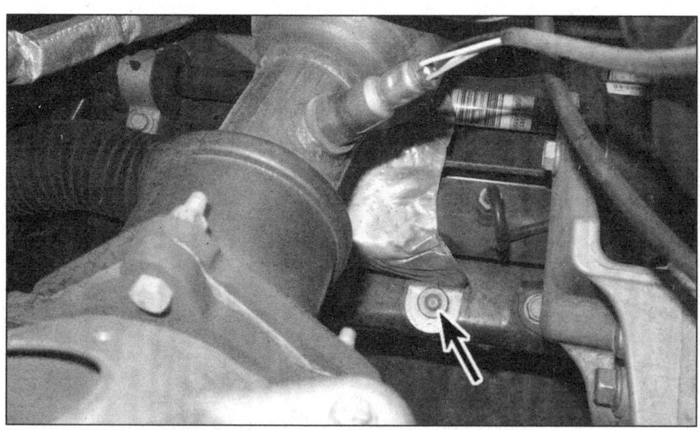

21.10b Heat shield bolt - left side

21.11 Power steering hose attachment points at the crossmember

Note: *If equipped with a column (automatic) shift, remove the shift cable from the steering column. Turn the ignition on, depress and hold the tab on the top of the interlock cable while pulling the cable from the ignition housing.*

7   Disconnect the electrical connections from the SCCM (Steering Column Control Module).

8   Position the tilt steering column in the up position, and lock it in place.

9   Disconnect any remaining electrical connectors coming from the large harness on the side of the steering column and any ground wires that may be attached to the steering column from the other side.

10   Remove the four steering column mounting fasteners, carefully lower the column, making sure nothing is still connected, and remove it.

Installation

11   Guide the steering column into position, then install the steering column mounting fasteners and tighten them to the torque listed in this Chapter's Specifications.

Note: *Begin the tightening sequence by starting with the left upper nut and working in a clockwise order.*

12   Connect the intermediate shaft and install the pinch bolt, tightening it to the torque listed in this Chapter's Specifications.

13   The remainder of installation is the reverse of removal. Reconnect the negative battery cable (see Chapter 5).

---

21   Steering gear - removal and installation

Warning: *Lock the steering wheel to keep it from moving while the steering shaft is disconnected or damage to the airbag system could occur when the vehicle is placed back in service. With the ignition key in the LOCK position, turn the steering wheel just enough to lock it or secure it with the seatbelt.*

Removal

1   Park the vehicle with the wheels pointing straight ahead. Disconnect the cable from the negative terminal of the battery (see Chapter 5).

2   Remove as much fluid as possible from the power steering fluid reservoir.

3   Loosen the wheel lug nuts, raise the vehicle, support it securely on jackstands, and remove the wheels.

4   Turn the steering wheel to the right until the intermediate shaft pinch bolt is accessible, then remove the bolt (see Section 20). Return the steering wheel to the straight ahead position, securing the steering wheel in place. Mark the intermediate shaft with the steering column and steering gear assembly before removing anything, then detach the intermediate shaft from the steering gear input shaft.

5   Disconnect both tie-rod ends from the steering knuckles (see Section 19).

6   Remove the through-bolt from the rear engine mount.

7   Remove the through-bolt from the front engine mount.

8   Remove any plastic retaining clips that hold the power steering hoses to any other wire harnesses or hoses mounted on the crossmember.

9   Unscrew the pressure and return lines from the steering gear by loosening the tube nut (see illustration).

10   Remove the steering gear heat shield mounting screws and remove the heat shield (see illustrations).

11   Remove the routing clamps for the power steering hoses that are attached to the crossmember (see illustration).

21.12a Steering gear mounting bolt - right side

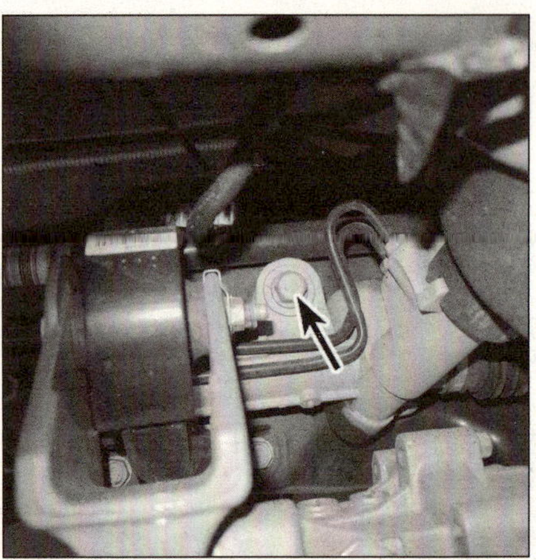

21.12b Steering gear mounting bolt - left side

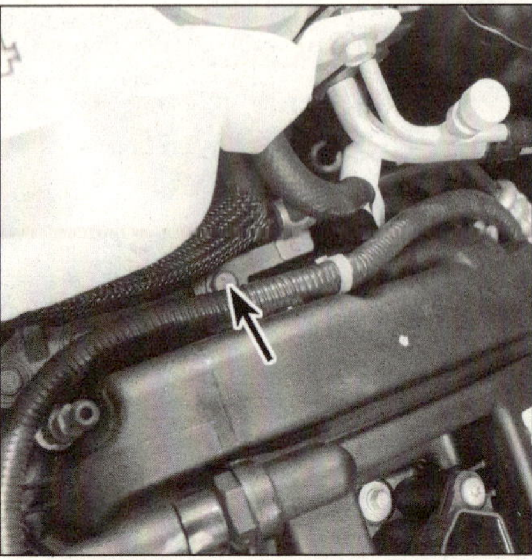

22.4 Pressure line hold-down bracket bolt

22.5 Power steering pressure line (A) and supply hose (B)

22.7 Power steering pump mounting bolts

12　Remove the two bolts securing the steering gear assembly to the crossmember (see illustrations).

13　Remove the front stabilizer bar brackets from the crossmember (see Section 2).

14　Support the crossmember with a floor jack.

15　Mark the position of the crossmember to the vehicle, then remove the four crossmember mounting bolts (see Section 24).

16　Lower the crossmember far enough to gain clearance for the steering gear assembly.

17　Remove any firewall seals that may be present while removing the steering gear.

Installation

18　Installation is the reverse of removal, noting the following points:

  a) *If a new steering gear is being installed, center the gear by turning the input shaft clockwise until it stops. Turn the input shaft counterclockwise and count the number of rotations until it stops. Divide that number by two and turn the input shaft clockwise that amount.*

  b) *Install the mounting bolts and tighten them to the torque listed in this Chapter's Specifications.*

  c) *Align the index marks on the steering gear shaft and intermediate shaft coupler before installing the bolt in the coupler.*

  d) *Install the fluid lines to the steering gear in the correct position and tighten them securely.*

  e) *Tighten the engine mount bolt, crossmember bolts, and reinforcement brackets to the torque listed in this Chapter's Specifications.*

  f) *Install the wheels and lug nuts. Lower the vehicle, then tighten the lug nuts to the torque listed in the Chapter 1 Specifications.*

  g) *Fill the power steering pump reservoir with the recommended fluid (see Chapter 1), then bleed the power steering system (see Section 23).*

  h) *Have the front wheel alignment checked and, if necessary, adjusted.*

22　Power steering pump - removal and installation

Removal

1　Disconnect the cable from the negative terminal of the battery (see Chapter 5).

2　Remove the fluid from the reservoir using a suction pump or equivalent.

3　Remove the engine cover.

4　Disconnect the power steering pressure line hold-down bracket from the front engine mount (see illustration).

5　Disconnect the pressure line and supply hose from the pump (see illustration).

6　Remove the drivebelt (see Chapter 1).

7　Remove the pump mounting bolts through the pulley openings (see illustration).

8　Remove the power steering pump.

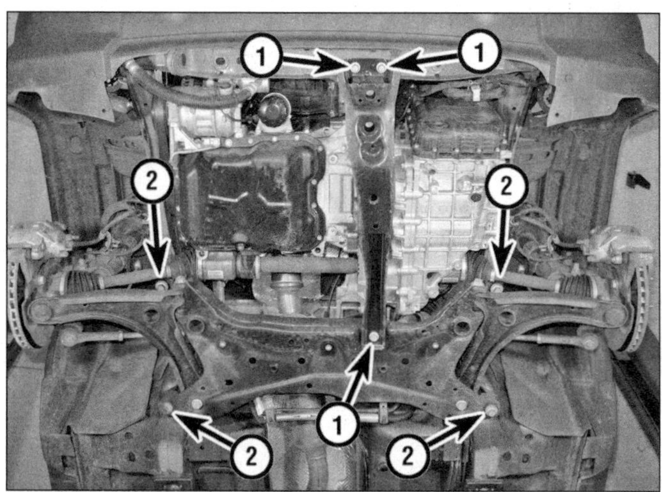

24.6 Crossmember details

1 Longitudinal crossmember mounting bolts
2 Main crossmember mounting bolts

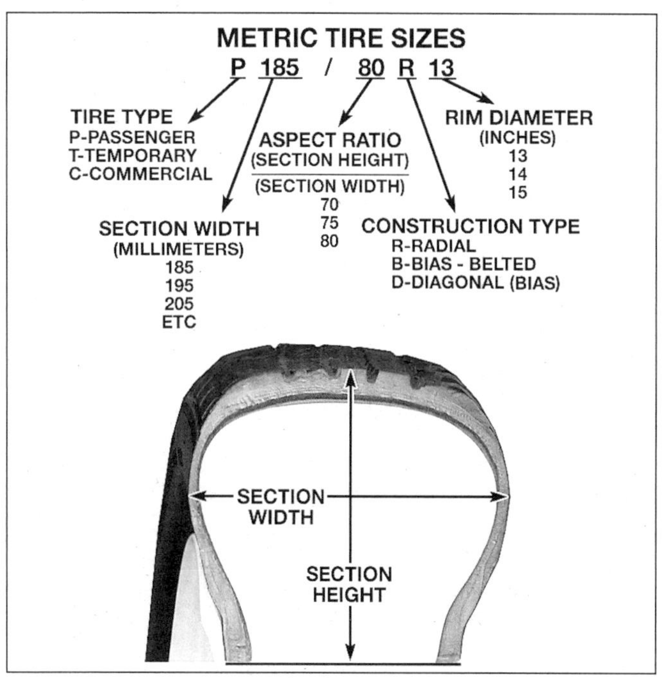

25.1 Metric tire size code

Installation

9   Installation is the reverse of removal.

10   Tighten the power steering pump mounting bolts to the torque listed in this Chapter's Specifications.

11   Tighten the pressure line-to-pump fitting securely.

12   Make sure the hoses are properly routed and all hose clamps are tightened securely.

13   Fill the power steering fluid reservoir with the recommended fluid (see Chapter 1).

14   Connect the negative battery cable (see Chapter 5).

15   Bleed the power steering system (see Section 23). Stop the engine, check the fluid level, and inspect the system for leaks.

23 Power steering system - bleeding

1   Following any operation in which the power steering fluid lines have been disconnected, the power steering system must be bled to remove all air and obtain proper steering performance.

2   With the front wheels in the straight ahead position, check the power steering fluid level (see Chapter 1).

3   Start the engine and allow it to run at fast idle. Recheck the fluid level and add fluid if necessary.

4   Bleed the system by turning the wheels from side to side, without hitting the stops. This will work the air out of the system. Maintain the proper fluid level as this is done.

5   When the air is worked out of the system, return the wheels to the straight ahead position and leave the vehicle running for several more minutes before shutting it off.

6   Road test the vehicle to be sure the steering system is functioning normally and noise free.

7   Recheck the fluid level to be sure it is correct; add fluid if necessary.

24 Crossmember - removal and installation

1   Loosen the front wheel lug nuts. Apply the parking brake, then raise the front of the vehicle and support it securely on jackstands. Block the rear wheels. Remove the front wheels.

2   Mark all four corners of the subframe to the vehicle (this will preserve alignment when assembling).

3   Remove the power steering hose fasteners from the subframe.

4   Disconnect the control arms from the steering knuckles (see Section 5).

5   Disconnect the stabilizer bar links from the stabilizer bar (see Section 2).

6   Remove the longitudinal (engine mount) crossmember (see illustration).

7   Remove the steering gear mounting bolts and the power steering line-to-crossmember bracket bolts (see Section 21). Once the gear is unbolted, tie it up out of the way.

8   Support the crossmember with a floor jack and remove the main crossmember mounting bolts.

9   Slowly lower the crossmember, making sure nothing is still attached.

10   If the subframe is being replaced, separate the control arms once it is on the ground (see Section 5).

11   Installation is the reverse of removal.

Tighten all fasteners to the torque listed in this Chapter's Specifications.

12   Have the wheel alignment checked and, if necessary, adjusted.

25 Wheels and tires - general information

1   All vehicles covered by this manual are equipped with metric-sized fiberglass or steel belted radial tires (see illustration). Use of other size or type of tires may affect the ride and handling of the vehicle. Don't mix different types of tires, such as radials and bias belted, on the same vehicle as handling may be seriously affected. It's recommended that tires be replaced in pairs on the same axle, but if only one tire is being replaced, be sure it's the same size, structure and tread design as the other.

2   Because tire pressure has a substantial effect on handling and wear, the pressure on all tires should be checked at least once a month or before any extended trips (see Chapter 1).

3   Wheels must be replaced if they are bent, dented, leak air, have elongated bolt holes, are heavily rusted, out of vertical symmetry or if the lug nuts won't stay tight. Wheel repairs that use welding or peening are not recommended.

4   Tire and wheel balance is important in the overall handling, braking and performance of the vehicle. Unbalanced wheels can adversely affect handling and ride characteristics as well as tire life. Whenever a tire is installed on a wheel, the tire and wheel should be balanced by a shop with the proper equipment.

26 Wheel alignment - general information

1   A wheel alignment refers to the adjustments made to the wheels so they are in proper angular relationship to the suspension and the ground. Wheels that are out of proper alignment not only affect vehicle control, but also increase tire wear. The front end angles normally measured are camber, caster and toe-in (see illustration). Toe-in is the only routine adjustment made. Both camber and caster are set at the factory and are not considered to be adjustable. However, camber can be slightly adjusted by using special adjustment parts from the manufacturer.

2   Getting the proper wheel alignment is a very exacting process, one in which complicated and expensive machines are necessary to perform the job properly. Because of this, you should have a technician with the proper equipment perform these tasks. We will, however, use this space to give you a basic idea of what is involved with a wheel alignment so you can better understand the process and deal intelligently with the shop that does the work.

3   Toe-in is the turning in of the wheels. The purpose of a toe specification is to ensure parallel rolling of the wheels. In a vehicle with zero toe-in, the distance between the front edges of the wheels will be the same as the distance between the rear edges of the wheels. The actual amount of toe-in is normally only a fraction of an inch. At the front end, toe-in is controlled by the tie-rod end position on the tie-rod; at the rear it's controlled by an adjuster cam on the inner end of the toe-link. Incorrect toe-in will cause the tires to wear improperly by making them scrub against the road surface.

4   Camber is the tilting of the wheels from vertical when viewed from one end of the vehicle. When the wheels tilt out at the top, the camber is said to be positive (+). When the wheels tilt in at the top the camber is negative (-). The amount of tilt is measured in degrees from vertical and this measurement is called the camber angle. This angle affects the amount of tire tread which contacts the road and compensates for changes in the suspension geometry when the vehicle is cornering or traveling over an undulating surface. On the front end it is adjusted using special camber adjusting bolts.

5   Caster is the tilting of the front steering axis from the vertical. A tilt toward the rear is positive caster and a tilt toward the front is negative caster. This is not considered to be adjustable on these vehicles.

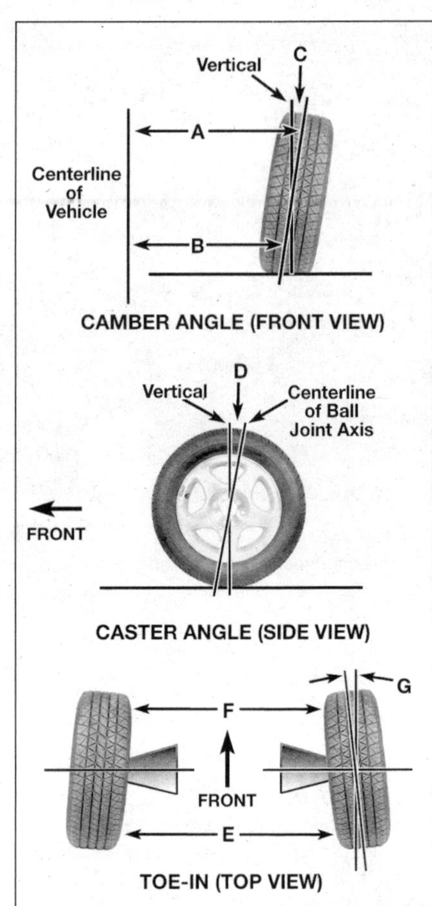

26.1 Wheel alignment details

A minus B = C (degrees camber)
D = caster (expressed in degrees)
E minus F = toe-in (measured in inches)
G = toe-in (expressed in degrees)

Chapter 11
Body

Contents

Specifications

Torque specifications   Ft-lbs (unless otherwise indicated)

Note: *One foot-pound (ft-lb) of torque is equivalent to 12 inch-pounds (in-lbs) of torque. Torque values below approximately 15 ft-lbs are expressed in inch-pounds, since most foot-pound torque wrenches are not accurate at these smaller values.*

Seats

Seat belt anchor bolts	24
Front seat mounting bolts	38
Rear seat back mounting bolts (rear)	34
Rear seat back mounting bolts (front)	59
Rear seat back mounting nuts (rear)	60
Rear seat belt buckle bolts	49
Rear seat cushion retaining bolts	60

1   General Information

Warning: *The models covered by this manual are equipped with Supplemental Restraint Systems (SRS), more commonly known as airbags. Always disable the airbag system before working in the vicinity of any airbag system components to avoid the possibility of accidental deployment of the airbags, which could cause personal injury (see Chapter 12).*

1   Certain body components are particularly vulnerable to accident damage and can be unbolted and repaired or replaced. Among these parts are the hood, doors, tailgate, liftgate, bumpers and front fenders.

2   Only general body maintenance practices and body panel repair procedures within the scope of the do-it-yourselfer are included in this Chapter.

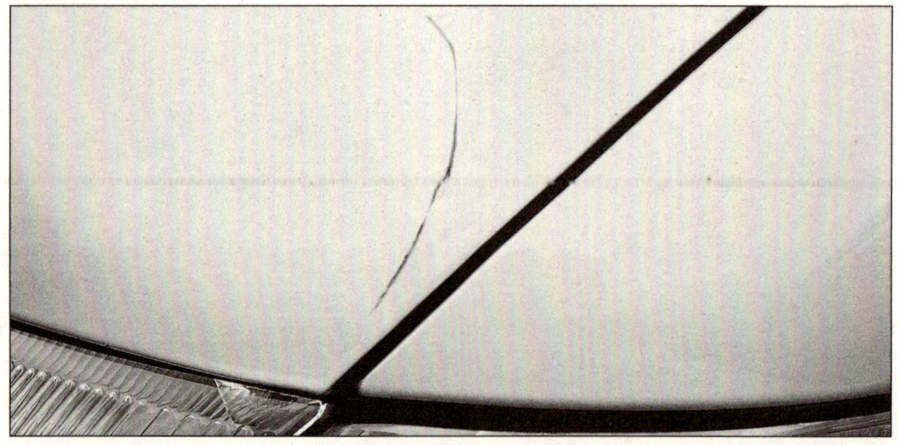

Make sure the damaged area is perfectly clean and rust free. If the touch-up kit has a wire brush, use it to clean the scratch or chip. Or use fine steel wool wrapped around the end of a pencil. Clean the scratched or chipped surface only, not the good paint surrounding it. Rinse the area with water and allow it to dry thoroughly

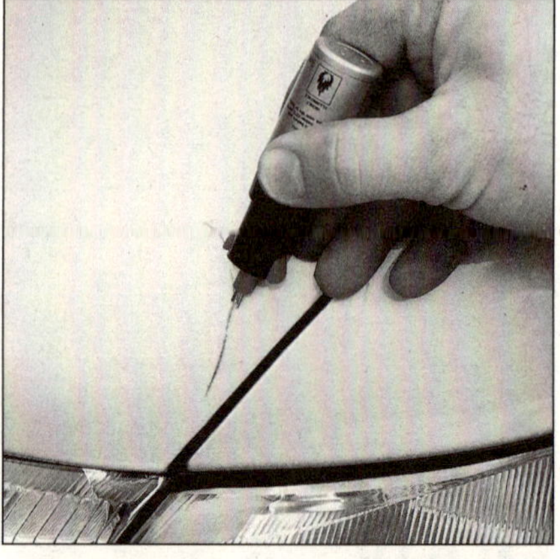

Thoroughly mix the paint, then apply a small amount with the touch-up kit brush or a very fine artist's brush. Brush in one direction as you fill the scratch area. Do not build up the paint higher than the surrounding paint

2 Repairing minor paint scratches

1 No matter how hard you try to keep your vehicle looking like new, it will inevitably be scratched, chipped or dented at some point. If the metal is actually dented, seek the advice of a professional. But you can fix minor scratches and chips yourself. Buy a touch-up paint kit from a dealer service department or an auto parts store. To ensure that you get the right color, you'll need to have the specific make, model and year of your vehicle and, ideally, the paint code, which is located on a special metal plate under the hood or in the door jamb.

3 Body repair - minor damage

Plastic body panels

1 The following repair procedures are for minor scratches and gouges. Repair of more serious damage should be left to a dealer service department or qualified auto body shop. Below is a list of the equipment and materials necessary to perform the following repair procedures on plastic body panels.

Wax, grease and silicone removing solvent
Cloth-backed body tape
Sanding discs
Drill motor with three-inch disc holder
Hand sanding block
Rubber squeegees
Sandpaper
Non-porous mixing palette
Wood paddle or putty knife
Wood paddle or putty knife
Curved-tooth body file
Flexible parts repair material

Flexible panels (bumper trim)

2 Remove the damaged panel, if necessary or desirable. In most cases, repairs can be carried out with the panel installed.
3 Clean the area(s) to be repaired with a

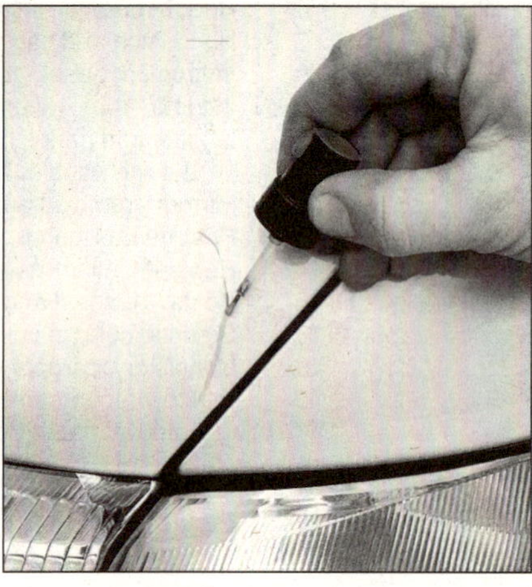

If the vehicle has a two-coat finish, apply the clear coat after the color coat has dried

wax, grease and silicone removing solvent applied with a water-dampened cloth.
4 If the damage is structural, that is, if it extends through the panel, clean the backside of the panel area to be repaired as well. Wipe dry.
5 Sand the rear surface about 1-1/2 inches beyond the break.
6 Cut two pieces of fiberglass cloth large enough to overlap the break by about 1-1/2 inches. Cut only to the required length.
7 Mix the adhesive from the repair kit according to the instructions included with the kit, and apply a layer of the mixture approximately 1/8-inch thick on the backside of the panel. Overlap the break by at least 1-1/2 inches.
8 Apply one piece of fiberglass cloth to the adhesive and cover the cloth with additional adhesive. Apply a second piece of fiberglass cloth to the adhesive and immediately cover the cloth with additional adhesive in sufficient quantity to fill the weave.
9 Allow the repair to cure for 20 to 30 min-

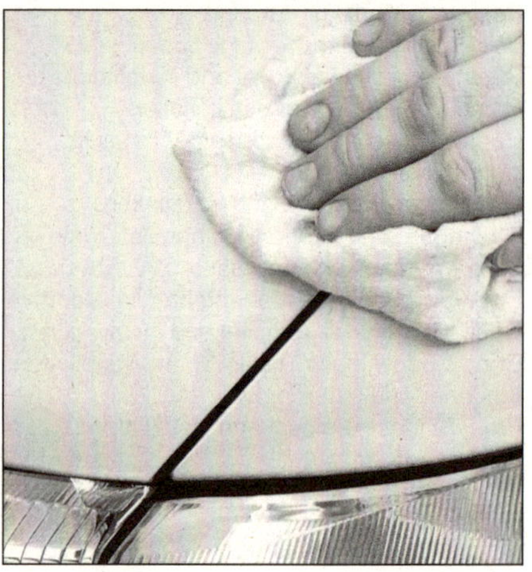

Wait a few days for the paint to dry thoroughly, then rub out the repainted area with a polishing compound to blend the new paint with the surrounding area. When you're happy with your work, wash and polish the area

utes at 60-degrees to 80-degrees F.
10 If necessary, trim the excess repair material at the edge.
11 Remove all of the paint film over and around the area(s) to be repaired. The repair material should not overlap the painted surface.
12 With a drill motor and a sanding disc (or a rotary file), cut a "V" along the break line approximately 1/2-inch wide. Remove all dust and loose particles from the repair area.
13 Mix and apply the repair material. Apply a light coat first over the damaged area; then continue applying material until it reaches a level slightly higher than the surrounding finish.
14 Cure the mixture for 20 to 30 minutes at 60-degrees to 80-degrees F.
15 Roughly establish the contour of the area being repaired with a body file. If low areas or

pits remain, mix and apply additional adhesive.

16   Block sand the damaged area with sandpaper to establish the actual contour of the surrounding surface.

17   If desired, the repaired area can be temporarily protected with several light coats of primer. Because of the special paints and techniques required for flexible body panels, it is recommended that the vehicle be taken to a paint shop for completion of the body repair.

Steel body panels

Repairing simple dents

18   When repairing dents, the first job is to pull the dent out until the affected area is as close as possible to its original shape. There is no point in trying to restore the original shape completely as the metal in the damaged area will have stretched on impact and cannot be restored to its original contours. It is better to bring the level of the dent up to a point that is about 1/8-inch below the level of the surrounding metal. In cases where the dent is very shallow, it is not worth trying to pull it out at all.

19   If the backside of the dent is accessible, it can be hammered out gently from behind using a soft-face hammer. While doing this, hold a block of wood firmly against the opposite side of the metal to absorb the hammer blows and prevent the metal from being stretched.

20   If the dent is in a section of the body which has double layers, or some other factor makes it inaccessible from behind, a different technique is required. Drill several small holes through the metal inside the damaged area, particularly in the deeper sections. Screw long, self-tapping screws into the holes just enough for them to get a good grip in the metal. Now pulling on the protruding heads of the screws with locking pliers can pull out the dent.

21   The next stage of repair is the removal of paint from the damaged area and from an inch or so of the surrounding metal. This is easily done with a wire brush or sanding disk in a drill motor, although it can be done just as effectively by hand with sandpaper. To complete the preparation for filling, score the surface of the bare metal with a screwdriver or the tang of a file or drill small holes in the affected area. This will provide a good grip for the filler material. To complete the repair, see the Section on filling and painting.

Repair of rust holes or gashes

22   Remove all paint from the affected area and from an inch or so of the surrounding metal using a sanding disk or wire brush mounted in a drill motor. If these are not available, a few sheets of sandpaper will do the job just as effectively.

23   With the paint removed, you will be able to determine the severity of the corrosion and decide whether to replace the whole panel, if possible, or repair the affected area. New body panels are not as expensive as most people think and it is often quicker to install a new panel than to repair large areas of rust.

24   Remove all trim pieces from the affected area except those which will act as a guide to the original shape of the damaged body, such as headlight shells, etc. Using metal snips or a hacksaw blade, remove all loose metal and any other metal that is badly affected by rust. Hammer the edges of the hole in to create a slight depression for the filler material.

25   Wire-brush the affected area to remove the powdery rust from the surface of the metal. If the back of the rusted area is accessible, treat it with rust inhibiting paint.

26   Before filling is done, block the hole in some way. This can be done with sheet metal riveted or screwed into place, or by stuffing the hole with wire mesh.

27   Once the hole is blocked off, the affected area can be filled and painted. See the following subsection on filling and painting.

Filling and painting

28   Many types of body fillers are available, but generally speaking, body repair kits which contain filler paste and a tube of resin hardener are best for this type of repair work. A wide, flexible plastic or nylon applicator will be necessary for imparting a smooth and contoured finish to the surface of the filler material. Mix up a small amount of filler on a clean piece of wood or cardboard (use the hardener sparingly). Follow the manufacturer's instructions on the package, otherwise the filler will set incorrectly.

29   Using the applicator, apply the filler paste to the prepared area. Draw the applicator across the surface of the filler to achieve the desired contour and to level the filler surface. As soon as a contour that approximates the original one is achieved, stop working the paste. If you continue, the paste will begin to stick to the applicator. Continue to add thin layers of paste at 20-minute intervals until the level of the filler is just above the surrounding metal.

30   Once the filler has hardened, the excess can be removed with a body file. From then on, progressively finer grades of sandpaper should be used, starting with a 180-grit paper and finishing with 600-grit wet-or-dry paper. Always wrap the sandpaper around a flat rubber or wooden block, otherwise the surface of the filler will not be completely flat. During the sanding of the filler surface, the wet-or-dry paper should be periodically rinsed in water. This will ensure that a very smooth finish is produced in the final stage.

31   At this point, the repair area should be surrounded by a ring of bare metal, which in turn should be encircled by the finely feathered edge of good paint. Rinse the repair area with clean water until all of the dust produced by the sanding operation is gone.

32   Spray the entire area with a light coat of primer. This will reveal any imperfections in the surface of the filler. Repair the imperfections with fresh filler paste or glaze filler and once more smooth the surface with sandpaper. Repeat this spray-and-repair procedure until you are satisfied that the surface of the filler and the feathered edge of the paint are perfect. Rinse the area with clean water and allow it to dry completely.

33   The repair area is now ready for painting. Spray painting must be carried out in a warm, dry, windless and dust free atmosphere. These conditions can be created if you have access to a large indoor work area, but if you are forced to work in the open, you will have to pick the day very carefully. If you are working indoors, dousing the floor in the work area with water will help settle the dust that would otherwise be in the air. If the repair area is confined to one body panel, mask off the surrounding panels. This will help minimize the effects of a slight mismatch in paint color. Trim pieces such as chrome strips, door handles, etc., will also need to be masked off or removed. Use masking tape and several thickness of newspaper for the masking operations.

34   Before spraying, shake the paint can thoroughly, then spray a test area until the spray painting technique is mastered. Cover the repair area with a thick coat of primer. The thickness should be built up using several thin layers of primer rather than one thick one. Using 600-grit wet-or-dry sandpaper, rub down the surface of the primer until it is very smooth. While doing this, the work area should be thoroughly rinsed with water and the wet-or-dry sandpaper periodically rinsed as well. Allow the primer to dry before spraying additional coats.

35   Spray on the top coat, again building up the thickness by using several thin layers of paint. Begin spraying in the center of the repair area and then, using a circular motion, work out until the whole repair area and about two inches of the surrounding original paint is covered. Remove all masking material 10 to 15 minutes after spraying on the final coat of paint. Allow the new paint at least two weeks to harden, then use a very fine rubbing compound to blend the edges of the new paint into the existing paint. Finally, apply a coat of wax

---

4   Body repair - major damage

1   Major damage must be repaired by an auto body shop specifically equipped to perform body and frame repairs. These shops have the specialized equipment required to do the job properly.

2   If the damage is extensive, the frame must be checked for proper alignment or the vehicle's handling characteristics may be adversely affected and other components may wear at an accelerated rate.

3   Due to the fact that all of the major body components (hood, fenders, etc.) are separate and replaceable units, any seriously damaged components should be replaced rather than repaired. Sometimes the components can be found in a wrecking yard that specializes in used vehicle components, often at considerable savings over the cost of new parts.

These photos illustrate a method of repairing simple dents. They are intended to supplement *Body repair - minor damage* in this Chapter and should not be used as the sole instructions for body repair on these vehicles.

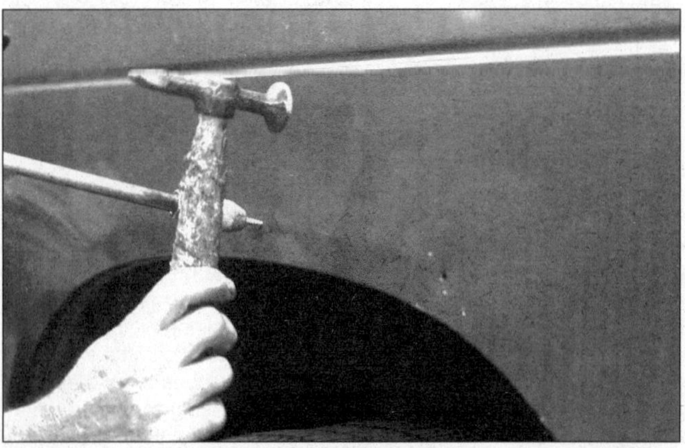

1 If you can't access the backside of the body panel to hammer out the dent, pull it out with a slide-hammer-type dent puller. Tap with a hammer near the edge of the dent to help 'pop' the metal back to its original shape, about 1/8-inch below the surface of the surrounding metal

2 Using coarse-grit sandpaper, remove the paint down to the bare metal. Clean the repair area with wax/silicone remover.

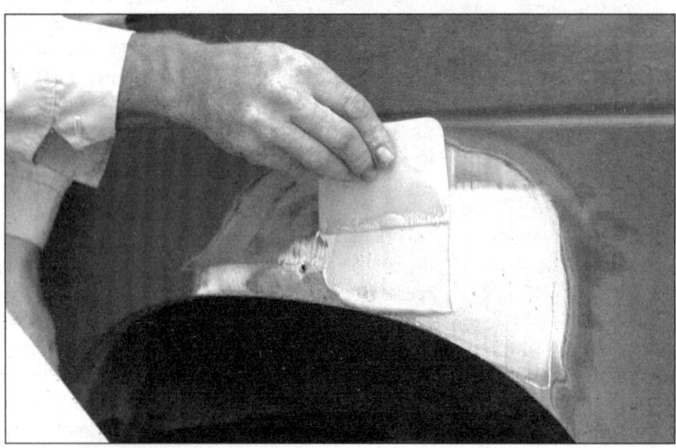

3 Following label instructions, mix up a batch of plastic filler and hardener, then quickly press it into the metal with a plastic applicator. Work the filler until it matches the original contour and is slightly above the surrounding metal

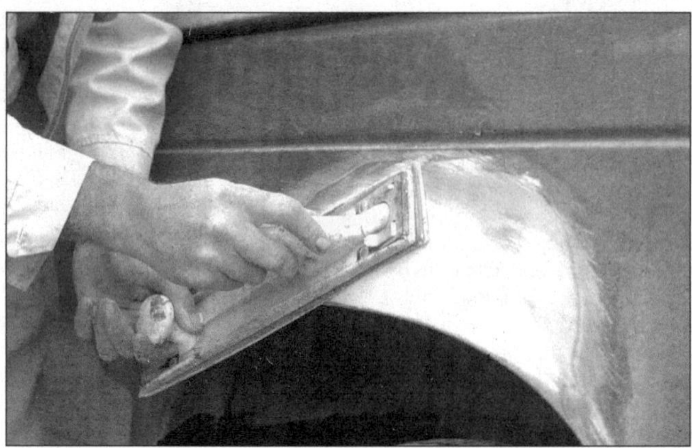

4 Let the filler harden until you can just dent it with your fingernail. File, then sand the filler down until it's smooth and even. Work down to finer grits of sandpaper - always using a board or block - ending up with 360 or 400 grit

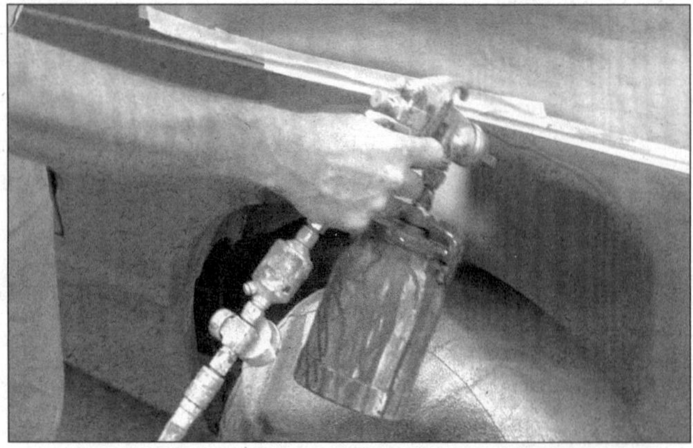

5 When the area is smooth to the touch, clean the area and mask around it. Apply several layers of primer to the area. A professional-type spray gun is being used here, but aerosol spray primer works fine

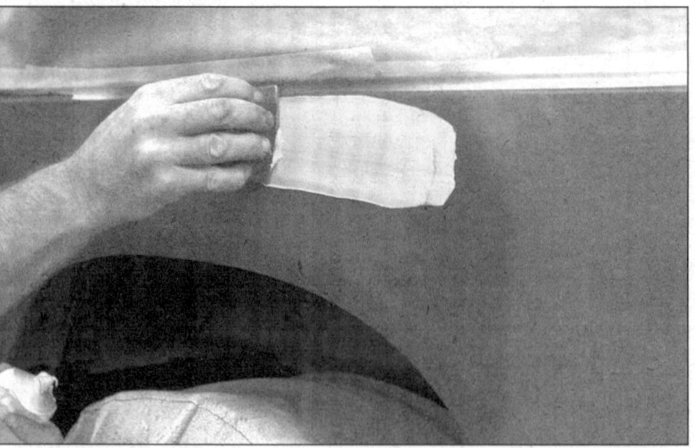

6 Fill imperfections or scratches with glazing compound. Sand with 360 or 400-grit and re-spray. Finish sand the primer with 600 grit, clean thoroughly, then apply the finish coat. Don't attempt to rub out or wax the repair area until the paint has dried completely (at least two weeks)

5 Fastener and trim removal

1   There is a variety of plastic fasteners used to hold trim panels, splash shields and other parts in place in addition to typical screws, nuts and bolts. Once you are familiar with them, they can usually be removed without too much difficulty.

2   The proper tools and approach can prevent added time and expense to a project by minimizing the number of broken fasteners and/or parts.

3   The following illustration shows various types of fasteners that are typically used on most vehicles and how to remove and install them (see illustration). Replacement fasteners are commonly found at most auto parts stores, if necessary.

4   Trim panels are typically made of plastic and their flexibility can help during removal. The key to their removal is to use a tool to pry the panel near its retainers to release it without damaging surrounding areas or breaking-off any retainers. The retainers will usually snap out of their designated slot or hole after force is applied to them. Stiff plastic tools designed for prying on trim panels are available at most auto parts stores (see illustration). Tools that are tapered and wrapped in protective tape, such as a screwdriver or small pry tool, are also very effective when used with care.

6 Upholstery, carpets and vinyl trim - maintenance

Upholstery and carpets

1   Every three months remove the floormats and clean the interior of the vehicle (more frequently if necessary). Use a stiff whiskbroom to brush the carpeting and loosen dirt and dust, then vacuum the upholstery and carpets thoroughly, especially along seams and crevices.

2   Dirt and stains can be removed from carpeting with basic household or automotive carpet shampoos available in spray cans.

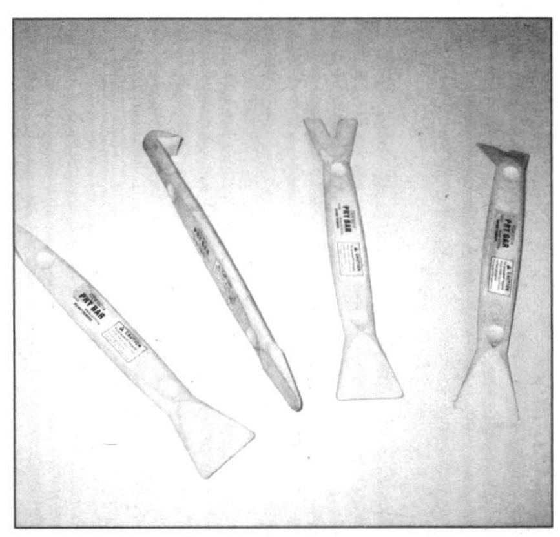

6.4 These small plastic pry tools are ideal for prying off trim panels

Follow the directions and vacuum again, then use a stiff brush to bring back the "nap" of the carpet.

3   Most interiors have cloth or vinyl upholstery, either of which can be cleaned and maintained with a number of material-

Fasteners

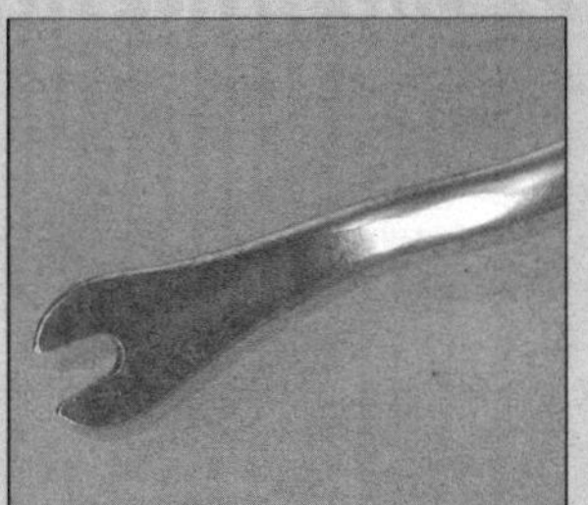

This tool is designed to remove special fasteners. A small pry tool used for removing nails will also work well in place of this tool

A Phillips head screwdriver can be used to release the center portion, but light pressure must be used because the plastic is easily damaged. Once the center is up, the fastener can easily be pried from its hole

Here is a view with the center portion fully released. Install the fastener as shown, then press the center in to set it

This fastener is used for exterior panels and shields. The center portion must be pried up to release the fastener. Install the fastener with the center up, then press the center in to set it

This type of fastener is used commonly for interior panels. Use a small blunt tool to press the small pin at the center in to release it . . .

. . . the pin will stay with the fastener in the released position

Reset the fastener for installation by moving the pin out. Install the fastener, then press the pin flush with the fastener to set it

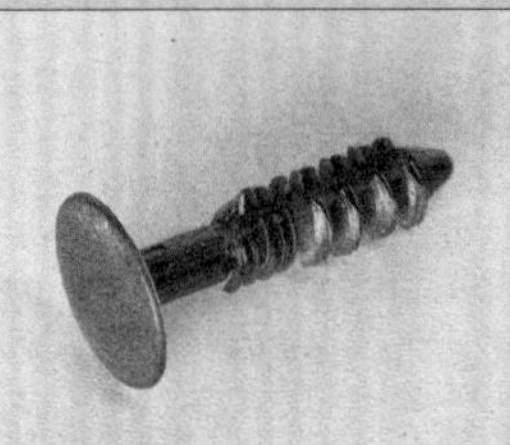

This fastener is used for exterior and interior panels. It has no moving parts. Simply pry the fastener from its hole like the claw of a hammer removes a nail. Without a tool that can get under the top of the fastener, it can be very difficult to remove

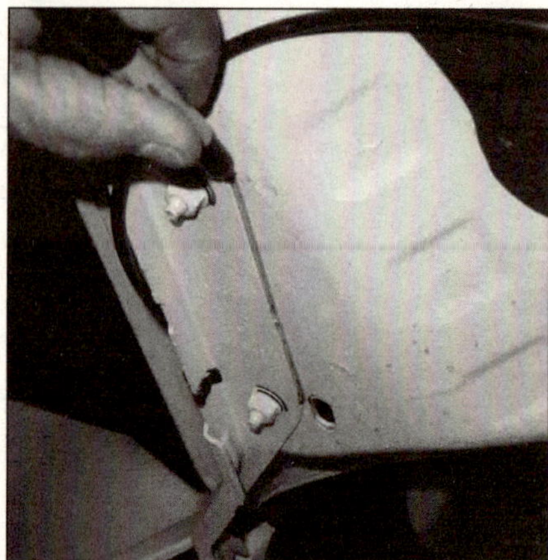

7.2 Before removing the hood, draw a mark around the hinge plates

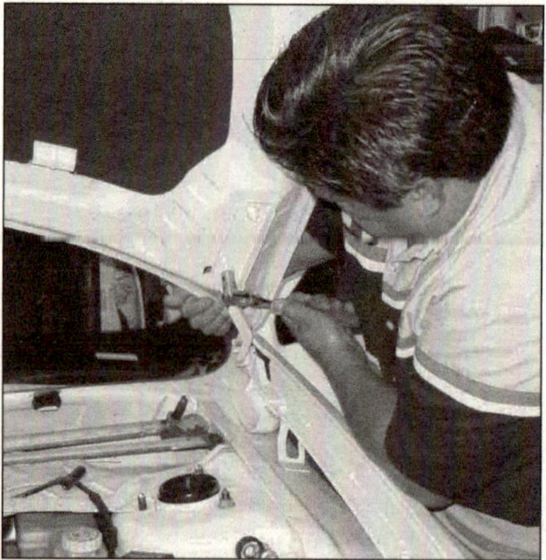

7.4 Support the hood with your shoulder while removing the hood bolts

7.11 Adjust the hood height by screwing the hood bumpers in or out

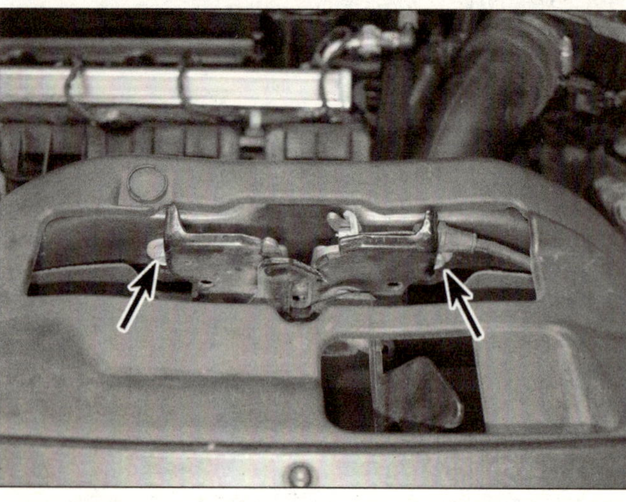

7.12 Mark the position of the hood latch, loosen the bolts and move the latch to adjust the hood in the closed position

specific cleaners or shampoos available in auto supply stores. Follow the directions on the product for usage, and always spot-test any upholstery cleaner on an inconspicuous area (bottom edge of a backseat cushion) to ensure that it doesn't cause a color shift in the material.

4   After cleaning, vinyl upholstery should be treated with a protectant.

Note: *Make sure the protectant container indicates the product can be used on seats - some products may make a seat too slippery.*

Caution: *Do not use protectant on vinyl-covered steering wheels.*

5   Leather upholstery requires special care. It should be cleaned regularly with saddle-soap or leather cleaner. Never use alcohol, gasoline, nail polish remover or thinner to clean leather upholstery.

6   After cleaning, regularly treat leather upholstery with a leather conditioner, rubbed in with a soft cotton cloth. Never use car wax on leather upholstery.

7   In areas where the interior of the vehicle is subject to bright sunlight, cover leather seating areas of the seats with a sheet if the vehicle is to be left out for any length of time.

Vinyl trim

8   Don't clean vinyl trim with detergents, caustic soap or petroleum-based cleaners. Plain soap and water works just fine, with a soft brush to clean dirt that may be ingrained. Wash the vinyl as frequently as the rest of the vehicle.

9   After cleaning, application of a high-quality rubber and vinyl protectant will help prevent oxidation and cracks. The protectant can also be applied to weather-stripping, vacuum lines and rubber hoses, which often fail as a result of chemical degradation, and to the tires. Chapter 11

---

7   Hood - removal, installation and adjustment

Note: *The hood is heavy and somewhat awkward to remove and install - at least two people should perform this procedure.*

Removal and installation

1   Use blankets or pads to cover the cowl area of the body and the fenders. This will protect the body and paint as the hood is lifted off.

2   Scribe alignment marks around the bolt heads and hinge attachment locations to insure proper alignment during installation - a permanent-type felt-tip marker also will work for this (see illustration).

3   Remove the top bolts holding the hood to the hinge and loosen the bottom bolts until they can be removed by hand.

4   Have an assistant on the opposite side of the vehicle support the weight of the hood. Simultaneously remove the bottom bolts holding the hood to the hinge and lift off the hood (see illustration).

5   Remove the under hood lamp wire connector to the engine compartment wire harness, if so equipped.

6   Disconnect the windshield washer hose from the hood.

7   Installation is the reverse of removal.

Adjustment

8   Front-and-back and side-to-side adjustment of the hood is done by moving the hood in relation to the hinge plate after loosening the bolts.

9   Scribe or trace a line around the entire hinge plate so you can judge the amount of movement.

10   Loosen the bolts or nuts and move the hood into correct alignment. Move it only a little at a time. Tighten the hinge bolts or nuts and carefully lower the hood to check the alignment.

11   Adjust the hood bumpers on the radiator support so the hood is flush with the fenders when closed (see illustration).

12   Mark the hood latch as a guide for adjustment (or removal and replacement). The hood latch assembly can also be adjusted up-and-down and side-to-side after loosening the bolts (see illustration).

13   The hood latch assembly, as well as the hinges, should be periodically lubricated with white lithium-base grease to prevent sticking and wear.

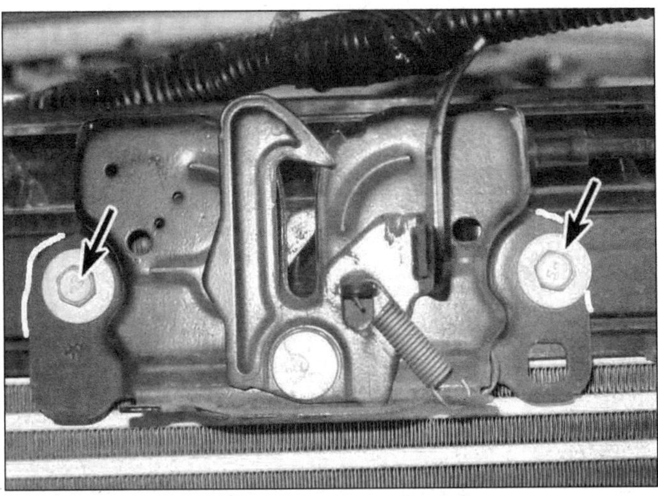

8.2 Mark the position of the hood latch, then remove the bolts

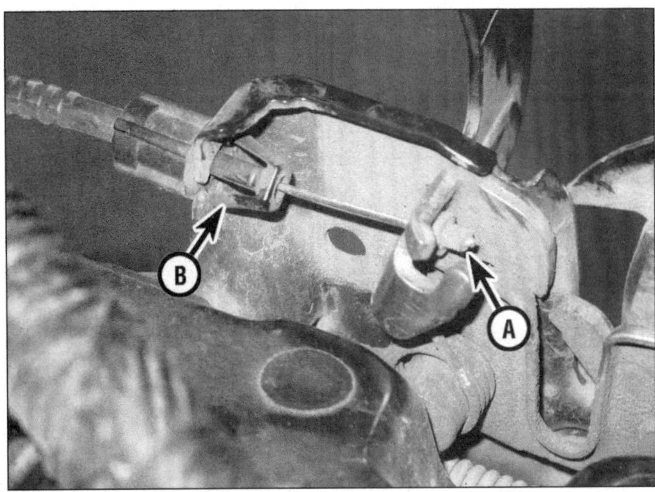

8.4 Release the cable end (A), then pinch the barb on the cable case (B) and slide it through

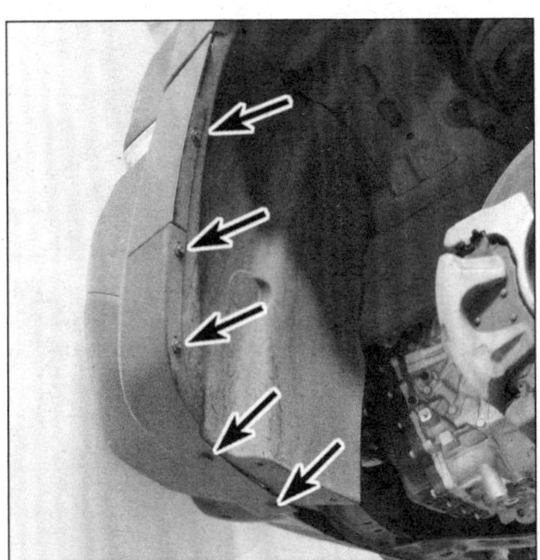

9.2 Remove the bumper cover-to-splash shield fasteners from both sides of the vehicle

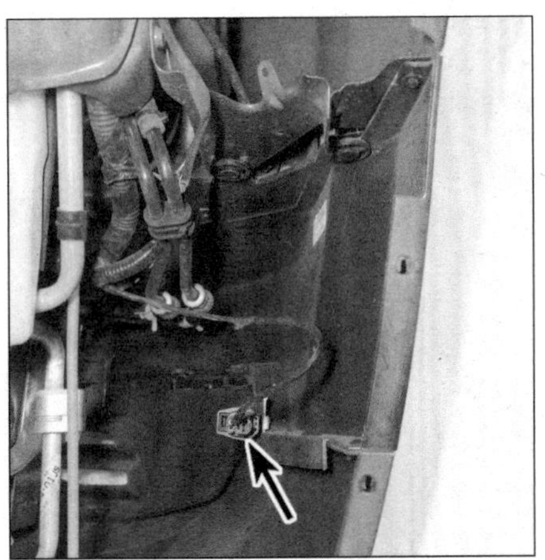

9.3a Remove the bumper cover lower electrical connector…

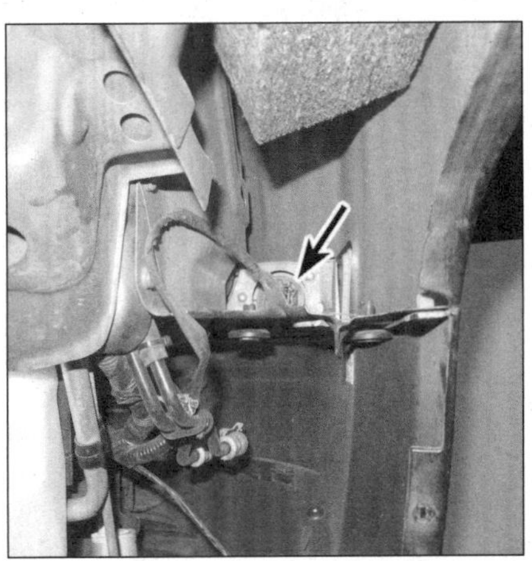

9.3b … then remove the upper electrical connector at the right side

8 Hood latch and cable - removal and installation

Latch

1   Remove the bolts holding the hood latch to the radiator support and detach the latch assembly.

2   Detach the hood release cable (see Step 4), then remove the latch from the radiator support (see illustration).

3   Installation is the reverse of removal.

Cable

4   Release the cable end, then slide the cable case sideways in the keyhole slot of the hood latch while pinching the barb on the cable case closed (see illustration). If it is difficult to release the cable end first, then it may be easier to reverse the order on these two steps.

5   Remove the cable from the latch.

6   In the passenger compartment (driver's side kick panel), remove the screws and detach the hood release handle. Disconnect the cable end from the hood release handle.

7   Under the dash, remove the rubber cable insulator from the hole in the dash panel.

8   Connect a long string or piece of wire to the engine compartment end of the cable, then detach the cable from any retaining clips and pull it through the firewall and into the passenger compartment.

9   Connect the string or wire to the new cable and pull it through the firewall into the engine compartment.

10   The remainder of installation is the reverse of removal.

9 Bumper covers - removal and installation

Front

1   Raise the front of the vehicle and support it securely on jackstands. Remove the under-vehicle splash shield.

2   Remove the fasteners (plastic push pins and screws) from both fenderwells that attach the front bumper cover to the splash shields (see illustration).

Note: *Depending on the model, there may be another electrical connector to disconnect at the left side of the bumper cover.*

3   With the right side splash shield free, reach in and disconnect the electrical connectors (see illustrations).

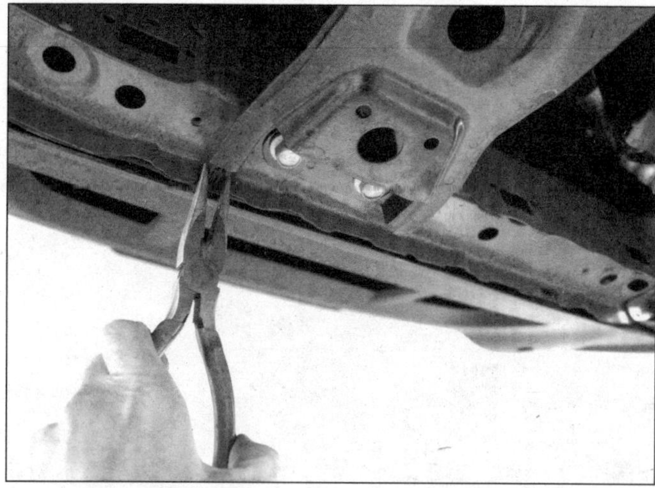

9.4 The lower fasteners can be disengaged easiest when you squeeze the clip ends together with a pair of needle nose pliers

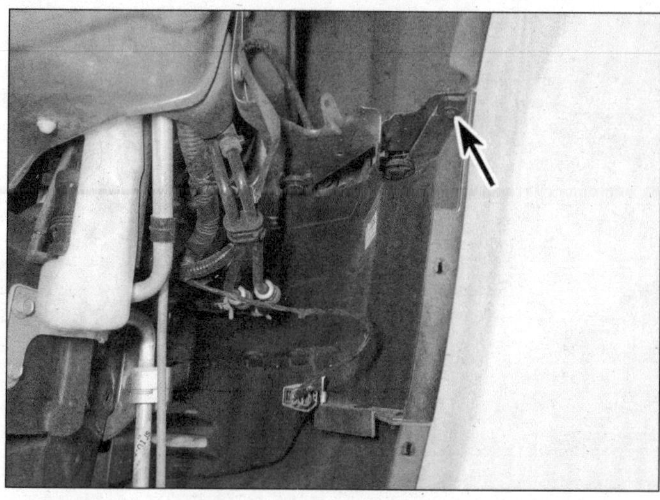

9.5 Remove the inside screws from each side of the bumper cover

9.6 Remove the screws and pushpins across the top edge of the bumper cover

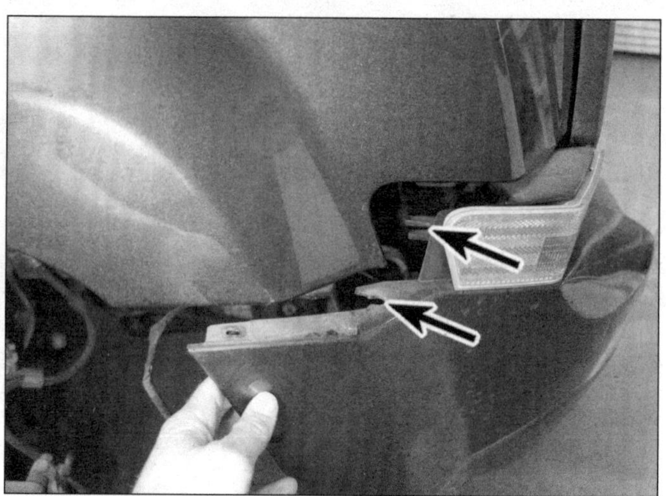

9.7 Finally, gently pull and disengage the bumper cover from the grommets at each side, then remove the bumper cover

9.9 Remove the lower pushpin fasteners

4   Disengage the fasteners along the bottom edge of the bumper cover (see illustration).

5   Remove this fastener from both sides, securing the edges of the bumper cover to the fenders (see illustration).

6   Remove the screws and pushpins securing the bumper cover to the fenders and upper radiator support (see illustration).

7   Gently pull the front bumper cover loose from the fender retaining clips at each side (see illustration). Then, with the help of an assistant, carefully guide the cover away from the vehicle, checking for any forgotten fasteners or electrical connections.

8   Installation is the reverse of removal.

Rear

9   Open the liftgate and remove the lower bumper cover fasteners (see illustration).

9.10 Remove the fasteners at the rear of the fenderwell

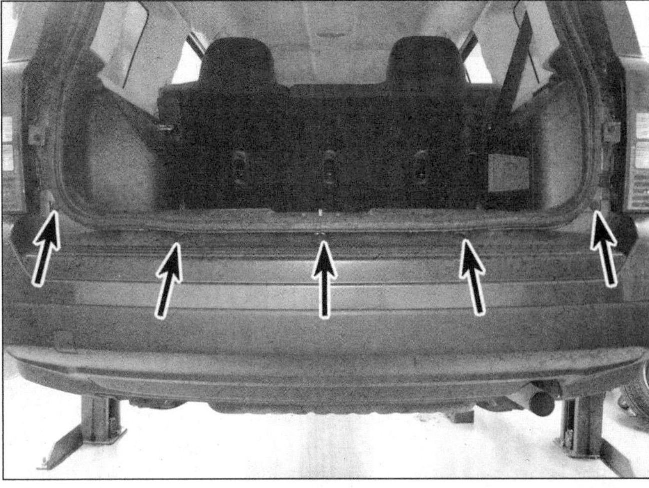

9.11 Remove the upper push pin fasteners, then remove the rear bumper cover

10   Remove the bumper cover fasteners from the fenderwell area at the rear (see illustration).

11   Remove the upper push pin fasteners (see illustration). Then, carefully pull the cover free. Slowly remove the cover while checking for any obstructions or fasteners that may have been missed.

12   Installation is the reverse of removal.

10   Bumpers - removal and installation

Front

1   Remove the front bumper cover (see Section 9).

2   Disconnect the horn electrical connector and unbolt it from the vehicle.

3   Detach the ambient air temperature sensor (mounted on the center of the bumper on the bottom side).

4   Pry out any wiring harness clips that are attached to the bumper.

5   Remove the bumper to frame bolts from both sides of the bumper.

6   Installation is the reverse of removal.

Rear

7   Open the liftgate and remove the rear bumper cover (see Section 9).

8   Remove the nuts securing the rear bumper to the frame and remove the rear bumper.

9   Installation is the reverse of removal.

11   Front fender - removal and installation

1   Remove the front bumper cover (see Section 9).

2   Remove the fasteners retaining the fender inner splash shield (see illustration)

and remove the splash shield. With the splash shield removed, remove any foam insulation that may be tucked up inside the fender.

3   Remove the fender-to-door pillar mount-

ing fasteners (see illustration).

4   Remove the lower fender bolts (just in front of the door) at the edge of the front door sill (see illustrations).

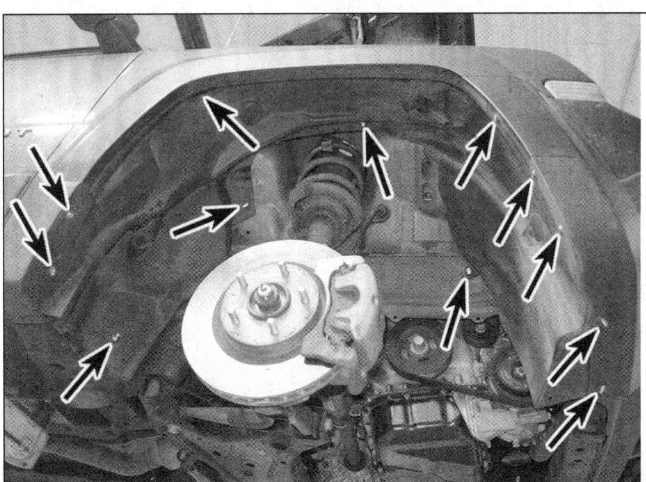

11.2 Remove the fender inner splash shield mounting fasteners and splash shield

11.3 Remove these fasteners from inside the rear of the fenderwell - peel back the foam to gain access

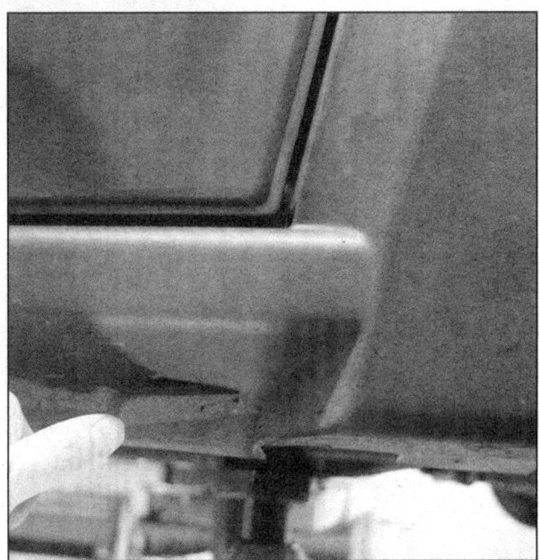

11.4a If equipped with a protective trim shield, remove the plastic fastener pin...

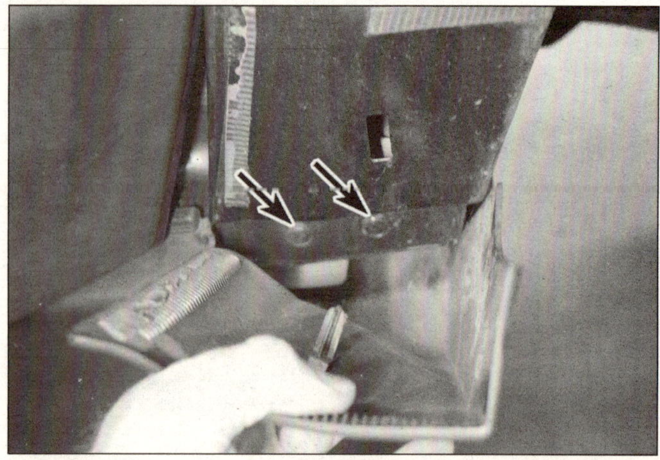

11.4b … then pull the splash shield down to gain access to the lower screws

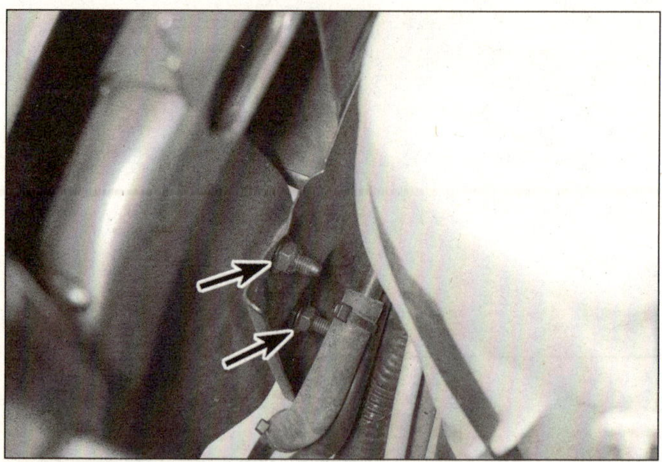

11.5 Remove the fasteners securing the front of the fender on the inside (working from the engine compartment)

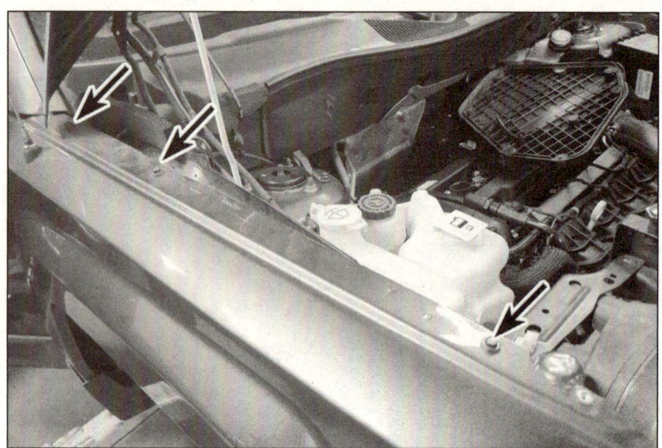

11.6 Remove the bolts across the top of the fender

12.3a Pull the hood seal off of the cowl cover and remove the pushpins…

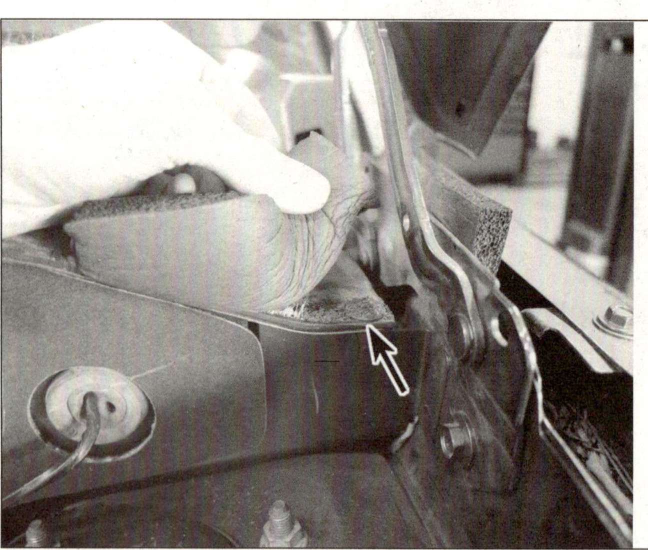

12.3b … then lift the foam at both sides to expose the plastic fasteners, and remove the fasteners

5   Remove the fender bolts at the front of the fender (see illustration).

6   Remove the fasteners along the top edge of the fender (see illustration).

7   Disconnect and remove the radio antenna (if equipped).

8   Detach the fender. It's a good idea to have an assistant support the fender while it's being moved away from the vehicle to prevent damage to the surrounding body panels.

9   Installation is the reverse of removal.

12   Cowl cover - removal and installation

1   Disconnect the cable from the negative battery terminal (see Chapter 5).

2   Remove the wiper arms (see Chapter 12).

3   Remove the hood seal and fasteners that attach the cowl cover to the body (see illustrations).

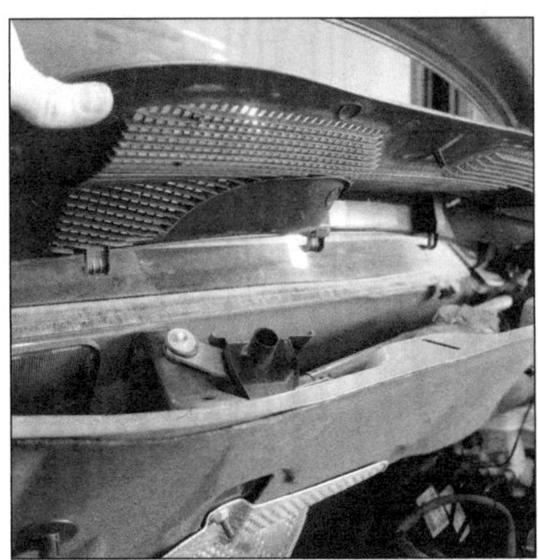

12.4 Pull the front of the cowl cover up and away from the windshield, then guide it out from the engine compartment

13.1a Pry out the protective cover and remove the screw…

13.1b … then pry the panel out from the door with a plastic trim tool, working around the perimeter…

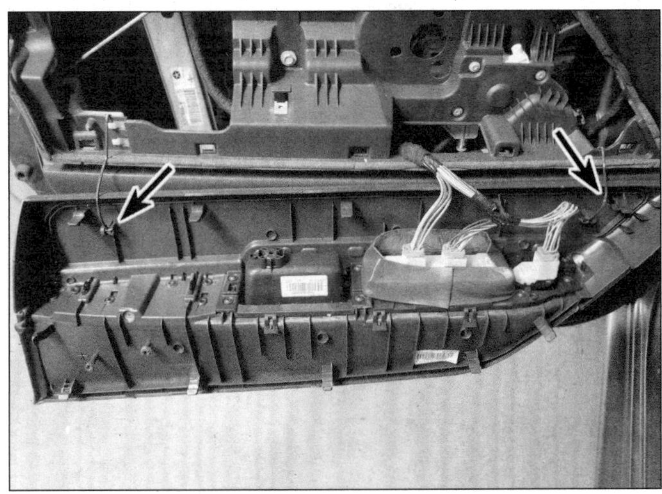

13.1c … allow the panel to hang by the tether straps and proceed with removing the main door panel

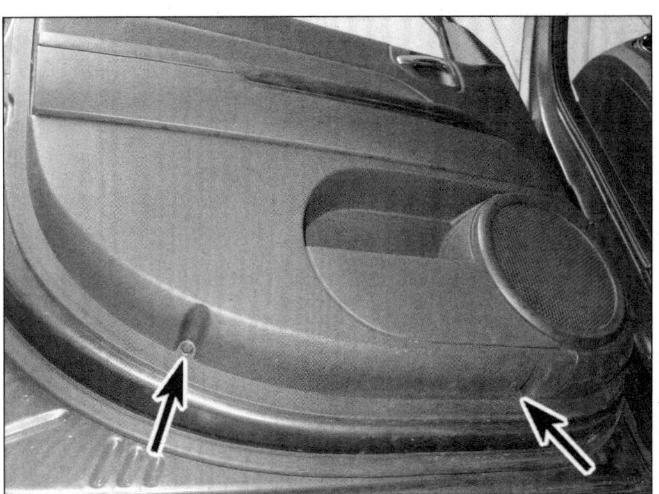

13.4 Remove the lower panel bolts

4   Lift the front of the cowl cover up and disengage the inner hooks from the windshield, then carefully maneuver it out of the vehicle (see illustration).

5   Installation is the reverse of removal.

13 Door trim panels - removal and installation

Note: *This procedure applies to front door trim panels - the rear door trim panels are similar in design.*

Switch assembly trim panel

1   Use a small flat-bladed screwdriver to pry out the cover inside the handle grip, then remove the door switch panel retaining screw. Working around the perimeter, pry the panel free and allow it to hang by the tether straps (see illustrations).

2   Installation is the reverse of removal.

Main door trim panel assembly (carrier plate)

3   Remove the switch assembly trim panel (see Step 1).

4   Remove the lower door trim panel bolts (see illustration).

5   Remove the speaker (see Chapter 12).

6   Remove the panel bolts next to the speaker opening (see illustration).

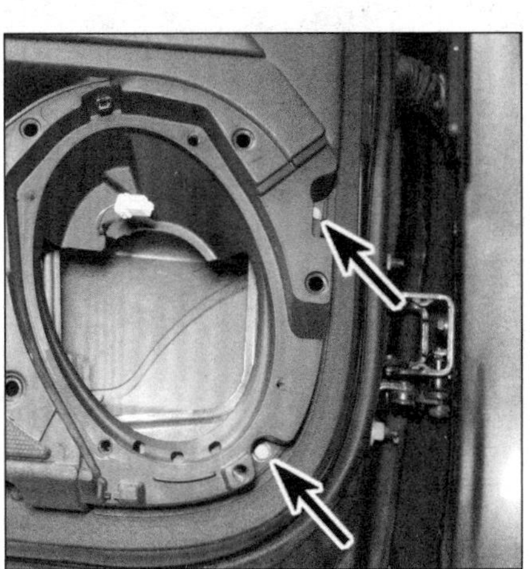

13.6 Remove the side panel bolts

13.7 Pry out the inside handle trim cover and remove the screw

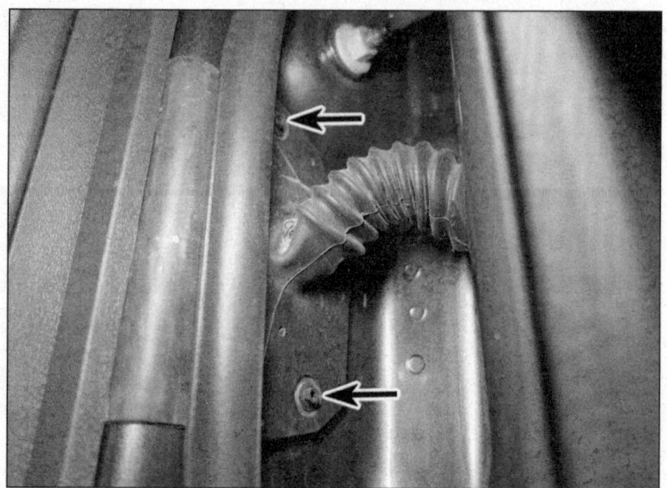

13.12 Remove the door wiring harness bracket screws

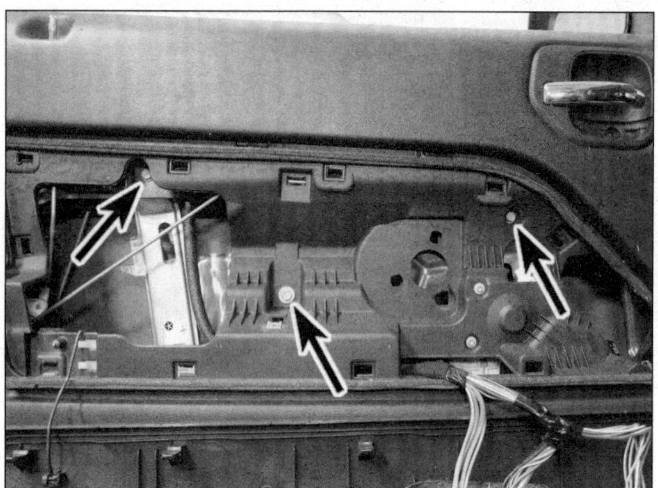

13.13 Remove the inner main panel bolts

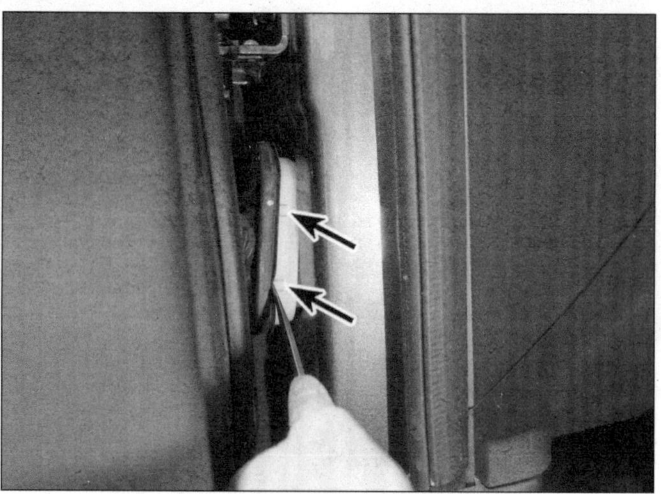

14.1a Release the tabs and pry the plastic connector housing from the jam…

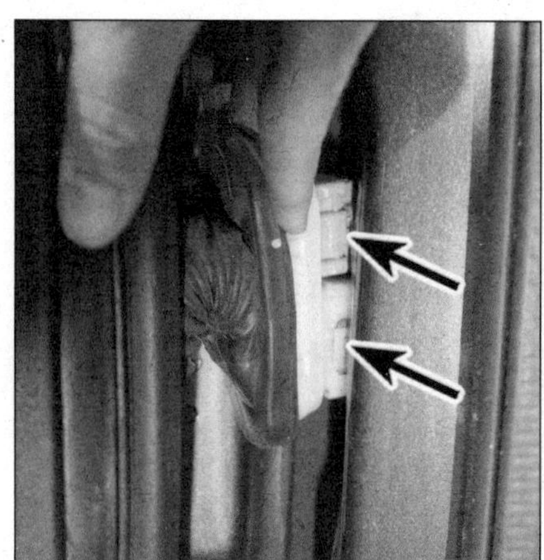

14.1b … then pull the connector housing out of the jam to disconnect the electrical connectors

7   Remove the small trim panel and retaining screw from behind the door handle (see illustration).

8   Remove the outside mirror trim panels (still working on the inside, see Section 18).

9   Remove the door window glass (see Section 16), then disconnect the cable from the negative battery terminal.

10   Disconnect the linkage rods from the door latch (leading from the outside handle) and remove the latch-to-door body bolts (see Section 15).

11   Disconnect the door main wiring harness connectors (see Section 14).

12   Remove the screws retaining the rubber connector conduit bracket to the door (see illustration), then slide the connectors through the rubber weatherstrip seal opening.

13   Remove the main panel bolts from inside the switch assembly panel opening (see illustration).

Note: *When removing the door panel assembly, the window regulator guides may have to be carefully worked free from the door body openings before the panel assembly can be fully removed.*

14   Lift the door panel assembly up, then carefully maneuver it out from the door, complete with the latch and window regulator guides.

15   Installation is the reverse of removal. Tighten all fasteners securely.

14 Door - removal and installation

Note: *Disconnect the cable from the negative battery terminal before beginning the procedure (see Chapter 5).*

1   Disconnect the door harness electrical connector from the body harness (see illustration).

14.3 While the door is safely supported, remove the lower nuts first, then the upper nuts

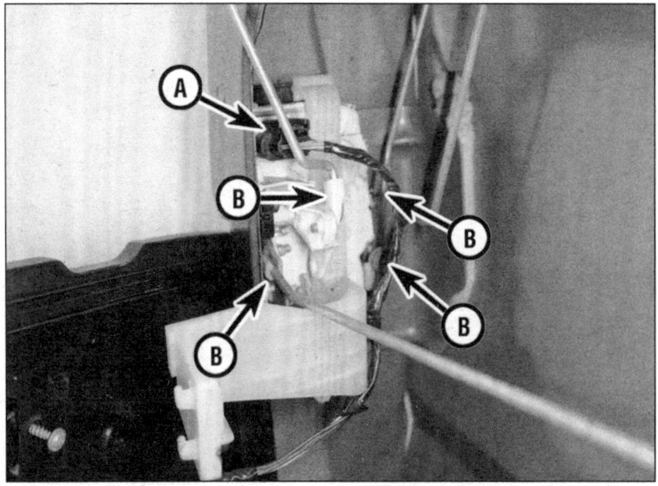

15.4 Disconnect the electrical connector (A), then separate the linkage rods from the latch (B)

2   Scribe around both the hinges with a marking pen, then place a jack under the door or have an assistant on hand to support it when the hinge fasteners are removed.
Note: *If a jack is used, place a towel between it and the door to protect the door's painted surfaces.*
3   Remove the fasteners holding the lower hinge to the door end frame. Keeping the door steady and balanced, remove the fasteners holding the upper hinge to the door end frame and carefully lift off the door (see illustration).
4   Installation is the reverse of removal. Align the hinge plates with the marks made during removal before tightening the fasteners.
5   Following installation of the door, check the alignment and adjust it if necessary as follows:

   a) *Up-and-down and in-and-out adjustments are made by loosening the hinge-to-door fasteners and moving the door as necessary.*
   b) *Forward-and-backward adjustments are made by loosening the hinge-to-body fasteners and moving the door as necessary.*
   c) *The door lock striker can also be adjusted both up-and-down and sideways to provide positive engagement with the lock mechanism. This is done by loosening the mounting screws and moving the striker as necessary.*

---

15 Door latch, lock cylinder and handle - removal and installation

---

Warning: *Models covered by this manual are equipped with a Supplemental Restraint System (SRS), more commonly known as airbags. Always disable the airbag system*

15.5 Remove the latch retaining bolts

before working in the vicinity of any airbag system component to avoid the possibility of accidental deployment of the airbag, which could cause personal injury (see Chapter 12).
Note: *The door lock actuator is part of the door latch. For an operating description and basic diagnostics see Chapter 12, Section 23 for further information.*
1   Disconnect the cable from the negative terminal of the battery (see Chapter 5).

Door latch

Note: *Although not absolutely necessary, replacement of the latch is easier when the main door panel (carrier plate) has been removed first.*
2   Remove the door switch assembly trim panel (see Section 13).
3   If easier access is needed, remove the

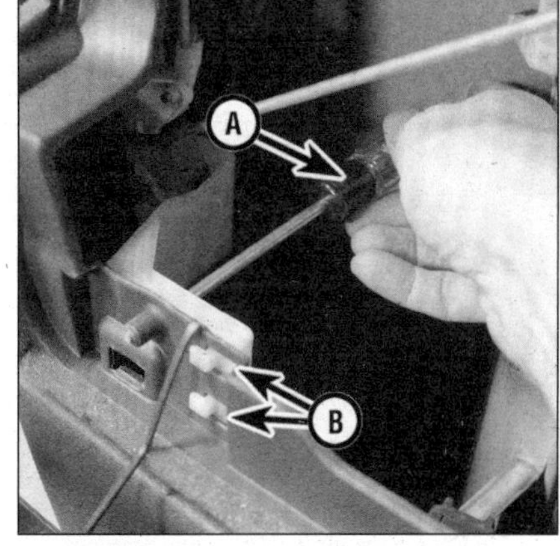

15.6 To separate the inner latch plastic from the door panel - unscrew the Torx bolt (A), then disengage the hooks (B)

main door trim panel (see Section 13).
4   Disconnect the latch electrical connector (and separate the wiring harness from the retaining clip), then disconnect the latch rods from the latch. The rods can be disconnected by first unsnapping and swiveling the colored plastic retainer off of the rod, then separating the rod from the retainer (see illustration).
5   Unscrew and remove the latch retaining bolts (see illustration).
6   Separate the inside latch plastic bracket from the door panel (see illustration), then remove the door latch.
7   Installation is the reverse of removal.

Outside handle

8   Remove the door switch assembly trim panel (see Section 13), letting it hang by the tether hooks.
9   Disconnect the latch rods from the door handle and lock cylinder, then remove the

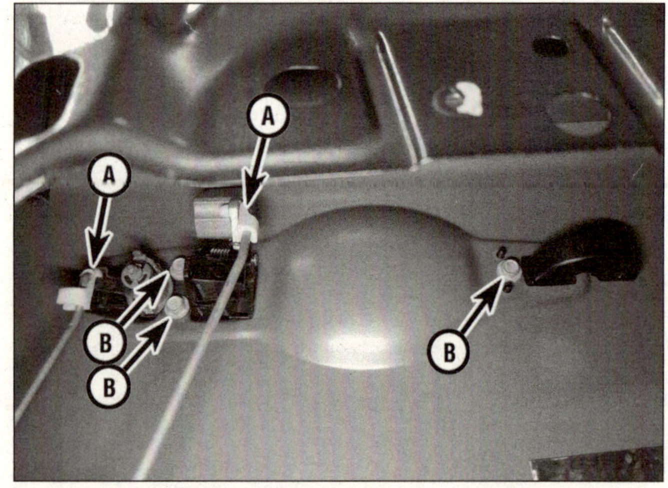

15.9 Disconnect the latch rods (A), then remove the retaining bolts (B)

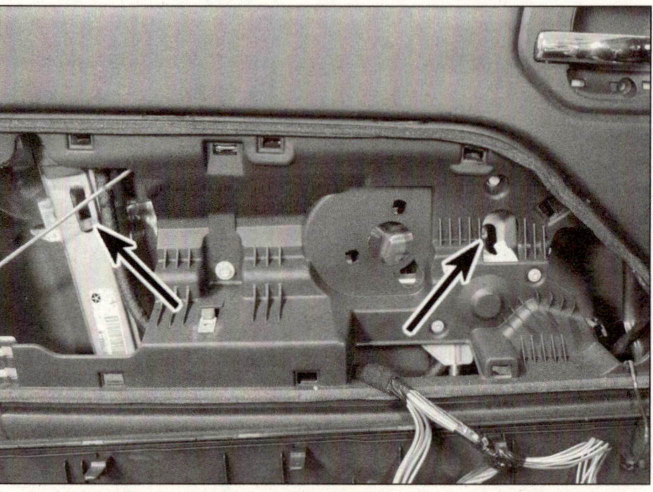

16.2a Adjust the window glass to this position - the window retaining clips should be visible through the slots

16.2b Close up view of the window glass retaining clip

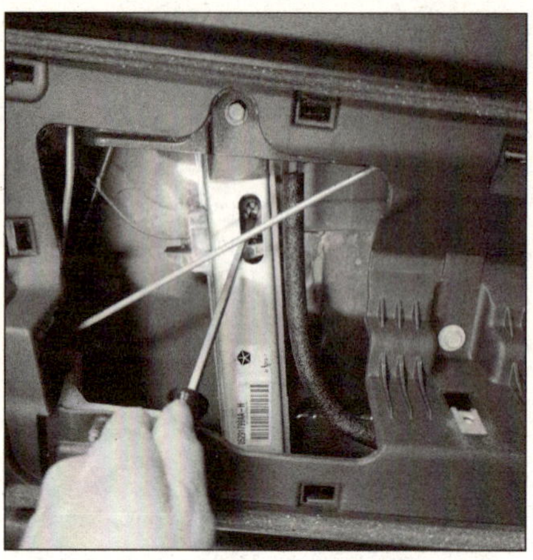

16.4 Press the plastic locking tabs inward

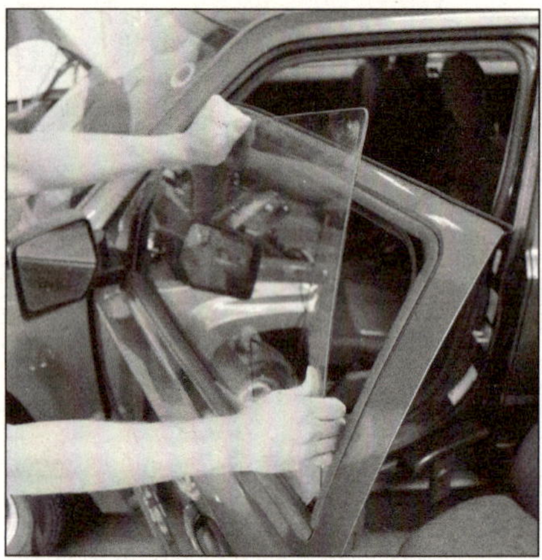

16.5 Once separated from the regulator track, carefully pull the window glass up and out of the door by hand

handle bolts (see illustration). The rods can be disconnected by first unsnapping and swiveling the plastic retainer off of the rod, then separating the rod from the retainer.

10   Installation is the reverse of removal.

Lock cylinder

11   Front door lock cylinder can be removed after removing the outside door handle from the vehicle. With handle removed, the lock cylinder slides out of the outside handle.

12   Installation is the reverse of removal.

16   Door window glass - removal and installation

Note: *This procedure applies to front and rear doors.*

1   Remove the door switch assembly trim panel and allow it to hang by the tether straps (see Section 13).

2   Raise or lower the window glass enough to access the tabs that secure the window to the window regulator tracks (see illustrations).

3   Once the tabs are visible through the slots, disconnect the cable from the negative battery terminal.

4   Use a flat tip screwdriver to press the tabs in on each side, releasing the glass from the window regulator track guides (see illustration).

5   Separate the glass from the channel, then lift the glass upward and out of the exterior opening at the top of the door, carefully tilting the glass as necessary to allow for removal (see illustration).

6   Installation is the reverse of removal.

17   Window regulator/power window motor assembly - removal and installation

1   Remove the main door trim panel (carrier plate) (see Section 13).

2   With the main door trim panel removed, the window regulator tracks should already be unbolted from the panel. Remove the window motor mounting bolts (see illustration), then remove the regulator and motor assembly from the door panel.

3   Installation is the reverse of removal. Transfer any working components onto the new regulator components as necessary. When installing, align the regulator track hooks into their respective locations on the door panel - the tracks should be oriented on the panel as shown (see illustration).

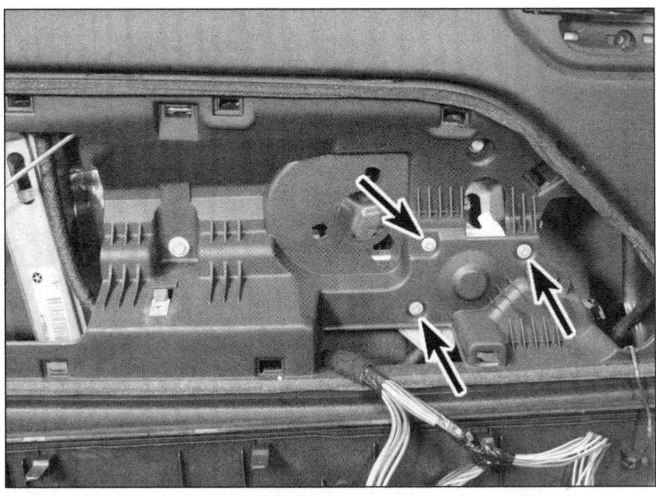

17.2 Remove the window motor (or hand crank) retaining bolts,
then remove the assembly

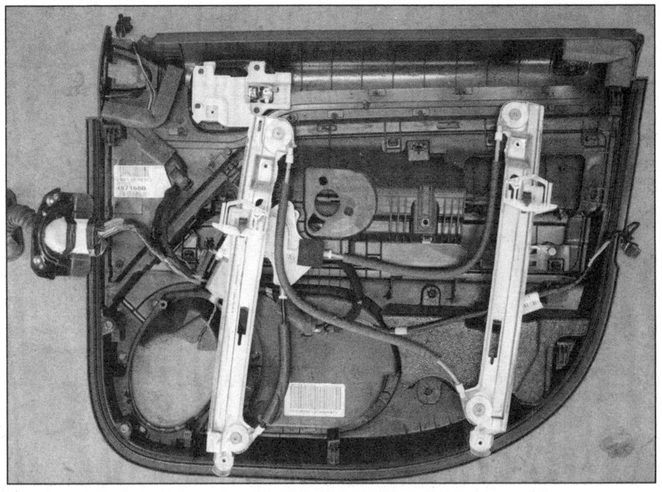

17.3 Inside view of installed regulator tracks and motor assembly
on the main door trim panel

18.1a Pry off the trim cover from the
corner of the door panel using a
trim tool...

18.1b ... then remove the door sail
trim panel

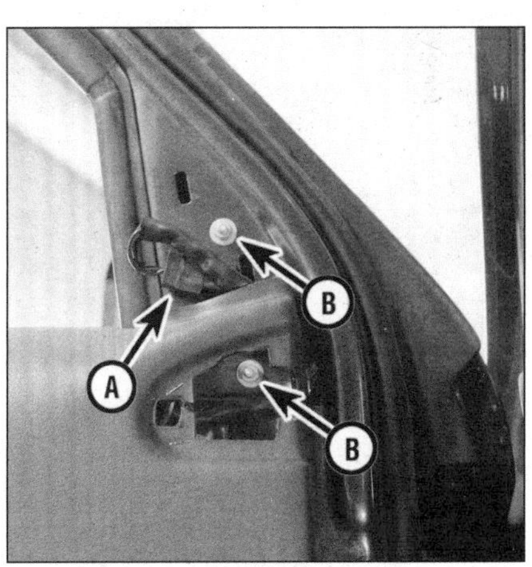

18.2 Disconnect the electrical
connector (A) and remove the outside
mirror mounting fasteners (B)

18   Mirrors - removal and installation

Outside mirrors

1   Use a pry tool to remove the side view mirror access trim panels from the door panel (see illustrations).

2   Disconnect the electrical connector and remove the outside mirror mounting fasteners (see illustration), then remove the mirror.

Note: *Hold the mirror as you remove the nuts securing it.*

3   Installation is the reverse of removal.

Inside mirror

4   If the vehicle is equipped with either the electrochromic or telematic mirror options, first disconnect the battery (see Chapter 5). Then disconnect the electrical connector at the back of the mirror.

5   Use a Philips head screwdriver to remove the set screw on the support/bracket used on the windshield (see illustration), then slide off the mirror.

Note: *If the mount plate itself has come off the windshield, adhesive kits are available at auto parts stores to re-secure it. Follow the instructions included with the kit.*

6   Installation is the reverse of removal.

18.5 Remove the inside mirror retaining
screw, then slide the mirror off the mount
plate and remove the mirror

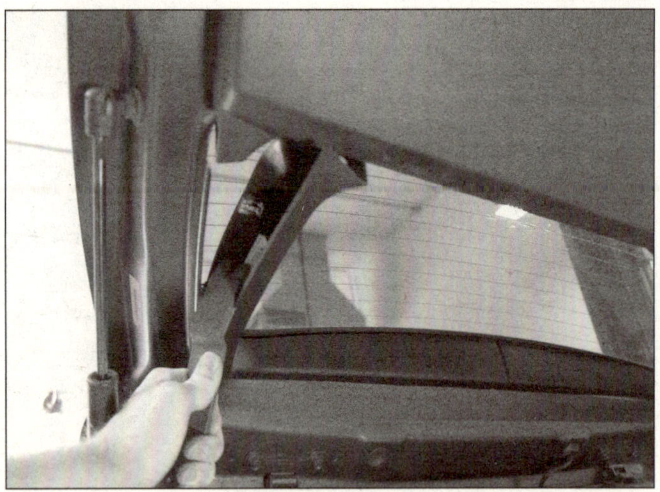

19.1a Pry off the left side trim panel first…

19.1b … then the right side panel

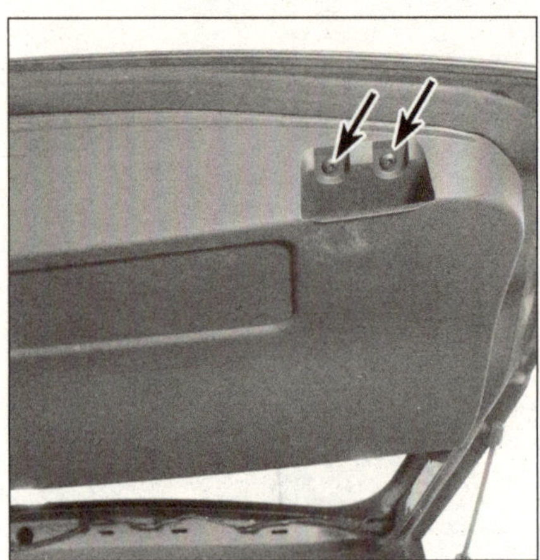

19.2a Remove the screws securing the panel…

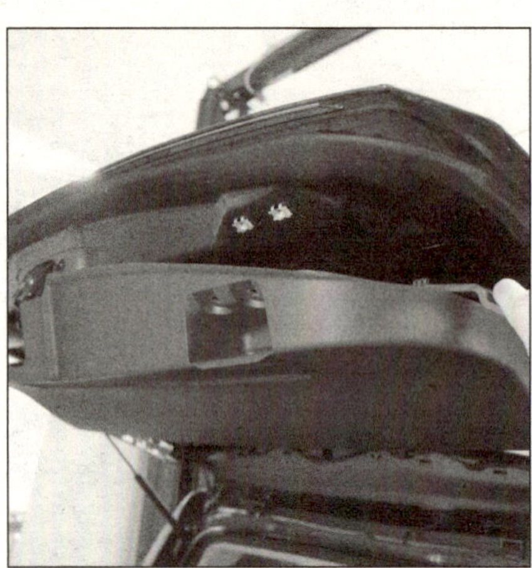

19.2b … then release the trim panel clips, working around the perimeter

19.5 Emergency access screw for the liftgate latch

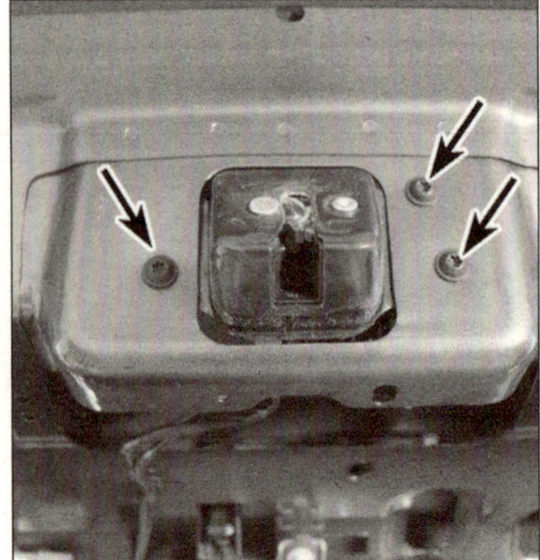

19.8 Remove the liftgate latch mounting bolts

19   Liftgate trim panel, latch, strut support shocks, lock cylinder, outside handle, and hinges - removal and installation

Note: *Disconnect the cable from the negative battery terminal (see Chapter 5).*

Trim paneling

1   Using a flat-bladed trim tool, work your way around the edge of the side trim panels until all of the pressure clips have released (see illustrations). Make sure to pry as close to the clips as possible to prevent breaking the plastic.
2   Remove the two screws securing the bottom edge of the rear liftgate panel. Work your way around the panel with a flat trim tool, releasing each of the pressure clips until all of them have been disengaged (see illustrations).
3   Remove the liftgate main trim panel. If equipped with a liftgate subwoofer system, disconnect the speaker electrical connector(s).
4   Installation is the reverse of removal.

Liftgate latch

5   If for some reason the liftgate latch does not operate due to a lack of electrical power, there is a mechanical backup. Remove this trim cap from the lower edge of the liftgate panel and insert a screwdriver into the Phillips slot. Rotate the screwdriver to unlock the latch (see illustration).

Replacement

6   Remove the liftgate trim panel (see Steps 1 through 3).
7   Mark the location of the latch to the liftgate by scribing or drawing a line around the latch.
8   Remove the latch mounting bolts (see illustration).
9   Pull the latch out, then disconnect the release cable from the latch by sliding the

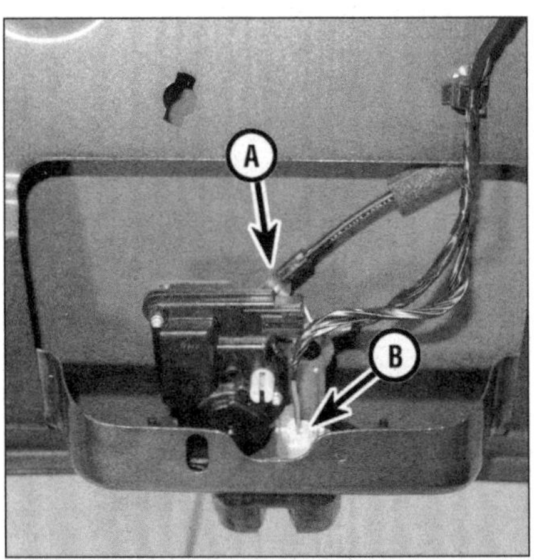

19.9 Once unbolted, pull the latch out enough to disconnect the release cable (A) and the electrical connector (B)

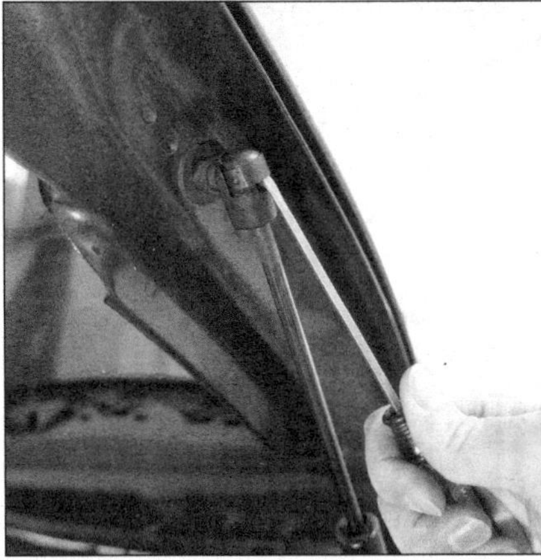

19.16 Pry the retaining clip outward to disengage the shock from the ball socket, then separate the shock end

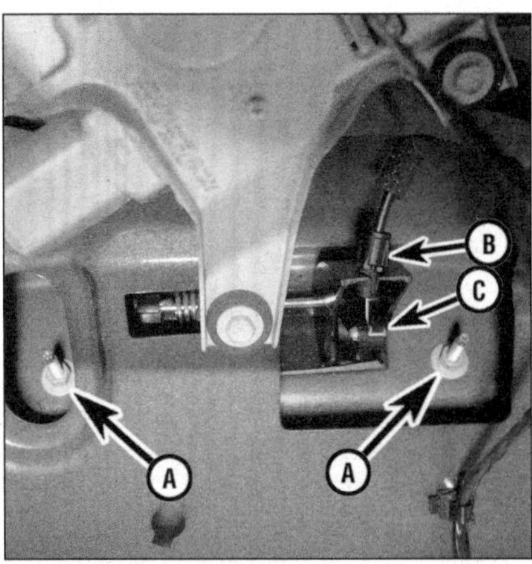

19.20 Remove the handle mounting nuts (A). To release the cable, compress the cable housing tabs with needle-nose pliers and slide it through the bracket hole (B), then disconnect the cable end by sliding it out of the slot (C)

cable housing out of the U-shaped bracket, then detach the cable end from the latch lever. Also disconnect the latch electrical connector (see illustration).

10   Disconnect the lock rod (if equipped).

11   Installation is the reverse of removal. Before tightening the bolts, align the latch to the marks drawn prior to removal.

Liftgate lock cylinder

12   Remove the liftgate trim panel (see Steps 1 through 3).

13   Disconnect the door lock actuator rod from the lock cylinder. The rod is disconnected by first unsnapping and swiveling the plastic retainer off of the rod, then pulling the rod out of the retainer.

14   Remove the nuts securing the lock cylinder to the liftgate.

15   Installation is the reverse of removal.

Strut support shocks

Warning: *Open the liftgate and have an assistant or an approved device safely support it as you replace the shocks.*

Caution: *The strut support shocks should be replaced in pairs.*

Note: *Have the replacement shock ready and at hand to install as soon as you remove the old one.*

16   With a small flat tip screwdriver, pry the retainer outward that secures the shock to the ball socket (see illustration), then disconnect the shock end from the socket. Repeat this for the shock's other end.

17   Check the condition of the ball sockets and replace them if necessary. Also make sure they are securely fastened.

18   To install, align the shock to the ball socket and push it firmly onto the socket. Be sure the shock is installed in the correct direction.

Outside release handle

19   Remove the liftgate trim panel (see Steps 1 through 3).

20   Remove the handle mounting nuts, then disconnect the cable from the handle (see

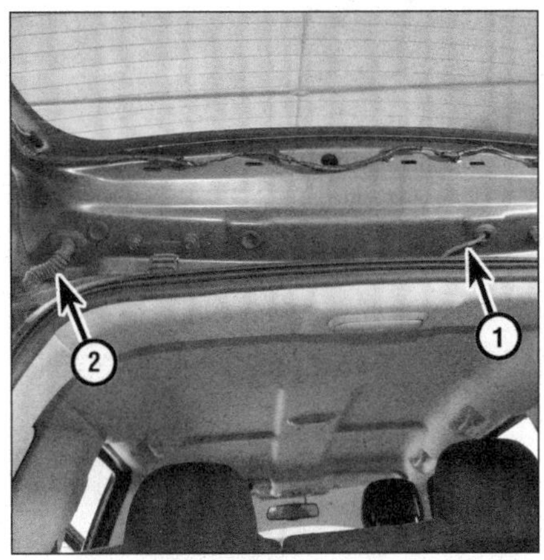

20.1 Disconnect the washer fluid line (1) and the liftgate harness electrical connector (2)

illustration) and remove the handle. Also disconnect the electrical connector, if equipped.

21   Installation is the reverse of removal.

Hinges

Note: *The liftgate hinges can be replaced without removing the entire liftgate - they can be replaced one at a time. An assistant or approved lifting device is still needed for this procedure.*

22   Safely support the liftgate, by means of an assistant or approved lifting/supporting device.

23   Disconnect the liftgate electrical harness connector and washer hose, then mark the hinge-to-liftgate location (see Section 20).

24   With the liftgate safely supported, remove the hinge-to-liftgate bolts (upper hinge bolts) from one hinge only.

25   Using caution not to distort the headliner, pull down the headliner enough to access and remove the nuts and bolt from the same hinge (lower hinge fasteners), then remove the hinge from the vehicle.

26   Install the replacement hinge and lower

20.2 Mark the hinge plate to liftgate placement for easier realignment

mounting fasteners. Tighten the fasteners securely, then reposition the headliner to its original form.

27   Install the hinge-to-liftgate bolts, the align the marks drawn previously and tighten the bolts securely.

28   Repeat this process for the other hinge, if necessary. The remainder of installation is the reverse of removal.

---

20   Liftgate - removal and installation

Warning: *Due to its heavy weight, it is recommended that the liftgate removal procedure is performed with the aid of an assistant.*

1   Open the liftgate, then disconnect the harness electrical connector and washer fluid line from the liftgate (see illustration).

2   To ensure correct realignment, mark the locations of the hinge plates in relation to where they are positioned on the liftgate (see illustration).

21.3a Remove the column cover screws…

21.3b … then separate the column cover halves and carefully guide the covers out for removal (steering wheel removed for clarity)

22.2 Pry the instrument panel end cap out to disengage the panel mounting clips (right side shown, left side identical)

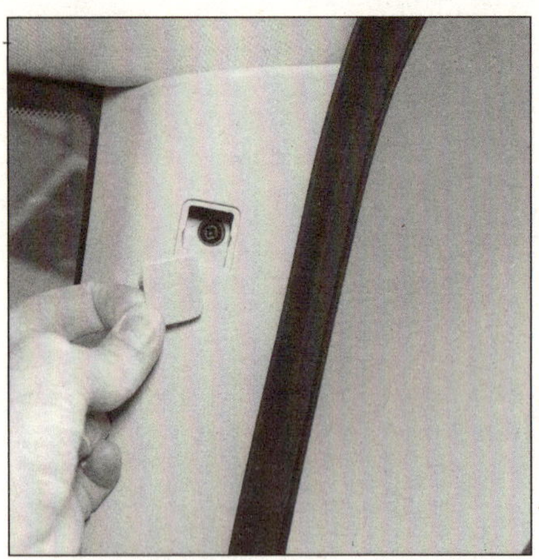

22.4a Pry off the trim cap and remove the A-pillar retaining screw…

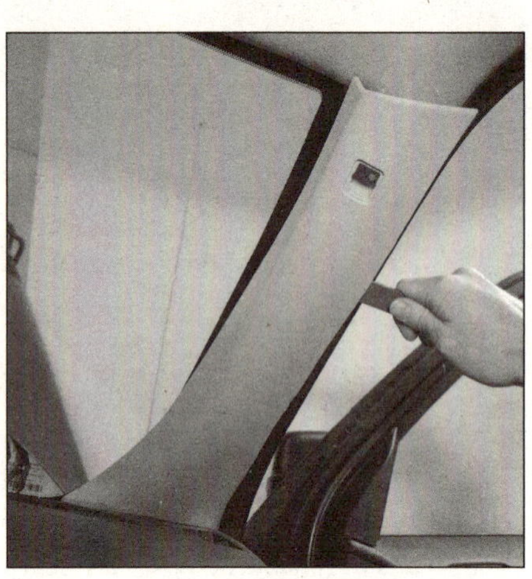

22.4b … then pry the A-pillar trim panel out to disengage it from the retaining clips…

22.4c … pull up on the A-pillar trim to disengage the tabs from the upper instrument panel slots

3   With the help of an assistant or two and/ or an approved supporting device, remove the liftgate support struts (see Section 19).

4   With the liftgate still safely supported, remove the hinge fasteners and remove the liftgate.

5   Check the condition of the liftgate hinges, and replace if necessary (see Section 19).

6   Installation is the reverse of removal.

21   Steering column covers - removal and installation

Warning: *Models covered by this manual are equipped with a Supplemental Restraint System (SRS), more commonly known as airbags. Always disable the airbag system before working in the vicinity of any airbag system component to avoid the possibility of accidental deployment of the airbag, which could cause personal injury (see Chapter 12).*

1   Remove the knee bolster cover and knee bolster (see Section 22).

2   Place the steering column tilt in the full downward position, locking it in place.

Note: *The two recessed screws are Torx head screws.*

3   Remove the column cover mounting screws that also hold the upper and lower halves together, then gently pry apart and separate the two halves for removal (see illustrations).

4   If the steering wheel has already been removed, be sure to tape the clockspring in place (see Chapter 10, Section 18).

5   Installation is the reverse of removal.

22   Dashboard and interior trim panels - removal and installation

Warning: *Models covered by this manual are equipped with a Supplemental Restraint*

System (SRS), more commonly known as airbags. Always disable the airbag system before working in the vicinity of any airbag system component to avoid the possibility of accidental deployment of the airbag, which could cause personal injury (see Chapter 12). Wait approximately two minutes after disconnecting the negative battery cable before proceeding.

1   Disconnect the cable from the negative terminal of the battery (see Chapter 5).

Instrument panel end caps

2   Use a trim tool to pry out and release the clips holding the end cap covers on the left and right sides of the instrument panel (see illustration).

3   Installation is the reverse of removal.

Defroster vent trim panel

4   Remove the retaining screw, then remove the A-pillar trim panels (see illustrations).

22.5 Use a plastic trim tool to pry along the defroster trim panel until all the clips have been disengaged

22.8 Slide the end of the dampener line bracket and disengage it from the glovebox door

22.9 Push in on both of the upper corners of the tray to release the stops, then lower the glove box down - unhook the glovebox hinge from the dash and remove it

22.11a Remove the lower screws first...

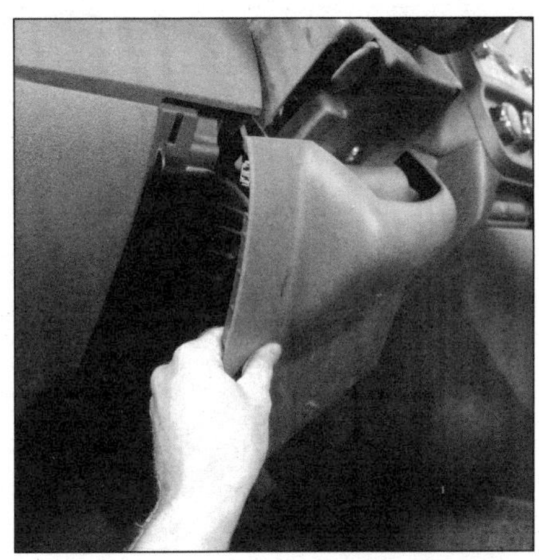

22.11b ... then, use a flat trim tool to release the pressure clips and remove the panel

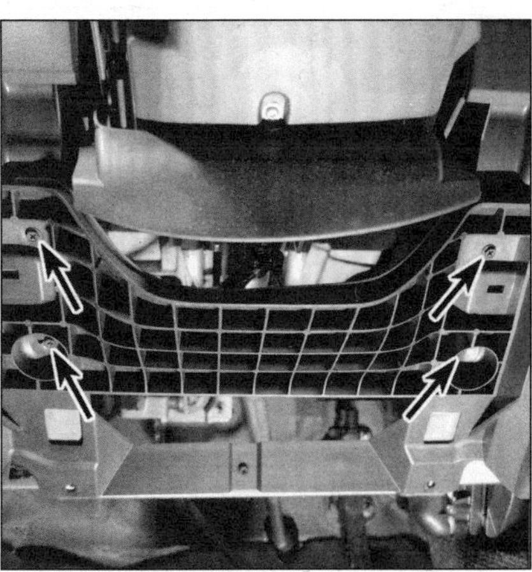

22.12 Location of the knee bolster screws

5   Pry along the defrost vent trim panel and remove it (see illustration).

6   Installation is the reverse of removal.

Center trim panel bezel (HVAC control assembly)

7   For the removal and installation of the heating and air conditioning control assembly, see Chapter 3, Section 11.

Glove box

8   Open the glove box, then disconnect the dampener line from the glove box door (see illustration).

9   Push in on the sides of the glove box tray to disengage the stops while lowering

(see illustration), then carefully unsnap and remove the glove box from the lower hinge.

10   Installation is the reverse of removal.

Knee bolster (driver's side)

11   Remove the knee bolster cover-to-instrument panel (see illustrations).

12   Remove the screws securing the knee bolster to the dash (see illustration).

13   Installation is the reverse of removal.

Close out panel - passenger side (under glove box)

14   Remove the two push pins securing the close out panel to the dash (see illustration).

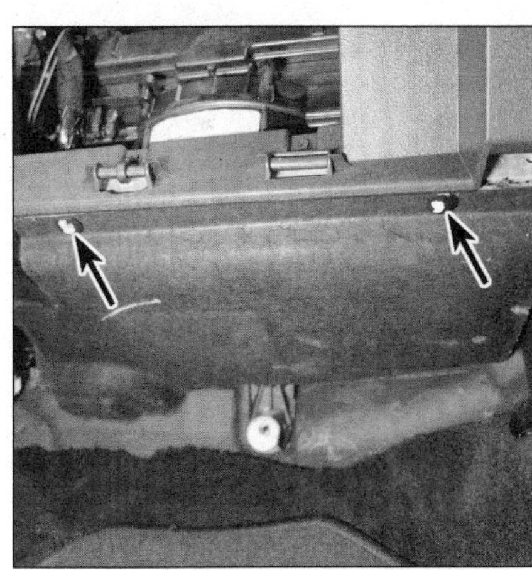

22.14 Remove the push pin clips with a trim tool

22.15 Lower the panel and slide it out from the rear section tab

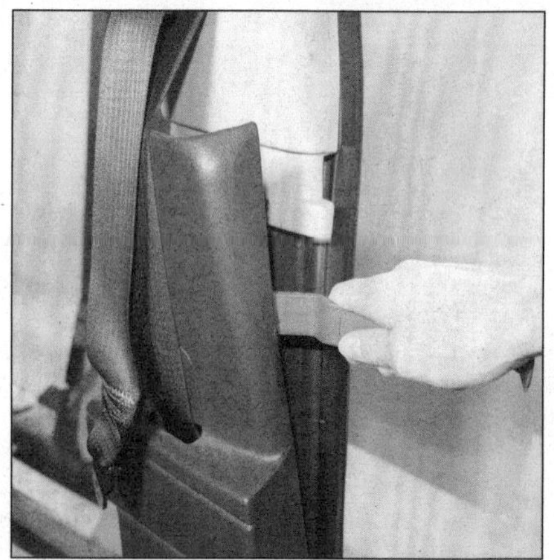

22.17a Pry the top edge of the lower B-pillar trim free from the upper B-pillar trim

22.17b Pry the lower-front of the B-pillar trim free from the door sill trim

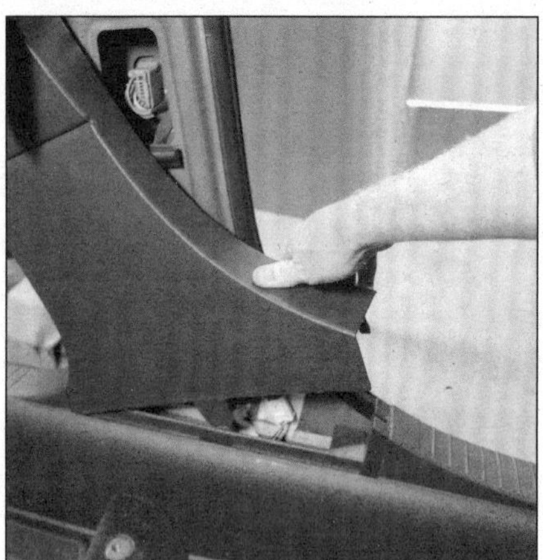

22.17c Lift off the lower B-pillar trim (Note the tab in the center must be aligned when reinstalling)

22.17d Pry up along the sill plate until all the pressure clips release

22.17e With all the pressure clips released, lift off the door sill plate and remove it

22.17f Remove the plastic retainer nut that secures the end of the kick panel

22.17g Pry the kick panel free to remove it - on the driver's side, work around the hood release handle

15   Lower the close out panel and slide it out from the rear tab (see illustration).

16   Installation is the reverse of removal.

Door sill plate trim, lower B-pillar trim, and kick panels

Note: *The seats have been removed for better photo clarity.*

Note: *To fully remove the lower B-pillar trim panel, the seat belt needs to be disconnected from the seat (see Section 24), and the upper seat belt adjuster anchor bolt needs to be removed in order to feed the belt through the panel.*

17   The sill plate trim and kick panels are held in place with pressure clips. However, they can not be properly removed unless the lower B-pillar trim is removed first. Follow the order of the accompanying photos listed below to remove the lower B-pillar trim, kick panel trim and the door sill plate trim (see illustrations).

18   Installation is the reverse of removal.

B-pillar upper trim panel

19   Remove the trim cover and adjuster anchor bolt securing the seat belt to the B-pillar.
20   Pry off the upper end of the lower B-pillar trim, enough to allow the upper B-pillar trim space for removal (see illustration 22.17a).
21   Using a firm grip along the edge of the upper B-pillar trim, pull outwards to release the pressure clips, then remove the panel.
22   Installation is the reverse of removal.

C-pillar trim

Note: *The C-pillar trim is located adjacent to the rear seat back.*
23   Remove the rear seat cushion (see Section 24).
24   Remove the D-pillar trim (see Steps 28-31 in this Section).
25   Remove the lower seat belt anchor bolt.
26   Pry out and release the C-pillar trim from all the pressure clips, then feed the seat belt through the slot and remove the panel.
27   Installation is the reverse of removal.

D-pillar trim

Note: *The D-pillar trim is located at the upper-rear of the vehicle.*
28   Remove the rear quarter trim panel (see Section 26).
29   Disconnect the seat belt anchor buckle from the center seat using a small screwdriver or car key to depress the locking tab.
30   Using a plastic trim tool, pry around the perimeter of the D-pillar trim panel until all the pressure clips have been released. Feed the seat belt through the slot and remove the D-pillar trim panel.
31   Installation is the reverse of removal.

Sun visor

32   The sun visors are held in place with two screws at the base. The inner visor catch uses a single screw securing it to the roof support bracket.
33   Remove the two screws securing the visor pivot to the roof support bracket. If equipped with a lighted vanity, pull the visor down about an inch to expose the wire connection. Disconnect the connector and remove the sun visor.
34   To remove the support catch of the visor, remove the single screw securing the catch and pull it straight down for removal.
35   Installation is the reverse of removal.

Overhead grab handle

36   On each side of the grab handle you'll find a plastic clip (it looks more like a screw cover). Use a small flat tipped screwdriver or equivalent to pry the plastic clip outward. With the clip pulled out, the grab handle should come off. If it is still attached, pull outward on the catch(es) as you gently pull outward on the grab handle.
37   To install - insert the grab handle into the slots of the roof support and headliner, then (while holding the grab handle in place) push the plastic catches back in until they are flush with the surface of the grab handle and the handle is secure.

Headliner

38   Disconnect the cable from the negative battery terminal (see Chapter 5).
39   Fold down the rear seat backs. Remove the driver's and passenger's seat headrests, then recline the seats as far as they will go. This should create enough room to allow the headliner to be maneuvered out of the vehicle.
40   Remove the A-pillar trim, then pry out and position aside the upper B and C-pillar trim panels accordingly to allow for headliner removal (see related Steps in this Section).
41   Remove the sun visors, sun visor support catches, and grab handles (see related Steps in this Section).
42   Remove the interior rearview mirror (see Section 18).
43   Disconnect the electrical connectors at the left and right side A-pillars, then free the wiring harness clips running up the pillars.

44   Open the liftgate and remove the push-pins securing the rear of the headliner. Pull down on the rear of the headliner and disconnect the dome light electrical connector. Also disconnect the rear windshield washer hose, if equipped.
45   If equipped with a sun roof, carefully pry out the headliner around the sun roof to release the retaining clips.
46   As the headliner is lowered, check to see if the rear washer hose (if equipped) is secured by any remaining clips to be detached.
47   Check for any electrical connections or harness clips that may still be attached, then guide the headliner out of the rear of the vehicle.
48   Installation is the reverse of removal.

Instrument panel upper trim cover

Warning: *Refer to airbag warning at the beginning of this Section or in Chapter 12.*
49   Make sure the negative battery cable has been disconnected.
50   Remove the left and right instrument panel end caps (see previous Steps in this Section).
51   Remove the A-pillar trim panels and the defroster vent trim panel (see previous Steps in this Section).
52   Remove the HVAC control assembly trim panel (see Chapter 3).
53   Remove the radio (see Chapter 12).
54   Remove the glove box (see previous Steps in this Section).
55   Working through the glove box opening, disconnect the passenger's side airbag electrical connectors and remove the airbag bracket mounting bolts (see illustration).
56   Remove the upper instrument panel cover securing screws (see illustrations).
Note: *The instrument panel upper cover may tend to get "hung-up" by the passenger airbag mounting studs at its final stage of removal - carefully free the studs while using caution not to crack any plastic.*

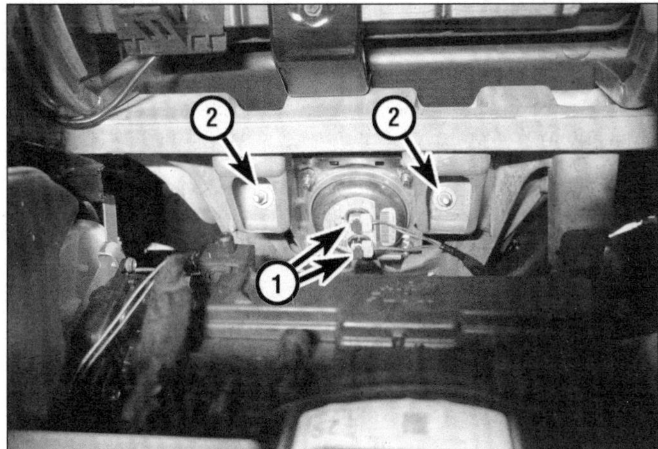

22.55 Release the connector locking tabs with a small screwdriver, then disconnect the airbag electrical connectors (1) and remove the airbag bracket mounting bolts (2)

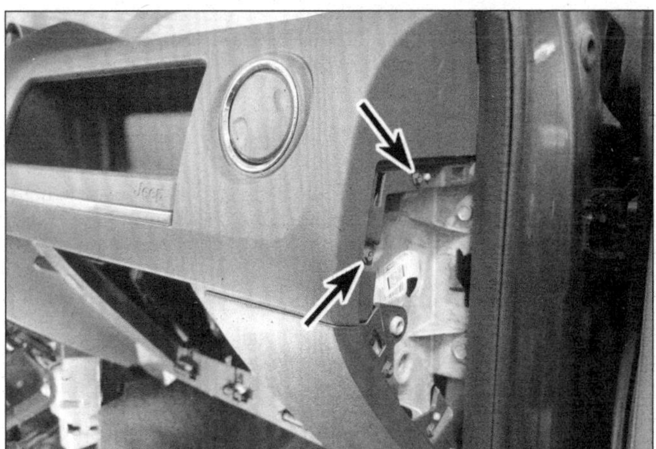

22.56a Remove the panel cover screws from the end cap openings (both sides)...

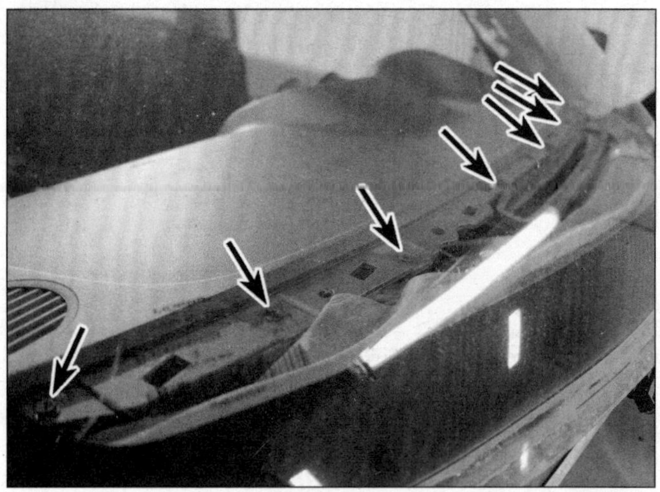

22.56b ... then the upper screws along the defroster trim panel opening...

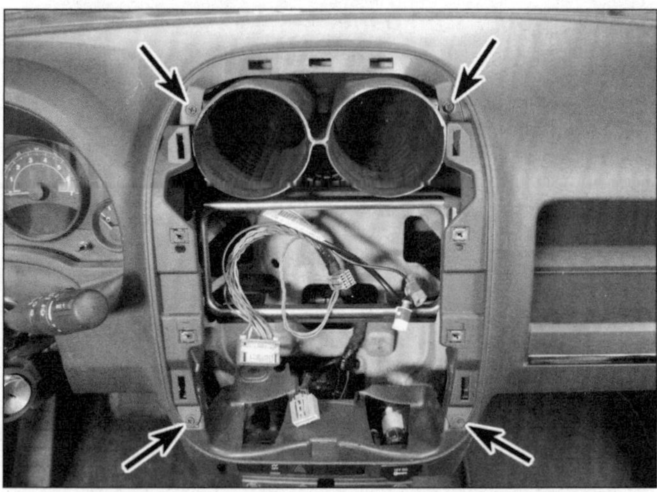

22.56c ... and finally, the screws at the center opening

22.57 Once the cover is free from all the retaining clips, carefully tilt it forward and up at each end and remove it from the vehicle interior

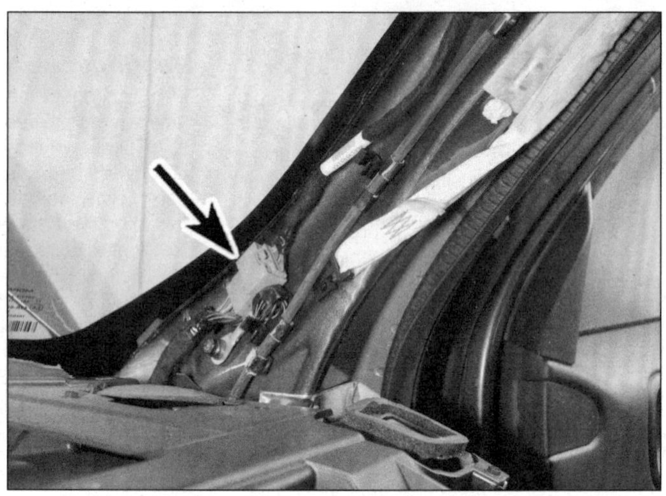

23.14 Disconnect the A-pillar connectors from each side

57　Pry out the upper instrument panel cover retaining clips along the perimeter, then carefully guide it out from the instrument panel (see illustration).

58　Installation is the reverse of removal. Tighten all fasteners securely.

23　Instrument panel - removal and installation

Warning: *Models covered by this manual are equipped with a Supplemental Restraint System (SRS), more commonly known as airbags. Always disable the airbag system before working in the vicinity of any airbag system component to avoid the possibility of accidental deployment of the airbag, which could cause personal injury (see Chapter 12). Wait approximately two minutes after disconnecting the negative battery cable before proceeding.*

Note: The instrument panel removal and installation procedure can be very difficult to perform and is not recommended for the novice mechanic - make sure you are comfortable with your mechanical abilities before attempting to start this procedure.

1　Disconnect the cable from the negative battery terminal (see Chapter 5).

2　Remove the driver's side and passenger's side instrument panel end caps (see Section 22).

3　Remove the center console and floor shifter housing (see Section 25).

4　Remove the transmission shifter assembly (see Chapter 7B).

5　Remove the door sill panels and kick panels (see Section 22).

6　Remove the knee bolster (see Section 22).

7　Remove the HVAC control assembly (see Chapter 3).

8　Remove the radio (see Chapter 12).

9　Remove the defroster trim panel (see Section 22).

10　Remove the under-glove box closeout panel (see Section 22).

11　Disconnect the blower motor and resistor electrical connectors (see Chapter 3).

12　Remove the A-pillar trim panels (see Section 22).

13　Remove the steering column (see Chapter 10).

14　Disconnect the electrical connectors from the A-pillars (see illustration).

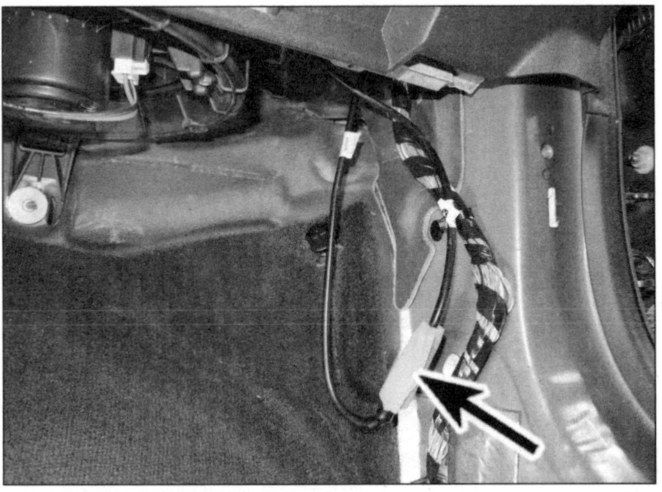

23.15 Disconnect the radio antenna connector

23.16 Center wiring harness clip locations

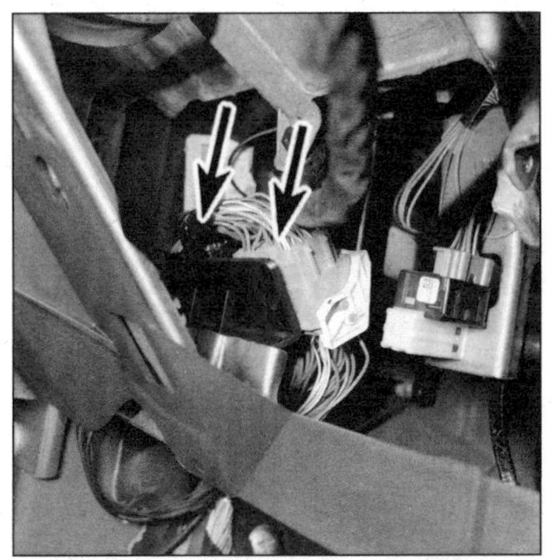

23.17 Main wiring harness connector locations near the driver's side kick panel - depress the locking tab and rotate the connector lever

23.18 Center instrument panel mounting bolts

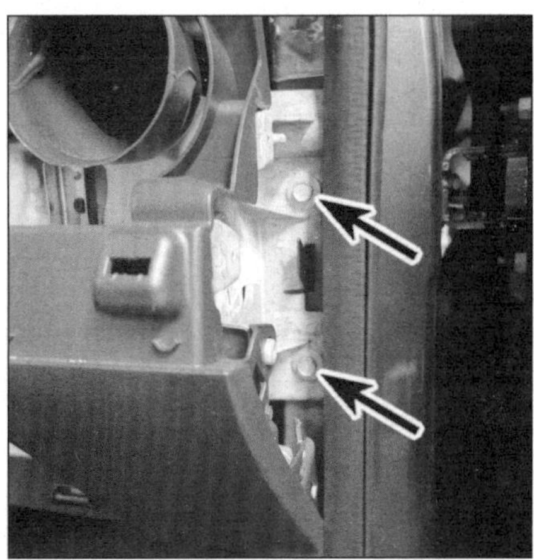

23.19a Remove the instrument panel mounting bolts from the passenger's side…

15   Disconnect the radio antenna connector from the passenger's side kick panel area (see illustration).

16   Detach the center wiring harness from the retaining clips (see illustration).

17   Working in the driver's side kick panel area, disconnect the main wiring harness connectors (see illustration), and also release the on-board diagnostic (OBD II) connector port from the bracket below.

18   Remove the instrument panel center mounting bolts from the radio opening (see illustration).

19   Remove the instrument panel side mounting bolts (see illustrations).

20   Remove the lower-center support bolts from each side (see illustration).

23.19b … and driver's side of the vehicle

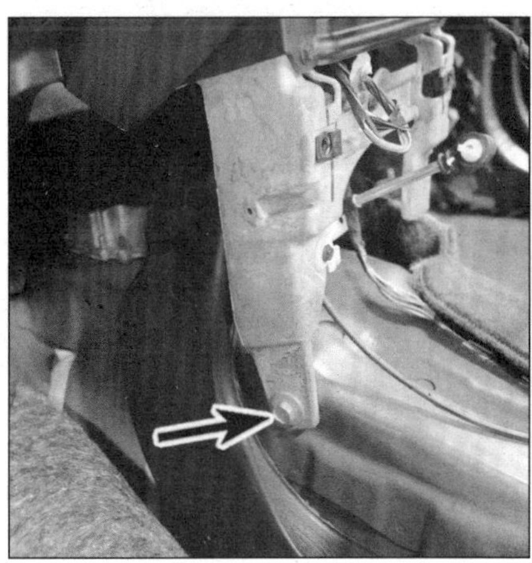

23.20 Remove the instrument panel lower-center support bolts (opposite side bolt not shown)

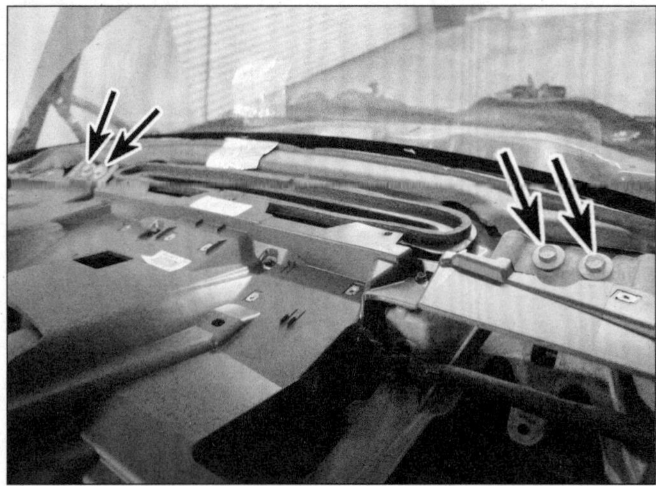

23.21 Remove the instrument panel upper bolts

24.2a Pry open the trim covers to expose the seat mounting bolts

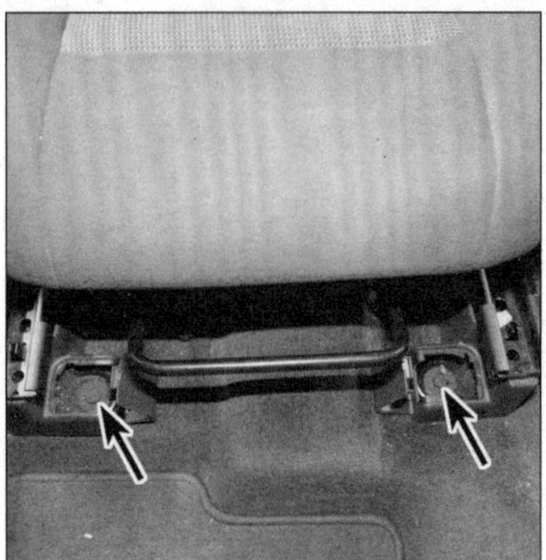

24.2b Location of the seat mounting bolts (front)

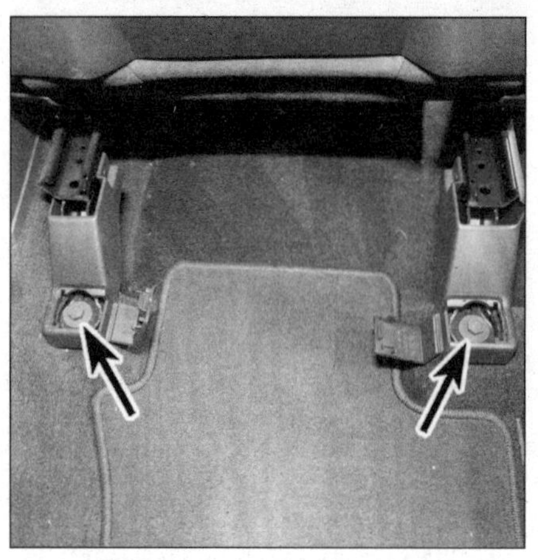

24.3 Location of the seat mounting bolts (rear)

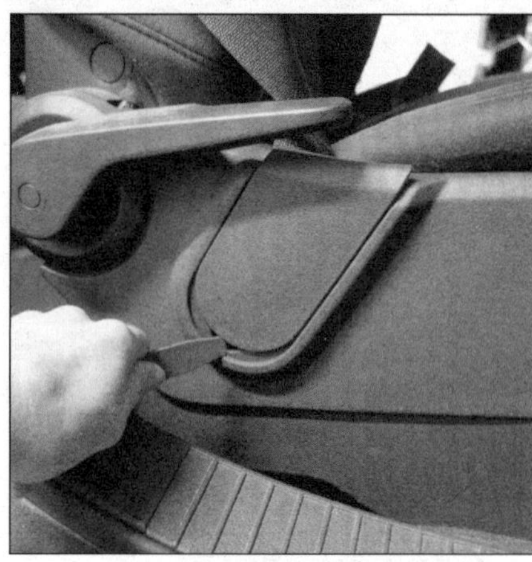

24.4a Carefully pry the trim cover upward…

24.4b … then pull it straight out to expose the seat belt anchor bolt

21   Remove the instrument panel upper bolts (see illustration).

22   With the help of an assistant, carefully guide the instrument panel out from the vehicle - double-checking that all electrical connections have been disconnected and wiring harness clips have been detached.

23   Installation is the reverse of removal.

24   Seats - removal and installation

Warning: *Models covered by this manual are equipped with a Supplemental Restraint System (SRS), more commonly known as airbags. Always disable the airbag system before working in the vicinity of any airbag system component to avoid the possibility of accidental deployment of the airbag, which could cause personal injury (see Chapter 12).*

Note: *For an operating instruction and basic diagnostics for the power seat system, see Chapter 12, Section 25 for further information.*

1   Disconnect the cable from the negative battery terminal (see Chapter 5).

Front seats

2   Slide the front seat all the way rearward and remove the mounting fasteners at the front (see illustrations).

3   Slide the seat all the way forward and remove the seat mounting fasteners at the rear (see illustration).

4   Use a flat tool and carefully pry upward (from the bottom) of the seat belt anchor trim (see illustrations). Remove the seat belt anchor bolt.

24.5 Slide out the red safety tab, then disconnect the airbag electrical connector (if equipped) and any other electrical connectors

24.8 Rear seat cushion mounting bolts

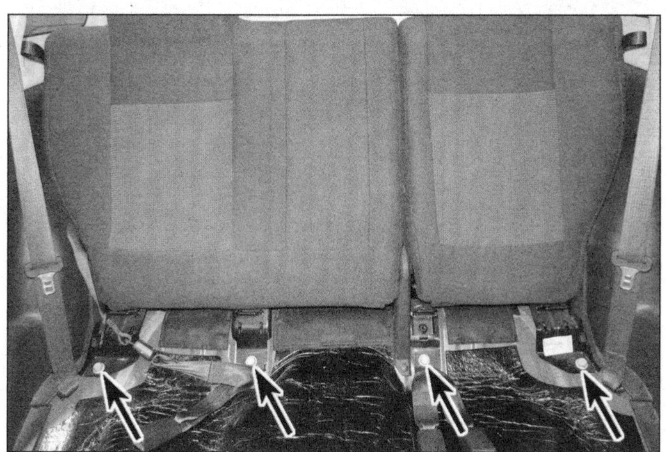

24.9 Seat belt anchor bolts are also the front seat back bracket bolts

24.10 Remove the mounting fasteners along the back side of the seats

5   Disconnect the electrical connector(s) from the seat (see illustration).
Note: *Do not handle the seat by the adjuster release bar, as the bar is spring loaded.*
6   Carefully guide the front seat out of the vehicle.
7   Installation is the reversal of removal. Tighten the seat mounting bolts and seat belt anchor bolts to the torque settings listed in this Chapter's Specifications.

Rear seats

8   Unbolt the seat cushion fasteners at each end (see illustration), then pull the front of the cushion up, disengage the rear, and remove the seat from the vehicle.
9   Remove the rear seat belt buckle and anchor fasteners (see illustration).
10   Fold the seats forward and remove the seat back mounting fasteners at the rear (see illustration).
11   Remove the seat back from the vehicle.
12   Installation is the reverse of removal.

Tighten the rear seat related fasteners to the torque settings listed in this Chapter's Specifications.

25 Center console and floor shifter housing - removal and installation

Warning: *Models covered by this manual are equipped with a Supplemental Restraint System (SRS), more commonly known as airbags. Always disable the airbag system before working in the vicinity of any airbag system component to avoid the possibility of accidental deployment of the airbag, which could cause personal injury (see Chapter 12).*

Center console

1   Remove the center console storage area carpet to expose the screws inside the bin (see illustration).

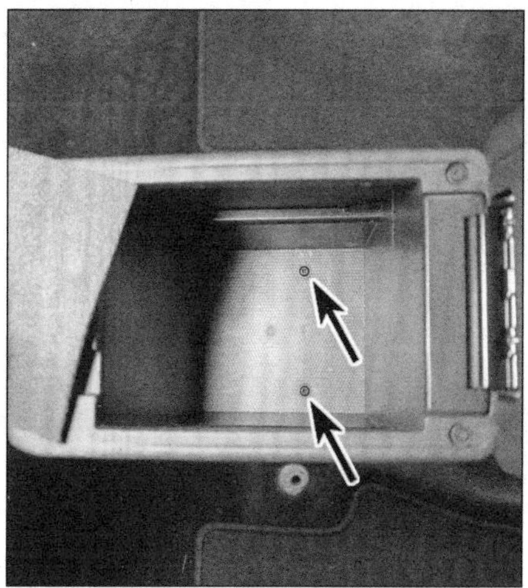

25.1 Remove the screws from inside the storage bin area

25.2 Remove the center console outer retaining screws on both sides (seat has been removed for clarity)

25.6 Center console electrical connector

25.10 Give the shift knob a sharp, upward pulling motion to remove it from the rod

25.11 Pry up the shifter trim panel with a trim tool and release the retaining clips

25.12 Remove the shifter housing trim mounting screws

2   Remove the outer screws from the center console (see illustration).
3   Raise the parking brake to its highest point.
4   Grasp the front edges of the console with both hands and pull out to release the pressure clips.
5   Lift the rear section up to release the rear pressure clips.
6   Lift the console up high enough to gain access to the electrical connections. Disconnect the electrical connector(s) (see illustration).
7   Remove the center console, guiding it out from the parking brake lever.
8   Installation is the reverse of removal.

Floor shifter housing trim paneling - removal and installation

Note: *The procedure listed is for automatic floor shift models. The manual transmission models are similar.*

9   Remove the center console (see previous Steps).
10   Pull up sharply on the shifter knob and remove it (see illustration).
11   Use a flat trim tool to remove the shift boot (manual) or trim panel bezel (automatic) from the shifter housing trim (see illustration).
12   Remove the shifter housing upper and lower retaining screws securing the housing to the shifter assembly (see illustration).
13   Remove the shifter housing trim panel.
14   Installation is the reverse of removal.

26   Rear quarter panel - removal and installation

1   Remove the cargo floor mat.
2   Remove the left or right door sill trim (see Section 22).
3   Open the liftgate and remove the rear liftgate sill trim with a flat trim tool, prying it up to release it from the pressure clips.
4   Fold down the rear seat back (of the side being worked on) and pry off the seat back latch hook trim cover.
5   If equipped with a rear cargo net, remove the cargo net hooks from the quarter panel area.
6   While grasping the edges of the quarter panel, pull straight out to release the pressure clips.
7   With all the clips released, check for any electrical connections or wire harnesses that may be attached to the back side of the quarter panel and remove or detach them.
8   Remove the quarter panel.
9   Installation is the reverse of removal.

Chapter 12
Chassis electrical system

Contents

1 General Information

1   The electrical system is a 12-volt, negative ground type. Power for the lights and all electrical accessories is supplied by a lead/acid battery, which is charged by the alternator.

2   This Chapter covers repair and service procedures for the various electrical components not associated with the engine. Information on the battery, alternator and starter motor can be found in Chapter 5.

3   It should be noted that when portions of the electrical system are serviced, the negative battery cable should be disconnected from the battery to prevent electrical shorts and/or fires.

2 Electrical troubleshooting - general information

1   A typical electrical circuit consists of an electrical component, any switches, relays, motors, fuses, fusible links or circuit breakers related to that component and the wiring and connectors that link the component to both the battery and the chassis. To help you pinpoint an electrical circuit problem, wiring diagrams are included at the end of this Chapter.

2   Before tackling any troublesome electrical circuit, first study the appropriate wiring diagrams to get a complete understanding of what makes up that individual circuit. Trouble spots, for instance, can often be narrowed down by noting if other components related to the circuit are operating properly. If several components or circuits fail at one time, chances are the problem is in a fuse or ground connection, because several circuits are often routed through the same fuse and ground connections.

3   Electrical problems usually stem from simple causes, such as loose or corroded connections, a blown fuse, a melted fusible link or a failed relay. Visually inspect the condition of all fuses, wires and connections in a problem circuit before troubleshooting the circuit.

4   If test equipment and instruments are going to be utilized, use the diagrams to plan ahead of time where you will make the necessary connections in order to accurately pinpoint the trouble spot.

5   The basic tools needed for electrical troubleshooting include a circuit tester or voltmeter (a 12-volt bulb with a set of test leads can also be used), a continuity tester, which includes a bulb, battery and set of test leads, and a jumper wire, preferably with a circuit breaker incorporated, which can be used to bypass electrical components (see illustrations). Before attempting to locate a problem with test instruments, use the wiring diagram(s) to decide where to make the connections.

Voltage checks

6   Voltage checks should be performed if a circuit is not functioning properly. Connect one lead of a circuit tester to either the negative battery terminal or a known good ground. Connect the other lead to a connector in the circuit being tested, preferably nearest to the battery or fuse (see illustration). If the bulb of the tester lights, voltage is present, which means that the part of the circuit between the connector and the battery is problem free. Continue checking the rest of the circuit in the same fashion. When you reach a point at which no voltage is present, the problem lies between that point and the last test point with voltage. Most of the time the problem can be traced to a loose connection. Note: Keep in mind that some circuits receive voltage only when the ignition key is in the Accessory or Run position.

Finding a short

7   One method of finding shorts in a circuit is to remove the fuse and connect a test light or voltmeter in place of the fuse terminals. There should be no voltage present in the circuit. Move the wiring harness from side-to-side while watching the test light. If the bulb goes on, there is a short to ground somewhere in that area, probably where the insulation has rubbed through. The same test can be performed on each component in the circuit, even a switch.

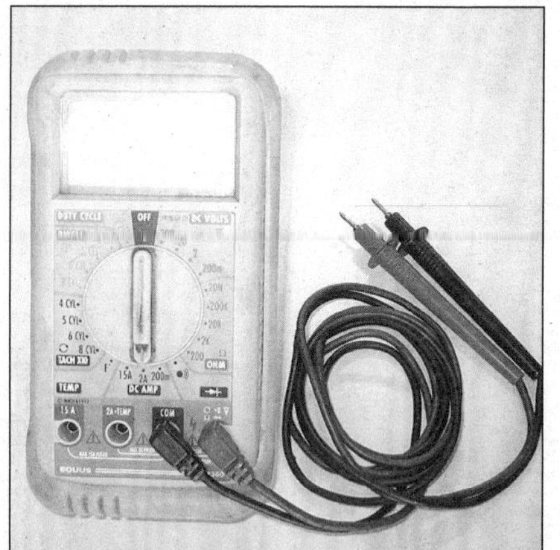

2.5a The most useful tool for electrical troubleshooting is a digital multimeter that can check volts, amps, and test continuity

Ground check

8   Perform a ground test to check whether a component is properly grounded. Disconnect the battery and connect one lead of a continuity tester or multimeter (set to the ohms scale), to a known good ground. Connect the other lead to the wire or ground connection being tested. If the resistance is low (less than 5 ohms), the ground is good. If the bulb on a self-powered test light does not go on, the ground is not good.

Continuity check

9   A continuity check is done to determine if there are any breaks in a circuit - if it is passing electricity properly. With the circuit off (no power in the circuit), a self-powered continuity tester or multimeter can be used to check the circuit. Connect the test leads to both ends of the circuit (or to the power end and a good ground), and if the test light comes on the circuit is passing current properly (see illustration). If the resistance is low

2.5b A simple test light is a very handy tool for testing voltage

(less than 5 ohms), there is continuity; if the reading is 10,000 ohms or higher, there is a break somewhere in the circuit. The same procedure can be used to test a switch, by connecting the continuity tester to the switch terminals. With the switch turned On, the test light should come on (or low resistance should be indicated on a meter).

Finding an open circuit

10   When diagnosing for possible open circuits, it is often difficult to locate them by sight because the connectors hide oxidation or terminal misalignment. Merely wiggling a connector on a sensor or in the wiring harness may correct the open circuit condition. Remember this when an open circuit is indicated when troubleshooting a circuit. Intermittent problems may also be caused by oxidized or loose connections.

11   Electrical troubleshooting is simple if you keep in mind that all electrical circuits are basically electricity running from the battery, through the wires, switches, relays, fuses

2.6 In use, a basic test light's lead is clipped to a known good ground, then the pointed probe can test connectors, wires or electrical sockets - if the bulb lights, the circuit being tested has battery voltage

2.9 With a multimeter set to the ohm scale, resistance can be checked across two terminals - when checking for continuity, a low reading indicates continuity, a high reading or infinity indicates high resistance or lack of continuity

3.1a The engine compartment fuse and relay box (TIPM)

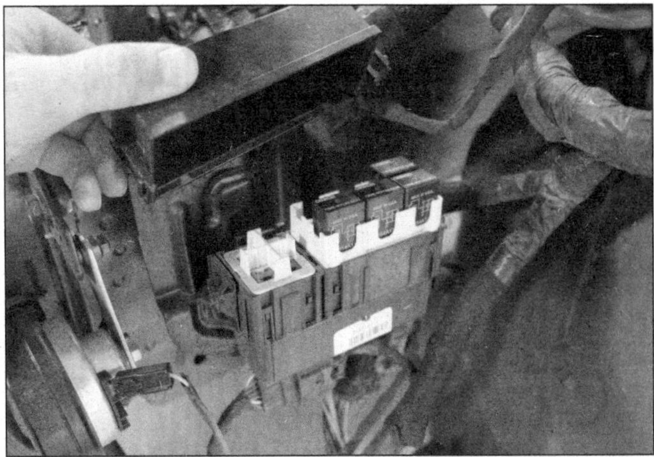

3.1b The secondary relay box is accessed through the fenderwell with the splash shield unfastened and pulled back (front bumper cover removed for photo clarity)

and fusible links to each electrical component (light bulb, motor, etc.) and to ground, from which it is passed back to the battery. Any electrical problem is an interruption in the flow of electricity to and from the battery.

3   Fuses and fusible links - general information

Fuses

1   The electrical circuits of the vehicle are protected by a combination of fuses, circuit breakers and fusible links. The main fuse/relay panel is located in the engine compartment, and the secondary relay panel (houses the brake lamp relay among a few other additional relays) is located at the left-front of the vehicle, next to the horn (see illustrations). On these vehicles, the fuse/relay box is referred to as the Totally Integrated Power Module (TIPM). Each of the fuses is designed to protect a specific circuit, and the various circuits are identified on the fuse panel itself.

2   Several sizes of fuses are employed in the fuse blocks. There are small, medium and large sizes of the same design, all with the same blade terminal design. The medium and large fuses can be removed with your fingers, but the small fuses require the use of pliers or the small plastic fuse-puller tool found in most fuse boxes.

3   If an electrical component fails, always check the fuse first. The best way to check the fuses is with a test light. Check for power at the exposed terminal tips of each fuse. If power is present at one side of the fuse but not the other, the fuse is blown. A blown fuse can also be identified by visually inspecting it (see illustration).

Note: *Not all fuses are energized with the key in the Off position. Turn the key to the On position, then check those fuses for voltage.*

4   Be sure to replace blown fuses with the correct type. Fuses (of the same physical size) of different ratings may be physically interchangeable, but only fuses of the proper rating should be used. Replacing a fuse with one of a higher or lower value than specified is not recommended. Each electrical circuit needs a specific amount of protection. The amperage value of each fuse is molded into the top of the fuse body.

5   If the replacement fuse immediately fails, don't replace it again or use a larger amperage fuse. More damage can occur until the cause of the problem is isolated and corrected. In most cases, this will be a short circuit in the wiring caused by a positive feed wire lead reaching ground potential before it has reached its module or component. Internal component failure or computer failure can also be a cause of a fuse to blow. Look for obvious signs of wire harnesses against metal components or near hot exahust. Abrasions to wiring harnesses are the most common electrical failures.

Fusible links

6   On these models, large, high-amperage fuses are used instead of traditional fusible links. They are located in the underhood fuse/relay box.

4   Circuit breakers - general information

1   Circuit breakers protect certain circuits, such as the power windows, power seats, windshield wipers, and seat heaters. Usually any high amperage and voltage system will generally have a breaker vs. a fuse as their protection device. Depending on the vehicle's accessories, there may be one or two circuit breakers, located in the fuse/relay box in the engine compartment.

2   Because the circuit breakers reset automatically, an electrical overload in a circuit

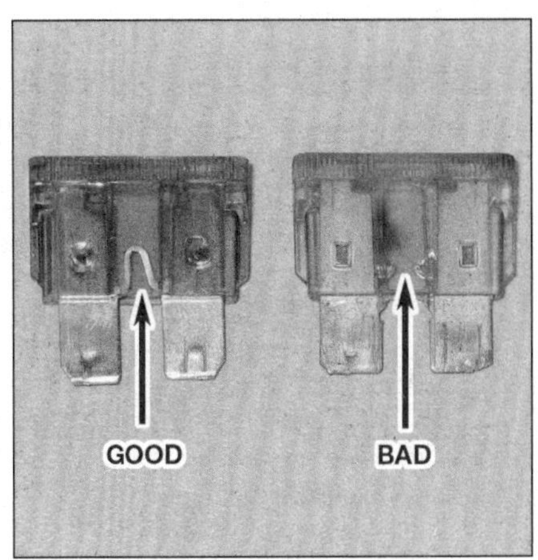

3.3 When a fuse blows, the element between the terminals melts

breaker-protected system will cause the circuit to fail momentarily, then come back on.

Caution: *Most breakers are silver in color and much larger than a standard fuse. If you suspect the breaker is the problem, be very careful touching the actual breaker. An electrical short generates a great deal of heat, so the breaker itself can be very hot to the touch. Proceed with caution when removing a hot breaker. If the breaker circuit is too hot, disconnect the battery and allow the breaker to cool down before removing it.*

3   For a basic check, pull the circuit breaker up out of its socket on the fuse panel, but just far enough to probe with a voltmeter. The breaker should still contact the sockets. With the voltmeter negative lead on a good chassis ground, touch each end prong of the circuit breaker with the positive meter probe. There should be battery voltage at each end. If there is battery voltage only at one end, the circuit breaker must be replaced.

4   Some circuit breakers must be reset manually.

5   Relays - general information

1   Several electrical accessories in the vehicle, such as the fuel injection system, horns, starter, and fog lamps use relays to transmit the electrical signal to the component. Relays use a low-current circuit (the control circuit) to open and close a high-current circuit (the power circuit). If the relay is defective, that component will not operate properly. Relays are mounted in the engine compartment fuse/relay box (see illustration 3.1a). Relays can be found in other locations; check your wiring diagram and component locator for exact locations.

Note: *Some relays are energized by a computer using a negative or positive feed. Do NOT bypass a relay from these connections unless you are sure of the source of the signal. Refer to the wiring diagram for the routing and exact location of these input voltages.*

6   Electrical connectors - general information

1   Most electrical connections on these vehicles are made with multiwire plastic connectors. The mating halves of many connectors are secured with locking clips molded into the plastic connector shells. The mating halves of some large connectors, such as some of those under the instrument panel, are held together by a bolt through the center of the connector.

2   To separate a connector with locking clips, use a small screwdriver to pry the clips apart carefully, then separate the connector halves. Pull only on the shell, never pull on the wiring harness, as you may damage the individual wires and terminals inside the connectors. Look at the connector closely before trying to separate the halves. Often the locking clips are engaged in a way that is not immediately clear. Additionally, many connectors have more than one set of clips.

3   Each pair of connector terminals has a male half and a female half. When you look at the end view of a connector in a diagram, be

Electrical connectors

Most electrical connectors have a single release tab that you depress to release the connector

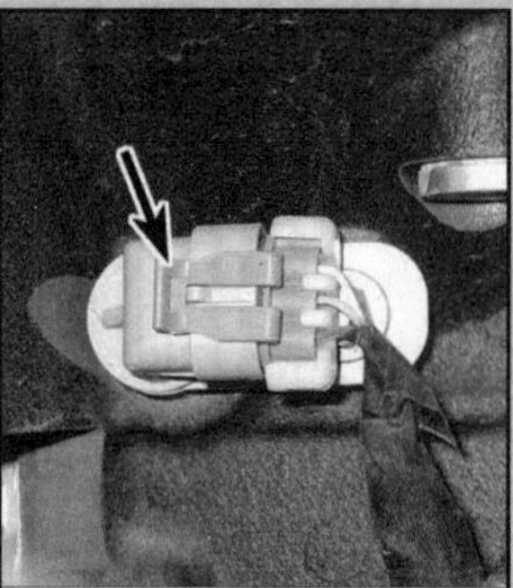

Some electrical connectors have a retaining tab which must be pried up to free the connector

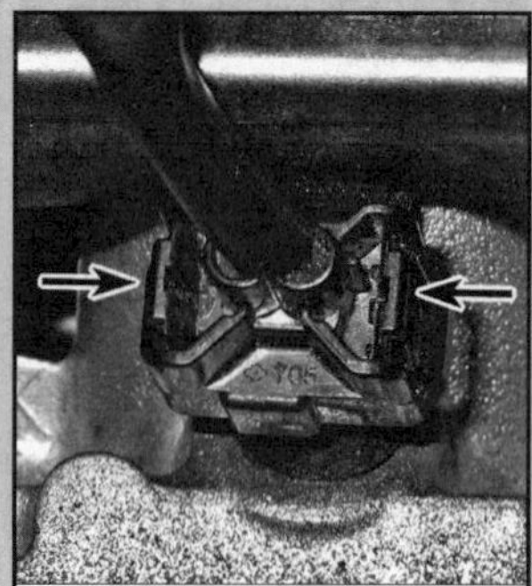

Some connectors have two release tabs that you must squeeze to release the connector

Some connectors use wire retainers that you squeeze to release the connector

Critical connectors often employ a sliding lock (1) that you must pull out before you can depress the release tab (2)

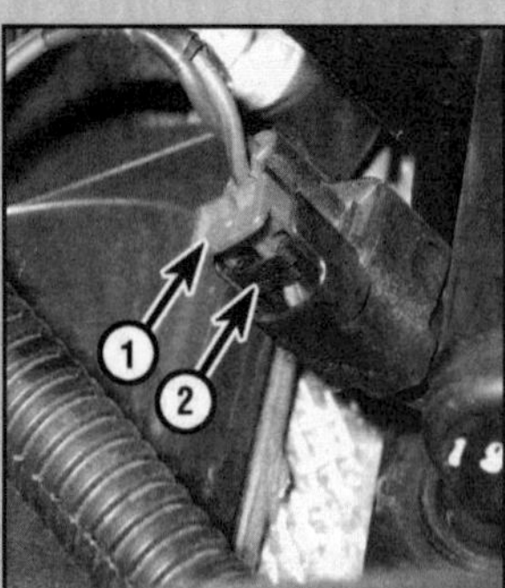

Here's another sliding-lock style connector, with the lock (1) and the release tab (2) on the side of the connector

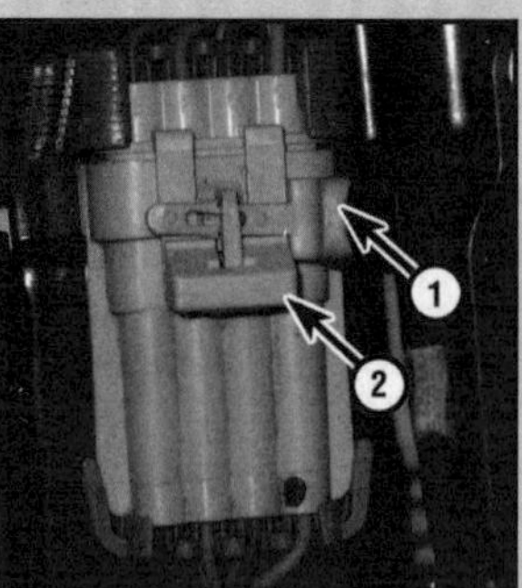

On some connectors the lock (1) must be pulled out to the side and removed before you can lift the release tab (2)

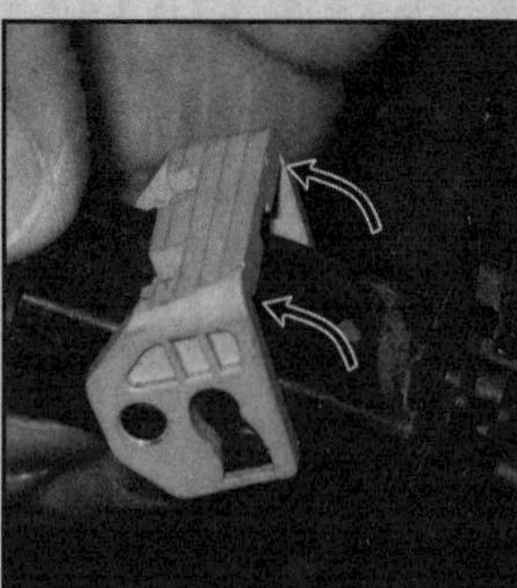

Some critical connectors, like the multi-pin connectors at the Powertrain Control Module employ pivoting locks that must be flipped open

sure to understand whether the view shows the harness side or the component side of the connector. Connector halves are mirror images of each other, and a terminal shown on the right side end-view of one half will be on the left side end-view of the other half.

4   It is often necessary to take circuit voltage measurements with a connector connected. Whenever possible, carefully insert a small straight pin (not your meter probe) into the rear of the connector shell to contact the terminal inside, then clip your meter lead to the pin. This kind of connection is called "backprobing." When inserting a test probe into a terminal, be careful not to distort the terminal opening. Doing so can lead to a poor connection and corrosion at that terminal later. Using the small straight pin instead of a meter probe results in less chance of deforming the terminal connector. "T" pins are a good choice as temporary meter connections. They allow for a larger surface area to attach the meter leads too.

7   Multi-function (turn signal) switch, wiper switch, and SCCM - replacement

Warning: *The models covered by this manual are equipped with a Supplemental Restraint System (SRS), more commonly known as airbags. Always disable the airbag system before working in the vicinity of any airbag system components to avoid the possibility of accidental deployment of the airbags, which could cause personal injury (see Section 26).*

Note: *The multi-function switch is on the left side of the steering wheel. This switch controls the interior lights as well as the exterior lighting systems. The portion of the switch that is visible (without removing the steering column trim) is NOT the actual switch but merely the operating knob for the systems. The actual switch is inside the steering column. There are no serviceable parts inside the knob or the*

switch assembly. Replace as a unit.

Note: *The multi-function switch controls headlights (both High and Low beam), fog lights (if applicable), park lights, turn signals, interior lamp defeat, interior lights, and panel light dimming control. Diagnosis of the multi-function switch requires special diagnostic tools. Refer to your local dealership or qualified independent repair shop.*

Note: *The multi-function switch works in conjunction with serial data signals. Do NOT attempt to bypass the switch with voltage or ground signals with a jumper wire. Testing of the leads is best performed with the proper scanning equipment.*

1   Disconnect the cable from the negative terminal of the battery (see Chapter 5).

Multi-function (turn signal) switch

2   Remove the upper and lower steering column covers (see Chapter 11).

3   Remove the single screw securing the multi-function switch (see illustration). Pull the switch straight out - enough to disengage the tabs - then disconnect the electrical connector and remove the switch.

4   Installation is the reverse of removal.

Steering column control module (SCCM)

Warning: *If the clockspring has become uncentered, refer to Chapter 10, Section 18 for the correct position initialization steps. The clockspring must be centered before the steering wheel is installed.*

5   The steering column control module (SCCM) is an integral part of the clockspring. The function of the SCCM is to carry the various data signals from the wiper switch, the multi-function switch, the horn, steering angle sensor, as well as a link between the driver's air bag and the air bag control module. It also serves as the turn signal canceling cam. The SCCM should not be disassembled or serviced - it should be replaced as a unit.

The wiper and multi-function switches can be replaced separately.

6   Rotate the steering wheel until the front wheels are pointed in the straight-ahead position.

7   Remove the steering wheel (see Chapter 10).

8   Remove the upper and lower steering column covers (see Chapter 11).

9   Insert a pin (referred to as a "grenade pin" or an appropriate sized drill bit or paper clip) into the locking hole of the clock spring. The hole is located at the 10 o'clock position. If a suitable pin is not available, tape the clockspring in place to prevent it from turning.

10   Remove the three screws securing the SCCM to the steering column, then disconnect the electrical connectors and remove the SCCM (see illustrations).

11   Installation is the reverse of removal.

Wiper switch

12   Remove upper and lower steering column covers (see Chapter 11).

7.3 Multi-function switch retaining screw location

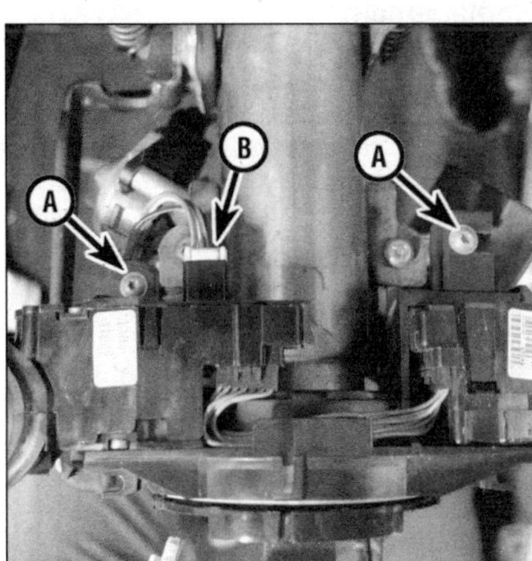

7.10a SCCM top view - Torx retaining screws (A) and electrical connector (B)

7.10b SCCM front view - Torx screw location (A)

7.10c SCCM bottom view - electrical connectors (B)

7.13 Wiper switch retaining screw location

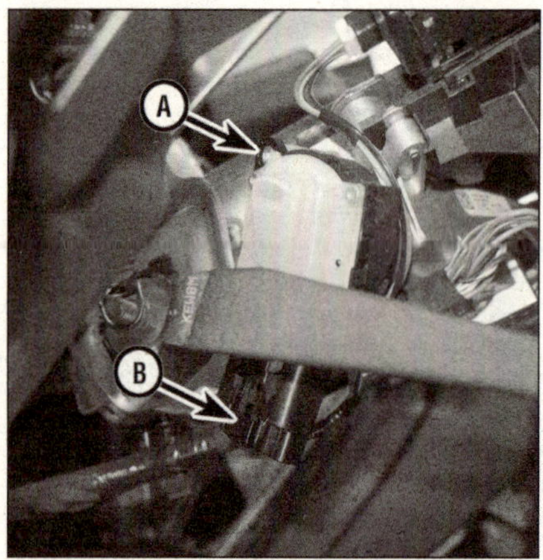

8.3 Remove the screw (A) and disconnect the electrical connector (B)

8.9 Insert a small screwdriver into the slot, press in on the release tab and pull out the lock cylinder

13   Remove the single screw securing the wiper switch to the SCCM (see illustration). Pull the switch straight out - enough to disengage the tabs - then disconnect the electrical connector and remove the switch.

14   Installation is the reverse of removal.

8   Ignition switch, lock cylinder, and immobilizer (SKREEM/WCM) - replacement

Warning: *The models covered by this manual are equipped with a Supplemental Restraint System (SRS), more commonly known as airbags. Always disable the airbag system before working in the vicinity of any airbag system components to avoid the possibility of accidental deployment of the airbags, which could cause personal injury (see Section 26).*

Ignition switch

1   Remove the upper and lower steering column covers (see Chapter 11).

2   Lock the steering column in the "full-down" position, then insert the key and posi-

tion it to the Run position.

3   Disconnect the electrical connector (releasing the safety tab on the connector first) and remove the screw securing the ignition switch to the steering column (see illustration), then pull the switch straight out of the housing.

4   Installation is the reverse of removal.

Lock cylinder

5   Remove the upper and lower steering column covers (see Chapter 11).

6   Lock the steering column in the "full-down" position, then insert the key and position it to the Run position.

7   Remove or position aside the wiper switch (see Section 7).

8   If necessary, remove the fastener for the SKREEM/WCM (see Steps in this Section), then unhook the tabs and slide the SKREEM/WCM back slightly to access the lock cylinder release tab.

9   Insert a small, flat screwdriver into the slot and depress the lock cylinder release tab. Pull the key and lock cylinder out together (see illustration).

10   To install, make sure the key is inserted and turned to the Run position, then align the slots of the lock cylinder to the housing and insert the cylinder until it locks in place. Turn the key to the Off position and check the operation of the key and cylinder. The remainder of installation is the reverse of removal.

Ignition switch immobilizer (SKREEM/WCM)

Description

11   SKREEM/WCM is an acronym for Sentry Key REmote Entry Module or Wireless Control Module, also known as the ignition switch immobilizer. It plays a key role in the alarm system, and contains receivers for the keyless entry and tire pressure monitor systems. It is equipped with a circular antenna that, when properly installed over the lock cylinder housing, communicates with a microprocessor chip inside the factory programmed key - thus allowing operation of the vehicle's ignition system.

Replacement

Note: *Before the vehicle can be driven, a diagnostic scan tool must be used to program the new SKREEM/WCM module to work with the factory specific keys. It is recommended to program at least two keys to work with the new module. When in doubt, see your nearest dealer service department to ensure that the module is programmed correctly.*

12   Remove the upper and lower steering column covers (see Chapter 11).

13   Remove or position aside the wiper switch (see Section 7).

14   Disconnect the electrical connector, remove the single screw securing the SKREEM to the lock cylinder housing, then carefully pry the retaining arms away from the lock cylinder housing and slide off the module (see illustration).

15   Installation is the reverse of removal.

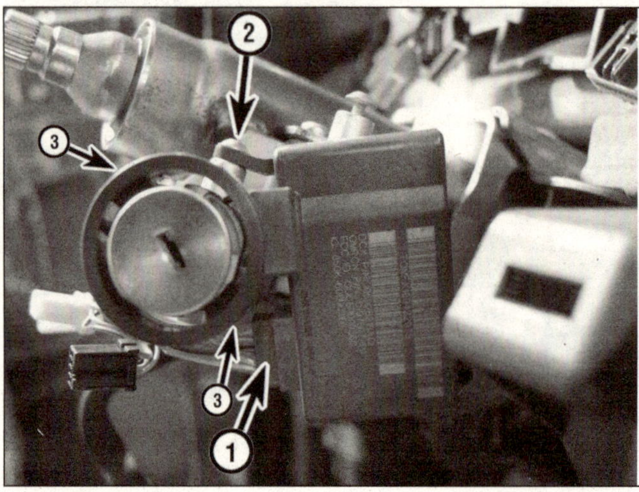

8.14 Disconnect the connector (1), remove the retaining screw (2), then gently pry out on the tabs (3) and slide off the immobilizer module

9.3 Instrument cluster mounting fasteners

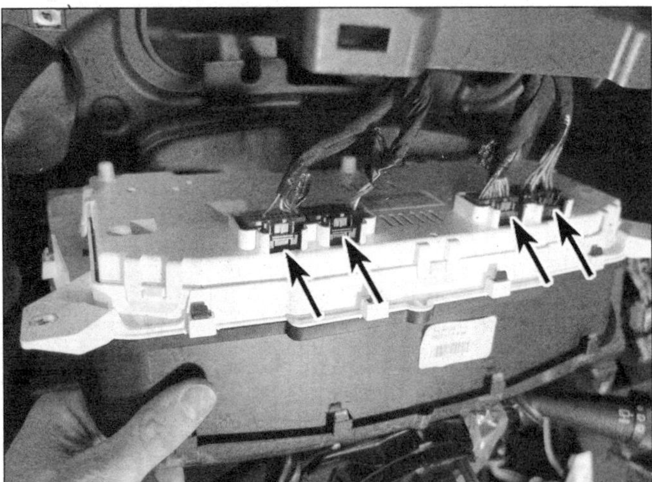

9.4 Disconnect the electrical connectors on the back of the instrument cluster

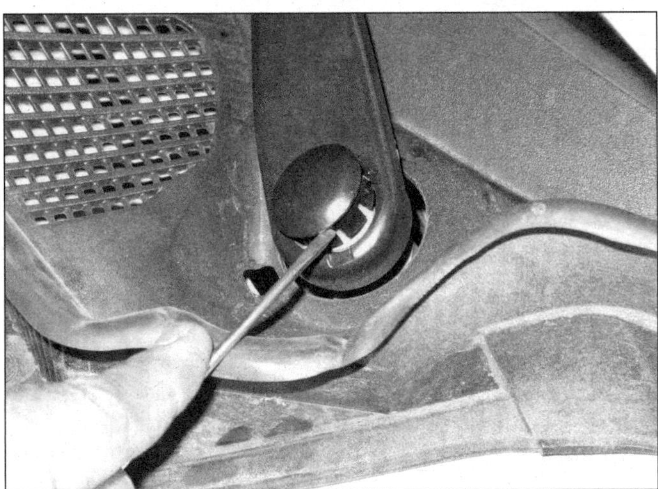

10.2 Pry off the caps, then remove the wiper arm nuts

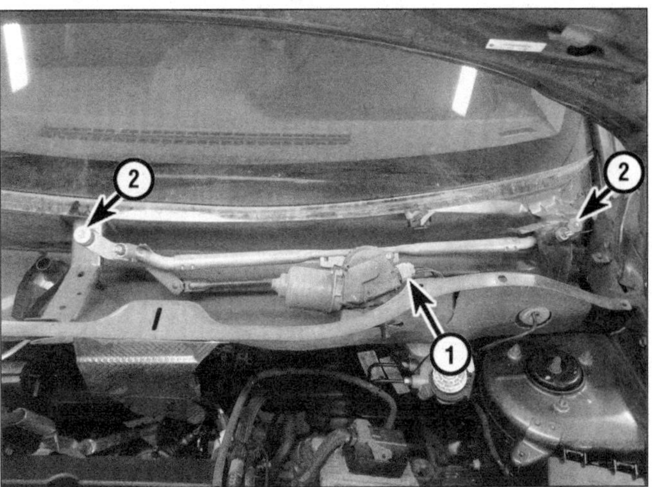

10.5 Disconnect the electrical connector (1), then remove the mounting fasteners (2) from the wiper motor assembly

9 Instrument cluster - removal and installation

Warning: *The models covered by this manual are equipped with a Supplemental Restraint System (SRS), more commonly known as airbags. Always disable the airbag system before working in the vicinity of any airbag system components to avoid the possibility of accidental deployment of the airbags, which could cause personal injury (see Section 26).*

1   Disconnect the cable from the negative battery terminal (see Chapter 5).

2   Remove the instrument panel upper trim cover (see Chapter 11, Section 22).

3   Remove the instrument cluster mounting fasteners (see illustration).

4   Disconnect the electrical connectors and remove the cluster (see illustration).

5   Installation is the reverse of removal.

10 Wiper motor - removal and installation

Front

1   Place the wipers in the Park position. Mark the location of the wiper arms before removing them. Disconnect the cable from the negative battery terminal (see Chapter 5).

2   Pry off the protective caps covering the wiper arm nuts, then remove the nuts that attach the wiper arms to their spindle shafts (see illustration).

3   Remove the wiper arms. If the arm is difficult to remove from the shaft, use a small two-jaw puller to loosen the arm, then wiggle the wiper arm free.

4   Remove the cowl cover (see Chapter 11).

5   Disconnect the wiper motor electrical connector, then remove the wiper transmission linkage assembly mounting fasteners (see illustration). Disengage the grommet from the wiper motor and remove the assembly from the cowl.

6   Remove the motor mounting bolts, then separate the wiper motor from the wiper transmission assembly. Mark the location of the wiper motor shaft to the pivot arms for correct installation. Transfer the motor onto the linkage and tighten the fasteners securely.

7   Installation is the reverse of removal. Before installing the cowl cover, operate the wiper motor and linkage without the wiper arms attached to ensure correct operation. Return the wiper motor to the Park position, then disconnect the negative battery cable and proceed with installation.

Rear

8   Disconnect the cable from the negative terminal of the battery (see Chapter 5).

9   Lift the wiper arm/blade off of the window, then remove the rear wiper arm. It is removed

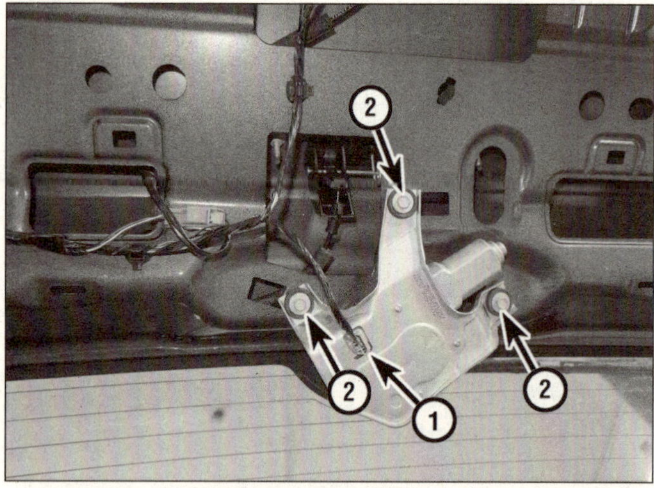

10.11 Disconnect the electrical connector (1), then remove the wiper motor mounting bolts (2)

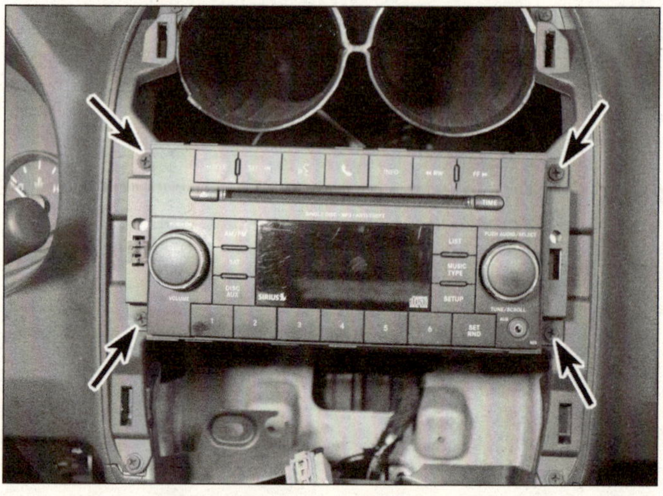

11.3 To detach the radio from the instrument panel, remove these four mounting screws

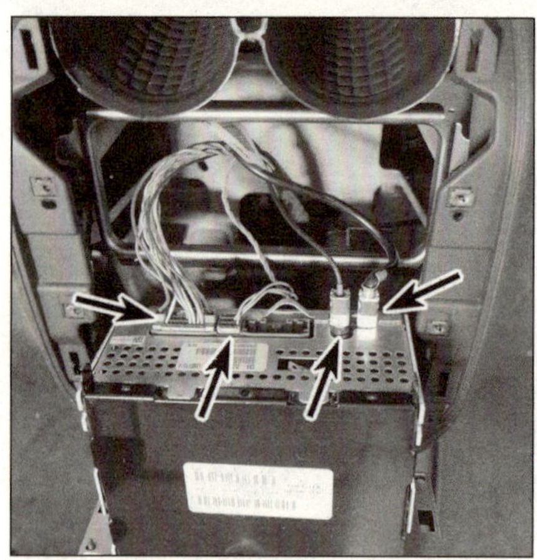

11.4 After pulling the radio out from the instrument panel, disconnect the electrical connectors and the antenna lead from the backside of the radio

11.7 Use a flat trim tool to remove the speaker cover

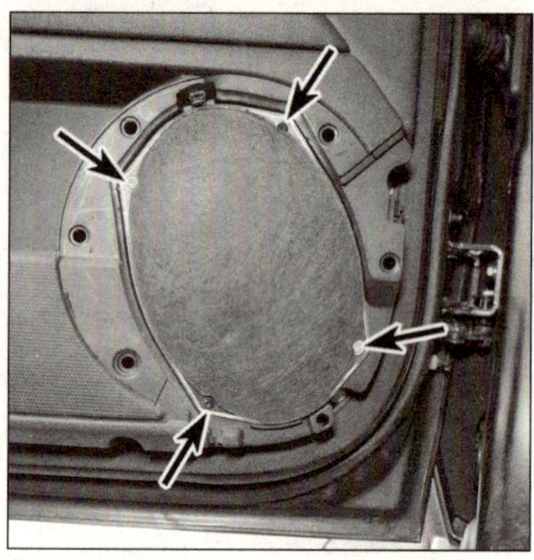

11.8 Speaker retaining screw locations

essentially the same as the front wiper arm (see related Steps in this Section).

10   Remove the liftgate trim paneling (see Chapter 11, Section 19).

11   Disconnect the electrical connector from the rear wiper motor, then remove the three bolts securing the wiper motor to the liftgate (see illustration).

12   Installation is the reverse of removal.

---

11   Radio and speakers - removal and installation

Warning: *The models covered by this manual are equipped with a Supplemental Restraint System (SRS), more commonly known as airbags. Always disable the airbag system before working in the vicinity of any airbag*
system components to avoid the possibility of accidental deployment of the airbags, which could cause personal injury (see Section 26).

1   Disconnect the cable from the negative battery terminal (see Chapter 5).

Radio

2   Using a trim tool, remove the radio trim bezel / HVAC control module (see Chapter 3, Section 11).

3   Remove the radio retaining screws (see illustration), then pull the radio out of the instrument panel.

Note: *When disconnecting the antenna connector(s), only pull on the connector body - do not pull on the wire itself or damage could occur.*

4   Disconnect the electrical connectors and the antenna lead from the backside of the

radio (see illustration) and remove the radio.

5   Installation is the reverse of removal.

Speakers

6   These models are equipped with up to five speakers (depending on the model's accessory package): one at each end on the top of the instrument panel, one in each door, a subwoofer mounted within the right-rear quarter panel, and a double-speaker assembly mounted in the liftgate.

Front door speakers

7   Pry the speaker cover from the door panel (see illustration).

8   Remove the four Torx screws securing the speaker to the door panel (see illustration).

9   Remove speaker from the door panel,

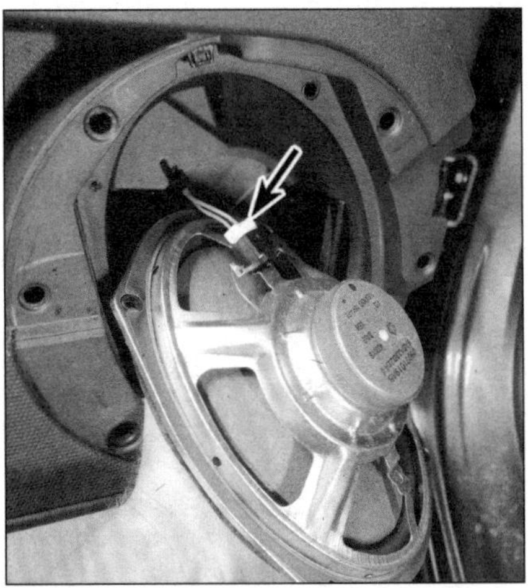

11.9 Speaker electrical connector

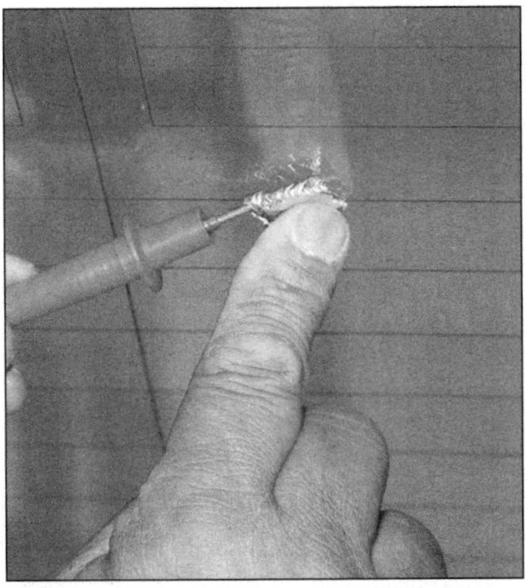

13.4 When measuring the voltage at the rear window defogger grid, wrap a piece of aluminum foil around the positive probe of the voltmeter and press the foil against the wire with your finger

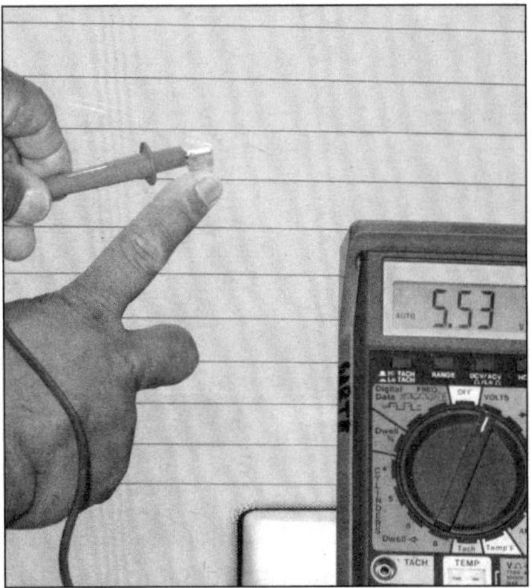

13.5 To determine if a heating element has broken, check the voltage at the center of each element. If the voltage is 5 or 6-volts, the element is unbroken; if the voltage is 10 or 12-volts, the element is broken between the center and the ground side; if there is no voltage, the element is broken between the center and the positive side

disconnect the electrical connector and remove the speaker (see illustration).

10   Installation is the reverse of removal.

Instrument panel speakers

11   Remove the instrument panel top cover (see Chapter 11, Section 22).

12   Remove the speaker mounting screws.

13   Pull out the speaker, disconnect the electrical connector and remove the speaker from the end of the instrument panel.

14   Installation is the reverse of removal.

Rear double-speaker assembly - liftgate

15   Open the liftgate and unscrew the speaker assembly mounting fasteners.

16   Disconnect the speaker electrical connector and remove the speaker assembly.

17   Installation is the reverse of removal.

Subwoofer (right-rear quarter panel area)

18   Remove the right-rear quarter panel trim (see Chapter 11).

19   Remove the subwoofer retaining fasteners securing it to the quarter panel.

20   Disconnect the subwoofer electrical connector and remove the subwoofer.

21   Installation is the reverse of removal.

12   Antenna - removal and installation

1   Disconnect the cable from the negative battery terminal (see Chapter 5).

Antenna mast

2   The antenna mast simply unscrews from the base. In most cases it can be unscrewed

by hand, but if necessary, use a pair of pliers to break it loose.

Antenna fixed base

3   The antenna base is mounted on the right front fender and is routed through the cowling and into the vehicle.

4   Remove the right-front fenderwell splash shield (see Chapter 11, Section 11).

5   The antenna cable has an inline connector under the passenger side kick panel (see Chapter 11, Section 23). Disconnect this electrical connector.

6   Remove the antenna mast, unscrew the antenna base retaining nut and remove the antenna base.

7   Installation is the reverse of removal.

Antenna (roof mounted, for satellite radio)

8   Lower the rear section of the headliner (see Chapter 11, Section 22) to gain access to the underside antenna dust cover.

9   The antenna is glued to the roof, and can be removed with a length of nylon string or fishing line. Starting at the front of the antenna (from beneath the dust cover), work the line back and forth using a 'sawing' motion until the perimeter of the antenna's adhesive has been covered.

Note: *This is more conveniently accomplished if the nylon string has handles attached to each end.*

10   Working from inside the vehicle, disconnect the antenna electrical connectors.

11   Using a flat-bladed screwdriver, release the antenna retaining tab on one side while pushing up on the antenna, then release the other tab. Remove the antenna from the roof.

12   Installation is the reverse of removal.

13   Rear window defogger - check and repair

1   The rear window defogger consists of a number of horizontal elements baked onto the glass surface.

2   Small breaks in the element can be repaired without removing the rear window.

Check

3   Turn the ignition switch and defogger system switches to the On position. Using a voltmeter, place the positive probe against the defogger grid positive terminal and the negative probe against the ground terminal. If battery voltage is not indicated, check the fuse, defogger switch and related wiring. If voltage is indicated, but all or part of the defogger doesn't heat, proceed with the following tests.

4   When measuring voltage during these tests, wrap a piece of aluminum foil around the tip of the voltmeter positive probe and press the foil against the heating element with your finger (see illustration). Place the negative probe on the defogger grid ground terminal.

5   Check the voltage at the center of each heating element (see illustration). If the voltage is 5 or 6-volts, the element is okay (there is no break). If there is not voltage, the element is broken between the center of the element and the positive end. If the voltage is 10 to 12 volts the element is broken between the center of the element and ground. Check each heating element.

6   Connect the negative lead to a good body ground. The reading should stay the same. If it doesn't, the ground connection is bad.

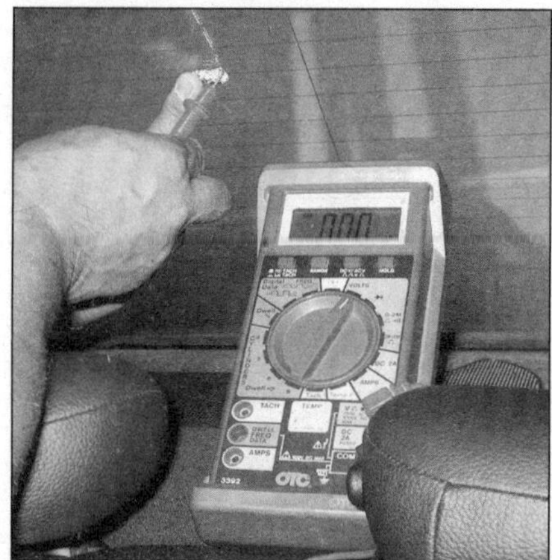

13.7 To find the break, touch the voltmeter negative lead to the defogger ground terminal, place the voltmeter positive lead with the foil strip against the heating element at the positive terminal end and slide it toward the negative terminal end. The point at which the voltmeter reading changes abruptly is the point at which the element is broken

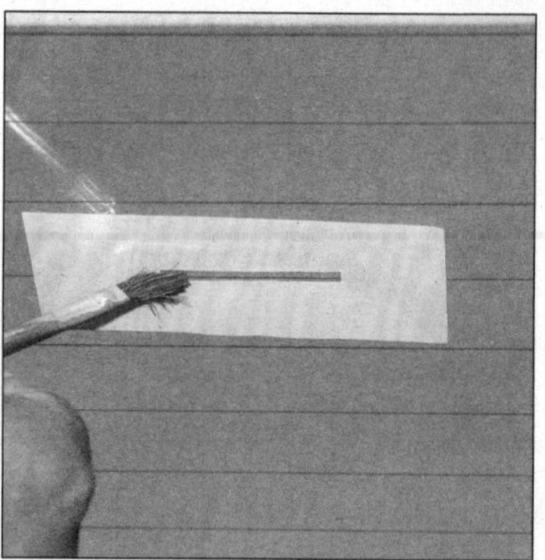

13.14 To use a defogger repair kit, apply masking tape to the inside of the window at the damaged area, then brush on the special conductive coating

14.3 Headlight housing mounting fasteners

---

14   Headlight housing - replacement

Warning: *These vehicles are equipped with halogen gas-filled headlight bulbs, which are under pressure and may shatter if the surface is damaged or the bulb is dropped. Wear eye protection and handle the bulbs carefully, grasping only the base whenever possible. Do not touch the surface of the bulb with your fingers because the oil from your skin could cause it to overheat and fail prematurely. If you do touch the bulb surface, clean it with rubbing alcohol.*

1   Disconnect the cable from the negative battery terminal (see Chapter 5).
2   Remove the front bumper cover (see Chapter 11).
3   Remove the headlight housing mounting fasteners (see illustration).
4   Pull the headlight housing forward enough to disconnect the electrical connectors from the housing, then remove the housing.
5   Installation is the reverse of removal. Adjust the headlights if necessary (see Section 16).

15.2a Unlock the safety clip, then press the main connector release tab...

15.2b ... and disconnect the electrical connector from the bulb

---

7   To find the break, place the voltmeter negative probe against the defogger ground terminal. Place the voltmeter positive probe with the foil strip against the heating element at the positive terminal end and slide it toward the negative terminal end. The point at which the voltmeter deflects from several volts to zero is the point at which the heating element is broken (see illustration).

Repair

8   Repair the break in the element using a repair kit specifically recommended for this purpose, available at most auto parts stores. Included in this kit is plastic conductive epoxy.
9   Be sure to have adequate ventilation and that the glass be at a moderate temperature. Do NOT try this repair on an extremely hot or cold glass. Glass should be at or near 72 degrees F (room temperature).
10   Prior to repairing a break, turn off the system and allow it to cool off for a few minutes.
11   Lightly buff the element area with fine steel wool, then clean it thoroughly with rubbing alcohol.
12   Use masking tape to mask off the area being repaired.
13   Thoroughly mix the epoxy, following the instructions provided with the repair kit.
14   Apply the epoxy material to the slit in the masking tape, overlapping the undamaged area about 3/4-inch on either end (see illustration).
15   Allow the repair to cure for 24 hours before removing the tape and using the system.

---

15   Headlight bulb - replacement

Warning: *Halogen bulbs are gas-filled and under pressure and might shatter if the surface is scratched or the bulb is dropped. Wear eye protection and handle the bulbs carefully, grasping only the base whenever possible. Don't touch the surface of the bulb with your fingers because the oil from your skin could cause it to overheat and fail prematurely. If you do touch the bulb surface, clean it with rubbing alcohol.*

Halogen headlight

1   Disconnect the cable from the negative battery terminal (see Chapter 5).
2   Disconnect the electrical connector from the back of the headlight housing (see illustrations).

15.3 Rotate the bulb about 30 degrees then pull straight out to remove it

16.1 Vertical adjustment screw location (right headlight shown, left headlight identical)

3   Rotate the headlight bulb counterclockwise and pull the bulb from the housing (see illustration).

4   When installing the new bulb, align the tabs on the bulb socket mounting flange with the slots in the housing. Installation is otherwise the reverse of removal.

Xenon (HID) headlights

Warning: *Some models use High Intensity Discharge (HID) bulbs instead of conventional halogen bulbs. According to the manufacturer, the high voltages produced by this system can be fatal in the event of shock. Also, the voltage can remain in circuit even after the headlight switch has been turned to Off and the ignition key has been removed. Therefore, for your safety, we don't recommend that you try to replace one of these bulbs yourself. Instead, have this service performed by a dealer service department or other qualified repair shop.*

16   Headlights - adjustment

Warning: *The headlights must be aimed correctly. If adjusted incorrectly, they could temporarily blind the driver of an oncoming vehicle and cause an accident or seriously reduce your ability to see the road. The headlights should be checked for proper aim every 12 months and any time a new headlight is installed or front-end bodywork is performed. The following procedure is only an interim step to provide temporary adjustment until the headlights can be adjusted by a properly equipped shop.*

1   The vertical headlight adjustment screw, located on the inside corner of the housing (see illustration), controls up-and-down movement of the beam.

2   There are several methods of adjusting the headlights. The simplest method requires a blank wall 25 feet in front of the vehicle and a level floor (see illustration).

3   Position masking tape on the wall in reference to the vehicle centerline and the centerlines of both headlights.

4   Measure the height of the headlight reference marks (in the centers of the headlight lenses) from the ground. Position a horizontal tape line on the wall at the same height as the headlight reference marks.

Note: *It may be easier to position the tape on the wall with the vehicle parked only a few inches away.*

5   Adjustment should be made with the vehicle sitting level, the gas tank half-full and no unusually heavy load in the vehicle.

6   Turn on the low beams. Turn the adjusting screw to position the high intensity zone so it is two inches below the horizontal line.

7   Have the headlights adjusted by a dealer service department at the earliest opportunity.

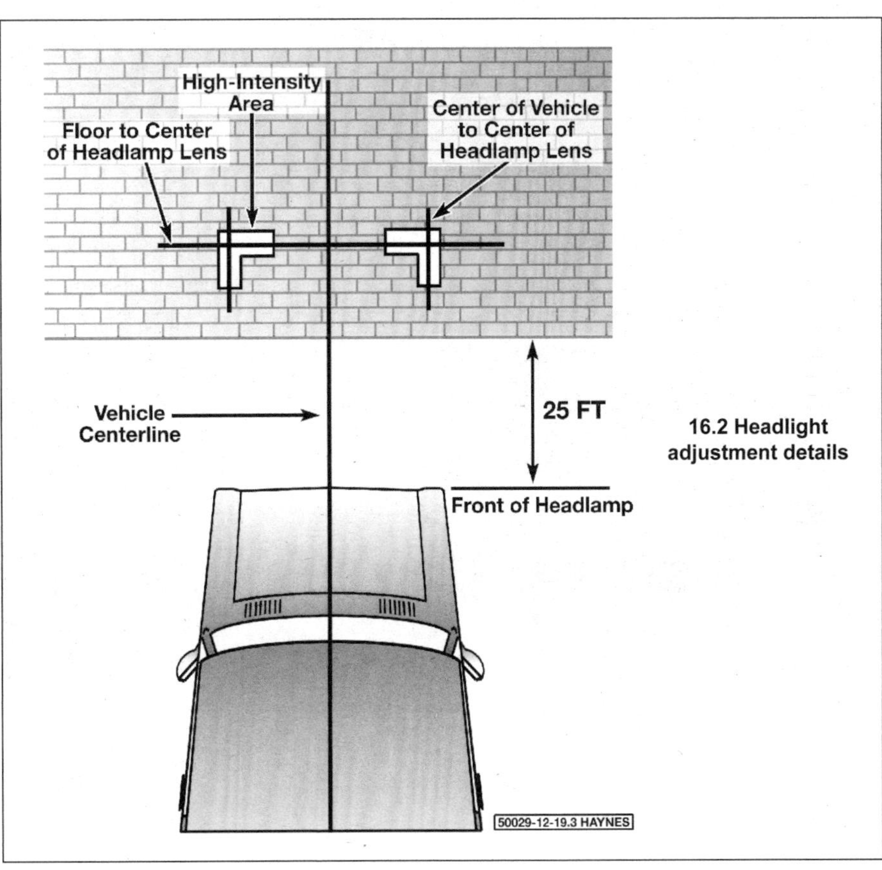

16.2 Headlight adjustment details

17   Bulb replacement

Exterior light bulbs

Note: *Disconnect the cable from the negative battery terminal (see Chapter 5).*

Front park and turn signal bulbs

1   Rotate the steering wheel to turn the vehicle wheels inward and away from the bulb being accessed.

2   Remove the fenderwell splash shield front fasteners (see Chapter 11, Section 11), then move aside the splash shield enough to access the park and turn signal bulb.

3   Disconnect the electrical connector from the bulb, then rotate the bulb holder counter-clockwise and pull it straight out of the housing.

4   Remove the bulb from the bulb holder.

5   Install the new bulb into the bulb holder.

6   The remainder of installation is the reverse of removal.

Fog light bulbs

Warning: *Halogen bulbs are gas-filled and under pressure and might shatter if the surface is scratched or the bulb is dropped. Wear eye protection and handle the bulbs carefully, grasping only the base whenever possible. Don't touch the surface of the bulb with your fingers because the oil from your skin could cause it to overheat and fail prematurely. If you do touch the bulb surface, clean it with rubbing alcohol.*

7   Loosen the wheel lug nuts. Raise the front of the vehicle and support it securely on jackstands. Remove the wheel for the side of the bulb being replaced.

8   Remove the fenderwell splash shield front fasteners (see Chapter 11, Section 11), then move aside the splash shield enough to access the fog light bulb.

9   Disconnect the bulb electrical connector.

Note: *Some models may have retaining screws to be removed from the fog light bulb housing, as well as latches to be disengaged.*

10   Using a wide-bladed screwdriver, care-fully pry between the fog lamp housing and retaining latch to unlock the latch. Repeat this for the remaining bulb retaining latches, then pull the bulb out of the fog light housing. The bulb and bulb bracket should come out of the fog light housing together as a unit.

11   Installation is the reverse of removal.

Center high-mounted brake light - (CHMBL)

Note: *The high-mounted brake light LEDs are an integral part of the housing and are not available separately.*

12   Remove the screws that fasten the CHMBL to the liftgate (see illustration).

13   Disconnect the electrical connector and rear windshield washer hose, then remove the center high-mounted brake light.

14   Installation is the reverse of removal.

Taillight bulbs

15   For the replacement of the taillight bulbs, follow the accompanying photos and captions in order:

16   Installation is the reverse of removal.

Bulb removal

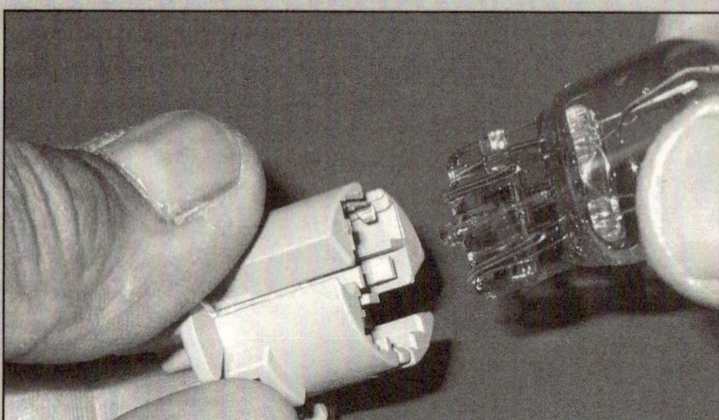

To remove many modern exterior bulbs from their holders, simply pull them out

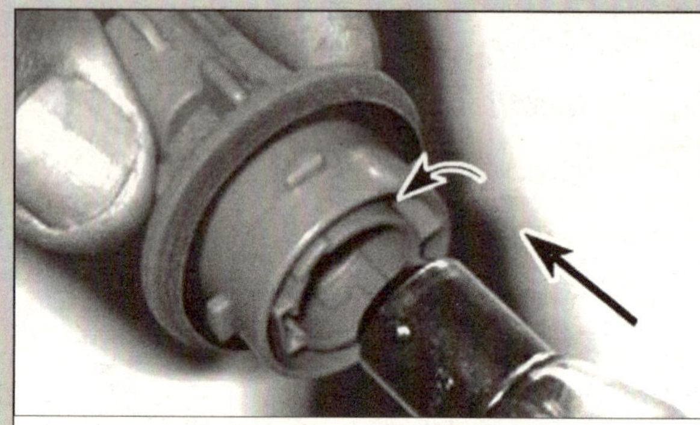

On bulbs with a cylindrical base ("bayonet" bulbs), the socket is spring-loaded; a pair of small posts on the side of the base hold the bulb in place against spring pressure. To remove this type of bulb, push it into the holder, rotate it 1/4-turn counterclockwise, then pull it out

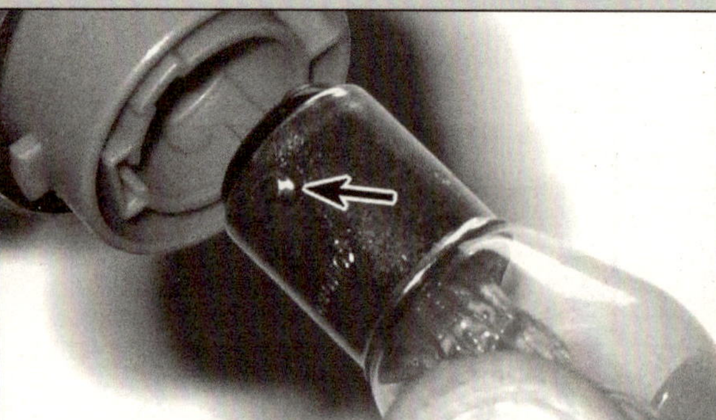

If a bayonet bulb has dual filaments, the posts are staggered, so the bulb can only be installed one way

To remove most overhead interior light bulbs, simply unclip them

License plate light bulbs

17   Reach under the liftgate outside handle and detach the lens cover by depressing the release tab, pivoting the cover downward, then sliding out the opposite end tabs to remove the cover.

18   Pull the bulb straight out of the socket to remove it.

19   Installation is the reverse of removal.

Interior lights

Instrument cluster illumination bulbs

20   The instrument cluster LEDs are an integral part of the cluster, and not separately serviceable. If the LEDs stop working, the cluster must be replaced (see Section 9).

17.12 Remove the two screws, pull the lens assembly out far enough to disconnect the washer hose and electrical connector, then remove the assembly

17.15a Open the liftgate and pry off the plastic taillight housing retainers

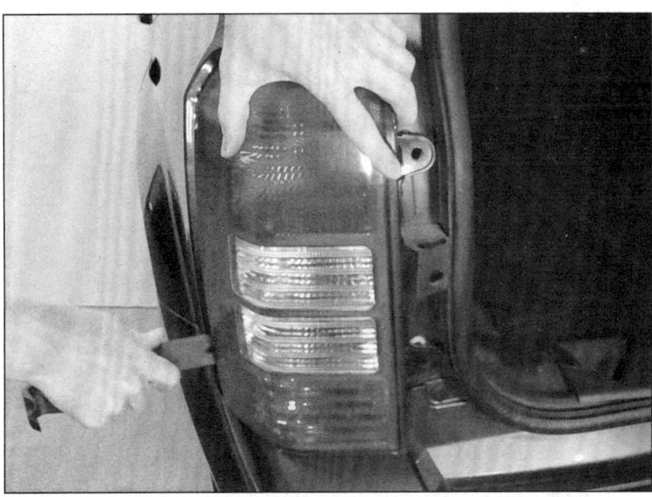

17.15b Using a flat trim tool, very carefully pry the studs inside of the lens housing free

17.15c Pull off the taillight housing and disconnect the electrical connectors

17.15d Rotate the necessary bulb holder counterclockwise, then pull it out of the housing

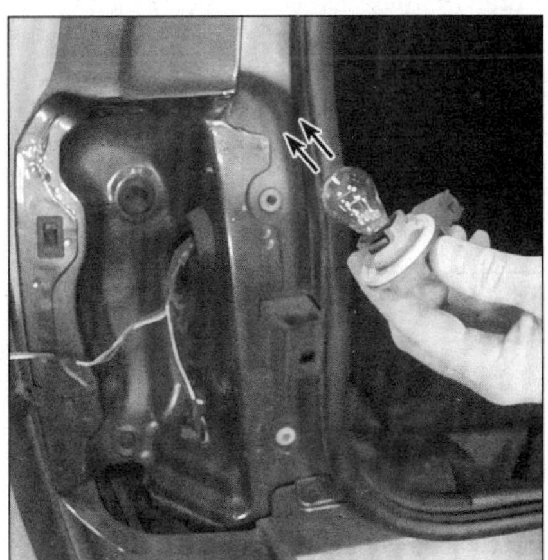

17.15e Pull the bulb straight out of the holder to remove it - to install, push it in firmly

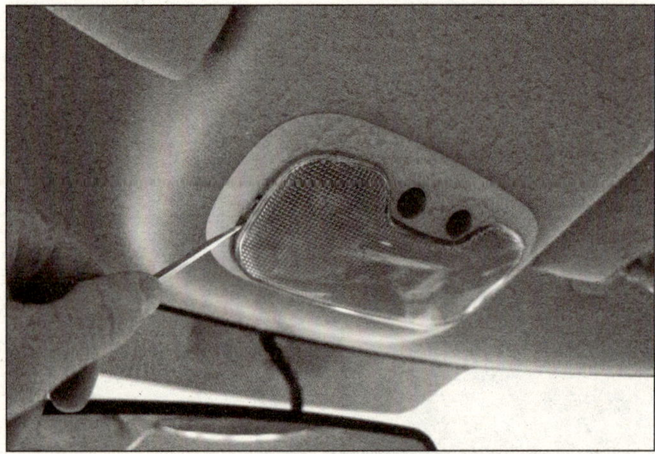

17.21a Carefully pry off the correct end of the lens to access the bulb(s)...

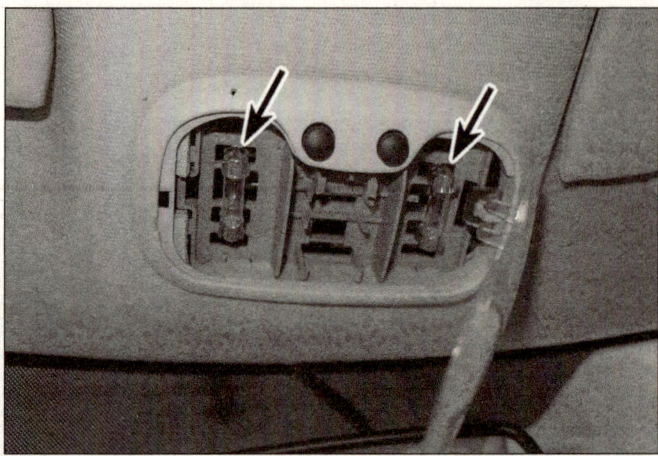

17.21b ... let the lens hang, and pull out the desired bulb from the metal sockets

18.2 Disconnect the electrical connector (1) and remove the fastener (2) securing the horn (front bumper cover removed for clarity - left side shown, right side similar)

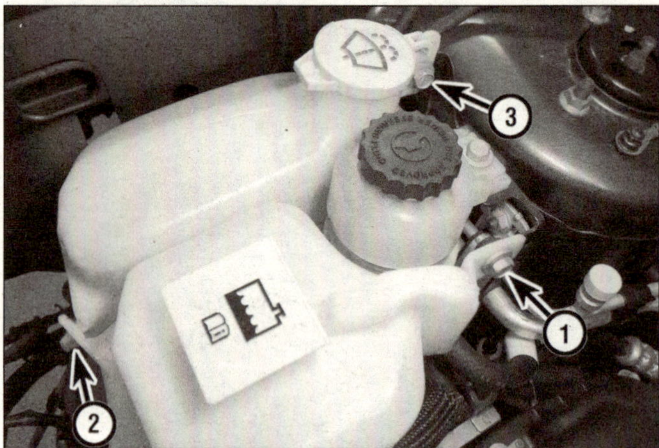

19.3 Remove the coolant reservoir bolt (1), separate the coolant reservoir from the washer reservoir (2), then remove the washer reservoir bolt (3)

Dome/reading lights

Note: *There should be a tiny slot imprinted to indicate the correct end for prying out the lens cover.*

21　Using a trim panel removal tool or a screwdriver, carefully pry off the end of the lens (see illustrations).

22　Installation is the reverse of removal.

18　Horn - replacement

Warning: *The models covered by this manual are equipped with a Supplemental Restraint System (SRS), more commonly known as airbags. Always disable the airbag system before working in the vicinity of any airbag system components to avoid the possibility of accidental deployment of the airbags, which could cause personal injury (see Section 26).*

Note: *There are two horns located in the front area of the vehicle - just outside of the main frame rail, behind the front bumper, on the*

right and left sides of the vehicle. The right side horn controls the high-note pitch, and the left side controls the low pitch.

1　Remove the fenderwell splash shield front fasteners (see Chapter 11, Section 11), then move aside the splash shield enough to access the horn.

2　Disconnect the electrical connector, then remove the horn mounting fastener and horn assembly (see illustration).

3　Installation is the reverse of removal.

19　Windshield washer fluid reservoir and pump - replacement

Warning: *The models covered by this manual are equipped with a Supplemental Restraint System (SRS), more commonly known as airbags. Always disable the airbag system before working in the vicinity of any airbag system components to avoid the possibility of accidental deployment of the airbags, which*

could cause personal injury (see Section 26).

Note: *Although it is not absolutely necessary, it may be easier to first remove the washer reservoir prior to replacing the pump, if greater access is needed.*

1　Disconnect the cable from the negative terminal of the battery (see Chapter 5).

2　Properly siphon out (or use a suction gun) to remove as much fluid as possible from the windshield washer fluid reservoir. If the fluid is still in good condition, it can be reused.

3　Remove the coolant reservoir mounting bolt, disengage the coolant reservoir from the windshield washer reservoir tab and position the coolant reservoir out of the way, using caution not to spill any coolant. Remove the windshield washer reservoir mounting bolt (see illustration).

Note: *It may be easier to first disconnect the pump hose connections from the location nearest the strut tower. Be sure to label the hoses to ensure that they are reconnected correctly.*

4   Lift the windshield washer reservoir up (disengaging it from its mounting grommet below) enough to access the connections at the pump. Disconnect the pump electrical connector, then label and disconnect the front and rear window fluid hose connections (see illustration). Use a towel or rag to soak up any residual fluid that may spill out.

Note: *On models with an automatic headlight leveling motor, remove the headlight housing mounting bolts and slide the housing forward enough to allow for clearance of the washer reservoir to pass through (see Section 14).*

5   To replace the pump, disconnect the electrical connector and hoses at the pump (if not already done) (see illustration 19.4) and lift the pump straight up to disconnect it from the reservoir inlet connection. Use caution not to damage the reservoir.

6   Remove the rubber seal / filter from the reservoir inlet. Discard the seal/filter, as a new one should be obtained for installation.

7   Installation is the reverse of removal.

20   Electric side view mirrors - general information

1   The electric rear view mirrors use two motors to move the glass; one for up and down adjustments and one for left-right adjustments.

2   The control switch has a selector portion which sends voltage to the left or right side mirror. With the ignition in the ACC position and the engine OFF, roll down the windows and operate the mirror control switch through all functions (left-right and up-down) for both the left and right side mirrors.

3   Listen carefully for the sound of the electric motors running in the mirrors.

4   If the motors can be heard but the mirror glass doesn't move, there's probably a problem with the drive mechanism inside the mirror. A loud but distinct clicking can be heard with most failures associated with the drive motors failing to move the actual mirrors. Power mirrors have no user-serviceable parts inside - a defective mirror must be replaced as a unit (see Chapter 11).

5   If the mirrors don't operate and no sound comes from the mirrors, check the fuses (see Section 3).

6   If the fuses are OK, remove the mirror control switch. Check the continuity of the switch with a multimeter, or if in doubt, have the switch continuity checked by a dealer service department or other qualified shop.

7   Check the ground connections.

8   If the mirror still doesn't work, remove the mirror and check the wires at the mirror for voltage.

9   If there's no voltage in each switch position, check the mirror and control switch for a disconnected (open) lead. It should be noted that a weak or loose connection is often overlooked as the problem. Be sure to check all electrical connections as well.

10   If there is voltage and grounds at the

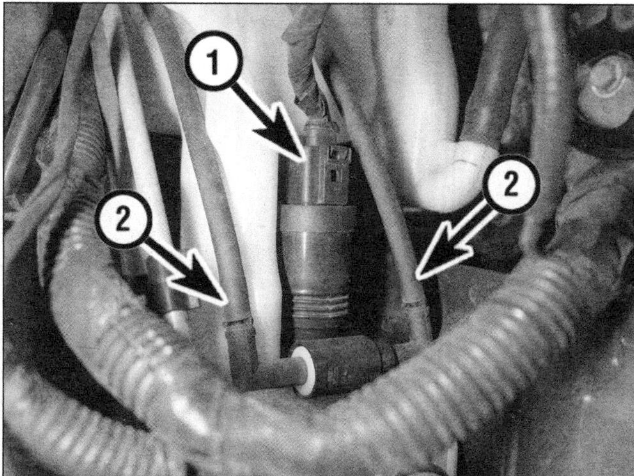

19.4 Disconnect the pump electrical connector (1) and hose connections (2)

leads on their respective positions and the mirror still does not respond, replace the mirror assembly.

11   For removal and installation instructions, see Chapter 11 for details.

21   Cruise control system – description and check

1   The cruise control system maintains vehicle speed with the Antilock Brake Module (ABM), Powertrain Control Module (PCM), instrument cluster, throttle actuator control motor, Brake switch, wheel speed sensors, control switches and associated wiring. There is no mechanical connection, such as a vacuum servo or cable. Some features of the system require special testers and diagnostic procedures that are beyond the scope of the home mechanic. Listed below are some general procedures that may be used to locate a common problem.

2   Check the fuses (see Section 3).

3   The brake light switch deactivates the cruise control system. Have an assistant press the brake pedal while you check the brake light operation. This still does not eliminate the brake switch as the fault, further testing of the brake switch wiring and connector will need to be done. Check the wiring diagram for the proper leads and voltage requirements for the cruise control section of the brake switch.

4   If the brake lights do not operate properly, correct the problem and retest the cruise control.

5   Check the wiring between the PCM and throttle actuator motor for any obvious opens or shorts and repair as necessary.

6   The cruise control system uses information from the PCM, including the wheel speed sensors, located on the knuckle of each wheel. Refer to Chapter 9 for more information on the wheel speed sensors.

Note: *If the ABS warning light is on, and it is due to a faulty wheel speed sensor, this can cause the cruise control system to not function.*

7   If after a few basic tests as described

or a test drive does not determine the problem, then take your vehicle to a dealer service department or a qualified independent repair shop for further diagnosis.

22   Power window system - description and check

1   The power window system operates electric motors, mounted in the doors, which lower and raise the windows. The system consists of the control switches, the motors, regulators, glass mechanisms, the Door Module and associated wiring.

2   The power windows can be lowered and raised from the master control switch by the driver or by remote switches located at the individual windows. Each window has a separate motor that is reversible. The position of the control switch determines the polarity and therefore the direction of operation.

3   The circuit is protected by a fuse and a circuit breaker. Each motor is also equipped with an internal circuit breaker; this prevents one stuck window from disabling the whole system. However, it should be noted that each door module will reverse the window direction if the current flow becomes greater than its preset values.

4   The power window system will only operate when the ignition switch is ON, and for a period of time after the ignition key has been turned Off (unless one of the doors is opened). In addition, many models have a window lockout switch at the master control switch which, when activated, disables the switches at the rear windows and, sometimes, the switch at the passenger's window also. Always check these items before troubleshooting a window problem.

5   These procedures are general in nature, so if you can't find the problem using them, take the vehicle to a dealer service department or other properly equipped repair facility.

6   If all the power windows won't operate, always check the fuse and circuit breaker first.

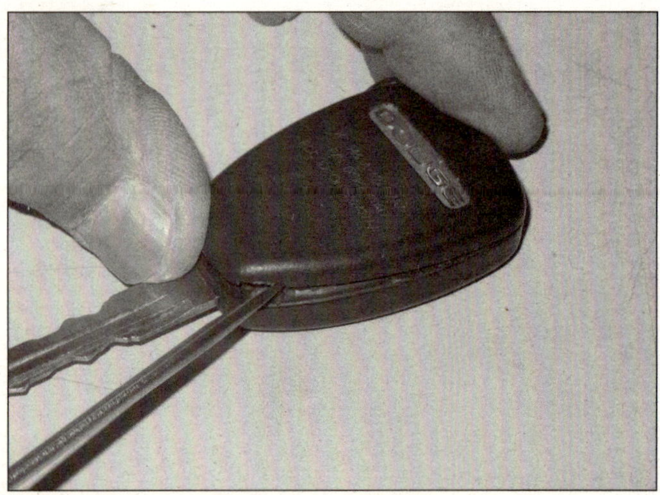

23.11 Using the emergency key or small screwdriver, carefully pry the halves apart

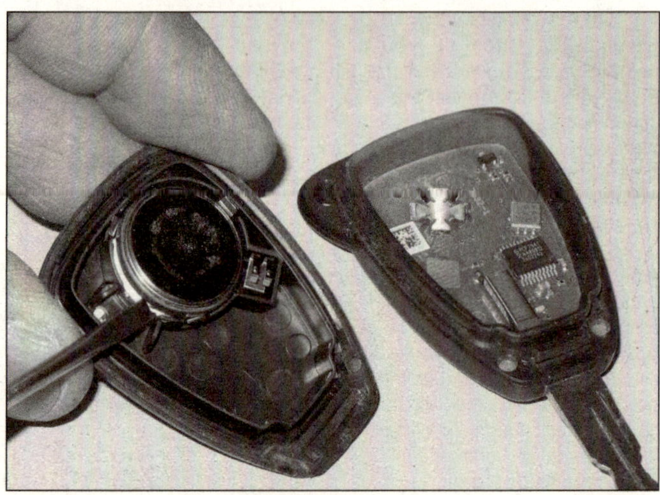

23.12 Remove the battery, noting which direction the battery faces

7   If only the driver's window is functioning, check to see if the master switch window lockout button - located on the driver's window switch panel - has been depressed.

8   If only one window is inoperative from the master control switch, check the wiring between the switches using the wiring diagram.

9   Window regulators can fail as well as the switches. If a motor is in question, remove the door panel and locate the wire connector to the motor. Check for voltage across the leads with the appropriate window switch depressed. If voltage is present and the motor does not move, chances are the motor itself has failed. Replace the window regulator assembly at that point.

10   Unusual noises from the door may indicate a problem not with the electrical side of the power window but with the track or guides. In most cases the track guide is sold as a window regulator assembly, which generally will come with a new motor as well. See Chapter 11 for window regulator removal.

Note: *If none of the basic tests yield an answer, see a dealership repair center or an independent repair shop and have it properly tested.*

23   Power door lock and keyless entry system - description and check

Note: *These models use input and output signals from various electronic components. These systems are linked to each other in several ways to the CCN (Cab Compartment Node), which allows simple and accurate troubleshooting, but only with a professional-grade scan tool. The door lock systems involve the ignition switch, wireless control module, instru-ment cluster, TIPM, door latches, door control switches and the respective door modules. Proper diagnostics requires special training and equipment. Have the vehicle diagnosed by a dealership service department or other qualified automotive repair facility.*

1   The power door lock system operates the door lock actuators mounted in each door. Diagnosis can usually be limited to simple checks of the wiring connections and actuators for minor faults that can be easily repaired.

2   Power door lock systems are operated by bi-directional solenoids which are part of the door latch. The lock switches have two operating positions: Lock and Unlock.

3   If you are unable to locate the trouble using the following general steps, consult your dealer service department or qualified independent repair facility.

4   Always check the circuit protection first. Some vehicles use a combination of circuit breakers and fuses. Refer to the wiring diagrams in this Chapter.

5   If all but one lock solenoids operates, remove the trim panel from the affected door (see Chapter 11). Using the wiring diagram, locate the positive voltage wire/connection that leads to the lock actuator and check for voltage while operating the lock. The lock actuator is an integral part of the door latch.

6   If the inoperative solenoid is receiving voltage, replace the solenoid or latch assembly.

7   If the inoperative solenoid isn't receiving voltage, check for an open or short in the wire between the lock solenoid and the instrument cluster.

8   If the above tests do not pinpoint the problem, take the vehicle to a qualified dealership repair facility or qualified independent shop with the correct scanning equipment for proper testing and repair.

Keyless entry system

9   The keyless entry system consists of a remote control transmitter that sends a coded infrared signal to a receiver, which then operates the door lock system.

10   Replace the battery when the transmitter doesn't operate the locks at a distance of ten feet. Normal range should be about 30 feet.

Key remote control battery replacement

Note: *The key remote control replacement battery is a CR2032 battery*

11   Use the tip of the emergency key, a plastic trim tool or coin to carefully separate the case halves (see illustration).

Caution: *Do not touch the battery terminals that are on the back of the transmitter housing or the printed circuit board. The transmitter contains "perchlorate material" that may require special handling for disposal. See www.dtsc.ca.gov/hazardouswaste/perchlorate for more information.*

12   Replace the battery. The battery number is Panasonic CR 2016 or equivalent (see illustration).

13   Snap the case halves together.

Note: *A good battery should have a 66 foot range from the vehicle. If equipped with a factory remote start system the range is increased to about 300 feet. The exact range depends on a lot of factors such as the location of obstructions, interfering radio frequencies, and high voltage power lines.*

Transmitter programming

14   Programming replacement transmitters requires the use of a specialized scan tool. Take the vehicle and the transmitter(s) to a dealer service department or other qualified repair shop equipped with the necessary tool to have the transmitter(s) programmed to the vehicle.

24 Daytime Running Lights (DRL) - general information

1   The Daytime Running Lights (DRL) system, which is required on new Canadian models and an option on models made for the United States, illuminates the headlights when the engine is running. The DRL system supplies reduced power to the headlights so they won't be too bright for daytime use, which also prolongs headlight life.

25 Power seats - general information and procedures

1   The power seat receives its voltage from a fuse in the Totally Integrated Power Module (TIPM) located in the engine compartment. The power seats can be operated in six different directions, not including the recliner (the recliner is on its own switch, incorporated with the seat switch).

Power seat system check

2   If the power seat fails to function properly, follow these test procedures:

3   Check under the seat for any obstructions or anything that might have pulled the electrical connections apart. Secure all electrical connections. If the connections are good and the seat still does not move, go to the next Step.

4   With engine off (to reduce noise level), operate seat controls in all directions and listen for any sounds coming from the seat motors.

5   A grinding sound when the motor is on indicates either a broken gear (usually plastic gears) or the cable between the motor and the seat transmission (if applicable) has stripped. If you do not hear any noise or motor movement, this could mean there is no voltage/ground to the motor assembly, or the motor/seat transmission assembly has frozen. A quick check is to leave a door open and watch the interior lights as you operate the switch. If the lights dim as you move the lever, but the seat fails to move, chances are it is stuck in that position for some reason.

6   Check the power seat fuse in the TIPM. If the fuse is good, proceed to the next Step.

7   Remove the power seat switch, and check for positive and negative signals on their respective terminals (following the appropriate wiring diagram). If switch is OK, check the leads between the switch and motor assembly. If the wires are OK and no signal is leaving the switch when moved to the appropriate position, replace it with a known good switch and recheck. If voltage is leaving the switch, wire connectors and harness are good, the track assembly will need to be replaced.

Track assembly replacement

8   Remove the driver's seat from the vehicle (see Chapter 11).

9   Remove the seat side trim and the fasteners securing the cushion to the track assembly. Remove all wiring harness connections and leads from the track assembly. Remove the seat back and the track assembly. Transfer any components that are going to be reused to the new seat.

10   Installation is the reverse of removal.

Power seat switch replacement

11   Disconnect the cable from the negative battery terminal (see Chapter 5), and isolate it from touching the terminal.

12   Remove the side cushion side shields. Disconnect the electrical connections. Using a small flat screwdriver, gently pry the four mounting tabs that secure the seat switch to the side shield.

13   Snap the switch onto the side shield. The remainder of installation is the reverse of removal.

Heated seat system - general information and procedures

Note: *It is recommended to also replace the Occupant Detection Sensor (ODS) when replacing the seat heater element(s).*

14   The seat heater circuit receives its power from a fuse in the TIPM mounted in the engine compartment. The system is designed to operate only with the key on. The seat heater system is controlled by the seat heater module mounted below the driver's seat. When the seat heater switch is depressed, a data message is sent via the LIN (Local Interface Network) to the instrument cluster (CCN - Cab Compartment Node). This message is then transferred to the seat heater modules. The module sends positive voltage from an internal solid state relay to the seat heater elements.

15   Both the seat heater module and the carbon fiber seat heater elements can be serviced by removing the seat. The seat heater module is bolted to the bottom of the lower cushion. To access the seat heater elements, the seat must be removed and the seat cushions must be disassembled. The elements can be peeled from the seat cushion and replaced separately, rather than having to replace the entire seat and/or cushions.

26 Airbag system - general information and precautions

Warning: *Before performing work near any airbag system components, disconnect the cable from the negative battery terminal (see Chapter 5), then wait at least two minutes for the back-up power supply to be depleted. Back-up power is supplied by a capacitor that takes about two minutes to fully discharge. During this two-minute interval, the SRS is still capable of deploying.*

General information

1   All models are equipped with a frontal-impact airbag system, which is referred to as the Supplemental Restraint System (SRS). The SRS is designed to protect the driver and the front seat passenger from serious injury in the event of a head-on or frontal collision. The SRS is controlled by the Occupant Restraint Controller (ORC), also referred to as the Airbag Control Module (ACM), which is mounted in the center of the vehicle, on the floor transmission tunnel, below the center of the instrument panel. The SRS uses an array of airbags to protect the front-seat occupants (and on models equipped with side curtain airbags, the rear seat passengers, too): the driver's airbag in the steering wheel; the passenger airbag, which is located in the right end of the instrument panel, beneath the instrument panel top pad and above the glove box; and, on models so equipped, the side curtain airbags, which are located above the side windows, in the outer edges of the headliner, between the A- and C-pillars. The SRS is activated by a pair of front impact sensors located on the front of the frame, just behind the bumper attachments. Other important components in the SRS include the clockspring (a wind-up coil that delivers battery voltage to the steering wheel airbag), and the AIRBAG readiness light on the instrument cluster.

2   In addition to the airbags, seat belt pretensioners are incorporated into the front seat belt retractor mechanisms. These are pyrotechnic (explosive) devices which retract the seat belts up to four inches when the airbag system is activated.

Driver's airbag

3   The airbag inflator module contains a housing incorporating the cushion (airbag) and inflator unit, mounted in the center of the steering wheel. The inflator assembly is mounted on the back of the housing over a hole through which gas is expelled, inflating the bag almost instantaneously when an electrical signal is sent from the system. The clockspring assembly on the steering column under the steering wheel carries this signal to the module. The clockspring assembly can transmit an electrical signal regardless of steering wheel position. The igniter in the airbag converts the electrical signal to heat and ignites the powder, which inflates the bag.

Passenger's airbag

4   The airbag is mounted in the right end of the instrument panel, beneath the instrument panel top pad and above the glove box. It consists of an inflator containing an igniter, a bag assembly, a reaction housing and a trim cover. The passenger airbag is considerably larger than the steering wheel-mounted unit and is supported by the steel reaction housing. The trim cover is textured and painted to match the instrument panel and has a molded seam that splits when the bag inflates.

Side-impact window airbags

5   Optional side-impact window airbags protect vehicle occupants in the event of a side impact. The side-impact window airbags are located above the windows, between the A- and C-pillars. If you're not sure whether your vehicle is equipped with side-impact window airbags, look for the words "SRS AIR-BAG" imprinted on a small identification trim button located above the B-and C-pillars.

6   Vehicles equipped with side-impact window airbags use six side-impact sensors: three on the left side of the vehicle and three on the right side. The front row side-impact sensors are located inside the B-pillars, above the front seatbelt retractors. The second-row side-impact sensors are located in the sliding door track openings, just ahead of the C-pillars. The third-row sensors are located behind the quarter-trim panels, between the C- and D-pillars, above the rear wheelwells.

Seat airbags

7   These airbags may be optional equipment on some models. They are located in the outside of the front seat backs.

Seat belt pre-tensioners

8   Some models are equipped with pyrotechnic (explosive) units in the front seat belt retracting mechanisms. During an impact that would trigger the airbag system, the airbag control unit also triggers the seat belt retractors. When the pyrotechnic charges go off, they accelerate the retractors to instantly take up any slack in the seat belt system to more fully prepare the driver and front seat passenger for impact.

9   The airbag system should be disabled any time work is done to or around the seats. **Warning:** *Never strike the pillars or floorpan with a hammer or use an impact-driver tool in these areas unless the system is disabled.*

Occupant Restraint Controller (ORC) or Airbag Control Module (ACM)

10   The ORC or ACM supplies current to the SRS in the event of a collision, even if battery power is cut off. The ORC/ACM checks the SRS every time the vehicle is started, and indicates that it is doing so by turning on the AIRBAG readiness light. If the SRS is operating properly, the ORC/ACM turns off the AIR-BAG readiness light. If it detects a fault in the system, the AIRBAG readiness light will remain on. If this condition occurs, take the vehicle to your dealer immediately for service.

Disarming the system and other precautions

Warning: *Failure to follow these precautions could result in accidental deployment of the airbag and personal injury.*

11   Whenever you are working in the vicinity of the driver's airbag in the steering wheel or any of the other airbags on your vehicle, DISARM THE SYSTEM. To disarm the system:

a) *Point the wheels straight ahead and turn the ignition key to the Lock position.*
b) *Disconnect the cable from the negative battery terminal (see Chapter 5). Isolate the cable terminal so it won't accidentally contact the battery post.*
c) *Wait at least two minutes for the back-up power supply to be depleted. Back-up power is supplied by a capacitor that takes about two minutes to fully discharge. During this two-minute interval, the SRS is still capable of deploying.*

12   Whenever handling an airbag, always keep the airbag opening (the trim side) pointed away from your body. Never place the airbag on a bench or other surface with the airbag opening facing the surface. Always place the airbag module in a safe location with the airbag opening facing up. **Warning:** *Never measure the resistance of any SRS component. An ohmmeter has a built-in battery supply that could accidentally deploy the airbag.*

13   Never dispose of a live airbag. Return it to a dealer service department or other qualified repair shop for safe deployment and disposal.

Component removal and installation

Driver's airbag and clockspring

14   Refer to Section 7 for the clockspring removal and installation procedures.

15   Refer to Chapter 10, Section 18 for driver's air bag removal and installation procedures.

Passenger's airbag

16   Refer to Chapter 11, Section 22 for the removal of the upper instrument panel cover.

17   With the upper instrument panel cover removed from the vehicle, remove the airbag retaining fasteners and slide them off the airbag.

18   Installation is the reverse of removal.

Other airbag modules

19   We don't recommend removing any of the other airbag modules. These jobs are best left to a professional.

---

27   Wiring diagrams - general information

---

1   Since it isn't possible to include all wiring diagrams for every year covered by this manual, the following diagrams are those that are typical and most commonly needed.

2   Prior to troubleshooting any circuits, check the fuse and circuit breakers (if equipped) to make sure they're in good condition. Make sure the battery is properly charged and check the cable connections (see Chapter 1).

3   When checking a circuit, make sure that all connectors are clean, with no broken or loose terminals. When unplugging a connector, do not pull on the wires. Pull only on the connector housings themselves.

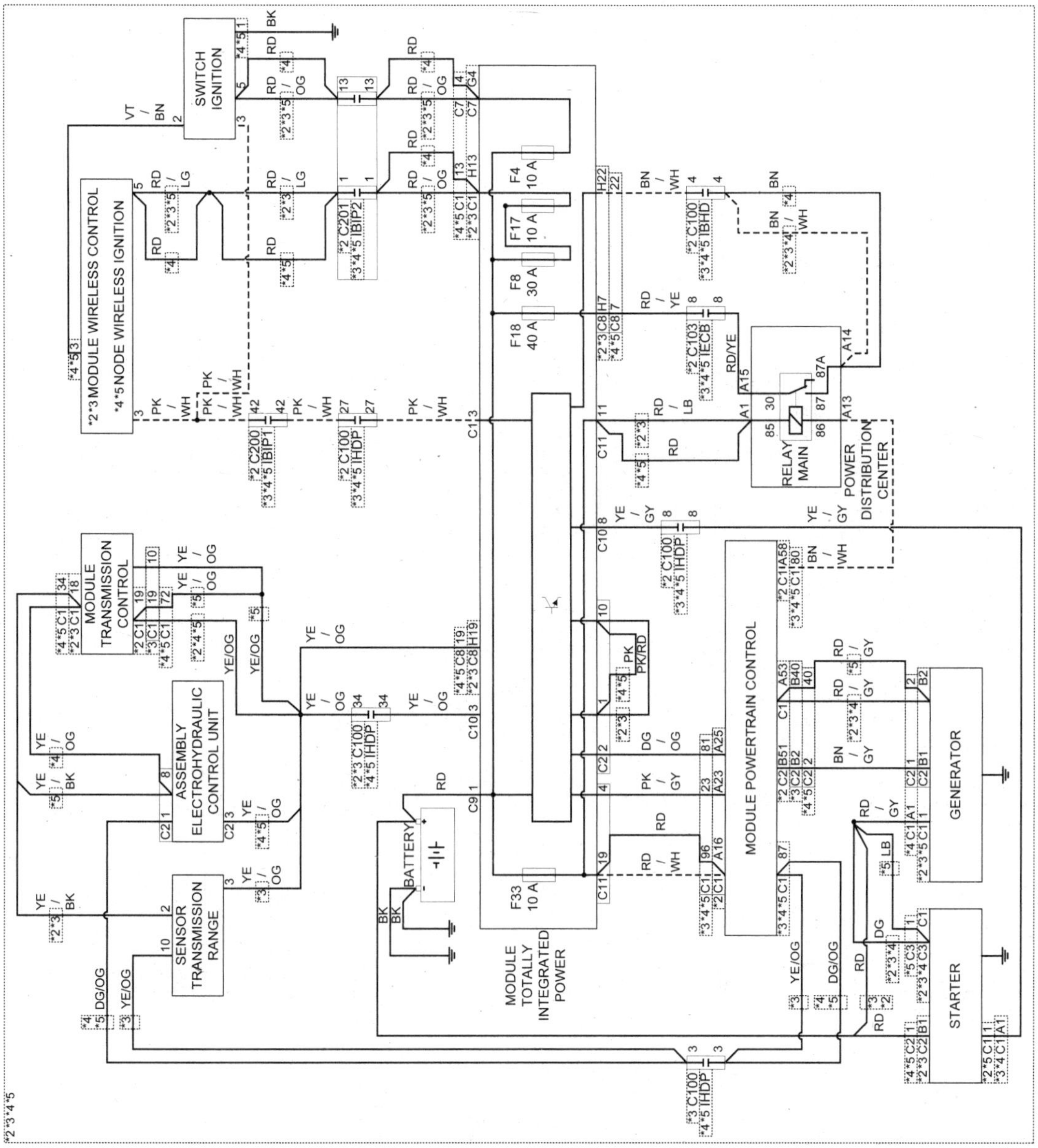

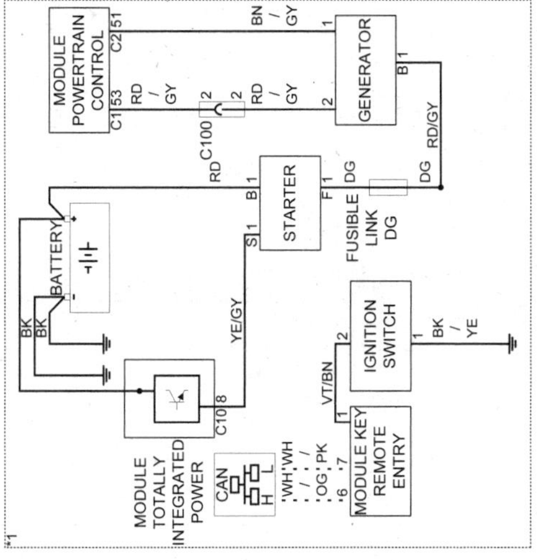

Starting and charging systems

*1 From 2007 to 2009
*2 From 2010 to 2013
*3 For 2014
*4 For 2015
*5 From 2016 to 2017

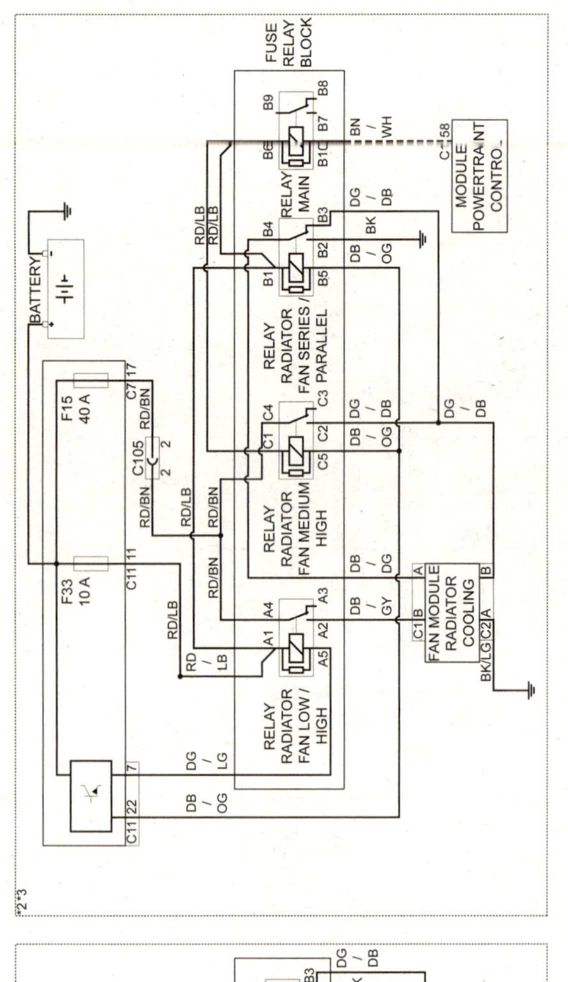

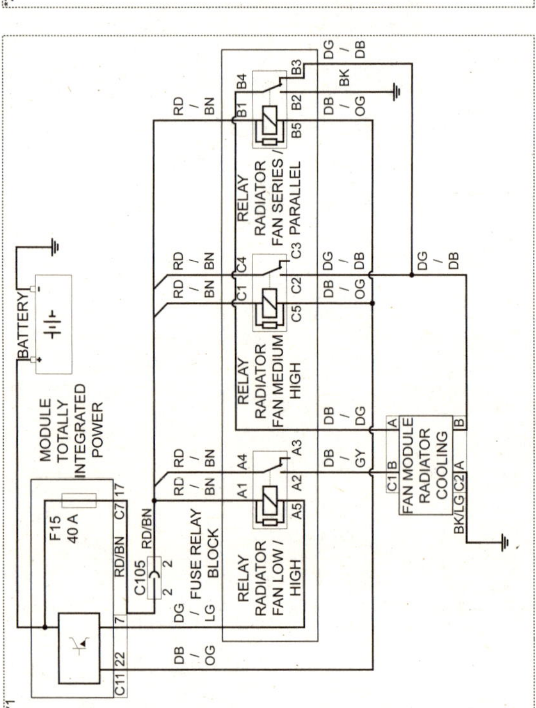

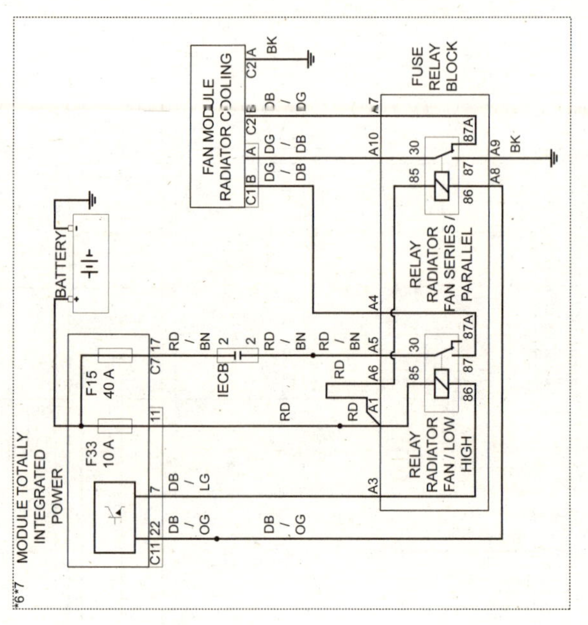

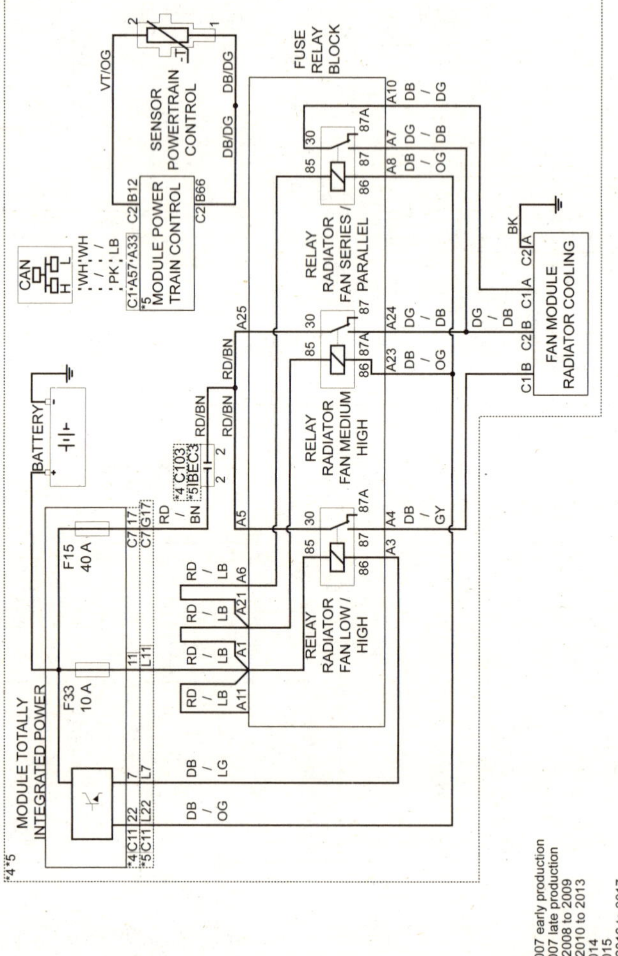

Engine cooling fan system

*1 For 2007 early production
*2 For 2007 late production
*3 From 2008 to 2009
*4 From 2010 to 2013
*5 For 2014
*6 For 2015
*7 From 2016 to 2017

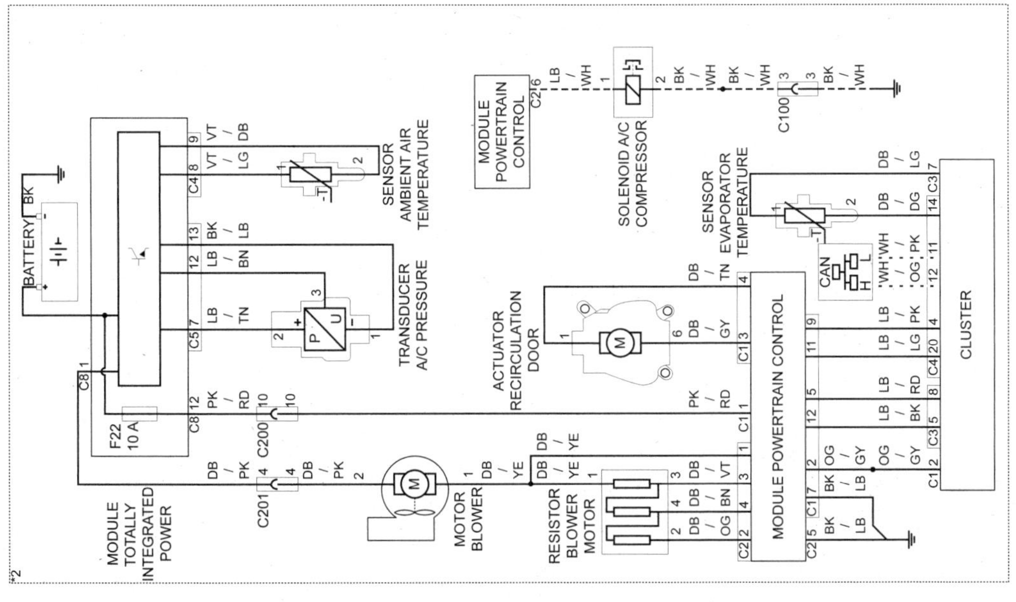

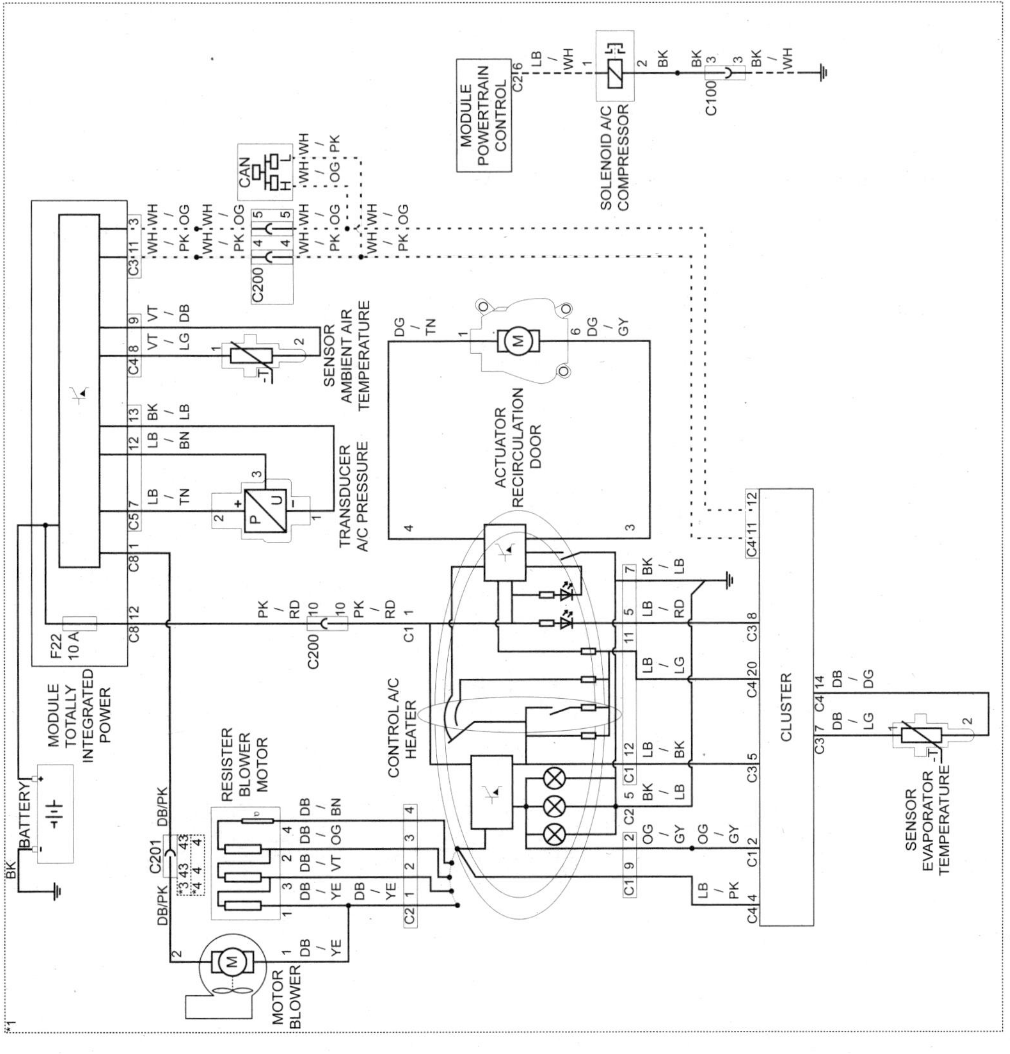

Heating and air conditioning systems - 2009 and earlier models

*1 For 2007
*2 From 2008 to 2009
*3 Early build
*4 Late build

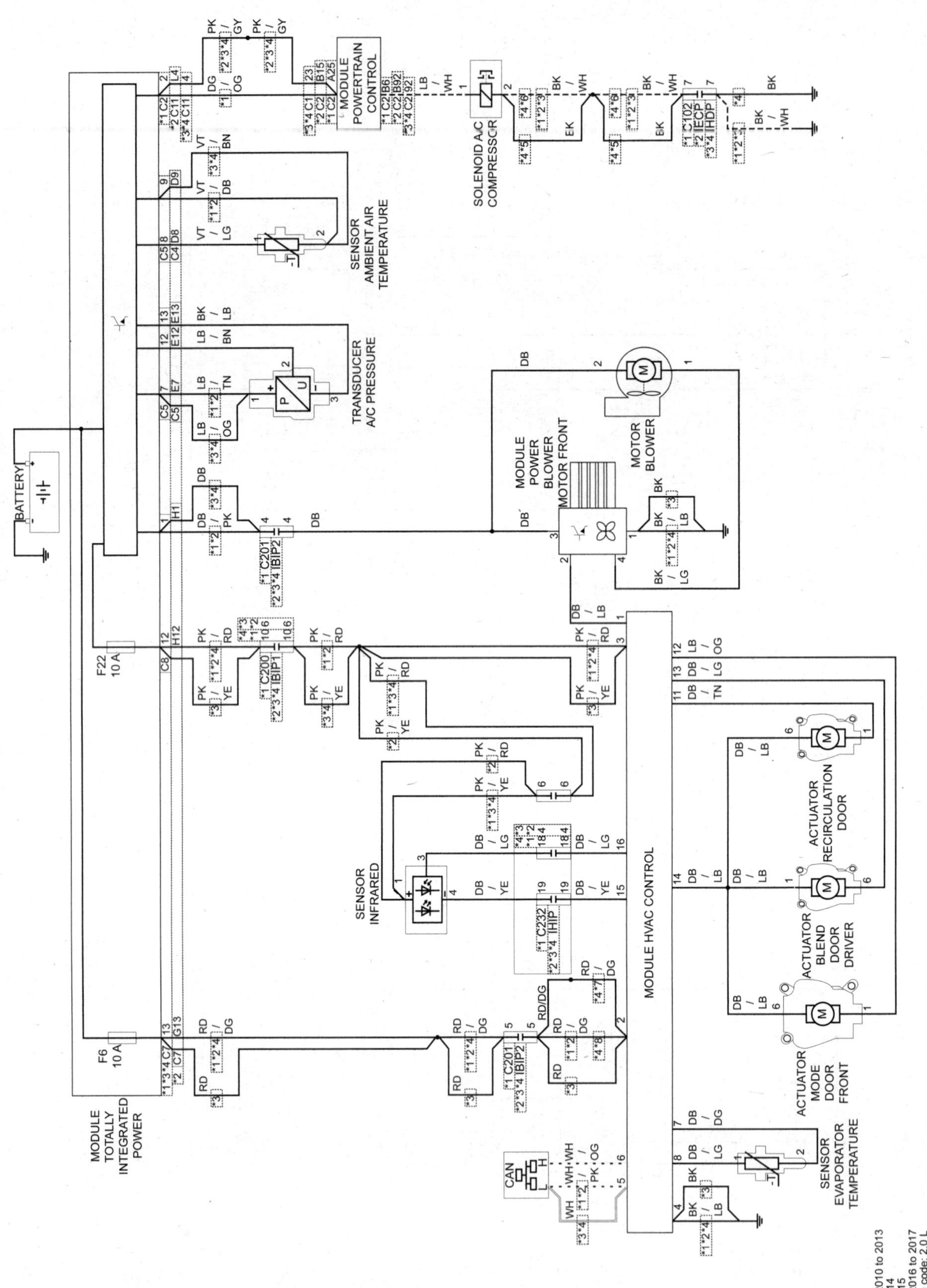

Heating and air conditioning systems - 2010 and later models

*1 From 2010 to 2013
*2 For 2014
*3 For 2015
*4 From 2016 to 2017
*5 Engine code: 2.0 L
*6 Engine code: 2.4 L
*7 With hands free
*8 Without hands free

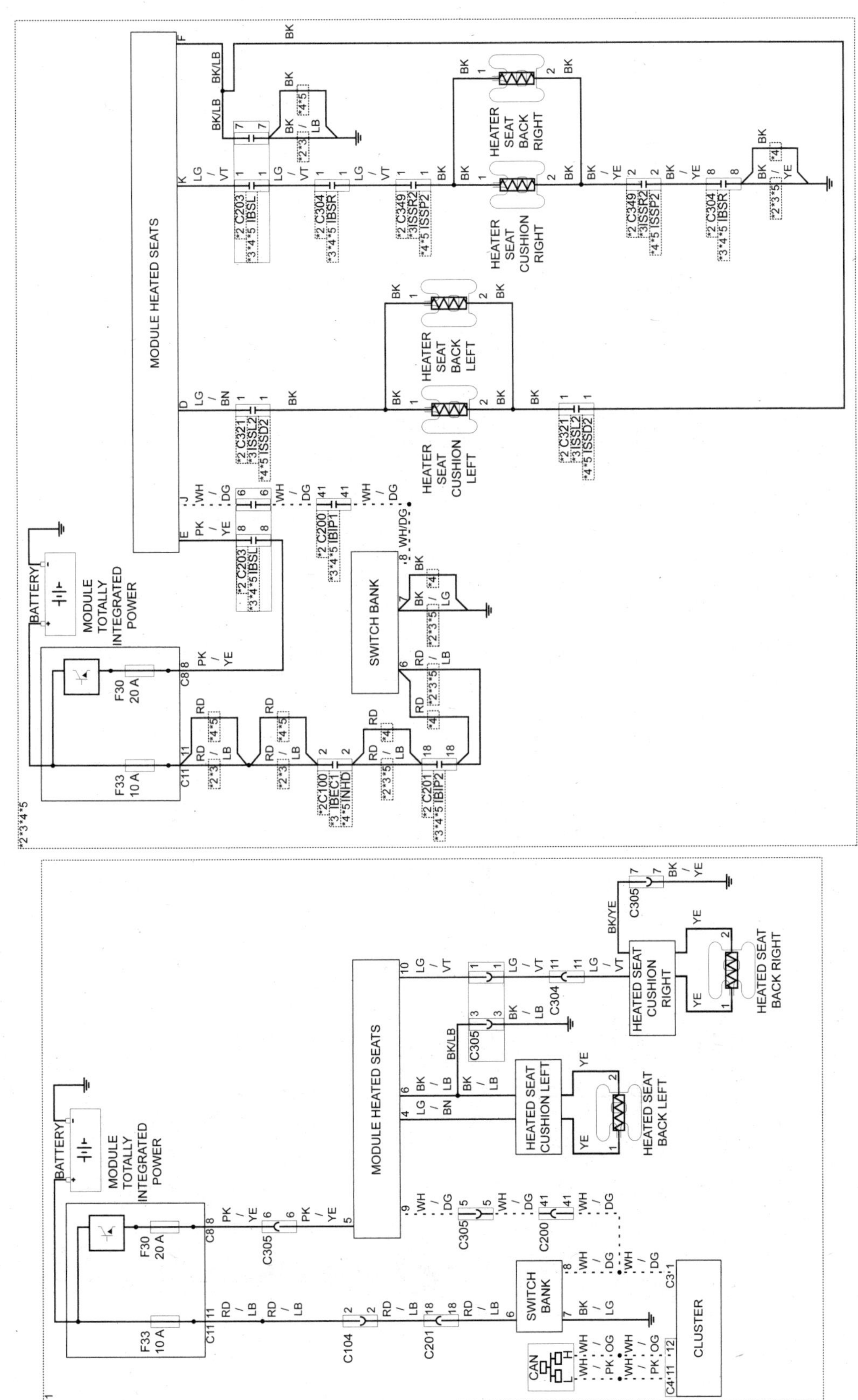

*1 From 2007 to 2009
*2 From 2010 to 2013
*3 For 2014
*4 For 2015
*5 From 2016 to 2017

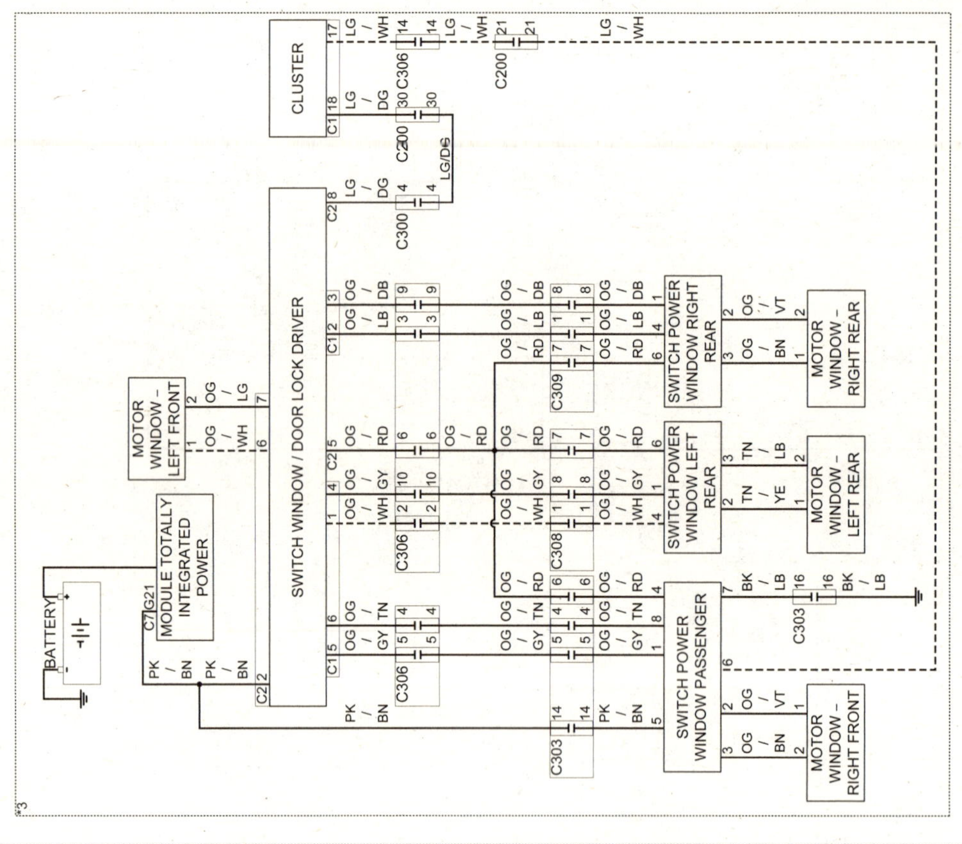

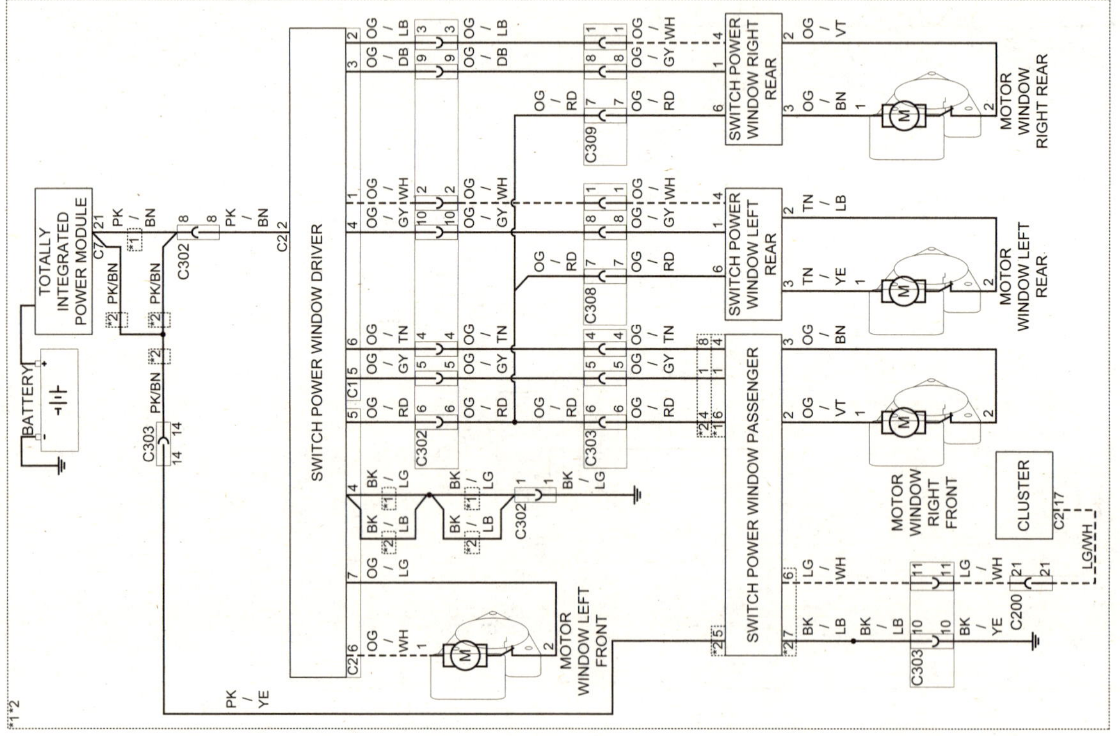

Power window system - 2013 and earlier models

*1 From 2007 to 2008
*2 For 2009
*3 For 2010 to 2013

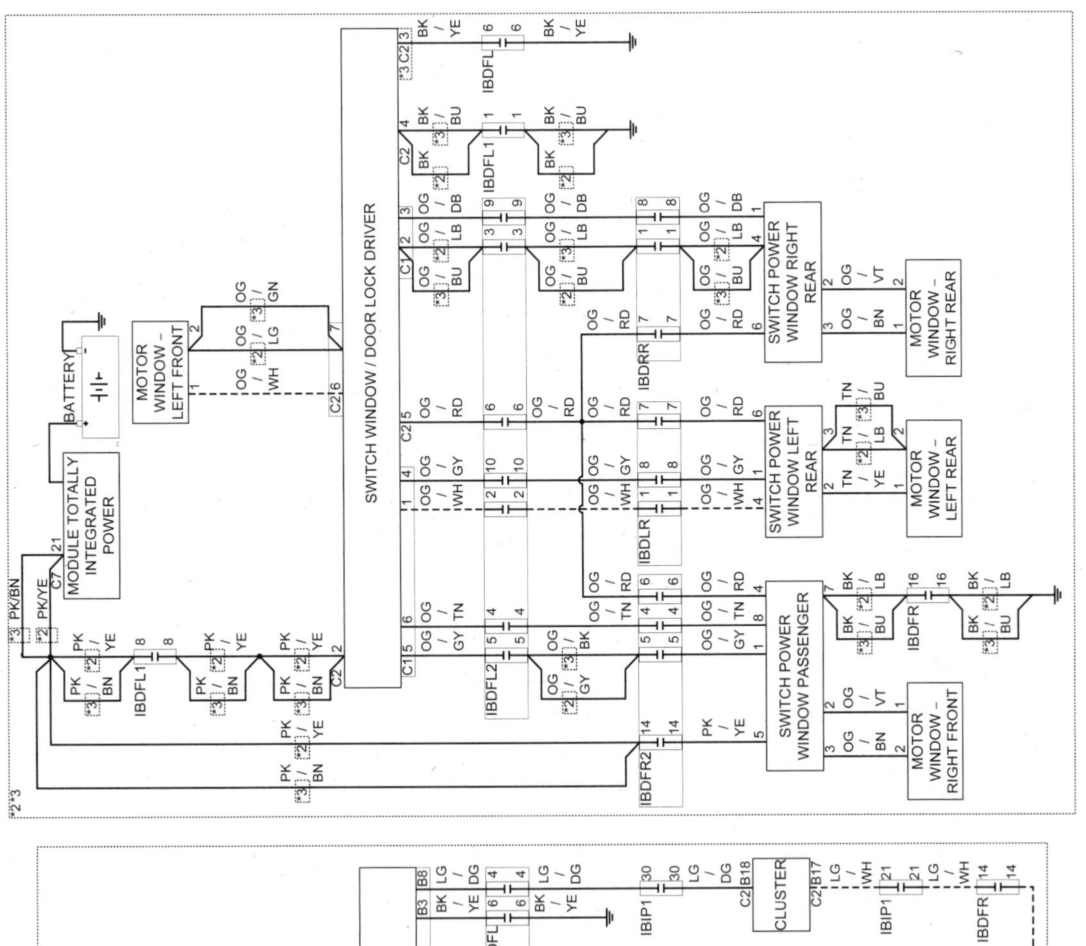

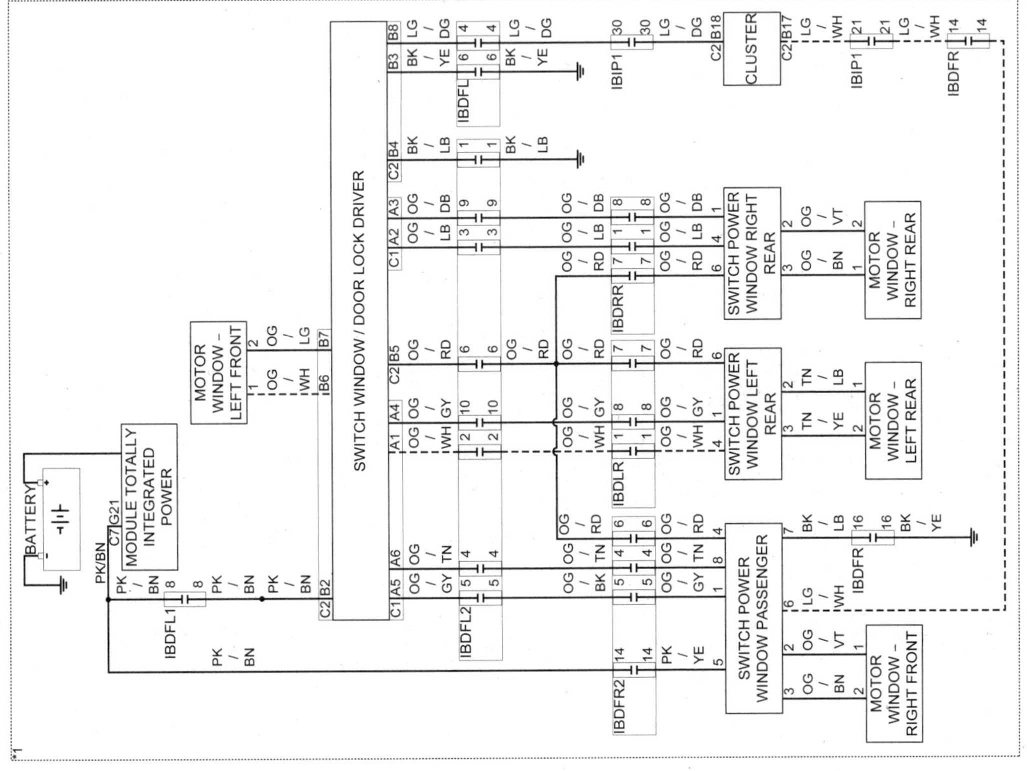

Power window system - 2014 and later models

*1 For 2014
*2 For 2015
*3 From 2016 to 2017

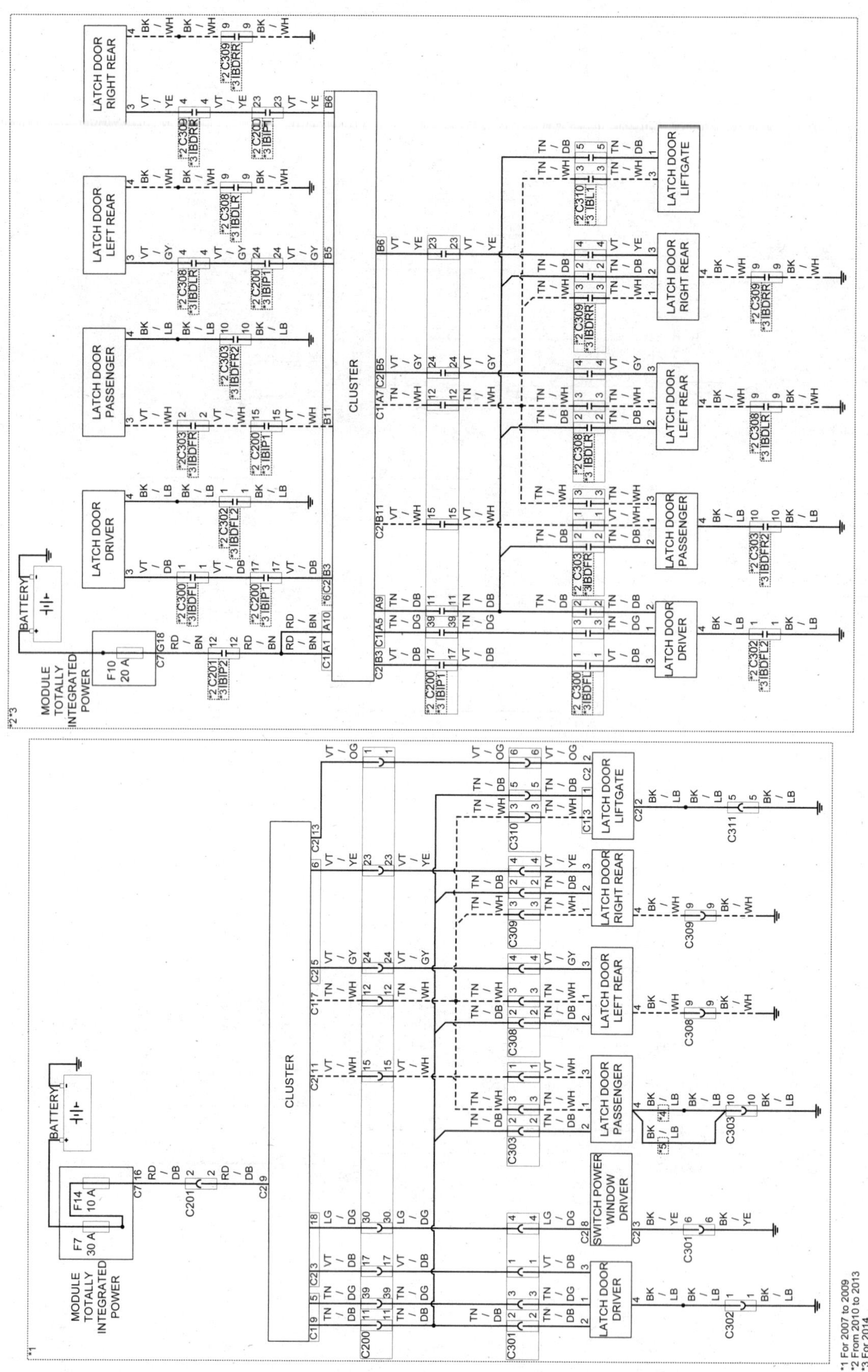

Power door lock system - 2014 and earlier models
*1 For 2007 to 2009
*2 From 2010 to 2013
*3 For 2014
*4 For heated mirrors
*5 Except heated mirrors
*6 Manual locks

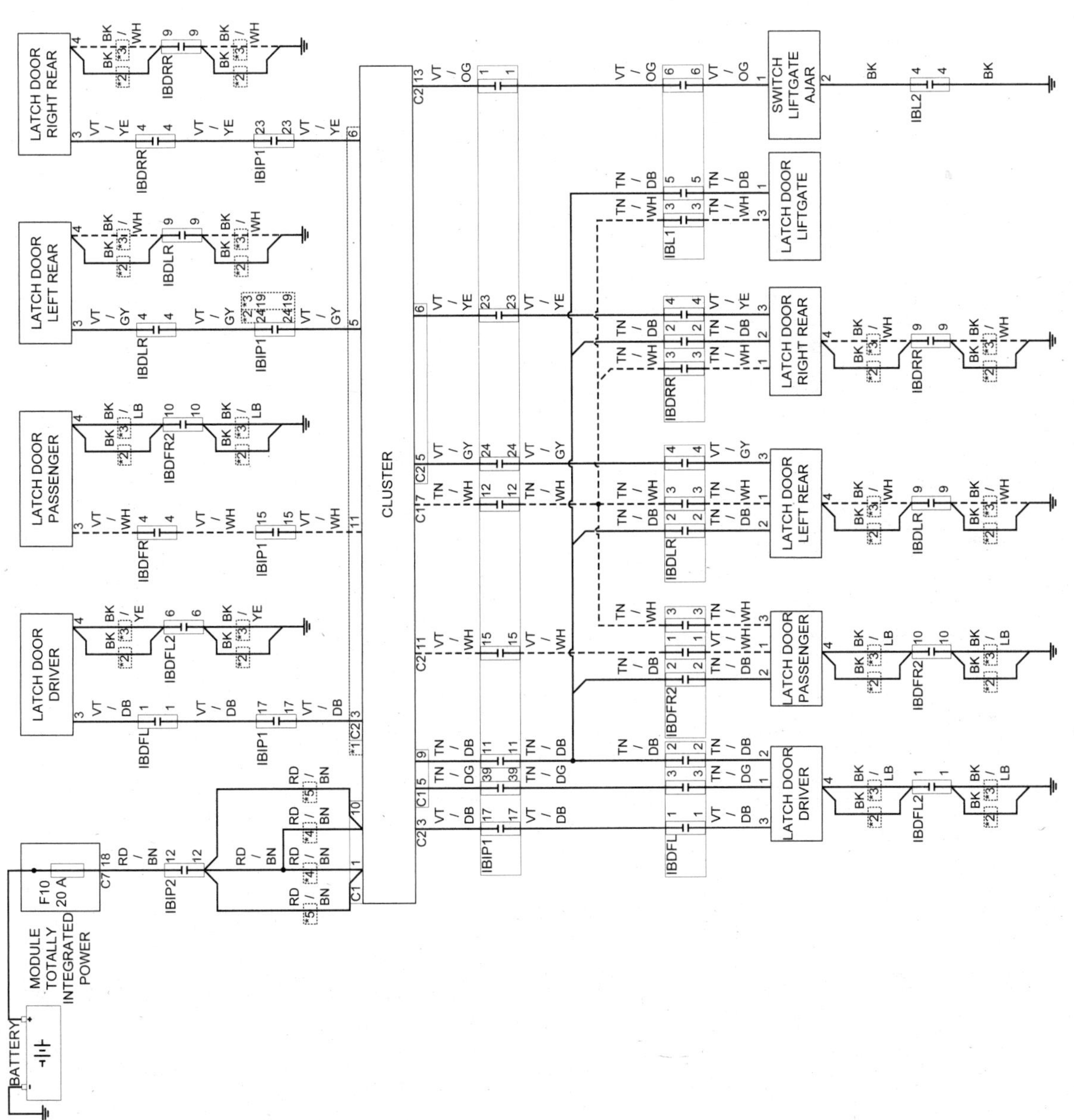

Power door lock system - 2015 and later models

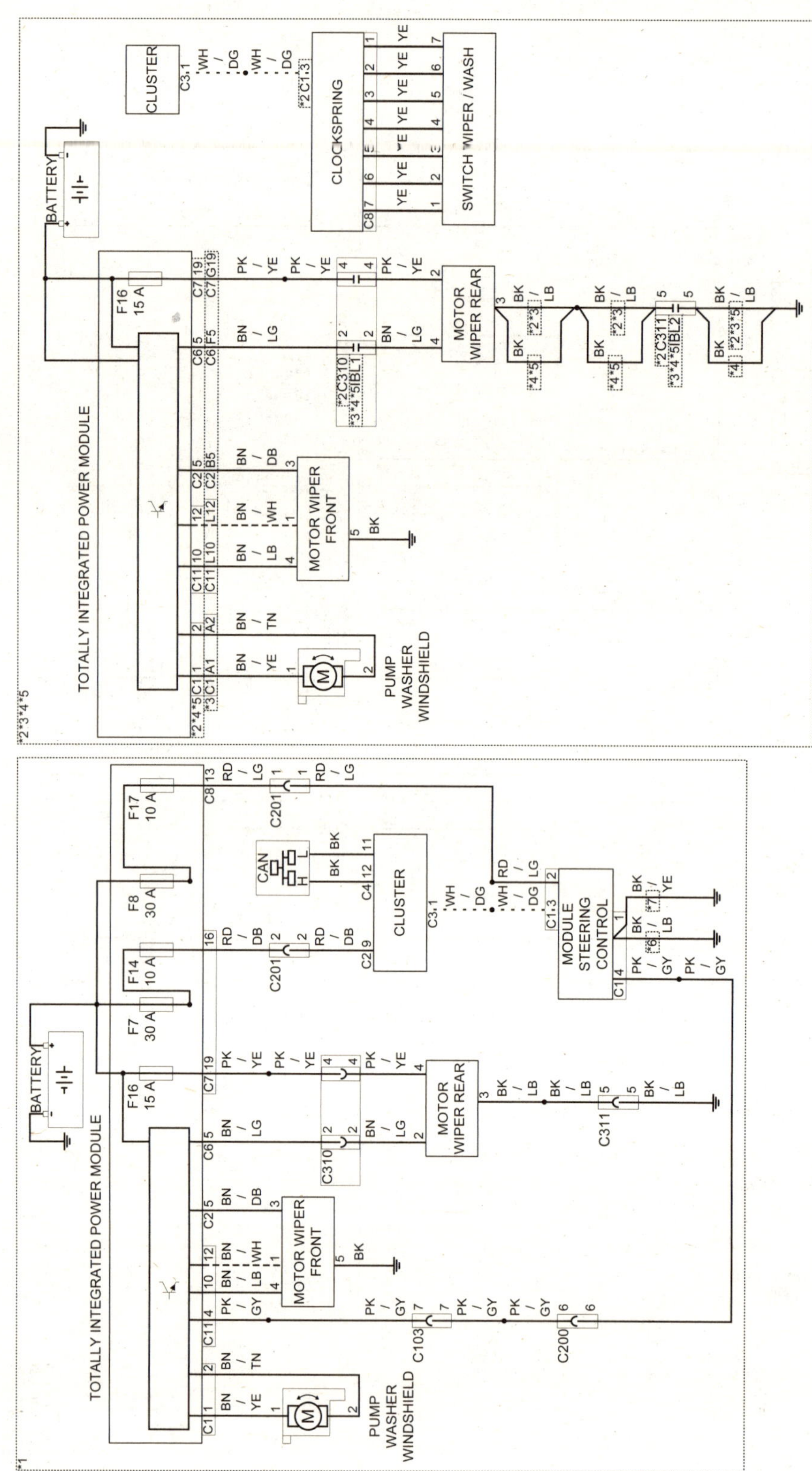

Windshield and rear wiper/washer systems

*1 From 2007 to 2009
*2 From 2010 to 2013
*3 For 2014
*4 For 2015
*5 From 2016 to 2017
*6 For base equipment
*7 Except base equipment

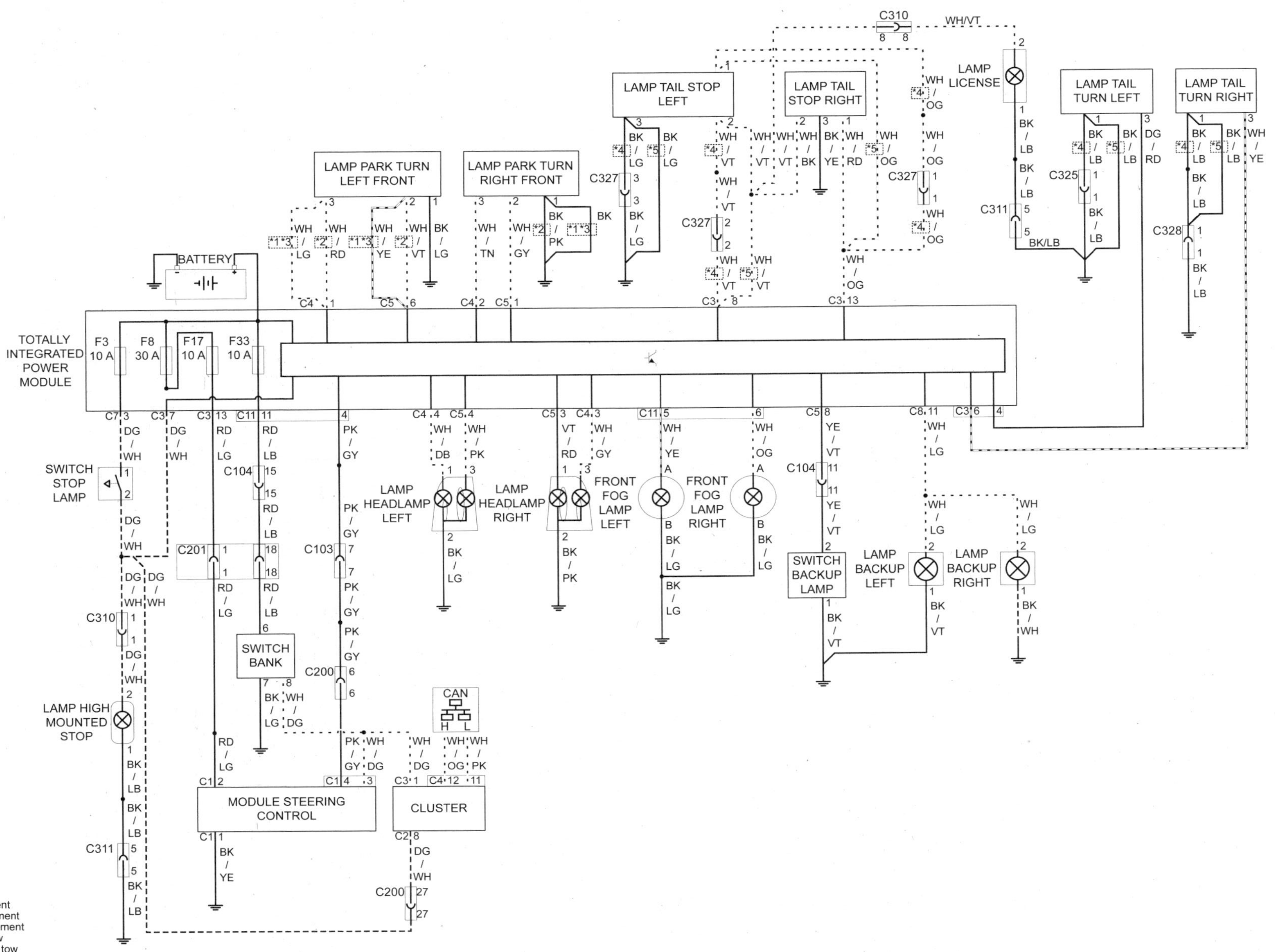

Exterior lighting system - 2009 and earlier models

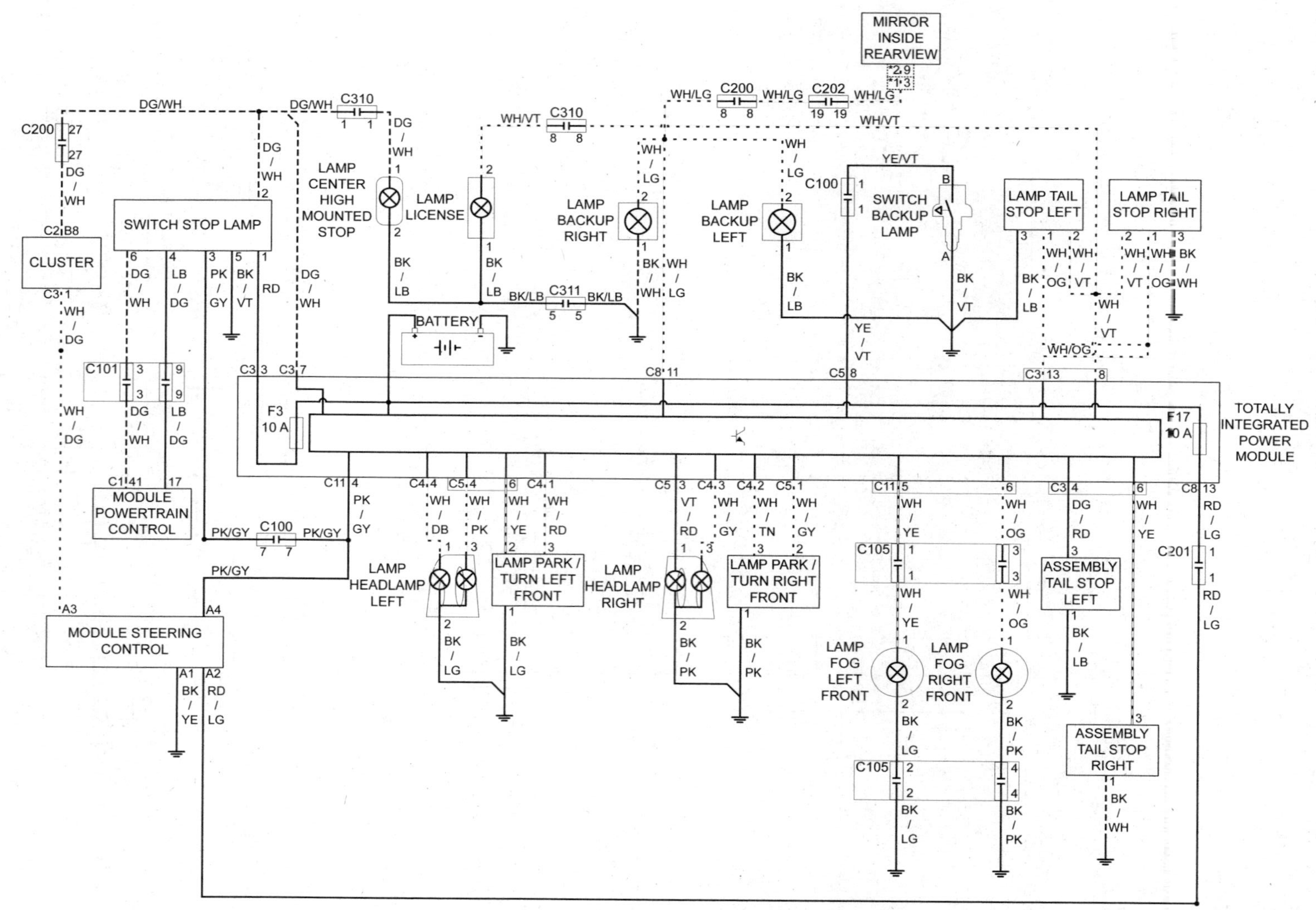

Exterior lighting system - 2010 through 2013 models

*1 Equipment code: base
*2 Equipment code: premium

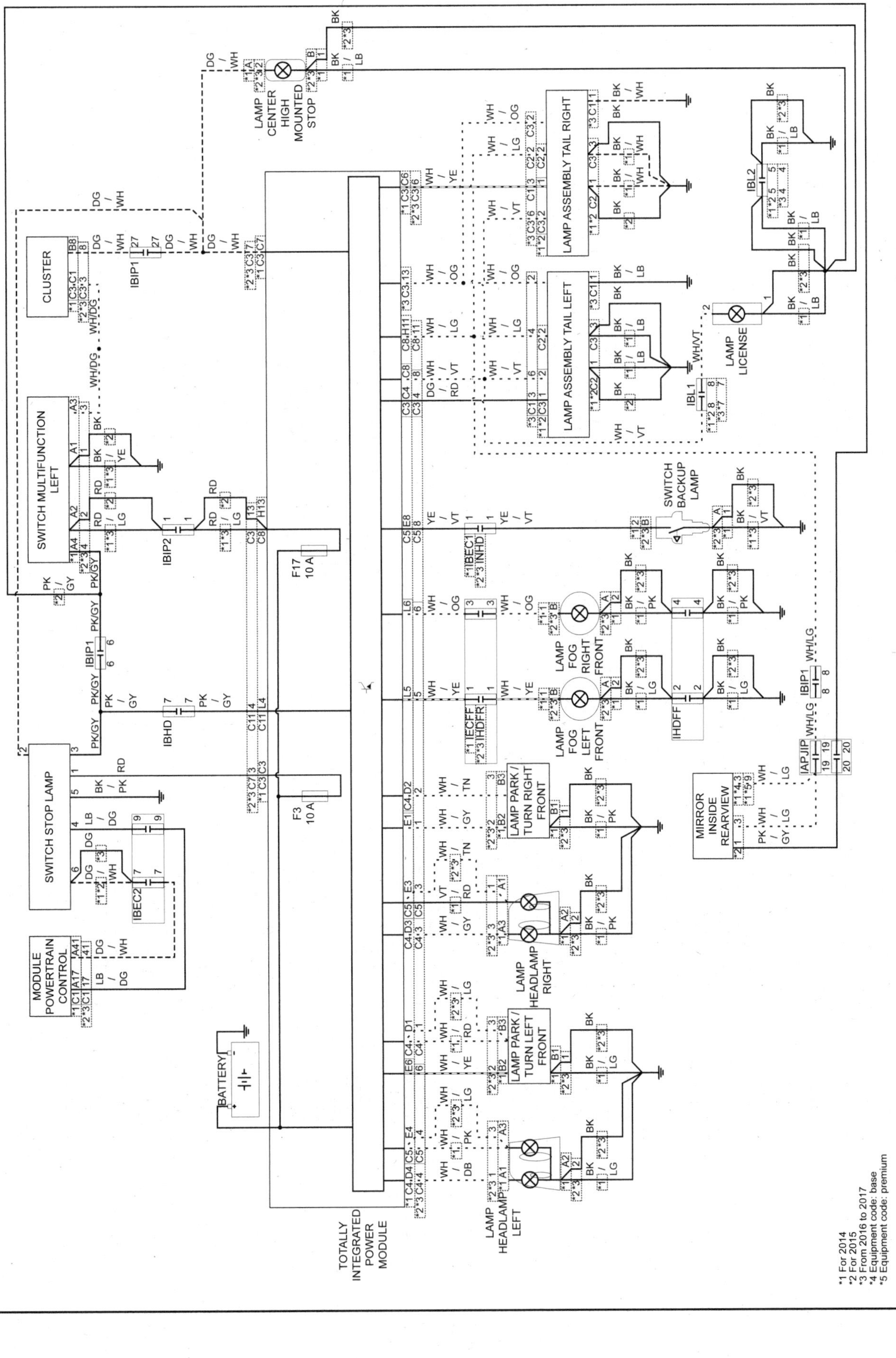

Exterior lighting system - 2014 and later models

*1 For 2014
*2 For 2015
*3 From 2016 to 2017
*4 Equipment code: base
*5 Equipment code: premium

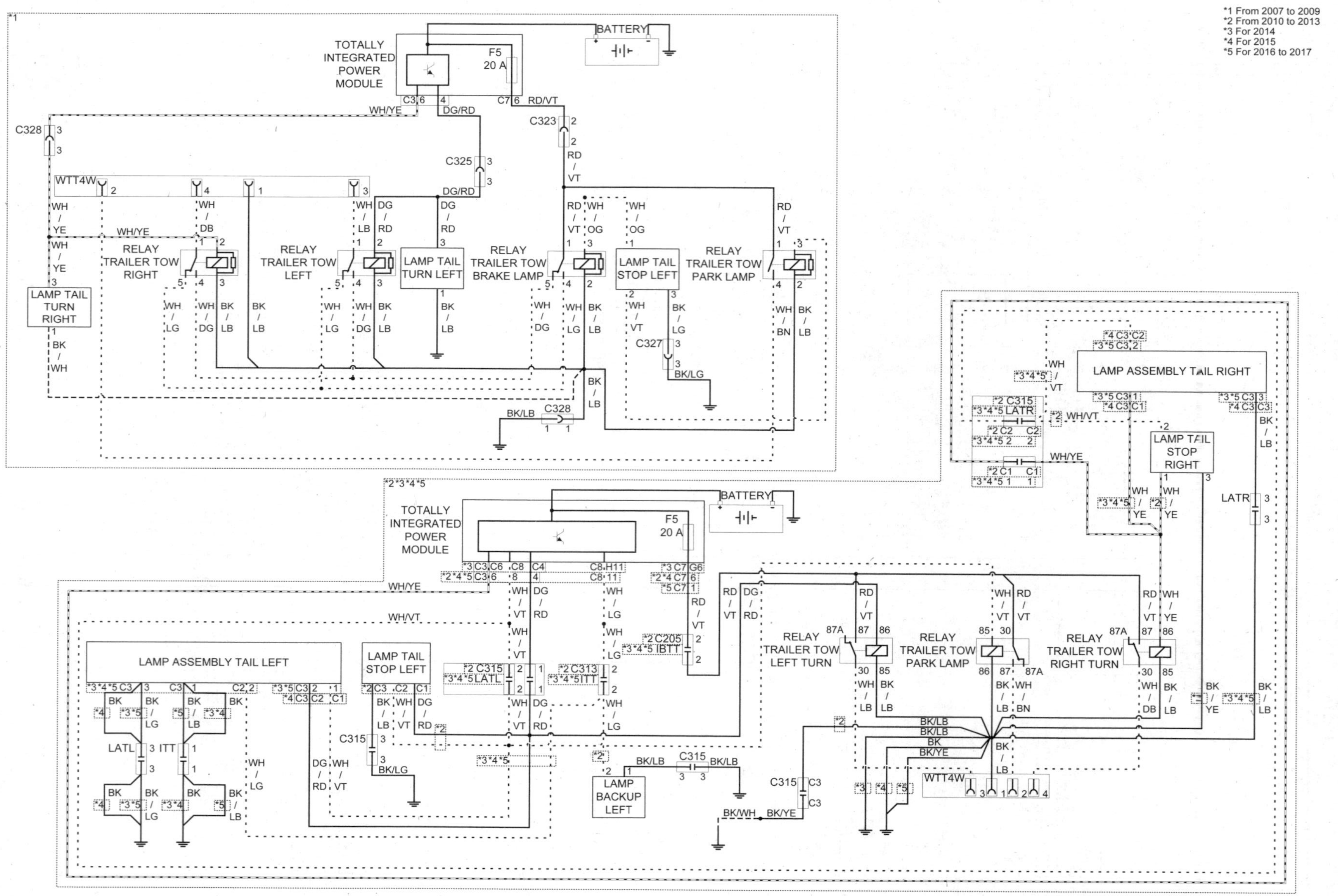

Exterior lighting system - trailer tow package

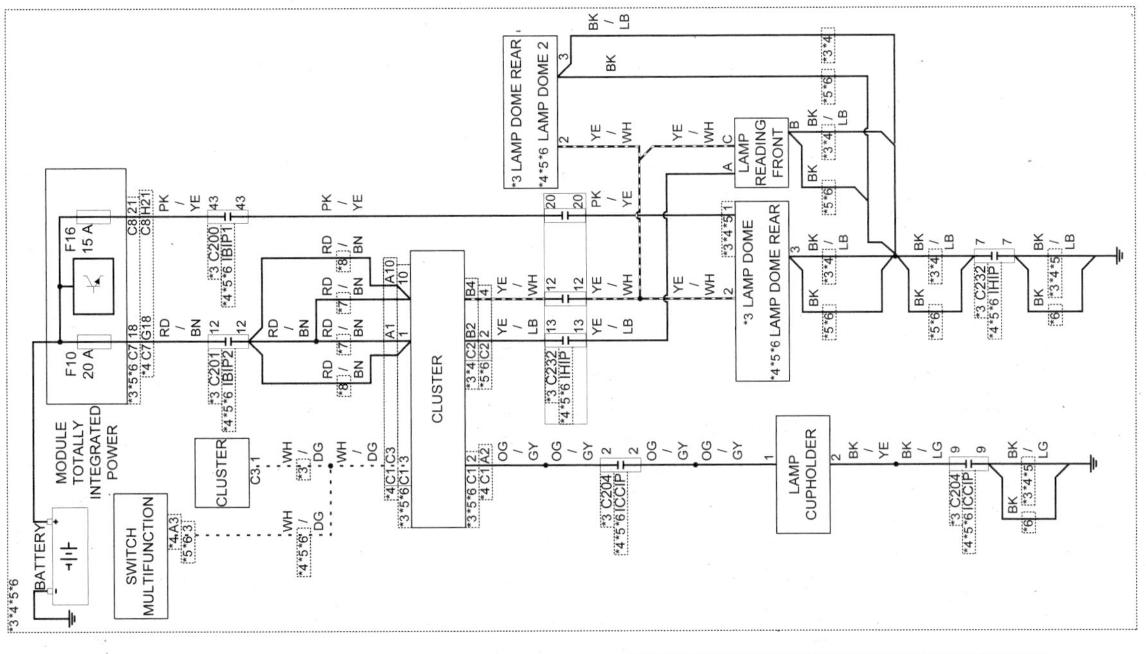

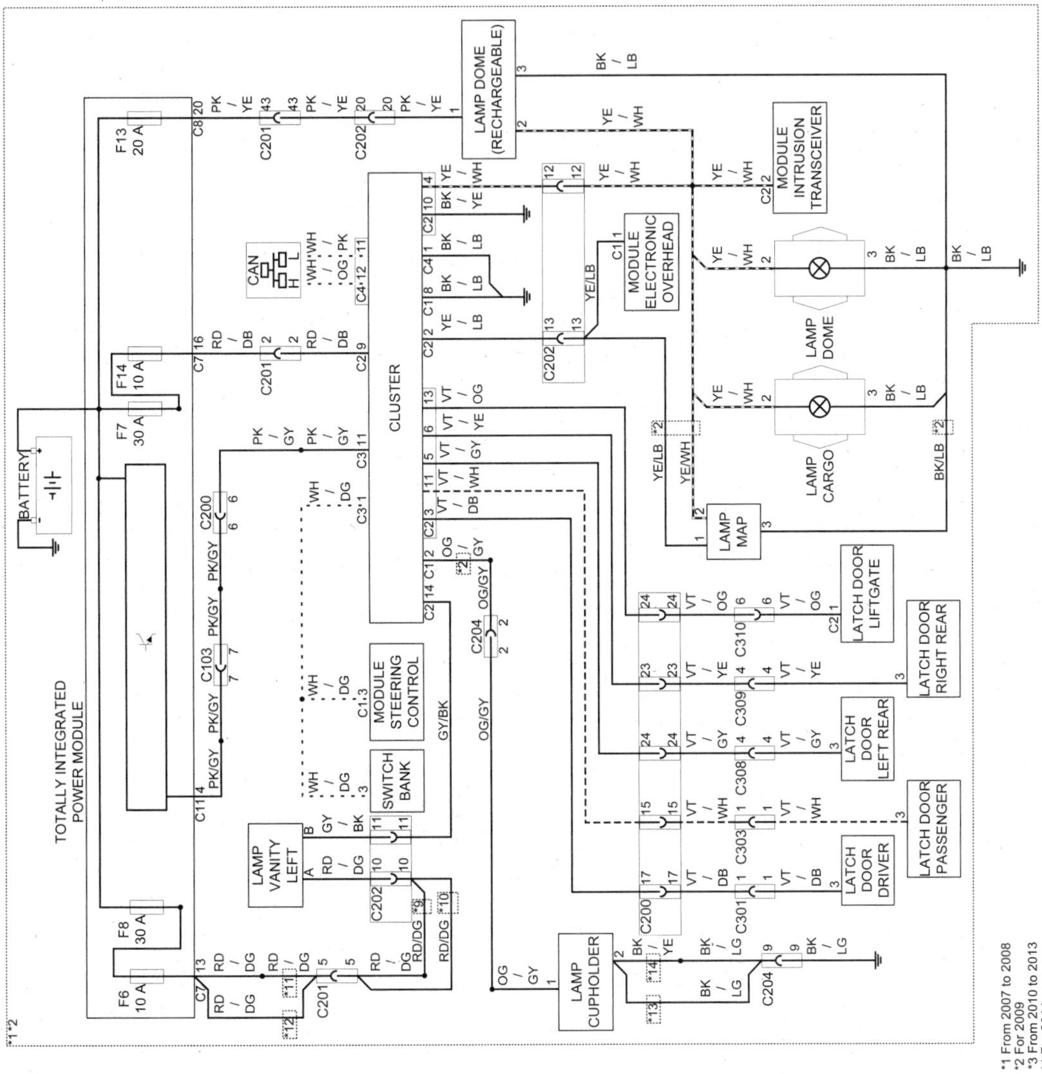

Interior lighting system
*1 From 2007 to 2008
*2 For 2009
*3 From 2010 to 2013
*4 For 2014
*5 For 2015
*6 From 2016 to 2017
*7 Early build
*8 Late build
*9 With hands free
*10 Without hands free
*11 Base equipment
*12 Except base equipment
*13 With AWD
*14 Without AWD

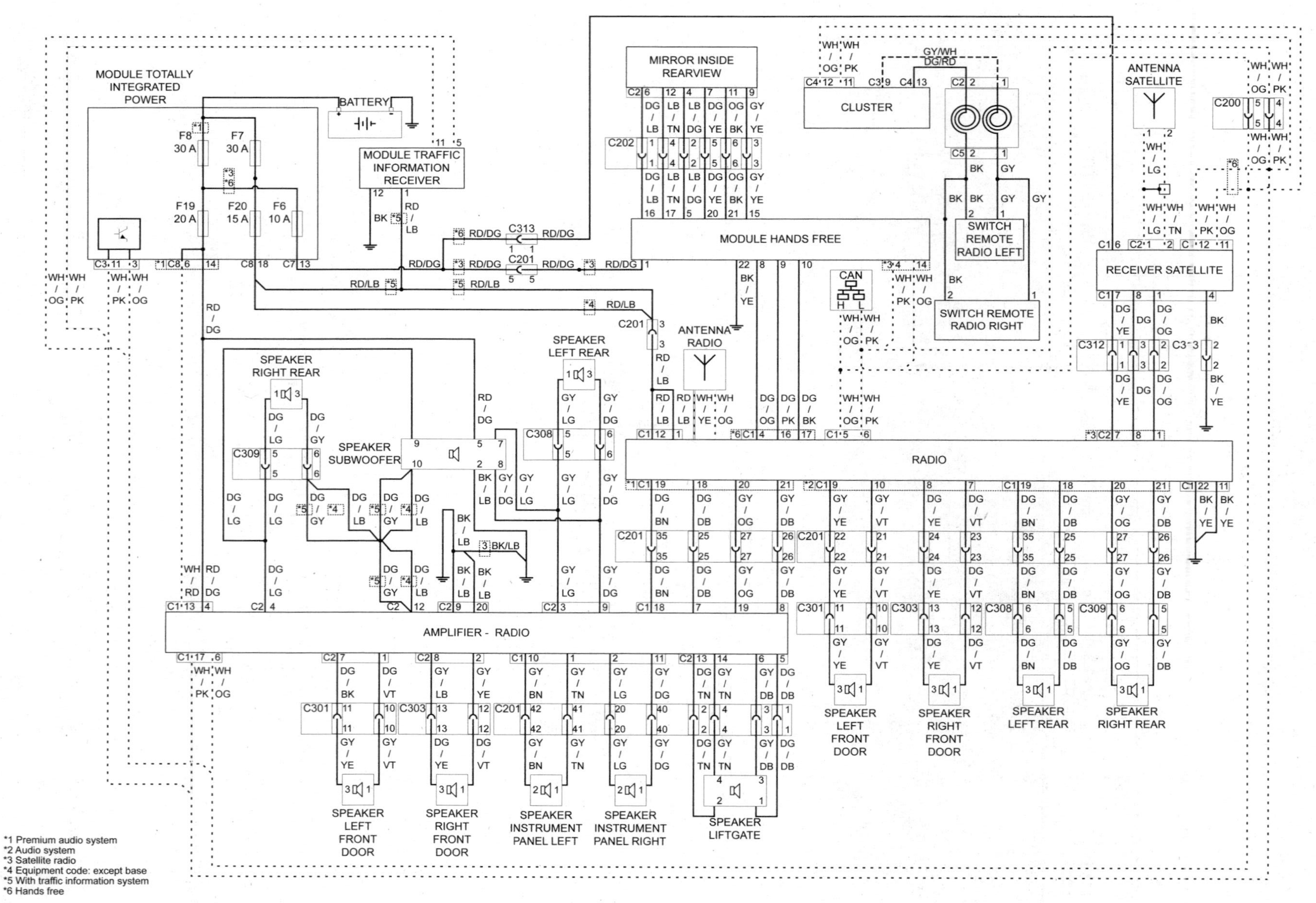

MODULE TOTALLY INTEGRATED POWER
BATTERY
F8 30 A
F7 30 A
F19 20 A
F20 15 A
F6 10 A
MODULE TRAFFIC INFORMATION RECEIVER
MIRROR INSIDE REARVIEW
CLUSTER
SWITCH REMOTE RADIO LEFT
SWITCH REMOTE RADIO RIGHT
ANTENNA SATELLITE
RECEIVER SATELLITE
MODULE HANDS FREE
CAN
ANTENNA RADIO
SPEAKER RIGHT REAR
SPEAKER LEFT REAR
SPEAKER SUBWOOFER
RADIO
AMPLIFIER - RADIO
SPEAKER LEFT FRONT DOOR
SPEAKER RIGHT FRONT DOOR
SPEAKER INSTRUMENT PANEL LEFT
SPEAKER INSTRUMENT PANEL RIGHT
SPEAKER LIFTGATE
SPEAKER LEFT FRONT DOOR
SPEAKER RIGHT FRONT DOOR
SPEAKER LEFT REAR
SPEAKER RIGHT REAR
*1 Premium audio system
*2 Audio system
*3 Satellite radio
*4 Equipment code: except base
*5 With traffic information system
*6 Hands free
Audio system - 2009 and earlier models

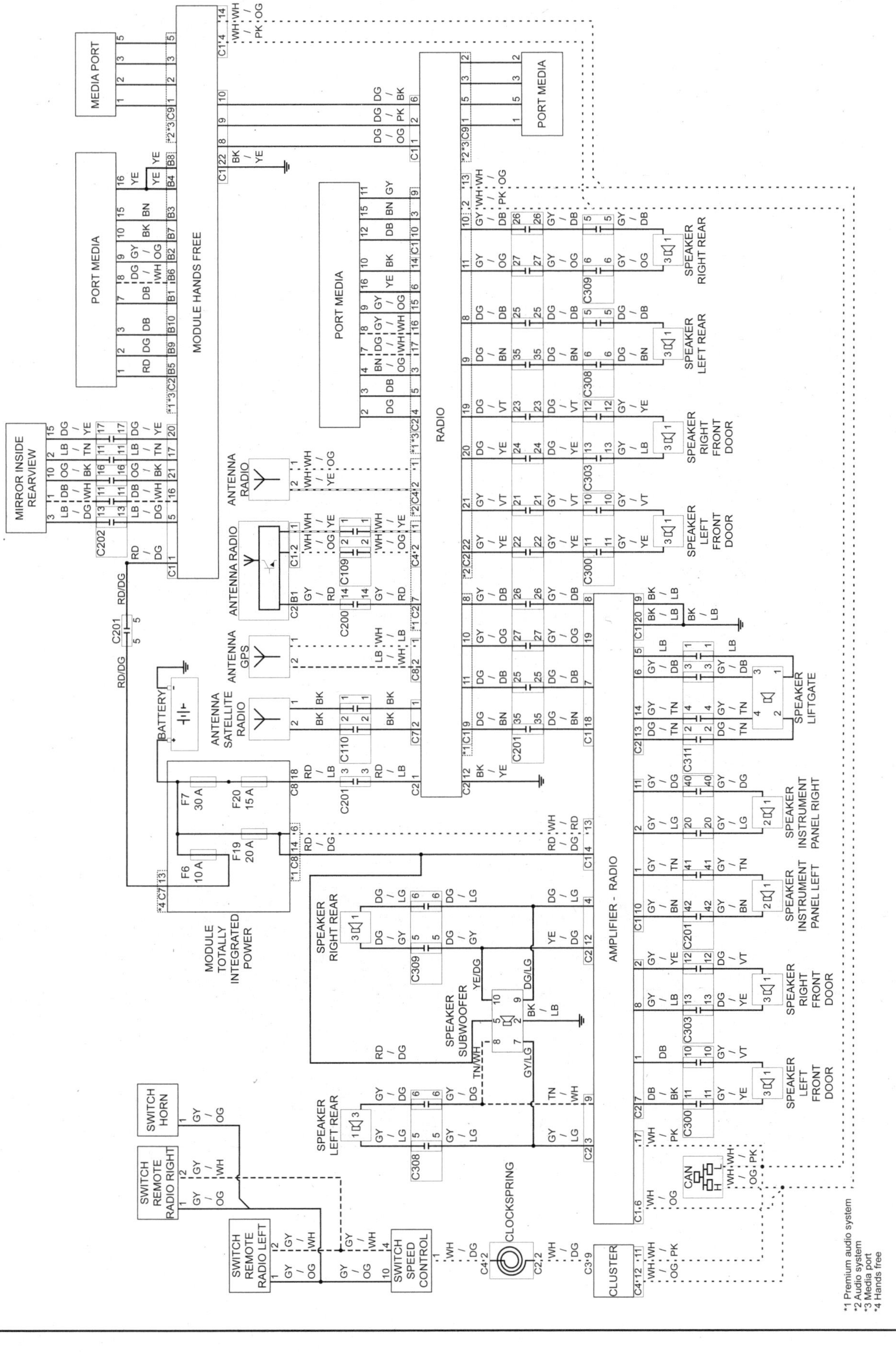

Audio system - 2010 through 2013 models

*1 Premium audio system
*2 Audio system
*3 Media port
*4 Hands free

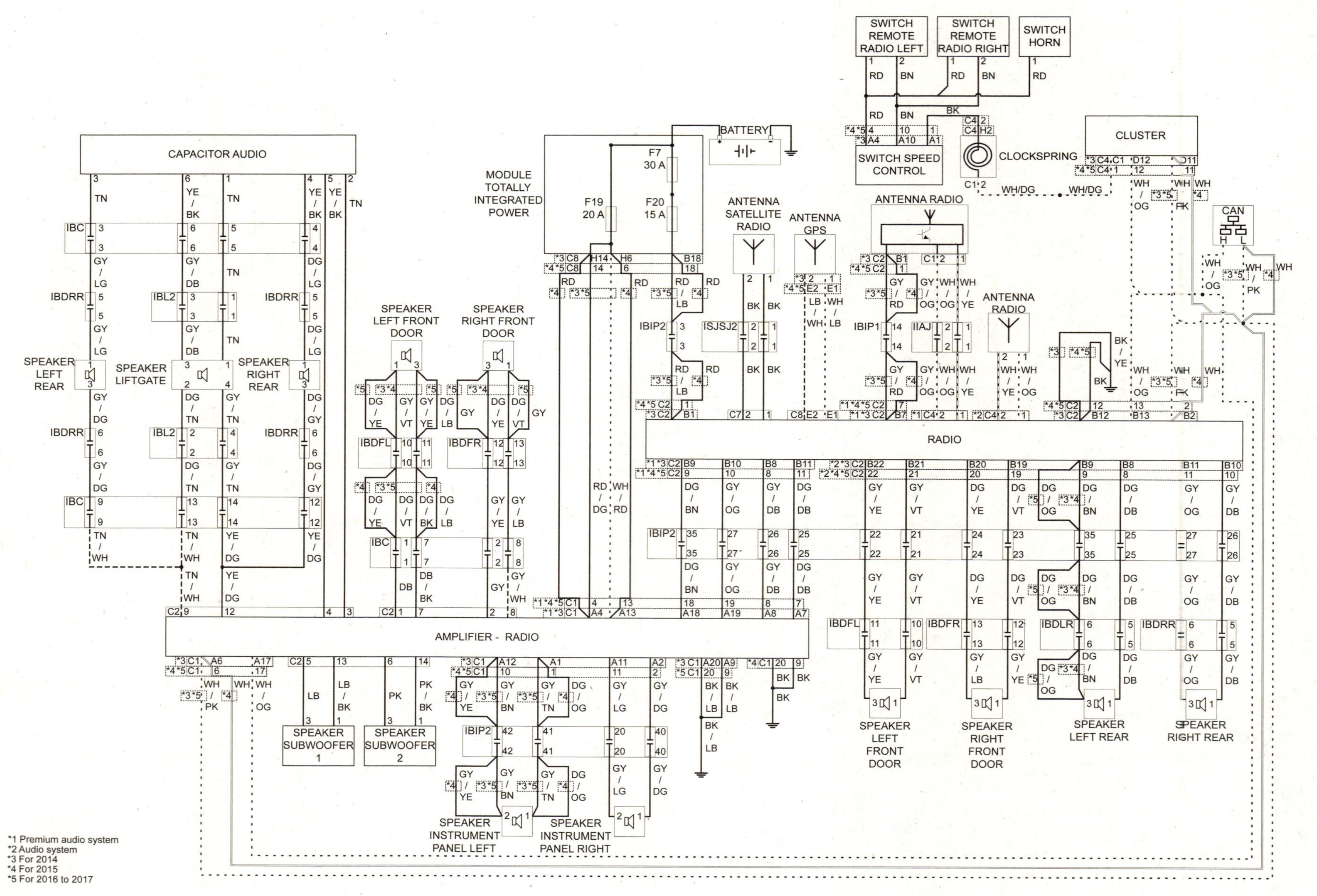

Audio system - 2014 and later models

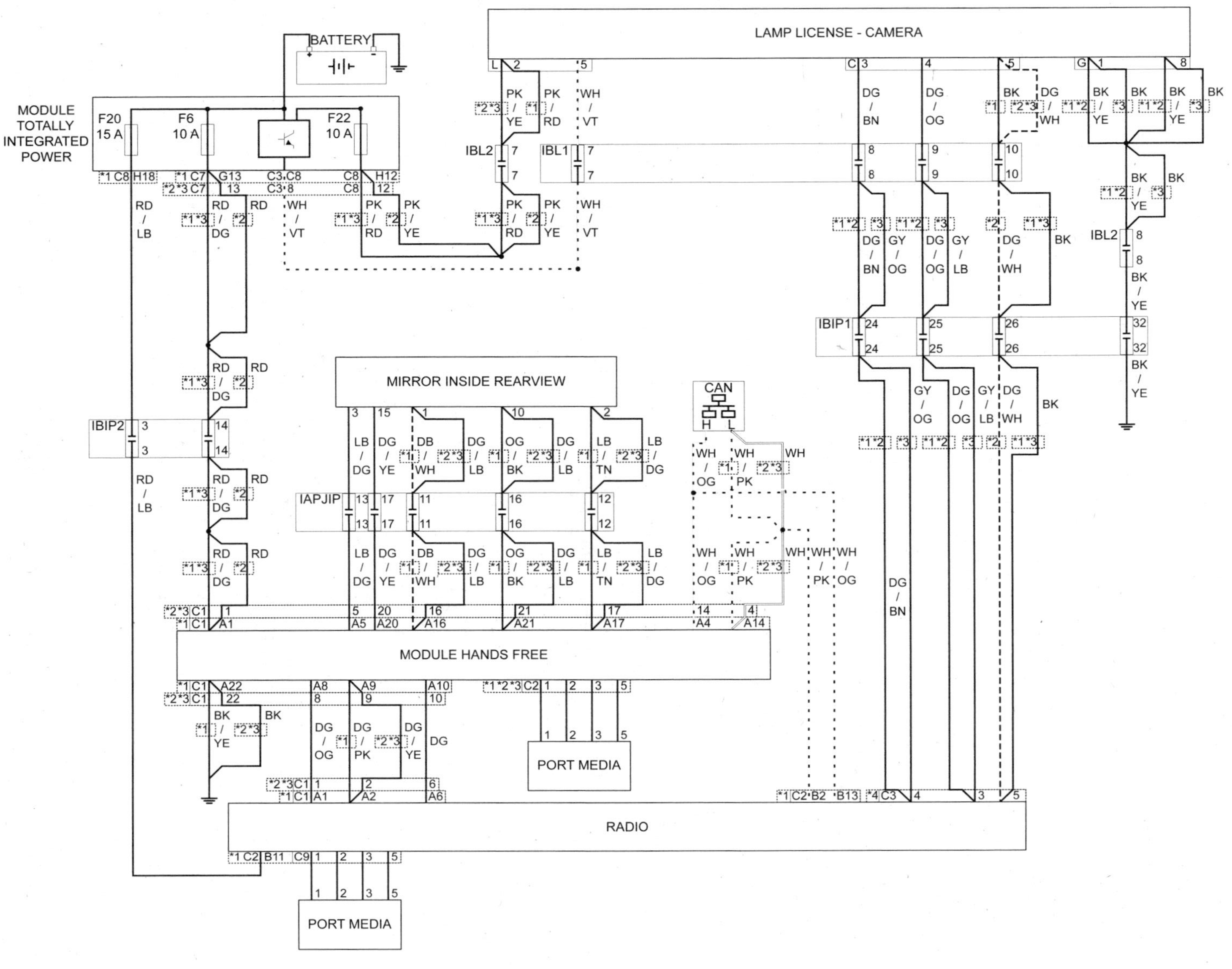

Hands-free system/back-up camera/audio port - 2014 and later models

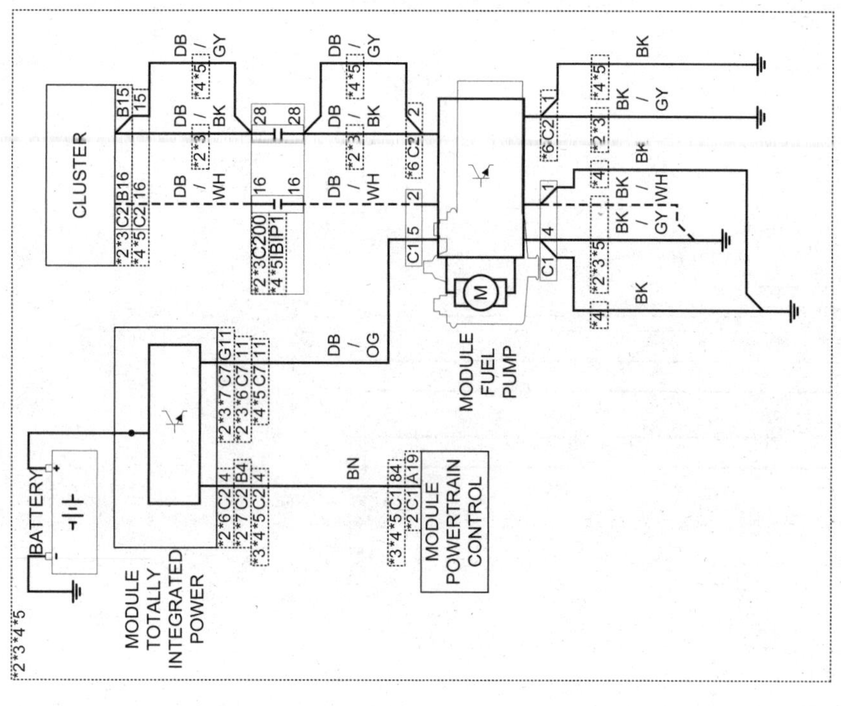

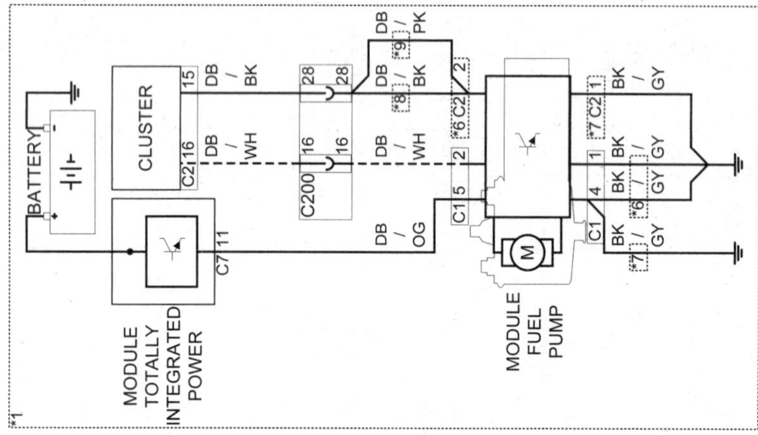

Fuel pump system

*1 From 2007 to 2009
*2 From 2010 to 2013
*3 For 2014
*4 For 2015
*5 From 2016 to 2017
*6 Equipment code: 4WD
*7 Equipment code: FWD
*8 Equipment code: Base
*9 Equipment code: Except Base

MODULE TOTALLY INTEGRATED POWER

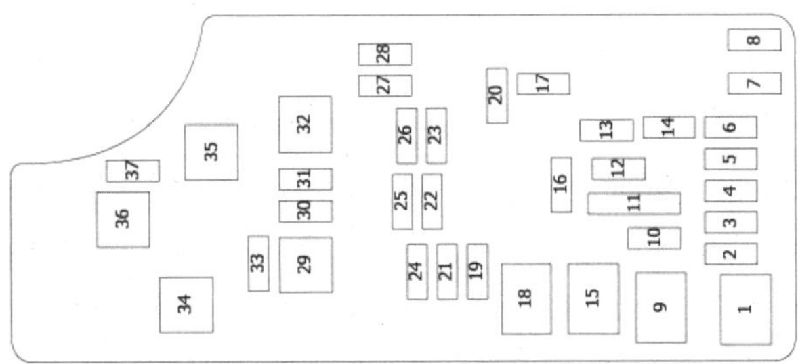

FUSE	VALUE	DESCRIPTION	OEM NAME
1	-	Not used	-
2	15 A	4WD control unit-if equipped	F2
3	10 A	Brake light switch	F3
4	10 A	Ignition switch	F4
5	20 A	Trailer towing -if equipped	F5
6	10 A	Steering control, Power mirror, Hands-free phone	F6
7	30 A	Power cut-off draw	F7
8	30 A	Power cut-off draw	F8
9	40 A	Electric seats	F9
10	20 A	Door lock control, Interior lighting	F10
11	15 A	Power outlet	F11
12	20 A	Power inverter -if equipped	F12
13	20 A	Rear power outlet or Cigarette lighter	F13
14	10 A	Interior lighting or Instrument cluster	F14
15	40 A	Radiator fan relay	F15
16	15 A	Interior lighting, Sunroof, Rear wiper motor	F16
17	10 A	Wireless control unit	F17
18	40 A	Auto shutdown relay	F18
19	20 A	Radio amplifiers	F19
20	15 A	Radio	F20
21	10 A	Alarm system - if equipped	F21
22	10 A	Air conditioning system, Compass unit	F22
23	15 A	Auto shutdown relay	F23
24	15 A	Electric sunroof - if equipped	F24
25	10 A	Heated mirror	F25
26	15 A	Auto shutdown relay	F26
27	10 A	Airbag control module	F27
28	10 A	Airbag control module, Occupant classification module	F28
29	-	Not used	-
30	20 A	Heated seats	F30
31	10 A	Headlamp washer - if equipped	F31
32	30 A	Engine automatic shutdown control	F32
33	10 A	ABS control unit, Powertrain control unit	F33
34	30 A	ABS valve	F34
35	40 A	ABS pump	F35
36	30 A	Headlight, Washer module, Smart glass	F36
37	25 A	Power inverter - if equipped	F37

FUSE RELAY BLOCK

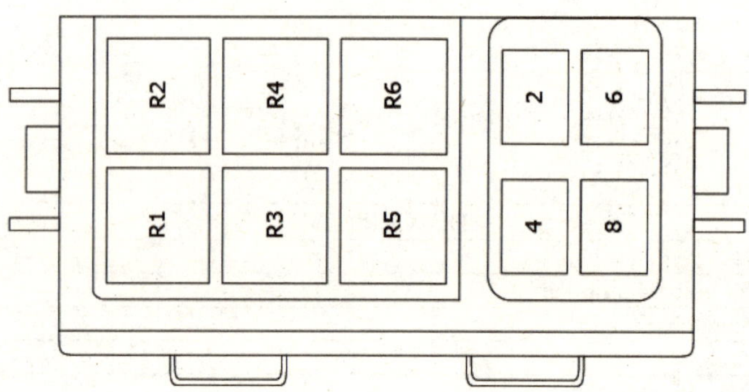

FROM 2007 TO 2013

RELAY	VALUE	DESCRIPTION	OEM NAME
R1	-	Radiator fan series	D838A
R2	-	Radiator fan high	D813A
R3	-	Lamp stop relay	D2583A
R4	-	Main relay	D907A
R5	-	Not used	-
R6	-	Radiator fan low	D812A
4	-	Not used	-
2	-	Not used	-
8	-	Not used	-
6	-	Not used	-

FROM 2014 TO 2017

RELAY	VALUE	DESCRIPTION	OEM NAME
R1	-	Radiator fan series parallel	D838A
R2	-	Radiator fan low	D813A
R3	-	Lamp stop	D2583A
R4	-	Main relay	D907A
R5	-	Fog lamps	D827A
R6	-	Not used	-
4	-	Not used	-
2	-	Not used	-
8	-	Not used	-
6	-	Not used	-

Index

U

V

W

Haynes Automotive Manuals

ACURA
- **12020** **Integra** '86 thru '89 **& Legend** '86 thru '90
- **12021** **Integra** '90 thru '93 **& Legend** '91 thru '95
  Integra '94 thru '00 - *see HONDA Civic (42025)*
  MDX '01 thru '07 - *see HONDA Pilot (42037)*
- **12050** **Acura TL** all models '99 thru '08

AMC
- **14020** **Mid-size models** '70 thru '83
- **14025** **(Renault) Alliance & Encore** '83 thru '87

AUDI
- **15020** **4000** all models '80 thru '87
- **15025** **5000** all models '77 thru '83
- **15026** **5000** all models '84 thru '88
  Audi A4 '96 thru '01 - *see VW Passat (96023)*
- **15030** **Audi A4** '02 thru '08

AUSTIN-HEALEY
Sprite - *see MG Midget (66015)*

BMW
- **18020** **3/5 Series** '82 thru '92
- **18021** **3-Series** incl. Z3 models '92 thru '98
- **18022** **3-Series** incl. Z4 models '99 thru '05
- **18023** **3-Series** '06 thru '14
- **18025** **320i** all 4-cylinder models '75 thru '83
- **18050** **1500 thru 2002** except Turbo '59 thru '77

BUICK
- **19010** **Buick Century** '97 thru '05
  Century (front-wheel drive) - *see GM (38005)*
- **19020** **Buick, Oldsmobile & Pontiac Full-size**
  (Front-wheel drive) '85 thru '05
  Buick Electra, LeSabre and Park Avenue;
  Oldsmobile Delta 88 Royale, Ninety Eight
  and Regency; **Pontiac** Bonneville
- **19025** **Buick, Oldsmobile & Pontiac Full-size**
  (Rear wheel drive) '70 thru '90
  Buick Estate, Electra, LeSabre, Limited,
  Oldsmobile Custom Cruiser, Delta 88,
  Ninety-eight, **Pontiac** Bonneville,
  Catalina, Grandville, Parisienne
- **19027** **Buick LaCrosse** '05 thru '13
  Enclave - *see GENERAL MOTORS (38001)*
  Rainier - *see CHEVROLET (24072)*
  Regal - *see GENERAL MOTORS (38010)*
  Riviera - *see GENERAL MOTORS (38030, 38031)*
  Roadmaster - *see CHEVROLET (24046)*
  Skyhawk - *see GENERAL MOTORS (38015)*
  Skylark - *see GENERAL MOTORS (38020, 38025)*
  Somerset - *see GENERAL MOTORS (38025)*

CADILLAC
- **21015** **CTS & CTS-V** '03 thru '14
- **21030** **Cadillac Rear Wheel Drive** '70 thru '93
  Cimarron - *see GENERAL MOTORS (38015)*
  DeVille - *see GENERAL MOTORS (38031 & 38032)*
  Eldorado - *see GENERAL MOTORS (38030)*
  Fleetwood - *see GENERAL MOTORS (38031)*
  Seville - *see GM (38030, 38031 & 38032)*

CHEVROLET
- **10305** **Chevrolet Engine Overhaul Manual**
- **24010** **Astro & GMC Safari Mini-vans** '85 thru '05
- **24013** **Aveo** '04 thru '11
- **24015** **Camaro V8** all models '70 thru '81
- **24016** **Camaro** all models '82 thru '92
- **24017** **Camaro & Firebird** '93 thru '02
  Cavalier - *see GENERAL MOTORS (38016)*
  Celebrity - *see GENERAL MOTORS (38005)*
- **24018** **Camaro** '10 thru '15
- **24020** **Chevelle, Malibu & El Camino** '69 thru '87
  Cobalt - *see GENERAL MOTORS (38017)*
- **24024** **Chevette & Pontiac T1000** '76 thru '87
  Citation - *see GENERAL MOTORS (38020)*
- **24027** **Colorado & GMC Canyon** '04 thru '12
- **24032** **Corsica & Beretta** all models '87 thru '96
- **24040** **Corvette** all V8 models '68 thru '82
- **24041** **Corvette** all models '84 thru '96
- **24042** **Corvette** all models '97 thru '13
- **24044** **Cruze** '11 thru '19
- **24045** **Full-size Sedans** Caprice, Impala, Biscayne,
  Bel Air & Wagons '69 thru '90
- **24046** **Impala SS & Caprice and Buick Roadmaster**
  '91 thru '96
  Impala '00 thru '05 - *see LUMINA (24048)*
- **24047** **Impala & Monte Carlo** all models '06 thru '11
  Lumina '90 thru '94 - *see GM (38010)*
- **24048** **Lumina & Monte Carlo** '95 thru '05
  Lumina APV - *see GM (38035)*
- **24050** **Luv Pick-up** all 2WD & 4WD '72 thru '82
- **24051** **Malibu** '13 thru '19
- **24055** **Monte Carlo** all models '70 thru '88
  Monte Carlo '95 thru '01 - *see LUMINA (24048)*
- **24059** **Nova** all V8 models '69 thru '79

- **24060** **Nova and Geo Prizm** '85 thru '92
- **24064** **Pick-ups** '67 thru '87 - Chevrolet & GMC
- **24065** **Pick-ups** '88 thru '98 - Chevrolet & GMC
- **24066** **Pick-ups** '99 thru '06 - Chevrolet & GMC
- **24067** **Chevrolet Silverado & GMC Sierra** '07 thru '14
- **24068** **Chevrolet Silverado & GMC Sierra** '14 thru '19
- **24070** **S-10 & S-15 Pick-ups** '82 thru '93,
  Blazer & Jimmy '83 thru '94,
- **24071** **S-10 & Sonoma Pick-ups** '94 thru '04,
  including **Blazer, Jimmy & Hombre**
- **24072** **Chevrolet TrailBlazer, GMC Envoy &**
  Oldsmobile Bravada '02 thru '09
- **24075** **Sprint** '85 thru '88 **& Geo Metro** '89 thru '01
- **24080** **Vans - Chevrolet & GMC** '68 thru '96
- **24081** **Chevrolet Express & GMC Savana**
  Full-size Vans '96 thru '19

CHRYSLER
- **10310** **Chrysler Engine Overhaul Manual**
- **25015** **Chrysler Cirrus, Dodge Stratus,**
  Plymouth Breeze '95 thru '00
- **25020** **Full-size Front-Wheel Drive** '88 thru '93
  K-Cars - *see DODGE Aries (30008)*
  Laser - *see DODGE Daytona (30030)*
- **25025** **Chrysler LHS, Concorde, New Yorker,**
  Dodge Intrepid, Eagle Vision, '93 thru '97
- **25026** **Chrysler LHS, Concorde, 300M,**
  Dodge Intrepid, '98 thru '04
- **25027** **Chrysler 300** '05 thru '18, **Dodge Charger**
  '06 thru '18, **Magnum** '05 thru '08 **&**
  Challenger '08 thru '18
- **25030** **Chrysler & Plymouth Mid-size**
  front wheel drive '82 thru '95
  Rear-wheel Drive - *see Dodge (30050)*
- **25035** **PT Cruiser** all models '01 thru '10
- **25040** **Chrysler Sebring** '95 thru '06, **Dodge Stratus**
  '01 thru '06 **& Dodge Avenger** '95 thru '00
- **25041** **Chrysler Sebring** '07 thru '10, **200** '11 thru '17
  Dodge Avenger '08 thru '14

DATSUN
- **28005** **200SX** all models '80 thru '83
- **28012** **240Z, 260Z & 280Z** Coupe '70 thru '78
- **28014** **280ZX** Coupe & 2+2 '79 thru '83
  300ZX - *see NISSAN (72010)*
- **28018** **510 & PL521 Pick-up** '68 thru '73
- **28020** **510** all models '78 thru '81
- **28022** **620 Series Pick-up** all models '73 thru '79
  720 Series Pick-up - *see NISSAN (72030)*

DODGE
- **400 & 600** - *see CHRYSLER (25030)*
- **30008** **Aries & Plymouth Reliant** '81 thru '89
- **30010** **Caravan & Plymouth Voyager** '84 thru '95
- **30011** **Caravan & Plymouth Voyager** '96 thru '02
- **30012** **Challenger & Plymouth Sapporro** '78 thru '83
- **30013** **Caravan, Chrysler Voyager &**
  Town & Country '03 thru '07
- **30014** **Grand Caravan &**
  Chrysler Town & Country '08 thru '18
- **30016** **Colt & Plymouth Champ** '78 thru '87
- **30020** **Dakota Pick-ups** all models '87 thru '96
- **30021** **Durango** '98 & '99 **& Dakota** '97 thru '99
- **30022** **Durango** '00 thru '03 **& Dakota** '00 thru '04
- **30023** **Durango** '04 thru '09 **& Dakota** '05 thru '11
- **30025** **Dart, Demon, Plymouth Barracuda,**
  Duster & Valiant 6-cylinder models '67 thru '76
- **30030** **Daytona & Chrysler Laser** '84 thru '89
  Intrepid - *see CHRYSLER (25025, 25026)*
- **30034** **Neon** all models '95 thru '99
- **30035** **Omni & Plymouth Horizon** '78 thru '90
- **30036** **Dodge & Plymouth Neon** '00 thru '05
- **30040** **Pick-ups** full-size models '74 thru '93
- **30042** **Pick-ups** full-size models '94 thru '08
- **30043** **Pick-ups** full-size models '09 thru '18
- **30045** **Ram 50/D50 Pick-ups & Raider and**
  Plymouth Arrow Pick-ups '79 thru '93
- **30050** **Dodge/Plymouth/Chrysler RWD** '71 thru '89
- **30055** **Shadow & Plymouth Sundance** '87 thru '94
- **30060** **Spirit & Plymouth Acclaim** '89 thru '95
- **30065** **Vans - Dodge & Plymouth** '71 thru '03

EAGLE
Talon - *see MITSUBISHI (68030, 68031)*
Vision - *see CHRYSLER (25025)*

FIAT
- **34010** **124 Sport Coupe & Spider** '68 thru '78
- **34025** **X1/9** all models '74 thru '80

FORD
- **10320** **Ford Engine Overhaul Manual**
- **10355** **Ford Automatic Transmission Overhaul**
- **11500** **Mustang** '64-1/2 thru '70 Restoration Guide
- **36004** **Aerostar Mini-vans** all models '86 thru '97
- **36006** **Contour & Mercury Mystique** '95 thru '00
- **36008** **Courier Pick-up** all models '72 thru '82

- **36012** **Crown Victoria &**
  Mercury Grand Marquis '88 thru '11
- **36014** **Edge** '07 thru '19 **& Lincoln MKX** '07 thru '18
- **36016** **Escort & Mercury Lynx** all models '81 thru '90
- **36020** **Escort & Mercury Tracer** '91 thru '02
- **36022** **Escape** '01 thru '17, **Mazda Tribute** '01 thru '11,
  & Mercury Mariner '05 thru '11
- **36024** **Explorer & Mazda Navajo** '91 thru '01
- **36025** **Explorer & Mercury Mountaineer** '02 thru '10
- **36026** **Explorer** '11 thru '17
- **36028** **Fairmont & Mercury Zephyr** '78 thru '83
- **36030** **Festiva & Aspire** '88 thru '97
- **36032** **Fiesta** all models '77 thru '80
- **36034** **Focus** all models '00 thru '11
- **36035** **Focus** '12 thru '14
- **36045** **Fusion** '06 thru '14 **& Mercury Milan** '06 thru '11
- **36048** **Mustang V8** all models '64-1/2 thru '73
- **36049** **Mustang II** 4-cylinder, V6 & V8 models '74 thru '78
- **36050** **Mustang & Mercury Capri** '79 thru '93
- **36051** **Mustang** all models '94 thru '04
- **36052** **Mustang** '05 thru '14
- **36054** **Pick-ups & Bronco** '73 thru '79
- **36058** **Pick-ups & Bronco** '80 thru '96
- **36059** **F-150** '97 thru '03, **Expedition** '97 thru '17,
  F-250 '97 thru '99, **F-150 Heritage** '04
  & Lincoln Navigator '98 thru '17
- **36060** **Super Duty Pick-ups & Excursion** '99 thru '10
- **36061** **F-150** full-size '04 thru '14
- **36062** **Pinto & Mercury Bobcat** '75 thru '80
- **36063** **F-150** full-size '15 thru '17
- **36064** **Super Duty Pick-ups** '11 thru '16
- **36066** **Probe** all models '89 thru '92
  Probe '93 thru '97 - *see MAZDA 626 (61042)*
- **36070** **Ranger & Bronco II** gas models '83 thru '92
- **36071** **Ranger** '93 thru '11 **& Mazda Pick-ups** '94 thru '09
- **36074** **Taurus & Mercury Sable** '86 thru '95
- **36075** **Taurus & Mercury Sable** '96 thru '07
- **36076** **Taurus** '08 thru '14, **Five Hundred** '05 thru '07,
  Mercury Montego '05 thru '07 **& Sable** '08 thru '09
- **36078** **Tempo & Mercury Topaz** '84 thru '94
- **36082** **Thunderbird & Mercury Cougar** '83 thru '88
- **36086** **Thunderbird & Mercury Cougar** '89 thru '97
- **36090** **Vans** all V8 Econoline models '69 thru '91
- **36094** **Vans** full size '92 thru '14
- **36097** **Windstar** '95 thru '03, **Freestar & Mercury**
  Monterey Mini-van '04 thru '07

GENERAL MOTORS
- **10360** **GM Automatic Transmission Overhaul**
- **38001** **GMC Acadia** '07 thru '16, **Buick Enclave**
  '08 thru '17, **Saturn Outlook** '07 thru '10
  & Chevrolet Traverse '09 thru '17
- **38005** **Buick Century, Chevrolet Celebrity,**
  Oldsmobile Cutlass Ciera & Pontiac 6000
  all models '82 thru '96
- **38010** **Buick Regal** '88 thru '04, **Chevrolet Lumina**
  '88 thru '04, **Oldsmobile Cutlass Supreme**
  '88 thru '97 **& Pontiac Grand Prix** '88 thru '07
- **38015** **Buick Skyhawk, Cadillac Cimarron,**
  Chevrolet Cavalier, Oldsmobile Firenza,
  Pontiac J-2000 & Sunbird '82 thru '94
- **38016** **Chevrolet Cavalier & Pontiac Sunfire** '95 thru '05
- **38017** **Chevrolet Cobalt** '05 thru '10, **HHR** '06 thru '11,
  Pontiac G5 '07 thru '09, **Pursuit** '05 thru '06
  & Saturn ION '03 thru '07
- **38020** **Buick Skylark, Chevrolet Citation,**
  Oldsmobile Omega, Pontiac Phoenix '80 thru '85
- **38025** **Buick Skylark** '86 thru '98, **Somerset** '85 thru '87,
  Oldsmobile Achieva '92 thru '98, **Calais** '85 thru '91,
  & Pontiac Grand Am all models '85 thru '98
- **38026** **Chevrolet Malibu** '97 thru '03, **Classic** '04 thru '05,
  Oldsmobile Alero '99 thru '03, **Cutlass** '97 thru '00,
  & Pontiac Grand Am '99 thru '03
- **38027** **Chevrolet Malibu** '04 thru '12, **Pontiac G6**
  '05 thru '10 **& Saturn Aura** '07 thru '10
- **38030** **Cadillac Eldorado, Seville, Oldsmobile**
  Toronado & Buick Riviera '71 thru '85
- **38031** **Cadillac Eldorado, Seville, DeVille, Fleetwood,**
  Oldsmobile Toronado & Buick Riviera '86 thru '93
- **38032** **Cadillac DeVille** '94 thru '05, **Seville** '92 thru '04
  & Cadillac DTS '06 thru '10
- **38035** **Chevrolet Lumina APV, Oldsmobile Silhouette**
  & Pontiac Trans Sport all models '90 thru '96
- **38036** **Chevrolet Venture** '97 thru '05, **Oldsmobile**
  Silhouette '97 thru '04, **Pontiac Trans Sport**
  '97 thru '98 **& Montana** '99 thru '05
- **38040** **Chevrolet Equinox** '05 thru '17, **GMC Terrain**
  '10 thru '17 **& Pontiac Torrent** '06 thru '09

GEO
Metro - *see CHEVROLET Sprint (24075)*
Prizm - '85 thru '92 see CHEVY (24060),
'93 thru '02 see TOYOTA Corolla (92036)
- **40030** **Storm** all models '90 thru '93
Tracker - *see SUZUKI Samurai (90010)*

(Continued on other side)

Haynes Automotive Manuals (continued)

*NOTE: If you do not see a listing for your vehicle, please visit **haynes.com** for the latest product information and check out our **Online Manuals!***

GMC
Acadia - *see GENERAL MOTORS (38001)*
Pick-ups - *see CHEVROLET (24027, 24068)*
Vans - *see CHEVROLET (24081)*

HONDA
42010 **Accord CVCC** all models '76 thru '83
42011 **Accord** all models '84 thru '89
42012 **Accord** all models '90 thru '93
42013 **Accord** all models '94 thru '97
42014 **Accord** all models '98 thru '02
42015 **Accord** '03 thru '12 & **Crosstour** '10 thru '14
42016 **Accord** '13 thru '17
42020 **Civic 1200** all models '73 thru '79
42021 **Civic 1300 & 1500 CVCC** '80 thru '83
42022 **Civic 1500 CVCC** all models '75 thru '79
42023 **Civic** all models '84 thru '91
42024 **Civic & del Sol** '92 thru '95
42025 **Civic** '96 thru '00, **CR-V** '97 thru '01
& **Acura Integra** '94 thru '00
42026 **Civic** '01 thru '11 & **CR-V** '02 thru '11
42027 **Civic** '12 thru '15 & **CR-V** '12 thru '16
42030 **Fit** '07 thru '13
42035 **Odyssey** all models '99 thru '10
Passport - *see ISUZU Rodeo (47017)*
42037 **Honda Pilot** '03 thru '08, **Ridgeline** '06 thru '14
& **Acura MDX** '01 thru '07
42040 **Prelude CVCC** all models '79 thru '89

HYUNDAI
43010 **Elantra** all models '96 thru '19
43015 **Excel & Accent** all models '86 thru '13
43050 **Santa Fe** all models '01 thru '12
43055 **Sonata** all models '99 thru '14

INFINITI
G35 '03 thru '08 - *see NISSAN 350Z (72011)*

ISUZU
Hombre - *see CHEVROLET S-10 (24071)*
47017 **Rodeo** '91 thru '02, **Amigo** '89 thru '94 & '98 thru '02
& **Honda Passport** '95 thru '02
47020 **Trooper** '84 thru '91 & **Pick-up** '81 thru '93

JAGUAR
49010 **XJ6** all 6-cylinder models '68 thru '86
49011 **XJ6** all models '88 thru '94
49015 **XJ12 & XJS** all 12-cylinder models '72 thru '85

JEEP
50010 **Cherokee, Comanche & Wagoneer Limited**
all models '84 thru '01
50011 **Cherokee** '14 thru '19
50020 **CJ** all models '49 thru '86
50025 **Grand Cherokee** all models '93 thru '04
50026 **Grand Cherokee** '05 thru '19
& **Dodge Durango** '11 thru '19
50029 **Grand Wagoneer & Pick-up** '72 thru '91
Grand Wagoneer '84 thru '91, Cherokee &
Wagoneer '72 thru '83, Pick-up '72 thru '88
50030 **Wrangler** all models '87 thru '17
50035 **Liberty** '02 thru '12 & **Dodge Nitro** '07 thru '11
50050 **Patriot & Compass** '07 thru '17

KIA
54050 **Optima** '01 thru '10
54060 **Sedona** '02 thru '14
54070 **Sephia** '94 thru '01, **Spectra** '00 thru '09,
Sportage '05 thru '20
54077 **Sorento** '03 thru '13

LEXUS
ES 300/330 - *see TOYOTA Camry (92007, 92008)*
ES 350 - *see TOYOTA Camry (92009)*
RX 300/330/350 - *see TOYOTA Highlander (92095)*

LINCOLN
MKX - *see FORD (36014)*
Navigator - *see FORD Pick-up (36059)*
59010 **Rear-Wheel Drive Continental** '70 thru '87,
Mark Series '70 thru '92 & **Town Car** '81 thru '10

MAZDA
61010 **GLC (rear-wheel drive)** '77 thru '83
61011 **GLC (front-wheel drive)** '81 thru '85
61012 **Mazda3** '04 thru '11
61015 **323 & Protogé** '90 thru '03
61016 **MX-5 Miata** '90 thru '14
61020 **MPV** all models '89 thru '98
Navajo - *see Ford Explorer (36024)*
61030 **Pick-ups** '72 thru '93
Pick-ups '94 thru '09 - *see Ford Ranger (36071)*
61035 **RX-7** all models '79 thru '85
61036 **RX-7** all models '86 thru '91
61040 **626 (rear-wheel drive)** all models '79 thru '82
61041 **626 & MX-6 (front-wheel drive)** '83 thru '92
61042 **626** '93 thru '01 & **MX-6/Ford Probe** '93 thru '02
61043 **Mazda6** '03 thru '13

MERCEDES-BENZ
63012 **123 Series Diesel** '76 thru '85
63015 **190 Series** 4-cylinder gas models '84 thru '88
63020 **230/250/280** 6-cylinder SOHC models '68 thru '72
63025 **280 123 Series** gas models '77 thru '81
63030 **350 & 450** all models '71 thru '80
63040 **C-Class:** C230/C240/C280/C320/C350 '01 thru '07

MERCURY
64200 **Villager & Nissan Quest** '93 thru '01
All other titles, see FORD Listing.

MG
66010 **MGB** Roadster & GT Coupe '62 thru '80
66015 **MG Midget, Austin Healey Sprite** '58 thru '80

MINI
67020 **Mini** '02 thru '13

MITSUBISHI
68020 **Cordia, Tredia, Galant, Precis & Mirage** '83 thru '93
68030 **Eclipse, Eagle Talon & Plymouth Laser** '90 thru '94
68031 **Eclipse** '95 thru '05 & **Eagle Talon** '95 thru '98
68035 **Galant** '94 thru '12
68040 **Pick-up** '83 thru '96 & **Montero** '83 thru '93

NISSAN
72010 **300ZX** all models including Turbo '84 thru '89
72011 **350Z & Infiniti G35** all models '03 thru '08
72015 **Altima** all models '93 thru '06
72016 **Altima** '07 thru '12
72020 **Maxima** all models '85 thru '92
72021 **Maxima** all models '93 thru '08
72025 **Murano** '03 thru '14
72030 **Pick-ups** '80 thru '97 & **Pathfinder** '87 thru '95
72031 **Frontier** '98 thru '04, **Xterra** '00 thru '04,
& **Pathfinder** '96 thru '04
72032 **Frontier & Xterra** '05 thru '14
72037 **Pathfinder** '05 thru '14
72040 **Pulsar** all models '83 thru '86
72042 **Roque** all models '08 thru '20
72050 **Sentra** all models '82 thru '94
72051 **Sentra & 200SX** all models '95 thru '06
72060 **Stanza** all models '82 thru '90
72070 **Titan pick-ups** '04 thru '10, **Armada** '05 thru '10
& **Pathfinder Armada** '04
72080 **Versa** all models '07 thru '19

OLDSMOBILE
73015 **Cutlass** V6 & V8 gas models '74 thru '88
For other OLDSMOBILE titles, see BUICK,
CHEVROLET or GENERAL MOTORS listings.

PLYMOUTH
For PLYMOUTH titles, see DODGE listing.

PONTIAC
79008 **Fiero** all models '84 thru '88
79018 **Firebird** V8 models except Turbo '70 thru '81
79019 **Firebird** all models '82 thru '92
79025 **G6** all models '05 thru '09
79040 **Mid-size Rear-wheel Drive** '70 thru '87
Vibe '03 thru '10 - *see TOYOTA Corolla (92037)*
For other PONTIAC titles, see BUICK,
CHEVROLET or GENERAL MOTORS listings.

PORSCHE
80020 **911** Coupe & Targa models '65 thru '89
80025 **914** all 4-cylinder models '69 thru '76
80030 **924** all models including Turbo '76 thru '82
80035 **944** all models including Turbo '83 thru '89

RENAULT
Alliance & Encore - *see AMC (14025)*

SAAB
84010 **900** all models including Turbo '79 thru '88

SATURN
87010 **Saturn** all S-series models '91 thru '02
Saturn Ion '03 thru '07- *see GM (38017)*
Saturn Outlook - *see GM (38001)*
87020 **Saturn L-series** all models '00 thru '04
87040 **Saturn VUE** '02 thru '09

SUBARU
89002 **1100, 1300, 1400 & 1600** '71 thru '79
89003 **1600 & 1800** 2WD & 4WD '80 thru '94
89080 **Impreza** '02 thru '11, **WRX** '02 thru '14,
& **WRX STI** '04 thru '14
89100 **Legacy** all models '90 thru '99
89101 **Legacy & Forester** '00 thru '09
89102 **Legacy** '10 thru '16 & **Forester** '12 thru '16

SUZUKI
90010 **Samurai/Sidekick & Geo Tracker** '86 thru '01

TOYOTA
92005 **Camry** all models '83 thru '91
92006 **Camry** '92 thru '96 & **Avalon** '95 thru '96
92007 **Camry, Avalon, Solara, Lexus ES 300** '97 thru '01

92008 **Camry, Avalon, Lexus ES 300/330** '02 thru '06
& **Solara** '02 thru '08
92009 **Camry, Avalon & Lexus ES 350** '07 thru '17
92015 **Celica Rear-wheel Drive** '71 thru '85
92020 **Celica Front-wheel Drive** '86 thru '99
92025 **Celica Supra** all models '79 thru '92
92030 **Corolla** all models '75 thru '79
92032 **Corolla** all rear-wheel drive models '80 thru '87
92035 **Corolla** all front-wheel drive models '84 thru '92
92036 **Corolla & Geo/Chevrolet Prizm** '93 thru '02
92037 **Corolla** '03 thru '19, **Matrix** '03 thru '14,
& **Pontiac Vibe** '03 thru '10
92040 **Corolla Tercel** all models '80 thru '82
92045 **Corona** all models '74 thru '82
92050 **Cressida** all models '78 thru '82
92055 **Land Cruiser** FJ40, 43, 45, 55 '68 thru '82
92056 **Land Cruiser** FJ60, 62, 80, FZJ80 '80 thru '96
92060 **Matrix** '03 thru '11 & **Pontiac Vibe** '03 thru '10
92065 **MR2** all models '85 thru '87
92070 **Pick-up** all models '69 thru '78
92075 **Pick-up** all models '79 thru '95
92076 **Tacoma** '95 thru '04, **4Runner** '96 thru '02
& **T100** '93 thru '08
92077 **Tacoma** all models '05 thru '18
92078 **Tundra** '00 thru '06 & **Sequoia** '01 thru '07
92079 **4Runner** all models '03 thru '09
92080 **Previa** all models '91 thru '95
92081 **Prius** all models '01 thru '12
92082 **RAV4** all models '96 thru '12
92085 **Tercel** all models '87 thru '94
92090 **Sienna** all models '98 thru '10
92095 **Highlander** '01 thru '19
& **Lexus RX330/330/350** '99 thru '19
92179 **Tundra** '07 thru '19 & **Sequoia** '08 thru '19

TRIUMPH
94007 **Spitfire** all models '62 thru '81
94010 **TR7** all models '75 thru '81

VW
96008 **Beetle & Karmann Ghia** '54 thru '79
96009 **New Beetle** '98 thru '10
96016 **Rabbit, Jetta, Scirocco & Pick-up**
gas models '74 thru '92 & Convertible '80 thru '92
96017 **Golf, GTI & Jetta** '93 thru '98, **Cabrio** '95 thru '02
96018 **Golf, GTI, Jetta** '99 thru '05
96019 **Jetta, Rabbit, GLI, GTI & Golf** '05 thru '11
96020 **Rabbit, Jetta & Pick-up** diesel '77 thru '84
96021 **Jetta** '11 thru '18 & **Golf** '15 thru '19
96023 **Passat** '98 thru '05 & **Audi A4** '96 thru '01
96030 **Transporter 1600** all models '68 thru '79
96035 **Transporter 1700, 1800 & 2000** '72 thru '79
96040 **Type 3 1500 & 1600** all models '63 thru '73
96045 **Vanagon Air-Cooled** all models '80 thru '83

VOLVO
97010 **120, 130 Series & 1800 Sports** '61 thru '73
97015 **140 Series** all models '66 thru '74
97020 **240 Series** all models '76 thru '93
97040 **740 & 760 Series** all models '82 thru '88
97050 **850 Series** all models '93 thru '97

TECHBOOK MANUALS
10205 **Automotive Computer Codes**
10206 **OBD-II & Electronic Engine Management**
10210 **Automotive Emissions Control Manual**
10215 **Fuel Injection Manual** '78 thru '85
10225 **Holley Carburetor Manual**
10230 **Rochester Carburetor Manual**
10305 **Chevrolet Engine Overhaul Manual**
10320 **Ford Engine Overhaul Manual**
10330 **GM and Ford Diesel Engine Repair Manual**
10331 **Duramax Diesel Engines** '01 thru '19
10332 **Cummins Diesel Engine Performance Manual**
10333 **GM, Ford & Chrysler Engine Performance Manual**
10334 **GM Engine Performance Manual**
10340 **Small Engine Repair Manual,** 5 HP & Less
10341 **Small Engine Repair Manual,** 5.5 thru 20 HP
10345 **Suspension, Steering & Driveline Manual**
10355 **Ford Automatic Transmission Overhaul**
10360 **GM Automatic Transmission Overhaul**
10405 **Automotive Body Repair & Painting**
10410 **Automotive Brake Manual**
10411 **Automotive Anti-lock Brake (ABS) Systems**
10420 **Automotive Electrical Manual**
10425 **Automotive Heating & Air Conditioning**
10435 **Automotive Tools Manual**
10445 **Welding Manual**
10450 **ATV Basics**

Over a 100 Haynes
motorcycle manuals
also available

10/22